£3.95

TUTORIALS IN MOTOR BEHAVIOR

ADVANCES IN PSYCHOLOGY

1

Editors

G. E. STELMACH

P. A. VROON

NORTH-HOLLAND PUBLISHING COMPANY
AMSTERDAM • NEW YORK • OXFORD

TUTORIALS IN MOTOR BEHAVIOR

Edited by
George E.STELMACH
Motor Behavior Laboratory
University of Wisconsin
Madison, U.S.A.

and

Jean REQUIN
Department of Experimental Psychobiology
Institute of Neurophysiology
and Psychophysiology of CNRS
Marseille, France

1980

NORTH-HOLLAND PUBLISHING COMPANY
AMSTERDAM • NEW YORK • OXFORD

ISBN: 0 444 85466 5

Publishers:
NORTH-HOLLAND PUBLISHING COMPANY
AMSTERDAM • NEW YORK • OXFORD

Sole distributors for the U.S.A. and Canada:
ELSEVIER NORTH-HOLLAND, INC.
52 VANDERBILT AVENUE
NEW YORK, N.Y. 10017

Library of Congress Cataloging in Publication Data
Main entry under title:

Tutorials in motor behavior.

    (Advances in psychology ; 1)
    Includes bibliographical references and indexes.
    1. Movement, Psychology of. 2. Motor learning.
I. Stelmach, George E. II. Requin, Jean. III. Series:
Advances in psychology (Amsterdam) ; 1) [DNLM: 1. Motor
activity--Congresses. 2. Motor skills--Congresses.
3. Behavior--Congresses. W1 AD798L v.2 / WE103 T966
1979]
BF295.T77   152.3'34   80-10905
ISBN 0-444-85466-5

PRINTED IN THE NETHERLANDS

Preface

This book grew indirectly out of an eleven day Advanced Study Institute
held at the Abbaye de Sénanque, June 10-21, 1979, in the south of France. As
with most Advanced Study Institutes, emphasis was placed on disseminating
advanced scientific knowledge and in developing a dialogue of cooperation
between scientists from different countries. The setting was most appropriate for this purpose as the twelfth century abbey provided a beautiful
peaceful setting for scholarly discussions. The Advanced Study Institute
was sponsored by the Scientific Affairs Division, North Atlantic Treaty
Organization and the U.S. Army Research Institute.

The text is intended to be a legacy of the Advanced Study Institute and to
document some of the best recent theory and data in the motor control and
learning area. The reputation of the authors is indicative of the quality
of the text's contents. By recording these contributions at this time I
hope to direct the course of motor control and learning, and perhaps reveal
to later generations of scientists some of the pitfalls that should be
avoided. With this perspective in mind the treatise brings together many
of the contemporary aspects of the very large, diverse and widely scattered
literature on motor control and learning.

Within a general theme, contributors were free to choose the contents of
their topic as well as their form of presentation without the usual constraints imposed by journals, textbooks or other edited volumes. Some
authors emphasized a particular set of their latest experiments, some preferred to give an overview of their special field, others focused on
theoretical issues. Some of the topics necessarily overlap and blend into
one another and some are dealt with in several parts of the volume, so that
a preliminary glance through the subject index may be worthwhile.

The text is partitioned into seven main sections with the topical organization rather arbitrary but intended to furnish the reader with a general
orientation of the material. A given topic, however, is covered in a comprehensive manner in which fundamental facts and concepts are presented
and important leads to journals and monographs of the specialized literature are provided. Part I of the book contains chapters on action control
systems that provide an emerging perspective on skilled behavior. An extensive series of papers on the control of segmental movement which utilized muscle length tension relationships is the focus of Part II. The
role of vision in the regulation and coordination of movement is dealt with
in Part III. Drawing on traditional information processing and neurophysiological techniques to probe the processes that lead to motor performance,
Part IV concentrates on stage analysis and motor preparation. The principal components of timing and sequencing of movements are considered in
Part V. Although a great deal of the text is concerned with motor control,
Part VI dwells on the cognitive aspects of motor behavior with most of the
chapters addressing learning and memory. The final part of the text elaborates on some of the emerging concepts in speech motor control.

I am indebted to many people for their aid in organizing and directing
this Advanced Study Institute and the resulting text. In the first place,
to my co-director Jean Requin for his superb administrative skills and
his technical staff at the CNRS who kept the institute running smoothly
and efficiently despite many obstacles. A special thanks is due to
Kees Michielsen, Vice President, North-Holland Publishing Company for his
constant advice and enthusiasm concerning the text. I would also like to
thank Les Szendrovits for reading the chapters to determine if they should
be edited and retyped, for assisting in the text organization, and for
providing the subject index. Finally, to my wife, Rosmary, whose constant
support during the early planning and organization of the Advanced Study
Institute and through the preparation of this text kept me from giving up
the task long ago.

GEORGE E. STELMACH
Madison, Wisconsin
November 1979

CONTENTS

CONTRIBUTORS AND PARTICIPANTS

Invited Contributors[1]

AGARWAL, G.C., Department of Systems Engineering, University of Illinois at Chicago Circle, Chicago, Illinois, 60680, U.S.A.

ARBIB, M.A., Center for Systems Neuroscience, University of Massachusetts, Amherst, Massachusetts, 01003, U.S.A.

BEAUBATON, D., C.N.R.S.-Institut de Neurophysiologie & Psychophysiologie 13274 Marseille Cedex 2, France.

BIZZI, E., Department of Psychology, Massachusetts Institute of Technology, Cambridge, Massachusetts, 02139, U.S.A.

BOYLLS, C.C., Department of Physiology, University of Bristol, Bristol, BS8 ITD, G.B.

BRUNIA, C.H.M., Department of Psychology, University of Tilburg, Tilburg, Holland.

BUTTERWORTH, B., Department of Experimental Psychology, University of Cambridge, Cambridge, CB2 3EB, G.B.

COOKE, J.D., Department of Physiology, University of Western Ontario, London, Ontario, Canada.

GLENCROSS, D.J., Department of Psychology, The Flinders University of South Australia, Bedford Park, 5044, Australia.

GOTTSDANKER, R., Department of Psychology, University of California, Santa Barbara, California, 93106, U.S.A.

HOLENDER, D., Départment de Psychobiologie Expérimentale, Institut de Neurophysiologie et Psychophysiologie du C.N.R.S., Marseille, France.

HOWELL, P., Department of Psychology, University College London, London, WC1E GBT, England.

JEANNEROD, M., Laboratoire de Neuropsychologie Expérimentale, Inserm U 94 69500, Bron, France.

KELSO, J.A.S., Haskins Laboratories, New Haven, Connecticut, 06510, U.S.A.

KUGLER, P.N., Department of Psychology, University of Connecticut, Storrs, Connecticut, U.S.A.

LEE, D.N., Department of Psychology, University of Edinburgh, Edinburgh, Scotland.

LEINONEN, L.M., Department of Physiology, University of Helsinki, Helsinki, Finland.

[1]P.N. Kugler did not attend nor present at the Advanced Study Institute.

MACNEILAGE, P.F., Department of Linguistics, University of Texas, Austin,
    Texas, 78712, U.S.A.
MARIN, O.S.M., Department of Neurology, Baltimore City Hospitals, Baltimore,
    Maryland, 21224, U.S.A.
MARTENIUK, R.G., Department of Kinesiology, University of Waterloo,
    Waterloo, Ontario, N22 3G1, Canada.
McLEOD, P., MRC Applied Psychology Unit, Cambridge, CB2 2EF England.
NEWELL, K.M., Institute for Child Behavior and Development, University of
    Illinois at Urbana-Champaign, Champaign, Illinois, U.S.A.
OSTRY, D.J., Department of Psychology, McGill University, Montreal,
    Quebec, H3A 1B1, Canada.
PAILLARD, J., C.N.R.S., Institut de Neurophysiologie & Psychophysiologie,
    13274, Marseille Cedex 2, France.
POSNER, M.I., Department of Psychology, University of Oregon, Eugene,
    Oregon, 97403, U.S.A.
REQUIN, J., Département de Psychobiologie Expérimentale, Institut de
    Neurophysiologie et Psychologie du C.N.R.S., Marseille, France.
ROSENBAUM, D.A., Bell Laboratories, Murray Hill, New Jersey, 07974, U.S.A.
ROUCOUX, A., Laboratoire de Neurophysiologie, University of Louvain,
    Brussels, Belgium.
SANDERS, A.F., Institute for Perception TNO, Soesterberg, The Netherlands.
SCHMIDT, R.A., Department of Physical Education, University of Southern
    California, Los Angeles, California, 90007, U.S.A.
SHAFFER, L.H., Department of Psychology, University of Exeter, Exeter,
    Devon, G.B.
SINGER, R.N., Movement Science-Physical Education Department, Florida
    State University, Tallahassee, Florida, 32306, U.S.A.
SMITH, J.L., Department of Kinesiology, University of California,
    Los Angeles, California, 90024, U.S.A.
STELMACH, G.E., Motor Behavior Laboratory, University of Wisconsin,
    Madison, Wisconsin, 53705, U.S.A.
TERZUOLO, C.A., Laboratory of Neurophysiology, University of Minnesota,
    Minneapolis, Minnesota, 55455, U.S.A.
TYLDESLEY, D.A., Interfakulteit Lichamelijke Opvoeding, Vrije Universiteit,
    Amsterdam, The Netherlands.
VAN GALEN, G.P., Psychological Laboratory of the University of Nijmegen,
    G525 GG Nijmegen, The Netherlands.
VIVIANI, P., Laboratoire du Physiologie du Travail, C.N.R.S., Department
    of Neurosensory Physiology, Paris, France,
WERTHEIM, A.H., Institute for Perception TNO, Soesterberg, The Netherlands.
WHITING, H.T.A., Interfakulteit Lichamelijke Opvoeding, Vrije Universiteit,
    Amsterdam, The Netherlands.
WING, A.M., MRC Applied Psychology Unit, Cambridge, CB2 2EF, England.

Co-Authors

AMATO, G., C.N.R.S.- Institute de Neurophysiologie & Psychophysiologie,
    13274 Marseille Cedex 2, France.
COHEN, Y., Department of Psychology, University of Oregon, Eugene, Oregon,
    97403, U.S.A.
CROMMELINCK, M., Laboratoire de Neurophysiologie, University of Louvain,
    Brussels, Belgium.
DUFRESNE, J.R., Laboratory of Neurophysiology, University of Minnesota,
    Minneapolis, Minnesota, 55455, U.S.A.

GORDON, B., Department of Neurology, Baltimore City Hospitals, Baltimore,
   Maryland, 21224, U.S.A.
GOTTLIEB, G.L., Department of Systems Engineering, University of Illinois
   at Chicago Circle, Chicago, Illinois, 60680, U.S.A.
HOLT, K.G., Department of Biobehavioral Sciences, University of Connecticut,
   Storrs, Connecticut, U.S.A.
HYVARINEN, J., Department of Physiology, University of Helsinki,
   Helsinki, Finland.
LARISH, D.D., Motor Behavior Laboratory, University of Wisconsin,
   Madison, Wisconsin, 53705, U.S.A.
MACKENZIE, C.L., Department of Kinesiology, University of Waterloo,
   Waterloo, Ontario, N22, 3G1, Canada.
PATASHNIK, O., Bell Laboratories, Murray Hill, New Jersey, 07974, U.S.A.
PERENIN, M.T., Laboratoire de Neuropsychologie Expérimentale, Inserm, U94
   69500, Bron, France.
PRABLANC, C., Laboratoire de Neuropsychologie Expérimentale, Inserm, U94
   69500, Bron, France.
SOECHTING, J.F., Laboratory of Neurophysiology, University of Minnesota,
   Minneapolis, Minnesota, 55455, U.S.A.
TROUCHE, E., C.N.R.S.-Institute de Neurophysiologie & Psychophysiologie,
   13274, Marseille Cedex 2, France.
TURVEY, M.T., Department of Psychology, University of Connecticut, Storrs,
   Connecticut, U.S.A.
WHITTAKER, S., Department of Experimental Psychology, University of
   Cambridge, Cambridge, CB2 3EB, G.B.

PART I

ACTION CONTROL SYSTEMS:
THEORY AND DATA

Tutorials in Motor Behavior
G.E. Stelmach and J. Requin (eds.)
© *North-Holland Publishing Company, 1980*

1

ON THE CONCEPT OF COORDINATIVE STRUCTURES AS DISSIPATIVE STRUCTURES: I. THEORETICAL LINES OF CONVERGENCE*

Peter N. Kugler[1], J. A. Scott Kelso[1,2] and M.T. Turvey[1]

Departments of Psychology[1] and Biobehavioral Sciences[2]
University of Connecticut, Storrs and
Haskins Laboratories, New Haven, Connecticut, U.S.A.

A model construct for coordination and control is pursued according to three related guidelines: (1) that it directly address Bernstein's problem of how to explain the regulation of the many biokinematic degrees of freedom with minimal recourse to an "intelligent regulator"; (2) that it be miserly on the number of explanatory principles, sui generis; and (3) that it be consistent with established strictures of non-equilibrium thermodynamics, that is, physical principles that inform biological design. Argument is given that a group of muscles constrained to act as a unit, a coordinative structure, is a member of the class of thermodynamic engines qua dissipative structures and that this membership gives a principled basis for understanding the characteristics of coordination and control.

1. Introduction

What should we take as the model construct by which to characterize the control and coordination of movement? Several candidates have presented themselves over the years: The linear chaining of reflexes or, more generally, the concatenation of stimulus-response connections; the musical-score metaphor of the past century transformed into the contemporary concept of central program; and the feedback, error-correcting mechanism fundamental to cybernetics and its allied disciplines. Our purpose in this essay (and its companion which follows) is to promote a lesser known candidate: We will give serious consideration to the idea that a group of muscles constrained to act as a unit is a member of the class of dissipative structures characterized by limit cycle oscillation and it is by virtue of this membership that the control and coordination of movement has the character that it has. We intend to show that this model construct of dissipative structure, in comparison to other candidate constructs, is more closely consonant with contemporary thought in biology, is a more principled basis for understanding the whys and wherefores of control and coordination and is more able to accommodate criterial findings about speech production and about the movement of limbs singly and in combination.

2. Bernstein's Problem

The deepening of inquiry over the past two decades into processes that mark animals as epistemic agents (as compared to animals considered only

*This work was supported by NIH grants HD 01994, NS 13617 and AM 25814

as biological or physical entities) has brought into sharp focus two
closely related problems which, for historical import, can be labeled
Hume's problem and Bernstein's problem.

An often-voiced and generally agreed upon argument is that there cannot
be a successful theory of psychology (or of physiology for that matter)
which does not include at its core the notion of representation. Representation, however, implies a user--an agent with goals, interests and
comprehension. That is, representation implies some entity--an animal-
analogue--very much like the entity--an animal--that we are attempting
to explain through the mechanism of representation. The infinite regress so enjoined undercuts the possibility of a successful psychology
or physiology. We can summarize the argument as follows: Viable theories
of psychology and physiology require the concept of representation, but
representation implies an animal-analogue which, in turn, implies an infinite regress; therefore, there can be no viable theories of psychology
or physiology (see Dennett, 1978).

There are two responses to this dilemma. One response is to seek a better
understanding of the causal and logical support for psychological and
physiological phenomena, one that renders representation superfluous (see
Gibson, 1979; Kugler, Kelso & Turvey, in press: Shaw and Turvey, in press;
Shaw, Turvey & Mace, in press; Turvey & Shaw, 1979). The other and more
frequent response is to pursue the possibility of self-understanding
representations so that no complete animal-analogue appears in the system.
The latter pursuit defines the problem of the seventeenth-century philosopher David Hume who sought to fashion a psychology on the notion of the
entrainment of ideas through the laws of association. Hume wanted ideas
to think for themselves, as it were.

Bernstein's problem is very much like Hume's problem--the difference is
simply one of emphasis. Whereas Hume focused on phenomena characteristically referred to as mental, Bernstein (1967) focused on movement. His
problem may be stated as follows: How can the very many degrees of freedom of the body be regulated in the course of activity by a minimally intelligent executive intervening minimally? Or, put differently, how can
the degrees of freedom be dissipated systematically at minimal computational cost? Whenever we are trying to understand a complex system we
are prone to attribute some portion, often large, of its intelligent
activity to the intelligence of a controller. That is to say, as theorists we take out a loan on intelligence, principally in the currency of
computational know-how, for the executive component of the system--a loan
that must eventually be repaid if the system is to be fully understood
(Dennett, 1971). Executive intelligence qua computational sophistication
cannot be an unanalyzable residual.

Bernstein's problem can be more readily appreciated by recasting it as a
list of principles to be followed for the problem's resolution: (a) keep
the number of free variables to be individually regulated at a minimum;
(b) keep the number of executive instructions per unit time at a minimum;
(c) keep the number of executive decisions about what kind of instruction
or command to issue at a minimum; (d) keep the number of executive decisions about when to issue an instruction or command at a minimum. The
list is far from exhaustive but it suffices for the present purpose. For
theorists sensitive to Bernstein's problem, the task is to identify a

style of organization that gives adequate realization to these principles and their cognates (Boylls, 1975; Fowler, 1977; Greene, 1972, 1975, 1978; Gurfinkel et al., 1971; Tomović & Bellman, 1970; Tsetlin, 1973; Turvey, 1977; Turvey, Shaw & Mace, 1978).

But there is one terribly important aspect of Bernstein's problem that we can not fail to address if we are to fully appreciate the style of organization that is being sought. It has to do with the definition of "costliness." Bernstein's problem is so stated as to emphasize the algorithmic or computational bases for the controlled dissipation of the body's degrees of freedom. As such the problem could be addressed (although there are strong hints that Bernstein himself did not believe it should) in formal terms, of mathematics and logic, without concern for the actual dynamics of the physico-chemical structure that must embody the solution.

Axiomatically, algorithms as effective procedures must be embodied and one might be satisfied with the claim that the "embodiment" is captured sufficiently by the particulars that define the universal Turing machine. There is a very strong inclination in the contemporary science of epistemic agents to define the costliness of a computation in strictly Turing machine terms--to worry about storage demands, speed, reliability and the like. Indeed one might use such cost variables to determine the tractability of algorithms. Thus, Stockmeyer and Chandra (1979) show that certain computational problems that are algorithmically solvable in principle would require a computer as large as the universe, composed of parts as small as the proton, running for as long as the age of the universe. Needless to say, such algorithms are deemed intractable.

But very little thought is required to appreciate that abstract automata formally equivalent to the Turing machine do not satisfy the natural constraints that must be met by any actual, evolved epistemic agent. (A Turing machine, it must be remembered, is a mathematical not a physical object.) The cost variables imposed on organisms by the laws of physics and biology are quite different from those formally placed on the workings of abstract automata: They are variables that bear no essential relation to the intuitive concept of algorithm for they are, in large part, variables relating to the exchange of energy and matter between an organism and its surroundings (Shaw & McIntyre, 1974).

It should be argued, therefore, that neither the "costliness" referred to in Bernstein's problem nor the solution to the problem can be conceptualized in a purely mathematical or logical vocabulary. Imperatively, the organization of control and coordination that we seek must include physical (read, dynamical) concerns as intrinsic to its style. To include them secondarily, perhaps as adjunct adjustments to purely formal constraints on algorithms, will not be sufficient; for it would assume too arbitrary a relation between an algorithm and the device by which it is executed (Shaw & McIntyre, 1974). Indeed, as the physical basis for control and coordination is better understood, algorithms as explicit logics may no longer be necessary for the resolution of Bernstein's problem.

3. The Primacy of Dynamics

It is a truism that biological processes exhibit order and form but how should

this truism be understood? A time-honored approach is well expressed in
the analogy drawn by Descartes between the body and mechanical gadgets
in which orderly events follow from the careful arrangement of rigid parts
such as levers, weights and wheels. On this machine analogy Descartes
sought to derive the orderly activity of the nervous system from the
anatomical arrangements of the body. Continuous with Descartes' machine
conception--as it has commonly been called (e.g. Kohlers, 1968; von
Bertalanffy, 1973)--are two later-day developments of considerable significance to students of movement, the feedback control systems of cybernetics (where control is based upon preestablished arrangements among
components) and their close relatives, the algorithmic machines of
Artificial Intelligence (where control is based upon preestablished
ordered arrangements of specific instructions).

In opposition to the machine conception is the understanding that it is
tendencies in dynamics--the free interplay of forces and mutual influences among components tending toward equilibrium or steady states--that
are primarily responsible for the order of biological processes. Beautiful examples abound of the form induced by dynamic principles(Thompson,1917;
1942; Stevens, 1974). For example, wherever spherical-like bodies of
uniform size with soft or deformable walls are packed together (so that
actual physical contact occurs at the boundary walls) they settle into
a hexagonal pattern (such as a honeycomb), a pattern in which surface
contact is least and potential energy is minimal. In such hexagonal
tessellation,where boundaries or interfaces are minimized, three-way 120
degree joints occur. But three-way joints arise not only in conditions
of close packing but under conditions of surface tension as with soap
bubbles, cracking as occurs with elastic surfaces such as mud, wrinkling
as occurs with fruits when they dehydrate and expansion as occurs when
buns in close proximity are baked together in the oven. Common to all of
these sources that produce the same pattern is the principle noted,
namely, minimum surfaces or more properly the minimization of work or
energy. It is important to note that the specific means by which the
three-way, 120 degree joint pattern or form is brought into being is not
as significant as how the constituent parts that become patterned relate
among themselves. Put simply, if the parts are free to vary and find
equilibrium, then they will arrange themselves in a configuration of
minimum free energy.

The contrast between the machine conception and the dynamic conception of
biological form and order is far from trivial. Clearly, the questions
emphasized by a student of natural systems and the investigatory procedures adopted are very much influenced by which of the two conceptions
are adhered to. It is true that the machine conception dominates the
interpretation of biological and physiological processes. There are,
however, very good reasons for believing that its application is often
ill-motivated and premature. The possibility that the phenomenon to be
explained is a phenomenon primarily owing to dynamics is often not explored or explored only superficially. In (perhaps larger) part the
favoritism shown the machine conception, particularly in contemporary
science, is due to the seductive fact that processes can be readily
described in formal and quasi-formal languages, languages that are consonant with the machine conception. In (perhaps lesser) part, the favoritism shown the machine conception is due to the fact that dynamics traditionally has been preoccupied with continuous motions in spaces evenly
populated with phase points (that is, with linear, conservative systems)

whereas the problems of biology are expressed as discontinuities in spaces unevenly populated with preferred stabilities (that is, the problems of non-linear, non-conservative systems). The extension of dynamics into the latter domain has been slow but it is gaining in impetus (see below and, for example, Eigen, 1971; Katchalsky & Curran, 1967; Morowitz, 1978; Onsager, 1931; Prigogine & Nicolis, 1971; Soodak & Iberall, 1978).

The allure of the machine conception is especially evident in debates on the role of DNA where a very popular conception is DNA as a program, a set of instructions, which order the epigenetic processes in a particular fashion. But two lines of argument--one that questions the relevancy of the problem conceptualization of DNA and one that questions its tract-ability--show that the allure of this program interpretation in particular and of machine-conception interpretations in general leads to convenient and easily imaged models of process but it does not, necessarily, lead to an understanding of process.

The following in paraphrase is an argument of Goodwin's (1970). The piv-otal points in the epigenetic process are those at which the cell, faced with several reasonable ways to differentiate, must select one. Pre-sumably, on the program notion, at such pivotal points the cell follows a sub-routine which identifies what to do if certain conditions hold. On this notion, therefore, the cell can be construed as computing its own state, examining the DNA program for what it should do next, and then changing state accordingly.

In actuality what goes on in a cell looks quite unlike the process just described. The state transitions that occur appear to arise from the mutual relations among the constituents that define the state of the cell. Goodwin (1970) describes it this way: Suppose that through the catalytic operation of enzyme E_1 two precursor metabolite molecules U and V give rise to a particular metabolite Y. And that through the catalytic opera-tion of enzyme E_2, precursors V and W give rise to metabolite Z. If U, V and E_1 are available in sufficient amounts but either W or E_2 is absent, then Y is formed; if, on the other hand, V, W and E_2 are present simul-taneously in sufficient amounts and either V or E_1 is absent then Z is formed. In this description there is no computation of cell state, no referring to DNA for instructions and no change of state based on instruc-tions. DNA does contribute significantly to epigenesis but in more modest and cooperative (rather than imperative) ways than expressed in the program conception; for example, it can be argued that it is partially responsible for the current state of the cell and that it participates with fellow cellular constitutents in determining the prior rate of synthesis of enzymes and other macromolecules.

Our second argument is from Gould (1970) and Rudwick (1964). The synthe-tic theory of evolution gives more than lip-service to the relation of form and function but it tends to approach form through concepts that are non-morphological such as gene-pool and genetical fitness (Rudwick, 1964). Moreover, the synthetic theory coupled with the machine conception invites one to think in terms of programs as responsible for form, that is to suppose, in the extreme, that each aspect of a complex form is the direct product of an individual genetic instruction. Such a proposal runs into the problem of degrees of freedom as is well recognized by Gould (1970) who, in reference to the form of sea urchins (echinoids) believes it "inconceivable" that each of several hundred echinoid plates, crinoid columnals and radular teeth could be the product of independent genetic commands. Resolution to the degrees of freedom problem in this context is sought in the direction promoted most notably by D'arcy Thompson (1917/

1942) which is to adhere to a strategy which recognizes that <u>physical forces directly influence form and that intricate final products might be fashioned on the basis of relatively simple constraints</u>. Thompson (1917/ 1942) was of the impression that many aspects of form, even as manifest in advanced species, are the direct consequence of physical forces--con- <u>figured according to an underlying geometry of stable arrangements</u>--acting on pliable material. A "curtain" metaphor cited by Gould (1970) is illu- minating: Intricate patterns of folds follow from specifying a few points of suspension.

Those who follow D'Arcy Thompson's thesis in principle, if not in detail, seek to identify either gradients (see Gould & Garwood, 1969 for a review) or a minimal number of rules (e.g. Raup, 1968; Rudwick, 1968), which in the context of freely operating forces will yield complex forms. The gradient approach is nicely captured in an example from Stevens (1976): If a circular slab of clay is depressed more at its periphery than at its center so that it grows faster at its periphery it will form a shallow shell-like structure with an undulating periphery; if depressed more at its center than at its periphery so that it grows faster at its center, it will form a bowl-like structure with a uniform periphery. And with reference to the "rules" perspective, Rudwick (1968) has shown that the odd-looking dorsal valve of the oldhaminid brachiopod (a shelled marine species popularly known as "lamp shells") can be generated by simply fol- lowing the rules: "Keep a minimum distance from other lobes" and "bud a new lobe when the previous one reaches a limiting length related to the shell edge."

While the "gradient" and "rules" perspectives look suspect in the face of developments in qualitative and non-equilibrium dynamics (see below) the thrust of the argument is clear: Biological form is largely due to a free interplay of forces and mutual influences among components and if one wished to persevere with the conception of DNA as program then this argu- ment suggests that the instructions in the program will be few in number and their content relatively simple. But we have already seen, in the pre- ceding argument of Goodwin's (1970), that DNA is understood more properly as constraining--not instructing--the epigenetic process. It is a common characteristic (though, perhaps, not a necessary one) of the machine con- ception that responsibility for the manifest order of a biological or physiological process be ascribed to a single entity. Thus, on this ma- chine conception, the question of why the state transitions in the pheno- type are ordered as they are is answered by saying that it is because the instructions in the DNA are ordered as they are. However, with the em- bracing of biology by dynamics and the appreciation for DNA as a con- straint, it becomes more apparent that the conditions for a biological process are not to be found invested in any single part of any special subset of parts but in the total organization. As Weiss (1961) and Goodwin ·(1970) would put it: The question of "what controls or coordi- nates?" a biological process should be answered with "the whole" rather than "the gene."

The tendency to explain a phenomenon (say, state transitions in the epi- genetic process) by investing the phenomenon in an independent device (say, the sequence of instructions in the DNA program) is in keeping with the style of scientific inquiry that has been dubbed "self-actional" by Dewey and Bentley (1949). The extreme consequence of this style of inquiry is a semantic regress (Shaw & Bransford, 1977)--each distinguishable phenom-

enon has an independent device as its source. The main general consequence is that many phenomena are read as sui generis, that is, they are
conceived as unique and fundamental and not explainable through an appeal
to other principles. But as anticipated above a very different style of
inquiry, dubbed transactional by Dewey and Bentley (1949) and coalitional,
on elaboration, by Shaw and Turvey (in press), is consonant with the
approach taken when a dynamic rather than a machine stance is adopted.
Roughly, this style of inquiry looks at the system in full, emphasizes
the mutuality of its "components," and tries to understand phenomena as
system properties.

The claim on which we are converging, ideally, is this: That the order
in biological and physiological processes is primarily owing to dynamics
and that the constraints that arise, both anatomical and functional,
serve only to channel and guide dynamics; it is not that actions are
caused by constraints it is, rather, that some actions are excluded by
them.

4.   Constraints Rather Than Instructions

The gist of the foregoing can be expressed differently in a way that is
more suited to the purpose of the present section. A formal system
account of a physical system process (qua biological, physiological or
psychological) necessarily requires discrete, serial operations and an
explicit representation of every aspect of the process, both frozen and
fluid. (Of course, a sequence of formalizations ordered in abstraction
can be assumed so that all aspects of the process are not made explicit
at one stage of description but are explicated over a succession of
stages). By way of contrast, in an actual physical system the operations
are mainly those of parallel and coordinated dynamics and many (if not
most) changes need no explicit description since they are taken care of
by the dynamical laws involving real space, time and energy. To paraphrase Pattee (1977), it is in the nature of real systems as opposed to
formal systems that they are necessarily special purpose instantiations
of logical operations which depend on a tacit "measurement" or "computations" process that does not have a detailed description anywhere--with-
in or without the system.

Our intent here is to put into perspective the machine conception of
control-cum-coordination as owing to fixed or relatively fixed instructional arrangements. In so doing we will highlight the contrast--touched
upon above--between constraints and programs,or synonymously,between what
might be termed declarative languages and imperative languages (Steele &
Sussman, 1978).

The coalitional style of inquiry advocated by Shaw and Turvey (in press)
claims that any naturally evolved system is comprised of two logically
dependent   components, the operational component (say, an organism) and
its context of constraint (say, the econiche), and that any explication
of systemic phenomena must be coordinated over four, mutually constrained
and closed, grains of analysis in the sense that no grain and neither
component is disproportionately accredited with responsibility for the
phenomenon. Crudely, the grains (from higher to lower) are the basis
grain, consisting of the dimensions or variables over which the system
is defined; the relation grain, consisting of the relations among the
variables; the order grain, consisting of the orderings that the vari-

ables take; and the value grain, consisting of the actual values that the
variables assume. Whenever explanation is not inclusive of all four
grains and not respectful of the mutualities among them, then the grain on
which explanation primarily rests tends to burgeon in the detail and in
the semantic richness required of its predicates. In particular, to fixate on a lower grain such as the order grain is to encourage more explanatory principles sui generis at the value grain than are scientifically
desirable [This reiterates in different form a major point of the preceding section; for a more elaborate discussion see Dewey & Bentley
(1949) and Shaw & Turvey (in press)].

We can now be more precise in our characterization of the formal machine
conception of order and form in biology: It emphasizes the order-grain to
the virtual exclusion of the grains above it. This is similarly true of
the control theory that is often applied to matters of biology. It assumes a value (with sui generis status) that defines a desired state of
affairs and then specifies how that value is achieved through an ordering
of commands. In the words of Yates, Marsh and Iberall (1973), modern control theory gives undue emphasis to the communication or small signal
aspects and ignores the "plant processes"--the high-power,energy converting machinery. The same criticism has been voiced, more particularly, for
popular accounts of hunger control (Friedman and Stricker, 1976), and
thermoregulation (e.g. Werner, 1977).

It is not a matter of happenstance that the machine conception of order
and form in biology is fixated at the order grain. Consonant with the
formal system approach referred to above, the currently popular programming languages are designed for expressing algorithms--that is to say,
they are languages of unidirectional computation in which the flow of information through the network is explicitly organized. Programming
languages with this characteristic may be labeled "imperative" languages
(Steele & Sussman, 1978). An imperative language, it seems to us, informs
an interpretation of control that is (i) logically deep in von Neumann's
(1959) sense of many formal mediating steps; (ii) separate from that which
is controlled. (Thus, in computers the "how" of computation is separate
from that which performs the computation; in control theory, the command-
algorithm is separate from the power flux that it modulates; in the neurophysiology of movement, the central nervous system as controller is held
conceptually separate from the skeletomuscular apparatus that performs the
movement); (iii) conceptually indistinct from coordination in that to explicitly organize the ordering of variables is to make "control" self-
sufficient and "coordination" redundant.

We began this section by remarking on the fact that in real physical
systems as contrasted with formal systems, explicit description of most of
the changes that transpire would be superfluous given the contribution of
dynamics. This fact, in and of itself, undercuts the relevance of imperative languages for systemic phenomena. In addition we registered our mis-
givings with explaining systemic phenomena at a single and lower grain of
analysis; not surprisingly, therefore, in our eyes any explanation fixated at the order grain of analysis must be suspect. There are two minimal
requirements for moving in the direction of a more adequate account of systemic phenomena--include a dynamic vocabulary and, relatedly, extend explanation to higher grains of analysis. The inclusion of the vocabulary
of equations of constraint and the concommitant extension to the relation-
grain of analysis reduces the detail and changes the semantic content of

the order grain. To anticipate, what emerges is a concept of control that
is: (i) logically less deep; (ii) less obviously segregated from that which
is controlled; and (iii) conceptually distinguishable from coordination.

5. Equations of Constraint

Consider a system of m independent dimensions. To define the position of
any one element within the system would require m coordinates; and if the
system were composed of n elements then a total of mn coordinates would be
needed to describe the system. The system would be said to have mn degrees
of freedom. If relations are now defined over the dimensions so that the
position of any one individual element must respect the positions of other
elements, then the number of coordinates needed to describe the system of
elements would be reduced. These relations--termed equations of con-
straint--reduce the degrees of freedom of a system according to the general
rule mn-c where c is the number of such equations.

How should equations of constraint be interpreted? The nature and origin
of constraints in biology are deep problems that only recently have been
carefully articulated (see Pattee, 1970, 1971, 1973, 1977). A full treatment of these problems cannot be given here but some important insights
can be distilled. As conventionally distinguished there are two types of
constraint--(relatively) time independent and (relatively) time dependent.
Pipes through which water flows exemplify the first type of constraint--
pipes permanently eliminate the motion of water perpendicular to the direction of flow. The second type, the time dependent, is the more interesting. Where an entity has the option of many alternative configurations or
trajectories--such as the cell in differentiating--then we speak of a time-
dependent, non-holonomic constraint that effectively selects one trajectory from among the virtual trajectories.

A constraint must have some distinguishable physical embodiment which means
that it is at one and the same time obedient to fundamental dynamical laws
and a constraint on them. If the degrees of freedom of the physical embodiment of a constraint were evaluated in microscopic detail they would
be seen to follow the same deterministic dynamical laws as the degrees of
freedom that the constraint is said to be selectively influencing. This
line of argument leads to an important understanding about constraints:
Constraints are distinct from the degrees of freedom they modulate _only_
in the sense that they are _alternative descriptions_ of those degrees of
freedom. This, in turn, leads to a further important understanding: If
the alternative description is to be distinct then it cannot be redundant,
that is, it cannot be simply an equivalent description of the dynamic details; and since it cannot be, most obviously, a more detailed description,
it must be a _less_ detailed description. For Pattee (e.g., 1973) the usefulness of a constraint is that it capitalizes on the dynamical context without including a description of that context. In the very simplicity of alternative descriptions resides their potential for selectively manipulating
complex dynamics. Thus--returning to DNA--as an alternative description
DNA is sparse in detail compared to the detail of the dynamics of epigenesis. DNA is "mute" on the tens-of-thousands of interacting degrees of
freedom that are involved in the structuring of amino acids and their manner of folding and operating as a rate-controlling enzyme (Pattee, 1977).

How do constraints arise spontaneously? It is useful to distinguish two
forms of this question. In one form we ask how definite structures or

regularities arise in physical systems that are initially homogeneous. In the other form we ask how it is possible for new dynamical restraints to originate in a physical system (at any scale) when the system's present state variables and dynamical equations completely determine the system's future state variables. A response to either form of the question must rest with an appreciation of the general nature of nonequilibrium systems.

6. Open Systems and Scaling Effects

Classical, equilibrium-oriented thermodynamics predicts that in isolated closed systems (that is, systems which exchange neither energy nor matter with their surroundings) things will run down to a state of maximum disorder, zero information, and loss of the ability to do work (cf. Bridgeman, 1941). This state is entropic equilibrium, and once in this state nothing new can emerge as long as the system remains isolated and closed. At this state the thermodynamic analysis is complete. The reversible quality of these systems is evident in the fact that if a perturbation occurs to the system at this state, the system responds by going through a succession of states, all of which are at entropic equilibrium. In short, the entire event occurs in a state space in which all points in the space are homogeneous with respect to entropic equilibrium. Each point in the space may be said to exhibit terminal point-stability or statically-stable stability. The concept of reversibility is reflected by the fact that there are no preferred points in the entropic state space: states may reverse themselves and still maintain entropic equilibrium. While some real events (such as very slow processes in the macroworld) are rather well described by classical equilibrium thermodynamics, most interesting events regarding living system are not among them.

An open system is markedly distinct from isolated closed systems in that it need not tend toward a state of thermodynamic equilibrium but more generally tends toward a steady state displaced from equilibrium (meaning that it has potential energy) that is maintained by a continual flow of free energy and matter into and out of the operational component of the system. Our reason for the tentative wording ("need not," "generally tends toward") in the preceding is to underscore the important fact that being an open system is not of itself sufficient to guarantee the critical property of biological systems that we are trying to understand, namely, the increasing order (lowering of entropy) or the appearance of new regularities (equations of constraint). A small temperature or concentration difference maintained across the operational component of an open system renders the system only slightly out of equilibrium and its tendency is to move as close as possible to maximum entropy, that is, away from structuralization. It is only when an open system is driven far from equilibrium that the spontaneous appearance of new structure and new organization becomes possible; a possibility that is realized if one further requirement is met--that nonlinearities be manifest in the relations among system components (Haken, 1977; Prigogine & Nicolis, 1971).

The emergence of (new) structure follows a set pattern. When the flux of energy and matter across the boundaries of the operational component of a system is low, the component is stable. However, when the flux is high and in excess of a critical value, the previous stability gives way to instability. Some of the fluctuations that were damped at the lower flux are amplified at the higher flux and carry or "enslave" the component as a whole to determine a new stability (Haken, 1977; Prigogine & Nicolis,

1971; Prigogine, Nicolis & Babloyantz, 1972). There are several fashionable examples of instability prefatory to a new structure or organization.

The Bénard or convection instability is manifest in a situation in which a
fluid layer is heated from below and kept as a fixed temperature above so
as to create a temperature gradient in opposition to the effects of gravitational force. At small values of this gradient heat is transported from
lower to upper regions by conduction and macroscopic motion is absent.
Random thermal motions of the molecules and a damping of convection currents characterize the state of the fluid. However, when the gradient
exceeds a critical value a convective, macroscopic motion occurs generally in the form of rolls or hexagons (for variations see Koschmeider,
1977). In short, out of an initial state that is completely homogeneous
there arises a well-ordered spatial pattern. Moreover, with further increases in the gradient the spatial pattern becomes oscillatory.

The Taylor instability, similarly a fluid phenomenon, is manifest in a
situation in which water is enclosed between two cylinders that can be
rotated in opposite directions. At rotation speeds below a critical value
the fluid flow is laminar; above that value the flow becomes turbulent
progressing toward stable, organized vortices.

The solid state laser provides a further example. Energy is pumped into a
rod of material in which specific atoms are embedded and at the two end-
faces of which are positioned mirrors. At small energy fluxes the laser
operates as a lamp--the atoms emit light wave tracks independently of each
other. When the energy flux exceeds a critical value, all the atoms oscillate in phase emitting a single and very large wave track of light.

In these examples we see that with a change of scale macroscopic structure
arises from a homogeneous state of affairs or from a state of affairs of
lesser structure. A new stability that arises beyond a critical scale
value may in turn give way to a further, different stability at higher
scale values. In both the Bénard and Taylor situations, at supercritical
values periodic pulsing characterizes the newer stabilities that replace
those that appear at the critical value. One might conjecture that the
origin of constraints--beginning as it must with low selectivity and imprecise function and gradually sharpening up to high specificity and narrow precise function (Pattee, 1973)--is interpretable, in part, as a
succession of instabilities (Prigogine & Nicolis, 1971).

At all events, as a tentative response to the question posed above we can
offer the proposal of Yates, Marsh and Iberall (1972) that at whatever
scale we choose to observe nature, new constraints or regularities arise
from an apparent continuum of "atomistic" particulars as a result of interactions among the particulars, constraints and a scale change in some
parameter.

7. Essential and Nonessential Variables

Following Gel'fand and Tsetlin (1962, 1971), it can be assumed that
the variables functionally linked by an equation of constraint or by
a system of such equations can be partitioned into two classes: Essential variables which determine the function's topological qualities
and nonessential variables which bring about marked changes in the value
of the function but which leave the topological qualities of the function unaltered. Importantly, the classification of variables into

essential and nonessential is not necessarily fixed--outside a range of
magnitudes a nonessential variable may become essential and vice versa
(see below). For Pattee, equations of constraint and the classification
of variables into essential and nonessential are lumped together as "control". Our intuition is that it is more prudent to dissociate the two.
We identify the classification of variables with control and the equations
of constraint with coordination. To conserve the topological qualities of
the relation enforced by a constraint requires that the essential variables
be kept fixed and to introduce variation in these qualities without
annihilating them requires that only the nonessential variables be changed.
Here then is the rationalization for the coordination/control distinction:
A constraint "coordinates" in the sense that it enforces (automatically)
a relationship among several variables; the partitioning into essential
and nonessential variables "controls" in the sense that it identifies the
means by which the relationship can be systematically modified--qualita-
tively and quantitatively.

8.   The Content of the Order Grain

To emphasize constraints and, therefore, to extend analysis to the relation grain is to farm out the causal responsibility that was exclusive
to the order grain. What consequences does this have for the order grain
of analysis? Recall the program conception of cellular state transitions;
basically, check with DNA for what to do when the state of the cell is
such-and-such. The program conception of DNA fixates the explanation of
the epigenetic process at the order grain and requires, therefore, that
the order grain be explicit on the type of state the cell is to assume and
the point in a temporal sequence at which it is to assume that state. In
raising the explanation to the relation grain (that is, the conception of
DNA as constraint) the preceding evaluation of the order grain is rendered inaccurate; the predicates of the order grain vis a vis the epigenetic
process can refer neither to systemic states nor to the order in which
they are to occur.

In terms of the distinction just drawn between coordination and control,
the relation grain is synonymous with coordination and the order grain is
synonymous with control. By this synonymity, the predicates of the order
grain are now semantically less fanciful referring only--at least under
the present analysis--to the classification of variables; and control is
logically less deep referring principally to changes in variables that
selectively influence functional dependencies automatically enforced at
the relation grain. These conceptual modifications, though roughly expressed, are consistent with the thrust of the coalitional style of inquiry which is to understand how systemic states and their order are not
explicitly represented as a priori facts of the system but rather arise,
from the mutualities among the grains, as necessary a posteriori facts
(Kripke, 1971) of the system.

Non-equilibrium phenomena of the kind described above hint at one way in
which systemic states may occur as necessary a posteriori facts without
an a priori, explicit description. Put differently, they hint at how an
organization or regularity can arise from within a system rather than
being imposed upon it (cf. Fitch & Turvey, 1978). (To reiterate, on the
machine conception of biological order, with its attachment to imperative
languages and its fixation at the order grain of analysis, organization
or regularity is more properly said to be owing to an agent or device that

is outside the system exhibiting the said organization or regularity.)
The point can be made in reference to a mammalian behavior. The stable
states of quadruped locomotion at low velocities have in common an asymmetry of limbs of the same girdle--they are always half a period out of
phase. At high velocities the stable states of quadruped locomotion are
characterized by an in-phase relation of limbs of the same girdle
(Grillner, 1975). The transition from an asymmetric gait to a symmetric
gait tends to occur abruptly (Shik & Orlovskii, 1976). It need not be
supposed that the differences among gaits are the effects of differences
among programs of instructions which prescribe the kinematic details.
The different gaits might well be interpreted as those quadruped stabilities, few in number (cf. Thom, 1975), that can arise pursuant to the
instabilities wrought by scaling up muscle power.

The general point is that locomotory patterns are to be explained by an
appeal to the concepts and tools that constitute non-equilibrium dynamics such as stability theory, bifurcation theory and fluctuation theory
(Haken, 1977; Landauer, 1978; Prigogine, Nicolis, Herman and Lam, 1975;
Thom, 1975) rather than by an appeal to formal programs of instructions.
This general point is illustrated all the more forcefully by the facts of
centipede locomotion. Thus, <u>Lithobius</u> (which normally moves its legs in
waves with adjacent legs out of phase by one-seventh of a step) displays
the asymmetric gaits of quadrupeds when all but two pairs of legs are
amputated indifferent to the number of segments separating the pairs.
Similarly, <u>Lithobius</u> displays the gaits of six-legged insects when all
but three pairs of legs are amputated (von Holst, 1973).

9. Dissipative Structures and Cyclicity

An open system with nonlinearities that is maintained far from equilibrium
is referred to as a "dissipative structure" (Prigogine and Nicolis, 1971).
Simply, such structures conserve stability at the price of energy dissipation and, therefore, contrast with the classical entities of equilibrium
thermodynamics which conserve energy and exhibit point or statical stability. What kind of stability do dissipative structures conserve? We
ought to expect the form of the answer to be suggested by living systems
so to them we turn for clues.

Consider two observations: Intracellular replication involves a (causal)
cycle of events--DNA-->RNA-->Protein-->DNA; the behavior of bacteria in a
life supporting medium is similarly cyclical--the bacteria grow and divide
repetitively. Neither observation is especially exotic. Cyclicity
appears to characterize many aspects of organismic behavior (Iberall, 1970;
1978). It was perhaps Goodwin (1963, 1970), who first took seriously the
understanding that biological systems belong to a class of systems that are
not stable in the classical point-stability sense but stable in relation
to a closed cycle of events. On elaboration this understanding leads to
a general principle, namely, that (the only) stability for a nonlinear
system whose processes degrade large amounts of free energy is a <u>dynamic
stability consisting of periodicities or cycles</u> (Minorski, 1962; Yates,
Marsh & Iberall, 1972).

To what kind of periodicity or cycle is the stability of dissipative structures referred? Consider the familiar mass-spring system in which the
moving mass is in contact with a non-ideal surface. It is a system that
exchanges energy among potential, inertial and frictional processes as it

displaces and it is a system that oscillates when certain relations hold
among these dissipative processes. It is commonly represented by the
linear, second-order equation:

$$M\ddot{x} + K\dot{x} + Sx = 0$$

where M is mass, K is the frictional coefficient, S is the stiffness coefficient and x is the displacement. More generally speaking, the equation is a representation of a decay or relaxation process; that is, it
expresses the fact that the system does not persist in doing what it is
doing (here, in this particular case, periodic displacing). For our mass-
spring system to persist in doing what it is doing, and, therefore, for
it to be more analogous to living forms, we would need to introduce a
forcing function, F(t). The above equation, so modified, then reads:

$$M\ddot{x} + K\dot{x} + Sx = F(t)$$

In the modified equation we have a component that can oscillate (represented by the left hand side) and our desire is to provide a means for its
continued oscillation. To this end a continuous forcing function is introduced. The problem now, however, is to identify a further mechanism,
one that guarantees the persistence of the forcing function. Other than
pursuing a strategy that mitigrates thermodynamic law, the provision of
a source of persistence for F(t) is doomed to infinite regression. For
it goes without saying that the forcing function does work and by thermodynamic law one cannot get something for nothing. The regress is avoided by letting energy be available in a constant, relatively "timeless"
manner and by letting the work accomplished by the constant energy source
be occasional (rather than continuous) and determined by the oscillatory
component. This is tantamount to letting the left hand side of the above
equation determine the form of the right hand side; that is, to the equating of persistent- or self-oscillation with a forced oscillation that is
produced by a force which depends on the nature of the self-oscillation
(cf. Andronow & Chaiken, 1949).

Consider the nature of clocks--periodic mechanisms with sustained oscillations. The three defining components of a clock are: (i) an oscillatory
component, for simplicity, a pendulum; (ii) a (continuous, for our purposes)
source of potential energy such as hanging weights or a wound spring; and
(iii) a device--an escapement--that correlates (i) and (ii). In a pendulum
clock the escapement is usually composed of two parts: an escape wheel with
teeth that is lined by a wheel train to the energy source and an oscillatory component linked with the pendulum and carrying two projections, called pallets, that engage alternatively with the teeth of the escape wheel.
At certain positions of the pendulum the wheel is allowed to escape (hence,
"escapement") through a distance (or pitch) of one tooth. The release of
the escapement wheel allows the hanging weights to descend a small distance
or the coiled spring to uncoil slightly thus converting a small amount of
potential energy into kinetic energy which is then "squirted," via the pallets, into the pendulum to keep it swinging. Generally, and ideally, the
release of the escapement and the consequent "squirting" occur close to the
pendulum's equilibrium point, that is where its kinetic energy is greatest.
The important feature of the clock, therefore, is that the periodic tapping of energy to sustain the clock's oscillation (its ticking) depends
solely on the position of the pendulum and not on time per se. In the
foregoing sense Yates and Iberall (1973) offer the construal of a

living system as an ensemble of "squirt" systems where the "squirtings" are made possible by degrading a good deal more free energy than is degraded in the drift toward equilibrium.

Our discussion has brought us to the following point: The stability of biological systems is in reference to cycles that are self-sustaining, non-conservative and non-linear. Cycles that meet these criteria are referred to as limit-cycles and among their important properties are numbered a tendency to a fixed amplitude and frequency no matter how disturbed, a tendency not to increase in amplitude when driven at their preferred frequency (that is, they are non-resonant) and a tendency to mutually entrain or synchronize (see Minorski, 1962; Oatley and Goodwin, 1971; Winfree, 1967).

In the foregoing remarks we have, in short, the motivation in many corners of contemporary theoretical biology for conceptualizing living systems, their component subsystems and their characteristic processes as ensembles of coupled and mutually entrained nonlinear oscillators, precisely, limit-cycles (Goodwin, 1970; Iberall, 1969; Nicolis & Prigogine, 1978; Walter, 1972; Yates, in press).

10.   Coordinative Structures as Dissipative Structures

Let us now collect these arguments with reference to Bernstein's problem It can be argued--and it has been by Bernstein and those who have pursued his point of view--that the problem of degrees of freedom is resolved in large part by a systematic linking together of muscles in such a manner that the set of individual muscles is reduced to a much smaller set of muscle collectives (e.g. Gelfand et al., 1971; Turvey, 1977). A muscle linkage or a coordinative structure, as we have come to call it (Kelso, Southard & Goodman, 1979; Kugler & Turvey, in press; Turvey, Shaw & Mace, 1978), following from, but different from Easton's (1972, 1978) original usage, may be given a slightly more precise definition: It is a group of muscles often spanning a number of joints that is constrained to act as a single functional unit.

A coordinative structure is an organization defined over a relative continuum of "atomistic" particulars--individual muscles. Thus, the contractile states of the extensor muscles at ankle, knee and hip can very independently of each other but they are, in the act of locomotion, so organized as to preserve a constant proportionality across variations in their individual values (Grillner, 1975; Shik & Orlovskii, 1976). This organization does not express a state of equilibrium maintained without effort but rather it expresses a (marginally) stable steady-state maintained by a flux of energy, that is, by metabolic processes that degrade more free energy than the drift toward equilibrium. In short, a coordinative structure is a "squirt" system or dissipative structure; it is, in Iberall's (1977) terms, a thermodynamic engine that draws energy from a high potential source, rejects some to a lower potential energy sink and does work in a periodic, limit-cycle fashion.

Above we described the clock as epitomizing squirt systems. Here we pursue that example in order to buttress the equating of coordinative structure and dissipative structure. As noted, the specifications of a clock's oscillatory component and escapement (for example, length of pendulum, pitch of escapement wheel) determine when the oscillatory component will be squirted with energy and the <u>duration</u> of a squirt. (Recall that the timing of squirts relates to the design specifications in a principled way, precisely, they are phased so that the resulting forcing function exactly offsets the energy loss averaged over each cycle.) It is also the case that the specifications of the oscillatory component and escapement determine the <u>amount</u> of an energy squirt. Owing to the linkage between the escapement wheel and the potential energy source, the degree of rotation of the escapement wheel per escape determines the distance through which the hanging weights descend or the amount by which the coiled spring uncoils. That is, the design specifications determine how much of the available potential energy is converted, pursuant to an escape, to kinetic energy.

Of course, as the hanging weights approach ground level or as the spring becomes more unwound the magnitude of the available potential energy will decrease and, in consequence, so should the magnitude of the sustaining pulses of kinetic energy. In the manufacturing of clocks precautions are taken (via contrivances) to insure that the tapping of potential energy yields constant injections of kinetic energy. For our purposes, however, we wish to consider the case where such precautionary measures are absent. That is to say, we wish to consider the kind of clock in which the <u>absolute</u> amount of kinetic energy injected into the oscillatory component varies with the <u>absolute</u> amount of potential energy that is made available for work. Our motive for introducing this caveat is to facilitate the parallelism between clocks and coordinative structures. The latter, necessarily, feed on a power source that is variable. Thus, the step cycles of locomotion partake of the energy released by the noradrenergic system; as this power source is scaled upwards the speed of locomotion increases.

Now in a clock where the magnitude of injected kinetic energy is sensitive to scale changes in the power supply we can expect the velocity and amplitude of the oscillatory component's motions to be likewise sensitive and to reflect these scale changes.

The design specifications, however, guarantee that certain features of the clock's behavior will hold invariant over increases and decreases in power. Thus, the timing and duration of squirts will be independent of their magnitude and will remain roughly the same relative to the time frame--here, a period of oscillation. Moreover, the magnitude of a squirt will be some fixed proportion of the magnitude of the power supply--the potential energy stored in the weights or spring.

The constraint on the dynamics of individual muscles and joints composing a coordinative structure can be likened to the design specifications of the clock's oscillatory component and escapement. And the chemical energy liberated to be used for maintaining the constraint can be likened to the clock's source of potential energy. On this metaphor, <u>a coordinative structure is an autonomous system in the conventional mathematical sense that the forcing function is not explicitly dependent on time</u>. The "timing" of impulses does not require a separate device but arises necessarily from the design specifications--the equations of constraint--of the muscle collective. The significance of the latter to Bernstein's problem is obvious.

The equation of coordinative structures and self-sustaining, thermodynamically real oscillators (such as clocks) has been established to this point solely on rational grounds. As we shall see, however, the equation is befitting the empirical results and provides a principled reason for them. The essence of the scale independencies just noted for the clock is that the form of the forcing function is logically independent of the power supply; and it is this very distinction which appears to mark the behavior of a group of muscles constrained to act as a functional unit.

In freely locomoting cats, increases in velocity result from increases in the absolute magnitude of muscle activity during the E3 phase (see Grillner, 1975) but these increases are not accompanied by changes in the timing of muscle activity relative to the step cycle (Engberg & Lundberg, 1969). Moreover, the scaling upwards of the electromyographic activity seems to grade evenly over the extensors so that fixed ratios of activity are maintained. With regard to postural maintenance, Nashner (1977) has observed that over wide variations in upright posture brought about by rotation of the ankles, the ratios and sequencing of electromyographic activity in the muscles of the ankle, knee and hip remain fixed. For movements of the forearm inertial variation seems not to affect the timing of activity in the agonist-antagonist synergy while pronouncedly influencing the overall magnitude of activity (Lestienne, 1979). Similarly, increases in stress and rate of speaking bring about changes in magnitude of electromyographic activity without altering the temporal relationship between onset of tongue body muscles (genioglossus) and offset of lip gesture (orbicularis oris group) (Harris, personal communication).

Taking a kinematic rather than electromyographic perspective there is the well-established feature of cursive handwriting that the timing of strokes remains fixed over changes in letter size and unexpected increases in friction between pen and paper (cf. Hollerbach, 1978; Denier van der Gon & Thuring, 1965). In like vein, following full-mouth tooth extraction and complete removal of the alveolar ridge speakers maintain transition time constant for lingual palatal contact for /t/ in the word /thats/ in spite of displacement and velocity changes in jaw and tongue tip (Zimmerman, Kelso & Lander, in press). Similarly, the timing relations of the upper limbs during the performance of a task involving different spatial demands remains invariant over changes in the magnitude of force produced by each limb (Kelso, et al., 1979a,b). Finally it is commonplace for the frequency of a movement to remain fixed over scale changes in the forces applied. Thus, insect flight is generally regulated through changes in the amplitude of wing beat with frequency of wing beat held invariant (see Srinivasan, 1977). Similarly, if a fish has to drag a load during swimming it will increase movement amplitude and thereby the force produced while maintaining the same frequency of undulatory motion (Webb, 1971).

In sum, a dissociation of power and timing and a fixed proportioning of activity characterize a set of relatively independent muscles that appear to be bound together, temporarily, as a unit. By the arguments given here these properties of a muscle collective are by no means exotic and arbitrary. They are, to the contrary, the necessary concomitants of a (universal?) thermodynamic design principle for autonomous systems. The ingredients of autonomy, as we have seen, are a time independent source of potential energy and a time-independent means that transforms that energy and does work in a periodic fashion. Given these ingredients, we might suppose, in the spirit of Thompson (1917/1942), Rashevsky (1950) and Thom

(1975) (see Kugler, Kelso & Turvey, in press), that there are relatively
few stable recipes. Thus self-sustaining devices can distinguish in many
ways materially (consider, for example, the material distinctions between
a grandfather clock and a coordinative structure) but they can distinguish
in very few ways functionally, if at all. The clock example, therefore,
should be viewed as exemplifying a function (common to both clocks and
coordinative structures) rather than as exemplifying a mechanism.

From the perspective of Bernstein's problem, designing locomotion in terms
of coupled limit cycle oscillators presents a distinct advantage. The
property to be underlined here is that of the mutual synchronization of
interacting limit cycle oscillators; mutual synchronization--entrainment--
is not possible for oscillators of the more familiar kind, namely, linear
harmonic oscillators. A fairly convincing argument can be made that in
locomotion the individual limbs function as distinct coordinative structures (Shik & Orlovskii, 1976) which, by the identity above, means distinct limit cycle oscillators. If a quadruped is locomoting in a given
gait and one of its limbs--for whatever reason--is momentarily perturbed
then (as long as the perturbation is not too extreme so as to precipitate
falling) the mutual entrainment of the limbs qua limit cycle oscillators
would restore the phase relations that preceded the perturbation. More
generally, mutual entrainment would guarantee the preservation of a gait
over that range of velocities (or muscle power) for which it is a stable
quadruped state. Of course, we can easily imagine the preservation of
gait to be owing to processes that iteratively refer to a set point or a
collection of set points. The elegant analysis of Shik and Orlovskii
(1965) is interpretable in such control theory terms (Fowler & Turvey,
1976).   However, we have given reasons for preferring explanatory principles which allow organization and regulation as necessary a posteriori
facts and which avoid attributing sui generis status to variables at the
value grain. Set points or reference signals, as noted, necessarily
assume sui generis status in control theory. There are a goodly number
of other rhythmic behavioral phenomena that appear to call out for interpretation in terms of coupled limit cycle oscillators. Many have been
reported by von Holst (1973) and their significance has not gone unnoticed
(e.g. Stein, 1977).

Let us proceed therefore to explore the thesis that where a group of muscles functions as a single, coherent unit it is a limit cycle oscillator.
And that limit cycle oscillation, characteristic as it is of dissipative
structures, identifies the model construct that we seek.

Limit cycle oscillation, by definition, arises in the context of nonlinearities and it will prove beneficial to our understanding of control
and coordination to dwell on the important distinction between linearity
and nonlinearity in systemic behavior. This distinction is a natural
extension of that drawn above between nonessential and essential variables.
We will in what follows identify linear with nonessential and nonlinear
with essential. These identities are somewhat eccentric but they permit
us to make the points we wish to make as well as indexing our current
(journeyman) understanding of the issues involved in the contrasting of
linear and nonlinear systems.

11. Linearity and nonlinearity

Let us begin with the notion of stability. Dynamical systems are modelled

as "systems" of differential equations. The solution to a differential
equation is, of course, not a number or set of numbers but a family of
functions. To study differential equations one proceeds along two routes,
the quantitative and the qualitative, with the latter the only course of
study for those equations--usually the most interesting--that resist
quantitative analysis. In pursuing the qualitative or geometric route
(first promoted by Poincaré) what becomes important is the phase portrait,
a study of the geometrical or structural characterization of the trajectories representing the range of solution graphs. The phase portrait permits the identification of qualitative properties of dynamical systems as
modeled by differential equations, for example, periodicities, equilibria
(as singular points), types of stable regions etc. One definition of
structural stability (cf. Andronov & Chaikin, 1949; Thom, 1970) follows:
A differential equation or a system of differential equations that is
structurally stable preserves the qualitative or topological characteristics of its entire phase portrait in the face of variations in its parameters. [See, however, Berlinski (1977) for an informed evaluation of
the stability concept.]

In the light of the foregoing, consider the linear harmonic oscillator
modeled by the equation given above, namely:

$$M\ddot{x} + K\dot{x} + Sx = 0$$

This system is structurally neutral in that a change in a dissipative
parameter may bring about marked changes in the topology of the system's
dynamical character. For example, in the absence of friction, solutions
are periodic; with friction solutions approach zero or infinity depending
on the parameter value. By contrast, in a system with nonlinearities such
as expressed by the celebrated van der Pol equation:

$$\ddot{x} - K(1 - x^2)\ \dot{x} + x - 0$$

for all positive values of the dissipative parameter K there is a topologically invariant limit cycle solution. A nonlinear system tends to be
structurally stable.

Speaking informally, a linear system is structurally neutral in the sense
that it has no preferred solution or set of solutions. The situation resembles that of a billiard ball on a smooth billard table--the ball will
remain at rest wherever it is placed. The phase space through which the
trajectories of a linear system are moved by varying the parameters is a
space that is flat and smooth like the billiard table--any location is as
good as any other. That is to say, the phase space can be populated evenly with trajectories; there are no locations, no attractor points, where
the trajectories become especially and consistently dense.

By way of contrast, and again speaking informally, a nonlinear system is
structurally stable in the sense that it has a preferred solution or set
of solutions. The trajectories of a nonlinear system move in a phase
space which is not flat and smooth but wrinkled and indented with attractor points or sets, like limit cycles, on which the trajectories consistently converge.

There is, importantly, a positive reading to be given to the structural
instability of a linear system: A different behavior follows from a

different setting of the system's parameters. The simple mass-spring
system is a topical illustration of this characteristic; the length at
which the spring equilibrates following a displacement is not fixed but
varies systematically with variations in mass, stiffness and friction.
One might say that a linear system exhibits a certain kind of precision
and a certain kind of flexibility in the sense that its behavior reflects
its parameterization. We wish to make something of this point--that a
linear system buys into precision and flexibility at the cost of structural stability in contrast to a nonlinear system which buys into structural stability at the cost of precision and flexibility.

The preceding has emphasized how a change in some aspect of a linear differential equation or a set of such equations affects the global topology
of its solution space. Let us now focus on the nature of the individual
trajectories in the solution space. It is standard procedure to treat
systems of linear differential equations in terms of linear transformations between two vector spaces and it is in this context, of abstract
vector spaces, that linearity as a concept is best appreciated. In the
mapping from one vector space to another, from "input" to "output," a
linear system possesses two defining properties: Superposition and proportionality. By superposition is meant that if several inputs are simultaneously applied to the system, their total effect is the same as that
resulting from the superposition of individual effects acting on each
input separately; in linear theory terms, $L(X_1 + X_2 \ldots + X_n) = L(X_1) +$
$L(X_2) + \ldots + L(X_n)$. And by proportionality is meant that if all the
inputs to a system are multiplied by the same factor, then the responses
are multiplied by the same factor; in linear theory terms, $L(\alpha X_1, \alpha X_2$
$\ldots \alpha X_n) = \alpha L(X_1, X_2 \ldots X_n)$. In brief, for a linear system there is
always a tight or "precise" coupling of input to output. The degrees of
freedom captured in the input are preserved in the output. This fundamental feature of a linear system is consonant with the phase space-as-
billiard table analogy--to paraphrase, for a linear system there are no
preferred outputs.

Neither proportionality nor superposition are properties of a nonlinear
system and this is consonant with the inhomegeneity of the phase space of
a nonlinear system. Because there are attractor points or sets identifying preferred outputs, the mapping from input to output by a nonlinear
system is many-to-one (more generally, many-to-few) in comparison to the
one-to-one mapping of linear systems. A nonlinear system is "imprecise"
in that it does not preserve at output the degrees of freedom at input.

To summarize, we have understood two major distinctions between linear and
nonlinear systems, namely, that they distinguish in their sensitivity to
parameter changes and in their coupling of inputs to outputs. It remains
for us to make one final but important point. The behavior of a nonlinear
system may be dramatically altered by the introduction of certain inputs
(defined in terms of amplitude or type of frequency) at certain times
(defined in terms of phase relationships). Thus at critical times an input with criterial properties may bring about a jump from one preferred
output or stability to another. Occasionally, therefore, a nonlinear system will appear to be closely coupled to its input when in fact there is
marked independence.

12. Essential and nonessential variables revisted

It is unquestionable that the dynamical systems of interest to biology involve nonlinearities; complexity begets nonlinearity, as Berlinski (1977) remarks and nonlinearity begets autonomy, as Prigogine (Prigogine & Nicolis, 1971; Prigogine, 1976) and Haken (1977) underscore. The fact of nonlinearity in the control and coordination of movement is duly recognized by the equating of coordinative structures with dissipative structures. However, if systems of muscles are necessarily nonlinear then are we not faced by a paradox? In the senses detailed above, a nonlinear system is stable but not precise whereas the activity of an animal in reference to its surroundings seems to demand a measure of both stability and precision.

If the periodicities of locomotion, the wavelike excursions in the successive joint changes within a limb and between limbs (see Arshavskii et al., 1965), were affected by slight variations in dissipative parameters than the integrity of locomotion as an act would be easily infirmed. As it is, the locomotory pattern is largely immune to wide variations in frictional forces, supplied by surface and by medium, and in the mass that is transported. In the extreme, cats swim as they walk (Miller, van der Burg & van der Meche, 1975), amphibious newts undulate identically in water and on land and donkeys (it seems) walk the same with and without heavy burdens. At the same time, however, it is patently obvious that these locomotory activities like other activities can be finely tailored to the exigencies of the environment (see Lee, this volume; Turvey & Remez, 1978). The question, therefore, is how do nonlinear systems that are basically imprecise though stable condense out--in a fashion suggestive of linear systems--kinematic details that are precisely related to environmental states of affairs? This question may be novel in the form that it takes but it is not novel in the fundamental concern that it expresses (viz., the tuning issue; Greene, 1972, 1975; Gurfinkel et al., 1971; Turvey, 1977).

Let us take another look at the linear/nonlinear distinction. Rather than viewing it as a distinction between systems let us view it as a distinction within a system, more precisely, a distinction between the behaviors of a system that would, by mathematical convention, be termed a nonlinear system. Imagine a differential equation in which some of the terms are products of variables or powers of variables and/or where one or more of the coefficients depend on the function or derivatives of the function being determined. Conventionally this is a nonlinear equation but the point to be emphasized is that there are distinctively different contributions to the dynamics of the system that the equation represents, some of which are nonlinear and some of which are linear. Put differently, all real systems contain nonlinearities but they also contain linearities which is to say that all real systems are both structurally stable and structurally neutral. How is the latter to be understood? To the global perspective on the concept of structural stability that was given above we will need to add a more local perspective. Imagine a (nonlinear) function of several arguments. The topology of the space that the function generates for variations in its arguments will be populated (unevenly) by points of inflection. A given path through the space can be termed structurally stable if the path contains an inflection point defining a preferred location and structurally neutral if the path contains no inflection points, that is, no points of preference. A family of struc-

turally stable paths that inflect at a common value identifies a structurally stable region; and, by the same token, a family of structurally
neutral paths identifies a structurally neutral region. Obviously, for a
region of the latter kind linear theory is the appropriate mathematical
tool.

It should be emphasized that an inflection point identifies a stable configuration of the system's dimensions, that is, a point about which the
dimensions will tend to configure subsequent to perturbation. Even in a
potential system, in which energy is a dimension (a system of the kind to
be examined in detail below), a point of inflection is not strictly energy
referential, say, a point of minimal energy dissipation; it is, more precisely, system or function referential in that it is a signature of the
system or function as a whole.

The foregoing remarks can be illustrated more clearly by considering the
function $z = f(x,y)$ plotted in Figure 1. (The precise nature of the
variables is immaterial to the illustration.) The gradient dynamics of

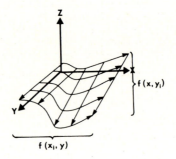

Figure 1

the manifold associated with the function $f(x,y)$ can be intuitively described as follows. There is a valley bordered by two chains of mountains
with geometric gradients which are not symmetrical. Starting with a point
of origin (x,y_i) on the y-axis a traveler moving in the direction of increasing x will move down a ramplike gradient, through a small valley,
and up an ascending slope. The traveler's path describes a phase portrait
associated with the function $f(x,y_i)$. Starting from a new y_i the traveler
again moves off the y-axis in the direction of increasing x and discovers
a new geometric path moving down a gentle slope, through a valley, and up
an ascending slope. Figure 2 describes a family of such paths where each
is associated with a different y_i. The important feature in this family
of curves is the invariant topological profile associated with each curve.
The topological invariance is geometrically portrayed in the inflection
point or valley revealed in each path. Thus the family of curves is

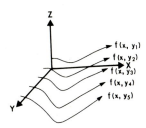

Figure 2

describable by a qualitatively invariant set of nonlinear differential
equations and they identify a local region in which the function is
"structurally stable".

Let us now consider the same function $f(x,y)$ from the perspective of the
y-variable, $f(x_i, y)$. Starting from a point (x_i,y) on the x-axis, a
traveler moving in the direction of increasing y journeys along a relatively flat geometric trajectory. Figure 3 describes a family of such
curves generated from various starting points on the x-axis, $f(x_i,y)$.
The family of curves generated from this orientation has a geometric profile that is topologically homogeneous. There are no inflection points
in these curves, no topological inhomogeneities. The paths form a family

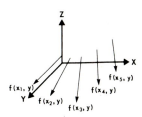

Figure 3

of curves describable by a set of linear differential equations. Furthermore, since there are no inflection points in the topological space, the
function is "structurally neutral" within the locally described region.
It is important to note that a family of linear equations need not describe a geometrically flat space. A family of linear equations could
describe a curving ascending or descending gradient with the only restriction being a prohibition of inflection points on the surface.

The partitioning of the function into components associated with linear
and nonlinear behavior is not necessarily "fixed". That is to say in one
region a variable may have a linear relationship to the function but in
another region its relationship to the function is nonlinear. Figure 4
describes a family of curves in which the behavior of the function undergoes a transformation from linear to nonlinear. The curves described by

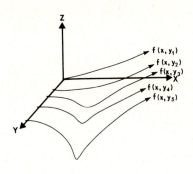

Figure 4

$f(x,y_1)$ and $f(x,y_2)$ behave linearly while the curves described by $f(x,y_3)$,
$f(x,y_4)$, $f(x,y_5)$ behave nonlinearly. At the same time, however, the
transformation need not be reflected in the other functional variables.
Figure 5 describes a function in which there is a functional transformation in the $f(x,y_i)$ relationship and yet no transformation in the $f(x_i,y)$
relationship. Recently, Thom (1975) has provided a systematic study of
these transition regions in his theory of "catastrophes". Catastrophes,
for Thom, are the dramatic and sudden "jumps" in behavior associated with
various topological transformations. These transformations occur when
systemic variables are "scaled-up" beyond certain limits. At these points
sudden qualitative changes occur in the system's behavior. This provides
part of the rationale for terming such regions "structurally unstable."
These regions are both exploited and avoided in the organization of natural functions. For example, in the case of an action potential in a
biological system, when the voltage gradient is driven beyond -70 mvolts
in the direction of zero a qualitative change occurs in the membrane's

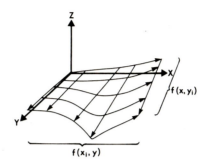

Figure 5

permeability allowing for an influx of sodium and thus depolarization. The behavioral catastrophe is associated with a qualitative change in the topological complexity of the underlying function. In this example the structurally unstable region is exploited by the biological system.

Let us now draw the identity between linear behavior and nonessential variables and nonlinear behavior and essential variables. As noted earlier essential variables determine the function's topological quali- ties, whereas nonessential variables determine the possible scalar trans- formations over the topological complexity. Following Gel'fand and Tsetlin (1962, 1971), we will consider a function "well-organized" when the function can be partitioned into these two classes of variables: essential and nonessential. For example, Figures 6 and 7 are not "well-

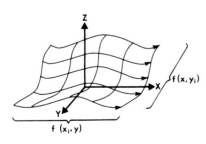

Figure 6

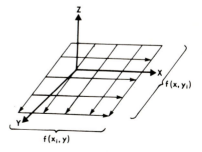

Figure 7

organized". Figure 6 defines a function composed of two essential variables, while Figure 7 defines a function composed of two nonessential
variables. Given the above identity, we can now say that linear variables
are associated with nonessential variables and therefore with control and
nonlinear variables are associated with essential variables and therefore
with coordination. Furthermore functions that are "well-organized" may
be said to be optimally organized with respect to components of control
and coordination. We proceed to consider this claim in more detail.

By coordination we refer to the function's regions of "structural stability" as specified by the topological properties of qualitative complexity.
For example, a function will maximally conserve stability when organized
at regions on the topological manifold specifying inflection points. Deviations from these regions will be associated with a decrease in functional stability and an increase in energy dissipation. Therefore, for
maximum conservation of stability and minimal dissipation of energy a
system is optimally organized around topological points of inflection.
As noted above, essential variables are associated with a system's coordination by virtue of the fact that they determine the inflection points
which specify points of maximum conservation of systemic stability.

By control we refer to the function's regions of "neutral stability" as
specified by the scalar properties associated with the nonessential variables. For example, stability will be minimally disrupted and energy dissipation minimally incurred at points on the topological manifold that preserve invariant the essential variables at inflection points. The advantage gained by the nonessential variable is flexibility. A system organized with only nonlinear variables results in either saddlepoints or
singularities around the inflection points. The result of this style of
organization is too much stability or marginal instability for the system.
In the case of the singularity, geometrically portrayed as a point on the
bottom of a conic projection, the function is so stable that deviations
in any direction will be resisted with a tendency to return to the singularity. In the case of a saddlepoint, geometrically portrayed as two orthogonally coupled horseshoes with one facing up and the other facing
down (the reader is reminded that the name "saddlepoint" comes from its
resemblance to a saddle), the function is unstable with any deviation away
from the intersection point in the direction of the variable pointing down,
while the function is stable for any deviation in the direction of the
variable facing upwards. In short, this style of organization has little
flexibility and only marginal stability. However, if a nonessential variable is introduced to complement the stability of an essential variable,
then flexibility is added to the functional organization. Since the nonessential variable defines a structurally neutral region in the manifold,
an organization can be realized in which the essential variable is "fixed"
at the inflection point while the nonessential variable moves through a
path which does not disturb the function's stability and minimally incurs
dissipation of energy.

Returning to Figure 1 we see that such an organization exists when the
function maintains the essential variable in the valley and movement up
the valley is specified by variations in the nonessential variable. This
style of organization involves the exploitation of stability specified by
the essential variable (that is, for maximum coordination maintain the
function in the valley), while introducing maximum flexibility for precision through deviation along the nonessential variable (that is, for
maximum control move the function through the valley).

13. The Behavior of a Force-driven Harmonic Oscillator

Let us now consider a natural dynamic function--that of a force-driven
harmonic oscillator--in terms of the above arguments for a linear/non-
linear style of organization. The dynamic behavior of the oscillatory
system is described by the following relation:

$$F = \frac{\theta LM}{\left[\frac{1}{(\omega_0^2 - \omega^2)^2 + 4\left(\frac{B}{2M}\right)^2\omega^2}\right]^{1/2}}$$

Driving force (F) = newtons
Amplitude (θ) = degrees
Length (L) = meters
Mass (M) = kilograms

Resonant frequency (ω_0) = hertz
Actual frequency (ω) = hertz
Damping coefficient (B) = kilograms/seconds
Gravity (G) = Meters/second^2

where: $\omega_0 = \frac{1}{2\pi \sqrt{L/G}}$

General examples of partial geometric manifolds associated with the above
functional organization are presented in Figures 8 and 9. The plotted

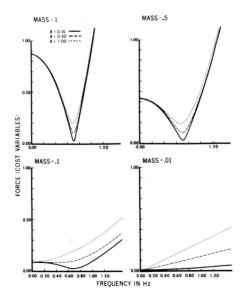

Figure 8

curves describe the system's behavior from the perspective of manipulation
on the frequency variable. For Figure 8, each curve represents different
parameter settings of the mass and damping coefficient variables. For
Figure 9, each curve represents different parameter settings of mass and
length variables. The parameters of amplitude, length and gravity are
held constant over each set of graphs. Since these graphs are plotted in
a two-dimensional space, a third dimensional variable is manipulated
between each of the three curves in each graph and a fourth dimensional
variable is manipulated between each of the four graphs in each series.

Let us begin by examining the geometric properties associated with the
curves in Figure 8. When viewed from a three-dimensional perspective,
the upper left graph of Figure 8 reveals a valley extending out towards
the viewer with asymmetrically ascending gradients to the left and right
of the valley. The x-axis represents frequency, the y-axis represents
force (or cost variables) and what would be the third-dimensional z-axis
(represented by the three separately plotted curves) indexes a damping
coefficient (B). A closer examination of the geometric properties reveals that the valley extending out to the viewer possesses a slightly
ascending slope in the direction of increasing damping coefficient.
Briefly, the three curves describe a family qualitatively similar to those
portrayed in Figure 2. Both families of curves depict nonlinear systems
and both functions are structurally stable in their respective local regions.

Moving from the upper left to the upper right graph in Figure 8, the
function has the parameter of mass changed from 1.0 kilograms to 0.5
kilograms. We notice that as the system's mass is reduced the slope of
the ascending gradients surrounding the valley is also reduced. Further
variations in the slope's geometric properties are associated with changes
in damping coefficient. As the damping coefficient increases, the slopes
of the corresponding geometric gradients decrease. The important property to note is that as the function changes its organization with new
parameter settings of mass and damping coefficient, there is a corresponding change in the underlying geometric properties. In particular,
decreases in slope are associated, on the one hand,with decreases in mass
and, on the other hand, with increases in damping coefficient. Let us
consider briefly the nature of the "slope". Not only is slope sensitive
to changes in mass and damping coefficient, but it is also sensitive to
a wide variety of combinations of the other variables that define the
system's dimensions such as amplitude, gravity and length. Since slope
is a "dimensionless" value, manipulation by the various dimensional variables imposes only "scale" changes on the value of the slope. In essence
slope specifies a critical ratio of the system's defining dimensions
where the ratio is a dimensionless number whose value is "system-scaled"
in association with changing system variables. We term such a ratio a
"system-scaled variable."

A second "system-scaled" variable is the geometric variable of inflection.
In Figure 8 the upper left and right graphs reveal a valley extending out
towards the viewer. The valley is formed by a series of inflection points
generated over a family of parameterizations on the damping coefficient.
We noted earlier that a function exhibiting stability of inflection
points within a local region is termed "structurally stable." With respect to the system's behavior, maximum stability and minimum energy dissipation is incurred when the system is organized with parameters specifying the region of the valley. For an oscillating system the region

specified by the valley is termed the region of "resonance." The variable
of inflection shares similar characteristics with the variable of slope.
Both slope and inflection have "dimensionless values" and both are "system-scaled variables." This becomes more apparent in the case of the inflection when we examine the lower left graph of Figure 8. Moving from
the upper right to the lower left graph the system's mass parameter has
been scaled down from 0.5 kilograms to 0.1 kilograms. Due to the scale
change the upper two curves of the lower left graph exhibit no inflections,
whereas the bottom curve still reveals an inflection property. This set
of curves is similar to those described in Figure 5. In both cases the
function describing the local regions are termed "structurally unstable."
The structurally instability is due to the annihilation of inflection
properties. Scaling down further on the mass parameter, the lower right
graph reveals a set of curves in which no inflection properties are present. Under this scale transformation all the inflection points are annihilated. This set of curves is similar to those described in Figure 3.
The function for both cases is termed "structurally neutral" since the local phase portrait in both cases is topologically homogeneous within the
entire local regions. Thus, as before with slope, the geometric property
of inflection is sensitive to scale changes in the parameter of mass. In
fact further scale changes in the inflection property are associated with
changes in damping coefficient, gravity and length. In short, the inflection point specifies a critical ratio of the system's defining dimensions
where the ratio is a dimensionless number whose value is "system-scaled"
in association with changing system variables.

Figure 9 is a set of graphs similar to those in Figure 8 except that instead of the damping coefficient changing within each graph, length is

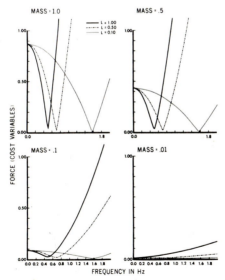

Figure 9

varied. The upper left graph describes a set of curves, each associated
with a different length oscillator. We note that each curve exhibits an
inflection point at a different frequency value. As we scale down on mass
from 1.0 kilograms to 0.5 kilograms, we see in the upper right graph that
scale changes have occurred in the slope variable but not in the inflection variable. Scaling mass down further to 0.1 kilograms reveals in the

lower left graph further changes in the slope variable with no change as
yet in the inflection variable. However, when the mass is scaled down to
0.01 kilograms in the lower right graph we now note that the inflection
variable has changed. In all three curves the inflection property has
been annihilated. We also note further changes in the slope variable.
Under this final transformation the system's resonance property is annihilated.

Let us conclude this section with a brief summary. Slope and inflection
are dimensionless geometric properties that are continuously scaled to
changing dimensions of the system. The nature of the change in the slope
variable is continuous while the nature of the change in the inflection
variable is discrete. We will argue in the following section that the
status of a variable in terms of essential and nonessential functional
components is distinguished on the basis of geometric information in a
vocabulary of dimensionless system-scaled variables. We have described
two such variables exhibited by the properties of slope and inflection.

14. Information as Form

Again, to bring our arguments into focus, we return to Bernstein's problem. Ideally, the model construct that is sought should be (1) an autonomous system in that the _energy_ flux by which the system is sustained
is determined by properties intrinsic to the system; and (2) a self-
organizing system in that the _information_ flux by which the system is
controlled and coordinated is, at one and the same time, determined by
the system's dynamics and modulatory of them. We have given a conceptualization of coordinative structure that is consonant with (1); our task
now is to pursue a conceptualization consonant with (2). In paraphrase,
and in the terminology of Pattee (1972, 1977), (2) above is the requirement that the sought-after model construct refer to a system that writes
and reads information about itself, that is to say, that it be a self-
describing,self-writing,and self-reading system. (The terms "writing"
and "reading" convey the flavor of the requirement--but they should not
be taken too literally.)

What is at issue, first and foremost, is the nature of the self-description. What are the predicates in terms of which a self-organizing system
describes itself? Suppose that the predicates are _quantitative_, precisely, values on the dimensions over which the system's dynamics are defined. It would follow, therefore, that at any given point in time the
self-description would be a set of values, a vector. But a vector space
as an information space is homogeneous: No vector can _of itself_ mean any
more or less to the system than any other vector. Any biasing of the
vector space, any ascription of meaning, would have to originate externally, that is, the semantics would have to be "added" to the information
space by a logically separable event such as a function which maps the
vectors to a memory or matches them with a reference. A very similar
conception of information to that just given is the popular simile of information as a finite sequence of symbols (like letters) taken from an
alphabet and organized by a linear syntax. This linguistic conception
suffers the same infirmity as the quantitative conception, namely, that
it is a purely formal description requiring a separate step of semantic
adumbration.

It would appear that the requirements of self-organization are ill-served by quantitative and linguistic interpretations of information (see Kugler et al., in press, for a more detailed discussion). A more suitable interpretation should be sought, one in which the formal description of a systemic state is not numerically distinct from the semantic description thereby avoiding a regress to an external, interpretative device.

Consider again a major theme of the foregoing section--that a "well-organized" function, a function that is both stable and flexible, is one in which the variables separate into nonlinear or essential and linear or nonessential. Assuming that the self-organizing system of present concerns is also a well-organized system then we can recognize that the interpretation of information that we seek should readily distinguish between essential and nonessential variables. Recall that the separation of variables is not fixed, not given a priori, but rather it is a distinction that is given a posteriori in the local aspects of the system's dynamics. In the analyses of the preceding two sections we saw how the two classes of variables may distinguish topologically. Membership in the classes is defined by topologies that are invariant over variations in dimensional values. On those analyses, therefore, we forward the tentative suggestion that the conception of information that we want is qualitative rather than quantitative; that information is, first and foremost, morphological--a form--and that the morphology of a system's dynamics is information about the system in the sense of specificity to the system. A separate, extra-dynamical step is therefore obviated. Information conceived morphologically may require detection but it does not require interpretation.

It is of no little significance that the specificity criterion for this conception of information is mandated by the ecological approach to perception, guided as it is by a commitment to realism (see Gibson, 1966, 1979; Mace, 1977; Shaw, et al., in press; Turvey & Shaw, 1979). It should also be recognized that it is a morphological approach to information that is being promoted by Thom (1972, 1975) and, moreover, that the need to focus on the geometry of dynamics has its precedent in the efforts of physicists to remove gravity from the list of global explanatory principles, sui generis (see Wheeler, 1962).

Let us highlight one of the many consequences of conceptualizing information morphologically. In Figure 1 an inflection point in the x variable is preserved over a range of variation in the y variable; in Figure 7 an inflection point in the frequency variable is preserved over a range of variation in the variables of mass and damping. In both cases there is a qualitative invariant even though the quantities, the coordinates, that mark the locations in the phase space are variable. Slope changes in a continuous quantitative fashion while inflection changes in a discrete quantitative fashion. As noted earlier, both slope and inflection are dimensionless system-scaled variables (see Bridgeman, 1922, for a simple and elegant account, and Lee this volume). The point to be appreciated is that morphological information is dimensionless and always system-scaled.

Now if we are to take the morphological approach seriously then we have to suppose that the proper perspective on the traditional channels of "information" for motor systems, the afferent paths, cannot be that they yield quantitative dimensional values to be referred to some preestablished dimensional quantity for their meaning and regulation. Rather, they must be viewed as contributing, together with the traditionally defined efferent paths and the muscles, to the form of a muscle system's dimensionless dynamics. In short, the efferents and afferents both contribute system-scaling variables. Put differently, the morphological perspective on information renders it unlikely that the contribution of traditionally defined afference is dimension specific. Moreover, it suggests that a collective of muscles will not be debilitated by the elimination of any given afferent source or even by the elimination of all afferent sources; although the stability and flexibility of the collective may be less than ideal. This is to say, that in the absence of the full complement of contributions to the information space, the topological characteristics specifying essential and nonessential dimensions will remain, but their system-scaling and articulation within the space may be less emphatic and, therefore, less "detectable."

This latter remark leads into one final contrast that would, under a more complete explication, be assiduously drawn. The distinction between nonlinear and linear is a formal mathematical distinction; that between essential and nonessential is a pragmatic distinction. Within a given range of variation a dimension may continue to meet the formal criteria for nonlinearity but it may not continue to meet the pragmatic criteria for essential. The essential/nonessential contrast owes an obligation to physical realities which the nonlinear/linear contrast does not. We are saying, in short, that the essential/nonessential distinction for a system is system referential and abides by the resolving power, the self-sensitivity, of the system.

15. A Geometrodynamic Perspective on Muscular Forces.

To reiterate, the hallmark of autonomy is that the energy flux, or forcing function, does not depend explicitly on time but rather on properties intrinsic to the system's design. The clock has been given as exemplary of self-sustaining thermodynamic engines: The form of the energy injections that maintain the clock's activity are determined by the design specifications of the escapement and oscillatory component. And, as noted, the design specifications of the clock are like a constraint which functionally and systematically binds a group of muscles--the behavioral effects in the two cases are qualitatively similar.

Focusing on the activity of a constrained collection of muscles, it behooves us to recognize two fluxes of force. There are, on the one hand the muscular forces and on the other hand the reactive, frictional, gravitational and contact forces into which the flux of muscular forces is inserted. The larger point of Bernstein's (1967) approach to movement was the necessity of considering the totality of forces, a point that others have duly expressed (e.g., Fowler and Turvey, 1978). Because the nonmuscular forces are in flux, the muscular forces cannot be prescribed temporally or quantitatively. To successfully effect a movement the animal must generate a flux of muscular forces that together with the flux of non-muscular forces suffices to achieve its aim.

How is a requisite flux of muscular forces generated? Or, putting the question into a specific form, one that is relevant to the discussion that follows, how does a group of muscles constrained to act as a functional unit maintain its integrity in the face of variations in the nonmuscular forces? The answer, in a sense, has already been given above--the flux of muscular forces is determined by the "design specifications" of the

system of muscles--but we have yet to acknowledge the full implications
of this answer. If a temporally constrained collection of muscles is an
autonomous, self-organizing system then the muscular forces that it
generates must be understood as arising from within the collective and
not as imposed from without. We have said this before, of course, but
the consideration just given to the morphological view of dynamics--geo-
metrodynamics as Wheeler (1962) terms it--permits a more explicit interpretation. In what follows we take a well known demonstration of systematic variation in the fluxes of muscular and nonmuscular force and give
it a purely geometric reading. In so doing we provide a way of interpreting discrete, non-oscillatory movements as products of a non-linear
oscillatory system.

Asatryan and Fel'dman (1965) and Fel'dman (1966 a,b) showed that the
maintenance of joint postures and motions could be understood as the
manifestation of an oscillatory device. In particular, they likened the
behavior of muscles at a joint to that of a controllable spring system.
Briefly, their model construct was a mass-spring system defined by the
equation $F = -s_0(1-y_0)$ where F is force, s_0 is the stiffness of the spring,
1 is the length of the spring and y_0 is the equlibrium length, that is,
the length at which force developed by the spring is zero. This simple
mass-spring system is controllable to the degree that the parameters s_0
and y_0 are adjustable. Changing y_0 with s_0 constant generates a set of
nonintersecting characteristic functions, $F(1) = -s_0(1-y)$, and changing
both parameters generates a set of functions $F(1) = s(1-y)$ that will pass
through all points in the plane defined by the cartesian product, F x 1.

Asatryan and Fel'dman's analysis was based on a qualitative comparison of
the geometric properties portrayed in their mechanographic analysis with
those geometric properties portrayed by the behavior of a mass-spring
system. In essence the analysis was meant to capture the abstract qualitative similarities relating the two systems. The mechanical instantiations of the systems were not of importance. In one case the mechanism
was composed of metallic coiled springs and weights with a mechanical
forcing component while in the other case the mechanism was composed of
nerve and muscle tissue with a metabolic forcing function. What Asatryan
and Fel'dman demonstrated was that these two radically different material
systems behaved in a "qualitatively" similar manner. Their suggestion
was that both systems might be sharing a "common" solution to a dynamic
problem. One functional difference between the two systems is that the
muscle/tissue system has increased flexibility through the freeing-up of
the stiffness and resting-length variables. What we would like to show
in the remainder of this section is how to reexamine the Asatryan and
Fel'dman plots in such a way that they reveal an underlying organization
similar to that of our dynamic model construct.

A first step is to change the plotting convention employed by Asatryan
and Fel'dman (see Figure 10). Instead of using a positive/negative convention to distinguish extension/flexion phases of movement, we will plot
all moment values with their actual value signs. In other words, if the
total moment increases (regardless if it is in the direction of flexion
or extension) the value will be plotted in the positive direction. The
result of using this convention is a family of curves similar to those
plotted in the upper left graph in Figure 9. Recall that that graph depicted a family of nonlinear curves associated with the behavior of a force-
driven harmonic oscillator; each curve distinguishes the behavior of an

oscillator of a different length, where each length exhibits a different "preferred" (i.e., resonant) frequency. When plotted in their original convention the data of Asatryan and Fel'dman generate a family of linear

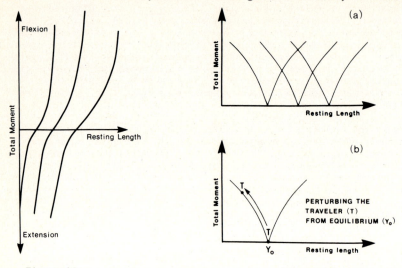

Figure 10   Figure 11

curves as Figure 10 shows. The family of curves in Figure 10 has a geometric profile in which there are no inflection points. For the collection of curves in Figure 10 the appropriate model construct is a linear system. As a member of the class of linear systems there are no regions of preferred stability. When plotted using the alternative convention, however, the data of Asatryan and Fel'dman generate a family of nonlinear curves with a geometric profile that is topologically inhomogeneous, the family of curves in Figure 11a. There are inflection points in the functional organization specifying the system's resting length. For the family of curves that follow from the alternative convention the appropriate model construct is a nonlinear system; there are preferred regions of stability. The geometric profile exhibits an inflection region at the resting length with ascending gradients on both sides. The slopes of these gradients specifies the system's stiffness parameter. (The importance of selecting the "appropriate" plotting convention cannot be over emphasized, for it forms the basis on which the model construct is established. The distinguishing properties are most readily revealed in a geometric analysis of the function's defining topological properties. These are revealed only when the proper plotting convention is used.)

We noted in the previous section that sensitivity to the geometric properties of a function's phase portrait is synonymous to sensitivity to information specific to the underlying dynamic organization of the function. Let us now return to our earlier "traveler" of geometric regions and see how it would behave according to the new "layout" of Asatryan and Fel'dman's data. Suppose an underlying organization of the system is set up such that a given resting length and stiffness is specified. The geometrodynamics associated with this organization is a manifold with a valley specified by the resting length and ascending sloping gradients specifying

stiffness. Let us further suppose that the traveler is at rest in the
valley. This condition is similar to Asatryan and Fel'dman's condition
of the subject maintaining a resting posture. If we now perturb the
traveler, by forcing it up one of the sloping walls, the traveler will
respond by returning to the valley, which for the traveler represents the
region of maximum stability and minimum energy dissipation (Figure 11b).
The "rate" (that is acceleration and velocity components) at which the
traveler returns will be specified by the steepness of the slope. Thus
perturbations to the traveler do not affect the underlying geographic layout but rather displace or relocate the traveler. Once the perturbing
influence is removed, the traveler once again tends to return to the
stable region in the valley. The information specifying the journey's
route is revealed in the geometrodynamics of the surrounding gradients
and equilibrium points, where the gradients and equilibrium points are
always "scaled" to the dimensions of the system (therefore eliminating
any "procedure" of recalibration). Such a style of organization is similar to our earlier discussion of linear and nonlinear systems. Reviewing
briefly, linear systems respond to any perturbation by moving to a new
location specific to the input perturbation. The mapping function from
"input" to "output" for a linear system possesses the defining properties
of superposition and proportionality. Put differently, there is a one-to-
one mapping relating input to output through some scalar function. Since
there are no "preferred" points in the phase portrait, the linear system
is free to move to any output region. A perturbed linear system does not
have any tendency to return to the state prior to perturbation. In contrast, non-linear systems are characterized by the presence of "preferred"
regions in the phase portrait. These points specify regions of maximal stability and minimal energy dissipation. Furthermore, there is a
many-to-few mapping function relating input to output such that the system always tends towards "preferred" regions in the output mode. When
these systems are perturbed, there is a tendency to return to preferred
regions. There is ample evidence to suggest that the style of organization characterizing the maintenance of simple postures is best modeled
with a nonlinear system (Asatryan and Fel'dman, 1965; Bizzi, Polit, and
Morrasso, 1976; Fel'dman, 1966a,b; Kelso, 1977; see accompanying paper).

16. A Geometrodynamic Perspective on Discrete Movement

Consider now what it means to produce a given movement rather than, more
simply, preserving a given posture. Curiously, on the geometrodynamic
perspective advanced here, the production of discrete movements is primarily owing to changes in the underlying "geometry" and only secondarily,
as a necessary consequence of the geometric change, owing to a change of
"forces". A limb in a given posture prior to a discrete single movement
means, by the analysis above, that a particular geometrodynamic organization holds over the relevant dimensions. To produce a movement is in
effect to change that underlying geometrodynamic organization. This
curious thesis is given a hearing through a further consideration of the
mechanographic analysis of Asatryan and Fel'dman.

Following Asatryan and Fel'dman, we would argue that while descriptions
of movements are generally made in the vocabulary of kinematics (that is,
distance, velocity and acceleration) movements are more likely regulated
in the vocabulary of dynamics (Fitch & Turvey, 1978). We stated above
that a stable postural arrangement could be maintained through the specification of stiffness and resting length parameters. Distance may be

regulated through the manipulation of the resting length while velocity
and acceleration may be regulated through the manipulation of stiffness.
Let us pursue in more detail how this might be accomplished.

Consider our traveler in a resting posture. It finds itself located in
a valley specifying its resting length and surrounded by ascending gradients with slope specifying stiffness. By changing the parameter of resting length, while holding stiffness constant, the traveler "suddenly"
finds its geographic layout changed (see Figure 12). It is no longer in
the bottom of a valley (T), but rather it is now on a sloping gradient
(T'), with a new valley off in the distance. This new geographic layout
possesses the "new" parameter setting specifying stiffness (in the slope
of the gradient) and resting length (in the new location of the valley).
Since stiffness has not changed, the slope of the new geographic layout
is the same as before the change. In fact, the actual coordinates (s, Y_0)
of the traveler's position have not changed, what changed was the geographic layout on which the traveler was positioned. In brief, the traveler's underlying geographic layout was "suddenly" changed by virtue of
a reparameterization of the resting length variable. Following the new
descending gradients, the traveler once again discovers a stable region
in the geographic valley.

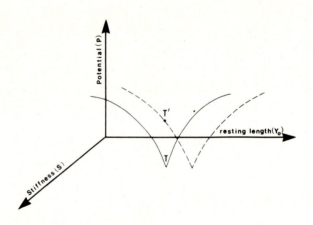

Figure 12

(Read P as a dynamic variable, such as total moment, to which the system
 is sensitive.)

Consider now the effects of perturbations on the traveler under the changing conditions associated with a simple movement (Figure 13). First,
suppose the traveler has its initial conditions changed after the under-

lying geographic layout has been changed to specify a different location
for the valley. In this case, changes in the initial conditions (such as
by a momentary perturbation) affect only the traveler's relative position
on the underlying geographic layout, they do not affect the geographic
layout itself. For example, before a reparameterization occurs the traveler is at rest in a geographic valley (T), suddenly a reparameterization
occurs and the traveler discovers that the underlying geographic profile
has changed. It is no longer in a valley, instead it is now located on a
sloping gradient (T') extending downwards towards a "new valley" (specifying a new resting length). Before the traveler starts its journey,
however, a sudden perturbation occurs, forcing the traveler a short distance either up or down the sloping gradient (T"). Put differently, the
initial conditions of the traveler's journey have been changed. Importantly the perturbation has no effect on the underlying geographic layout. Therefore, since the geographic layout remains unaltered, the
final resting position of the traveler remains the same. Regardless of
the nature of the perturbation (within certain limits) the final resting
position is invariant. More commonly, such a style of organization is

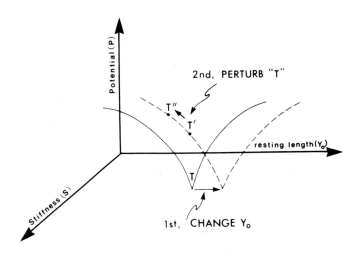

Figure 13

said to possess the property of "equifinality" (that is, the ability to
reach the same final condition from various initial conditions). Second,
perturbation during the movement similarly only temporarily relocates the
traveler. Since the underlying geographic layout is not altered by the
perturbation, the traveler again ends its journey in the same final location. Finally, if an external moment is added to the system during the
movement, but not removed, then the traveler will end its journey at a
resting length deviating from the geographic valley by a distance determined by the external moment and the sloping gradient surrounding the
valley (that is, the stiffness parameter). The deviation from the valley

is "maintained" by the external moment. As before, the underlying layout
is not changed but in this condition the external moment adds a bias to
the traveler's disposition, the result being a relative shift in the resting condition predicated upon the biasing nature of the external moment.

Summing briefly, the underlying principle for perturbations is: Perturbations influence the disposition of the traveler but not the underlying
geographic layout. When a perturbation is introduced and removed after
the underlying geographic parameters have been established and before the
end of the movement, then the traveler always ends its journey in the
same stable valley region. If, however, a persistent change in the traveler's disposition occurs (such as the addition of a constant external
moment), then the final resting location is specific to the underlying
geographic layout but now with reference to the traveler's new disposition. Put differently, any change in the traveler's disposition
"biases" the final resting location.

From the above arguments the production of discrete movements (and, similarly complex movements) is primarily owing to a change of "geometry,"
a reparameterization of a geographic layout. A limb in a given posture
maintains its postural integrity by virtue of an invariant geometrodynamic organization and movement production is the event consequent to a
change in that underlying geometrodynamic organization.

Concluding Remarks

Our efforts in this essay have been directed at defining a model construct in terms of which the control and coordination of movement might
be understood. Three related guidelines have shaped the direction taken.
First, that the model construct identify a system whose internal degrees
of freedom regulate themselves with minimum recourse to an 'intelligent
regulator'. Second, that the model construct require a minimum number of
design principles, sui generis. And finally, that the principles of biological design characterizing the model be mandated by physical principles. In accordance with these guidelines we have suggested that a
group of muscles constrained to act as a functional unit, a coordinative
structure, is a member of the class of thermodynamic engines qua dissipative structures.

A dissipative structure is a physical system characterized by the ability
to autonomously manifest spatio-temporal self-organization. This manifestation requires:

  1. A reservoir of potential energy from which (generalized)
      work can arise.

  2. A microcosm of elements with a stochastic fluctuating
      nature (such as a collective of muscles or at a lesser
      scale, the fluctuating nature of an interneuronal pool
      as is manifest in tremor, see accompanying paper).

  3. The presence of nonlinear components.

  4. A scale change such that a nonlinear component is critically
      amplified (in the sense that the system's own dimensions now
      resist the previously dominant effects of the initial and
      boundary conditions).

If these requirements are met, then the possibility exists for a transition from the stochastic steady-state situation to a spatially structured
steady-state situation or a time-dependent, limit cycle regime characterized by homogeneous oscillations or by propagating waves. The regimes
are stable, by virtue of the 'amplified nonlinear component', and maintained, by virtue of 'dissipation of energy'. As such the manifestation
of these 'open' systems is achieved by drawing spontaneously on potential
energy sources at their boundaries. Under these conditions the system
feeds on the potential energy source, is stable in the nonlinear sense,
and dissipates energy (that is, there is a greater loss of order in the
surround than gain of order by the system itself--the behavior of the
system is 'lossy' with respect to energy). This behavior is prototypical
of thermodynamic engines in that the mean states of the internal variables are characterized by 'fluxes' and 'squirts' of energy that become
constrained by nonlinear components so as to behave in a limit cycle manner. The temporal ordering of the 'squirts' is nonspecific (many-to-few
mapping) with respect to the stable spatio-temporal structures that are
manifest within the system. Thus stable structure, owing to the nonlinear components, may arise and be maintained with minimum specification
of internal details. In contrast, for linear components the degrees of
freedom captured in the input are conserved (map one-to-one) in the output. Thus structure, owing to linear components, may arise and be maintained but it requires a full complement of detail in the energy 'fluxes'
specifying the nature of the arising structure. A dissipative structure
is 'well-organized' when it manifests a functional relationship exhibiting properties of both linear and nonlinear components. Under this style
of organization, the system reveals qualities of precision and stability.
Information specifying linear and nonlinear components, more pragmati-
cally, nonessential and essential components, is made directly available
when the system undergoes dynamic transformations. The information is
morphological, manifest as gradients and equilibrium points in the system's dynamics. If the information specifies only nonlinear components
then the system is stable in the face of perturbations to the point of
prohibiting (useful) variation; if, on the contrary, the information
specifies only linear components, then the system is variable in the face
of perturbation to the point of indifference with respect to stability.
In sum, pragmatic coordination and control is realized only when the information specifies sources of stability and precision, respectively.

References

[1] Andronov, A., and Chaikin, C. E. Theory of Oscillations (Princeton
     Univ. Press, N. J., 1949).
[2] Asatryan, D., and Fel'dman, A. Functional tuning of the nervous
     system with control of movement or maintenance of a steady posture--
     1. Mechanographic analysis of the work of the joint on execution of
     a postural task, Biophys. 10 (1965) 925-935.
[3] Arshavsky, Yu. I., Kots, Ya. M., Orlovsky, G. N., Rodionov, I. M.,
     and Shik, M. L. Investigation of biomechanics of running by the dog,
     Biophys. 10 (1965) 665-672.
[4] Berlinski, D. On Systems (MIT Press, Boston, Mass., 1976).
[5] Bernstein, N. The Coordination and Regulation of Movements (Pergamon
     Press, London, 1967).
[6] Bertalanffy, L. von, General Systems Theory (Penguin Univ. Press.
     Harmondsworth, England, 1973).

[7]   Bizzi, E., Polit, A., and Morasso, P. Mechanisms underlying achievement of final head position, Jrnl. Neurophys. 39 (1976) 435-444.

[8]   Boylls, C. C. A theory of cerebellar function with applications to locomotion. II. The relation of anterior lobe climbing fiberfunction to locomotion behavior in the cat. COINS Technical Report 76-1, Dept. of Comp. and Info. Sc., Univ. of Mass. (1975).

[9]   Bridgeman, P. W. Dimensional Analysis (Yale Univ. Press, New Haven, Conn.,1922).

[10] Bridgeman, P. W. The Nature of Thermodynamics (Harvard Univ. Press, Cambridge, Mass., 1941).

[11] Denier van der Gon, J. J. and Thuring, J. P. The guidance of human writing movements, Kybernetik, 2 (1965) 145-148.

[12] Dennett, D. C. Intentional Systems, Jrnl. Phil. 118 (1971) 87-106.

[13] Dennett, D. C. Brainstorms: Philosophical Essays on Mind and Psychology (Bradford Books, Montgomery, VT., 1978).

[14] Dewey, J. and Bentley, A. F. Knowing and the Known (Beacon, Boston, 1949).

[15] Easton, T. A. On the normal use of reflexes, Amer. Sci. 60 (1972) 591-599.

[16] Easton, T. A. Coordinative structures--the basis for a motor program, in: Landers, D., and Christina, R. (eds.), Psychology of Motor Behavior and Sport (Human Kinetics Publishers, Illinois, 1978).

[17] Eigen, M. Self organization of matter and the evolution of biological macromolecules, Die Naturwissenschaften, 58 (1971) 465-523.

[18] Engberg, I. and Lundberg, A. An electromyographic analysis of muscular activity in the hindlimb of the cat during unrestrained locomotion, Acta. Physio. Scand., 75 (1969) 614-630.

[19] Fel'dman, A. G. Functional tuning of the nervous system with control of movement or maintenance of a steady posture--II. Controllable parameters of the muscles. Biophys. 11 (1966) 565-578(a).

[20] Fel'dman, A. G. Functional tuning of the nervous system during control of movement or maintenance of a steady posture--III. Execution by man of the simplest motor tasks, Biophys. 11 (1966) 766-775(b).

[21] Fitch, H. and Turvey, M. T. On the control of activity: Some remarks from an ecological point of view, in: Landers, D. and Christina, R. (eds.), Psychology of Motor Behavior and Sport (Human Kinetics, Urbana, Illinois, 1978).

[22] Fowler, C. A. Timing control in speech production (Indiana Univ. Linguistics Club, Bloomington, 1977).

[23] Fowler, C. A., and Turvey, M. T. A simulation of the Shik-Orlovskii Model, unpublished manuscript. Dept. of Psychol. Univ. of Connecticut (1976).

[24] Fowler, C. A. and Turvey, M. T. Skill acquisition: An event approach with special reference to searching for the optimum of a function of several variables, in: Stelmach, G. E. (ed.), Information Processing in Motor Control and Learning (Academic Press, New York, 1978).

[25] Friedman, M. I. and Stricker, E. M. The physiological psychology of hunger: A physiological perspective, Psych. Rev., 86, 6 (1976) 409-431.

[26] Gelfand, I. M., Gurfinkel, V. S., Tsetlin, M. L., Shik, M. L.: Some problems in the analysis of movements, in: Gelfand, I. M. et al. (eds.), Models of the Structural-Functional Organization of Certain Biological Systems (MIT Press, Cambridge, Mass., 1971).

[27] Gelfand, I. M., and Tsetlin, M. L. Some methods of control for complex systems, Russ. Math. Surv. 17 (1962) 95-116.

[28] Gelfand, I. M. and Tsetlin, M. L.: Mathematical modeling of mechanisms of the central nervous system, in: Gelfand, I. M., et al. (eds.), Models of the Structural-Functional Organization of Certain Biological Systems (MIT Press, Cambridge, Mass., 1971).

[29] Gibson, J. J. The Senses Considered as Perceptual Systems (Houghton Mifflin, Boston, 1966).

[30] Gibson, J. J. The Ecological Approach to Visual Perception (Houghton Mifflin, Boston, 1979).

[31] Goodwin, B. C. Temporal Organization in Cells (Academic Press, New York, 1963).

[32] Goodwin, B. Biological stability, in: Waddington, C. H. (eds.) Towards a Theoretical Biology (Aldine, Chicago, 1970).

[33] Gould, S. J. Evolutionary paleontology and the science of form, Earth Sci. Rev. 6 (1970) 77-119.

[34] Gould, S. J. and Garwood, R. A. Levels of integration in mammalian dentitions: An analysis of correlations in Nesophorites Micrus (Insectivora) and Oryzomys Covesi (Rodentia), Evolut. 23 (1969) 276-300.

[35] Greene, P. H. Problems of organization of motor systems, in: Rosen, R. and Snell, F. (eds.) Progress in Theoretical Biology Vol. 2 (Academic Press, N. Y., 1972).

[36] Greene, P. H. Strategies for heterarchical control--an essay. I. A style of controlling complex systems, unpublished manuscript. Dept. of Comp. Sci., Illinois Inst. of Tech. Chicago, 1975.

[37] Greene, P. H. Technical Report 78-12, Dept. of Comp. Sci., Illinois Inst. of Tech. (1978).

[38] Grillner, S., Locomotion in vertebrates. Central mechanisms and reflex interaction, Physio. Rev. 55 (1975) 247-304.

[39] Gurfinkel, V. S. et al., Concerning tuning before movement, in: Gelfand, I. M., et al. (eds.), Models of the Structural-Functional Organization of Certain Biological Systems. (MIT Press, Cambridge, Mass., 1971).

[40] Haken, H. Synergetics: An introduction (Springer Verlag, Heidelberg, 1977).

[41] Hollerbach, J. J., A study of human motor control through analysis and synthesis of handwriting, Ph.D. Thesis, Dept. of Elect. Eng. and Comp. Sc., M.I.T. (August, 1978).

[42] Holst, E. von. The Behavioral Physiology of Animals and Man (University of Miami Press, Coral Cables, Fla., 1973).

[43] Iberall, A. A personal overview, and new thoughts in biocontrol, in: Waddington, C. H. (ed.), Toward a Theoretical Biology, 2 (Aldine, Chicago, 1969).

[44] Iberall, A. Periodic phenomena in organisms seen as non-linear systems, Theoria to theory 4 (1970) 40-53.

[45] Iberall, A. S. A field and circuit thermodynamics for integrative physiology: I. Introduction to general notion, Am. J. Physiol./ Reg., Integ. Comp. Physiol., 2 (1977) R171-R 180. II. Power and communicational spectroscopy in biology, Am. J. Physiol./Reg., Integ., Comp. Physiol. 3 (1978) R3-R19. III. Keeping the books--a general experimental method, Am. J. Physiol./Reg., Integ. Comp. Physiol. 3 (1978) R85-R97.

[46] Katchalsky, A., and Curran, P. F. Nonequilibrium Thermodynamics in Biophysics (Harvard Univ. Press, Cambridge, Mass., 1967).

[47] Kelso, J. A. S. Motor control mechanisms underlying human movement production. Jrnl. Exp. Psychol.: Hum. Perc. Perf. 3 (1977) 529-543.

[48] Kelso, J. A. S., Southard, D. L., and Goodman, D. On the nature of interlimb coordination, Science, 203 (1979) 1029-1031(a).

[49] Kelso, J. A. S., Southard, D. L., and Goodman, D. On programming and coordinating two-handed movements, Jrnl. Exp. Psychol.: Hum. Perc. Perf. 5 (1979) 229-238(b).

[50] Koschmieder, E. L. Instabilities in fluid dynamics, in: Haken, H. (ed.), Synergetics: A Workshop (Springer-Verlag, New York, 1977).

[51] Kohler, W. The task of Gestalt Psychology (Princeton Univ. Press, Princeton, N. J. 1969).

[52] Kripke, S. Identity and necessity, in: Munitz, M. (ed.), Identity and Individuation (N. Y. Univ. Press, N. Y., 1971) 135-164.

[53] Kugler, P. N., Kelso, J. A. S., and Turvey, M. T. On the control and coordination of naturally developing systems, in: J. A. S. Kelso & J. Clark (Eds.) Development of Human Motor Skill (John Wiley, New York, London, in press).

[54] Kugler, P. N. and Turvey, M. T. Two metaphors for neural afference and efference, Beh. Br. Sc., in press.

[55] Landauer, R. Stability in the dissipative steady state, Phys. Today (Nov. 1978) 23-30.

[56] Lestienne, F. Effects of inertial load and velocity on the braking process of voluntary limb movements, Exp. Brain Res. 35 (1979) 407-418.

[57] Mace, W. M. Gibson's strategy for perceiving: Ask not what's inside your head but what your head's inside of, in: Shaw, R. and Bransford, J. (eds.) Perceiving, Acting, and Knowing (Erlbaum, Hillsdale, N. J., 1977).

[58] Miller, S., van der Burg, T., van der Meche, F. G. A. Locomotion in the cat: Basic programs of movements, Brain Res. 91 (1975) 239-253.

[59] Minorsky, N. Nonlinear Oscillations (D. van Nostrand, Princeton, 1962).

[60] Morowitz, H. J. Foundations of Bioenergetics (Academic Press, New York, 1978).

[61] Nashner, L. M. Fixed patterns of rapid postural responses among leg muscles during stance, Exp. Brain Res. 30 (1977) 13-24.

[62] Neuman, J. von. The Computer and the Brain (Yale Univ. Press, New Haven, Conn. 1959).

[63] Nicolis, G. and Prigogine, I. Self-organization in nonequilibrium systems: From dissipative structures to order through fluctuations (Wiley Interscience, New York, 1978).

[64] Oatley, K. and Goodwin, B. C. The explanation and investigation of biological rhythms, in: Colquhoun, W. P. (ed.), Biological Rhythms and Human Performance (Academic Press, New York, 1971).

[65] Onsager, L. Reciprocal relations in irreversible processes, I., Phys. Rev. 37 (1931) 405.

[66] Pattee, H. Physical problems of heredity and evolution, in: Waddington, C. H. (ed.) Towards a Theoretical Biology, 3 (Aldine, Chicago, 1970).

[67] Pattee, H. H. Physical theories of biological coordination, Quart. Rev. Biophys. 4, 243 (1971) 255-276.

[68] Pattee, H. H. Laws and constraints, symbols and languages, in: Waddington, C. H. (ed.), Towards a Theoretical Biology (Aldine, Chicago, 1972).

[69] Pattee, H. H. Physical problems of the origin of natural controls, in: Locker, A. (ed.) Biogenesis, Evolution, Homeostasis (Springer-Verlag, Heidelberg, 1973).

[70] Pattee, H. H. Dynamic and linguistic complementarity at the cellular level. Paper presented at conference in honor of M. Polanyi (Skidmore College, N.Y., 1977).

[71] Pattee, H. H. Dynamic and linguistic modes of complex systems, Intern. J. Gen. Systems 3 (1977) 259-266.

[72] Prigogine, I. Order through fluctuation: self-organization and social systems, in: Jantsch, E. and Waddington, C. H. (eds.), Evolution and Consciousness: Human systems in Transition (Addison-Wesley, Reading, Mass., 1976).

[73] Prigogine, I. and Nicolis, G. Biological order, structure and instabilities, Quart. Rev. Biophys. 4 (1971) 107-148.

[74] Prigogine, I., Nicolis, G., and Babloyantz, A. Thermodynamics of evolution, Phys. Today 25 (1972) Nos. 11 and 12.

[75] Prigogine, I., Nicolis, G., Herman, R., and Lam, T. Stability, fluctuations, and complexity, Cooperative Phenomena 2 (1975) 103-109.

[76] Rashevsky, N. Mathematical Biophysics; Physico-mathematical Foundations of Biology (Dover Pub., New York, 1950).

[77] Raup, D. M., Theoretical morphology of echinoid growth, in: Macurda, D. B. (ed.), Paleobiological Aspects of Growth and Development: A Symposium, J. Paleontol. 42(5) 1968, 50-63 (suppl.): Paleontol. Soc. Mem., 2 (1968).

[78] Rudwick, M. J. S. The inference of function from structure in fossils, Brit. J. Phil. Sci. 15 (1964) 27-40.

[79] Rudwick, M. J. S. Some analytic methods in the study of ontogeny in fossils with accretionary skeletons, in: Macurda, D. B. (ed.) Paleobiological Aspects of Growth and Development, A Symposium, J. Paleontol. 42(5) 1968, 35-49 (suppl.); Paleontol. Soc., Mem. 2 (1968).

[80] Shaw, R. and Bransford, J. Introduction: Psychological approaches to the problem of knowledge, in: Shaw, R. and Bransford, J. (eds.), Perceiving, Acting and Knowing: Toward an Ecological Psychology. Erlbaum, Hillsdale, N.J., 1977) 1-42.

[81] Shaw, R. and McIntyre, M. Algoristic foundations to cognitive psychology, in: Weimer, W. and Palermo, D. (eds.) Cognition and the Symbolic Processes (Erlbaum, Hillsdale, N.J., 1974).

[82] Shaw, R. and Turvey, M. T. Coalitions as models for ecosystems: A realist perspective on perceptual organization, in: Kubovy, M. and Pomerantz, J. (ed.), Perceptual Organization (Erlbaum, Hillsdale, N. J., in press).

[83] Shaw, R., Turvey, M. T. and Mace, W. Ecological psychology: The consequence of a commitment to realism, in: Weimer, W. and Palermo, D. (eds.) Cognition and the Symbolic Processes, II. (Erlbaum, Hillsdale, N. J., in press).

[84] Shik, M. L. and Orlovskii, G. N. Coordination of the limbs during running of the dog. Biophys. 10 (1965) 1148-1159.

[85] Shik, M. L. and Orlovsky, G. N. Neurophysiology of locomotor automatism, Physiol. Rev. 56 (1976) 465-501.

[86] Soodak, H., and Iberall, A. S. Homeokinetics: A physical science for complex systems, Science 201 (1978) 579-582.

[87] Srinivasan, M. V. A visually-evoked roll response in the housefly: open-loop and closed-loop studies, Jrnl. Comp. Physio. 119 (1977) 1-14.

[88] Steele, G. L. and Sussman, G. S.   Constraints, MIT Artificial
     Intelligence Lab. memo no. 502 (Nov. 1978).
[89] Stein, P. S. G.   Application of the mathematics of coupled oscilla-
     tor systems to the analysis of the neural control of locomotion,
     Fed. Proc. Vol. 36, No. 7 (June 1977, 2056-2059.
[90] Stevens, P. S.   Patterns in Nature (Little Brown, Boston, Mass.:
     1974).
[91] Stockmeyer, L. J. and Chandra, A. K.   Intrinsically difficult pro-
     blems, Sci. Amer. 240 (1979) 140-159.
[92] Thom, R.   Topological models in biology, in: Waddington, C. H.
     (ed.) Towards a Theoretical Biology, 3 (Aldine, Chicago, 1970).
[93] Thom, R.   Structuralism and biology, in: Waddington, C. H. (ed.)
     Towards a Theoretical Biology, 4 (Aldine, Chicago, 1972).
[94] Thom, R.   Structural stability and morphogenesis (Benjamin, Reading,
     Mass., 1975).
[95] Thompson, D. A. W., On Growth and Form (2nd Ed.) (Cambridge, England,
     1942, Orig. Ed. 1917).
[96] Tomović, R. and Bellman, R.   A systems approach to muscle control.
     Math. Biosc. 8 (1970) 265-277.
[97] Tsetlin, M. L.   Automata Theory and Modeling in Biological Systems.
     (Academic Press, New York, 1973).
[98] Turvey, M. T.   Preliminaries to a theory of action with reference to
     vision, in: Shaw, R. and Bransford, J. (eds.), Perceiving, Acting
     and Knowing: Towards an Ecological Psychology (Erlbaum, Hillsdale,
     N. J., 1977).
[99] Turvey, M. T. and Remez, R. E.   Visual control of locomotion in
     animals: an overview, in: Proceedings of Conference on Interre-
     lations among the communicative senses, Asilomar, California
     (Sept. 29-Oct. 2, 1978) 275-295.
[100] Turvey, M. T. and Shaw, R. The primacy of perceiving: An ecological
     reformulation of perception for understanding memory, in: Nilsson,
     L-G (Ed.) Perspectives on Memory Research: Essays in Honor of
     Uppsala University's 500th Anniversary (Erlbaum, Hillsdale, N.J.,
     1979).
[101] Turvey, M. T., Shaw, R. and Mace, W.   Issues in a theory of action:
     Degrees of freedom, coordinative structures and coalitions, in:
     Requin, J. (ed.), Attention and Performance, VII (Erlbaum, Hillsdale,
     N. J., 1978).
[102] Walter, C. F.   Kinetic and thermodynamic aspects of biological and
     biochemical control mechanisms, in: Kun, E., and Grisolia, S. (eds.)
     Biochemical Regulatory Mechanisms in Eukaryotic cells (Wiley-Inter-
     science, New York, 1972)
[103] Webb, P. W.   The swimming energetics of trout. I. Thrust and power
     output at cruising speeds. Jrnl. Exp. Biol. 55 (1971) 489-520.
[104] Weiss, P.   The cell as unit, J. Theor. Biol. 5 (1963) 389-397.
[105] Werner, J. Mathematical treatment of structure and function of the
     human thermoregulatory system, Bio. Cyber. 25 (1977) 93-101.
[106] Wheeler, J. A. Geometrodynamics (Academic Press, New York, 1962).
[107] Winfree, A. T.   Biological rhythms and the behavior of populations of
     coupled oscillators, J. Theoret. Biol. 16 (1967) 15-42.
[108] Yates, F. E.   Physical biology: A basis for modeling living systems,
     Jrnl. Cyber. Info. Sci. (in press).
[109] Yates, F. E. and Iberall, A. S.   Temporal and hierarchical organi-
     zation in biosystems, in: Urquhart, J. and Yates, F. E. (eds.),
     Temporal Aspects of Therapeutics (Plenum, New York, 1973).

[110] Yates, F. E., Marsh, D. J., and Iberall, A. S. Integration of the whole organism: A foundation for a theoretical biology, in: Behnke, J.A. (ed.), Challenging Biological Problems: Directions Towards their Solutions (Oxford Univ. Press, New York, 1972).
[111] Zimmerman, G., Kelso, J. A. S. and Lander, L. Articulatory behavior pre and post full mouth tooth extraction and total alveoloplasty: A cinefluorographic study. Jrnl. Sp. Hear. Res., in press.

Tutorials in Motor Behavior
G.E. Stelmach and J. Requin (eds.)
© *North-Holland Publishing Company, 1980*

2

ON THE CONCEPT OF COORDINATIVE STRUCTURES AS DISSIPATIVE STRUCTURES:
II. EMPIRICAL LINES OF CONVERGENCE*

J. A. Scott Kelso[1,2], K. G. Holt[2], P. N. Kugler[1] and M. T. Turvey[1]

Haskins Laboratories, New Haven, Connecticut
and
Departments of Psychology[1] and Biobehavioral Sciences[2]
University of Connecticut, Storrs, U. S. A.

In this paper we pursue the argument that where a group of
muscles functions as a single unit the resulting coordinative structure, to a first approximation, exhibits behavior
qualitatively like that of a force-driven mass-spring system. Data are presented illustrating the generative and
context-independent characteristics of this system in tasks
that require animals and humans to produce accurate limb
movements in spite of unpredictable changes in initial
conditions, perturbations during the movement and functional
deafferentation. Analogous findings come from studies of
articulatory compensation in speech production. Finally we
provide evidence suggesting that one classically-defined
source of information for movement, namely proprioception,
may not be dimension-specific in its contribution to coordination and control.

I. Introduction

In the first paper we have given a detailed theoretical argument suggesting that a group of muscles organized as a single functional unit is necessarily a thermodynamic engine, a dissipative structure, with the behavioral properties of a non-linear oscillator. That a constrained collection of muscles might well exhibit a likeness to oscillatory mechanisms was intuited some years ago by Bernstein (1947; see also Greene,
1978) and was advanced, on empirical grounds, by Fel'dman via a (now
classical) mechanographic analysis of arm movements (Asatryan & Fel'dman,
1965; Fel'dman, 1966a,b). Fel'dman's departure point was that the muscles
at a joint behave, on a first approximation, as a linear mass-spring system. His analysis revealed, however, that the behavior was more closely
approximated by a non-linear oscillatory system and we have shown, in the
preceding essay, how data such as Fel'dman's can be given an interpretation in the qualitative dynamics of a non-linear system. It remains,
however, a simpler convention to address some aspects of the behavior of
a constrained muscle collective in terms of the "first approximation" and
in large part the evidence to be reported below is an elaboration of the
mass-spring perspective.

*This work was supported by N.I.H. Grants NS 13617, AM 25814 and HD 01994.

Before proceeding with a presentation of this evidence however, it is
worth noting an important, but easily missed aspect of a mass-spring system that serves to bridge the two papers and preserve their unitary theme.
We refer to the realization that a mass-spring system is intrinsically
rhythmic or cyclic even though it does not have to behave rhythmically or
cyclically. This claim can be readily established by reconsidering (for
exemplary purposes only) the second-order differential equation of motion
for a simple mass-spring system, $m\ddot{x} + c\dot{x} + kx = 0$ where x is the displacement of the system from equilibrium and $\dot{x}$ and $\ddot{x}$ are its velocity and acceleration respectively. The type of motion produced is dependent upon
the intrinsic relationship between mass (m), stiffness (k) and the linear
damping constant (c). Thus where $c^2 = 4$ mk critical damping occurs; the
mass moves quickly to the equilibrium point without ever passing through
it. Where $c^2 < 4$ mk light damping occurs and the system oscillates with
amplitude of oscillation decreasing with time. Finally, in heavy damping
$c^2 > 4$ mk and the system does not oscillate nor does it reach the equilibrium position (Volterra & Zachmanoglou, 1965). Accepting that real systems do not persist in the absence of a periodic forcing function (cf.
Yates & Iberall, 1973), the message nevertheless is clear: a mass-spring
system is a concrete example of a system that can oscillate or not depending on its parameterization. Thus, there is no need to conceive discrete
and cyclical behaviors as arising from separate mechanisms. They are, in
fact, different manifestations of the same underlying organization.

In the first part of this paper, then, we extend the observation that an
oscillatory system analysis provides an apt account of the well-known
ability of the human motor system to precisely produce limb movements to
designated targets using a variety of movement trajectories and without regard to initial conditions. Second, we argue that it provides a much more
parsimonious explanation of the "immediate adjustment" phenomenon in speech
production than explanations currently in vogue. Third we shall discuss
evidence, based primarily on our joint replacement studies that suggests
it is unlikely that afferent information, as traditionally defined in the
motor systems literature, is dimension-specific.

2. The Production of Single Trajectory Movements

A major characteristic of a mass-spring system is that it is intrinsically
self-equilibrating; once set in motion the spring will always come to rest
at the same resting length or equilibrium position. Neither an increase
in initial deflection of the spring from its resting length nor temporary
perturbations will prevent the achievement of the equilibrium point, a
property known for open systems as equifinality (von Bertalanffy, 1973).
Support for this account comes from experiments in which subjects were required to hold a steady angle at the elbow joint against a resistance and
not to make adjustments when loads were added or removed. A systematic
change in load resulted in a systematic change in joint angle (steady-
state position) which was predictable as the behavior of a non-linear
spring (Asatryan & Fel'dman, 1965). The question arises as to how such a
spring might be controlled to produce different steady state positions.
According to Fel'dman (1966; see also Houk, 1978) this can be accomplished
by adjusting certain parameters, 'tuning' the spring, prior to movement.
In this account, the nervous system sets the values of resting length, λ,
by adjusting the length-tension relationships of the muscles involved. If
the length of the muscle, χ, varies from the resting length, movement takes

place. If $\chi > \lambda$ an active tension develops in the muscle and if $\chi < \lambda$
the muscle is relaxed. The invariant character of the muscle is, therefore, the dependence of tension on length for any fixed value of λ. Thus,
the only static parameter which need be set for voluntary movement in
Fel'dman's model is resting length: namely, the length of the muscles for
which differences in tension in opposing muscles sum to zero. On the
other hand, kinematic changes in rate, acceleration and periodicity in
the joint muscle collective are brought about by altering the dynamic
properties of stiffness and damping.

Recent data fit this perspective quite well, at least on a posteriori
grounds. For example, Bizzi and his colleagues (e.g. Bizzi, Dev, Morasso
& Polit, 1978; Polit & Bizzi, 1978; see also Bizzi this volume) have shown
for both head and arm movements that normal and rhizotomized monkeys can
accurately achieve learned target positions even when constant and brief
load perturbations were applied during the movement trajectory. They argue that the controlled variable must be an equilibrium point specified in
terms of the length-tension relationships in agonist and antagonist muscles. Similarly, a consistent outcome in human experiments has been the
superior accuracy of attaining final position over amplitude from variable
starting positions: a finding that extends to functionally deafferented
subjects (Kelso, 1977) as well as patients in whom positional detectors
in the joint capsule have been surgically removed (Kelso, Holt & Flatt,
Note 1; see below). These results are not easily accommodated by currently popular closed-loop, feedback (e.g., Adams, 1977) or open-loop,
programming accounts (e.g., Keele, in press). For example, although a
closed-loop model could handle the finding that achievement of final
position is possible in spite of changes in limb position prior to movement or the introduction of abrupt changes in load during execution, it
is at a loss when the same findings can be demonstrated under deafferented
conditions. Similarly, central programs that do not require ongoing feedback monitoring may handle deafferentation findings, but go awry when confronted with unforeseen changes in movement context. It seems more appropriate therefore to view terminal location as a steady-state position
specified by the tuned parameters of the spring: it is thus impervious
to unpredictable changes in initial conditions. Amplitude production, on
the other hand, involves a change in the equilibrium point as a function
of task demands, and hence a reparameterization of the spring function.

In our recent work we have set out to determine--on an a priori basis--
whether any of the observed kinematic characteristics that arise in localization violate the mass-spring model (cf. Kelso & Holt, in press).
Specifically our tack was to introduce sudden and unexpected torque
loads--which acted to drive the limb (in this case the index finger) in
the opposite direction--and observe consequent effects on localization.
In these experiments, we were not particularly concerned in providing a
detailed analysis of the various reflex responses to changed loading conditions (see Desmedt, 1978 for numerous studies). Rather we wished to
elucidate the effects of changing dynamic parameters and consequent kinematic variation on the attainment of a specified steady-state position.
Subjects performed extension movements of the index finger on a device
that allowed precise measurement of movement around the metacarpophalangeal joint. An electronic control system supported the programming of
D. C. torque motor output with respect to movement of the finger (max. =
81.6 oz. in.). The location (joint angle) at which the perturbation was
triggered as well as its duration (100 msec throughout) could be con-

trolled directly by the experimenter from the electronic panel. A potentiometer mounted over the axis of motion provided information regarding the
position and velocity of movement. Electromyographic activity was recorded from the right extensor digitorum and flexor digitorum superficialis
via Beckman silver-silver disk type surface electrodes.

Experiment 1 proceeded in two phases. The first, acquisition trials, consisted of 30 extension movements to a to-be-learned target position (50°
movement from the starting position which remained constant throughout at
20° flexion). Quantitative knowledge of results (KR) was provided by the
experimenter. Following the acquisition phase there were 18 test trials
(without KR) of which half were perturbed via the programmable torque
motor. The locations of the perturbation were designated as short (applied
after 10° of movement), medium (after 25°) or long (after 40°). There were
three trials at each of the three perturbation locations, and these were
randomly ordered amongst the 18 test trials. The subjects (n = 12) were
informed that on some of the trials a perturbation would occur and that
they should move through it in attempting to reach the learned location.
Deviations from the target position were recorded. By convention an undershoot was signed negative (-) and an overshoot was signed positive (+).
Absolute (unsigned), constant (signed) and variable error (standard deviation around mean constant error) were used for analysis purposes. During
acquisition there were obvious improvements in performance and these were
borne out statistically (p < .05).

The test trial data for constant and variable error are shown in Figure 1
indicating no significant differences between perturbed and non-perturbed
responses. Examination of the raw data revealed that nine of the 12 sub-

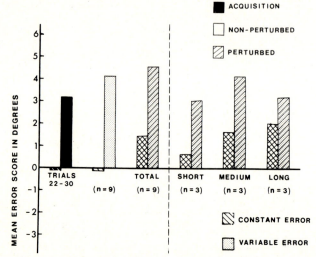

Figure 1 - Mean constant and variable errors (in degrees) for the last nine
           acquisition trials as well as perturbed and non-perturbed con-
           ditions. Perturbations were brief torque loads applied at three
           different loci during the movement.

jects showed little or no decrement in performance as a result of perturbations. No significant effects were observed for any of the dependent
variables between the three perturbation loci. Somewhat surprisingly
there was kinematic variability in velocity, movement time and oscillations, a result which either points to variability in at least one of the
dynamic parameters of stiffness and damping or to the fact that we are
looking at a system which is reliable but "dirty" (cf. Greene, in press).
In fact, of the 12 subjects nine demonstrated both critical and light
damping characteristics and none showed heavy damping (for actual examples
see Figure 2).

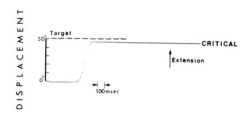

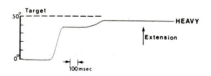

Figure 2. Actual records of one subject performing finger extension
           movements to a learned target. Figure illustrates light,
           critical and heavy damping.

There was a tendency towards critical damping in non-perturbed trials
(76%) while in perturbed trials there was a slight tendency for light
damping. We might have expected that in a learned motor activity these
parameters would be maintained constant from trial to trial. Since the
task demanded only target attainment, however, the movement patterns by
which this goal was achieved probably played a less significant role.
Clearly, the system can afford several variations in parameter specification for achieving the steady-state.[1]

We confirmed the equifinality result in a second experiment in a variation of the theme employed in Experiment 1. In this case, instead of inject- ing a brief torque load during the movement, we applied a constant load at the beginning of the movement and released it at unpredictable points during the trajectory. Thus the subjects (n =10), after learning the target position as before, performed a set of nine test trials (without knowledge of results), six of which were perturbed and three of which were not. The load was held constant throughout the 50 deg. extension move- ment (70% max. torque output), until its sudden release at one of three points during the movement (after 10, 25 or 40 deg.). Perturbed and non- perturbed test trials were randomly interspersed for each subject and de- viations from the target position noted as before.

A mass-spring model, consonant with the theoretical analysis provided in the previous paper, predicts that the unexpected addition of an external load should lead to an initial undershooting of the target. Once the ex- ternal force is removed however, and provided the parameters of the sys- tem have not been changed, the limb will move to the desired resting length. This is exactly what happened in Experiment 2. Examples of actual recordings from two subjects are shown in Figure 3 and the error data for the ten subjects are presented in Table 1. None of the dif- ferences between perturbed and non-perturbed conditions proved significant for either absolute or constant error ($p > .10$). There was an overall tendency to undershoot the target position in both perturbed and non- perturbed trials but no differences were significant as a function of lo- cus of release.

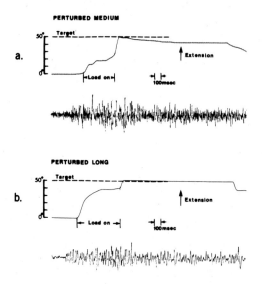

Figure 3.   Actual recordings of two different subjects performing a learned movement when a load is suddenly applied at the beginning of the movement and released unpredictably dur- ing the trajectory. EMG is from extensor digitorum.

Table I

Means and standard deviations (in deg.) of absolute and constant error
for non-perturbed and perturbed (load release) movements (N =10).

Means		Non-Perturbed[a]	Perturbed[b] Total	Short	Perturbed[c] Medium	Long
Absolute	M	5.97	6.73	5.75	6.70	7.75
Error	SD	4.76	4.23	5.21	4.56	4.83
Constant	M	-4.75	-4.32	-3.79	-4.49	-4.70
Error	SD	5.86	6.38	6.61	6.44	7.85

a   Means of 3 trials per subject
b   Means of 6 trials per subject
c   Means of 2 trials per subject

The finding that equally accurate performance was obtained in perturbed
and non-perturbed trials in both Experiments 1 and 2 strongly supports
the stability property that is characteristic of non-linear oscillatory
systems. Although comparisons are somewhat tenuous, our results appear
even more favorable for the concept than those obtained for arm movements
in monkeys where the errors are quite large (see Figure 2, Polit & Bizzi,
1978). In addition, this is the first time to our knowledge that equifinality in the face of unpredictable perturbations has been observed
in human subjects (see also Kelso, 1977).

The foregoing results do not, of course, rule out the possibility of
fast-acting peripheral feedback loops (e.g., Cooke & Eastman, 1977;
Evarts & Granit, 1976) that may have served to modify the movement during
its execution. A major prediction of our model-construct however, is
that a read-out of conventionally defined proprioceptive information (see
Section 4 below) is not a necessary condition for the achievement of the
equilibrium position. We therefore examined this issue by injecting load
perturbations during the localization movements of individuals who had
joint and cutaneous information removed using the wrist cuff technique
(see Merton, 1964; Goodwin, McCloskey & Matthews, 1972; Kelso, 1977 for
details). The advantage of this procedure is that muscle function is
preserved in the long finger flexors and extensors that lie high in the
forearm while sensory inputs to the hand itself are effectively eliminated.[2]

In this experiment (see Kelso & Holt, in press, for detailed account) we
built-in a replication of the first experiment and thus followed its procedure exactly. After the acquisition phase (30 trials with knowledge
of results) subjects performed nine perturbed and non-perturbed trials
(together designated pre-cuff trials) which were given in random order
and with knowledge of results withdrawn. On completion of this phase,
subjects were removed from the apparatus and the wrist cuff applied and
inflated as discussed in detail elsewhere (Kelso, 1977). The subject's
arm and hand were then replaced in the apparatus in the same posture as
before. Following the establishment of sensory cut-off using the same
criteria as our earlier work (Kelso, 1977) subjects performed a further

56   J.A. SCOTT KELSO ET AL.

18 trials in the absence of knowledge of results half of which were perturbed at three different loci.

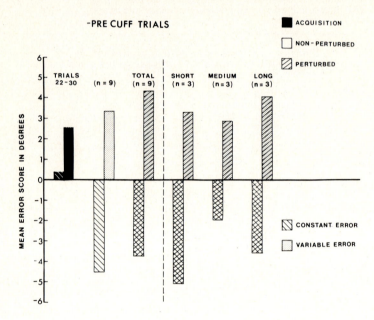

Figure 4.   Mean constant and variable errors (in degrees) for acquisi-
            tion, perturbed and non-perturbed trials prior to applica-
            tion of the wrist cuff.

The results of the acquisition and pre-cuff phases replicated the previous
studies in virtually all respects. Collectively these results are shown
in Figure 4 for variable and constant error. The only departure from the
previous findings was a very modest, but significant increase in variability between perturbed and non-perturbed trials (in the order of 1°).
For cuff trials, a comparison of non-perturbed and perturbed trials revealed significant differences for constant and variable error. The mean
constant error for non-perturbed trials was larger and more positive than
that for perturbed trials and the latter also showed greater variability.
As Figure 5 reveals, however, these differences are very modest indeed,
and in fact are orders of magnitude less than the boundary conditions set
by Polit and Bizzi (1978) for accurate arm movements in monkeys (12 to
15°). Neither pre-cuff nor cuff trials revealed differential error effects as a function of perturbation locus. It should be emphasized that
it is not legitimate to compare the accuracy data shown in Figures 4 and
5 due to the substantial time lapse that was necessary for the pressure
cuff to exert its effect (between 1 and 1.5 hr.). Although it is not
possible to completely discount the possibility of proprioceptive influences on target accuracy, the modest increase in error is likely
accounted for by the time delay combined with the absence of knowledge
of results regarding performance.

Qualitative differences in EMG activity (extensor digitorum) were exam-
mined in pre-cuff and cuff trials. Examples are given in Figure 6 along

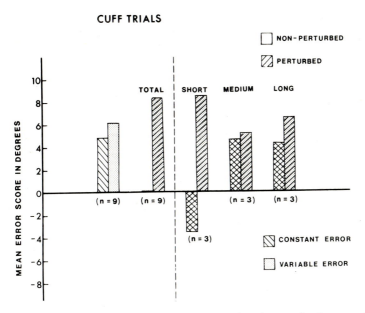

Figure 5. Mean constant and variable errors (in degrees) of perturbed
           and non-perturbed trials under wrist cuff conditions.

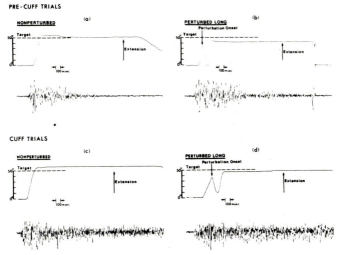

Figure 6. EMG activity of extensor digitorum and movement traces of
           perturbed and non-perturbed conditions with (c and d) and
           without wrist cuff (a and b).

with accompanying displacement records illustrating perturbed and non-perturbed movements. As shown in Figure 6(b) there is an increase in agonist EMG activity following perturbation onset due presumably to proprioceptive stimulation and consequent initiation of fast acting reflex loops (e.g. Evarts, 1973). In cuff performance, however, electrical activity was constant throughout the movement and signs of stretch reflex function were largely absent (Figure 6(c) and 6(d)). A notable observation was that the activity of the antagonist muscle (not shown here) was close to baseline during pre-cuff trials but highly active during and after achievement of the equilibrium point in cuff conditions.

One final and interesting aspect of the results was that movements in the wrist cuff condition were slower ($\underline{M}$ = 260°/sec, $\underline{SD}$ = 80°/sec) and movement patterns more consistent than in pre-cuff trials. This may well be related to the observed increase in EMG activity in flexor and extensor muscle groups during cuff movements which was combined (in not necessarily a causal way) with a perceived increase in effort in all subjects. One might suppose that an increase in the conjoint activity of flexors and extensors will have consequences qualitatively similar to increases in the stiffness parameter of a mass-spring system (Fel'dman, 1966). Given a constant damping parameter and increased stiffness, a mass spring system will convert from lightly damped to critically damped (Volterra & Zachmanoglou, 1965), thus suggesting a reason why all our subjects showed critical damping in cuff trials.

In summary, these data which are only briefly summarized here bear out aspects of the theoretical analysis of the system's dynamic organization discussed in the previous paper (Kugler, Kelso & Turvey, this volume) and strongly suggest a mode of coordination and control that has behavioral consequences qualitatively similar to those of a non-linear oscillatory system. Perhaps the most important characteristic of a non-linear system is its stability in the face of perturbations (see Part I) which emerges as the predominant feature in our data. Thus the limb terminates at the steady state originally specified despite unexpected and abrupt load disturbances, functional deafferentation and both of these in conjunction. Harkening back to the geometrodynamic perspective of Part 1, we note that this outcome is exactly that predicted by the traveler journeying on a curve whose geometry defines a valley positioned at the resting length of the system and with ascending walls whose slope indexes stiffness. While our manipulations may be seen to force the traveler up the sloping walls of the curve they do not change the tendency of the traveler to return to the valley or stable region of systemic organization. Moreover, our empirical findings are continuous with earlier work (Kelso, 1975; 1977) and, corroborated by recent neurophysiological data, provide a broad basis of experimental support for the model construct proposed here (see also Bizzi, this volume and Cooke, this volume).

3. The Immediate Adjustment Phenomenon in Speech Production

Let us now consider the foregoing analysis of limb movements in relation to an intriguing phenomenon in speech production, namely, how talkers can spontaneously adjust the movement patterns of their articulators in response to various types of disruption yet still produce intelligible acoustic output. Speech researchers have examined this phenomenon quite closely with the intent of discovering the nature of underlying adaptive mechanisms. The broader question of interest concerns, of course, the issue of context-independency in speech control--the fact that any single phoneme-phoneme transition places unique mechanical demands on the articulators involved--a problem discussed in some detail by MacNeilage (1970) and others (cf. Abbs, 1979; Perkell, 1979).

Consider the intuitive example of the pipe-smoker talking with his/her teeth clenched firmly on the pipe (cf. MacNeilage, 1970). To produce the open vowel /a/ requires some type of compensation for the fact that normal downward mandibular movement does not take place. For example, when speaking with a raised jaw, the normal trajectory of tongue movement is impeded by the fixed mandible. How does the talker accommodate such induced changes? At least two possible explanations seem to be immediately excluded. Lindblom, Lubker and Gay (in press) confirming the earlier work of Lindblom and Sundberg (1971) found that subjects were able to produce natural, steady state vowels with the jaw fixed in an unnatural physiological state by a bite-block without the need for acoustic feedback. "Normal-range" formant patterns were produced in the first glottal pitch-pulse of speech before any auditory information could have assisted the discovery of the appropriate articulator organization. While these studies suggest that adjustment was immediate and that acoustic feedback was insignificant they are not conclusive because they allow the subject to search for the appropriate positioning of the tongue before the production of the sound. Hence compensatory search behavior could feasibly occur before the onset of a measurable acoustic output. A recent study by Fowler and Turvey (Note 2) seems to preclude the articulatory search interpretation. The logic behind the experiment was simply this: In response to a visually presented vowel, a subject will typically require some time to organize the appropriate response. An extensive period of training should ensure a reasonably reliable measure of vocal reaction time under normal conditions. If a bite block is now inserted, and subjects employ an articulatory search strategy before producing an acoustic signal, then vocal reaction time should increase over non bite-block conditions. Preliminary analysis of the data reveals that this is not the case. Moreover, it matters not whether subjects performing under bite block conditions are instructed to maintain reaction time within normal bounds or whether the time stress is removed altogether. Vocal reaction times are the same in each as are the acoustic frequencies of the first and second formant patterns. There is then no speed-accuracy trade-off in the two groups. Thus, articulatory organization does indeed appear to be spontaneous and immediate under bite-block conditions.

How then can such a totally novel and unfamiliar task be produced so rapidly and without any apparent trial and error? What type of system could take into account such dramatic changes in context? An open-loop interpretation can be readily dispensed with for reasons we have outlined earlier (see also, MacNeilage, 1970; Schmidt, 1975). Similarly, a classical closed-loop, servomechanism using peripheral feedback to continually update motor commands to produce a desired state--would be much too slow to account for bite-block phenomena (but see arguments below for dynamic speech case). An alternative espoused by Lindblom and his colleagues (Lindblom et al. in press; Lindblom, McAllister & Lubker, 1977), proposes that the peripheral feedback loop is replaced by a simulation component that derives the sensory consequences of the motor command before it is executed. An internal comparison between the sensory goal and the simulated sensory consequences yields an error which can provide the basis for subsequent motor commands. This type of predictive simulation is

variously referred to as dynamic loop (Eccles, 1973) or model-referenced
control (e.g., Arbib, 1972 and this volume; Ito, 1970). To account for
their bite block findings, Lindblom et al. (in press) argue that since
the predictive component precedes peripheral phonetic output it can provide the system with a simulated set of sensory error signals before the
actual motor pattern is sent to the musculature. Thus the system in their
words 'learns' from its simulated mistakes before they can exert their
effects on the periphery.

Aside from the fact that this model ignores the conjoint problems of degrees of freedom and context-conditioned variability (Bernstein, 1967;
Turvey, Shaw & Mace, 1978) as well as the logical problems associated with
any servomechanism whether peripherally or internally based (cf. Fowler
& Turvey, 1978), it is not consistent with recent data. For example, one
interpretation of predictive simulation is that the simulation requires
additional computation time to achieve a match between the simulated sensory consequences and the desired state. Given this interpretation it is
difficult to imagine why longer than normal reaction times were not realized under bite block conditions in the Fowler and Turvey (Note 2)
study. Perhaps more damaging to the simulation model, however, is the
finding that vowels whether isolated or inserted in dynamic speech material (e.g. "it's a /pip/ again"), can be produced without any serious
acoustic consequences under bite block conditions combined with anesthesia (bilateral sensory blockage of the temporomandibular joint and extensive application of topical anesthetic to structures in and around the
oral cavity) and the presence of auditory masking noise (Kelso & Tuller,
Note 3). This result is obviously incompatible with a model that proposes
the generation of "appropriately revised motor commands on the basis of
the feedback positional information available before onset of phonation"
(Lindblom et al., in press). If such were the case, much more dramatic
effects of sensory interference on acoustic output should have been
evident, but this was not so.

The model construct proposed here promises a more elegant account of the
immediate adjustment phenomenon. Given a set of variables (such as the
components of the vocal tract) constrained to act as unit, the resultant
system has properties qualitatively like those of a non-linear oscillatory system. By virtue of its dynamic configuration such a system is
capable of attaining its goal -- which is intrinsic to the device --
from any starting point. Furthermore, if certain variables are fixed
as a result, for example, of a bite block, the non-frozen variables will
assume values appropriate to the constrained relation (see Fowler, Rubin,
Remez & Turvey, in press, for the details of this account). Consonant
with the theoretical analysis of the preceding paper and the experimental
analysis presented in Section 2 of this paper, computationally defined
sensory imputs are not a necessary condition for the operation of a group
of muscles constrained to act as a functional unit. In theory, at least,
our proposed model construct is equally applicable regardless of whether
disruptions are static and anticipated (e.g., bite block) or time-varying
and unanticipated. Thus Abbs and his colleagues have performed a number
of recent studies (cf. Abbs, 1979 for review) in which anticipated
disturbances to the lips and jaw were introduced during ongoing speech.
"Compensatory responses" of short latency (25-50 msec) were observed in
the articulator muscles to which loads were applied as well as in others
contributing to the same vocal tract goal. For example, loads applied to

the jaw yielded compensatory adjustments in both inferior and superior
orbicularis oris muscles in order to preserve ongoing articulation (e.g.,
Folkins & Abbs, 1975). In proposing a model to account for such
immediate adjustment phenomena, Abbs (1979) suggests that ..."while it is
plausible to consider parallel pre-adjustment of multiple motor commands
(through some sort of efferent copy), in response to steady-state,
anticipated disturbances (Lindblom et al., in press) rapid adjustment
to dynamic, unanticipated loads appears to require an afferent feedback
control capability " (p. 323).

Notice that Abbs' proposal is suggestive of two possibly distinct
mechanisms for responses to perturbations--one for anticipated disruptions
(a predictive simulation mechanism) and one for unanticipated disruptions
(a closed-loop, peripheral feedback mechanism). The present analysis
views such a distinction as redundant: rather, immediate adjustment
to perturbations of either kind is the necessary outcome of a dynamic
system in which a collective of muscles is constrained to act as a unit.
One final point is worthy of emphasis. The attainment of a goal for our
model construct--producing a vowel,for example--is conceptually distinct
from equating the production of a vowel with a spatial target. Vowel
attainment is not determined by a set-point or reference value as in a
closed-loop servo-mechanism. Granted, the production of a particular
vowel may be seen as one member of a class of gestures that aims toward
some specific vocal tract shape. But to equate this view of "vowels as
gestures" with a "targets" model is to miss the obvious difference
between a curve and its assymptotes (Fowler, et al., 1979). Moreover,
the achievement of a particular vocal tract shape is a consequence of
the vowel production system's parameterization: parameters are intrinsic
to the system and do not constitute an externally defined set point which
causally determines the system's behavior.

4.   Information as intrinsic to the model construct

An oscillatory system does not require the availability of ongoing feedback to be used for comparison purposes with some desired state like a
typical servomechanism. In a mass-spring system for example, there is no
feedback monitoring or comparison procedure and hence no need to introduce
special mechanisms for these purposes. What, then is the role of information in the ongoing control of movement? Clearly an adequate treatment of
this issue requires a longer story than we can tell here (but see Kugler,
Kelso & Turvey, in press). To be brief, we present some data that is relevant to the question of what information does: we take as an example, that
information which is typically thought to be germane to movement, namely,
kinesthetic stimulation.

One, not uncommon, view among psychologists is that kinesthetic information, primarily from joint receptors, serves to establish an internal referent of movement somewhere in the brain that can be used to elaborate
motor commands and even as a basis for motor learning. Physiological
models (usually of cerebellar function) incorporate this notion and extend
it as an explanation of highly learned behavior. Thus, when the "internal
model" or "perceptual referent" has been firmly established by the feedback
and feedforward consequences of movement, the need for kinesthetic stimulation diminishes and "automatization" occurs (cf. Eccles, 1973; Ito,
1970).

Early physiological work on slowly adapting joint receptors in the cat's
knee joint (e.g., Boyd & Roberts, 1953; Skoglund, 1956) seemed to pave the
way for the view that kinesthetic stimulation is angular specific and
served to establish spatial coordinate systems and the like (cf. Russell,
1976). Single neurons from joint receptors were shown to fire maximally
at particular joint angles and with a sensitive range of 15 ot 30 deg.
Such findings have led to the assumption that "receptor firing functions
for joint receptors are stored in the perceptual trace[3]...Theoretically,
learned timing is now seen as a consequence of an image of the firing
functions for joint receptors stored in the perceptual trace, and learned
position is the storage of which joint receptors have fired." (Adams,
1977, p. 514-515). Aside from the fact that recent and more expansive
physiological data discount the earlier findings (for review see Kelso,
1978; Lee & Kelso, in press), from our perspective the "image" is no more
a list of receptor firing functions than is the plan for an act a list of
commands to muscles.

In the previous paper it was argued that the distinction between variables
of control and coordination is not a fixed one, but rather is topologically defined by the system's dynamics. The argument, in brief, was that
the informational predicates are qualitative rather than quantitative in
nature. Moreover, information is conceived as information about the current state of the system's dynamics in the sense of information specific
to the system's dynamics. For example, information regarding the properties of a surface (e.g. its sponginess or compliance) not only informs
the individual of the surface attributes (e.g. soft or hard) but specifies
in a complementary way, what the stiffness of the muscular system for
postural support must be.

Experimentally, it can be shown that dimension-specific information--at
least about joint angle--does not appear to be crucial to the perception
and control of human movement. Briefly, we examined the movement production of 13 patients during a period from two days to four weeks following
total joint replacement of the metacarpophalangeal joints (see Kelso. Holt
& Flatt, 1979, Note 1). The operation involves complete surgical removal of the joint capsule--the supposed seat of position and movement detec-
tors--and replacement of the articular surfaces. One experiment examined
finger positioning accuracy under conditions where the starting position
changed from trial to trial. Patients moved actively to various angles
of finger flexion that defined criterion movements and then were passively
returned to different starting positions. Under one condition the patient
was asked to reproduce the final position of the criterion movement; in
another condition the patient was required to reproduce the original distance or amplitude (see Kelso, 1977 for a detailed account of this paradigm). The findings which are shown in Table 2 were very clear: final
position was much more accurate than amplitude and, as revealed by both
constant and absolute error was hardly affected by changes in initial conditions. Moreover, amplitude performance reflected a bias to reproduce
location. Even though task demands required the production of amplitude,
the motor system appears to be predisposed to achieve final position.
More important, the level of error in joint replacement patients was readily comparable with normal levels in 12 subjects (mean absolute error =
4.40 deg.).

One way of interpreting the differences between location and amplitude

TABLE 2

Mean errors (in degrees) for amplitude and location conditions
as a function of changes in starting position in patients (N=13)
following total metacarpophalangeal joint replacement.

		Amplitude		Location	
		Absolute Error	Constant Error	Absolute Error	Constant Error
[a]Starting Position$_1$	M	5.71	3.67	3.67	1.36
	SD	3.17	5.23	2.05	3.66
Starting Position$_2$	M	9.19	8.34	4.29	-0.19
	SD	5.47	6.26	2.54	4.41

[a]The starting position was either 5 deg (SP$_1$) or 15 deg (SP$_2$)
beyond the original starting position of 20 deg flexion, i.e.,
in 15 deg and 5 deg flexion respectively.

conditions is that there is a location code based on information provided
by some type of peripheral receptor or set of receptors. Reproduction of
location may then be viewed as a matching of receptor inputs to the stored
referent or spatial code. Reproduction of amplitude however is more difficult in that the change in starting position requires an additional
subtractive process relative to the spatial code. Thus to reproduce accurately, a new spatial code must somehow be derived to take into account
the change in starting position (e.g. Stelmach & McCracken, 1978).

But an alternative, more parsimonious account and one that is entirely
consonant with an oscillatory system analysis, equates the achievement of
location with the steady state of the system determined only by its dynamic organization. Note how the two interpretations discussed here differ
in perspective. In the former, kinematic details, such as the position
coordinates of the limb are represented in some internal reference system.
In contrast , a system that is like a mass-spring system cannot be said
to represent a kinematic detail such as final position; to the contrary,
the dynamic parameters determine the kinematic consequences.

With reference to the present data, the argument that a muscle system behaves qualitatively like a mass-spring system clearly negates reliable
reproduction of amplitude (a kinematic detail) from variable initial conditions. Furthermore, the finding that accurate positioning is possible
in the absence of slowly adapting joint afferents dampens enthusiasm for
the view that angular specific receptors contribute to the development of
a spatial code. While such receptors have typically been regarded as con-
tributing--or not contributing--specific types of kinematic information
(e.g. position, rate) to a central interpreting device, our predisposition
is to suppose that peripheral receptor information is not dimension-
specific. Instead, their function may be to tune or modulate lower-level
spinal centers (interneuronal pools) so that simple, undifferentiated
supra-spinal signals may exert optimum facilatory effects on the muscles
served by such pools.

The research of Aizerman and his colleagues (e.g. Aizerman & Andreeva, 1968; Chernov, 1968; Litvintsev, 1972), has provided evidence for this tuning viewpoint with reference to kinesthetic stimulation in such activities as postural adjustment, pain avoidance and precision aiming. In the latter task, for example, the subject is instructed to maintain the position of the radio-carpal joint consonant with a point on an oscilloscope screen whose gain factor is increased such that a 1 to 2 min. angle takes the point beyond screen limits (Chernov, 1968). During 'precision aiming' the electromyographic envelopes of the two muscle antagonists display alternating peaks at around 10 Hz. These peaks oscillate such that when the joint is moved in one direction a large peak arises approximately once a period (around 100 msec). It should be emphasized that both muscles pull at 10 Hz, but one is apparently biased to have a slightly higher amplitude than the other and so the limb moves. An identical result holds for rapid shaking of the wrist joint: only the amplitude of oscillation changes. To account for these and other findings Aizerman and Andreeva (1968) coin the term simple search mechanism whose central elements are a set of randomly interconnected neurons in the spinal cord, the random interneuron pool (RIP) and a mathematical function which, in the case of precision aiming, depends on the magnitude and velocity of joint angle (or, more precisely the muscle states that define these values).

The RIP output is determined by the number of interneurons, N_e, excited at any moment. In response to an impulse volley the value of N_e increases to a maximum defining the magnitude of the RIP 'peak' and then drops to a mean value about which it oscillates. The resting state of the autonomous RIP therefore corresponds to this value and the oscillation itself constitutes tremor. Clearly the background state of the RIP can affect the magnitude of the 'peak'; the actual duration of the descending signal or its intensity characteristics have little effect. Thus, during the task of 'precision aiming' non-differentiated impulses are sent simultaneously to both muscle antagonists involved in controlling joint angle. Peaks of muscular activity therefore arise in both muscles, but the larger peak arises in the muscle that is at that moment extended; that is muscle spindle inputs from the temporarily extended muscle lower the background state of the interneuronal pool and thereby insure that the extensor obtains the stronger peak. If one such peak serves to change joint angle in the direction of extension, the flexor muscle is lengthened: thus, on the next downward signal, the stronger peak occurs in the flexor and so the cycle is repeated.

Perhaps a more intuitive example comes from the maintenance of posture (Litvintsev, 1972). If a person in a relaxed position is pushed in the back, the muscle spindles in the gastrocnemius and hamstring muscle groups will be stretched. An undifferentiated supraspinal command pulse results in the activation of only those muscles whose spindle inputs define the background state of the interneuronal pool. Consequently, selective activation of the stretched muscles automatically gives rise to forces that preserve vertical posture. It seems imminently possible that kinesthetic stimulation in general (and not just muscle spindle inputs alone) serves a similar "tuning" function.[4] One obvious advantage of the simple search mechanism is that it obviates the need to select which muscles to contract; rather selective contraction occurs by virtue of the state of the interneuronal pools. Notice also that oscillation in the interneuronal pools is not some aberrant characteristic to be regulated. It is, instead an

intrinsically periodic process that appears to be _exploited_ for movement
control purposes. But even more important for the present discussion is
the proposal--borne out in part by the data presented here and the
Aizerman type of analysis--that kinesthetic "information" does not provide
quantitative values on certain kinematic variables to some interpreting
device. Rational considerations and a commitment to the primacy of dynamics persuade us that "information," however conceived is not likely
to be something that contributes to a reference mechanism whose goal resides outside the system itself.

5. Concluding remarks

In this paper as in its predecessor we have attempted to provide a principled basis for coordination and control, one that recognizes and emphasizes constraints on the free variables of a system as the necessary requirement for coordinated movement. True to Bernstein's problem, we have
promoted a model construct that for us takes out the least loan on intelligence by minimizing the number of so-called "executive" decisions and the
requirements for on-line control. Control and coordination arise we believe from the synergic relations among muscles: to a first approximation
this synergy or coordinative structure is a force-driven oscillatory system with the qualitative characteristics of a mass-spring. More properly
it is, as Yates, Marsh and Iberall (1972) remark, the minimal assembly of
components that sustains periodic energy transformations (power fluxes)
and information fluxes (see also Part 1).

Let us acknowledge in these final comments that of the data we have presented in favor of the model construct, none are individually persuasive.
Collectively, however, they provide a compelling basis of support for an
oscillatory system proposal while at the same time supplying empirical
reasons for questioning machine-type theories of the conventional cybernetic and artificial intelligence kind. An oscillatory system conception
brings with it, however, its own unique set of questions. For instance,
it is not easy to distinguish the roles of efferent and afferent information, at least as they are classifically defined. Servomechanisms, in
contrast have an appeal to some in this regard: afference is input to a
referent value and the consequent comparison (error) determines what the
efferent output or correction will be. Efference and afference are conceptually distinct. But as we have taken pains to establish, a system
such as a mass-spring is not a servo-mechanism and it would be erroneous
to describe it as one. There is no afference to be monitored and compared nor errors to be computed and corrected. The system behaves as it
does by virtue of its dynamic organization which is intrinsic to the system.

Elsewhere we have argued that where a collective of muscles functions as a
unit the efferent-afferent distinction becomes superfluous. Thus if muscles are linked synergistically, information about the current state of a
given muscle (afference) is also, by virtue of the linkage, a specification
of the states of other muscles (efference) to which it is functionally
linked (cf. Kugler & Turvey, in press). Different theories of motor control place undue importance on either efference (e.g. motor programs) or
afference (closed-loop systems); in contrast, the constraint (geometrodynamic) perspective assigns primacy to neither but equal priority to both.
Such a perspective is much more in line with the functional organization
of the nervous system revealing interactions at all levels of the neuraxis

and the fact that the Bell-Magendie law is now extinct (cf. Smith, 1978). In addition, it is consonant with the view expressed many years ago by Sperry (1952) amd more recently emphasized by Diamond (1979) that the classical post-central (sensory)- precentral (motor) cortex distinction does not fit the actual patterning of information flux in the cortex. Both "afferent" and "efferent" paths can be linked, for example, to post central cortex thus enabling this structure to perform both a "sensory" and a "motor" function. Our suspicion therefore, is that inquiry into the control and coordination of movement may be ill-served by the traditional distinction between sensory and motor (see Evarts, Bizzi, Burke, DeLong & Thach, 1971). In fairness, however, we should admit that the details of the informational support for an organization of muscles that is qualitatively like an oscillatory system such as a mass-spring system presents a major challenge.

A dominant theme throughout this paper--in acknowledgement of Bernstein's problem--has been to minimize the number of executive instructions and to keep those instructions simple in content. Multivariable systems may be optimally controlled via a small set of autonomously regulated variables constrained in such a way that just a few parameters are required. In this claim we mirror for movement, Runeson's (1977) requirement for "smart" perceptual devices that register directly a complex variable--a complex particular (Pittenger, Shaw & Mark, 1979; Turvey & Shaw, 1979)--yet consist of only a few specialized components which are capable of solving problems that repeatedly occur. There are a number of valid comparisons between our model construct as a "smart" motor device and the type of perceptual mechanism envisaged by Runeson (1977).

The guiding philosophy behind our approach to understanding motor systems should by now be blatently apparent: Reject the introduction of new mechanisms and principles until, at least, the laws of dynamics have been fully explored. As Yates and Iberall (1973) emphasize, as did others in the past (e.g. von Bertalanffy, 1953; Weiss, 1941), it has been much easier to explain living (and we would say movement) systems in terms of a deus ex machina outside the system than to discover causality and start-up processes within the dynamic organization of the system itself. If nothing else in this paper and its companion we have given notice as to where our bets are placed.

Reference Notes

[1]Kelso, J. A. S., Holt, K. G., & Flatt, A. E.   Towards a theoretical reassessment of the role of proprioception in the perception and control of human movement. Manuscript in review.

[2]Fowler, C. A. & Turvey, M. T. Manuscript in preparation.

[3]Kelso, J. A. S. & Tuller, B. Manuscript in preparation.

Footnotes

[1]This is readily apparent from the intrinsic relationship between c^2 and 4 mk in the equation of motion for a simple mass-spring system (see earlier discussion).

[2]Three independent sources of evidence speak to the viability of the wrist cuff technique as a tool in reducing mechanoreceptive information. First,

passive displacements of the metacarpophalangeal joint up to an estimated 90°/sec went undetected. Second, subjects when instructed to produce a movement but prevented from doing so, consistently perceived that they had executed the movement. If muscle afferent information were capable of accessing consciousness, this would be an unlikely finding. Third, it has been consistently verified that the loss of background facilitation from joint and cutaneous sources using this procedure depresses stretch reflex function (e.g., Marsden, Merton & Morton, 1972; Merton, 1974).

[3]In Adams' (1977) words, "the perceptual trace is a learned reference of correctness for the movement based on feedback from response-produced stimuli" (p. 514).

[4]It may be the case that visual and auditory information serve a similar tuning function via a form of reflex input into the interneuronal pools. There is evidence, admittedly preliminary in nature, that may be viewed as supportive of such a notion for vision (e.g. Thoden, Dichgans & Savidis, 1977) and for audition (e.g. Melville-Jones, Watt & Rossignol, 1973).

References

[1]   Abbs, J. H. Speech motor equivalence. The need for a multi-level control model, in: Proceedings of the Ninth International Congress of Phonetic Sciences 1979, Vol. II. (Inst. of Phonetics, Copenhagen, 1979).
[2]   Adams, J. A. Feedback theory of how joint receptors regulate the timing and positioning of a limb, Psychol. Rev. 84 (1977) 504-523.
[3]   Aizerman, H. A., and Andreeva, E. A., Simple search mechanism for control of skeletal muscle. Autom. Rem. Cntrl. 29 (1968) 452-463.
[4]   Arbib, M. A. The metaphorical Brain. Wiley-New York, 1972).
[5]   Asatryan, D. G. and Fel'dman, A. D. Functional tuning of the nervous system with control of movement or maintenance of a steady posture - I. Mechanographic analysis of the work on the joint on execution of a postural task. Biophys. 10 (1965) 925-935.
[6]   Bernstein, N. The coordination and regulation of movement (Pergamon, New York, 1967).
[7]   Bizzi, E., Dev, P., Morasso, P., Polit, A. Effects of load disturbance during centrally initiated movements. Jrnl. Neurophys. 41 (1978) 542-556.
[8]   Boyd, I. A. and Roberts, T. D. M. Proprioceptive discharges from stretch receptors in the knee-joint of the cat. Jrnl. Physiol. Lond. 122 (1953) 38-58.
[9]   Chernov, V. I. Control over single muscles of a pair of muscle-antagonists under conditions of precision search. Autom. Rem. Cntrl. 29 (1968) 1090-1101.
[10]   Cooke, J.D. and Eastman, M. J. Long-loop reflexes in the tranquilized monkey, Exp. Br. Res. 27 (1977) 491-500.
[11]   Desmedt, J. E. (ed.) Cerebral Motor Control in Man: Long Loop Mechanisms (Karger, Basel, 1978).
[12]   Diamond, I. T. The subdivisions of neocortex: A proposal to revise the traditional view of sensory, motor and association areas, in: Sprague, J. M., and Epstein, A. N. (eds.), Progress in Psychobiology and Physiological Psychology, Vol. 8 (Academic Press, New York, 1979).

[13] Eccles, J. C. Understanding the Brain (McGraw-Hill, New York, 1923).
[14] Evarts, E. V. Motor cortex reflexes associated with learned movement, Science 179 (1973) 501-503.
[15] Evarts, E. V. and Granit, R., Relations of reflexes and intended movements, Prog. Br. Res. 44 (1976) 1-14.
[16] Evarts, E. V., Bizzi, E., Burke, R. E., Delong, M., and Thach, W. T. The central control of movement, Neurosc. Res. Prog. Bull. 9 (1971) 1-170.
[17] Fel'dman, A. G. Functional tuning of the nervous system with control of movement or maintenance of a steady posture - II. Controllable parameters of the muscles, Biophys. 11 (1966) 565-578(a).
[18] Fel'dman, A. G. Functional tuning of the nervous system with control of movement or maintenance of a steady posture - III. Mechanographic analysis of the execution by man of the simplest motor tasks, Biophys. 11 (1966) 766-775(b).
[19] Folkins, J. and Abbs, J. H. Lip and jaw motor control during speech, Jrnl. Speech. Hear. Res. 19 (1975) 207-220.
[20] Fowler, C. A., Rubin, P., Remez, R. E. and Turvey, M. T. Implications for speech production of a general theory of action, in: Butterworth, B. (ed.), Language Production (Academic Press, New York, in press).
[21] Fowler, C. A., and Turvey, M. T. Skill acquisition: An event approach for the optimum of a function of several variables, in: Stelmach, G. E. (ed.), Information Processing in Motor Control and Learning (Academic Press, New York, 1978).
[22] Goodwin, G. M., McCloskey, D. I., and Matthews, P. B. C. The contribution of muscle afferents to kinesthesia shown by vibration induced illusion of movement on the effects of paralyzing joint afferents, Brain 95 (1972) 705-748.
[23] Greene, P. H. Technical Report 78-12, Dept. of Comp. Sci., Illinois Inst. of Technol. (1978).
[24] Greene, P. H. Strategies for heterarchical control--an essay. I. A style of controlling complex systems, Intern. Jrnl. Man-Mach. Stud., in press.
[25] Houk, J. C. Participation of reflex mechanisms and reaction time processes in the compensatory adjustments to mechanical disturbance, in: J. E. Desmedt (ed.), Cerebral Motor Control in Man: Long Loop Mechanisms (Karger, Basel, 1978).
[26] Ito, M. Neurophysiological aspects of the cerebellar motor control system. Inter. Jrnl. Neurol. 7 (1970) 162-176.
[27] Keele, S. W. Behavioral analysis of motor control, in: V. Brooks (ed.), Handbook of Physiology, Motor Control Volume (American Physiol. Soc., Washington, in press).
[28] Kelso, J. A. S. Planning, efferent and receptor components in movement coding. Ph.D. dissertation, Univer. Wisconsin, Madison. (December, 1975).
[29] Kelso, J. A. S. Motor control mechanisms underlying human movement reproduction. Jrnl. Exptl. Psychol: Hum. Perc. Perf. 3 (1977) 529-543.
[30] Kelso, J. A. S. Joint receptors do not provide a satisfactory basis for motor timing and positioning. Psychol. Rev. 85 (1978) 474-481.
[31] Kelso, J. A. S. and Holt, K. G. Exploring a vibratory systems analysis of human movement production, Jrnl. Neurophys., in press.
[32] Kugler, P. N. and Turvey, M. T. Two metaphors for neural afference and efference, Behav. Br. Sci., in press.

[33] Kugler, P. N., Kelso, J. A. S. and Turvey, M. T. On the control and
      coordination of naturally developing systems, in: Kelso, J. A. S. and
      Clark, J. (eds.), Development of Human Motor Skill (Wiley, New York,
      in press).
[34] Lee, W. A., and Kelso, J. A. S. Properties of slowly adapting joint
      receptors do not readily predict perception of limb position, Jrnl.
      Hum. Move. Stud. in press.
[35] Lindblom, B. and Sundberg, J.   Acoustical consequences of lip,
      tongue, jaw and larynx movement, Jrnl. Acoust. Soc. Am. 50 (1971)
      1166-1179.
[36] Lindblom, B., Lubker, J., and Gay, T. Formant frequencies of some
      fixed mandible vowels and a model of speech motor programming by
      predictive simulation, Jrnl. Phon. in press.
[37] Lindblom, McAllister, R., and Lubker, J. Compensatory articulation
      and the modeling of normal speech production behavior, Paper pre-
      sented at Symposium on Articulatory Modeling, Grenoble, France (July,
      1977).
[38] Litvintsev, A. I. Vertical posture control mechanisms in man, Autom.
      and Rem. Contr. 33 (1972) 590-600.
[39] MacNeilage, P. The motor control of serial ordering in speech,
      Psychol. Rev. 77 (1970) 182-196.
[40] Marsden, C.D., Merton, P. A. and Morton, H. B., Servo action in
      human voluntary movement. Nat. Lond. 238 (1972) 140-143.
[41] Melvill-Jones, G., Watt, D. G. D. and Rossignol, S. Eighth nerve
      contributions to the synthesis of locomotor control, in: Stein, R.
      G., Pearson, K., Smith, R., and Redford, J. (eds.), Control of
      Posture and Locomotion (Plenum, London, 1973).
[42] Merton, P. A. Human position sense and sense of effort. Homeo-
      stasis and feedback mechanisms. 18th Symp. Soc. Exp. Biol.
      (Cambridge Univ. Press, Cambridge, 1964).
[43] Merton, P. A. The properties of the human muscle servo, Br. Res. 71
      (1974) 475-478.
[44] Perkell, J. A. On the use of orosensory feedback: An interpretation
      of compensatory articulation experiments, in: Proceedings of the
      Ninth International Congress of Phonetic Sciences, Vol. II (Institute
      of Phonetics, Univ. Copenhagen, 1979).
[45] Pittenger, J. B., Shaw, R. E., and Mark, L. S. Perceptual informa-
      tion for the age level of faces as a higher order invariant of growth,
      Jrnl. Expt. Psychol.: Hum. Perc. Perf. 5 (1979) 478-493.
[46] Polit, A., & Bizzi, E. Processes controlling arm movements in mon-
      keys, Science 201 (1978) 1235-1237.
[47] Runeson, S. On the possibility of "smart" perceptual mechanisms,
      Scand. Jrnl. Psychol. 18 (1977) 172-179.
[48] Russell, D. G. Location cues and movement production, in: Stelmach,
      G.E. (ed.), Motor Control: Issues and Trends (Academic Press, New
      York, 1976).
[49] Schmidt, R. A. A schema theory of discrete motor skill learning,
      Psychol. Rev. 82 (1975) 225-260.
[50] Skoglund, S. Anatomical and physiological studies of knee joint in-
      nervation in the cat. Act. Physiol. Scand. Monog. Suppl. 124
      (1956) 1-99.
[51] Smith, J. L. Sensorimotor integration during motor programming, in:
      Stelmach, G. E. (ed.) Information processing in motor learning and
      control (Academic Press, New York, 1978).
[52] Sperry, R. W. Neurology and the mind-brain problem, Amer. Sci.
      40, 291-312.

[53] Stelmach, G. E. and McCracken, H. D. Storage codes for movement information, in: Requin, J. (ed.), Attention and Performance VII (Erlbaum, Hillsdale, 1978).

[54] Thoden, V., Dichgans, J. and Savidis, T. Direction specific opto-kinetic modulation of monosynaptic hind limb reflexes in cats, Exp. Br. Res. 30 (1977) 155-160.

[55] Turvey, M. T. and Shaw, R. E. The primacy of perceiving: An ecological reformulation of perception for understanding memory, in: Nilsson, L. G. (ed.), Perspectives on Memory Research: Essays in Honor of Uppsala University's 500th Anniversary (Erlbaum, Hillsdale, 1979).

[56] Turvey, M. T., Shaw, R. E. and Mace, W. Issues in the theory of action, in: Requin, J. (ed.), Attention and Performance, VII (Erlbaum, Hillsdale, 1978).

[57] Volterra, E. and Zachmanoglou, E. C., Dynamics of Vibrations (Merrill, Ohio, 1965).

[58] von Bertalanffy, L. Problems of Life (Harper, New York, 1953).

[59] von Bertalanffy, L. General System Theory. (Penguin, England, 1973).

[60] Weiss, P. Self differentiation of the basic pattern of coordination, Comp. Psychol. Monog. 17 (1941) 29-96.

[61] Yates, F. E., Marsh, D. J., and Iberall, A. S. Integration of the whole organism: A foundation for theoretical biology, in: Behnke, J. A. (ed.), Challenging Biological Problems: Directions towards their solutions (Oxford Univ. Press, New York, 1972).

[62] Yates, F. E., and Iberall, A. S. Temporal and hierarchical organization in biosystems, in: Urquart, J. and Yates, F. E. (eds.), Temporal Aspects of Therapeutics (Plenum, New York, 1973).

Tutorials in Motor Behavior
G.E. Stelmach and J. Requin (eds.)
© *North-Holland Publishing Company, 1980*

3

INTERACTING SCHEMAS
FOR MOTOR CONTROL*

Michael A. Arbib
Center for Systems Neuroscience
University of Massachusetts
Amherst, MA 01003, USA

Motor activity must be guided by perception of the environment,
and itself affects that perception. We give an overview of
the way in which interacting schemas may be posited in the
visual perception of the structure of the environment, the
planning of a course of action, the integration of effectors
in the execution of the plan, and the updating of plan and
perception as the organism moves -- a continuing action/per-
ception cycle. To show how some simple processes of this kind
may be played out over neural structures, we review behavioral,
physiological and anatomical data on visuomotor coordination
in frog and toad, and discuss related computational models.

Underlying most behaviors are complex internal processes, providing integrative mechanisms and representations for the spatio-temporal organization
of behavior. In the first part of this paper, we sketch a set of representations and mechanisms which could mediate visually-guided behavior. An
extended account of this analysis of perceptual structures and distributed
motor control, together with extended citations of the literature, may be
found in [2]; while its relation to visually-guided robot locomotion is
presented in [4]. The second part of the paper shows that certain portions
of the general analysis can be related to anatomical, physiological and
behavioral experiments, by presenting several studies on visuomotor coordination in frog and toad.

PART 1. THE GENERAL FRAMEWORK

We propose that the following internal structures and processes are neces-
sitated by the visual control of locomotion: the representation of the
environment, the updating of that representation on the basis of visual
input, the use of that representation by programs which control the locomotion; and the cycle of integrated perception and action. We seek functional units whose cooperation in achieving visuomotor coordination can be
analyzed and understood irrespective of whether they themselves are further
decomposed in terms of neural nets or computer programs. Our style of
analysis will seek to decompose functions into the interaction of a family
of simultaneously active processes called schemas, which will serve as
building blocks for both representations and programs.

---

*Preparation of this paper was supported in part by NIH grant NS14971-01.

1.1 Multi-level Programs and the Action/Perception Cycle

The control of locomotion may be specified at varying levels of refinement:
the goal of the motion; the path to be traversed in reaching the goal; the
actual pattern of footfalls in the case of a legged animal; and the detailed pattern of motor or muscle activation required for each footfall.
It is well-known that the fine details of activation will be modified on
the basis of sensory feedback, but we stress that even the path-plan will
be continually modified as locomotion proceeds. For example, locomotion
will afford new viewpoints which will reveal shortcuts or unexpected obstacles which must be taken into account in modifying the projected path. We
thus speak of the action/perception cycle -- the system perceives as the
basis for action; each action affords new data for perception.

1.2 Motor Schemas

In terms of "units independent of embodiment" we may seek to postulate
basic motor processes for, e.g., locomoting which, given a path plan as
input, will yield the first step along that path as output. Another such
unit would direct a hand to grasp an object, given its position as input.
We refer to such units of behavior as "motor schemas". Our analysis will
descend no further than the level of motor schemas, and will leave aside
details of mechanical or neuromuscular implementation. Our claim will be
that crucial aspects of visuomotor coordination can be revealed at this
level of aggregation.

1.3 Representing the Environment as a Schema-Assemblage

The raw pattern of retinal stimulation cannot guide locomotion directly.
Rather, it must be interpreted in terms of objects and other "domains of
interaction" in the environment. We also use the term "schema" for the
process whereby the system determines whether a given "domain of interaction" is present in the environment. The state of activation of the
schema will then determine the credibility of the hypothesis that
which the schema represents is indeed present; while other schema parameters will represent further properties such as size, location, and motion
relative to the locomoting system.

Consider a schema that represents, say, a chair; and consider an environment that has two chairs in plain view. It is clear that two copies of the
chair-schema -- or, at least, two separate sets of chair-schema-parameters
-- will be required to represent the two chairs. We refer to these two
copies as separate "instantiations" of the same schema, each with its own
set of parameter values. We may thus view the internal representation of
the environment as an assemblage of spatially-tagged, parametrized, schema
instantiations.

1.4 Segmenting and Structuring the Changing Retinal Input

Object-representing schemas will not be driven directly by retinal activity,
but rather by the output of segmentation processes which provide an intermediate representation in terms of regions or segments (usually corresponding to the surfaces of objects) separated from one another by edges, and
characterized internally by continuities in hue, texture, depth and velocity.
As locomotion proceeds, and as objects move in the environment, most of
these regions will change gradually, and the segmentation processes must be

equipped with a dynamic memory which allows the intermediate representation to be continually updated to provide current input for the object-schemas, so that the schema-assemblage representing the environment will be kept up-to-date.

1.5 Distributed Control

Note that a schema is both a process and a representation. The formation and updating of the internal representation is viewed as a distributed process, involving the parallel activity of all those schemas which receive appropriately patterned input. The resultant environmental representation interacts with those processes which represent the system's goal structures to generate the plan of action -- exemplified by the projected path in the case of locomotion -- which can provide the input to the various motor schemas that directly control behavior.

1.6 Planning

We may view the schema-assemblage -- the structure of perceptual schemas which relates the animal to its environment -- as a spatial structure which has temporal characteristics (e.g. representing the motion of objects relative to the animal). We shall shortly discuss the possible nature of "coordinated control programs" which can coordinate the activation of motor schemas. Such a program serves to control the temporal unfolding of movement, but has spatial characteristics since interaction with objects will usually depend on their position in the environment.

There is no simple stimulus-response relationship here. Perception of an object (activating perceptual schemas) involves gaining access to motor schemas for interaction with it, but does not necessarily involve their execution. While an animal may perceive many aspects of its environment, only a few of these can at any time become the primary locus of interaction. A process of planning is required to determine the plan of action, the appropriate program of motor schema activation, on the basis of current goals and the environmental model. Perception activates, while planning concentrates. Coming upon unexpected obstacles can alter the elaboration of higher-level structures -- the animal continually makes, executes and updates its plans as it moves.

1.7 Adaptive Controllers

We suggest that a motor schema be thought of as a control system, continually monitoring feedback from the system it controls to determine the appropriate pattern of action to achieve the motor schema's goals (which will, in general, be subgoals within some higher-level coordinated control program). Since the controlled system may itself be variable, the motor schema must contain an "identification algorithm" to estimate the relevant parameters of the controlled system (for example, a grasp schema needs to know the position, size and orientation of what is to be grasped). This identification procedure may be viewed as a perceptual schema embedded within a motor schema. We stress, however, that this identification algorithm has both a "short-term" and a "long-term" component -- determining parameters relevant to the current controlled system, and determining parameters relevant to the controller's general control strategy.

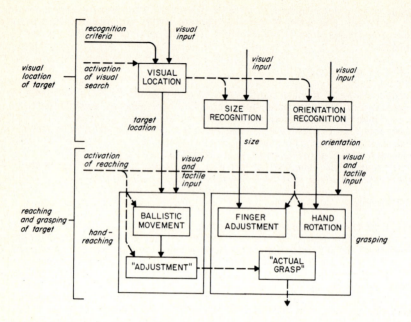

Fig. 1. A hypothetical coordinated control program for visually
directed grasping. The perceptual schemas atop the figure serve
as identification procedures for the motor schemas in the control
program of the lower half of the figure. (--- → control path;
⟶ data path)

1.8 Coordinated Control Programs

The language of "coordinated control programs" addresses the description of
the coordinated phasing in and out of the brain's manifold control systems.
While certain basic programs are "hard-wired" (as in the cases considered
in Part 2 of the present paper) most programs are generated as the result
of an explicit planning process. We exemplify this notion by the hypothetical program of Figure 1 for a human's grasping an object.

The spoken instructions given to the subject drive the planning process
that leads to the creation of the appropriate plan of action -- which we
here hypothesize to take the form of the distributed control program shown
in the lower half of the figure, involving the interwoven activation of
motor schemas for reaching and grasping. Activation of the program (broken
arrows convey "activation signals") is posited to simultaneously initiate a
ballistic movement toward the target and a preshaping of the hand during
which the fingers are adjusted to the size of the object and the hand is
rotated to the appropriate orientation (solid arrows indicate transfer of
data). When the hand is near the object, feedback adjusts the position of
the hand, and completion of this adjustment activates the actual grasping
of the hand about the object.

The perceptual schemas hypothesized in the upper half of the figure need not be regarded as a separate part of the program. Rather, they provide the identification algorithms required to pass parameter values to the motor schemas. This analysis of visual input locates the target object within the subject's "reaching space"; and extracts the size and orientation of the target object and feeds them to the control surface of the grasping schema. When the actual grasping movement is triggered, it shapes the hand on the basis of a subtle spatial pattern of tactile feedback. (For data on visuomotor mechanisms in reaching within extrapersonal space, and a careful review of the relevant literature, see [19].)

1.9 Feedforward

We view feedforward both as a means whereby a controller can "pre-empt" the effect of disturbances, and as a strategy that generates large control signals that rapidly bridge large discrepancies in desired output. In discrete-activation feedforward, each activation of the feedforward controller returns the controlled system to the "right ballpark" in which feedback can operate effectively. In co-activation feedforward, feedforward control is continually active to provide the appropriate control signal required to maintain the desired output, with feedback serving to refine this approximation.

Holmes [15] studied motor behavior in patients with damage to one side of the cerebellum. The overall program for control of the trajectory appears unimpaired by cerebellar damage, but "the speed of the affected limb [moving to a target] is often unchecked till the object is reached or even passed, and then the error is corrected by a series of jerky secondary movements ..." I suggest that we might characterize the deficiency as a loss of the feedforward required to initiate active deceleration perhaps halfway through the movement to avoid overshooting. Interestingly, a common strategy in these cerebellar patients seems to involve voluntary superposition of a conscious feedforward control which is less accurate than the cerebellar mechanism it replaces.

A useful experiment would test the hypothesis that each movement is pre-shaped on the basis of what comes next -- another predictive component in addition to feedforward. It is well-known that the utterance of a given phoneme is highly context-dependent. To get similar data on limb movement, we need to consider EMG and cine data on pointing at a target as a function of whether or not the subject is told to hold at the target before moving again, and as a function of the location of the next target.

1.10 Skill Acquisition

While the neural mechanisms for "planned" coordinated control of motor schemas (as distinct from the "hard-wired" systems to be discussed in Part 2) seem to be beyond the range of current experimental investigation, the notion of coordinated control program does make contact with the motor skills literature. For example, the work of Pew [22] may be interpreted as showing that the feedback provided to a subject learning a motor skill may be of little use when the overall structure of a coordinated control program has yet to be learnt, no matter how appropriate it may be for fine-tuning specific motor schemas within the program. Since we may posit that a system will learn best with feedback suited to its current learning strategy, study of the relative effectiveness of different types of feed-

back during skill acquisition may provide useful data for inferring what
the strategy might be.

1.11 Schmidt's Schemas

Schmidt [24, 25] has developed a notion of schema appropriate for the
control of a single motion. The schema is broken into two parts. The
"recall schema" is essentially the feedforward component of a motor schema
in our sense: it controls a complete rapid movement, even though environmental feedback may later signal errors. The "recognition schema" is responsible for the evaluation of response-produced feedback. It seems to
combine on-line feedback to improve the accuracy of the present movement
with identification procedures which may operate even after a movement is
completed to better tune the schema for its next activation.

PART 2.   VISUOMOTOR COORDINATION IN FROG AND TOAD

2.1 Maps as Control Surfaces

A notable characteristic of brains is the orderly mapping from one neural
layer to another, be it the retino-topic mapping from retina to the many
visual systems, or the somatotopic mapping of motor cortex to the musculature. We suggest that such a map may be viewed as a "control surface", so
that it is spatio-temporal patterns in such a map that provide input to
some control system in the brain. Where Pitts and McCulloch [23] modelled
the output layers of superior colliculus as a control surface for eye movements, Braitenberg and Onesto [5] gave a scheme for the conversion of
spatial input pattern to a timing distribution of control signals for a
ballistic movement. Such models led to the idea that a plausible subsystem
for vertebrate nervous systems may be a layered motor controller in which
position of the input on the control surface encodes the target to which
the musculature will be sent. Further, we might expect that -- akin to the
result of merging the Pitts-McCulloch scheme with the Braitenberg-Onesto
scheme -- if an array of points is activated on the input surface, the
system will move to the position which is the "center of gravity" of the
positions encoded by that array.

2.2 A Model of Frog Snapping

Ingle [16] studied the snapping behavior of the frog when confronted with
one or more fly-like stimuli. He found that in a certain region around the
head, the presence of a fly-like stimulus will elicit a snap; that is, the
frog will turn so that its midline is pointed at the "fly", and "zap" it
with its tongue. When confronted with two "flies", either of which was
vigorous enough that alone it would have elicited a snapping response, the
frog could exhibit one of three reactions: it could snap at one of them,
it could not snap at all, or it might snap at the "average fly". Didday
[7, 8] provided a simple model of such "choice behavior" based on data
available in 1970.   We present it not as state-of-the-art, but rather
to provide a clear example of the processing of structured stimuli to provide the input to a motor controller of the kind posited above. The task,
then, was to design a network which can take a position-tagged array of
"foodness" intensity from tectal neurons which modulate signals from the
Group II "bug detector" cells of Lettvin et al. [21] with that from other
layers, and ensure that usually only one region of activity will influence
the motor control systems. The model maintains the spatial distribution of

information, with new circuitry introduced whereby different regions of
the tectum so compete that in normal circumstances only the most active
will provide an above-threshold input to the motor circuitry. To achieve
this effect, we first introduce a new layer of cells in close correspondence to the "foodness layer", but whose activity is to yield the input to
the motor circuitry. In some sense, then, it is to be "relative foodness"
rather than "foodness" which describes the receptive field activity appropriate to a cell of this layer.

Didday's transformation scheme from "foodness" to "relative foodness"
employs a population of what we shall call S-cells in topographic correspondence with the other layers. Each S-cell inhibits the activity that
cells in its region of the "relative foodness layer" receive from the corresponding cells in the "foodness" layer by an amount that increases with
increasing activity outside its region. This ensures that high activity in
a region of the foodness layer only "gets through" if the surrounding areas
do not contain sufficiently high activity to block it.

When we examine the behavior of such a network, we find that plausible in-
terconnection schemes yield the following properties:
1) If the activity in one region far exceeds the activity in any other
   region, then this region will eventually "overwhelm" all other regions,
   and the animal will snap at the space corresponding to it.
2) If two regions have sufficiently close activity, then:
   (a) If both regions are very active they may both overwhelm the other
       regions and simultaneously "take command" with the result that the
       frog snaps between the regions.
   (b) However, in many cases these two active regions will simply "turn
       down" each other's activity, and that in other regions, so much that
       neither is sufficient to "take command" and the frog will remain
       immobile, ignoring the two "flies".

One trouble with the circuitry as so far described is that the build-up of
inhibition on the S-cells precludes the system's quick response to new
stimuli. For example, in case 2(b) above, if one of those two very active
regions were to suddenly become more active, then the deadlock should be
broken quickly, but in the network so far described, the new activity cannot easily break through the inhibition built up on the S-cell in its
region. In other words, there is hysteresis. Didday thus introduced what
we shall call an N-cell for each S-cell. The job of an N-cell is to monitor temporal changes in the activity in its region. Should it detect a
sufficiently dramatic increase in the region's activity, it then overrides
the S-cell inhibition to enter the new level of activity into the relative
foodness layer. With this scheme, the inertia of the old model is over-
come, and the system can respond rapidly to significant new stimuli.
Didday hypothesized that the S-cells and N-cells modelled the sameness and
newness cells, respectively, that had been observed in the frog tectum.
Regrettably, no experiments have been done to test this hypothesis. We
note here two specific experiments suggested by the model: (i) Present two
fly-like stimuli in TP(thalamus/pretectum)-ablated, behaving frogs. If the
postulated lateral interaction is mediated by TP inhibition of tectum, then
the frogs should always snap at the average fly, even for large separations;
but if it is mediated solely within tectum, selection should persist.
(ii) Another experiment would test the hypothesis that pre-selection occurs
at the tectal level rather than along the motor outflow. Present two unilateral fly-like stimuli to a behaving frog whose descending tecto-fugal

pathways have been partially interrupted, with stimulus A mapping away from the interruption, while stimulus B corresponds to interrupted motor outflow. If competition takes place at the tectal-TP level, then snapping at A should occur with the same frequency as in the normal, while there would be no response in those cases where a normal would respond to stimulus B. But if competition is downstream from the tectum, the animal should respond as if to stimulus A presented alone.

In any case, the wealth of experimental data on visuomotor coordination have led to the development of new models which extend the methodology of the Didday model, rather than incorporating the model directly [3]. In the remainder of the paper, we review some of the data the new models encompass, but first place the Didday model within a broader context.

2.3 Competition and Cooperation in Neural Nets

The above model of prey-selection is an example of a broad class of models of what may be called competition and cooperation in neural nets. In the Dev stereopsis model [6] we have competition along the disparity dimension and cooperation along the other dimension to cleanly segment the activity of disparity-tuned visual neurons responding to a random-dot stereogram. In the S-RETIC model of mode-selection by the reticular formation [20], the cooperation dimension is the row of modules, and competition is between modes rather than disparities. The Didday model can be regarded as the limiting case where there is only a competition dimension, namely that of bug location. Such informal observations laid the basis for a rigorous mathematical analysis of competition and cooperation in neural nets [1].

2.4 Cooperative Computation of Controllers

The prey-selection model provided a simple example of how a single task may be controlled in a distributed way, based on a structured stimulus array rather than a lumped input. In the simplest case of interaction of multiple controllers, the process of coordination simply "turns off" all but one of the controllers -- as when a frog either snaps at prey or flees a predator. In more complex situations, the activity of one controller will modulate the activity of another. Whether as experimentalists or modellers, our focus is on "chunks" of both brain and behavior which are sufficiently restricted to provide a coherent focus of investigation. Yet many of the properties of such "chunks" are governed by the rich interplay with other subsystems and involvement in other behaviors. Thus our models will have to be open-ended, able to interface with models of other subsystems. Ingle [18] has argued for the utility of the frog in the analysis of such interactions. Five of the visual functions of the frog are pre-catching (a model for which we have already described), threat-avoidance, barrier negotiation, phototactic orientation and visual stabilization. In each case we may trace a different "visual map", providing a control surface for a distinct (yet not independent) layered motor controller. "Many types of visual representation of the world can be used to define the objects and spatial relations necessary for fine-tuning of a given motor sub-system" [18]. Here is an example [17] of process coordination which should provide a fruitful basis for future experiments and modelling: Certain frogs preferentially respond to the approach of a large dark object (a "predator stimulus") by leaping away. For these "good avoiders", the jumping direction is highly predictable as a compromise between the forward direction and that directly away from the stimulus. Yet when a black stationary barrier is set within

the frog's preferred jump path, the frog escaping the "predator" will
jump to one side or other of the barrier.

2.5 Prey-Enemy Pattern Recognition

Ewert has conducted a variety of behavioral, physiological and lesion experiments to determine aspects of the interaction between the tectum and
other brain regions (especially pretectum and thalamus) in determining
whether a moving object is treated by the toad as prey or enemy (see [11]
for a review). Where normal toads will jump away from any large moving
object, toads with thalamic-pretectal lesions [9] were uninhibited in their
snapping at moving objects of all sizes, and would orient and snap at their
own limbs, at another toad, or even at the experimenter's hand. A more
analytic series of behavioral experiments [10] showed that elongation of a
moving stimulus in the direction of movement increased the normal toad's
prey-catching responses; whereas elongation orthogonal to the direction of
movement decreased, and eventually inhibited, its prey-catching. However,
in the case of the toad with thalamus and pretectum lesioned, orthogonal
elongation yielded no such effect. These behavioral experiments have been
complemented by physiological recordings [13, 14] in which tectum type 2
neurons were seen to give responses to elongated rectangles quantitatively
similar to the "prey-catching responses" measured behaviorally -- with the
correspondence holding both in the normal toad and in the animal with pre-
tectal/thalamic lesions. Moreover, small-field-units were found in PT
(pretectum/thalamus) where response increased with elongation of a rectangular stimulus orthogonal to the direction of motion.

These observations were the basis for a model of the prey-enemy recognition
system [12] which used Fourier analysis to determine the transfer functions
of the tectum type 2 cells and PT small-field-units so as to fit the experimental data (though not taking into account any size-constancy mechanisms
that may exist). Their study looks at several alternative schemes for inhibitory interactions between the two "form filters" in generating orienting and avoiding responses.

The value of this model is its account of interaction between tectum and
thalamus/pretectum in determining whether the toad will treat a single
stimulus as "prey" or "enemy"; but the model can only handle a single stimulus. By contrast, the Didday model (admittedly for frog) addresses the
problem of handling multiple stimuli, but treats the tectum in isolation.
(The full thesis [7] does offer an ad hoc account of how features from
different ganglion cells may be combined in determining "overall foodness".)
The models are thus complementary, and should be subsumed in an analysis of
the animal's behavior in complex structured environments.

REFERENCES

[1] Amari, S. and Arbib, M.A., Competition and cooperation in neural nets, in: Metzler, J. (ed.), Systems Neuroscience (Academic Press, New York, 1977), p. 119-165.

[2] Arbib, M.A., Perceptual structures and distributed motor control, in: Brooks, V.B. (ed.), Handbook of Physiology, Section on Neurophysiology, Volume III: Motor Control (American Physiological Society, 1980).

[3] Arbib, M.A., Cromarty, A.S. and Lara, R., Modelling studies of visuomotor coordination in frog and toad (to appear).

[4] Arbib, M.A. and Lawton, D.T., Internal processes in the visual control of locomotion, in: Ingle, D.J., Mansfield, R.J.W. and Goodale, M.A. (eds.), Advances in the Analysis of Visual Behavior (The MIT Press, in press).

[5] Braitenberg, V. and Onesto, N, The cerebellar cortex as a timing organ, in: Proc. Congresso di Inst. di Medicina Cibernetica (Naples, 1969) p. 239-255.

[6] Dev, P., Computer simulation of a dynamic visual perception model, Int. J. Man-Mach. Stud. 7 (1975) 511-528.

[7] Didday, R.L., The Simulation and Modelling of Distributed Information Processing in the Frog Visual System, Ph.D. Thesis, Stanford Univ., (1970).

[8] Didday, R.L., A model of visuomotor mechanisms in the frog optic tectum, Math. Biosci. 30 (1976) 169-180.

[9] Ewert, J.-P., Untersuchungen über die Anteile zentralnervöser Aktionen an der taxisspezifischen Ermüdung beim Beutefang der Erdkröte (Bufo Bufo L.), Z. Vergl. Physiol. 57 (1967) 263-298.

[10] Ewert, J.-P., Zentralnervöse Analyse und Verarbeitung visueller Sinnesreize, Naturwiss. Rundsch. 25 (1972) 1-11.

[11] Ewert, J.-P., The visual system of the toad: Behavioral and physiological studies on a pattern recognition system, in: Fite, K.V. (ed.), The Amphibian Visual System, A Multidisciplinary Approach (Academic Press, New York, 1976) p. 141-202.

[12] Ewert, J.-P. and von Seelen, W., Neurobiologie und System-Theorie eines visuellen Muster-Erkennungsmechanismus bei Kröten, Kybernetik 14 (1974) 167-183.

[13] Ewert, J.-P. and von Wieterscheim, A., Musterauswertung durch Tectum- und Thalamus/Praetectum-Neurone im visuellen System der Kröte (Bufo Bufo L.), J. Comp. Physiol. 92 (1974) 131-148.

[14] Ewert, J.-P. and von Wieterscheim, A., Der Einfluss von Thalamus/ Praetectum-Detekten auf die Antwort von Tectum-Neuronen gegenüber visuellen Mustern bei der Kröte (Bufo Bufo L.), J. Comp. Physiol. 92 (1974) 149-160.

[15] Holmes, G., The cerebellum of Man, Brain 62 (1939) 1-30.

[16] Ingle, D., Visual releasers of prey-catching behavior in frogs and toads, Brain Behav. Evol. 1 (1968) 500-518.

[17] Ingle, D., Spatial vision in anurans, in: Fite, K.V. (ed.), The Amphibian Visual System (Academic Press, New York, 1976) p. 119-141.

[18] Ingle, D., A functional approach to the many visual systems dilemma, (to appear).

[19] Jeannerod, M. and Biguer, B., Visuomotor mechanisms in reaching within extrapersonal space, in: Ingle, D.J., Mansfield, R.J.W. and Goodale, M.A. (eds.), Advances in the Analysis of Visual Behavior (The MIT Press, in press).

[20] Kilmer, W.L., McCulloch, W.S. and Blum, J., A model of the vertebrate central command system, Int. J. Man-Mach. Stud. 1 (1969) 279-309.

[21] Lettvin, J.Y., Maturana, H., McCulloch, W.S. and Pitts, W.H., What the frog's eye tells the frog's brain, Proc. IRE 47 (1959) 1940-1951.

[22] Pew, R.W., Levels of analysis in motor control, Brain Res. 71 (1974) 393-400.

[23] Pitts, W.H. and McCulloch, W.S., How we know universals, the perception of auditory and visual forms, Bull. Math. Biophys. 9 (1947) 127-147.

[24] Schmidt, R.A., A schema theory of discrete motor skill learning, Psychol. Rev. 82 (1975) 225-260.

[25] Schmidt, R.A., The schema as a solution to some persistent problems in motor learning theory, in: Stelmach, G.E. (ed.), Motor Control: Issues and Trends (Academic Press, New York, 1976) p. 41-65.

Tutorials in Motor Behavior
G.E. Stelmach and J. Requin (eds.)
© *North-Holland Publishing Company, 1980*

4

CEREBELLAR STRATEGIES FOR MOVEMENT COORDINATION

C.C. BOYLLS

Department of Physiology
Medical School
University of Bristol
Bristol, England

The role of the cerebellar flocculus in tuning optokinetic
and vestibulo-ocular reflexes in monkeys and rabbits is explored
with the aid of several simple, lumped-system models. One of
these is then suitably recast into a form recognizably
applicable to vermal and paravermal cerebellar regions in their
efforts to coordinate the locomotion of cats. The mechanisms
examined indicate that movement commands could be forwarded by
the cerebellum with, in particular, phase shifts appropriate to
the correction of ongoing performances.

Introduction
        The present report addresses the question, how can we apply what is
known of the cerebellar tuning of oculomotor reflexes to the cerebellar
tuning of anything else? I have specifically in mind the coordination of
decerebrate locomotion in cats, since the question first occurred during
experiments using such preparations (4,5). Microstimulation was being
employed to activate a climbing fiber pathway to the cerebellar vermis; and
as this was done, the cats adopted new postures which they retained for
some tens of seconds following stimulation. Earlier, Barmack and Hess
(reviewed in ref. 2) had microstimulated to excite climbing fibers in the
cerebellar flocculus of awake rabbits. Rather than postural changes, they
observed instead a nystagmus, but again with a prolonged time course. The
flocculus is as richly associated with eye movement as the vermis is with
limbs and trunk, so seeing the eyes move was no surprise. However, there
seemed to be a common thread in the cat and rabbit results: The climbing
fiber was implicated in a prolonged biasing action of some sort in either
situation. It suggested a common coordinational strategy for their use in
moving either eyes or legs. Other results now indicate that, besides
having a homogeneous cortical cytoarchitecture, the flocculus projection
onto the vestibular nuclear complex (41) may follow a zonal template akin
to the rigid 'compartmentalization' of vermal corticonuclear pathways
(e.g., ref. 11). Discharge frequencies of interpositus nucleus neurons can
encode elbow joint velocities during voluntary forelimb flexions in cats
(7) in a way analogous to the encoding of head, eye, and retinal-image
velocities in vestibular nuclear neurons of various species (cf.,refs. 17,
36-38). Although not yet rigorously tied to the cerebellum, the programming of rapid isometric force adjustments in cats is said to follow the
"pulse-step" regime (14) characteristic of saccadic eye movement (27). Limb
proprioception can itself cause visual motion illusions (20), and opto-
kinetic-like reactions (nystagmus, after-nystagmus, and vection; ref.6).
        We thus present 4 simple, lumped-system models illustrating features
of cerebellar oculomotor tuning, followed by a final model of "locomotion"
dependent upon the former. The models are designed to illustrate concepts

and to test logic – not to fit curves. Much detail is necessarily omitted.
Hopefully the novelty remains.

Basic Mechanisms of Gaze-Stabilizing Oculomotor Reflexes

        Gaze, the position of the eyes relative to earth-fixed coordinates,is
stabilized against movements of the head by a number of mechanisms. From
the standpoint of their cerebellar tuning, the best known of these are the
vestibulo-ocular (VOR) and optokinetic (OKR) responses. The former utilizes
the damped accelerometers of the semicircular canals to counterrotate the
eyes in some proportion to head movement. The latter detects whole-field
motion of the visual scene across the retina ("retinal slip"), attempting
its nullification by driving the eyes in the same direction.
        Current analytical approaches to the VOR and OKR (e.g. refs.23,29)
treat them as symbiotic: The VOR is considered to be an "open-loop"
mechanism which adjusts gaze quickly, but in a somewhat approximate fashion.
The OKR has the closed-loop advantage of being able to see what it has
accomplished, and the disadvantage of being slow. Thus, the OKR in some
sense could be used to take up any slack in the VOR. This is the first of
several assumptions embodied in the simple diagram of Fig.1, freely
abstracted from a model by Robinson (29)

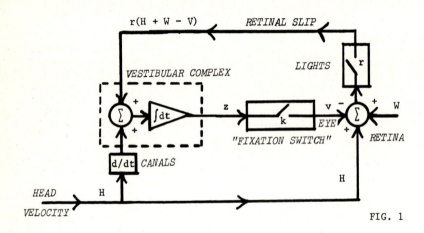

FIG. 1

        It is simplest to run through Fig.1 starting at the "retina", a
summing junction where eye velocity, v, is subtracted from head velocity,
H, and any added velocity of the visual field, W, not due to head movement
to yield the net retinal slip velocity, H + W – v, the stimulus to the OKR.
With lights on and eyelids open, switch r is closed (r = 1) and the retinal
slip signal makes its way to a variety of places. One of these appears to
be the vestibular nuclear complex (18,36), whose integrity seems essential
for proper OKR elaboration (1,35). Here (ignoring the illustrated canal
input for a moment) a curious process reveals itself. The discharge
frequencies of vestibular neurons receiving the slip input not only encode
the magnitude of slip, but also – it appears – something like the time-
integral of slip (cf. ref. 37). Such is the rationale for the integrator
shown in Fig.1's "vestibular complex". The neural construction of that
integrator will be touched upon below. Normally z would then emerge
directly as eye velocity, v. However, recent findings (38) demonstrate

that z can be decoupled from v when an animal (monkey)fixates targets in a visual world rotating with its head (a so-called VOR/OKR "conflict situation", the OKR fighting the VOR's attempts to move the eyes). Here the observed v is zero (21) while z does strange, non-zero things shortly to be of interest. We account for this decoupling in Fig.1 by the temporary artifice of a "fixation switch" controlled by k. k = 1 allows eye movement; k = 0 allows fixation (in VOR/OKR conflict only). As in other models (23,29), we leave the computing of eye position from OKR (and VOR) v's to another integrator (32) assumed to be remote from the circuitry under consideration.

Fig.1's "VOR" segment is not a loop at all, of course, since the response is allegedly open-loop. Instead, canal input, H, is transmitted via n. VIII to the vestibular complex where it is thought to sum more or less algebraically with retinal slip inputs in vestibular nuclear neurons (cf. ref. 39). It then shares the OKR pathway to eye velocity. That path is also assumed to include the same integrating function featured in the OKR loop (29) - hence the inclusion of a differentiator at the canal level in Fig.1, lest VOR-generated eye velocities end up proportional to head positions, rather than velocities. Robinson's recent model (29) treats canal function much more accurately; however, Fig. 1's approximation is quite sufficient for the present discussion.

A better understanding of Fig.1's operation can be got by writing down the dynamical equations it implies. We'll do this in terms of vestibular-complex output, z, since eye behaviour is always calculable from it, but not vice-versa. Thus, we have

$$\frac{1}{rk}\dot{z} = -z + \frac{1}{k}H + \frac{1}{rk}\dot{H} + \frac{1}{k}W \qquad (1)$$

where v, H, and W are functions of time and a superscripted dot signifies the time-derivative operator. Assuming r = k = 1 (i.e., normal VOR/OKR symbiosis), we see immediately that in the steady-state (z = H = 0), z = v = H + W, ensuring gaze stability

For future reference we now need to consider Fig.1's behaviour in two special experimental conditions. The first is the OKR to a constant W (k = r = 1). From eq. 1, v (= z) is seen to reach W exponentially with a time constant of one unit, while the vestibular-complex integrator charges to W. Switching off the lights (r = 0) at this point should cause the eyes to retain their achieved velocity for a "long" time, since the integrator now has no means of discharging. Of course, such optokinetic after-nystagmus (OKAN) is well-known in many species (8,10,12,16,26,28,33, 35,37), and in fact suggested the existence of an OKR integrator in the first place (10). If we want to preempt OKAN, we must present another W (often W = 0, a fixed scene). The eye velocity and integrator activity will then exponentially decay, again with a one-unit time constant.

The second experimental condition of interest for Fig.1 is VOR/OKR conflict - that is, r = 1, k = 0 (eyes fixed), and H = -W (visual world rotates with head). Here we calculate from eq.1 the ostensible output of the vestibular complex, z, to be simply H. That is, the discharge frequencies of vestibular neurons will track head velocity.

As it happens, experimental results don't bear out some of these expectations, perhaps because Fig.1 lacks a cerebellum:

Cerebellar Regulation of the VOR and OKR

The cerebellar flocculus and nodulus have long been hypothesized as a nexus where visual cues cause long-term modifications of the VOR (e.g., refs. 13,22). Here we will sidestep that issue and ask instead, are they

involved with immediate modifications as well? One example of such a
modification occurs during VOR/OKR conflict (see previous section), where
the eyes remain fixed in the orbit despite head movement. Using monkeys,
several investigators (21,24) have compared the behaviors of floccular
Purkinje cells during conflict with their activity during both the VOR in
the dark, and the OKR.   Classically, the flocculus is supposed to receive
a substantial mossy fiber input from n. VIII (cf. ref.30). It was thus
surprising when Purkinje discharges were found to be almost unresponsive
to dark-VOR stimulation.   By contrast, strong firing frequency modulation
roughly in-phase with head velocity and seemingly driven by canal
afferents appeared during VOR/OKR conflict.   It was conjectured that this
modulation was helping to retain visual fixation by "cancelling" the
simultaneous canal afferent input to the vestibular nuclei (21). When the
eyes alone moved during a visual tracking task, it was found that Purkinje
cells were also modulated, this time in a (posited) antiphasic relationship
with vestibular nuclei, a relationship that would facilitate eye movement
by the latter. This final observation suggested that the flocculus
receives an "efference copy" of the eye movement command (21,24).   The
need for a head-velocity component in the flocculus mix, presumably from n.
VIII, was also recognized to account for the VOR/OKR conflict data (21).
A synthesis of these hypotheses is shown in Fig.2:

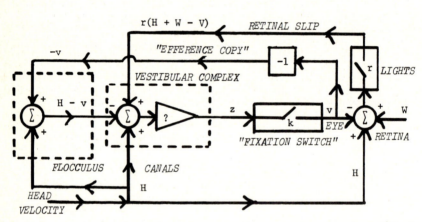

FIG. 2

     The "flocculus" of Fig.2 receives two inputs (both ostensibly mossy
fiber, since VOR/OKR modulation of climbing fibers appears scant in monkey
flocculus; refs. 21, 24). One input is the posited "efference copy",
shown with the sign reversal necessary to induce antiphasic vestibular and
Purkinje activity during the OKR. Note that the arrangement has a
regenerative potential, tending to prolong eye movements already underway.
As several reports point out (21,23), this could be the substrate for the
"integrator" of Fig.1, hence its reduction to a ? in Fig.2. A n.VIII input has also been introduced into the flocculus. Since that H adds
algebraically to any "-v" efference copy (a fact for which Lisberger and
Fuchs provide indirect evidence; ref. 21), this is sufficient to account
for Purkinje cell behavior in dark-VOR and VOR-suppressed conditions. The

scheme does require H, not its derivative, at the flocculus, so the canal-differentiator of Fig.1 has been retired. Miles and Fuller (24) have proposed that retinal slip also reaches flocculus Purkinje cells to enable the latter to compute earth-fixed velocities of visual targets. Such inputs may (and likely do) exist (21); but their illustrated observations (24) seem adequately dealt with by Fig.2.

Fig.2 does present several difficulties, however. The first can be seen under "normal VOR/OKR" conditions - i.e., when the two reflexes are supposedly cooperating (W = 0). Retinal slip then equals H-v; but because canal and eyeball efference-copy are combined in the Purkinje cell, the latter is also producing a surrogate "H-v" (perhaps of philosophical interest). If the eye is moving as commanded, then there is the potential for Purkinje inhibition to cancel the retinal slip input to the vestibular complex. The OKR contribution to the performance is diminished leaving an open-loop VOR that may or may not be up to the gaze-stabilizing task on its own. Recent anatomical evidence (19) also casts some doubt upon the number of n. VIII fibers actually reaching the flocculus. Quite possibly the "head velocity" input derives from another source (see below).

The second problem with Fig.2 is purely interpretive and relates to an idea mentioned above: Is the implied positive-feedback loop, involving eye velocity efference copy and the flocculus, responsible for the time-integration effects seen in the VOR-OKR (not to mention smooth-pursuit tracking and the like; refs. 23,29). The problem is that flocculectomy (8), and even cerebellectomy (28) seem to leave the integrator intact (at least as assessed by OKAN). Thus, the integrator appears to rely on extra-cerebellar circuitry.

The flocculus may in fact be more useful in *discharging* the integrator than in constructing it; Cohen and colleagues (8) "charged" the integrator using constant-velocity motion of the visual field (constant W in eq.1, previous section). They compared the time-constant of this charging with that of the integrator's subsequent discharge by a fixed visual scene (W = 0), finding discharge to be much faster. Recall that this contradicts the predicted behavior of Fig.1. In Cohen's interpret-ation (26), it was as though conditions calling for visual fixation closed a "switch" through a negative-feedback pathway across the OKR integrator, through which the integrator could discharge. In a different set of experiments, Cohen and coworkers (33) have demonstrated that lesions of the flocculus prevent the suppression of vestibular nystagmus by a fixed visual world. This nystagmus is in part generated by canal mechanics, but is ostensibly sustained using the OKR integrator (cf. Fig.1 and refs.26, 29). Perhaps, then, the "discharge switch" not only generalizes to the VOR, but also involves the flocculus. How? The simplest solution is to have it become part of an integrator-discharging pathway, as shown in Fig.3.

The operation of this circuit is straightforward enough. When the "discharge switch" is open, the circuit is identical with that of Fig. 1. When it is closed - which has been linked here with k = 0, implying no eye movement (fixation) - the integrator discharges through the flocculus and vestibular complex. It is easy to see, assuming Purkinje inhibition, p, to be "large" (p > 1), that closing the discharge switch has the effect of shortening the system time-constant from unity to 1/p. For periodic inputs switch closure will be marked by a phase-advance of the observed z relative to the switch-open state. That last point will come up again shortly.

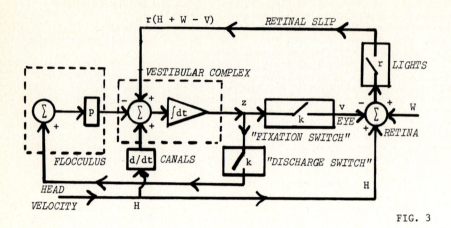

FIG. 3

Adjustment of VOR/OKR Dynamics by the Flocculus and Its Afferents

Taking a cue from the "discharge switch" ideas just discussed, I will assume that the flocculus rides herd on the ability of the VOR/OKR integrator to charge, according to whether such charging suits environmental conditions. Furthermore, the integrator discharge pathway of Fig. 3 could, by hypothesis, be identified with the mossy fiber afferent projection to the flocculus which arises from vestibular nuclear neurons themselves (secondary vestibular afferents; ref. 40 for review). But there is nothing in that direct path which could function as a "switch" - at least until the flocculus is reached. At the floccular level, however, "switching" could readily be accomplished by regulating the ability of Purkinje cells to respond to those afferents.

In the rabbit there is evidence to indicate that flocculus climbing fibers may serve such a regulatory function. Their inactivation by lesioning during the OKR causes an immediate phase-advance in the OKR responses of vestibular nucleus neurons (Barmack, personal communication), as though the "discharge switch" were now closed. The fibers are well known to react to retinal slip (31), usually a cue for allowing integration to occur; and it recently has been demonstrated in rat (9) that their activation very effectively suppresses Purkinje discharges (i.e., essentially setting p = 0 in Fig. 3 and opening the integrator-discharge pathway). The prolonged OKAN-like nystagmus elicitable in rabbits by climbing fiber volleys was mentioned above (Introduction; ref. 2).

The destruction of flocculus climbing fibers almost completely abolishes the OKR in rabbits (2), perhaps because of the release of floccular inhibition of vestibular neurons. However, a recent preliminary announcement (Robinson; ARVO, 1979) indicated that this maneuver had rather less effect on the monkey OKR. We recall in fact that climbing fibers of monkey flocculus are only weakly modulated by OKR/VOR stimuli, most of the Purkinje activity seeming to arise from mossy fibers (Fig. 2). It may be, then, that monkeys can call upon an additional, rather more subtle strategy for regulating integration by means of the flocculus - a strategy perhaps in the style of Fig. 4:

Fig. 4's scheme retains the mossy fiber (secondary vestibular afferent) integrator-discharge pathway of Fig. 3. However, we now see that its

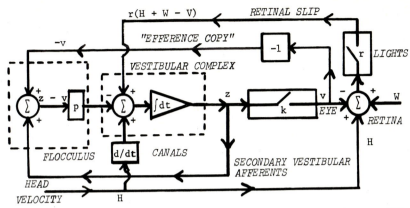

FIG. 4

action can be nullified at appropriate times by another conjectural mossy
system, essentially the "efference copy" path of Fig. 2. The integrator
thus comes into play when two conditions are satisfied: The eyes have to
be commanded to move by H and/or retinal slip; and they have to actually
move – k non-zero. Note that the system can produce OKAN, since when the
integrator generates a z in the dark, both z and –z (the latter in the form
of a –v efference copy) cancel in the flocculus and prevent the integrator's discharge. But if the sudden presenting of a fixed visual environment causes fixation (k = 0 and thus v = 0), z from the integrator goes unopposed in the flocculus. The integrator thus discharges quickly, and one
sees what seems to be the "discharge switch" in action.

Fig 4 is also consistent with some of the observations mentioned in
conjunction with Fig. 2. For example, during the VOR in the dark (eyes
moving, k = 1), canal input generates a z at the integrator, but which at
the flocculus is again nullified by the –z efference copy. Purkinje cells
thus are little modulated by the head oscillation. But when the eyes are
fixated by a visual scene moving in synchrony with the head, the oscillatory z is seen alone in the same cells. It will be in phase with head velocity, as actually observed. At this point it is interesting to recall
the "use" for that flocculus response: It was to cancel the canal input
to the vestibular complex and so prevent the latter from destabilizing the
fixed eyes (as obvious from Fig. 2). We might ask, therefore, what does
Fig. 4 predict for z under that condition; and how does the prediction compare with the actual behaviors of vestibular nuclear neurons?

We can tackle the first point by writing down the dynamics of z as
was done in eq. 1 for Fig. 1. For the general situation we have

$$\frac{1}{rk + p(1-k)}\dot{z} = -z + \frac{r}{rk + p(1-k)}H + \frac{1}{rk + p(1-k)}\dot{H} + \frac{r}{rk + p(1-k)}W \qquad (2)$$

Notice that for k = r = 1 (i.e., eyes moving, lights on, etc.), eq. 2 is
identical with eq. 1, and Fig. 4 equivalent to Fig. 1 behaviorally. Similarly, with the lights out but eyes still moving (r = 0, k = 1; dark-VOR
conditions), both models predict that z = v = H. We are interested, however, in the VOR/OKR conflict situation, where the eyes are fixated (k = 0)

and the visual world rotates with the head (H = −W). Recall that here the model of Fig. 1 predicts that z = H (because for it, this environment is equivalent to the no-retinal-slip condition found in the dark). The system of Fig. 2 says that z = 0 (or z = aH, where a is near zero; this is where the flocculus doesn't quite cancel canal input in the vestibular nuclei). Fig. 4 predicts something more complex, namely

$$\frac{1}{p}\dot{z} = -z + \frac{1}{p}\dot{H}$$

which, for p large enough to discharge the integrator quickly during fixation, can be approximated by

$$z = \frac{1}{p}\dot{H}$$

In other words, z exhibits a small-amplitude modulation phase-advanced relative to H − in some contrast with its larger-amplitude modulation in-phase with H during the dark-VOR. It has been known for some time that the discharge frequencies of many vestibular nuclear neurons fluctuate in phase with head velocity during the monkey dark-VOR (e.g., ref. 17), as indicated by all of our previous models. But Waespe and Henn recently examined those neurons' behaviors during VOR/OKR conflict (38). Discharge frequencies were of reduced amplitude and phase-advanced relative to the dark-VOR.

This is a good place to stop to consider some rather more general questions about cerebellar function raised by the discussion of Figs. 3 and 4. We've made a hypothesis that a subdivision of cerebellar cortex, the flocculus, is part of a variable-gain feedback pathway imposed around an extra-cerebellar, time-integrating process seen in the vestibular complex. When the feedback is strong, vestibular output essentially replicates the time-course of vestibular input (e.g., Ḣ, in the case of the canals); when it is weak, vestibular output is the time-integral of that input. In rabbits, the integrator is "released" through the climbing fibers when retinal slip is present; and in monkeys, through the presence of efference copy when movement is underway. Thus, in either species, *motor command signals pass through the cerebellar complex and are phase shifted (with gain-change) pursuant to both environmental factors and the "desire to move"*.

Is it possible to employ some of this thinking in analyzing the coordination by non-floccular cerebellar subdivisions − the anterior lobe vermis, for example − of non-oculomotor behaviors, such as cat locomotion? This report concludes with a simple suggestion to that end.

A Suggestion for Locomotor Coordination by the Cat's Cerebellum

The suggestion is simply to consider the implications of a particular *algebraic equivalent* (without W) of Fig. 4, which is illustrated in Fig. 5. Fig. 5 obviously has had some remodeling and relabeling compared with Fig. 4, but 4's variable names have been retained to help make the algebraic equivalency more clear. The equivalence also implies that "interpositus complex" outflow, z, will be governed by eq. (2) (less W), provided that k behaves discretely (0 or 1). Thus, H from a "spinal locomotor pattern generator" (PG) again becomes v, an output velocity (of a "hindlimb" in this example) when k = 1. We have kept Fig. 5 in the velocity domain given the velocity correlations of "real" cat interpositus neurons (7). There is rather more to discuss, of course, and in doing so I will have to assume some knowledge of locomotor circuits and behavior (of which there are many reviews; e.g., refs. 3,15,25, and Smith, this volume).

Let's begin with how Purkinje input is derived. In Fig. 4 it stemmed

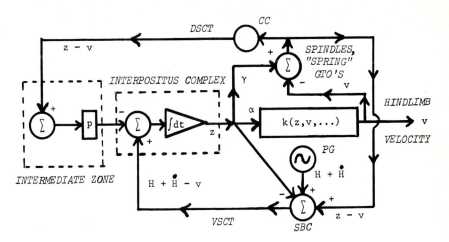

FIG. 5

from the difference between a "potential" movement command in the vestibular nuclei (z) and the "actual" efference copy, v. Here in Fig. 5 we have
merely moved down the command hierarchy one step and made z the efference
and v the *achieved* result. But given traditional notions about α-γ linkage
and the like, this seems a quantity readily derived from spindle afferents.
For the hindlimb there also exist Clarke's column neurons (CC) ready to intercept spindle information and to transmit it via the dorsal spinocerebel-
lar tract (DSCT) directly to the cerebellar cortex (Fig. 5). The current
popularity of so-called "spring models" of neuromuscular mechanics (cf.
Bizzi, Cooke, Kelso, and others, this volume) suggests that perhaps z - v
is additionally encoded in (derivatives of) the *tensions* of springlike muscles (z deriving from the "zero-length" or "equilibrium" command; v from
the actual muscle length, etc.). In other words, z - v could also be reported by Golgi tendon organs (GTO's), whose information additionally is
represented in the DSCT. Much can be made theoretically of GTO's and spindles speaking a similar language under the aegis of spring models, but it
can't be done here. Naturally, there is nothing to keep the z - v system
of Fig. 4 out of Fig. 5 as well. The cerebellar nuclei are well supplied
with their own renditions of "secondary vestibular afferents" in the form
of recurrent mossy fiber collaterals (e.g., ref. 34), although the origin
of -v then becomes more of a mystery (joint afferents?). We won't deal now
with the numerous cutaneous afferents influencing the cerebellum.

       In Fig. 4, retinal slip is delivered to the vestibular complex direct-
ly, along with Ḣ from the canals. In Fig. 5 we synthesize the lot within
the spinal border cells (SBC's) originating, in part, the ventral spino-
cerebellar tract (VSCT). As in the real cat, the synthesis is achieved by
combining a PG input, input from peripheral receptors (spindles, GTO's),
and "descending supraspinal control" in the form of z emanating ultimately
from the cerebellum.

       From the analysis of Fig. 4, we know that for k = 1, z is proportion-
al to H; while for k = 0, z varies with Ḣ. But in Fig. 5, k can be viewed
as describing, in part, *the progress of actual movement*: k = 1 implies

that movement is tracking H, and cerebellar outflow then equals in fact, H. However, $0 \leq k < 1$ can denote varying degrees of resistance to movement. The cerebellar response is to produce, as k diminishes, an increasingly phase-advanced version of the motor command, H. This, of course, is the strategy one might well employ to make v catch up with H, provided k is an appropriate function of z (it's shown as a generalized function of many things in Fig. 5).

I would suggest, then, that when the vermal and paravermal regions of the cerebellum are viewed as a simple lumped system (i.e., Fig. 5), DSCT-like pathways use peripheral (and possibly efference-copy) information to control the type of temporal filter the cerebellum presents to the motor commands it is to forward (in parallel with other centers, of course). Phase lag in movement implies phase-lead in command, and presumably vice-versa.

We need now to introduce spino-olivocerebellar pathways (climbing fibers) into Fig. 5; but that cannot be done until proper account is taken of the spatial geometry of the cerebellar complex and the spatial distribution of muscles in mutable synergic groups. A start, into which the present ideas can be merged, has been made elsewhere (3,5), and continues.

My sincere thanks to Drs. D.M. Armstrong and R.F. Schild for their advice and encouragement. Supported by the Medical Research Council of Great Britain.

References

(1) Azzena, G.B., Azzena, M.T., and Marini, R., Optokinetic nystagmus and the vestibular nuclei, Exp. Neurol. 42 (1974) 158-168.
(2) Barmack, N.H., Immediate and sustained influences of visual olivo-cerebellar activity on eye movement, in: Talbot, R.E., and Humphrey, D.R. (eds.), Posture and Movement: Perspective for Integrating Sensory and Motor Research on the Mammalian Nervous System (Raven Press, New York, 1979) 123-168.
(3) Boylls, C.C., A theory of cerebellar function with applications to locomotion. II. The relation of anterior lobe climbing fiber function to locomotor behavior in the cat. COINS Technical Report 76-1, Dept. of Computer and Infor. Sci., Univ. of Mass. (Amherst, 1976).
(4) Boylls, C.C., Prolonged alterations of muscle activity induced in locomoting premammillary cats by microstimulation of the inferior olive, Brain Res. 159 (1978) 445-450.
(5) Boylls, C.C., Contributions to locomotor coordination of an olivocerebellar projection to the vermis in the cat: Experimental results and theoretical proposals, in: Courville, J., Lamarre, Y., and deMontigny, C. (eds.), The Inferior Olivary Nucleus: Anatomy and Physiology (Raven Press, New York), in press.
(6) Brandt, T., Büchele, W., and Arnold, F., Arthrokinetic nystagmus and ego-motion sensation, Exp. Brain Res. 30 (1977) 331-338.
(7) Burton, J.E., and Onoda, N., Dependence of the activity of interpositus and red nucleus neurons on sensory input data generated by movement, Brain Res. 152 (1978) 41-63.
(8) Cohen, B., Matsuo, V., and Raphan, T., Quantitative analysis of the velocity characteristics of optokinetic nystagmus and optokinetic after-nystagmus, J. Physiol. (Lond.) 270 (1977) 321-344.
(9) Colin, F., Desclin, J., and Manil, J., Quantitative relationship between simple spike firing pattern and evoked complex spikes of cerebellar Purkinje cells after acute chemical destruction of the

inferior olive, J. Physiol. (Lond.), in press.
(10) Collewijn, H., An analog model of the rabbit's optokinetic system, Brain Res. 36 (1972) 71-88.
(11) Courville, J., and Diakiw, N., Cerebellar corticonuclear projection in the cat. The vermis of the anterior and posterior lobes, Brain Res. 110 (1976) 1-20.
(12) Dichgans, J., Optokinetic nystagmus as dependent on the retinal periphery via the vestibular nucleus, in: Baker, R., and Berthoz, A. (eds.), Control of Gaze by Brain Stem Neurons (Elsevier, New York, 1977) 261-267.
(13) Dufossé, M., Ito, M., Jastreboff, P.J., and Miyashita, Y., A neuronal correlate in rabbit's cerebellum to adaptive modification of the vestibulo-ocular reflex, Brain Res. 150 (1978) 611-616.
(14) Ghez, C., and Vicario, D., The control of rapid limb movement in the cat. II. Scaling of isometric force adjustments, Exp. Brain Res. 33 (1978) 191-202.
(15) Grillner, S., Locomotion in vertebrates: Central mechanisms and reflex interaction, Physiol. Rev. 55 (1975) 247-304.
(16) Hightower, D., Honrubia, V., and Ward, P.H., Experimental studies of optokinetic nystagmus. IV. Rabbits, Ann. Otol. 80 (1971) 455-463.
(17) Keller, E.L., and Kamath, B.Y., Characteristics of head rotation and movement-related neurons in alert monkey vestibular nucleus, Brain Res. 100 (1975) 182-187.
(18) Keller, E.L., and Precht, W., Persistence of visual responses in vestibular nucleus neurons in cerebellectomized cat, Exp. Brain Res. 32 (1978) 591-594.
(19) Korte, G.E., and Mugnaini, E., The cerebellar projection of the vestibular nerve in the cat, J. comp. Neurol. 184 (1979) 265-278.
(20) Lackner, J.R., and Levine, M.S., Visual direction depends on the operation of spatial constancy mechanisms: The oculobrachial illusion, Neurosci. Letts. 7 (1978) 207-212.
(21) Lisberger, S.G., and Fuchs, A.F., Role of primate flocculus during rapid behavioral modification of vestibuloocular reflex. I. Purkinje cell activity during visually guided horizontal smooth-pursuit eye movements and passive head rotation, J. Neurophysiol. 41 (1978) 733-763.
(22) Melvill Jones, G., Plasticity in adult vestibulo-ocular reflex arc, Phil. Trans. R. Soc. Lond. B 278 (1977) 319-334.
(23) Miles, F.A., and Evarts, E.V., Concepts of motor organization, Ann. Rev. Psychol. 30 (1979) 327-362.
(24) Miles, F.A., and Fuller, J.H., Visual tracking and the primate flocculus, Science 189 (1975) 1000-1002.
(25) Orlovsky, G.N., and Shik, M.L., Control of locomotion: a neurophysiological analysis of the cat locomotor system, in: Porter, R. (ed.), Neurophysiology II, International Review of Physiology (University Park Press, London, 1976) 10: 281-317.
(26) Raphan, T., Cohen, B., and Matsuo, V., A velocity-storage mechanism responsible for optokinetic nystagmus (OKN), optokinetic afternystagmus (OKAN) and vestibular nystagmus, in: Baker, R., and Berthoz, A. (eds.), Control of Gaze by Brain Stem Neurons (Elsevier, New York, 1977) 37-47.
(27) Robinson, D.A., The mechanics of human saccadic eye movement, J. Physiol. (Lond.) 174 (1964) 245-264.
(28) Robinson, D.A., Adaptive gain control of vestibuloocular reflex by the cerebellum, J. Neurophysiol. 39 (1976) 954-969.

(29) Robinson, D.A., Vestibular and optokinetic symbiosis: An example of explaining by modelling, in: Baker, R., and Berthoz, A. (eds.), Control of Gaze by Brain Stem Neurons (Elsevier, New York, 1977) 49-58.

(30) Shinoda, Y., and Yoshida, K., Neural pathways from the vestibular labyrinth to the flocculus in the cat, Exp. Brain Res. 22 (1975) 97-111.

(31) Simpson, J.I., and Alley, K.E., Visual climbing fiber input to rabbit vestibulo-cerebellum: a source of direction-specific information, Brain Res. 82 (1974) 302-308.

(32) Skavenski, A.A., and Robinson, D.A., Role of abducens neurons in vestibuloocular reflex, J. Neurophysiol. 36 (1973) 724-738.

(33) Takemori, S., and Cohen, B., Loss of visual suppression of vestibular nystagmus after flocculus lesions, Brain Res. 72 (1974) 213-224.

(34) Tolbert, D.L., Bantli, H., and Bloedel, J.R., Multiple branching of cerebellar efferent projections in cats, Exp. Brain Res. 31 (1978) 305-316.

(35) Uemura, T., and Cohen, B., Effects of vestibular nuclei lesions on vestibulo-ocular reflexes and posture in monkeys, Acta Oto-laryng. (Stockh.) Suppl. 315 (1974).

(36) Waespe, W., and Henn, V., Neuronal activity in the vestibular nuclei of the alert monkey during vestibular and optokinetic stimulation, Exp. Brain Res. 27 (1977) 523-538.

(37) Waespe, W., and Henn, V., Vestibular nuclear activity during optokinetic after-nystagmus (OKAN) in the alert monkey, Exp. Brain Res. 30 (1977) 323-330.

(38) Waespe, W., and Henn, V., Conflicting visual-vestibular stimulation and vestibular nucleus activity in alert monkeys, Exp. Brain Res. 33 (1978) 203-211.

(39) Wallace, M., Blair, S.M., and Westheimer, G., Neural pathways common to vestibular and optokinetic eye movements, Exp. Brain Res. 33 (1978) 19-25.

(40) Wilson, V.J., Physiological pathways through the vestibular nuclei, Int. Rev. Neurobiol. 15 (1972) 27-81.

(41) Yamamoto, M., Localization of rabbit's flocculus Purkinje cells projecting to the cerebellar lateral nucleus and the nucleus prepositus hypoglossi investigated by means of the horseradish peroxidase retrograde axonal transport, Neuroscience Letts. 7 (1978) 197-202.

Tutorials in Motor Behavior
G.E. Stelmach and J. Requin (eds.)
© *North-Holland Publishing Company, 1980*

5

PROGRAMMING OF STEREOTYPED LIMB MOVEMENTS BY SPINAL GENERATORS

Judith L. Smith

Neuromotor Control Laboratory
Brain Research Institute
University of California
Los Angeles, California

During the past decade the capacity of the isolated mammalian spinal cord
to generate rhythmic, stereotyped movements of the hindlimbs, such as locomotion (Grillner, 1973) and scratching (Berkinblit, et al 1978) has been
the subject of intense investigation in several laboratories, including
our own.* The concept of spinal generators, posited to be a series of interneuronal networks, is examined, and the role of these networks in programming locomotion, segmental reflexes and other stereotyped movements of
the hindlimbs is discussed with respect to the chronic spinal cat.
Although treadmill locomotion of cats transected at T_{12}- T_{13} and curarized
is normal in many respects (Grillner and Zangger, 1979), there are some
abnormalities. The extensive interaction of peripheral and supraspinal
signals during the control of normal locomotion, provides for optimal control, and a model of multilevel control is required to explain the animal's
ability to move effectively.

WHAT IS THE MOTOR CAPACITY OF THE CHRONIC SPINAL CAT?

The Preparation

The motor capacity of the chronic spinal animal, with low thoracic transection that renders the lumbosacral cord isolated from the rostral neuraxis,
is enhanced by two factors: age at which the animal is transected and the
application of a daily program of exercise and therapy.

Age. With respect to the age of spinalized animals, Shurrager and
Dykman (1951) reported that of 10 cordotomized cats, transected from 2 days
to 12 weeks, four of the five best were 14 days old or less at transection,
and of four of the five poorest animals were 21 days or older. Grillner
and his colleagues (Grillner, 1973; Forssberg, et al 1974, 1977) also
found that kittens, 6-14 days old, adapted well to spinalization. In fact
this group noted that operated kittens increased in weight parallel with
unoperated controls in the same litter.

In our own laboratory (Smith, et al 1979; Edgerton, et al 1979), we have
transected eight kittens at two weeks and eight cats at 12 weeks of age.
With proper therapy and exercise programs (see below), both groups gained
recovery of hindlimb functions, as judged by treadmill performance. We
have not experimented with cats transected after the third month of age,
and the literature is not clear as to the ability of adult mammals to re-

─────────────────────
*The following colleagues worked collectively towards gathering and analy-
zing the data presented from our laboratory: K. Dahms, V.R. Edgerton,
B. Hibl, N. Meyerott, P. Reback, C. Sabin and L. Smith. The research was
supported by an Easter Seal grant and USPHS Grant NS 10423.

cover motor functions of the hindlimbs after spinal transection. Sherrington (1906, 1910), in the course of his historic studies on reflexes of
adult cordotomized cats, seemed convinced that adult spinal cats were unable to locomote. Presently a few investigators, including Lorne Mendell
at Duke University and Lynn Eldridge at the University of California-Los
Angeles, are using chronic spinal cats, transected as adults, as experimental animals and maintaining them from 3 to 8 months. Neither investigator (personal communication) has observed these animals to stand spontaneously or to perform any other gross motor patterns with the hindlimbs.
In fact the hindlimbs of the transected adult cat most often are called
"paralyzed" or "flaccid". Traditionally, however, investigators have not
provided therapies or exercise programs for the adult cat that have proven
to be so effective in stimulating the recovery of hindlimb function of
kittens.

Daily program of therapy and exercise. Shurrager and Dykman (1951)
were the first group to recognize the value of daily therapy and exercise
for cordotomized cat. With even the youngest kitten, transected at two
days of age, electrocutaneous stimulation was applied to hindlimbs 24 hours
after surgery. All spinalized animals were stimulated a minimum of an
hour daily with shock of sufficient intensity to elicit full flexion con-
tractures of the limb. In addition to electroshock treatment, the hindquarters were massaged and washed every second day, and the animals were
housed in boxes filled with paper excelsior which enabled them to move
about without dragging their hindlimbs on a hard surface and provided intermittent cutaneous stimulation which encouraged movement of the hindlimbs.

Grillner (1973) exercised kittens transected 6-14 days on a motorized
treadmill for about 30 minutes daily, beginning two weeks after surgery.
At this time, about 30 days postnatal, normal kittens exhibit adequate
standing and imperfect walking with slight ataxia and hypermetria (Villablanca & Olmstead, 1979). The forelimbs and thorax of the transected
kittens were held over the treadmill in one hand, while the hindpaws were
placed on the belt. To prevent the kitten's hindquarters from falling
from side-to-side, the tail was gently supported with the other hand.
Particular attention was taken to see that the animal supported as much of
the weight of the hindquarters as possible, otherwise stepping became irregular and weak.

Nesmeyanova (1977) has reported on the extensive work of several Russian
investigators, who have treated chronic spinal dogs over a 20 year period.
Daily treatment of massage, electrocutaneous stimulation which systematically evoked motor reflexes of the extremities, and passive movements of
all joints of the hindlimbs were used. Untreated dogs showed less improvement than the treated animals, with respect to recovery of polysynaptic
reflexes and spontaneous weight bearing. In addition, drugs such as pyro-
genal and trypsin, were administered to reduce the scar formation and to
promote regeneration of descending and ascending axons. Scar formations
at the transection site were reduced, and isolated axons were seen to pen-
etrate through the scar. Weak restoration of the scratch reflex, elicited
by stimulating the skin rostral to the lesion, was often correlated with
the presence of axons penetrating through the scar to the opposite spinal
stump. Regeneration of axons and restoration of proper spinal reflexes
were not observed in dogs without the use of drugs.

In this chapter, the motor capacity of the transected cat will be discussed

exclusively in terms of the isolated lumbosacral cord. Evidence will be presented that recovery of spontaneous standing and locomotion are not dependent on axonal regeneration. The question as to whether regeneration is
possible after spinalization has been debated; see Clemente (1972) for a
review.

Air Stepping

In 1913, Sherrington, describing what he called "reflex stepping", reported that after spinal transection at the top of the lumbar region, alternating flexion and extension was started by merely lifting the animals so
that the hindquarters hung vertically. Sherrington noted that extension
at both hips was the primary condition favoring air stepping, and that
passive extension of the ankle or the knee alone or together, but without
the hip, did not initiate stepping.

From 1911 to 1914, Graham Brown studied what he called "narcosis progression" of guinea pigs and cats. Under conditions of ether or chloroform
narcosis, the hindlimbs of the normal cat, placed prone, exhibited reciprocal stepping that was very rhythmical and very similar to the air stepping
observed by Sherrington. After a rapid transection of the spinal cord at
the "lower thoracic segments", narcosis stepping continued from rates of
0.6 to 2.5 c/sec. Brown noted that at the ankle, stepping movements were
controlled primarily, if not exclusively, by the the contraction and relaxation of the flexor (tibialis anterior); he saw no evidence that the lateral gastrocnemius, a fast ankle extensor, participated. In cat and guinea
pig, narcosis progression was generally that of bilateral alternation,
such as that seen during walking and trotting. At the fastest rates of air
stepping, both hindlimbs often moved in synchrony, similar to galloping.

Shurrager and Dykman (1951) reported that rhythmical stepping of the hindlegs occurred spontaneously a few hours after spinal transection. They
also observed that when the kitten was held in the air, the legs made stepping movements even though the forelimbs were still. Grillner (1973) reported that 1 to 2 days after spinalization, the hindlimbs showed alternate movements typical of locomotion when kittens 6 to 9 days old were held
over a treadmill. These alternate movements were evident at a stage when
the eyes had not yet opened, and when the limbs had not yet developed the
force necessary to weight bear.

We (Smith, et al 1979) have found air stepping to be extremely easy to elicit in all of our cordotomized kittens. When chronic spinal cats are held
vertically, with hindlimbs pendent, air stepping is evoked without exception. The rhythm varies from 2.5-5 c/s and flexors and extensors are alternatively active, with the soleus, the slow extensor, more active than
the gastrocnemius, the fast extensor (Fig. 1A). We have also observed
rhythmic stepping with the cat lying supine and laterally to one side.
Thus, although passive hip extension may be one way to trigger the rhythmic
movements, other nonspecific afferent signals, produced by rubbing the
lower abdomen, or gently twisting the tail, also trigger these automatic
movements.

Treadmill Locomotion.

Sten Grillner's (1973) pioneering work on exercising spinalized kittens on
a small motorized treadmill has provided invaluable information about the
locomotor capabilities of the isolated lumbosacral cord. All eight of the
spinalized kittens from his laboratory were exercised daily on the mill,
and all developed the ability to locomote with a muscle force sufficient to

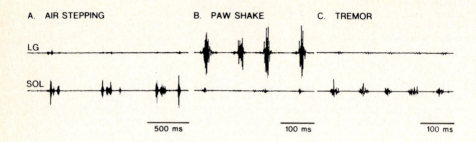

Figure 1: These activity patterns are typical of LG and SOL during air step-ping, paw shakes and tremor while weight supporting.

support the weight of the suspended hindquarters. The step cycle of the limbs, divided into stance and swing phases, varied with the speed of the treadmill belt that ranged from 0.10 to 1.0 m/s. The entire step cycle, paw contact to paw contact, decreased from 900 to 450 ms: the stance phase showed similar decreases from 600 to 200 ms, while the swing phase was relatively constant at about 300 ms. It is difficult to compare this data to normal cats locomoting on a treadmill, because the treadmill speeds of 0.1 to 1.0 m/s are at the lower end of the range used for normal adult cats (Smith, et. al 1976; Wetzel, et al 1976). If however, the duration of the stance phase is plotted in a log-log fashion, the relation between speed and stance is linear, suggesting a power function (Grillner, 1973).

Grillner's published data (Grillner 1973; Edgerton, et al 1976) is based on cats selected because they exhibited the most normal treadmill stepping (personal communication). In our laboratory, we have studied eight chro-nic cats with T_{12} lesions; each had a characteristic mode of treadmill walking; yet, all were successful in weight-bearing (Smith, et al 1979). The cats, transected at 2 days or 12 weeks and exercised daily on the treadmill, were tested 5 or 6 months postsurgery at speeds of 0.3 to 0.9 m/s. Kittens were hand-held over the treadmill until they were large enough to wear a thoracic jacket that was attached to plexiglass supports above the treadmill (Fig. 2A). With respect to the two components of the step cycle, the percentage of time devoted to the swing phase was quite variable. For example, one cat (Fig. 2:171) devoted proportionately little time to the swing phase at slow speeds, using a quick catchstep to keep up with the belt. Another cat (173), conversely, devoted nearly 51% of the step cycle to the swing phase, even at the slower speeds (Fig. 2B). These two chronic spinal cats do not represent the extreme range of our data, they simply illustrate two individualized adaptations. More studies of this nature are needed to determine the variation in treadmill locomo-tion elicited during the recovery process.

Gait Conversions. Paw contact patterns, recorded by viewing frames of high speed 16mm film, revealed that changes in treadmill speeds elicited typical gait patterns for the hindlimbs (Zernicke & Smith, manuscript in preparation). At the slower speeds, one hindpaw was placed on the belt usually 250-290 ms before the other hindpaw was lifted off for the swing phase (Fig. 3A). This is typical of normal walking, in which the period of double hindlimb support is about one third of the step cycle (Wetzel & Stuart, 1976). At intermediate speeds, a trot-like pattern emerged, such that lift-off of one paw occurred 40 to 60 ms before or after the other paw

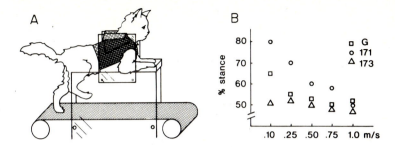

Figure 2: The chronic spinal cats 2-4 mo. wore a thoracic jacket that was
attached to the plexiglass walls of the treadmill. The cat's position
was adjusted so that the weight of the hindquarters could be supported
by the hindlegs (A). As the treadmill speed was increased from 0.10 to
1.0 m/s, the cat's gait changed, indicative of the % of the step cycle
devoted to the stance phase of the step cycle. Data from three cats are
plotted, two from our laboratory (171, 173) and one from Grillner's (G)
laboratory (Grillner, 1973).

was placed on the belt (Fig. 3B). At the fastest speeds, galloping was
elicited in intermittent epochs; that is, galloping sequences were interspersed with trotting and were usually limited to 8-10 step cycles (Fig.
3C). During these periods contact and lift-off of the hindpaws were
asymmetrical and closely resembled the transverse and rotatory gallops described by Grillner (1973; 1975) and Wetzel & Stuart (1976).

Kinematics. Displacements of the hip, knee and ankle joints have been
described by Grillner (1973) and his associates (Edgerton, et al 1976,
Forssberg, et al 1977) in an attempt to identify the four phases of the
step cycle outlined by Philippson (1905) during treadmill locomotion.
Both the ankle and the knee joints showed two subcomponents during the
swing phase: flexion (F) when the limb was brought forward and upward, and
extension (E), when the limb was moved forward and downward to touch the
belt (Fig. 4). During the stance phase, the yield, or E_2, was initiated
with paw contact and terminated when the limb began to extend during push-
off or E_3 (Fig. 4). The yield phase (E_2) was often missing or greatly minimized when the transected cat locomoted on the mill (Fig. 4). The absence
and or reductions of yield phase, produced a tilting action as the weight
was rocked from side-to-side. It is possible that the yield phase is reduced because the cat is not assuming the weight of the limb properly. Unfortunately we have no data on the kinetics of the limb action and do not
know if the weight support approximates that required during normal treadmill stepping.

Electromyography. Grillner (1973) and his associates (Forssberg, et al
1977) have recorded the activity patterns of selected hindlimb muscles of
the hip, knee and ankle in order to determine the temporal relationships.
The extensor muscles of the knee and ankle are active 30-50 ms prior to paw
contact and terminate 50-100 ms prior to lift-off, or the beginning of the
swing phase. Flexor muscles, such as the tibialis anterior (TA), are active briefly at the beginning of F, while two-joint muscles that may have
both flexor and extensor functions at different joints, commonly have two
epochs of activity: one at F and one at E_1. These data closely match the
electromyography patterns of normal cats locomoting on a treadmill

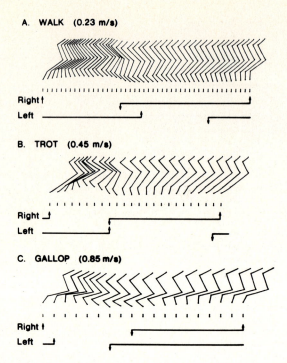

Figure 3: Limb kinematics and paw-contact patterns for one chronic spinal
cat during treadmill locomotion are shown. 16mm film was digitized and
each vertical line indicates a single frame or 20 msec (see text for
detail).

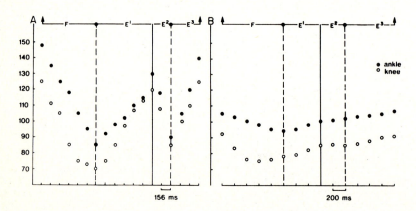

Figure 4: Displacement of the ankle and knee joints during a rapid gallop
of a normal cat (A) and a slow gallop of a chronic spinal cat (B). Notice
the lack of the yield, or E^2 phase in B, as well as the diminished range
of motion during all phases of the step cycle.

(Rasmussen, et al 1979; Engberg & Lundberg, 1969).

Our laboratory (Smith, et al 1979) has recently measured the peak amplitude of the rectified-average (RA) EMG of two ankle extensors during treadmill locomotion. At speeds of 0.13 to 0.90 m/s, which elicited the entire
range of gaits from a slow walk to a slow gallop, the peak amplitude of the
RA-EMG, which in normal adults is correlated with peak tendon forces measured in vivo (Walmsley, et al 1978), increased about 20% for the soleus and
about 300% for the LG (Fig. 5). This data suggest that spinal centers are
capable fully of recruiting motor units to adjust for kinetic demands without supraspinal influence.

Reflexes in Chronic Spinal Animals

    Myotatic. Nesmeyanova (1977) tested the patella reflex in chronic
spinal dogs, some of which had received daily electrocutaneous shock and
physical therapy. Neither the treated, nor the control spinal dogs exhibited changes in the responses to tendon taps as judged by the latency of
onset, or the amplitude of the myopotentials. In monkeys with spinal cord
hemisections at T_8, the ipsilateral knee jerk and Archilles tendon jerk
gradually developed 2 to 3 weeks after surgery and reached a maximum in
about six weeks and persisted in an exaggerated state for several months at
which time the monkeys were sacrificed (Akoi, 1976).

    Nociceptive. Sherrington's (1910) pioneer work on limb reflexes of
spinal dog and cat provided a full description of the flexion reflex and
its accessory reaction, the crossed-extensor reflex. The pair of reflexes
are easily elicitable from the skin of the hindlimb, especially when a pain-
ful stimulus is presented to the paw. Nesmeyanova (1977) reported that
chronic spinal dogs, treated with mild electrical stimulation or massage,
exhibited both the flexor and crossed-extensor reflexes, while in the untreated chronic spinal dogs, the pair of reflexes was "irregular, if present".

    Extensor Thrust. Sherrington (1910) reported that a light touch of the
plantar cushion of the spinal dog's hind paw elicited a "sudden forcible
extension of the limb". The rapid extension was called the "direct extension reflex" or extensor thrust. Sherrington found that applications of
either cold, heat or chemical reagents were ineffective per se to evoke the
reflex, as were noxious mechanical stimuli. Sherrington also noted that
the "broad harmless pressure" may evoke extension followed by flexion "as
if to shake off the irritation".

    Paw Shaking. Smith and her colleagues (1979, 1980) have studied the
"shaking" reflex in normal and chronic spinal cats. The shaking reflex was
elicited by sticking tape on the plantar pads, or by squirting water on the
hindpaw. The frequency of the shakes in normal and chronic cats was 10 to
14 c/s: flexion and extension of the ankle and knee occured rhythmically.
In normal cats the hind limb was abducted at the hip during the reflex,
while in spinal cats there was no abduction. In normal cats and cats transected at 12 weeks, the extensor activity at the ankle during "paw shaking"
was limited to the fast extensors, while the slow extensor was silent (Fig.
1B).

    Tactile Placing. In 1951, Shurrager and Dykman observed that a chronic
spinal cat held up so that the legs were pendent "will lift and place the
paw on a table top if the hind legs contact the edge of the table". This
placing reaction or tactile placing reflex was thought earlier (Bard,
1933), and even more recently (Amassian, et al 1972), to depend on supra-

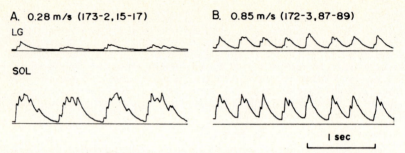

A. 0.28 m/s (173-2,15-17)   B. 0.85 m/s (172-3,87-89)

LG

SOL

I sec

Figure 5: Rectified-averaged (RA) electromyography of LG and SOL during two
   treadmill speeds that elicited a slow walk (A) and a slow gallop (B).
   Peak amplitude of the RA-EMG increased 20% for SOL and 290% for LG.

spinal structures. Recently Forssberg, et al (1974) studied tactile placing
reaction of chronic spinal kittens that were exercised daily on a treadmill.
All kittens exhibited the tactile placing reflex when they were held in the
air. If the kittens were locomoting on the treadmill, the response to a
light tap on the dorsum of the paw varied according to the phase of the
step cycle. A stimulation during the swing phase evoked a flexion response
with a concomitant crossed extension reflex (Fig. 6). If delivered during
the stance phase, the same stimulus induced an increase in ipsilateral extension (Forssberg, et al 1977).

Spontaneous Quadrupedal Standing and Locomotion.

For over a century there have been descriptions in the literature of chronic
spinal animals, with low thoracic or high lumbar transections, that were
able to rise up on their hindlimbs and maintain a quadrupedal stance without assistance. As early as 1905, Philippson showed a film of a chronic dog
standing by raising up on its hindquarters. In 1946, Kellogg, Deese and
Pronko reported standing in chronic spinal dogs, some of which could weight-
bear for several minutes. Similarly, in 1951, Shurrager and Dykman described spinal animals (cats and dogs) that rose "with heads forward", which
helped to dispell the notion, promoted earlier by investigators, notably
Magnus (1912), that in order to rise or to maintain balance, spinal animals
had to shift their center of gravity by lowering their heads. Shurrager
and Dykman (1951) reported that during quadrupedal standing, the trunk of
the cordotomized cats had a noticeable concavity of the vertebral column,
while the hindlimbs often assumed a wide stance. These authors also noted
that when thrown gently off balance, the animals made adequate postural adjustments with the hindlimbs. In addition transected cats were shown
"fast walking with head up" and maintaining "balance while turning" (see
their Fig. 2,3). A "goodness of walking" ranking for the 10 transected
animals, correlated negatively with age of transection, but positively with
the amount of induced exercise the animal had experienced. Shurrager &
Dykman (1951) noted that movement seemed to be initiated anterior to transection. They suggested that once the forepart was in motion, receptors of
the hindlegs were stimulated, producing the walking responses posterior to
transection.

Cate (1962) placed chronic spinal (T_{11}) cats in a wheeled carriage, so that
the "soles of the hind feet" rested on the floor, while the forelimb rested
on a elevated board that was part of the carriage. While in the carriage,

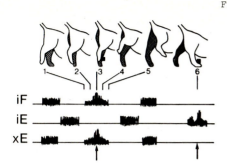

Figure 6: Tactile placing reactions of chronic spinal cat during the swing phase (3) and the stance (6) phase of treadmill locomotion. A crossed extensor reflex (iF and xE) is elicited during the swing phase, while an ipsilateral extensor thrust (iE) is elicited during stance. Schematic EMG is representative of data presented by Forssberg, Grillner and Rossignol (1977).

none of five cats showed stepping movements with their hindlimbs as long as the wheeled carriage was motionless. Even when the hindlimbs were stimulated by pinching, walking was not elicited. When the carriage was pulled forward by the experimenter, stepping in both hindlimbs was observed which persisted as long as the apparatus was pulled forward.

Of the eight transected kittens that Grillner (1973) trained daily on the treadmill, one walked and galloped with ease when the tail was held to provide some lateral stability, while three used their hindlimbs regularly during walking, but "always had some difficulty". Half of these treadmill-trained cats did not use their hindlimbs at all during overground locomotion, but simply dragged their hindlimbs behind them, even when the hindquarters were assisted by pulling up on the tail.

Of the 16 chronic cats that we have maintained, six showed good spontaneous weight support and locomotion; two of these six received no daily exercise on the treadmill. Cats were recorded standing for 3-4 min., during which time the postural muscle such as the soleus were active while more phasic muscles, such as the lateral gastrocnemius were silent (Smith, et al 1979). In one sequence filmed (Smith & Edgerton, 1979), the chronic cat stepped in some water with the left hindpaw; the paw was immediately lifted and shook, and then replaced as the cat initiated a turn. Weight transfer was efficient and smoothly executed.

WHAT NEURONAL MACHINERY IS REQUIRED FOR PATTERN GENERATION?

Isolated Cord With Deafferentation

In an abstract published in 1974, Grillner and Zangger reported that rhythmical stepping could be elicited in a chronic spinal cat, in which both hindlimbs had been acutely deafferented by the transection of dorsal roots L_3-S_4 (Fig. 7A). Rhythmic movements generated by the isolated cord preparation were absent unless tonic input was provided by continuous stimulation of the dorsal roots (DR), dorsal column (DC), or by injecting the animal with clonidine or DOPA. To eliminate phasic information from ventral root afferents (Coggeshall, et al 1974), Grillner and Zangger (1974) used curarized preparations and studied "fictive" locomotion as evidenced by recordings from muscle nerves, ventral (VR) filaments or α-MN directly (Fig. 7B).

In a recent article, Grillner & Zangger (1979) fully explored fictive

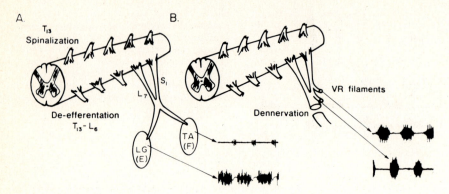

Figure 7: With spinalization (T13) and deafferentation caudal to the cordotomy, rhythmic and alternate contractions of an ankle flexor (TA) and
   extensor (LG) are programmed by the spinal generators, even when no contraction (as in B) is permitted after dennervation or curarization.

locomotion of the acute spinalized, deafferented-curarized cat, or the
spinalized curarized cat. After an injection of the noradrenergic precursor, DOPA, a rhythmic alternating discharge pattern, recorded from muscle
nerves, started spontaneously in 14 of 25 spinalized, curarized cats.
In six, continuous electrical stimulation of DR or DC was required, and in
five no rhythmic activity could be obtained.

   Limb Coordination. The most common type of interlimb coordination of
the curarized cat was that of alternation, as judged by the reciprocal
action of homologue muscle nerves from the two sides. When DR or DC stimulation increased, the burst pattern of muscle pairs changed from alternation to synchrony, typical of a halfbound. Step cycles, measured as the
time interval between the midpoints of two successive bursts from the same
muscle, varied from 0.8 sec. to 6.0 sec., while the bursts of flexor (F)
and extensor (E) muscles ranged from 0.5 to < 3.0 sec. Decreases in period
length, or fictive step cycle, were associated with decreased F and E
bursts, but F burst exhibited a more constant value, reflected by significantly flatter regression lines when period lengths were plotted against
burst durations (see Fig. 6 of Grillner & Zangger, 1979). The duration of
the step cycles and muscle bursts were appreciably longer than those recorded for the chronic spinal cat (Grillner, 1973; Smith, et al 1979), in
which the step cycle was always < 1 sec, and the F burst averaged about
350 ms, while the extensor burst varied from 300 to 600 ms depending on the
speed of the treadmill (see Fig. 2B).

It is possible that phasic inputs from limb proprioceptors and exterocep-
tors are responsible, in part for an adequate stepping frequency. Frequency modulation has been attributed to proprioceptors of the locust wing
(Wilson & Gettrup, 1963). Removal of the stretch and lift receptors of the
locust wings caused no qualitative alteration in pattern of the output, but
a decrease in wing-beat frequency. Phasic feedback information from the
stretch receptors was shown to be lost in an averaging process and to
serve only a tonic function in maintaining the excitability of the central
oscillators. In the cat the rhythm of scratching, another automatic move-

ment believed to be controlled by spinal generators (Deliagina, et al 1975), is generally unaffected by deafferentation or curarization. However, deafferentation always resulted in a change of limb posture and an increase of amplitude of oscillation. Certainly in the curarized cat, there is a frequency shift during fictive locomotion, but the general quality of the endogenous motor pattern and the temporal patterning of muscle activity appears unchanged.

Muscle Synergies. During rhythmic activity of the curarized preparation, transition from flexor to extensor activity was generally reciprocal with intervals of 0-250 ms. However, Grillner & Zangger (1979) did observe some co-activity which is seldom if ever observed in the chronic spinal cat during efficient treadmill locomotion (Grillner, 1973; Smith, et al 1979). One group of muscles, the bifunctional hamstrings, have shown some activity alterations with deafferentation. The semitendinosus (ST) of the deafferented cat, spinal (Forssberg & Grillner, 1973; Grillner & Zangger, 1974, 1975, 1979), and mesencephalic (Perret & Cabelguen, 1976) preparations tended to show only one period of activity; either during the swing phase as a pure flexor, or during the stance phase, as a pure extensor. During normal overground stepping, the ST exhibits two bursts of activity at walk and trot speeds: one during the end of E_3 that extends into F and one at the end of E_1, that continues into E_2 (Enberg & Lundberg, 1969; Rasmussen, et al 1978). What role phasic afference plays in determining the role of biarticular muscles is not clear, but it is apparent that the spinal generators have a variety of options.

Synergistic muscles of a single limb were generally tightly coupled, but "exceptional patterns of activity" were noted. For example, rhythmic alternate activity occurred in a knee flexor, simultaneously with tonic activity of an ankle flexor, and flexors at a single joint were active without extensors, or vice versa. These abnormal patterns, recorded during fictive locomotion, suggest that the generators for each limb could be subdivided into small units, controlling a few muscles at a single joint. Occasionally, Grillner & Zangger (1979) observed alternating activity on one side of the body only, whereas the other was silent, displayed tonic efferent activity, or irregular rhythmic activity. These observations and those of Kulagin and Shik (1970), who had decerebrate cats walk with RT and LT limbs on different treadmill belts driven at different speeds with a 2:1 ratio, suggest that each hindlimb has a collection of generator networks that can be controlled independently. Such independence would be required for the normal animal to turn, where the limbs opposite the direction of the turn must exert greater force and range of motion than the limbs adjacent to the direction of the turn.

Control of α and γ-MNs. In the same type of curarized-spinal preparation, α-motoneurons (MN) have been recorded intracellularly during fictive locomotion (Edgerton, et al 1976). Active α-MNs exhibited periods of depolarization, in which there was spike activity, followed by an interval of hyperpolarization. The hyperpolarization currents may be the result of rhythmically active Ia inhibitory neurons that are known to be influenced by spinal generators (Feldman & Orlovsky, 1975) as well as the Ia afferents of the antagonist muscle (Sjostrom & Zangger, 1976). The membrane potential of some α-MNs oscillated in phase with the activity in the corresponding VR filament, but without action potentials. Thus the spinal generator facilitated many α-MNs, but actual recruitment depended on several factors including the "size principle" (Henneman, et al 1974). In chronic spinal cat, as in the normal, SOL α-MNs appear to be maximally recruited during all gaits, while recruitment of LG α-MNs is correlated with the speed of the treadmill belt (Smith, et al 1977, 1979). According to Walmsley, et al (1978), only slow-twitch fibers need to be recruited during a slow walk, while the largest tension producing units, which are composed of fast-twitch fatigue fibers, are not required until the gallop.

In 1967, Severin and his colleaques showed that in a stable mesencephalic preparation, induced to locomote by stimulating the cuneiform nucleus of the midbrain, that once an α-MN is recruited its frequency of firing is constant even though the speed of locomotion increases. If this is true, increased muscular force is determined by recruiting inactive units.

Sjostrom and Zangger (1976), demonstrated in curarized cats that α and γ-MNs of both flexors and extensors of the hindlimb were co-activated by the spinal generators, potentiated by DOPA. These authors also studied the firing patterns of Ia afferents of the TA and SOL during induced locomotion in which the muscles of the spinal prepartation contracted isometrically from a lengthened position. The discharge of the spindle primaries increased approximately 150 ms before the tension increased in the homonymous muscle. Perret and Buser (1972) recorded primary and secondary spindles afferents from the SOL and medial gastrocnemuis (MG) of acute decorticate cats during locomotion which was elicited by natural stimulation. Both Ia and group II afferents of immobilized, deafferent muscles discharged simultaneously with the rhythmic tension increases of the homonyous muscle. There is evidence that in the decorticate, deafferent preparation, that both static and dynamic fusimotors are recruited during spontaneous locomotion (Perret & Bethoz, 1973).

The efficiency of α-γ co-activation during normal locomotion has been studied by Prochazka, et al (1977) and Loeb and Duysens (1978). Both groups have recorded the activity of spindle afferents from dorsal root ganglia or DR of L_7 and S_1 in freely moving cat locomoting over ground and on a treadmill. Discharge pattern of triceps surae afferents during walking and trotting steps were consistent with the notion that spinal generators activate γ-MNs. During the swing phase (F), Ia activity was evoked by passive muscle stretch, but during E_1, when the muscle shortens, Ia is silenced, despite gamma bias. Generally the greatest discharge was recorded during E_2, when the muscle is actively stretched during the yield. During E_3, when the muscle shortened actively, the afferent was not usually silenced, suggesting strong static γ-bias during this phase (Lennerstrand & Thoden, 1968). Different discharge patterns from two spindle primaries from a single muscle, recorded simultaneously (Loeb & Duysens, 1978), suggest that fusimotor recruitment during locomotion may be as selective as the recruitment of α-MNs.

What is the Role of Afference?

In the previous section, the capacity of the spinal generator to control locomotion without phasic afference from the stepping limbs was considered. Locomotor rhythm, albeit slow, appropriate timing of extensors and flexors of both hindlimbs and gait changes do not require phasic input. What, then is the role of phasic afference during locomotion?

Joint Receptors. The afference from passive movements of a single hip joint in a spinalized curarized cat, injected with DOPA, is powerful enough to engage the central rhythm generator of the ipsilarteral limb to follow the frequency of the imposed hip movements (Anderson, et al 1978). During passive hip flexion, nerve filaments of de-efferented flexors of the knee

(ST) and ankle (TA) were active during hip flexion, and the efferent burst of these nerve filaments followed induced frequencies of 0.13 to 2.2 c/s. Similarly ankle extensors were active during periods of extension, with one exception, when the range of hip extension was greater than 80 degrees, flexor rather than extensor activity was initiated. The position of the hip joint of the ipsilateral limb appears to be one of the key factors in initiating the swing phase (Grillner & Rossignol, 1978).

Our knowledge of the responses of and reflexes mediated by joint receptors is limited primarily to the slowly adapting receptors located within the joint capsule and collateral ligaments of the knee joint of cat (Clark & Burgess, 1975; Grigg, 1975) and primate (Grigg & Greenspan, 1977). During passive positionings and passive movements of the knee, slowly adapting joint receptors of the lateral (LAN), medial (MAN), and posterior (PAN) articular nerves supplying the knee, discharge primarily during the last 30 degrees of flexion or extension and not during the intermediate range. The rate of discharge is relatively linear with respect to the passive torque required to maintain an angular displacement.

Responses of the majority of joint receptors are initiated or enchanced by isometric contraction of muscles about the knee joints, such as the vastii, hamstrings and gastrocnemius (Grigg, 1975). Under these conditions, some joint afferents are activated at intermediate joint angles (Grigg & Greenspan, 1977). These recent studies suggest that slowly adapting mechanoceptors within articular tissues have characteristics that are not appropriate for signaling static or dynamic limb positioning. Rather joint torque, influenced by passive structures and active muscular forces, is detected.

The reflex effects mediated by joint receptors have received little study. Initial studies by Cohen and Cohen (1956) suggested that knee flexion increased flexor tone and decreased extensor tone, while knee extension had the exact opposite effects. Recent experiments by Grigg, et al (1978) appear to confirm these early studies. Changes in the magnitude of evoked monosynaptic reflexes (MSR) were observed in relation to changes in passive knee positions, with hindlimbs that were denervated except for specific articular nerves. Reflexes mediated by fibers of the PAN produced an increase in MSRs of vastii muscles and elicited a decrease in hamstring MSRs during passive knee extension. The magnitudes of the increase or decrease was related directly to the passive joint torques. During locomotion PAN discharge would most likely peak during the stance phase, when knee extensors are contracting and the knee joint is extending. During this phase, PAN mediated reflexes would enhance extensor activity and thereby support the output of the spinal generator.

Muscle Receptors. Both tendon organs and spindle afferents discharge during the contractions of their homonymous muscle (Severin, et al 1967; Prochazha, et al 1977 and Goslow, et al 1973). The spindle afferents, Ia and II, are biased by γ-MNs that are co-active with α-MNs during locomotion. Both of these afferents have monosynaptic connections with homonymous pools of α-MNs, and therefore do not have to work through an interneuronal network (Stauffer, et al 1976; Watt, et al 1976). However, during fictive locomotion, the amplitude of the Ia EPSP increases during the active phase and generally di- and trisynaptic EPSPs were observed only during this phase (Schomberg & Behrends, 1978). These results suggest that the transmission of multineuronal pathways, in particular, depend upon the phase of the step cycle. Also it is possible also that primary afferent depolarization of central Ia terminals by other sensory neurons (Willis, et al 1976), is governed by spinal generators.

The Golgi tendon organ afferents, group IB, are also active with the homonymous muscle, and their influence on the pool of α-MNs is primarily one of
inhibition (Watt, et al 1976). Houk (1979) has suggested that the afference from spindles and tendon organs work co-jointly to regulate muscle
stiffness, defined as the ratio of force change to length change. It is
true that inherent mechanical properties of muscle tissue (i.e. inertial,
viscous and elastic) provide stiffness that does not require reflex regulation (Bizzi, et al 1978), but the mechanical properties of muscle are
highly nonlinear, and feedback from proprioceptors may help to compensate
for these nonlinear features (Nichols & Houk, 1976). During the E_2 phase,
when the extensors of the hindlimb are actively lengthening, myotatic reflexes have more than enough time to contribute to setting or regulating
muscle stiffness. The time interval for the E_2 phase is about 175 ms for
a slow walk and about 55 ms for a fast trot-gallop (Goslow, et al 1973b).
Torque pertubations produce typical muscle responses at minimal latencies
of 8-15 ms for the "jerk" response and 25 to 40 ms for the so-called functional stretch reflex in spinal and normal cat (Ghez & Shinoda, 1978). So,
although the stretch reflex does not initiate extensor contraction during
stepping (Engberg & Lundgerg, 1969), myotatic reflexes may help to regulate
muscle stiffness and ensure that the muscular force is well adapted to the
terrain.

Cutaneous. The regulatory role of cutaneous input from the paw was
questioned in 1910 by Sherrington when he reported that severance of all
the nerve trunks innervating the four paws up to and above the wrists and
ankles of the intact animal (cat, dog) produced little deficit during overground locomotion. Sherrington did report, however, that these animals
tended to stand and walk with the toes flexed underneath the planta, and
that no correction of the mal-position was made. Although the position may
have been due to motor paralysis of the short extensors of the toes, Sher-
tington observed that severance of the muscle nerve alone did not produce
the underturning. These early observations were of particular interest to
our laboratory staff when both of the two chronic spinal cats that failed
to improve with treadmill training, walked on the dorsum of the paw (Smith,
Smith, Edgerton, unpublished observations). Neither cat achieved weight
support on the treadmill, although both would air step, and both produced
weak alternate movements when suspended over the treadmill. It is our
opinion that proper cutaneous input is important for several aspects of
stepping, and there is some evidence to support this concept.

When a short train of weak electrical shocks are delivered to the planta of
the hindpaw at the beginning of the stance phase, a long and intense discharge of the ipsilateral ankle extensor is elicited (Duysens & Pearson,
1976). The prolonged extension of the ipsilateral leg is associated with
a delay in the onset of the flexor burst that initiates the swing phase and
thus the natural step cycle is prolonged up to 30%. These results can be
interpreted functionally in terms of resistance and compressional forces
met by the plantar pad. As these forces increase, so does the extensor
activity. If, on the other hand, a weak stimuli is applied to the plantar
pads during the swing phase, the flexor on-going burst increases in amplitude and duration, while the following extensor burst is decreased, causing
the step cycle to shorten as much as 20% (Forssberg, et al 1977). Such a
movement would insure that the cat could quickly clear a small object
should the plantar surface brush against an obstacle.

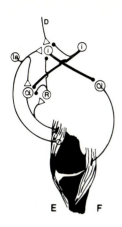

Figure 8: Schematic view of the interaction between Ia inhibitory interneurons (i) and Renshaw cells (R) with extensor (E) and flexor
(F) motor pools. Activity of the E 1A afferent would excite R via the recurrent collateral, and thereby disinhibited the flexor
α-MN to facilitate the switch from E to F
activity. If this model is correct, MN firing fictive stepping would be produced
through disinhibition, and the depolarization
giving rise to MN firing would be accompanied
by reduced membrane conductance, as compared
to the conductance when the membrane was hy-
perpolarized during the non-active phase.
Menzies, et al 1978 found an increased rather
than a decreased conductance associated with
the depolarizing phase of the step cycle,
suggesting that excitation and just not disinhibition occured.

When tape is applied to the plantar surface of a chronic spinal cat (Smith,
et al 1979) , vigorous shaking of the hindleg is initiated immediately
(Fig. 1B). Locomotion of both legs cease and often the taped limb will be
pulled rigidly forward, with flexion at the hip and extension at the knee
and ankle with toes fanned. Stepping is resumed only after the tape has
been removed. Thus it seems that prolonged excitation of low threshold
cutaneous input from plantar pads may completely over-ride the rhythmic
oscillation of the spinal generators.

Tactile placing in the chronic spinal cat also provides evidence of the
efficiency of cutaneous input in the regulation of spinal generators. As
illustrated in Fig. 6, stimulation of the paw dorsum during the swing
phase, elicits flexion (Forssberg, et al 1977). This forceful flexion
initiated by knee flexion within 8-11 ms, is followed by an equally forceful extension in normal (Prochazha, et al 1978) and chronic spinal cats
(Forssberg, et al 1977). Simultaneously contralateral extensors contract
more forcefully within 12-14 ms. During the gallop, the crossed-extensor
effect is absent, suggesting that this cutaneous reflex is gait dependent.
Conversely, when the dorsum of the paw is lightly stimulated during the
stance phase, on-going extensor activity of the ipsilateral limb is greatly
enhanced and is followed by a similar augmentation of ipsilateral flexor
activity during the swing phase. This acceleration of F and E activity may
shorten the step cycle as much as 20% (Forssberg, et al 1977). At treadmill speeds up to 1.5 m/s, the point at which flexor enhancement is **altered**
to extensor enhancement, changed from 50% to 80% of the normalized step
cycle. Thus the "phase-dependent reflex reversal" (Forssberg, et al 1977),
has been correlated with gait characteristics, in which the swing phase, or
period of flexor enhancement, becomes relatively longer as locomotion
velocity increased.

WHAT IS THE NATURE OF THE SPINAL GENERATORS?

Probably the most accurate statement that can be made today about the
nature of the spinal generator is that it is a neuronal network of unknown
design. Of the interneurons that are active and rhythmically modulated in
relation to fictive locomotion (Edgerton, et al 1976) and fictive

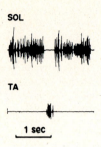

SOL

TA

1 sec

Figure 9: EMG of SOL recorded during treadmill locomotion at 0.28 m/s shows cyclic "packaging" of myopotentials during each epoch of activity at 12-14 c/s. This cyclic bursting is similar to postural tremor that is observed when the spinalized cat supported the weight of the hindquarters during quadrupedal standing. Similar packets were seen during flexor bursts (110-5, 889).

scratching (Berkinblit, et al 1978), most are located in Rexed lamina VII. Interneurons in this region which have been identified by physiological and/or anatomical methods include Ia inhibitory interneurons (Jankowska and Lindstrom, 1972), Ib inhibitory interneurons (Lucas & Willis, 1974) and Renshaw cells (Jankowska & Lindstrom, 1971; Van Keulen, 1979). It has been proposed that the Ia inhibitory interneuron and the Renshaw cell constitute part the spinal generator, because collectively they could provide an automatic mechanism for switching between antagonist MN pools during locomotion (Fig. 8). Such a model is reminiscent of Brown's (1914) concept of half-centers, and if correct, motoneuron firing during locomotion would be the result of disinhibition. Recent experiments by Menzies, et al (1978) suggest that this design alone cannot constitute the generator network.

Other neural structures, including the dendritic bundles of α-MNs, have been implicated in the programming of alternate movements (Scheibel & Scheibel, 1970a), and deserve some attention. At birth, these bundles are rudimentary in the lumbosacral cord, and their development is coeval with the development of walking (Scheibel & Scheibel, 1970b). Preliminary findings from our laboratory (Reback, 1979) question the importance of bundles, since they do not form in kittens cordotomized at 2 weeks, and they appear to degenerate in cats transected at 12 weeks of age. Both groups of cats, however, perform adequately on the treadmill if they are exercised daily (see previous section). However, the EMG of selected ankle muscles (Fig. 9) often show abnormal packaging with separated bursts of activity from 12 to 14 c/s within a single epoch of extensor and flexor activity (Fig. 9). These packets are similar to postural tremor that is seen when the transected cat is standing and supporting the weight of the hindlimb (Fig. 1C). It has been suggested that dendritic bundles mediate synchronization of the MN pool (Gogan, et al 1974), and it appears that motor pools of the transected cats lack the synchronization that normally fills in the EMG epoch.

It is beyond the scope and length of this chapter to discuss or to speculate about appropriate neural circuitry for the spinal generators. Grillner (1975), Gurfinkel and Shik (1977) and Stein (1978) provide excellent reviews on this topic. The latter review relates the more recent work on the mammalian cord to the more extensive investigations on the designs of pattern generators and command signals that coordinate stereotyped movements in the invertebrate. Undoubtedly, the elucidation of these circuits in the mammalian spinal gray, and their interaction with supraspinal and peripheral inputs, will provide a challange to spinal cord physiologists for the next century.

REFERENCES

Amassian, V.E. Weiner, H. and Roseblum, Neural systems subserving the tactile place reaction: a model for the study of higher level control of movement, Brain Res. 40 (1972) 171-178.

Bard, P. Studies on the cerebral cortex. 1. Localized control of placing and hopping reaction in the cat and their normal management by small cortical remnants, Arch Neurol. Psychiat. 30 (1933) 40-74.

Anderson, O. Grillner, S., Lindquist, M., Zomleffer, M. Peripheral control of the spinal pattern generators for locomotion in cat, Brain Res. 150 (1978) 625-630.

Aoki, M.S., Mori, S. and Fujimori, B. Exaggeration of knee-jerk following spinal hemisection in monkeys, Brain Res. 107 (1976) 471-486.

Berkinblit, M.B., Deliagina, T.G., Feldman, A.F., Gelfand, I.M. and Orlovsky, G.N. Generation of scratching. I. Activity of spinal interneurons during scratching, J. Neurophysiol. 41 (1978) 1040-1057.

Bizzi, E. Dev., P., Morasso, P. and Polit, A. Effect of load disturbances during centrally initiated movements, J. Neurophysiol. 41 (1978) 542-556.

Brown, T.G. The phenomenon of "narcosis progression" in mammals, Proc. Roy. Soc. London, Ser. B. 86 (1913) 140-164.

Brown, T.G. On the nature of the fundamental activity of nervous centres; together with an analysis of the conditioning of rhythmic activity in progression, and a theory of the evolution of function in the nervous system, J. Physiol. 48 (1914) 18-46.

Cate, J. ten. Innervation of locomotor movements by the lumbosacral cord in birds and mammals, J. Exp. Biol. 39 (1962) 239-242.

Clark, F.J. and Burgess, P.R. Slowly adapting receptors in cat knee joint: can they signal joint angle? J. Neurophysiol. 38 (1975) 1448-1463.

Clemente, C. Neuronal degeneration and regeneration, in: Regenerative Phenomena in the CNS (Los Angeles: UCLA Brain Information Service, 1972).

Coggeshall, R.E., Coulter, J.D. and Willis, W.D. Unmyelinated in the ventral roots of the cat lumbosacral enlargement, J. Comp. Neurol. 153 (1974) 39-58.

Cohen, L.A. and Cohen, M.L. Arthrokinetic reflex of the knee, Am. J. Physiol. 184 (1956) 433-437.

Deliagina, T.G., Feldman, A.G., Gelfand, I.M. and Orlovsky, G.N. On the role of central program and afferent inflow in the control of scratching movements in the cat, Brain Res. 100 (1975) 297-313.

Duysens, J. and Pearson, K.G. The role of cutaneous afferents from the distal hindlimb in the regulation of the step cycle of thalamic cats, Exp. Brain Res. 24 (1976) 245-256.

Edgerton, V.R., Grillner, S., Sjostrom, A., and Zangger, P. Central generation of locomotion in vertebrates, in: Herman, R.M., et al (eds.), Neural Control of Locomotion (New York, Plenum, 1976).

Edgerton, V.R., Smith, L.A. and Eldred, E. Muscle and motor unit properties of exercised and non-excercised chronic spinal cats, Neurosc. Abst. 5 (1979, in press).

Engberg, I. and Lundberg, A. An electromyographic analysis of muscular activity in the hindlimb of the cat during unrestrained locomotion, Acta. Physiol. Scand. 75 (1969) 614-630.

Feldman, A.G. and Orlovsky, G.N. Activity of interneurons mediating reciprocal Ia inhibition during locomotion. Brain Res. 84 (1956) 181-194.

Forrsberg, H. and Grillner, S. The locomotion of the acute spinal cat injected with clondine i.v., Brain Res. 50 (1973) 184-186.

Forssberg, H., Grillner, S., and Sjostrom, A. Tactile placing reactions in chronic spinal kittens, Acta Physiol. Scand. 92 (1974) 114-120.

Forrsberg, H., Grillner, S., and Rossignol, S. Phase dependent reflex reversal during walking in chronic spinal cats, Brain Res. 85 (1977) 121-139.

Ghez, C. and Shinoda, Y. Spinal mechanisms of the functional stretch reflex, Exp. Brain Res. 32 (1978) 55-68.

Gogan, P., Gueritaud, G., Horcholle-Bousavit, G. and Tyc-Dumont, S. Electronic coupling between motoneurons in the abducens nucleus of the cat, Exp. Brain Res. 21 (1974) 139-154.

Goslow, G.E., Stauffer, E.K., Nemeth, W.C. and Stuart, D.G. The cat step cycle: responses of muscle spindles and tendon organs to passive stretch within the locomotor range, Brain Res. 60 (1973) 35-54.

Grigg, P. Mechanical factors influencing response of joint afferent neurons from cat knee, J. Neurophysiol. 38 (1975) 1473-1484.

Grigg, P. and Greenspan, B.J. Response of primate joint afferent neurons to mechanical stimulation of knee joint, J. Neurophysiol. 40 (1977) 1-8.

Grigg, P., Harrigan, E.P. and Fogarty, K.E. Segmental reflexes mediated by joint afferent neurons in cat knee, J. Neurophysiol. 41 (1978) 9-14.

Grillner, S. Locomotion in the spinal cat, in: Stein, R.B. (ed.), Control of Posture and Locomotion (New York, Plenum Press, 1973).

Grillner, S. Locomotion in vertebrates: central mechanisms and reflex interaction, Physiol. Rev. 55 (1975) 247-307.

Grillner, S. and Rossignol, S. On the initiation of the swing phase of locomotion in chronic spinal cats, Brain Res. 146 (1978) 269-277.

Grillner, S. and Zangger, P. Locomotor movements generated by the deafferented spinal cord, Acta Physiol. Scand. 91 (1974) 38-39A.

Grillner, S. and Zangger, P. How detailed is the central pattern generation for locomotion? Brain Res. 88 (1975) 367-371.

Grillner, S. and Zangger, P. On the central generation of locomotion in the low spinal cat, Exp. Brain Res. 34 (1979) 241-262.

Gurfinkel, V.S. and Shik, M.L. The control of posture and locomotion, in: Gyikov, A.A., Tankov, N.T. and Kosarov, D.S. (eds), Motor Control (New York, Plenum Press, 1977).

Henneman, E., Clamann, H.P., Gillies, J.D. and Skinner, R.D. Rank order of motoneurons within a pool: law of combination, J. Physiol. London 37 (1974) 1338-1349.

Houk, J.C.   Regulation of stiffness by skeletomotor reflexes, Ann Rev. Physiol. 41 (1979) 99-114.

Jankowska, E. and Lindstrom, S.   Morphological identification of Renshaw cells, Acta Physiol. Scand. 81 (1971) 428-430.

Jankowska, E. and Lindstrom, S.   Morphology of interneurones mediating la reciprocal inhibition of motoneurones in the spinal cord of the cat, J. Physiol. Lond. 226 (1972) 805-824.

Kellog, W.N., Deese, J. and Pronko, N.H.   On the behavior of the lumbo-spinal dog, J. Exp. Psych. 36 (1946) 503-511.

Kulagin, A.S. and Shik, M.L.   Interaction of symmetrical limbs during con-trolled locomotion, Biophysics 15 (1970) 171-178.

Loeb, G.E. and Duysens, J.   The unit activity of primary and secondary afferents from cat hindlimb muscle spindles during normal walking, Neurosc. Abst. 4 (1978) 300.

Lucas, E. and Willis, W.D.   Identification of muscle afferents which acti-vate interneurons in the intermediate nucleus, J. Neurophysiol. 37 (1974) 282-293.

Lennerstrand, G. and Thoden, U.   Static fusimotor single-fibre activation of primary and secondary endings, Acta Physiol. Scand. 74 (1968) 30-49.

Magnus, R. and de Kleign, A.   Die abhangigheit des tonus der extremitaten muskeln von der kopfspellung, Pflugers Arch. 145 (1912) 455-476.

Menizes, J.E., Albert, C. and Jordan, L.M.   Testing model for the spinal generator, Neurosc. Abst. 4 (1978) 383.

Nesmeyanova, T.A.   Experimental Studies in Regeneration of Spinal Neurons (Wiston & Sons, Washington, D.C., 1977).

Nichols, T.R. and Houk, J.C.   Improvement in linearity and regulations of stiffness that results from actions of stretch reflex.   J. Neurophysiol. 39 (1976) 119-142.

Perret, C. and Buser, P.   Static and dynamic fusimotor activity during locomotor movements in the cat, Brain Res. 40 (1973) 165-169.

Perret, C. and Berthoz, A.   Evidence of static and dynamic fusimotor ac-tions on the spindle response to sinusoidal stretch during locomotor acti-vity in the cat, Exp. Brain Res. 18 (1973) 178-188.

Perret, C. and Cabelguen, J.M.   Central and reflex participation in the timing of locomotor activations of a bifunctional muscle, the semitendi-nosus, in the cat, Brain Res. 106 (1976) 390-395.

Phillipson, M.   L'autonomic et al centralisation dans le systeme nerveux des animaux, Trav. Lab. Physiol. Inst. Solvay, Bruxelles 7 (1905) 1-208.

Prochazka, A., Westerman, R.A. and Ziconne, S.P.   la afferent activity dur-ing a variety of voluntary movements in the cat, J. Physiol. London 268 (1977) 423-448.

Prochazka, A., Sontag, K.H. and Wand, P.   Motor reactions to pertubations of gait: proprioceptive and somesthetic involvement, Neurosc. Letters 7 (1978) 35-39.

Rasmussen, S., Chan, A.K. and Goslow, G.E.   The cat step cycle: electro-myographic patterns for hindlimb muscles during posture and unrestrained locomotion, J. Morphol. 155 (1978) 253-270.

Reback, P. The effect of cordotomy on dendrite bundles and treadmill walking in kittens, Neurosc. Abst. 5 (1979, in press).

Schomberg, E.D. and Behrends, H.B. The possibility of phase-dependent
monosynaptic and polysynaptic la excitation to homonymous motonerones during fictive locomotion, Brain Res. 143 (1978) 533-537.

Scheibel, M.E. and Scheibel, A.B. Organization of spinal motoneuron dendrites, Exp. Neurol. 28 (1970a) 106-112.

Scheibel, M.E. and Scheibel, A.B. Developmental relationship between
spinal motorneuron dendrite bundles and patterned activity in the hindlimb
of cats, Exp. Neurol. 29 (1970b) 328-335.

Severin, F.V., Orlovsky, G.N. and Shik, M.L. Work of the muscle receptors
during controlled locomotion, Biophysics. 12 (1967) 575-586.

Severin, F.V., Shik, M.L. and Orlovsky, G.N. Work of the muscles and
single motoneurones during controlled locomotion, Biophysics. 12 (1967)
762-772.

Sherrington, C.S. The Integrative Action of the Nervous System (New York,
Scribner, 1906).

Sherrington, C.S. Flexion-reflex of the limb, crossed extension reflex,
and reflex stepping and standing, J. Physiol. Lond. 40 (1910) 28-121.

Sherrington, C.S. Nervous rhythm arising from rivalry of antagonistic reflexes: reflex stepping as outcome of double reciprocal innervation, Proc.
Roy. Soc. Lon., Ser. B. 86 (1913) 233-261.

Shurrager, P.S. and Dykman, R.A. Walking spinal carnivores, J. Comp.
Physiol. Psych. 44 (1951) 252-262.

Sjostrom, A. and Zangger, P. Muscle spindle control during locomotor movements generated by the deafferented spinal cord, Acta Physiol. Scand. 97
(1976) 281-291.

Smith, J.L. and Edgerton, V.R. Chronic Spinal Cat: Reflexes, treadmill and
spontaneous play: a 16mm film, UCLA Productions, 1979.

Smith, J.L., Edgerton, V.R., Betts, B. and Collatos, T.C. EMG of slow and
fast ankle extensors of cat druing posture, locomotion and jumping, J.
Neurophysiol. 40 (1977) 503-513.

Smith, J.L., Betts, B., Edgerton, V.R. and Zernicke, R.F. Rapid ankle extension during paw shakes: selective recruitment of fast ankle extensors,
J. Neurophysiol. (in press) 1980.

Smith, J.L., Smith, L.A., and Dahms, K.L. Motor capacities of the chronic
spinal cat: recruitment of slow and fast extensors of the ankle, Neurosc.
Abt. 5 (1979, in press).

Stauffer, E.K., Watt, D.G.D., Taylor, A., Reinking, R.R. and Stuart, D.G.
Analysis of muscle receptor connections by spike-triggered averaging. 2.
spindle group II afferents, J. Neurophysiol. 15 (1976) 1393-1402.

Stein, P.S.G. Motor systems, with specific reference to the control of
locomotion, Ann. Rev. Neurosc. 1 (1978) 61-82.

Van Keulen, L.C.M. Axon trajectories of Renshaw cells in the lumbar spinal
cord of the cat, as reconstructed after intracellular staining with horse-

radish peroxidase, Brain Res. 167 (1979) 157-162.

Villablanca, J.R. and Olmstead, C.E.   Neurological development of kittens, Develop. Psych. 12 (1979) 101-127.

Walmsley, B., Hodgson, J.A. and Burke, R.E.   Forces produced by medial gastrocnemius and soleus muscles during locomotion in freely moving cats, J. Neurophysiol. 41 (1978) 1203-1216.

Watt, D.G.D., Stauffer, D.K., Taylor, A., Reinking, R.M. and Stuart, D.G. Analysis of muscle receptor connections by spike-triggered averaging. 1. Spindle primary and tendon organ afferents, J. Neurophysiol. 39 (1976) 1375-1392.

Wetzel, M.C. and Stuart, D.G.   Ensemble characteristics of cat locomotion and its neural control, Prog. Neurobiol. 7 (1976) 1-99.

Willis, W.D., Nunez, R. and Rudomin, P.   Excitability changes of terminal arborizations of single 1a and 1b afferent fibers produced by muscle and cutaneous conditioning, J. Neurophysiol. 39 (1976) 1150-1159.

Wilson, V.J. and Gettrup, E.   A stretch reflex controlling wing beat frequency in grasshoppers, J. Exp. Biol. 40 (1963) 171-185.

Tutorials in Motor Behavior
G.E. Stelmach and J. Requin (eds.)
© *North-Holland Publishing Company, 1980*

6

PARIETAL ASSOCIATION CORTEX OF THE MONKEY
AS REVEALED BY CELLULAR RECORDINGS

L.M. Leinonen and J. Hyvärinen

Department of Physiology
University of Helsinki
Helsinki, Finland

The review summarizes some of the results from cellular
recordings in posterior parietal and parieto-temporal
association cortices of awake, behaving macaque monkeys.
Neurons in these areas respond to somesthetic, visual
and auditory stimuli and are active during the monkey's
own eye, face, limb and head movements. Cellular recordings suggest that the association cortex is intra-areally
differentiated for the analysis of sensory information
evoked by movements of different body parts and as a
whole the area functions as an integrator of this information.

INTRODUCTION

This review deals with recent results from cellular recordings in the
posterior parietal association cortex of the macaque monkey.[1] The cellular
discharges in the monkey's parietal association cortex are related to the
spatial control of the movements of the eyes, arms, hands, face and head.
The use of these body parts is in many respects similar in man and monkey.
Like man the monkey uses its arm and hand when reaching for attractive
visual targets, when taking hold of small objects with the forefinger and
thumb and when exploring novel objects. It fixates its gaze on attractive
objects and avoids fixating a threatening individual which it is, however,
able to observe using the periphery of the visual field. The monkey turns
its head towards the target to be observed but it does not do this when it
does not want to reveal its interest in the object. Like man the monkey
uses its facial musculature for expressive movements signaling threat,
fear, excitement and pleasure. These types of motor behaviors develop
during the first years of social life in the monkey as they do in man.
The behavioral similarities in the use of the arms, hands, eyes, face and
head in the monkey and man suggest that neuronal discharges related to
these types of motor behaviours in the monkey could be recorded also in
some parts of the posterior parietal association cortex in man. This view
is further supported by clinical observations in man and by ablation
studies in the monkey which show that a lesion in the posterior parietal
association cortex produces many similar symptoms in man and monkey. The
similar symptoms, reported by several investigators[2], are: 1. Deterioration
of movements of arm and hand; abnormal posture, refusal to use delayed and
slow movements, spatial error in reaching and grasping for objects under
visual and tactual guidance. 2. Deterioration of eye movements (hardly
studied in the monkey); error in fixation. 3. Deterioration of discrimination of contralateral stimuli; unresponsiveness to visual and/or soma-
esthetic stimuli, unresponsiveness to contralateral visual, somesthetic
and auditory stimuli on bilateral simultaneous stimulation, deterioration
of somesthetic recognition of three dimensional objects.

This review deals with area 7 of Brodmann and area Tpt of Pandya and
Sanides (1973) (Fig. 1, upper part). Area 7 has been divided on histological grounds into two parts by Vogt and Vogt (1919, areas 7a and 7b) and
von Bonin and Bailey (1947, areas PG and PF). The temporo-parietal association cortex, area Tpt of Pandya and Sanides is histologically similar to
area 7 (Pandya and Sanides, 1973) and has its functional features (Leinonen
et al. in prep.). The anatomical connections of area 7 and Tpt reveal that
these areas receive information from the association cortices of all
sensory modalities, from the frontal association cortex, the premotor areas
(Pandya and Kuypers, 1969) and from some of the thalamic nuclei, the
pulvinar and the ventrolateral nucleus (Baleydier and Mauguiere, 1977), and
that these areas with their efferents to the premotor cortex (Pandya and
Kuypers, 1969), the caudate nucleus, the superior colliculus, the ventro-
lateral nucleus (Kaas et al. 1977), and the pyramidal tract (Peele, 1942)
may also directly influence the functions of the motor system.

A signal needs 70 ms or more to pass from the periphery to area 7 or from
area 7 to the periphery (latency of visually evoked responses 70-120 ms,
Yin and Mountcastle, 1977; of somesthetically evoked responses 100 ms,
Robinson and Goldberg, 1978; latency of saccades from beginning of the activity 73-150 ms and latency of arm movements 100 ms, Mountcastle et al.
1975). This is a long time compared, for instance, with the response
latencies of about 20 ms measured in the primary sensory cortices, and it
shows the high level of the central processing that takes place in area 7.

Differences in the research methods

Table 1 summarizes some results from single cell recordings made in areas 7
and Tpt of awake behaving macaque monkeys. The investigations referred to
have been carried out in four different laboratories using considerably
different methods. Mountcastle, Robinson and Sakata with their co-workers
observed cellular discharges primarily during experimentally conditioned
eye or arm movements whose beginning and direction were signalled by light
stimuli. Hyvärinen and his coworkers observed systematically the relationships between cellular discharges and natural behavior and stimuli. This
method has its drawbacks but it is useful when searching new relationships
between neuronal activity and the monkey's behavior.

Results common for the different laboratories

Regardless of the differences in the paradigms, the different laboratories
have obtained many similar results: the neurones in area 7 are active
during visually guided arm, hand and eye movements and they respond to visual, cutaneous and proprioceptive stimuli and some cells respond to stimulation of several sensory systems.

Differences in results obtained in different laboratories

The main differences in the results of the different investigations are the
following: 1. The number of isolated but undrivable neurones was greater in
the laboratories where mainly experimentally conditioned tasks were used
than in the laboratory where natural behavior was observed. 2. The investigators in Mountcastle's laboratory stated that most neurones did not
respond to sensory stimulation but discharged only during conditioned arm
or eye movements. Investigators in Hyvärinen's laboratory stated that most
neurones responded to sensory stimulation and the rest discharged during the

Table 1

Results from cellular recordings in area 7 and Tpt

Investigation	Drivable neurones	Un-drivable neurones	Neurones discharging during active movements			Neurones responding to stimuli				
			eyes	arms	other	visual	skin	muscle joint	sound	several
Mountcastle et al. 1975	377	21%	60%	33%		+	+	+		+
Lynch et al. 1977	907	29%	81%	15%						
Yin and Mountcastle 1977	350					28%				
Robinson and Goldberg 1978	165	11%	(38%)	(44%)		+	+	+		+
Robinson et al. 1978	195	12%	(33%)	(19%)		14%		22%		
Sakata et al. 1978			20%			+				
Hyvarinen and Poranen 1974	193	7%	36%	47%		+	+			6%
Leinonen et al. (1,2,3) 1979	425	1%	7%	20%	face 7%	14%	12%	23%		16%
Leinonen et al. in prep. (Tpt)	197	-		1%	head 4%	1%	10%	14%	54%	17%

Vestibular, thermal, nociceptive, gustatory or olfactory stimuli have not been used.

monkey's own movements. Robinson et al. reported that all neurones
discharging during conditioned arm or eye movements also responded to
sensory stimulation. 3. In Mountcastle's laboratory most neurones discharged during eye movements and in the laboratory of Hyvärinen most
neurones discharged when the monkey reached for and manipulated an object
with its hand. 4. The finding that a cell was activated by several types
of stimuli was exceptional in the laboratory of Mountcastle but common in
the laboratory of Hyvärinen. These differences are due to the different
methods, differences in conceptualizing the behavioral situation as well
as to differences in the locations of the targets within area 7.

Methodological differences as a source of differences in the results

The differences in the methods, especially in the number of qualitatively
different stimuli used, are the probable cause of the different proportions
of isolated but undrivable neurones. The differences in the proportion of
neurones responding to sensory stimulation are due both to differences in
the method of stimulation and to the differences in the conceptualization
of the results from the neuronal activity that appears to be related only
to movements.

The difficulties in finding an adequate stimulus for a neurone are demonstrated by the following examples. Sakata et al. showed that some of the
neurones discharging during tracking eye movements in a certain direction
discharged also when the gaze was stationary but the background moved in
the direction opposite to the optimal tracking direction. Also Robinson
et al. showed that some neurones discharged during tracking movements in a
certain direction but also when a visual stimulus moved in the opposite
direction while the monkey's eyes were stationary.

Differences in the conceptualization as a source of difference in the
results.

All investigators have observed neurones which discharge 100-150 ms prior
and during movements towards a conditioned (visual) target. Lunch et al.
and Sakata et al. showed that neurones discharging during certain eye
movements did not discharge similarly in the dark during the same eye
movements. Hyvärinen and Poranen and Mountcastle et al. observed that
random arm movements were not preceeded by cellular discharges in area 7.
Thus, the movement-related neurones which were considered not to be re-
sponsive to sensory stimuli discharge only during movements towards the
target. By natural or experimental conditioning the monkey has learned
that the target is to be looked at, to be touched and that it is within its
reach. Movements related to the activity of some parietal neurones are
thus always preceeded by a complex analysis: pattern recognition, analysis
of the information content of the pattern and localization of the pattern.
It is probable that not only the movements but also the discharges of
movement-related neurones depend on these stimulus properties, that is, the
neurones respond to some features of the stimulus. This is supported by
the statement of Robinson et al. that any cell that fires in association
with a movement can be driven by a passive sensory stimulus, frequently by
the identical stimulus that is the target of the movement.

Thus, it seems that all neurones in area 7 respond to sensory stimulation
but discharges of some neurones are also in a particular way dependent on

the probability of the subsequent motor activity. It is therefore useful
to describe the neurones as stimulus-related and movement-related. The
results of different investigations would probably be more comparable if
the classification were done on the following grounds: 1. A movement-related neurone responds only to a stimulus which in certain conditions
(external and those internal ones that can be inferred from the monkey's
behavior) will most probably evoke a movement towards itself (the stimulus). If the movement occurs the neurone continues to discharge until the
movement reaches the stimulus. 2. A stimulus-related neurone responds to
a stimulus which usually evokes no motor response in the monkey. Also the
discharges of stimulus-related neurones depend on the focus of attention,
state of arousal and emotional state of the monkey. For instance, it has
often been observed in Hyvärinen's laboratory that when the monkey's
attention is diverted to some other stimulus the discharges to the adequate
stimulus diminish or sometimes even disappear. The stimulus-related
neurones may discharge during all kinds of movements which activate the
receptive fields of the neurones whereas the movement-related neurones
discharge only during movements of a certain body part towards a conditioned stimulus.

Role of movement-related neurones

Mountcastle and his coworkers showed that movement-related neurones signal
the direction of eye movements (in reference to the head). When Mountcastle et al. examined neurones discharging during visually guided arm
projections they noticed that the cellular activity was neither related
to the exact execution nor to the direction of the movement (in reference
to the body). These discharges might, however, signal whether the movement
is towards the target or not. The analysis of the location of the target,
which is a prerequisite for signalling the direction of movement towards
it, depends on the direction of the gaze or direction of eye movement.
Mountcastle et al. proposed that the signals of movement-related neurones
are used for the guidance of motor activity.

Robinson and Goldberg argued against Mountcastle's idea of motor command by
stating that all movement-related neurones respond to stimuli also in the
absence of movement. They showed this by an experiment in which the monkey
made conditioned arm or eye movements, triggered by a light signal, towards
a conditioned visual target; the movement-related neurones discharged after
the triggering stimulus although the monkey occasionally did not make the
conditioned movement. Robinson and Goldberg said that as the discharges
were not followed by a movement these cells did not command the movement.
However, their experiment shows only that the discharges of these neurones
were not sufficient for the occurrence of an observable movement. It is
possible that the discharges activated some part of the motor system.
Their experiments, as well as those performed by other investigators,
suggest that the activity of the movement-related neurones in the posterior
parietal cortex is a necessary antecedent for accurate guidance of movements directed towards a stimulus. The activity occurs at the same
time as the attention is directed towards the signal and the movement is
initiated. Thus, the cellular activity may be a neural counterpart for
these psychological phenomena. However, the discharges of these cells are
related only to the use of a certain body part(s). Because the discharges
of these neurones are almost always associated with the movements it is
possible that they activate parts of the motor system.

Differences in results due to differences in regions recorded within area 7

The differences in the location of the target within area 7 account for
some of the differences in the results obtained from this area. Multiple
and single cell recordings in different parts of area 7 made in Hyvärinen's
laboratory have revealed that the parietal association cortex, although it
is functionally uniform in some respects, shows high intra-areal differentiation in some other respects. The common features for the parts of
area 7 and Tpt examined are: 1. some neurones are movement-related in the
sense described earlier, 2. most neurones respond to stimuli which usually
trigger no certain movement in the monkey and the receptive fields of these
neurones are large, covering, for example, almost the whole visual field or
the skin of an entire body part, 3. half of the neurones are bilateral, that
is, they respond to stimuli on both sides of the body or are active during
movements of both halves of the body, 4. some cells respond to stimulation
of different sensory systems.

The intra-areal differentiation of the posterior parietal association cortex
is demonstrated by the following findings: in the medial part of area 7
most neurones discharge during visual stimulation or eye movements
(Hyvärinen and Shelepin, 1979), in the anterolateral part during movements
and stimulation of the face (Leinonen and Nyman, 1979), in the lateral part
during movements and stimulation of the limbs (Leinonen et al. 1979,
Leinonen, in prep.), and in area Tpt during stimulation and movements of the
head (Leinonen et al. in prep.), Figure 1, lower part.

The differences in the locations of the targets within area 7 probably explain why the proportion of cells related to eye movement varied from
7 to 81% in different studies.

Intra-areal differentiation in posterior parietal association cortex

The functional characteristics of the lateral parts of area 7 and Tpt,
which have been examined in detail in Hyvärinen's laboratory, are described
shortly in the following.

In the face area around the anterior end of the intraparietal sulcus the
movement-related neurones discharge during reaching movements made with the
lips and sometimes also with the arms towards a visual or somesthetic
target, during active bringing of objects to the mouth with the hand, and
a few cells discharge during convergent eye movements. Most cells are
stimulus-related, they respond to touching or palpation of the face,
passive bringing of the hand towards the face or to visual stimuli moving
towards the face within 30-50 cm. Some cells respond to several of these
stimuli. Most cells in the face area discharge while the monkey brings an
object to the mouth and reaches for an object with its lips.

In the arm area, posterior to the face area, the movement-related neurones
discharge when the monkey reaches for and grasps objects under visual
guidance, a few when the animal is tracking an object with the eyes. In
this area most neurones are stimulus-related responding to touching or
palpation of the arms, stroking of the skin in a certain direction,
passive movement of the limb in a certain direction,(for instance from left
to right in reference to the body and to the visual field irrespective of
the actual movement of the joint), visual stimuli moving in a certain

tangential direction within the animal's reach, visual stimuli moving
towards the arms and hands, and some cells respond to several of these
stimuli. When the same cell responds to limb movement, stroking of the
skin and to visual stimuli the effective stimuli always have the same
direction of movement. Most cells in the arm area discharge during
reaching movements of the arms. A few cells are active during grasping
with legs under tactual guidance; reaching with legs under visual guidance
could not be studied in our experimental conditions.

Parietal association cortex of the monkey

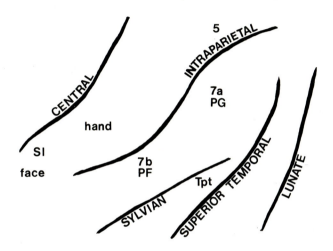

Analysis and control of movements in area 7 and Tpt

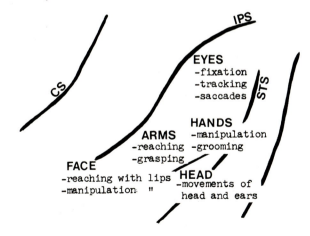

Figure 1

In the postero-lateral part of area 7 the movement-related neurones are active during grasping and manipulation with hands with or without visual guidance. Here most cells are stimulus-related, they respond to touch or compression on the hands, palpation of muscle bellies in the forearm, visual stimuli approaching the hands within about 30-50 cm and to objects rotating in the visual field. Some cells respond to several of these stimuli. Most cells in this area are active during hand movements, such as grasping, manipulation and grooming which is an important mode of social behavior in the monkey.

In area Tpt the movement-related neurones discharge during the monkey's head movements. Most neurones are stimulus-related and respond to sounds with a certain angle of incidence, visual stimuli moving in the periphery of the visual field or approaching the temple, touching or palpation of the temple, neck and back and to passive rotation of the head in a certain direction. Effective acoustic stimuli for these cells are noisy sounds with rapid intensity modulations like sounds generated by rubbing hands together or uttering human consonants /k/, /p/, /t/, /r/, and /s/.

General properties of effective stimuli within one subarea

The effective stimuli for each functionally different subarea are located on or near one body part. All the critical features of these stimuli are also produced by active movements of this body part. The active movements usually result in simultaneous occurrence of effective stimuli within several sensory systems. It seems that one subarea extracts information of the order in which the receptors are stimulated so that signals from several sensory systems repeatedly occurring at the same time or successively associate and become equivalent. When the operational spaces of two separate body parts overlap in the objective world, the information evoked by movements of different body parts integrates. This is exemplified by such stimulus combinations as passive bringing of the hand towards the mouth and touching of the lips which can activate the same cell.

Discussion

The findings from cellular recordings agree with the results of ablation studies; both suggest that functions of the parietal association cortex are necessary for the intersensory analysis of spatial relationships and for the accurate guiding of movements towards targets located in the receptive fields of different sensory systems. The intra-areal differentiation suggests that area 7a takes part in the analysis of extrapersonal space whereas area 7b takes part in the analysis of personal space. In the monkey the posterior parietal cortex takes part in the analysis of short term spatial relationships. In man the posterior parietal association cortex takes part also in the analysis of the logical relationships between communicative signs, which makes it possible for man to analyze information simultaneously over a wide temporal and spatial range.

The intra-areal differentiation suggests that lesions in different parts of area 7 and Tpt would result in different symptoms. A lesion in area 7a, the eye area, would cause disorders in eye movements, a lesion in the arm area of area 7b would cause inaccuracy in reaching under visual or tactual guidance, a lesion in the hand area of area 7b would result in difficulties in recognition of three dimensional objects and grasping with hand under visual and tactual guidance, a lesion in area Tpt would cause unresponsiveness to sensory stimuli in the contralateral half of a sensory space on bilateral simultaneous stimulation. All these symptoms have been observed in ablated monkeys.

The results from cellular recordings suggest that a lesion around the intraparietal sulcus would cause defects in bringing the food to the mouth, in reaching movements of the lips and in facial expressions. Such symptoms have never been described in the monkey, presumably because the lesions have not included the face area. The results of cellular recordings also suggest that a lesion in area Tpt would cause difficulties in the localization of a sound source. Errors in the localization of a sound source in the half of the auditory space contralateral to the lesion in area Tpt has been described only in man (Heilman and Valenstein, 1972).

The intra-areal differentiation revealed by cellular recordings is also in accordance with electric stimulation studies which showed that stimulation of different parts of the posterior parietal association cortex resulted in movements of different parts of the body (von Bechterew 1911, Vogt and Vogt 1919, Lilly, 1958).

Footnotes

1. A review based on the experiments made in the laboratory of Mountcastle has been written by Darian-Smith et al. 1979.
2. Holmes 1918, Ruch et al. 1938, Peele 1944, Semmes Blum et al. 1950, Denny-Brown and Chambers 1958, Bates and Ettlinger 1960, Ettlinger and Kalsbeck 1962, Heilman et al. 1971, Heilman and Valenstein 1972, Ratcliff et al. 1977, Faugier-Grimaud et al. 1978, LaMotte and Acuna 1978.

References

1. Baleydier, C. and Mauguiere, F., Pulvinar-lateroposterior afferents to cortical area 7 in monkeys demonstrated by horseradish peroxidase tracing technique, Exp. Brain Res. 27(1977) 501-507.
2. Bates, J.A.V. and Ettlinger, G., Posterior biparietal ablations in the monkey, Arch. Neurol. 3 (1960) 177-192.
3. Bechterew, W. von, Die Functionen der Nervencentra (Verlag von Gustav Fisher, Hena, 1911)
4. Bonin, G. von and Bailey, P., The Neocortex of Macaca Mulatta (University of Illinois Press, Urbana, 1947)
5. Darian-Smith, I., Johnson, K.O. and Goodwin, A.W., Posterior parietal cortex: relations of unit activity to sensorimotor function, Ann. Rev. Physiol. 41 (1979) 141-157.
6. Denny-Brown, D. and Chambers, R.A., The parietal lobe and behavior, Res. Publ. Ass. nerv. ment. Dis. 36 (1958) 35-117.
7. Ettlinger, G. and Kalsbeck, J.E., Changes in tactile discrimination and in visual reaching after successive and simultaneous bilateral posterior parietal ablations in the monkey, J. Neurol. Neurosurg. Psychiat. 25 (1962) 256-268.
8. Faugier-Grimaud, S., Frenois, C. and Stein, D.G., Effects of posterior parietal lesions on visually guided behavior in monkeys, Neuropsychologia 16 (1978) 151-168.

9. Heilman, K.L., Pandya, D.N., Karol, E.A. and Geschwind, N., Auditory inattention, Arch. Neurol. 24 (1971) 323-325.
10. Heilman, K.M. and Valenstein, E., Auditory neglect in man, Arch.Neurol. 26 (1972) 32-35.
11. Holmes, G., Disturbances of visual orientation, Brit. J. Opththal. 2 (1918) 449-516.
12. Hyvärinen, J. and Poranen, A., Function of the parietal associative area 7 as revealed from cellular discharges in alert monkeys, Brain 97 (1974) 637-692.
13. Hyvärinen, J. and Shelepin. Y., Distribution of visual and somatic functions in the parietal associative area 7 of the monkey, Brain Res. 169 (1979) 561-564.
14. Kaas, J.H., Lin, C.S. and Wagor, E., Cortical projections of posterior parietal cortex in owl monkeys, Comp. Neurol. 171 (1977) 387-408.
15. LaMotte, R.H. and Acuna, C., Defects in accuracy of reaching after removal of posterior parietal cortex in monkeys, Brain Res. 139 (1978) 309-326.
16. Leinonen, L., Hyvärinen, J., Nyman, G. and Linnankoski, I., Functional properties of neurons in lateral part of associative area 7 in awake monkeys, Exp. Brain Res. 34 (1979) 299-320.
17. Leinonen, L., and Nyman, G., Functional properties of cells in antero-lateral part of area 7, associative face area, of awake monkeys. Exp. Brain Res. 34 (1979) 321-333.
18. Lilly, J.C., Correlations between neurophysiological activity in the cortex and short-term behavior in the monkey (Macaca mulatta), in: Harlow, H.F. and Woolsey, C.N. (eds), Biological and Biochemical Bases of Behavior (The University of Wisconsin Press, Madison, 1958)
19. Lynch, J.C., Mountcastle, V.B., Talbot, W.H. and Yin, T.C.T., Parietal lobe mechanisms for directed visual attention, J. Neurophysio. 40 (1977) 326-389.
20. Mountcastle, V.B., Lynch, J.C., Georgopoulos, A., Sakata, H. and Acuna, C., Posterior parietal association cortex of the monkey: command functions for operations within extrapersonal space, J. Neurophysiol. 38 (1975) 871-908.
21. Pandya, D.N. and Kuypers, H.G.J.M., Cortico-cortical connections in the rhesus monkey, Brain Res. 13 (1969) 13-36.
22. Pandya, D.N. and Sanides, F., Architectonic parcellation of the temporal operculum in rhesus monkey and its projection pattern, Z. Anat. Entwickl.-Gesch. 139 (1973) 127-161.
23. Peele, T.L., Acute and chronic parietal lobe ablations in monkeys, J. Neurophysiol. 7 (1944) 269-286.
24. Peele, T.L., Cytoarchitecture of individual parietal areas in the monkey (Macaca mulatta) and the distribution of the efferent fibers. J. Comp. Neurol. 77 (1942) 693-738.
25. Ratcliff, G., Ridley, R.M. and Ettlinger, G., Spatial disorientation in the monkey, Cortex 13 (1977) 62-65.
26. Robinson, D.L., Goldgerg, M.E. and Stanton, G.B., Parietal association cortex in the primate: sensory mechanisms and behavioral modulations, J. Neurophysiol. 41 (1978) 910-932.
27. Robinson, D.L. and Goldberg, M.E., Sensory and behavioral properties of neurons in posterior parietal cortex of the awake, trained monkey, Fed. Proc. 37 (1978) 2258-2261.
28. Ruch, T.C., Fulton, J.F. and German, W.J., Sensory discrimination in monkey, chimpanzee and man after lesions of the parietal lobe, Arch. Neurol. & Psychiat. 39 (1938) 919-938.

29. Sakata, H., Parietal neurones with dual sensitivity to real and in-
    duced movements of visual target, Neurosci. Lett. 9 (1978) 165-169.
30. Semmes Blum, J., Chow, K.L. and Pribram, K.H., A behavioral analysis
    of the organization of the parieto-temporal preoccipital cortex,
    J. Comp. Neurol. 93 (1950) 53-100.
31. Vogt, C. and Vogt, O., Allgemeinere Ergebnisse unserer Hirnforschung,
    J. Psychol. Neurol. (Lpz.) 25 (1919) 279-462.
32. Yin, T.C.T. and Mountcastle, V.B., Visual input to the visuomotor
    mechanisms of the monkey's parietal lobe, Science 197 (1977)
    1381-1383.

PART II

CONTROL OF SEGMENTAL MOVEMENT

Tutorials in Motor Behavior
G.E. Stelmach and J. Requin (eds.)
© *North-Holland Publishing Company, 1980*

7

CENTRAL AND PERIPHERAL MECHANISMS IN MOTOR CONTROL

Emilio Bizzi
Department of Psychology
Massachusetts Institute of Technology
Cambridge, Massachusetts

Recent experiments concerning the control of forearm
movements in man and monkeys have disclosed some of the
processes subserving visually guided movements. These
results are relevant to the question of what is being
controlled by motor commands, and have indicated that
movement may take place through a process involving the
selection of a set of length-tension curves, i.e., by
establishing an equilibrium point between agonist and
antagonist muscles. In my presentation I will attempt
to establish how these processes are relevant to the
organization of more complex arm trajectories. The
role of proprioceptive feedback during the execution of
these movements will be examined with respect to trajectory formation and reprogramming.

Introduction

In my presentation I will discuss some of the processes that subserve the
execution of visually evoked movements in monkeys. To begin with, I would
like to make two assumptions. First I will assume that the forces that
control arm movements result from "commands" that are, to a great extent,
precomputed in some part of the central nervous system (CNS). This assumption is based on observations made in deafferented animals which have
demonstrated open-loop reaching (Bizzi et al., 1976; Polit and Bizzi, 1979;
Taub et al., 1965, 1966, 1975). It should be stressed that while acknowledging the capacity to make arm trajectories after deafferentation, I
certainly do not intend to minimize the great importance of sensory feedback originating from the moving limb. As it will be shown later, sensory
feedback is crucial in setting up the appropriate pattern of neural commands.

My second assumption is that muscles moving a body segment can be thought
of as springs whose resting length can be set at some value and by damping
elements. In fact, springs and muscles have a fundamental property in
common: they produce force as a function of length (Asatryan and Feldman,
1965; Feldman, 1974a, 1974b).

Given these two assumptions, i.e., that commands are preprogrammed and that
a limb can be represented as pairs of springs acting across joints in the
agonist-antagonist configuration, the question is: what kind of control
signals may be generated by the central nervous system in order to execute
trajectories? To answer this question I will examine the evidence derived
from experiments in which visually triggered head and arm movements were
studied.

The head movements were part of the monkey's coordinated eye-head response
to the presentation of a visual stimulus (Bizzi et al., 1971). Both head
and arm movements were subjected to various force disturbances. I will
review first the results obtained by applying a constant torque load to
the head.

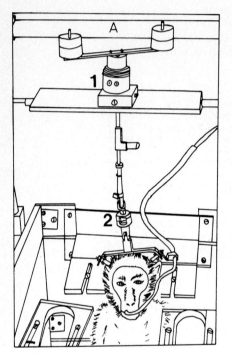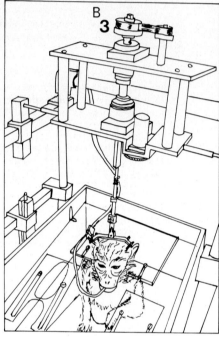

Fig. 1. Schematic representation of the equipment used to
monitor horizontal head movements. In both A and B the load
is coupled to the shaft by means of a clutch, 1, which is
engaged by a triggering circuit which monitors the EMG signal.
In A, weights at the top of the drawing and the length of the
arms determine the inertial load. In B, several different
constant-load springs, 3, can be used in order to vary force
load. 2, strain gauge glued over the shaft. (From Bizzi et
al., J. Neurophysiol. 39 (1976) 435-444.)

When this type of load was applied, a constant degree of head undershoot
was observed. In the intact animal, while the constant load was being
applied, there was an increase in electromyographic (EMG) activity, presumably due to an increase in muscle spindle and tendon organ activity.
As shown in Fig. 2, in spite of these changes in the flow of proprioceptive
activity, the head reached its "intended" final position after the constant
load was removed. In fact, the final head position was equal (on average)
to that reached when the load had not been applied, suggesting that the
program for final position was maintained during load application and was
not readjusted by proprioceptive signals acting at segmental and suprasegmental levels. On the basis of these results Bizzi and collaborators

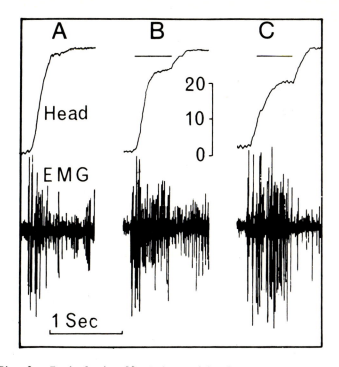

Fig. 2. Typical visually triggered head movements in chronically vestibulectomized monkey to appearance of target at 40°
but performed in total darkness. A shows an unloaded movement.
In B, a constant-force load (315 g·cm) was applied at the
start of the movement resulting in an undershoot of final
position relative to A, despite increase in EMG activity. In
C, a constant-force load (726 g·cm) was applied. Note head
returns to same final position after removal of the load.
Vertical calibration in degrees; time marker is 1 s; EMG
recorded from left splenius capitis. (From Bizzi et al., J.
Neurophysiol. 39 (1976) 435-444.)

(Bizzi et al., 1976) concluded that the central program establishing final
position is not dependent on a readout of proprioceptive afferents generated during the movement, but is preprogrammed. It should be stressed
that the load disturbances were totally unexpected and that the monkeys
were not trained to move their head to a certain position, but choose to
program a head movement together with an eye movement in order to perform
a visual discrimination task (Bizzi et al., 1976). Because only rarely
any evidence of reprogramming after the initiation of a trial was observed,
Bizzi et al. (1976) were in a favorable condition to observe the effect of
an unexpected proprioceptive feedback while a program calling for a given
final position was maintained by the animal. It is not known, of course,
whether requiring the animal to achieve a given final head position would

have led to different results.

In a second set of experiments Bizzi et al. (1976) examined the effect of stimulating proprioceptors only during the dynamic phase. To this end they used as a stimulus a load which modified the trajectory but did not represent a steady-state disturbance. This was done by using an inertial load. As a result of the sudden and unexpected increase in inertia during centrally initiated head movement, the following changes in head trajectory, relative to unloaded movement, were observed: first, a slowing down of the head, followed by a relative increase in velocity (due to the kinetic energy acquired by the load being transmitted to the decelerating head), culminating in an overshoot; finally, the head returned to the intended position (Fig. 3).

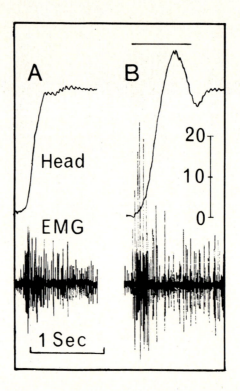

Fig. 3. Typical head responses of a chronically vestibulectomized monkey to sudden appearance of target at -40°. A shows an unloaded movement, whereas in B a load of approximately 6 times the inertia of the head was applied at the start of the movement, as indicated by the force record. Both movements were performed in total darkness, the light having been turned off by the increase in EMG (splenius capitis). Peak force exerted by the monkey is approximately 750 g·cm; head calibration is in degrees; time marker is 1 s. (From Bizzi et al., J. Neurophysiol. 39 (1976) 435-444.)

The changes in head trajectory brought about by the sudden and unexpected increase in head inertia induced corresponding modifications in the length and tension of neck muscles. The agonist muscles were, in fact, first subjected to increased tension because the application of the load slowed down the process of muscle shortening, then the shortening of the same muscles was facilitated during the overshoot phase of the head movement induced by the kinetic energy of the load. Such loading and unloading did, of course, provoke the classical muscle spindle response presumably mediated by group IA and group II afferent fibers which, in turn, affected the agonist EMG activity. Figure 3B shows that there was first a greater increase in motor unit discharge during muscle stretch than would have occurred if no load were applied, followed by a sudden decrease in activity at the beginning of the overshoot phase.

Therefore, during a head movement, an unexpected inertial load induced a series of waxing and waning proprioceptive signals from muscle spindles, tendons and joints, but the intended head position was eventually reached even in the complete absence of other sensory cues (visual and vestibular). This observation, together with those on the effect of constant-torque loads, suggests that the central program establishing final head position is not dependent on a readout of proprioceptive afferents generated during the movement but, instead, is preprogrammed.

To provide a further test of the hypothesis that final head position is preprogrammed, Bizzi et al. (1976) investigated how chronically vestibulectomized monkeys reached final head position without visual feedback when they were deprived, in addition, of neck proprioceptive feedback. The goal here was to observe how monkeys moving their heads in an "open-loop" mode were able to deal with the application of constant torque applied during centrally initiated movements.

Figure 4 shows that following the unexpected application of a constant-torque load at the beginning of a visually triggered movement, the posture attained by the head was short of intended final position. It should be emphasized that the target elicited the movement, but there was no target light to guide the orienting head movement and that these animals were chronically vestibulectomized. After the removal of the constant torque, the head attained a position that was found to be equal to the one reached by the head in the no-load case. When the disturbance was an inertial load, as expected, no change in final head position was found. The head trajectory, however, was disturbed by this type of load in the deafferented animal. Because of the open-loop condition, the head overshoot shown in Fig. 5 must have been corrected by an increase in tension generated not by an increase in alpha motor outflow to antagonist muscles, but by the intrinsic length-tension properties of the muscle tissue. The effectiveness of this mechanism is, of course, dependent on the central programming of alpha activity to both agonists and antagonists which determines the stiffness of these muscles (Grillner, 1972).

These results indicate that the head motor system behaved qualitatively in the same way before and after deafferentation with respect to head position.

I believe that the results of these experiments contribute to our understanding of the mechanism whereby movement is terminated and a newly acquired position is maintained. If one assumes that the "program" for head movements and posture specifies a given level of alpha motoneuron

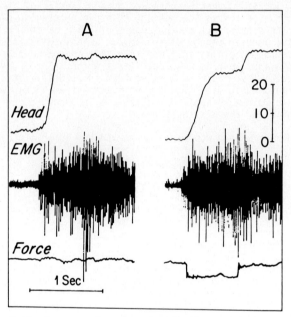

Fig. 4. Typical movements of a chronically vestibulectomized monkey with sectioned dorsal roots (C_1-T_3) made open-loop (in total darkness). In B, constant-force load (315 g.cm) was applied at the start of movement, resulting in an undershoot while the load was on. Similarity of EMG pattern in A and B shows lack of a stretch reflex. Peak force in B approximately 315 g.cm. Vertical calibration in degrees. (From Bizzi et al., J. Neurophysiol. 39 (1976) 435-444.)

activity to both agonist and antagonist muscles, and that the firing of these neurons will determine a particular length-tension curve in each muscle, then it must be concluded that the final resting position of the head is determined by the length-tension properties of all of the muscles involved. This hypothesis explains both the head undershoot when a constand load is applied, and the attainment of the intended final head position following the removal of the load, shown in Figs. 2 and 4, respectively. Although the process of selecting a new equilibrium between the length-tension properties of agonists and antagonists should result in movement and attainment of a new head position, it should be clear that these experiments do not rule out the presence of other, parallel processes. It is possible, for instance, that the dynamic changes are controlled through separate mechanisms.

In a complementary set of experiments involving arm movements, Polit and Bizzi (1979) extended the previously described findings on the final position of the head. Adult rhesus monkeys were trained to point to a target light with the forearm and to hold the arm in that position for about one

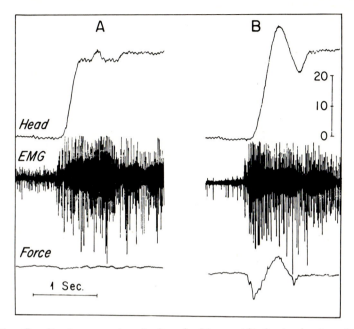

Fig. 5. Head movements of chronically vestibulectomized monkey
with dorsal roots C_1-T_3 sectioned. In both cases the eliciting
stimulus was turned off just before the start of the movements
so that the performance was accomplished open-loop. A shows an
unloaded movement. In B, a load of approximately 4 times the
inertia of the head was applied at the start of the movement.
Note lack of evidence of a stretch reflex (compare with Fig
3B) in EMG. Peak force exerted by the monkey in B is approximately 375 g·cm. Vertical calibration is in degrees. EMG
recorded from splenius capitis. Compare overshoot in B with
that in Fig. 3B, but note that there the load is 50% larger.
(From Bizzi et al., J. Neurophysiol. 39 (1976) 435-444.)

second in order to obtain a reward. The monkey was seated in a primate
chair, and its forearm was fastened to an elbow apparatus which permitted
flexion and extension of the forearm about the elbow in the horizontal
plane (Fig. 6). A torque motor in series with the shaft of this apparatus
was used to apply positional disturbances to the arm. The experiments
were conducted in a dark room to minimize visual cues; at no time during
an experiment was the animal able to see its forearm. At random times,
the initial position of the forearm was displaced. In most cases, the
positional disturbance was applied immediately after the appearance of the
target light and was stopped just prior to the activation of the motor
units in the agonist muscle. Hence, when the motor command specifying a
given forearm movement occurred, the positional disturbance had altered
the length of the agonist and antagonist muscles, and the proprioceptive
stimulation resulting from this disturbance had altered their state of

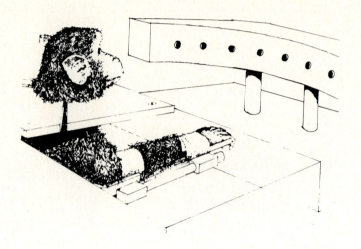

Fig. 6. Monkey set up in arm apparatus. Arm is strapped to
splint, which pivots at elbow. Target lights are mounted in
perimeter arc at 5° intervals. During experimental session,
the monkey was not permitted to see its arm, and the room was
darkened. (From Polit and Bizzi, J. Neurophysiol. 42 (1979)
183-194.)

activation. In spite of these changes, the intended final arm position was
always reached; this was true whether the torque motor had displaced the
forearm further away from, closer to, or even beyond the intended final
position. There were no significant differences among the final positions
achieved in these three conditions. Naturally, the attainment of the
intended arm position in this experiment could be explained by assuming
that afferent proprioceptive information modified the original motor command. However, the results of previous work on final head position suggest
an alternative hypothesis: that the motor program underlying arm movement
specifies, through the selection of a new set of length-tension curves, an
equilibrium point between agonists and antagonists that correctly positions
the arm in relation to the visual target. To investigate this hypothesis,
Polit and Bizzi (1979) retested the monkey's pointing performance after it
had undergone a bilateral C_1-T_3 dorsal rhizotomy. They could elicit the
pointing response very soon after the surgery (within 2 days in some of the
animals), even though they observed no spontaneous arm movements other than
an occasional quick, flinging movement in response to a threat. The forearm was again displaced (at random times) immediately after the appearance
of the target light and released just prior to the activation of motor
units in the agonist muscles. Because the arm was not visible to the
animal and the proprioceptive activity could not reach the spinal cord,
The arm reached its intended final position "open loop". A fact corroborated by lack of any sign of reflex response or reprogramming in the EMG
activity. For each target position, t-tests were performed to test for
differences between the average final position of movements with undisturb-

ed and the loaded disturbed initial positions. No significant differences were found. This finding suggests that what is programmed is an intended equilibrium point, resulting from the interaction of agonist and antagonist muscles. The results when a constant force was applied with the torque motor throughout the arm movement add further support to this idea. The arm undershoot which we observed in this case suggests that the intended equilibrium point of the arm muscles was modified, in a predictable way, by the application of an external force.

If one assumes that no radical change in motor programming occurred during the days immediately following the rhizotomy, it can be concluded that visually triggered arm and head movements are subserved by a process that specifies a new intended equilibrium point between agonists and antagonists rather than amplitude or duration of movement. The fact that immediately after undergoing deafferentation, the monkey was able to execute accurate forearm movements in response to any one of 12 visual targets to which it had been trained to respond before the operation strongly implies that "programs" were released when the targets were presented.

The successful execution of the hypothesized "programs" in the deafferented animal is contingent upon the animal's knowing the position of the arm relative to the body. Whenever the usual spatial relationship between the animal and the arm apparatus was changed, the monkey's pointing response to the target was inaccurate. This change was achieved in two ways. One way consisted in applying a constant torque load in the direction that flexes the arm. Thus, movements toward targets requiring flexion were aided, whereas movements requiring extension were hindered. In both cases the monkey had to adjust its motor output to avoid overshooting or undershooting the target. The intact monkeys were able to make essentially normal movements within a few attempts.

The behavior of the deafferented monkey was in marked contrast to that of the intact monkey when bias loads were applied to the arm. Typically, the monkey would attempt to make a movement to a target, but would overshoot or undershoot the target, become very upset at its failure to get a reward, and stop performing. Its arm would, of course, be pushed in the direction of the maintained load, causing a shift in the preferred position in between the trials.

A second type of manipulation involved shifting the center of rotation of the elbow rest 1 or 2 inches forward from the monkey's body, a maneuver that caused a change in the canonical position of the arm. This procedure also changed the joint angle required to point at the different lights (see Fig. 7).

The intact animal had little difficulty dealing with this novel posture and, as in the case of the bias loads, adjusted to it in a few movements. The deafferented monkey, on the other hand, performed poorly in this posture. The dramatic inability of the deafferented monkey to execute accurate pointing responses in an unusual postural setting underscores the great importance of afferent feedback in the control of movement.

Conclusions

One of the main points dealt with in this presentation is that a certain class of head and arm movements depend on neural patterns which are pro-

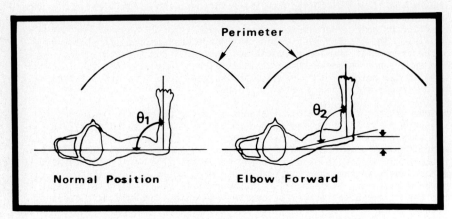

Fig. 7. Schematic representation of postural manipulation
performed in intact and deafferented monkeys. The normal
position of the manipulandum is shown on the left. The
diagram on the right shows that moving the elbow forward
causes the normal relation between joint angle and target
light to be changed. (From Polit and Bizzi, J. Neurophysiol.
42 (1979) 183-194.)

grammed prior to movement initiation. What is being preprogrammed is a
process that is capable of controlling final head and arm position independently of initial position. This finding can be explained by postulat-
ing that the motor program specifies, through the selection of a set of
length-tension properties in agonist and antagonist muscles, an equilibrium
point between these two sets of muscles that correctly positions the arm
and the head in relation to the visual target. Recent electromyographic
(EMG) recording in man indicated the central commands specifying an
equilibrium point between agonists and antagonists specify new levels of
activity in both sets of muscles (Lestienne et al., 1978, 1979). While the
EMGs associated with a given position are variable, the ratio between EMGs
is constant for each position (Lestienne et al., 1978).

The view that the processes underlying movement involves a shift in
equilibrium point between agonists and antagonists may be illustrated by
reference to a simple mechanical analog. Assume that the muscles moving a
body segment can be represented by a pair of springs acting across a hinge
in the agonist-antagonist configuration. If the CNS were to specify a new
length-tension relationship for one of the springs, movement would occur
until a new equilibrium point of the two opposing springs were reached.
According to this hypothesis, movements are at the simplest level transitions in posture.

This view ought to be qualified. First, although we may have detected a
process underlying arm and head movements, it is certainly not the only
process that occurs during the movement. It is quite clear that the arm
and head movements that monkeys use to reach a given position can vary in
velocity. Consequently, the mechanism by which an intended posture is
achieved must coexist with a mechanism specifying intended arm velocity.

The program underlying final arm position, as well as the postulated independence of the process controlling velocity, indicates that a number of parallel processes underlie arm movement and that motor control may be thought to be organized in a modular fashion.

One of the goals of the studies of Bizzi and collaborators was to develop some perspectives on the role of afferent feedback during voluntary movements (Bizzi et al., 1976; Bizzi et al., 1978; Polit and Bizzi, 1979). They showed that in the deafferented animal the successful execution of forearm programs released by target presentation was contingent on the animal's knowing the position of its arm relative to its body. Whenever the usual spatial relationship between the animal and the arm apparatus was changed or a constant bias load was applied, the monkey's pointing response was inaccurate. The intact monkeys, in contrast, were able to compensate quickly for any variations in their accustomed position with respect to the arm apparatus. The dramatic inability of the deafferented monkey to execute accurate pointing responses in an unusual postural setting or when a constant bias load was applied underscores the great importance of afferent feedback in updating and adjusting the execution of learned motor patterns when posture is changed. These findings emphasize the widespread influence and importance of afferent impulses in the control of voluntary movement. They suggest that, in addition to contributing to the classical spinal and supraspinal reflex loops, which may servo assist movement (Marsden et al., 1976a, 1976b; Vallbo, 1973; Wilson, 1961), provide load compensation (Allum, 1975; Bizzi et al., 1978; Conrad et al., 1974), and/or linearize muscle properties (Nichols and Houk, 1973, 1976), the afferent system may affect, in a manner that is not yet understood, a reorganization of the central processes that are released when targets are presented (Hoyle, 1975). It is perhaps of interest to comment that while servo assistance or load compensation can occur during a single centrally driven movement, the postulated reorganization has a longer time scale encompassing a few movements.

This research was supported by National Institutes of Neurological Diseases and Stroke Research Grant NS09343, National Aeronautics and Space Administration Grant 22-009-798 and National Eye Institute Grant NIH-1-P30-EY02621.

References

[1] Allum, J.H.J., Responses to load disturbances in human shoulder muscles: the hypothesis that one component is a pulse test information signal, Exp. Brain Res. 22 (1975) 307-326.

[2] Asatryan, D.G. and Feldman, A.G., Biophysics of complex systems and mathematical modesl. Functional tuning of nervous system with control of movement or maintenance of a steady posture. I. Mechanographic analysis of the work of the joint on execution of a postural task, Biophysics 10 (1965) 925-935.

[3] Bizzi, E., Dev, P., Morasso, P. and Polit, A., The effect of load disturbances during centrally initiated movements, J. Neurophysiol. 41 (1978) 542-556.

[4] Bizzi, E., Kalil, R.E. and Tagliasco, V., Eye-head coordination in monkeys: evidence for centrally patterned organization, Science 173 (1971) 452-454.

[5] Bizzi, E., Polit, A. and Morasso, P., Mechanisms underlying achievement of final head position, J. Neurophysiol. 39 (1976) 435-444.

[6] Conrad, B., Matsunami, C., Meyer-Lohmann, J., Wiesendanger, M. and Brooks, V.B., Cortical load compensation during voluntary elbow movements, Brain Res. 81 (1974) 507-514.

[7] Feldman, A.G., Change of muscle length due to shift of the equilibrium point of the muscle-load system, Biofizika 19 (1974a) 534-538.

[8] Feldman, A.G., Control of muscle length, Biofizika 19 (1974b) 749-751.

[9] Grillner, S., The role of muscle stiffness in meeting the changing postural and locomotor requirements for force development of the ankle extensors, Acta Physiol. Scand. 86 (1972) 92-108.

[10] Hoyle, G., Neural mechanisms underlying behavior of invertebrates, in: Gazzaniga, M.S. and Blakemore, C. (eds.), Handbook of Psychobiology (Academic, New York, 1975).

[11] Lestienne, F., Polit, A. and Bizzi, E., Transition from movement to posture: an electromyographic (EMG) study, Abst. 8th Ann. Meeting Soc. for Neurosci., St. Louis, 1978.

[12] Lestienne, F., Polit, A. and Bizzi, E., From movement to posture, in: Nadeau, C.H., Newell, K.M., Roberts, G.C. and Halliwell, W. (eds.), The Skillfulness in Movement: Theory and Application (Human Kinetics Publishers, Champaign, Ill., 1979, in press).

[13] Marsden, C.D., Merton, P.A. and Morton, H.B., Servo action in the human thumb, J. Physiol. (Lond.) 257 (1976a) 1-44.

[14] Marsden, C.D., Merton, P.A. and Morton, H.B., Stretch reflexs and servo actions in a variety of human muscles, J. Physiol. (Lond.) 259 (1976b) 531-560.

[15] Nichols, T.R. and Houk, J.C., Reflex compensation for variations in the mechanical properties of a muscle, Science 181 (1973) 182-184.

[16] Nichols, T.R. and Houk, J.C., The improvement in linearity and the regulation of stiffness that results from the actions of the stretch reflex, J. Neurophysiol. 39 (1976) 119-142.

[17] Polit, A. and Bizzi, E., Characteristics of motor programs underlying arm movements in monkeys, J. Neurophysiol. 42 (1979) 183-194.

[18] Taub, E., Bacon, R.C. and Berman, A.J., Acquisition of a trace-conditioned avoidance response after deafferentation of the responding limb, J. Comp. Physiol. Psychol. 59 (1965) 275-279.

[19] Taub, E., Ellman, S.J. and Berman, A.J., Deafferentation in monkeys: effect on conditioned grasp response, Science 151 (1966) 593-594.

[20] Taub, E., Goldberg, I.A. and Taub, P., Deafferentation in monkeys: pointing at a target without visual feedback, Exp. Neurol. 46 (1975) 178-186.

[21] Vallbo, Å.B., The significance of intramuscular receptors in load compensation during voluntary contractions in man, in: Stein, R.B., Pearson, K.G., Smith, R.S. and Redford, J.B. (eds.), Control of Posture and Locomotion (Plenum, New York, 1973).

[22] Wilson, D.M., The central nervous control of flight in a locust, J. Exp. Biol. 38 (1961) 471-490.

Tutorials in Motor Behavior
G.E. Stelmach and J. Requin (eds.)
© *North-Holland Publishing Company, 1980*

8

ON THE THEORETICAL STATUS OF TIME

IN MOTOR PROGRAM REPRESENTATIONS

Richard A. Schmidt
Departments of Physical Education and Psychology
University of Southern California
Los Angeles, California

Abstract

Evidence suggests that motor programs for both gait
and learned responses are abstract representations
containing sequencing, phasing (relative timing), and
relative force. Various parameters can be applied to
produce slightly different expressions of an invariant
pattern. However, phasing does not appear to be a
part of programs for unidirectional actions, and a
tentative model to explain these aspects of programming is offered.

It has long been recognized that for humans and other animals to perform
skilled activities--be they "innate" responses such as locomotion and feeding behaviors, or learned such as in throwing a ball--the system as a
whole appears to determine not only the sequences of muscle contractions
and relaxations as well as the force with which each is contracted, but
also the timing structure of the series of contractions. One of the important questions that confronts the area of motor behavior is how these
obviously critical features of responses are determined by the system. In
this paper I would like to address how one of these aspects of responding--
the determination of the _time_ of the contractions and relaxations--appears
to be controlled. In doing this, I will examine some of the literature
from the neurological control of gait as well as some of the behavioral
studies that provide implications for how our models should be conceptualized. Finally, I will propose that there is a distinct discontinuity
between two classes of responses with respect to the role of time and
the mechanisms thought to control them. I begin by examining some of the
thinking on the neurological control of gait, with specific reference to
the role of time in this control process.

SEQUENCING AND TIMING IN GAIT

There has never been very much disagreement about the fact that, in skilled
actions, the muscles and limbs that they control seems to display distinct
patterns that are structured in time. There was, however, early disagreement about _why_ this timing behavior was displayed, and the ideas tended to
fall into two distinct categories (see Grillner, 1975; Wetzel & Stuart,
1976): (a) reflex chaining versus (b) central programming.

Reflex-Chaining Hypothesis

According to this early idea, some central event would initiate an action (perhaps by contracting the first muscle in the sequence), and the feedback from this contraction would serve as a trigger for the next action in the sequence; the feedback from this action would trigger the next, and so on until the entire sequence had been run off. In such a view, sequencing and timing are structured into the action indirectly, in that a given muscle acts when it is triggered by the action that was to precede it in the sequence. This idea was a popular one for stereotyped actions like gait, where the connections were thought to be "hardwired" genetically; with respect to learned responses such as throwing a ball, these connections were thought to be acquired through practice (e.g., James, 1890).

While this notion provided a logical explanation for the control of sequencing and timing, the hypothesis has suffered severely from a number of lines of evidence. Certainly the most damaging is the common finding that movements can be performed nearly normally when the responding limb is deafferented (e.g., Bickel, 1897, and Hering, 1897, both cited by Grillner, 1975; Lashley, 1917; Taub, 1976; Taub & Berman, 1968). The number of different studies showing essentially this is very large, many species having been used (including humans), and the conclusion seems to hold for movements that can be considered as genetically defined (ambulation) as well as for movements that are acquired with practice. Theoretically, if there is no afferent information from the responding limb, and movements can occur nearly normally, considerable doubt exists that the movement is controlled via reflex chains as the hypothesis suggests. Such thinking led quickly to the idea that the limbs were controlled by some central mechanism, or program, that contained the necessary sequencing and timing information.

MOTOR-PROGRAM VIEWS

Apparently, Brown (1914) was the first to propose that the sequencing and timing of the impulses necessary for action were "contained" in a central mechanism, and a number of more specific hypotheses have been postulated since then (see Grillner, 1975; Wetzel & Stuart, 1976). The problem involved how a set of neurons could be interconnected so that (a) rhythmic actions among limbs would be produced such as in gait, and (b) the contractions of the various muscles involved in a single action (e.g., in the swing phase in gait) could be initiated at the proper time in that sequence. Essentially, the models all have a central "clock" that is capable of "metering out" time, so that the system can activate the proper muscles and actions at the proper moment.

Some examples of this early thinking about central movement generators are provided in Figure 1 (after Grillner, 1975). At the left is Brown's original idea. The movement was thought to start with the tonic excitation of a neuron(s) connected to both the flexor and extensor groups. While it is not clear how the oscillating pattern could begin under this view, once it is underway the excitation of the flexor neuron(s) also provides inhibition to the extensor neuron(s) until the former neurons fatigue. This fatigue reduces both the firing of the flexor neuron(s) and the inhibition to the extensor neuron(s), causing the extensor muscles to act; this process is reversed again so that the activation is shifted to the flexors, and so on. In this way, the model provides for the sequencing and timing of action, and the impulses to the muscles can be said to be "metered out" over time as a result of the durations of the fatigue and nerve-conduction processes.

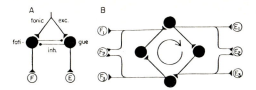

Figure 1. Two models of pattern generators for gait (after Grillner, 1975).

Other models of this process are, of course, possible, and in the right
side of Figure 1 is another mentioned by Grillner. Here, the action is
initiated by input to one of the neurons in the loop, it triggers the next
neuron, etc.; the action around the loop continues until the first is activated again. If certain muscle groups are neurologically connected to
certain places in the loop, then when the activity is in that part of the
loop the particular muscle group will be in action, and it will be quiescent when the control is in some other part of the loop. By having the
various participating muscle groups connected at the "proper" places in
the loop, the model is capable of generating sequencing and timing of the
various muscles involved in the action.

Finally, such models do not imply that the central pattern generator defines every aspect of the movement sequence. There is ample evidence to
show that the numerous afferent sources can act to modify the motor output
somewhat, so that what is manifested in the movement is not necessarily
exactly what was specified by the pattern generator. Grillner (1975,
p. 297) makes this point well when he says,

> Perhaps it is useful to regard the relevant reflexes as
> prepared (emphasis mine) to operate but without any ef-
> fect as long as the movement proceeds according to the set
> central program. At the same instant when the locomotor
> movements are disturbed (small hole, a slippery surface,
> etc.) the reflexes come into operation to compensate.

Thus, Grillner sees no difficulty in having a response be defined by a
central pattern generator or program, and yet having the actions in the
limbs modified somewhat by afferent information. In many ways, this is
the notion I had in mind when I discussed "errors in execution" for
skilled actions (Schmidt, 1976).

LEARNED VERSUS INNATE ACTIONS

Among those of us who concentrate on responses that can be considered
learned (e.g., throwing, pole vaulting, etc.) there has been far more
skepticism about the notion of central control of movement (see, e.g.,
Stelmach,1976) than there has been among the people concerned with animal
work; with the latter group, central generators are rather well accepted,
and the problem has, in many ways, become one of working out the details
of how these programs operate (e.g., Davis, 1973). It is for my colleagues
in the former group that I wanted to include this small (and incomplete,
by necessity) section on central pattern generators. I don't think that

we who study learned motor responses from behavioral points of view fully recognize the weight of evidence suggesting that the concept of a central pattern generator is important for explaining the evidence about the control of gait. Also, for me at least, the idea that sequencing and timing can be modeled with such simple systems as those presented in Figure 1 gives a great deal of encouragement that the more complex systems in human skilled movement will be someday modeled in the same basic way.

But this forbidden fruit has a few brown spots. The evidence which so strongly supports the notion of central generators has used responses that must be considered as genetically defined, such as ambulation (the most frequent class of behavior), grooming, feeding, and the like. Typically, although not universally, the movements of interest to motor-behavior workers cannot be considered as innate (e.g., doing a somersault). and one must question the generality of the central-generator notion to the performance of such learned acts. As a working hypothesis, I assume that the programs that define a throwing pattern are fundamentally like those that define more innate patterns like gait, but this assumption could be incorrect. Next, to consider motor programs for throwing implies that such programs be modifiable via practice (i.e., we need to learn how to throw).[1] How can we conceptualize such modification to programs? Can we imagine that there could be changes (as a result of experience) in the number of connecting neurons (Figure 1) between one that controls one muscle and another neuron that controls another muscle, so that the time between the two contractions is changed slightly? Such subtle changes seem to be required in perfecting a golf swing. How shall we consider the fact that movements become more consistent with practice? Do the motor programs have "noise" in them which prevents their accurate execution when they are poorly learned, or do we gradually reduce the number of such programs from among which we choose, thereby increasing consistency? Can we think of these learned programs as being located largely in the cord as programs for gait appear to be (see Grillner, 1975, for evidence on this point)? If so, then we must entertain the possibility that there is much more motor learning that occurs in the cord. What are the implications of these realizations for our "information-processing" models of motor learning? I certainly don't have many good answers to these questions, but they nevertheless seem important to raise if only to point out some of the future directions that our work must take if we are to be concerned with the control of learned motor responses.

MOTOR PROGRAMMING IN LEARNED ACTS

Space here does not permit a full treatment of the development of the motor-program idea for learned responses, but the area has been reviewed by a number of authors (e.g., Keele, 1968; Klapp, 1977a; Schmidt, 1975, 1976); an especially good modern review is by Keele (in press). Essentially two lines of support have been provided. First, there was the idea that animal locomotion (and other similar responses mentioned in the previous sections) was not dependent on feedback from the responding limbs, and thus central programs were indicated in order to explain how sequencing and timing could be controlled. This argument was strengthened by human evidence that the processing of information leading to a new movement was slow, requiring 150 to 200 msec for the new action to begin. This kind of feedback processing, if it were to be employed in the ongoing control of a rapid motor act like throwing, would be too slow to be effective until that act is completed. Both of these lines of evidence have led to the idea that movements must be controlled by some sort of central program that has the same general capabilities for sequencing and timing as the central programs appear to have for gait. Those who call the program notion a "default argument" (e.g., Pew, 1974) fail to appreciate that a theory about any phenomenon must be an argument "by default"; we use a theory (like motor programming) because all of our other theories (e.g., reflex chaining) fail to explain the data. It seems to me that this is a perfectly proper way in which to reason.

A second line of research, begun by Henry and Rogers (1960) and extended by Klapp (1977a) and his colleagues, has recognized that programs must be prepared before the movement, and thus this activity should require time and/or mental effort (attention). Recent work has shown that the more "complex" the movement to be made (in terms of the number of separate actions or reversals in direction), or the longer its duration, the longer is the RT required to initiate it. This RT technique seems to allow the examination of motion in terms of the processes involved in selecting and/or executing a program.

An important difficulty for this kind of program notion as it was stated for human skills was that it assumed that there must be a separate program for every movement the person was to make; throwing a light and heavy ball requires different muscular action, and hence different motor programs. MacNeilage (1970), Pew (1974), and I (Schmidt, 1975, 1976) were concerned that this kind of model assumes that the system must have nearly infinite storage capability for programs, and we each proposed ways in which the program idea could be modified to reduce this "storage problem." This difficulty led Pew (1974) and I (Schmidt, 1975, 1976) to propose that a given program could be varied slightly (e.g., to throw different distances) by providing different parameters that would affect program execution. That is, we proposed that the program should be considered as generalized, so that certain invariant features emerged in the responses while other features were allowed to change. In the next sections, the evidence for this notion is examined.

Generalized Motor Programs

Armstrong (1970) had subjects learn movements of a lever through a particular pattern defined in space and time; its duration was either 3 or 5 sec, and its space-time pattern is shown in Figure 2. Armstrong noticed that if the subject made a particular movement too rapidly, he tended to make the entire movement too rapidly, not just certain parts of it. This effect is seen in Figure 2, where the speeded-up movement is compared to the pattern that the subject was attempting to produce. The response appears to be compressed in time, such that the relative time to any portion of the response (e.g., a peak) is constant across variations in movement speed; that is, the time to a peak divided by the overall movement time seems to be a constant.

This evidence suggested to Pew (1974) and later to me (Schmidt, 1975, 1976) that there might be an underlying representation of this movement which manifests itself as a set of invariant properties, even when the movement might vary in other ways. The evidence I have seen seems to support a view in which these invariant features are (a) the phasing (or relative

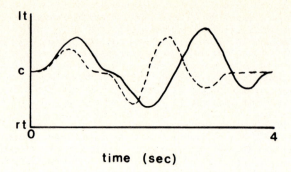

time (sec)

Figure 2. A space-time pattern which was the goal response (solid line)
          and a response that appeared to be compressed in time (broken
          line) (from Armstrong, 1970).

timing) inherent in the sequence, (b) the sequencing of elements, and (c)
the relative force, or the relation among the various forces produced by
the different contractions in the sequence. If we assume that these aspects
of a response are represented in an abstract program, the addition of certain parameters should allow this basic pattern to be produced with slight
variations such as those found by Armstrong. I have reviewed the evidence
for this view elsewhere (Schmidt, 1976), but a brief discussion of the
kinds of parameters that seem possible will be useful here.

Movement time. In addition to the work by Armstrong (1970), a number of
authors have examined movements under "speeded-up" conditions, searching
for those aspects of a response that remained invariant while speed
changed. Summers (1977) and Shapiro (1977, 1978) had subjects learn sequences of button presses or wrist movements, respectively, each of which
had complex spatial and timing characteristics. Shapiro (1978) showed
that when subjects were asked to speed up the wrist movement pattern, they
could do so without disturbing the phasing characteristics, which extends
Armstrong's work to "commanded" changes in MT. But even more interesting
was the fact that when both Summers and Shapiro asked their subjects to
speed-up the movements, and at the same time to disregard the phasing that
they had learned earlier, the phasing still remained in the faster movements. This evidence is in keeping with the view that sequencing and
phasing are (perhaps inseparable) invariant features in the program, with
MT as a parameter that is added to affect the program's operation as a
whole.

Similar suggestions have been made about the programs for gait. For example, the implication is that trotting in horses is a single program with
invariant sequencing, phasing, and relative force, but that the horse can
trot faster or slower by applying a movement-speed parameter. In the model
in right of Figure 1, the implication is that the speed of conduction
around the loop of neurons that constitutes the "clock" can be increased or
decreased by changing the excitability of the various cells (Grillner,
1975).

Force. A second parameter can be thought of as an overall "gain" parameter that affects all of the contractions proportionally, although the
evidence for this parameter comes more from logical grounds than it does
from experimentation. The idea is that throwing a heavy and a light object through the same trajectory to a target requires the same movement
speed, but greater forces of contraction are required in order to achieve
it. A parameter of force seems to be required to increase while holding
the MT parameter constant. Also, there are many responses in which the
force and MT parameters appear to be correlated; for example, when I throw
a ball faster, I must go through the sequence of contractions not only more
rapidly, but also with greater force.

Merton (1972) has compared the handwriting done in the usual paper-and-
pencil size against the same words written on a blackboard some 10 times
larger, and then reduced in size photographically. The patterns are very
similar, and there is little difficulty in determining that the writing
is "the same." This suggests that the writing is done with different
force parameters in these two cases, so that the relative space and time
components of the response can remain constant, while the absolute size
of the movement can vary; increasing the amount of force in, for example,
an up stroke increases the distance the pen travels in the same period of
time, thereby increasing the size of the writing. Wing (1978) has taken
this idea further by proposing that the up-down and right-left movements
of the fingers are two separate dimensions controlled by the program, with
a third component being the steady translation of the limb rightward via
shoulder rotation.

Muscle selection. From Merton's example, it is interesting to note that
the smaller writing was done by the fingers primarily, while the blackboard writing was done with the elbow and shoulder, with the fingers being
relatively fixed. This evidence suggests that the particular muscles are
not specified by the program, but that the program is more abstract with
muscle selection being a parameter that can be applied to a given program
to produce the "same" movement in various limbs.

Using very different paradigms, Klapp (1977b) and Zelaznik, Shapiro, and
Carter (unpublished) have shown that if the subjects are told in advance
about which of two patterns they are to make when a reaction signal comes
on, but they are not precued as to which muscles with which to make the
response, subjects can shorten the RT (compared to RT in the no-precue
condition). The interpretation is that the program can be selected ahead
of time, thereby saving time during RT, while the choice of muscle will be
done after the reaction signal. Thus, the muscle with which the move is
to be made seems to be a kind of parameter, and is not "in" the motor program for the action. Also, Shapiro (1978), in the context of her research
cited above, has shown that the movement pattern can be suddenly trans-
ferred to the left hand, while retaining the invariant features of the
response (i.e., phasing and sequencing), again suggesting that the program
is not muscle-specific.

A final line of evidence comes from recent investigations using two-handed
aiming movements (Kelso, Southard, & Goodman, 1979; in press). Using the
very old (Woodworth, 1903) idea that two mirror-image movements appear to
be very easy to control simultaneously, Kelso et al. show that the initiation time, the termination time, the time of maximum acceleration and

velocity, etc., are remarkably similar (but not constant exactly) across
hands. Even when the movements are to be made with different amplitudes,
they also tend to be performed with similar times in the variables just
noted. In my terms, the program for action that determines sequencing,
phasing, and relative force has remained invariant across hands; in order
to make the movements travel different distances at the same time, the
force parameter is applied separately to the two limbs. Schmidt, Marteniuk
and MacKenzie (cited in Schmidt, Zelaznik, Hawkins, Frank, & Quinn, in
press), also using two-handed movement, have provided additional evidence
about the role of parameters in limb movements. These two-handed movements
have a number of features that make them particularly profitable to study
(see Schmidt et al., in press), and we feel that this paradigm is certainly
worthy of consideration by those interested in movement programs.

Other parameters. We can probably think of other ways that movements can
be varied while retaining the invariant features; but it is not clear
whether these other parameters are fundamentally different from those just
mentioned, or whether they are merely special cases of them. For example,
we appear to be able to throw a ball overhead, sidearm, or "three-quarters,"
all with the same pattern; perhaps the parameter here is the angle of the
arm with the torso. Also, Marteniuk (personal communication) has mentioned
evidence that basketball shooting at different distances is accomplished by
changing the amount of knee bend and body lean; more bend before the knee-
extension phase and more body lean are associated with greater shooting
distances, with the shot itself being nearly invariant.

IMPULSE-VARIABILITY THEORY

The preceding ideas about generalized motor programs and parameters were
the basis for a number of theoretical ideas; one of these was the idea of
schema learning (Schmidt, 1975) where the schema was a learned rule for
selecting the parameters of the generalized motor program. But more germane to this paper are ideas about variability in movement. If the programs "contains" sequencing, phasing, and relative force, and parameters
must be added in order to completely specify the motor response, then
variability in the selection of these parameters and/or in the execution
of the program should affect the variability in the response in predictable
ways. These ideas are presented in detail elsewhere (Schmidt, Zelaznik, &
Frank, 1978; Schmidt et al., in press), but a few highlights of this
series of studies will serve to make the point that the notion of the generalized motor program can be extended to produce models that account for
a wide variety of motor performance data.

Impulse Variability

When I make a movement from one place to another, there is an acceleration
in the direction of the target, the acceleration is turned off, and there
is a deceleration as the limb approaches the target. These force-time
patterns (impulses), according to physical principles, determine the nature
of the movement; and, variability in these impulses will also produce variability in the trajectories over which the limb travels and/or in the endpoint that the limb achieves. This line of thought led us to consider two
kinds of variability--(a) variability in the forces produced by the system, and (b) variability in the time over which the forces are active.
Surprisingly, we were able to find very little evidence from behavioral

work, and no evidence from neurophysiological work, that had considered the determinants of <u>variability</u> in the impulses that produce action.

<u>Force variability</u>. We suspected that the variability (within-person SD) in the forces produced would be proportional to the amount of force produced. We examined this relation by having subjects make ballistic "shots" of force against a static strain gauge, attempting to "shoot" a dot on an oscilloscope to a target. We varied the amounts of force from 100 gm to about 13 kg in two experiments, and the results of the first experiment are presented in Figure 3. The within-subject (across trials) SD of the forces plots nearly linearly with the amount of force that the subject is to produce; this effect appears similar to a kind of Weber-fraction, but for movement outputs rather than for sensory inputs. This suggested that as the subjects move farther (with a given MT), the force should increase proportionally with distance, as should its variability (Figure 3), and hence variability of the movement output should increase proportionally with distance as well.

<u>Time variability</u>. Earlier work with finger tapping (Michon, 1967), with RT (Gottsdanker, personal communication), and with piano playing (Michon, personal communication) all suggested that the variability in an interval to be estimated or produced was nearly proportional to that interval length. We supposed that the same relation would hold for the variability in the length of an impulse for acceleration or deceleration, but conducted one experiment to check this assumption. Subjects moved a lever back and forth in time to a metronome set at 200, 300, 400, or 500 msec per movement. We recorded the impulses from a strain gauge, and measured the SDs of their durations. In Figure 4 are the SDs of the impulse durations as a function of the MT; the relation is both linear and proportional, with an intercept of only -4 msec. Apparently, some aspect of the mechanism that defines the time of impulses has a variability that is proportional to its mean duration.

Amplitude and Movement-Time Effects

The above ideas lead directly to the statement of a model that describes the relation between the movement distance, the MT, and the resulting movement accuracy (defined as the effective target width, W_e--the SD of the movement endpoints about their own mean). For aiming movements, where the muscular impulse for deceleration is not the only force acting to stop the limb at the target (the remainder being the force associated with hitting the target), increasing the movement distance increases the force, which increases force variability and the variability in the movement endpoint. Likewise, decreasing the MT (a) increases the time variability because more force has to be produced, but also (b) decreases the time variability because the time of action of the impulse is shorter. Considering the effect of MT and movement amplitude (A) jointly as they affect W_e, Schmidt et al. (1978; in press) have proposed the following model:

$$W_e = \underline{a} + \underline{b}(A/MT). \tag{1}$$

This notion is a strict programming model, which assumes that no feedback corrections are taking place within the MT, and relies only on the relation between force and force variability and time and time variability. It deals with the same variables as does Fitts' (1954) law, but the models are

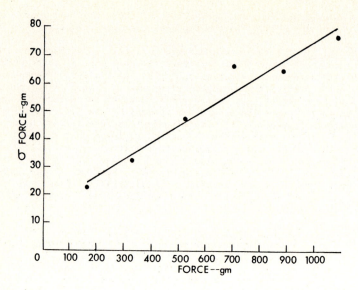

Figure 3.   The relationship between force and the within-subject varia-
           bility in force (from Schmidt et al., 1978, in press).

quite different and probably apply to different kinds of movement, with our
model applying to more rapid responses.

An initial test of this model was provided with aiming movements. We used
three movement distances (10, 20, and 30 cm) and three MTs (140, 170, and
200 msec) combined factorially, and Figure 5 presents the W_es as a function
of the ratio of A and MT.   The relation appears to be quite linear, with
the correlation between A/MT and W_e being .98 for these data points.
Schmidt et al. (in press) go on to extend this idea to two additional para-
digms--a rapid-timing paradigm wherein the subject moves through a given
distance in a given time (analogous, perhaps to the timing involved in
batting a baseball) and reciprocal lever movements done in time to a
metronome.   In both cases, the data obtained fit the predictions from the
model rather well. Also, the model predicts that added mass (which is
predictable to the subject) should have no effect on the accuracy of
movement, and one experiment using the rapid-timing paradigm shows nearly
no effect of an added mass that triples the muscular impulse necessary to
produce the action. Taken together, the model seems to be able to account
for a number of diverse findings from at least three paradigms, and seems
to have its strongest appeal in those movements that can be considered as
programmed.

PHASING IN UNIDIRECTIONAL MOVEMENTS

The foregoing model is concerned with the relations between the forces produced in movement, their variabilities, and the resulting variability in
the movement output. While it makes no assumptions about the nature of the

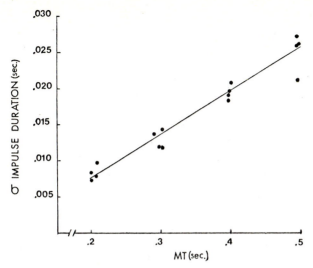

Figure 4. The relationship between movement time and the within–subject
variability of the impulse duration (from Schmidt et al., 1978,
in press).

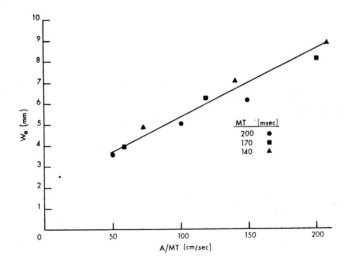

Figure 5. The relation between the ratio of the amplitude (A) and the
movement time (MT) and the effective target width (W_e) (from
Schmidt et al., 1978, in press).

underlying control processes (except to say that they are programmed) it
is certainly logical (in view of the model and of the work on the control
of gait) to suggest that the motor program activates the impulse for acceleration, it turns it off after the overall movement time is approximately at its midpoint, and activates the impulse for deceleration; thus, this
impulse-timing hypothesis has the phasing of unidirectional actions specified directly by the motor program.

But this hypothesis is challenged by another view of limb control apparently originally proposed by Crossman and Goodeve (1963). According to this
view, phasing is not represented in the motor program for one-directional
actions at all, but the limb moves to a position defined by the equilibrium
point between the torques produced by the agonist and antagonist muscle
groups. For a given level of excitation, the length-tension relationships
for the agonist and antagonist groups specify a unique angle where the
torques are equal (see also Turvey, 1977), and the limb achieves this position via the spring-like characteristics of the muscles acting on the mass
of the bone. This mass-spring view, as it came to be called, holds that
the limb moves to a new position via the specification of a new equilibrium point, achieved by changing the level of excitation to one or both of
the opposing muscle groups. Thus, this view denies that phasing of agonist and antagonist contractions is involved in these motions, and it suggests that reflex-based corrections to achieve the target need not be used
(although they may be, under certain conditions). To support their argument, Crossman and Goodeve showed that human limb movements were biased in
the direction of an unexpected torque applied half-way through a rapid positioning response (and it was not corrected when vision was absent, which
argues against a model of feedback-based corrections). This biasing effect
of the added load would be expected if the muscular system were operating
to achieve an equilibrium point.

This idea was (apparently independently) studied by Asatryan and Fel'dman
(1965) and Fel'dman (1966a, 1966b), who provided a detailed basis for the
idea and supporting evidence for it (see also Turvey, 1977). But the
ideas did not seem to attract very much attention (at least among the
people whose work I read), probably because of the relatively obscure
places that they were published (Crossman & Goodeve's paper was distributed
only to those attending a meeting, plus a few others), or perhaps because
this period was one in which the ideas about reflex-based corrections
seemed to dominate the thinking of workers in movement control. However,
Bizzi and his colleagues (Bizzi, Polit, & Morasso, 1976; Bizzi, Dev,
Morasso, & Polit, 1978; Polit & Bizzi, 1978, 1979) have provided a great
deal of recent evidence for this mass-spring view, and the support for it
has shaken our belief in the impulse-timing hypothesis for unidirectional
actions. Consider a situation in which the initial position of a limb or
the load applied to it is suddenly and unexpectedly changed prior to a
movement. Under the impulse-timing view, if the initial location of the
limb were suddenly changed, the program would produce the impulses to the
agonist and antagonist as planned, and the movement endpoint would be shifted by approximately the amount that the initial position was. However,
Bizzi and colleagues found that deafferented monkeys moved to the intended
target even though the initial position was shifted--sometimes even shifted
to a position past the target! Also, if the limb is suddenly loaded iner-
tially, the impulse-timing view predicts that the agonist and antagonist
contractions will occur for the pre-programmed durations; but because the
limb will now be going less rapidly, the limb will stop short of the target.

Bizzi and colleagues found that the limb achieved the intended target position in these conditions, again with deafferented monkeys. Both of these
sets of findings (if they hold in humans) argue strongly against an impulse-timing view of motor programming in (at least) unidirectional actions,
and tend to support the mass-spring view of movement control.

McGown and I (Schmidt & McGown, 1979) conducted a number of experiments
that, taken together, strongly support the mass-spring notion, while argue-
ing against our own ideas about the phasing of time in these responses.
Using intact humans, the first three experiments involved rapid angular
(either 30 or 40°, depending on the study) positioning of a lever. To control movement speed, we provided MT to the subjects as knowledge of results,
with the goal MT being 150 to 200 msec in different experiments. The subjects trained with this MT for 100 trials, attempting to reduce the variability in movement distance and duration. Then, in a separate series of
150 responses, we randomly inserted 15 trials wherein the resistance to the
lever was unexpectedly changed (unpredictable to the subjects) before the
movement began, with the changed resistance persisting throughout the remainder of that movement.[2] In the first experiment, we either added or
subtracted 455 gm placed 33 cm from the pivot of the lever, with the movements being done in the horizontal plane. In the second experiment, the
change in mass was the same (i.e., 455 gm) but the movements were in the
vertical plane. In the third experiment we changed the spring resistance
to the movement in the horizontal plane; the spring was attached so that
an added force of about 2 kg was required to move the lever from the starting position, and a force of 4.1 kg was required to hold it at the target.
In each of these cases, the predictions from the mass-spring and the impulse-timing views are considerably different, and I will explain these
predictions as I present the results in the next section.

Mass Varied in Horizontal Movements

First consider the experiment in which the subjects were moving the lever
horizontally to a target, with a mass either being added or subtracted unexpectedly. The impulse-timing theory holds that the impulse for acceleration will be shut off (by the motor program) when the preplanned impulse
duration has expired, and the impulse for deceleration will have the same
duration as well. But, because the mass to be moved is now unexpectedly
larger (or smaller) the limb will travel a shorter (longer) distance in
that fixed time, and the movement will be short (long) in its final endpoint. A mass-spring view, on the other hand, predicts that the limb will
reach the preprogrammed equilibrium point between the agonist and antagonist muscles, but will be slower (faster) in arriving because of the heavier
(lighter) mass in the "switch" trials.

Table 1A contains the essential results for this experiment. Considering
the "mass-added" portion of the experiment, suddenly increasing the mass
(in the "switch trials") caused a large lengthening of MT (from 187 to 278
msec), strongly present for both subjects. At the same time, there was
a slight increase in the distance moved (a CE shift from 6.36° to 6.81°),
but this effect was quite small and in opposite directions for the two
subjects. Considering next the "mass-subtracted" portion of the study,
suddenly decreasing the mass caused large reductions in MT (from 214 to
180 msec), present in both subjects. There was again nearly no change in
movement extent, with the two subjects again showing small and opposite
effects for CE.[3]

Table 1. Mean movement time and constant error for "normal" and "switch"
trials in four experiments (Schmidt & McGown, 1979).

		NORMAL TRIALS	SWITCH TRIALS
A. Horizontal, Mass Varied			
Mass Added	MT	187	278
	CE	+6.36	+6.81
Mass Subt'd	MT	214	180
	CE	+5.78	+6.28
B. Vertical Mass Varied			
Mass Added	MT	202	243
	CE	+15.82	+10.40
Mass Subt'd	MT	196	155
	CE	+7.83	+15.79
C. Horizontal, Spring Varied			
Spring Added	MT	188	170
	CE	+3.16	-3.04
Spring Subt'd	MT	177	247
	CE	-1.42	+11.00
D. Reversal, Mass Varied			
Mass Added	MT	165	174
	CE	+2.84	+.03
Mass Sub't	MT	163	161
	CE	+1.50	+6.83

Note: MT=movement time, CE=constant error, positive CEs are overshoots, errors are in degrees, and time is in milliseconds.
For "normal" trials in the resistance-added conditions, the
resistance is removed; for "normal" trials in the resistance-
subtracted condition, the resistance is present.

Taking both parts of the study together, the data are in strong opposition
to the impulse-timing view which predicts that there should be under- or
overshooting (for mass-added and mass-subtracted conditions, respectively),
with no change in MT. To the contrary, there were strong shifts in MT,
with no shifts in CE. These results are at least consistent with the mass-
spring view, since the limb appears to arrive at the preprogrammed target
location regardless of the mass that is applied to it.

The MT aspect of these results seems clearly to provide difficulties for
a motor-program view that holds that impulse durations are "metered-out"
via the program. But the results of the movement endpoint variable
(i.e., CE) are somewhat equivocal, in that they can be explained easily
by assuming that the limb is guided to the endpoint location by the gamma
system (or by some other feedback-based mechanism). The next two experiments bear on this latter issue.

<u>Mass Varied in Vertical Movements</u>

The second experiment involved exactly the same paradigm, but the movements
of the lever were in the vertical plane. The mass that was added (or subtracted) was identical to that in the first experiment. Note, however,
that adding mass in the vertical dimension adds 455 gm to the force needed
to hold the lever in the horizontal position at the target (while it did
not do so in the horizontal plane); and thus, according to the mass-spring
view, the equilibrium point should be shifted in the direction of the added
force (i.e., downward) for the "mass-added" portion of the experiment, and
be shifted upward for the "mass-subtracted" portion. A feedback view
would, of course, predict that the limb would reach the target, and this
experiment seemed to provide a basis for deciding between these two views,
as well as providing an additional test of the impulse-timing view.

The essential results are provided in Table 1B. For the "mass-added"
portion of the study, increasing the mass unexpectedly caused again large
lengthening of MT (from 202 to 243 msec), with similar effects for both
subjects. However, contrary to the findings from the previous experiment,
adding mass caused undershooting relative to the "normal" trials, with a
CE shift from 15.82° to 10.40°). Here, subjects always overshot the target
slightly, but they did so by about 5.4° less when the mass was added.
Next, considering the "mass-subtracted" portion of the data, suddenly subtracting mass caused a shortening of MT (from 196 to 155 msec) which was
present for both subjects. Subtracting mass caused more overshooting, as
the CEs increased from 7.83° to 15.79°, with similar affects for both subjects. Here, subjects always overshot, but they did so about 7.9° more
when the mass was subtracted.

This second experiment, which used the same mass-change technique as the
first experiment, but with movements in the vertical plane, also argues
strongly against the impulse-timing theory, since the MTs were lengthened
or shortened when the mass was added or subtracted, respectively. But it
also argues against a feedback view for explaining how the limb arrives at
its final position, since adding mass caused undershooting, and subtracting
it caused overshooting. This finding is nicely in keeping with the mass-
spring view since, in this view, the changed mass has the effect of shifting the equilibrium point between the agonist and antagonist; and the resultant shifts were fairly large (either 5.4 or 7.9°) and consistent across
subjects.

Spring Tension Varied in Horizontal Moves

In the third experiment, the paradigm was the same as in the previous two,
except that spring tension was either added or subtracted unexpectedly.
The essential results are in Table 1C. The effect of adding the spring unexpectedly was to shorten the MT slightly from 188 to 170 msec, which was
present in both subjects. With respect to movement distance, adding the
spring shortened the movement considerably, resulting in a CE shift from
3.16° past the target (spring off) to 3.04° short of the target (spring on).
The shorter movement distance when the spring was added is probably the
cause of the shortened MT. With respect to the "spring-subtracted" portion
of the study, removing the spring caused a lengthening of MT from 177 to
247 msec. The movements were longer, with a CE shift from 1.42° short of
the target to 11.00° beyond it. This lengthened movement distance is
likely the cause of the lengthened MT in this condition.

The effects of added or subtracted spring tension on the movement endpoint
support the mass-spring notion, and provide additional evidence against the
idea that the terminal position is achieved by some kind of feedback process. Finally, the fact that the MTs changed with the change in spring
tension suggested that an impulse-timing theory of discrete movements is
incorrect; the fact that the added resistance can influence when the move
comes to a stop--even though spring tension actually shortened MT--is
particularly damaging to the theory.

PHASING IN MULTI-DIRECTIONAL MOVEMENTS

The foregoing evidence seems to provide a dilemma about how we conceptualize the programming of phasing. On the one hand, the evidence from movements that contain many segments strung together (e.g., Armstrong, 1970;
Summers, 1976; Shapiro, 1977, 1978) or many parts performed nearly simultaneously (e.g., trills on the piano) seems to say that phasing and sequencing are closely linked--perhaps even inseparable. On the other hand,
if we wish to consider the first half and the second half of a positioning
response as two separate serial "components," then the evidence presented
in the last section suggests that the phasing of these segments is not
determined in advance by the programs. One obvious difference between the
two kinds of movements just described is that the former have multiple
limbs being active and/or at least one change in direction; the single positioning responses have neither, having only a single limb with no changes
in direction. To test the view that the impulse-timing view might be applicable only to the first category, McGown and I did another experiment,
using a movement reversal.

Movement Reversals

In this experiment, the paradigm was the same as in the previous studies,
with mass being added to a lever (or subtracted in other subjects) unexpectedly. The difference was that the movement was in this case a flexion
followed by an extension of the elbow. The subject was to time the reversal so that the lever came as close to a target as possible, and then he was
to move back through the starting position so the overall MT (from start
and back to start) was approximately 300 msec. We were interested in the
effect of added (or subtracted) mass on the location of the reversal. If
phasing is not "in" the program for this action, the limb would go to the

same position, but the time to reversal would be either shortened or
lengthened depending on whether the mass was subtracted or added. On the
other hand, the impulse-timing view would hold that the timing of the onset of the extensor muscles is defined by the program; if the mass were
added unexpectedly, the limb would have traveled less distance by this
time, and the reversal point would be shifted in the direction of being too
short.

The major findings are in Table 1D. When the mass was suddenly added, the
average MT (to the reversal) increased from 165 to 174 msec; but this effect was small, was in different directions for the two subjects, and it
cannot be regarded as a stable finding. On the other hand, adding the mass
shortened the distance to the reversal point, with the average change being
from 2.84° to .03°; both subjects showed an effect in the same direction,
but they were quite different in magnitude. When mass was subtracted, the
results were essentially opposite in sign to the above. There was a very
slight shortening of MT to reversal, but again this effect was only 2 msec,
and was in different directions for the two subjects. Subtracting mass
caused more overshooting, increasing CE from 1.50 to 6.83°.

Taken together, this last experiment supports our hypothesis that, in
multidirectional movements, the motor program determines the time of impulse onset and offset. When the movement had a reversal, the MT to the
reversal point was not systematically affected by adding mass to the limb,
whereas the location of the reversal was biased strongly. This pattern of
results was completely different from that shown in the first three experiments with unidirectional movements. There, the MTs were biased strongly,
while the movement endpoints were not. We (Schmidt & McGown, 1979) interpret this pattern of results to mean that the role of time in motor-program
representations is fundamentally different in unidirectional and two-directional movements.

PHASING IN MOTOR PROGRAMS

Given the pattern of evidence in the literature (including that just presented), how are we to conceptualize the role of time in motor-program representations. One view is that the motor program specifies a target location (defined by the equilibrium point between agonist and antagonist
tensions) for single-direction moves, and that time is not represented in
the program for such actions at all. The reason that there are certain
temporal regularities in such actions is merely a result of the spring-like
effects of the muscles acting on the bones to provide a consistent pattern
of events spread across time. Seen in this way, the program for a unidirectional movement need not "meter out" time at all, and our evidence suggests that it does not.

Next consider a response with a change in direction. Here, a specification
of a single equilibrium point by the program seems no longer to be adequate
to define the entire response, and our fourth experiment suggests that the
time of the reversal is specified by the program (Table 1D). The flexors
were activated to move the limb in the direction of the reversal point, but
the extensors appeared to be activated at a particular time after the movement initiation, regardless of whether or not the limb had ever achieved
the reversal point aimed for. [These results also argue against Adams'
(1977) view that the timing of one action in a sequence is tied to a

particular joint angle of another limb involved in the sequence.] Thus, in these two-directional movements, the role of phasing in the program may be to determine when a new equilibrium point is to be specified. In these responses, we argue that an initial equilibrium point is specified that is far beyond the actual reversal point, and this action is initiated. After the flexors have been in action, the program specifies exactly when this equilibrium point should be abandoned, and when a "new" one "behind" the limb in the direction of extension should be adopted. The limb slows, reverses its direction, and accelerates toward this "new" equilibrium point. Such a model would explain our finding that the time to reversal would shift, as the mass to be moved was changed suddenly. In multidirectional movements, such as those used by Armstrong (1970) and Shapiro (1977, 1978), the role of phasing would be to define when each of a series of equilibrium points would be specified, and their findings are also in keeping with this hypothesis.

How can such a model of programming explain movements where there is more than one joint operating (e.g., in piano playing where all of the fingers operate in coordination with each other)? It could be that each of the finger moves (e.g., a press down, or a pull up) is defined by an equilibrium point, but the distribution of these equilibrium points across time is defined by the phasing in the motor program. [This is a common situation in skills, since all of the joints involved in pole vaulting (for example) must be coordinated with each other so that they move at the proper places at the proper times.] This view is not very different from that of MacNeilage (1970) for the control of speech. In his target hypothesis, MacNeilage suggested that the speech system determines target locations of the relevant musculature, and that these targets are achieved by the follow-up servo mechanisms such as has been proposed by Merton (1972). However, recent evidence indicates that the motor system does not operate in the way Merton has suggested, with a more effective idea being that of alpha-gamma coactivation (e.g., Smith, 1976). At first, this realization caused a rapid loss of interest in the target hypothesis, since the mechanism on which his hypothesis was based had lost a great deal of creditibility. But now with the findings of Bizzi and his colleagues, together with our findings reported here, there appears to be a way in which the musculature can achieve a target without having to rely on follow-up servos, and the MacNeilage hypothesis seems to be as healthy as ever. That view solves a number of difficult theoretical problems in the control of speech (and of other movements), and I believe that it should be reconsidered in the light of this new evidence.

A reasonable view of this evidence would be as follows. When a single-direction movement is required, either alone or in conjunction with other single-direction movements (e.g., in piano playing), the program specifies equilibrium points for each; the phasing in the program has nothing to do with the adoption of each equilibrium point, but rather determines when the limb will begin to adopt each. Thus, any time there is a reversal in direction, the motor program will determine the time of this reversal, but the actual kinematics of the limb's achieving the equilibrium point will be defined by the mechanical properties of the contracting musculature. Such a view minimizes the role of reflex corrections in guiding the limb along its path through space, and emphasizes the idea that the mechanical properties of muscles on their way to a new equilibrium point may be able to account for a great deal of the phenomena we see in the trajectories of limbs during skilled human actions.

References

Adams, J. A. Feedback theory of how joint receptors regulate the timing
    and positioning of a limb. Psychological Review, 84 (1977), 504-523.

Armstrong, T. R. Training for the Production of Memorized Movement
    Patterns. Technical Report No. 26, Human Performance Center, University
    of Michigan, 1970.

Asatryan, D. G., & Fel'dman, A.G. Functional tuning of the nervous system
    with control of movement or maintenance of a steady posture. I.
    Mechanographic analysis of the work on the joint on execution of a
    postural task. Biophysics, 10 (1965), 925-935.

Bizzi, E., Dev, P., Morasso, P., & Polit, A. Effect of load disturbances
    during centrally initiated movements. Journal of Neurophysiology, 41
    (1978), 542-556.

Bizzi, E., Polit, A., & Morasso, P. Mechanisms underlying achievement of
    final head position. Journal of Neurophysiology, 39 (1976), 435-444.

Brown, T. G. On the nature of the fundamental activity of the nervous
    centers; together with an analysis of the conditioning of rhythmic acti-
    vity in progression, and a theory of the evolution of function in the
    nervous system. Journal of Physiology (London), 48 (1914), 18-46.

Cooke, J. D. Dependence of human arm movements on limb mechanical proper-
    ties. Brain Research, 165 (1979), 366-369.

Crossman, E. R. F. W., & Goodeve, P. J. Feedback control of hand-movement
    and Fitt's (sic) law. Paper presented at the Experimental Psychology
    Society meeting, July, 1963.

Davis, W. J. Neuronal organization and ontogeny in the lobster swimmeret
    system. In R. B. Stein, K. G. Pearson, R. S. Smith, & J. B. Redford
    (Eds.), Control of Posture and Locomotion. (Plenum, New York, 1973).

Fel'dman, A. G. Functional tuning of the nervous system with control of
    movement or maintenance of a steady posture. II. Controllable paramet-
    ers of the muscles. Biophysics, 11 (1966), 565-578. (a)

Fel'dman, A. G. Functional tuning of the nervous system with control of
    movement or maintenance of a steady posture. III. Mechanographic
    analysis of the execution by man of the simplest motor tasks.
    Biophysics, 11 (1966), 766-775. (b)

Grillner, S. Locomotion in vertebrates: Central mechanisms and reflex
    interaction. Physiological Reviews, 55 (1975), 247-304.

Henry, F. M., & Rogers, D. E. Increased response latency for complicated
    movements and a memory drum theory or neuromotor reaction. Research
    Quarterly, 31 (1960), 448-458.

James, W. Principles of Psychology (2 vols). (Holt, New York, 1890).

Keele, S. W. Movement control in skilled motor performance. Psychological
    Bulletin, 70 (1968), 387-403.

Keele, S. W. Behavioral analysis of motor control. In V. Brooks (Ed.), Motor Control (Handbook of Physiology). In press.

Kelso, J. A. S., Southard, D. L., & Goodman, D. On the coordination of two-handed movements. Journal of Experimental Psychology: Human Perception and Performance, in press.

Kelso, J. A. S., Southard, D. L., & Goodman, D. On the nature of human interlimb coordination. Science, 203 (1979), 1029-1031.

Klapp, S. T. Reaction time analysis of programmed control. Exercise and Sport Sciences Reviews, 5 (1977), 231-253. (a)

Klapp, S. T. Response programming, as assessed by reaction time, does not establish the commands for particular muscles. Journal of Motor Behavior, 9 (1977), 301-312. (b)

Lashley, K. S. The accuracy of movement in the absence of excitation from the moving organ. American Journal of Physiology, 43 (1917), 169-194.

MacNeilage, P. F. Motor control of serial ordering of speech. Psychological Review, 77 (1970), 182-196.

Merton, P. A. How we control the contraction of our muscles. Scientific American, 226 (1972), 30-37.

Michon, J. A. Timing in Temporal Tracking. (Institute for Perception RVO-TNO, Soesterberg, The Netherlands, 1967).

Pew, R. W. Human perceptual-motor performance. In B. H. Kantowitz (Ed.), Human Information Processing: Tutorials in Performance and Cognition. (Erlbaum, New York, 1974).

Polit, A., & Bizzi, E. Processes controlling arm movements in monkeys. Science, 201 (1978), 1235-1237.

Polit, A., & Bizzi, E. Characteristics of motor programs underlying arm movements in monkeys. Journal of Neurophysiology, 42 (1979), 183-194.

Rack, P. M. H. The significance of mechanical properties of muscle in the reflex control of posture. In Excitatory Synaptic Mechanisms. (Universitetsforlaget, Oslo, 1970).

Schmidt, R. A. A schema theory of discrete motor skill learning. Psychological Review, 82 (1975), 225-260.

Schmidt, R. A. Control processes in motor skills. Exercise and Sport Sciences Reviews, 4 (1976), 229-261.

Schmidt, R. A., & McGown, C. The role of phasing in motor program representations for arm movements. Manuscript in preparation, 1979.

Schmidt, R. A., Zelaznik, H.N., & Frank, J. S. Sources of inaccuracy in rapid movement. In G. E. Stelmach (Ed.), Information Processing in Motor Control and Learning. (Academic Press, New York, 1978).

Schmidt, R. A., Zelaznik, H. N., Hawkins, B., Frank, J. S., & Quinn, J. T., Jr., Motor-output variability: A theory for the accuracy of rapid motor acts. Psychological Review, in press.

Shapiro, D. C. A preliminary attempt to determine the duration of a motor program. In D. M. Landers & R. W. Christina (Eds.), Psychology of Motor Behavior and Sport. (Urbana, IL, Human Kinetics Publishers, 1977).

Shapiro, D. C. The Learning of Generalized Motor Programs. Unpublished Ph.D. dissertation, University of Southern California, 1978.

Smith, J. L. Fusimotor loop properties and involvement during voluntary movement. Exercise and Sport Sciences Reviews, 4, (1976), 297-333.

Stelmach, G. E. Motor Control: Issues and Trends. (Academic Press, New York, 1976).

Summers, J. J. The role of timing in motor program representation. Journal of Motor Behavior, 9, (1977), 49-60.

Taub, E. Movement in nonhuman primates deprived of somatosensory feedback. Exercise and Sport Sciences Reviews, 4, (1976), 335-374.

Taub, E., & Berman, A. J. Movement and learning in the absence of sensory feedback. In S. J. Freedman (Ed.), The Neuropsychology of Spatially Oriented Behavior. (Dorsey Press, Homewood, IL, 1968).

Turvey, M. T. Preliminaries to a theory of action with reference to vision. In R. Shaw & J. Brandsford (Eds.), Perceiving, Acting, and Knowing. (Erlbaum, Hillsdale, NJ, 1977).

Wetzel, M. C., & Stuart, D. G. Ensemble characteristics of cat locomotion and its neural control. Progress in Neurobiology, 7, (1976), 1-98.

Wing, A. M. Response timing in handwriting. In G. E. Stelmach (Ed.), Information Processing in Motor Control and Learning. (Academic Press, New York, 1978).

Woodworth, R. S. Le Mouvement. (Doin, Paris, 1903).

Footnotes

1. The animal motor-behavior work is disappointing to me in this one
    regard. I know of no work that uses responses that can be considered
    "learned" in the sense that pole-vaulting is learned in humans. That
    is not to say that learning is not involved in most animal experiments;
    but invariably, the animal is taught to produce a response that is al-
    ready represented by a program (a button press, an arm movement) in
    response to a signal. Never, it would seem, is the animal taught to
    perform a new motor act that is not already a part of his <u>repertoire</u>.

2. Half of the subjects had "normal" trials that were unresisted, with
    "switch" trials having the resistance added; the other half of the sub-
    jects had "normal" trials that were resisted, with "switch" trials
    having the resistance subtracted. There were two subjects in each
    "half" of each experiment.

3. Our strain-gauge records show that there is an <u>immediate</u> increase in
    muscle force when the load is added. This can be seen by comparing the
    unloaded and unexpectedly loaded movements. That such a load compensa-
    tion is immediate, and cannot be explained by reflex-based corrections,
    has been found previously (e.g., Rack, 1970), but this fact has not
    been generally recognized among my own colleagues.

Tutorials in Motor Behavior
G.E. Stelmach and J. Requin (eds.)
© *North-Holland Publishing Company, 1980*

9

EGOCENTRIC REFERENTS IN HUMAN LIMB ORIENTATION*

George E. Stelmach
Douglas D. Larish
Motor Behavior Laboratory
University of Wisconsin

Abstract

Testing the hypothesis that spatial localization is
made on the basis of an abstract spatial code, rather
than on stored proprioceptive information, orientation
of the unseen limb was contrasted under same and
switched limb movement conditions. In Experiments 1
and 2, movements were executed in the midline vertically
upward and horizontally away, respectively. The results
of both experiments revealed that same limb accuracy was
superior only at farther target positions, and it was
hypothesized that orientation of the limb could be
mediated by a spatial location code if movements remained within the confines of an egocentric reference
system. To test this tentative assertion more directly,
Experiment 3 examined same and switched limb performance
in two-dimensional space. At locations defined a priori
as inside egocentric space, absolute movement accuracy
and amplitude error failed to differentiate between same
and switched limb localization. At locations defined
a priori as outside egocentric space the same limb condition prevailed. Meanwhile, irrespective of spatial
position directional error revealed that same limb
orientation was superior to switched limb orientation.
The amplitude error findings were interpreted to mean
that body referent points inside egocentric space allow
for the parameterization of the necessary length-tension
relationships in the agonist and antagonist muscles of
either limb. The direction findings were explained in
light of previous data demonstrating systematic perceptual errors in estimating the objective referents.

Without question the accurate orientation of the body in physical space is
an all-important faculty essential to our very existence. In this regard,
the relationship between orientation and action is an important one. When
the body, or any part of the body, becomes misaligned or disoriented compensatory motor activity ensues. These actions can be either reflexive or

*The present research was supported by grants from the Research Committee
of the Graduate School, University of Wisconsin-Madison, Project No.
190400, Biomedical Research Support Grants 144-G805 and 144-J432, and Air
Force Grant AFOSR-78-3691 awarded to G. E. Stelmach.

voluntary, such as in postural adjustments (Gottlieb, Agarwal, & Stark, 1970), but they ultimately realign the body or body segment in an advantageous equilibrial state. Furthermore, the successful execution of numberous goal-directed actions relies on the maintenance of an optimal equilibrial state. Such behaviors vary from the simplicities of limb orientation, to the complexities of geographical orientation. Orientation also encompasses the perception of stimulus position in relation to objective environmental spatial referents and/or anatomical spatial referents (Howard & Templeton, 1966). Spatial orientation, then, depends on a high degree of predictability afforded by anatomical and ecological invariances (Paillard & Brouchon, 1968).

Although many features of spatial orientation are recognized, one of the most widely acclaimed is the space coordinate system (Bernstein, 1967; Gross, Webb, & Melzack, 1974; Pick, 1970; Howard & Templeton, 1966; Lashley, 1951; Luria, 1966; MacNeilage, 1970; Paillard & Brouchon, 1968; Reisser and Pick, 1976; Russell, 1976). This system is proposed as a model or representation of physical space, within which invariant descriptors (anchor points) correspond to objective spatial positions (Attneave & Benson, 1968). The constructed relationships between anchor points and spatial positions are integrated during the orienting process. In other words, a number of anchor points or referents maintain an invariant relationship, which in turn defines the current spatial schema. The locale of spatial positions or targets is defined with respect to these absolute coordinates and when it becomes necessary to orient to a specific position or target the anchor points are thought to facilitate this action.

The importance of a spatial coordinate system or spatial schema is to introduce invariant relationships that afford predictability. Consequently, space coordinate systems have long been given a mediating role in the control and regulation of motor action. Lashley (1951; pg. 126) stated that such a system provides "a possible basis for some serial actions through the interaction of postural and timing mechanisms." Howard and Templeton (1966; pg. 7) add that "spatially coordinated behavior is construed as the development and maintenance of a repertoire of response patterns which are moulded and conditioned by the spatial characteristics of the body and of the physical world in such a way that objectives may be rapidly and accurately achieved." MacNeilage (1970) has also proposed a theory of speech production which relies on established relationships between spatial positions of the articulatory apparatus and a space coordinate system. More recently, Russell (1976) has extended MacNeilage's target hypothesis to include motor acts of limbs. Russell asserts that achievement of a desired spatial position or target is not accomplished via the storage of direct sensory consequences from preliminary movements. Rather, limb position information, signalled by the sensory receptors in the joint-muscle complex, is transformed in conjunction with the space coordinate system, to a spatial location code. When a motor act to a location is repeated all that needs be done is to determine the current position of the limb and retrieve the location's spacial coordinates. Next, one simply "generates afresh" the neural commands required to achieve the desired spatial location (MacNeilage & MacNeilage, 1973; pg. 434).

For the target hypothesis to be a viable explanation of motor control it must be shown that spatial location can be accessed in memory, independent from movements responsible for its initial storage, and that accurate movements can be reproduced from starting positions and directions not

associated with initial storage (Russell, 1976). In the much cited work
of Laabs (1973), Stelmach, Kelso, and Wallace (1975), and Bizzi, Polit,
and Morasso, (1976), it has indeed been shown that varied start positions
have no affect on limb localization. A more convincing argument could be
made however, if accurate orientation is demonstrated under conditions
where it is difficult or impossible to rely on specific proprioceptive information. Such evidence was provided by Wallace (1977). In this study
subjects performed horizontal arm movements along a linear positioning
apparatus under two movement conditions; same limb and switched limb reproduction. In the switched limb condition criterion and reproduction movements were executed by different limbs. Wallace argued that such a procedure makes it difficult to rely on direct proprioceptive information during
reproduction, thus permitting an assessment of the target hypothesis. In
Experiment 1, on switched limb trials a location was approached from different directions. The results revealed same limb performance to be more
accurate than switched limb performance; failing to support the target
hypothesis. In a second experiment, however, a location was approached
from the same direction on switched limb trials. By keeping direction
constant, same and switched limb accuracy was found to be equivalent; partially supporting the target hypothesis.

In general, this study implies that accurate limb orientation need not be
executed on the basis of remembered sensory consequences. Rather, accurate
motor actions can be guided by stored or predicted spatial locations. From
the perspective of economy, such an assertion is appealing as it permits a
certain degree of flexibility in the central nervous system's ability to
use the knowledge provided by the spatial code. This point is important
because the adaptive capabilities displayed in the orienting process
require this same flexibility.

Although Lashley (1951), Paillard and Brouchon (1968), and Wallace (1977)
refer to a spatial coordinate system, none of these authors considers the
possibility of different types of reference systems. However, two general
categories of reference systems have been recognized: their distinction
with respect to motor control should be made. The first is an egocentric
reference system and the second is an exocentric reference system (Howard
and Templeton, 1966; Pick, 1973; Reisser and Pick, 1976). When positioning an object or another part of the body, the egocentric system utilizes
anchor points defined entirely with respect to the body schema, whereas
the exocentric system involves orienting actions made on the basis of
objective environmental anchor points and gravity (Howard and Templeton,
1966). Localizing a limb to the midline or the straight ahead position
(e.g., Werner, Wagner, and Bruell, 1953) is an example of egocentric orientation and visually adjusting a rod to the gravitational vertical under
varying degrees of body and room tilt (Asch and Witkin, 1948) is an example of exocentric orientation.

With the acknowledged importance of spatial orientation and the apparent
importance of the space coordinate system to orientation, it is surprising
to find little or no experimental evidence corroborating such an assertion.
The present study is an attempt to provide such data within the context of
egocentric space and human limb orientation. The first two experiments
were conducted simply to examine the relationship between same and switched
limb localization in the median and mid-transverse planes of the body.
From the perspective of closed-loop theory (e.g., Adams, 1971), one of the

more traditional explanations of motor control, it is unlikely that the
switched limb condition would attain the degree of accuracy as the same
limb condition. Closed-loop theory assumes that the memory trace of pre-
ceeding movements regulates the actions of future movements. Furthermore,
this trace is specific to the conditions of the defined movement. In the
switched limb instance, however, no such memory trace is available for
movement reproduction. Consequently, orientation with the contralateral
limb will be at a disadvantage. In direct contrast, from a target hypothesis perspective same limb reproduction will have no special advantage
over switched limb reproduction, since it is reasonable to argue that the
system controlling the limb can use the spatial code to orient. Thus,
same and switched limb accuracy should be comparable.

One Dimension Experiments

METHOD

Procedure. Twelve right-handed subjects executed criterion and reproduction movements on a vertical positioning apparatus for Experiment 1 and
eleven subjects executed similar movements on a Numonics Graphic Digitizer
arranged so that movements could be made in the horizontal plane for
Experiment 2. Subjects wore conventional dark glasses and headphones to
preclude extraneous visual and auditory cues.

After entering the testing chamber, subjects were seated so that the
midline was directly in front of the movement track and the movement range
could be completed with both arms. A familiarization period followed
during which the movement tasks and verbal commands were explained. All
four limb combinations were considered unnecessary since previous research
has shown that performance accuracy of the two same-limb combinations
(right-right and left-left) is equivalent and the performance accuracy of
the two switched-limb combinations (right-left and left-right) is equivalent (Larish, Stelmach, & McCracken, 1979; Wallace, 1977). A verbal
command cued subjects to move to a target. After contacting the target,
the termimal position was maintained for two seconds and then the subjects
were cued to return their hands to the base of the apparatus. The experimenter returned the apparatus to its original start position, which remained constant throughout the experiment, and then issued the reproduction
command for the same or opposite arm. The reproduction movement was to be
made directly to the defined location, avoiding subsequent adjustments once
the movement was terminated.

Subjects performed 30 same limb trials and 30 switched limb trials during
the testing period. Within each movement type, movements to each of five
locations (10, 25, 35, 50, 60 cm) recurred six times. All trials were
presented in a mixed list fashion, thus avoiding any problems associated
with sequence or order effects. As a consequence of this procedure subjects had no indication of the task to be performed on any trial until the
reproduction command was given. Reproduction errors at each location were
recorded to the nearest millimeter and combined for inspection of constant
error (CE), absolute error (AE) and variable error (VE). The design thus
corresponded to a completely within-subjects 12 x 2 x 6 (subjects x task x
location) factorial. The error data, however, were not analyzed using the
F-statistic as a screening device. Rather, based on the predictions made
earlier the data were analyzed on the basis of planned orthogonal

comparisons (see Kirk, 1973). Six directional comparisons were performed between the means of same and switched limb trials at each location. Since these comparisons were orthogonal the per comparison alpha level was set at .01. Directional comparisons were deemed appropriate since traditional motor control theories predict switched limb performance will be the least accurate of the two. Further, support for the target hypothesis, in the present framework, depends upon acceptance of the null hypothesis. If the null hypothesis is not proven in error, even after a liberal statistical test, then it is less likely a Type I error has been committed, thus giving more credibility to the target hypothesis.

For Experiment 2 the general procedures, instructions, and verbal commands paralleled those from the previous experiment. Movements, however, were executed in the mid-transverse plane horizontally away from the body. One further difference involved the target positions. Because of mechanical limitations in reach, the locations were 10, 20, 30, 40, and 50 cm. The basic analysis also remained invariant; planned orthogonal, directional comparisons were made with each tested at alpha = .01.

RESULTS - VERTICAL EXPERIMENT

In all three error measures the critical value to be exceeded for significance was $t(5,55) = 2.40$, $p < .01$. For CE, the analysis revealed that same limb reproduction was more accurate than switched limb reproduction only at the 50 and 60 cm targets. Unexpectedly, at the 25 cm target switched limb accuracy was better than same limb accuracy. For AE, performance of the same limb condition was superior to that of the switched limb condition only at the 50 and 60 cm targets. Finally, for VE the analysis yielded one significant comparison and it showed same limb reproduction was the most accurate at the 60 cm target.

TABLE 1

Vertical Locations in cm

LIMB		10	25	35	50	60
SAME	CE	1.93	2.10	2.13	0.65	0.20
	AE	2.10	2.62	3.38	2.53	1.85
	VE	1.50	2.62	2.95	2.58	1.69
SWITCHED	CE	2.18	0.69	1.82	-2.00	-1.35
	AE	2.54	2.53	3.49	3.49	3.79
	VE	1.60	2.24	3.21	2.60	3.51

RESULTS - HORIZONTAL EXPERIMENT

The critical value necessary for significance was $t(4,44) = 2.42$, $p < .01$. The CE analysis revealed that same limb accuracy was superior at the two far targets, 40 and 50 cm. Again unexpectedly, switched limb performance was more accurate than same limb performance. This situation occurred at the 20 and 30 cm targets. For the 30 cm target this result is difficult to evaluate because the positive magnitude of same limb errors is nearly

equivalent to the negative magnitude of switched limb errors. Finally, the
superiority of the same limb reproduction at the 40 and 50 cm targets was
also found in AE and VE.

TABLE 2

Horizontal Locations in cm

LIMB		10	20	30	40	50
SAME	CE	2.25	3.71	1.15	-0.65	-0.44
	AE	2.81	3.98	2.73	1.89	1.65
	VE	1.28	1.83	2.21	1.74	1.51
SWITCHED	CE	3.29	2.15	-0.70	-3.08	-3.31
	AE	3.52	2.89	2.43	4.01	4.02
	VE	1.76	2.04	2.05	2.54	2.36

DISCUSSION OF ONE DIMENSION EXPERIMENTS

The striking feature of both experiments is the consistent superiority of
same limb reproduction at the far-most locations. Indeed, such results
were unexpected, yet are consistent enough to warrant speculation. Perhaps
the role of body reference points is much more important than has been
previously acknowledged. Although many have theorized about the possible
role of body reference points, to our knowledge, no research has explicitly
demonstrated that they assist kinesthetic spatial coding. The present
results address themselves directly to this issue. The closer target positions can be said to be within the boundaries of an individual's egocentric,
body based reference system, thus establishing a robust spatial location
code that is effectively used by both limbs. In contrast, the more distant
locations lie outside the boundaries of the egocentric reference system,
and consequently lack the necessary knowledge afforded by the supplemental
body reference points. While the ipsilateral limb maintains accurate
performance via repeated sensory feedback, the contralateral limb is forced
to rely upon a less than optimal spatial code, eventuating in a performance
decrement. Such an interpretation is strengthened by the fact that the
50 and 60 cm targets in Experiment 1 were above the head; a position where
additional body reference points would be unavailable.

The difference between the limb conditions at the far targets appears to be
due to the function of same limb accuracy increasing and switched limb accuracy decreasing. The general pattern of results reveals that the same limb
errors progressively increase for movement lengths up to 35 cm (Vertical
Experiment) and 30 cm (Horizontal Experiment), with a subsequent decrease
in error for movement lengths of 50 and 60 cm, (Vertical Experiment) and 40
and 50 cm (Horizontal Experiment). Meanwhile, switched limb errors increase
for movement lengths up to 35 cm (Vertical Experiment) and 30 cm (Horizontal
Experiment), with errors for longer movement lengths remaining at this level
or elevating slightly. These results might be considered unusual, in that
one might expect increasing errors with increasing movement length, however,
a similar pattern of results is reflected in data presented by Diewert
(1976) and Larish, Stelmach, and McCracken (1979). Further, Luria (1967)
has also cited evidence that extreme ranges of flexion and extension are
more easily specified than intermediate ranges.

Perhaps this pattern of localization errors is related to the mechanical
degrees of freedom (Bernstein, 1967) of the reaching apparatus involved in
the orientation action. Complete flexion or extension of the limb is
accompanied by a corresponding reduction in the variation possible in the
musculature and joints. In other words, when the limb is fully extended
its position can vary only in one direction, towards flexion. Due to
structural constraints, the system is unable to specify further extension.
Alternatively, when the limb maintains an intermediary position both flexion and extension movements are possible, therefore, the control system
must be able to specify both, and consequently the system has more freedom
to vary. In the present context, as the limb extends to the longer targets
the degrees of freedom the system must be concerned with reduce accordingly. One can argue that such reductions make it easier to code and re-
specify the essential parameters controlling the orienting act, thus accounting for the increased accuracy of the same limb condition. Why
doesn't switched limb accuracy also decrease? In this instance, the
parameterization of the system must rely on a less than optimal spatial
code because there is a lack of precise body reference points. As a result,
the parameterization process lacks sufficient information to function efficiently. Therefore, error in the switched limb condition would be unable
to decrease with movement length.

An implication of the present logic is that not only will same limb
accuracy prevail outside the reference system, but switched limb reproduction errors outside the reference system will be greater than inside the
reference system. An ANOVA was performed on the data to examine this
hypothesis on a purely post hoc basis. Specific interest focused on the
limb by target interaction, and when significant at $\alpha \leq .01$ a set of
complex contrasts tested the inside-outside prediction via Sheffé's test.
All contrasts were also tested at $\alpha \leq .01$. For both same and switched
limb reproduction, the three targets hypothesized to be inside egocentric
space were compared against the two targets hypothesized to be outside
egocentric space. In the Vertical experiment, the two-way interaction was
significant for CE, AE, and VE: F (4,44) = 4.64, 6.02, and 4.37, respectively. For switched limb reproduction, the complex contrasts in all error
measures were significant and they showed that accuracy inside the reference system was greater than outside the reference system. For same limb
reproduction, inside-outside errors were equivalent in VE, whereas, outside errors were smaller in CE and AE. In the Horizontal experiment, the
limb by target interaction was significant for CE and AE; F (4,40) = 6.76
and 7.96, however, VE failed to reach significance: F (4,40) = 1.56, p >.01.
As in the previous experiment, switched limb errors were lowest inside the
reference system and same limb errors were lowest outside the reference
system. The switched limb results, indeed, provide further support to the
current speculation regarding the egocentric reference system.

In the first two experiments, same limb accuracy prevailed only at the
farthest targets. Rather than invoking the preferred hypothesis of egocentric space and body referent points, these findings could be interpreted
as a movement length effect. That is, the closer targets and shortest
movement lengths were always inside the reference system and the farthest
targets and longest movement lengths were always outside the reference
system. To rule out movement length as a contributing factor, an experiment was conducted in which same and switched limb movements began with the
arm fully extended above the head and movements were executed in a vertical

downward manner. Movement lengths of 10, 25, 35, 50, and 60 cm were
again used.

The egocentric referent hypothesis predicts that same-switch differences
will occur for the shorter movement lengths, which are now outside the
reference system, and no differentiation will occur for the longer movement lengths, which are now inside the reference system. In contrast,
the movement length hypothesis predicts same-switch differences for the
50 and 60 cm movements. Analysis of the data showed that same and switched
limb accuracy was equivalent at all target locations. Even though these
data failed to support the referent hypotheses outright, they seem to rule
out movement length as the sole description of the results at the farthest
targets in the previous experiments.

                        Two Dimension Experiments

Although the data support the foregoing analysis, they are by no means
determinate, especially since it is a post hoc account. The next logical
step is to examine reproduction ability inside and outside the egocentric
reference system. In this third experiment the same-switched limb reproduction paradigm was used, except that three targets were selected to
represent positions within the bounds of the reference system, and three
targets were selected to represent positions outside the bounds of the
reference system. Providing our interpretations are correct, the expected
pattern of results is obvious: same and switched limb accuracy will be
equivalent when limb orientation remains inside the egocentric reference
system, whereas, same limb accuracy will be superior when limb orientation
is beyond the influence of the reference system. In addition, switched
limb accuracy inside the reference will be superior to that outside the
reference.

METHOD

Procedure. Twelve right-handed participants were recruited from the
University of Wisconsin-Madison. The Numonics digitizer was again used,
however, spatial locations were no longer restricted to one-dimension. The
fixed track from the Horizontal experiment was removed and targets in two
dimensions were chosen. Further, the digitizer was interfaced with a PDP8e
computer, which recorded the X-Y coordinates of subject's terminal position
and computed measures of radial, amplitude and directional error.

The basic instructions and verbal commands remained unchanged from the
earlier experiments. In this experiment, however, four limb combinations,
rather than two, were introduced; right-right (RR), left-left (LL),
right-left (RL), and left-right (LR). The LL and LR combinations were included because data concerning movement accuracy in two dimensions for all
four combinations were unavailable. During criterion movements subjects
guided the stylus inside a movable track, .5 cm wide and 55 cm long, until
a mechanical stop was contacted. During the reproduction phase, the track
was removed and movement excution proceeded unrestricted by directional
constraints. The start position was invariant, corresponding to a point
that intersected the midline and the base of the movement range. Three
spatial targets were designated as within the reference system. Target 1
corresponded to a point 20 cm in front of the midline; this point was selected as it represents a location used in the second experiment. Targets 2

and 3 corresponded to locations 15 cm to the left and right of the midline and 20 cm from the base of the apparatus at a straight line distance of 26 cm from the start position. These were considered inside the reference system because they were approximately in line with the shoulders and could be coded in conjunction with this body reference point. Three targets were designated to be outside the reference system. Target 4 was placed 40 cm in front of the midline and it was the point at which same and switched limb performance became differentiated in Experiment 2. Targets 5 and 6 were placed 35 cm to the left and right of the midline, at a straight line distance of 41 cm from the start position. The latter two locations were defined as outside the reference system because they were nearly 20 cm beyond each shoulder, and it would be difficult to code these points in conjunction with some body referents.

Figure 1. Graphic of experimental arrangement and target locations.

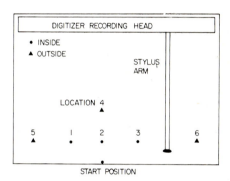

RESULTS

Radial Error. The first question of interest was whether differences existed within a particular limb condition. That is, were there differences in reproduction accuracy between RR vs. LL and RL vs. LR? The limb x target interaction was significant, F (15,165) = 1.90 p < .05, however, Tukey post hoc tests revealed only one significant difference; LR errors were less than RL errors at location 5. Since consistent limb differences were not present in the data this factor was dropped from subsequent analyses, such that RR and LL scores were averaged for one same limb mean and RL and LR scores were averaged for one switched limb mean. To test the primary questions of interest another ANOVA was conducted, with particular interest focused on the limb x target interaction, which did reach significance, F (5,55) = 4.92, p < .01. Tukey tests were used to compare same and switched limb reproduction accuracy at each criterion target. These results showed that same limb reproduction was superior only at the three targets defined as outside egocentric space. The analysis of the inside-outside comparisons using Scheffé showed that switched limb errors were significantly less at the three targets defined as inside the reference system, whereas, no differentiation was evident for same limb reproduction.

Amplitude Error. Although the limb x target interaction was significant, F (15,165) = 5.94, p < .01, post hoc analysis revealed a lack of consistent limb differences. The only difference present was beteeen RL and LR at location 5. Consequently, the same collapsing procedure used for radial error was employed, and again the limb x target interaction for the averaged scores was significant, F (5,55) = 3.86, p < .01. For the same limb-switched limb comparisons the results were identical to those of radial error; same limb accuracy prevailed only at locations defined as outside egocentric space. As for the inside-outside comparison, within the switched limb condition no differences were found and within the same limb condition errors outside the reference system were less than inside.

TABLE 3

Same and Switched Limb Errors as a Function of Targets

	Movement Locations					
	Inside				Outside	
Radial Error - (cm)						
	1	2	3	4	5	6
Same	4.64	4.43	5.07	3.41	4.73	4.06
Switched	5.66	4.91	5.16	5.86	7.00	6.26
Amplitude Error - (cm)						
Same	3.74	4.14	4.28	2.07	1.73	2.58
Switched	3.87	3.96	3.57	3.07	4.43	3.53
Directional Error - (degrees)						
Same	4.48	2.69	4.56	3.33	4.07	3.71
Switched	7.54	5.79	5.77	6.25	6.65	6.49

Directional Error. The ANOVA testing for limb differences failed to show any differentiation, the limb x target interaction was non-significant, F (15,165) < .1, p > .05. Also non-significant was the limb x target interaction on the averaged scores, F (5,55) < 1, p > .05. The main effect, however, revealed that same limb reproduction was more accurate than switched limb reproduction. Inspection of Table 3 clearly shows that same limb accuracy was superior at all target locations. Since the limb x target interaction failed to reach significance the inside-outside comparisons could not be computed.

DISCUSSION OF THE TWO DIMENSION EXPERIMENT

The rationale for this third experiment was that if body reference points facilitate proprioceptive coding it would be possible to differentiate same and switched limb accuracy by directly manipulating the availability of these reference points. It was argued, on logical grounds, that the shoulders define the lateral boundary of egocentric space and could also be used as anchor points. Moreover, on the basis of previous experiments 30 cm was defined as the approximate straight ahead boundary of egocentric space. A two-dimensional reproduction paradigm was used, in which it was possible to include locations defined a priori as either inside or outside the reference system. It was predicted that same and switched limb orientation would be equivalent inside the reference system, whereas, and in direct contrast, same limb orientation accuracy would prevail outside the reference system. Three related movement dimensions of localization accuracy were examined: absolute location accuracy, movement length (amplitude) accuracy, and angular (directional) accuracy.

Radial error and amplitude error convincingly support the stated predictions. Same and switched limb performance parallel each other inside the reference system and same limb performance is definitely more accurate outside the reference system. Directional error, however, is less amenable with the experimental hypothesis; same limb reproduction is superior at five of the six spatial targets. Although one would like to believe that spatial referents facilitate all dimensions of the orienting act, body anchor points evidently fail to enhance direction information.

Can these apparent discrepancies be reconciled with the present notions of human limb orientation? In our view, amplitude and direction errors are determined by two independent factors in a manner specified by Fel'dman (1966, 1974). Amplitude reproduction is controlled by an equilibrium point established by the agonist and antagonist muscles during the criterion movement. Fel'dman (1966, 1974) states that limb movements are controlled by two independent systems. The first specifies the properties of dynamic movement and the second specifies the static, equilibrial properties of the joint. The latter system is of, primary concern since it is directly involved in achieving a desired spatial position. Fel'dman likened the process of limb positioning to that of a spring. Operationally, regardless of how a spring is stretched, when the forces acting on the spring are released it always assumes an established equilibrial status. Not only is this hypothesis appealing, but its explanatory power is confirmed by neurophysiological evidence concerning alpha-gamma coactivation (McCloskey, 1978; Vallbo, 1974 a, b). Moreover, this concept has been frequently invoked to explain limb localization in monkeys (Bizzi, this text; Bizzi, Dev, Morasso, and Polit, 1978; Polit and Bizzi, 1978; Bizzi, Polit, Morasso, 1976) and location reproduction in humans (Kelso, 1977; Kelso and Turvey, this text).

The spring loading hypothesis is certainly compatible with the movement length data (amplitude reproduction) in the present context. It appears that when a two-dimensional spatial target is well coded, via body referent points, the movement control system can parameterize the length-tension properties of either limb equally well, even though the relationship among agonist and antagonist muscles may change from criterion to reproduction movements (e.g., as in switched limb movements to locations 1 and 3). In other words, the spatial location code is well-defined inside the egocen-

tric reference system, thereby, facilitating the length-tension setting
of the opposite limb. Without the additional referent points the settings
in the contralateral limb cannot be accomplished effectively.

Direction error can best be addressed by inquiring whether subjects' perceived or subjective referents correspond directly to the actual objective
referents. If asked to position the limb in front of the midline, or to
any other body referent, how accurate will an individual be? Any disparities between the objective and subjective referents will adversely
affect direction accuracy in switched limb reproduction. Wallace (1976)
presented evidence that subjects are, in fact, unable to position either
limb directly in front of the midline. In movements initiated from the
horizontal left and right, subjects underestimated the midline with both
limbs. Average errors were on the magnitude of 2-3 cm, showing larger
inter-individual variation. McFarland, Werner, and Wapner (1962) and
Werner, Wapner, and Breull (1953) also provide corroborative evidence,
implying that although one relies on body referent points the objective
referents are misperceived. Finally, Gross, Webb, and Melzack (1974)
showed systematic perceptual errors when subjects were required to match
the unseen limbs in space.

Such systematic misperceptions between objective and subjective referents
would surely inflate switched limb direction error, yet same limb direction
error would be unaffected by this factor. Inferring from the Wallace data,
if a limb is passively positioned to the midline, and one is asked to judge
its location, the estimate is likely to be beyond the midline. Furthermore, such perceptual errors would also exist when asked to position a
limb in line with any other body referent. These errors should also be
systematic in the sense that they will be equivalent across any number of
body reference points. That is, when the right limb is involved, biases
would be to the left of all referents and corresponding targets, and when
the left limb is involved, biases would be to the right of all referents
and corresponding targets. As an example, consider the RL combination to
location 1. First, at the start position the right limb is perceived left
of the midline and the initial coding of the target is based on a subjective referent displaced an equivalent amount to the left of the actual
target. Second, at the start position the left limb is perceived right of
the midline and the perceived shoulder referent is displaced to the right
of the target by an equivalent amount. As a result, reproduction by the
left will leave the limb to the right of the objective target, thereby
inducing direction error. Amplitude error remains unaffected because the
straight line distance between the perceived and objective start and
terminal positions is invariant. The perceptual biases affect the angular
relationship of objective and subjective spatial referents and not their
absolute movement length. A qualitative examination of algebraic direction errors for the two switched limb combinations at locations 1 through
4 (see Table 4) indicate that this explanation gives an accurate description of the data. Based on the foregoing analysis, RL errors at these
locations should be clockwise in direction, whereas LR errors at these
locations should be counter-clockwise in direction. In all eight instances
the data conform exactly to this pattern.

TABLE 4

Algebraic Direction Error (Degrees) for the Switched
Limb Combinations as a Function of Targets

LOCATION	LIMB	
	RL	LR
1	−5.89	2.76
2	−2.76	5.19
3	−2.86	2.02
4	−0.49	4.77
5	−3.09	0.33
6	1.69	5.80

Note: A positive number indicates errors left of the target
and a negative number indicates errors right of the target.

One possible challenge to the above interpretations must be considered.
The data of the third experiment may be the result of distortions in the
straight ahead body alignment, which is an artifact solely at distant
targets. As a function of trying to reach these target positions, the
limb approaches full extension, and in doing so torsional rotation of the
upper body is induced about the vertical midline axis. Torsion is pre-
cluded at shorter movement lengths inside the reference system, therefore,
it makes no contribution to localization error. Although some distortion
is present in the same limb movements outside the system, the effect
remains constant, thus, having no real consequence for localization error.
The torsional artifact has its primary effect on switched limb movements
outside the egocentric reference system. Right arm movements to locations
4 and 5 create counter-clockwise trunk rotation and left arm movements to
locations 4 and 6 create clockwise trunk rotation. It is possible that
these opposing distortions have some adverse effect on reproduction
accuracy.

If the foregoing analysis is correct, torsion would have its greatest
impact on direction error. More specifically, during right limb reproduction, the counter-clockwise rotation should shift direction errors away
from the midline. Similarly, during left limb reproduction, the clockwise rotation should also shift direction errors away from the midline.
For location 4 the results do indeed corrspond to these expectations. At
locations 5 and 6 the findings are less complimentary. Direction error
was virtually nil for the LR combination at location 5 and was towards
the midline for the RL combination at location 6. Further, such an interpretation predicts greater direction error at location 4, relative to
location 2, and again the data fail to strongly support this position (see
Tables 3 and 4). Thus, while this explanation may be a tenable alternative, supplementary experiments are needed before a definite decision can
be reached. Finally, it should be pointed out that such an explanation
has no bearing on amplitude error, since the upper body rotation should
not disrupt the length-tension settings of the muscles in the limb itself.

General Discussion

The present experiments were designed to investigate the importance of the space coordinate system in proprioceptive spatial coding using the switched limb technique (Hermelin and O'Conner, 1975; Wallace, 1977). The one dimension experiments began by examining the generality of MacNeilage's (1970) target hypothesis. For vertical movements executed in the median plane and horizontal movements executed in the mid-transverse plane the data yielded similar results. It was found that accurate limb orientation, mediated by the postulated spatial location code (MacNeilage and Mac-Neilage, 1973; Russell, 1976), is restricted to instances when target positions are situated relatively close to the body. The subsequent explanation is that when locations are specified within an egocentric reference system (Howard and Templeton, 1966; Reisser and Pick, 1966) the spatial location code is efficiently developed and this development is primarily determined by supplemental body reference points. When the referents are available the coding and transformation processes function optimally, eventuating in precise localization with either limb. In marked contrast, when the augmented reference points are unavailable, the coding and transformation processes result in a deficient spatial code. Thus, at positions outside the boundary of the egocentric system switched limb accuracy is poorer than same limb accuracy. It appears that in this instance specific proprioceptive cues are more reliable than the spatial code alone.

The two dimensional experiment sought to evaluate this preliminary interpretation by directly comparing localization performance at spatial positions defined as inside and outside the influence of the egocentric reference system. The results for absolute location accuracy and amplitude accuracy concurred with the above interpretation since same and switched limb errors were equivalent when targets were inside the system. Unfortunately, all dimensions of the orienting act failed to support the above interpretation. Direction error differentiated same and switched limb performance at five of the six targets. The above findings suggest, therefore, that body referent points inside the egocentric reference system facilitate only the specification of the length-tension relationships between agonist and antagonist muscles. Due to systematic perceptual errors in estimating the objective referents (Cross, Webb, and Melzack, 1974; Wallace, 1976; McFarland, Werner, and Wapner, 1962; Werner, Wapner, and Breull, 1953) direction estimation is adversely affected during switched limb orientation, accounting for the large directional errors.

Taken as a whole the present data addresses a number of important issues regarding spatial orientation and the egocentric reference system. The results of Wallace (1977), which showed that movement control is not necessarily dependent upon direct proprioceptive cues, have been replicated, at least under the specific conditions of the present experiments. In doing so, we have generated additional support for the basic spirit of MacNeilage's (1970) target hypothesis. At the same time, however, restrictions on the generality of this control have been identified. On the basis of the data, one is compelled to believe that efficient motor control by the spatial code is possible only when localization is made within the egocentric reference system. Although the role of a space coordinate system and body reference points have been postulated, to the best of our know-

ledge, the direct role of these factors have never been explicitly implicated in an experimental study. This study has initially delineated the
external boundaries of an egocentric, body-based reference system. Future
experimentation needs to be more specific since the boundaries, especially
the horizontal, may be greatly influenced by height, arm length, and
shoulder width. At the same time, these variables could provide a partial
account for the large individual differences in limb orientation accuracy.
These experiments also demonstrate the functional importance of body
reference points. When available, the accuracy of spatial positioning
proceeds independent of the movement originally responsible for creating
the spatial location code. Moreover, when these body reference points
are unavailable, accurate spatial positioning becomes _dependent_ on direct
kinesthetic information.

These results also point out that more specificity is needed when referring
to the spatial schema or referent system. Typically, distinctions between
types of reference systems have been disregarded. For example, one is
unable to discern whether Russell (1976) refers to an egocentric or exocentric reference system in his elaboration of MacNeilage's target hypothesis. Such a distinction is not a trivial one. Benton (1969) reviews a
number of studies concerning spatial disorders, suggesting that the type of
disorder is dependent upon the type of reference system disrupted. Howard
and Templeton (1969) also make a clear distinction between the two reference systems. We are not advocating complete functional independence because both conceivably influence an orienting act. Rather, since so little
is known about each system's operational characteristics, it may be more
advantageous to initially examine them independently. Finally, although
the data reported is preliminary in nature, we are compelled to maintain
that the spatial reference system concept has a good deal of functional
utility and merits continued examination.

References

[1] Adams, J.A. A closed-loop theory of motor learning. _Journal of Motor Behavior_, 1971, _3_, 111-150.

[2] Asatryan, D.G., & Fel'dman, A.G. Functional tuning of the nervous system with control of movement of maintenance of a steady posture: I. Mech-anographic analysis of the work of the joint on execution of a postural task. _Biophysics_, 1965, _10_, 925-935.

[3] Asch, S.E., & Witkin, H.A. Studies in space orientation: II. Percep-tion of the upright with displaced visual fields and with body tilt. _Journal of Experimental Psychology_, 1948, _38_, 455-477.

[4] Attneave, F., & Benson, B. Spatial coding of tactile stimulation. _Journal of Experimental Psychology_, 1968, _81_, 216-222.

[5] Benton, A.L. Disorders of spatial schema. In P.J. Vinken and G.W. Bruyn (Eds.), _Handbook of Clinical Neurology: Disorders of Higher Nervous Activity, Vol. 3_, Amsterdam: North Holland Publishing, 1969.

[6] Bernstein, N.A. The Co-ordination and Regulation of Movements. New York: Pergamon Press, 1967.

[7] Bizzi, E. Central and peripheral mechanisms in motor control. In G.E. Stelmach and J. Requin (Eds.), Tutorials in Motor Behavior, North Holland Publishing Company, Amsterdam, 1980 (In Press).

[8] Bizzi, E., Dev, P., Morasso, P., & Polit A. Effect of load disturbance during centrally initiated movements. Journal of Neurophysiology, 1978, 41, 542-556.

[9] Bizzi, E., Polit, A., & Morasso, P. Mechanisms underlying achievement of final head position. Journal of Neurophysiology, 1976, 39, 435-444.

[10] Diewert, G.L. The role of vision and kinesthesis in coding of two dimensional movement information. Journal of Human Movement Studies, 1976, 3, 191-198.

[11] Fel'dman, A.G. Functional tuning of the nervous system with control of movement or maintenance of a steady posture: II. Mechanographic analysis of the execution by man of the simplest motor tasks. Biophysics, 1966, 11, 766-775. (b)

[12] Fel'dman, A.G. Change in the length of the muscle as a consequence of a shift in equilibrium in the muscle-load system. Biophysics, 1974, 19, 534-538. (a)

[13] Gottlieb, G.L., Agarwal, G.C., & Stark, L. Interaction between voluntary and postural mechanisms of the human motor system. Journal of Neurophysiology, 1970, 33, 365-381.

[14] Gross, Y., Webb, R., & Melzack, R. Central and peripheral contributions to localization of body parts: Evidence for a central body schema. Experimental Neurology, 1974, 44, 346-362.

[15] Hermelin, B., & O'Connor, N. Location and distance estimates by blind and sighted children. Quarterly Journal of Experimental Psychology, 1975, 27, 295-301.

[16] Howard, I.P., & Templeton, W.B. Human Spatial Orientation. London: Wiley, 1966.

[17] Kelso, J.A.S. Motor control mechanisms underlying human movement reproduction. Journal of Experimental Psychology: Human Perception and Performance, 1977, 3, 529-543.

[18] Kelso, J.A.S. & Turvey, M.T. The concept of the coordinative cycle. In G.E. Stelmach and J. Requin (Eds.), Tutorials in Motor Behavior, North Holland Publishing Company, Amsterdam, 1980 (In Press.).

[19] Kirk, R.E. Experimental Design: Procedures for the Behavioral Sciences. Belmont, CA: Wadsworth Publishing Company, Inc., 1968.

[20] Laabs, G.E. Retention characteristics of different reproduction cues in motor short-term memory. Journal of Experimental Psychology, 1973, 100, 168-177.

[21] Larish, D.D., Stelmach, G.E., & McCracken, H.D. The generalizability of preselection. In G.C. Roberts and K.M. Newell (Eds.), Psychology of Motor Behavior and Sport-1978. Champaign, Ill: Human Kinetics Publishers, 1979.

[22] Lashley, K.S. The problem of serial order behavior. In L.A. Jeffress (Ed.), Cerebral Mechanisms in Behavior. New York: Wiley, 1951.

[23] Luria, A.R. Human Brain and Psychological Processes. New York: Harper and Row Publishers, 1966.

[24] MacNeilage, P.F. Motor control and serial ordering of speech. Psychological Review, 1970, 77, 183-196.

[25] MacNeilage, P.F., & MacNeilage, L.A. Central processes controlling speech production in sleep and waking. In F.J. McGuigan (Ed.), The Psychophysiology of Thinking, New York: Academic Press, 1973.

[26] McCloskey, Kinesthetic sensibility. Physiological Reviews, 1978, 58, 763-820.

[27] McFarland, J.H., Werner, H., & Wapner, S. The effect of postural factors on the distribution of tactual sensitivity and the organiza-tion of tactual-kinesthetic space. Journal of Experimental Psychology, 1962, 63, 148-154.

[28] Paillard, J., & Brouchon, M. Active and passive movements in the calibration of position sense. In S.J. Freedman (Ed.), The Neuro-psychology of Spatially Oriented Behavior. Homewood, Ill: Dorsey Press, 1978.

[29] Pick, H. L. Systems of perceptual and perceptual-motor development. In J. P. Hill (Ed.), Minnesota Symposia on Child Psychology (Vol. 4). Minneapolis: University of Minnesota Press, 1970.

[30] Reisser, J.J., & Pick, H.L. Reference systems and the perception of tactual and haptic space. Perception and Psychophysics, 1976, 19, 117-121.

[31] Russell, D.G. Spatial location cues and movement reproduction. In G.E. Stelmach (Ed.), Motor Control: Issues and Trends. New York: Academic Press, 1976.

[32] Stelmach, G.E., Kelso, J.A.S., & Wallace, Preselection in short-term motor memory. Journal of Experimental Psychology: Human Performance and Perception, 1975, 1, 745-755.

[33] Vallbo, A.B. Afferent discharge of human muscle spindles in non-contracting muscles: Steady state impulse frequency as a function of joint angle. Acta Physiol. Scandanavia, 1974, 90, 303-318, (a).

[34] Vallbo, A.B. Human muscle spindle discharge during isometric volun-
     tary contractions: Amplitude relations between spindle frequency
     and torque. Acta Physiol. Scand., 1974, 90, 319-336, (b).

[35] Wallace, S.A. The coding of location: A test of the target hypothe-
     sis. Unpublished Doctoral Dissertation, University of Wisconsin,
     Madison, 1976.

[36] Wallace, S.A. The coding of location: A test of the target hypothe-
     sis. Journal of Motor Behavior, 1977, 9, 157-169.

[37] Werner, H., Wapner, S., & Bruell, J.H. Experiments on sensory tonic
     field theory of perception: VI. Effect of position of head, eyes,
     and object on position of the apparent median plane. Journal of
     Experimental Psychology, 1953, 46, 293-299.

Tutorials in Motor Behavior
G.E. Stelmach and J. Requin (eds.)
© *North-Holland Publishing Company, 1980*

10

A PRELIMINARY THEORY OF TWO-HAND
CO-ORDINATED CONTROL

R.G. Marteniuk* and C.L. MacKenzie
Department of Kinesiology
University of Waterloo
Waterloo, Ontario, Canada

A two-hand co-ordinated control model is presented based on
data collected on subjects who performed both unimanual and
bimanual lateral movements to a target. The overall pattern
of results strongly suggests three basic control processes.
The first two, specifications of equilibrium points (length-
tension ratios) and intensities (force-time) to the limbs are
independent control processes, both of which are modified by
a hand/hemisphere asymmetrical organizational process. The
model predicts that interference, in the form of both inhibition and facilitation effects in two-hand movements occur as
a result of subcortical and spinal level interactions. These
interference effects are manifested in terms of the movement
times of the limbs and the constant errors about the targets.

INTRODUCTION

Interest in how the two hands are controlled in simultaneous movements has
been expressed for a considerable amount of time (Babinski, 1902 as reported
in Hausmanowa-Petrusewicz, 1959; Woodworth, 1899). A review of research in
this area shows two themes: first, is an approach geared towards understanding why the control of the two hands appears to be exactly the same
when performing simultaneous, symmetrical movements; and, second, a line of
investigation concerned with explaining the just as apparent interference
and facilitation effects in simultaneous hand movements.

The first approach is typified by Woodworth's (1899) statement that it is
easily observable that simultaneous movements with the two hands are easy
to execute in almost an identical manner. More recently, this work has
been extended by Kelso, Southard, and Goodman (in press) who postulate that
for simultaneous movements of the two hands, control is through one "coordinative structure" or motor program. Their evidence for this claim is the
very similar time and kinematic properties (specifically, the starting
times, the times to peak velocity and acceleration, and arrival times on
targets) of the two limbs as they execute movements to both equally and
unequally displaced targets. These authors further postulate that the
invariance of the two limbs is due to the common "structural prescription"

---

*This research was partially supported through a research grant to the first
author from the Natural Sciences and Engineering Research Council of Canada.
The second author wishes to acknowledge support by the same Council.

of time while the "metrical prescription", force, is left to vary. The
latter is necessary to account for the fact that the two limbs, when moving
unequal distances, have similar time histories but the limb moving the
greater distance must generate a greater impulse (i.e., greater force over
time) in order to arrive at the target at the same time as the other limb.

Interference in bimanual activity is demonstrated by Cohen (1970). He found
that a sequence of rhythmic, alternating wrist flexion-extension movements
performed by one limb was interfered with when rapid movements were executed by the contralateral limb. While this interference was attributed to
capacity interference effects (i.e., exceeding the capacity of the central
feedback processing mechanism), a later study by Preilowski (1975) dismissed the capacity interference explanation in favour of a structural
interference one.

Preilowski's interpretation of observed interference effects in bilateral
movement is based on ipsilateral efferent influences. If non-homologous
muscle groups are involved in bilateral movement the contralateral innervation (from one hemisphere) would be different from the ipsilateral innervation (from the other hemisphere) and interference between these two types
of innervation would result. Preilowski's results support the idea that
the site of this interference is lower than the cortical level and probably
both in brain stem and spinal cord areas. Anatomical evidence would tend
to support this conclusion (Brinkman and Kuypers, 1972; Hartman-von
Monakow, Akert and Künzle, 1979).

The purpose of the present research is to understand both the apparent ease
(i.e., non-interference) and interference of simultaneous manual activity.
In order to explain this activity, however, the underlying parameters of
movement commands must be elucidated. We (Marteniuk and MacKenzie, in
press) support the view that any discussion of these parameters must be
based on internal variables related to the structure and function of the
central nervous system. Thus, such variables as number of responding limbs,
spatial location, direction of movement, and force-time (impulse) production become important when attempting to understand bilateral manual
activity.

Two recent pieces of work support the above claim and will have rather
direct application to understanding our view of simultaneous manual activity. First, is the work of Schmidt and his colleagues (Schmidt, Zelaznik
and Frank, 1978) who have shown that the accuracy and speed with which
single hand movements can be made to a target can be explained by considering only the characteristics of the produced impulse (force over time).
Thus, at least for the rapid movements studied by Schmidt et al., one need
only consider the internal variable of impulse to understand how movements
in space are made. This is in sharp contrast to previous work which
attempted to explain these types of movements in terms of their amplitude
and the experimenter defined target size. These latter variables, which
we (Marteniuk and MacKenzie, in press) have called external variables have
little validity in explaining the underlying control processes of movement.

The second line of research which bears heavily on our consideration of
bilateral manual activity and which is also based on a consideration of
internal variables is the work of Bizzi and his co-workers (Bizzi and Polit,
in press; Bizzi, Polit and Morasso, 1976). In their work on monkeys, they

showed quite convincingly that single arm movements are subserved by a process that specifies an equilibrium point between agonist and antagonist
musculature. This equilibrium point can be thought of as a length-tension
ratio between the agonists and antagonists of the responding limb that,
when achieved, results in termination of the movement.

From the work of Schmidt et al. and Bizzi et al. we might postulate that
for single hand movement, the subject begins by specifying an equilibrium
point in the arm to be moved. This would occur through visual inspection
of the task parameters. Once the equilibrium point is set, the movement
is initiated by the subject supplying the appropriate impulse to the limb.
The size of the impulse, or the intensity of the movement, would be determined by task requirements and experimenter imposed instructions concerning
the required speed-accuracy characteristics. In our view then, for rapid
single arm movements, the only two parameters which must be specified in
movement control are intensity and length-tension ratios. More importantly,
we maintain that the dependent measures that correspond to these two parameters are: movement time which, given a constant distance to move,
reflects the size of the impulse; and, constant error (the algebraic sum of
the end point error) which measures the subject's perceived movement amplitude. Note that movement amplitude is the result of the setting of a
length-tension ratio in the responding limb and thus constant error
reflects the bias a subject has in translating a position in space to a
length-tension ratio.

The present paper will present a summary of a series of studies designed to
elucidate the mechanisms of bilateral manual activity (Note 1). A model
will be presented which predicts that this type of activity can be understood by considering impulse generation and the setting of equilibrium
points in the two limbs. Further, the model predicts that structural
interference of impulses to the two limbs (due to neural interaction)
results in the observed facilitation and degradation effects on movement
time and, either a type of perceptual interference or structural interference results in systematic biases in the setting of the equilibrium
points of the two limbs as reflected by changes in constant error.

METHOD

Ten undergraduate students performed simultaneous two-hand lateral movements away from the midline of the body. In addition, one-hand control
movements were required for all conditions of two-hand movements. Movement
amplitudes used for both one and two-hand movements were 10 and 30 cm.
Further, the styli .the subjects were using to hit the target could be light
(50 gm;NW) or heavy (350 gm;W). In total there were 20 experimental conditions, 4 of which included the left and right single hand controls for each
amplitude and stylus weight. The 16 two-hand conditions included all combinations of stylus weight and amplitude across the 2 hands (i.e., ranging
from W10-W10 to W10-NW10 to W30-NW10).

Subjects were instructed to move as quickly and accurately as possible. For
the two-hand conditions no instructions were given concerning the simultaneity of the movements. Each trial was initiated by a "ready" command from
the experimenter, followed one sec later by a warning light, and then 1-3
sec later the stimulus light was presented. Each subject was given five
practice trials and 10 test trials for each condition. Dependent measures

were reaction time (RT), movement time (MT, effective target width (W$_e$)
defined as the standard deviation of the horizontal errors about the one
mm diameter target, and constant error (CE) which was defined as the
arithmetic mean of the algebraic errors in the horizontal dimension.

RESULTS

To best illuminate the underlying processes of bilateral movements the data
will be analyzed in two parts. First, data from one-hand movements will be
compared to the two-hand data with identical task requirements for the two
hands (i.e., the two hands were required to travel the same amplitude and
the stylus weight was the same). The second analysis is concerned with
comparing the above two-hand same conditions to conditions of two-hand
movement where the amplitude and/or stylus weight were/was different
between the two hands.

Single hand vs two-hands same. Table 1 presents all dependent measures of
interest and, as well, all significant effects found from the analysis of
variance.

Table 1

SINGLE HAND VS 2 HANDS SAME

EFFECT	REACTION TIME (msec)	MOVEMENT TIME (msec)	W$_e$ (mm)	CE (mm)
1 HAND VS 2 HANDS SAME	*	**	n.s.	n.s.
1 hand	255	201	9.73	1.62
2 hands same	263	214	10.41	2.71
DISTANCE	n.s.	**	**	*
10 cm	257	175	8.64	3.38
30 cm	260	241	11.89	.95
MASS	p~.05	**	n.s.	*
50 g(NW)	254	197	10.43	2.84
350 g(W)	263	218	10.00	1.50

** $p < .01$
* $p < .05$

For RT, the only significant effect ($p < .05$) was for the one-hand vs two-
hand contrast. Initiation of two-hand movements were eight msec slower
than for one-hand movements. MT, on the other hand, had three significant
effects: one for hands alone vs hands together ($p < .01$); another ($p < .01$)
for the amplitude manipulation of 10 cm vs 30 cm; and, the final one ($p < .01$)
for the weight of the stylus (50 gm vs 350 gm).

For W_e, only the distance manipulation proved to be significant (p<.01) with the 10 cm movement resulting in less variability. Finally, two significant effects for CE resulted from the analysis. In one, the distance effect (p<.01) resulted in the 10 cm being overshot and the 30 cm movement resulting almost in zero CE. The other effect (p<.01) saw a weighted stylus resulting in less constant error than an unweighted one.

Two-hands same vs two-hands different. The significant effects from the analysis of variance are summarized in Table 2. For RT, while there were main effects of amplitude and stylus weight these two variables both entered into significant interactions with hands (left vs right) both with p<.01. The analysis of MT gave identical statistical results as those for RT. However, both W_e and CE exhibited only a distance by hand interaction (p<.01 for both).

Table 2

2 HANDS SAME VS 2 HANDS DIFFERENT

	MASS BY HAND INTERACTION **		DISTANCE BY HAND INTERACTION **	
	LEFT	RIGHT	LEFT	RIGHT
	NW	NW	10	10
Reaction Time	262	261	259	259
Movement Time	200	201	181	178
(CE;W_e)			(4.2;8.8)	(4.2;8.1)
	W	W	30	30
Reaction Time	260	263	257	259
Movement Time	230	224	249	248
(CE;W_e)			(2.7;12.9)	(-0.8;12.2)
	NW	W	10	30
Reaction Time	255	264	259	254
Movement Time	217	219	206	226
(CE;W_e)			(13.7;10.1)	(-3.1;12.8)
	W	NW	30	10
Reaction Time	257	250	259	266
Movement Time	220	207	231	199
(CE;W_e)			(2.7;13.0)	(11.6;8.5)

** p<.01 for all dependent measures recorded

NW - stylus weight of 50 g   10 - 10 cm
 W - stylus weight of 350 g   30 - 30 cm

Kinematic analysis. In view of the significant effects that stylus weight and amplitude had on MT, it was decided to test one subject on the identical apparatus but, at the same time, through the use of light emitting diodes (LEDs) and photographic analysis, determine the displacement, velocity, and acceleration characteristics of his movements. Identical testing procedures were used except an amplitude of 20 cm was added and only two-hand movements were used. Digitization of the X,Y coordinates of each

flash of the LED (a frequency of one flash per 10 msec was used) gave a
series of these coordinates for each movement of each hand. These displacement data were then differentiated (data were filtered at 6 Hz) to
obtain velocity and then double-differentiated to obtain acceleration.

From the above data, times to peak velocity, peak acceleration, and peak
deceleration for horizontal displacement were calculated for each hand for
each trial. The means and standard deviations of these peak times were
calculated within each of the experimental conditions. Table 3 presents
these latter data.

Table 3

MEANS (SDs) OF TIMES TO PEAK MAGNITUDES (msec)

	LEFT HAND			RIGHT HAND		
CONDITION	VEL.	ACC.	DEC.	VEL.	ACC.	DEC.
NW20-NW20	75.71 (10.16)	20.00 (6.79)	135.00 (19.50)	85.00 (10.19)	27.14 (6.11)	143.57 (15.98)
W20- W20	88.57 (11.51)	21.43 (6.63)	177.86 (28.60)	97.14 (13.26)	27.86 (9.75)	198.21 (20.15)
W20-NW20	101.62 (12.20)	32.67 (11.00)	186.00 (25.01)	93.33 (11.75)	22.67 (7.04)	168.67 (20.66)
NW30-NW10	107.14 (11.39)	42.14 (10.51)	179.29 (16.39)	85.00 (17.21)	24.67 (10.60)	144.00 (19.93)
W30-NW10	100.77 (16.05)	28.46 (15.73)	203.08 (38.87)	81.15 (6.50)	22.31 (7.25)	141.54 (23.04)
W30- W10	107.33 (16.68)	31.33 (9.15)	225.33 (59.50)	88.67 (12.32)	28.00 (10.82)	156.67 (31.09)

These results confirm the above MT analysis in that there are rather different peak times when the two hands are moving different amplitudes or
with different weighted styli. It is only in the NW20-NW20 and W20-W20 conditions that peak times between the hands show some correspondence. Finally,
correlations of these peak times between hands (e.g., peak velocity of left
hand with peak velocity of right hand) showed the velocities, accelerations, and decelerations to be practically unrelated. Only two of the 18
correlations were significant (p<.05), with the range from r=.02 to r=.56.

DISCUSSION

While the main purpose of this work is to explain the nature of bimanual
control, the discussion would be only partially complete if the mechanisms
underlying its organization and initiation were not also included. For this
reason, RT results were of interest and several meaningful results occurred.

From Table 1, two results are noteworthy. First is the fact that the time
to initiate two hands is longer than the time to intiate one hand movements.
Second, although not apparent from Table 1, the RT for left and right hands,
in both the hands alone and the hands same conditions, were virtually identical. The nearly identical reaction times for left and right hands in
both distance and mass conditions are seen in the top half of Table 2 and
these results are in agreement with Kelso et al. (in press). At first
glance these data appear to argue for one control process (a motor program)
governing the organization of both hands. The only difference between the
one-hand and two-hand conditions would be that a more complex program is
necessary for the two-hand same movements, resulting in a longer RT.

The above analysis, however, is insufficient to answer the question of why
bilateral activity is more complex than unimanual movement. It may be because two limbs are involved, two impulses must be organized, two equilibrium points must be set, or some combination of these variables. An
answer, however, can be obtained by comparing RT for bimanual movements
with the same task requirements to RT for bimanual movements with different
task requirements for the two hands.

The above analysis of RT data is presented in Table 2 and, as reported in
the results section, a hands by distance and a hands by mass interaction
resulted. These interactions revealed that when the two hands are making
movements with different task requirements RT is longer in the hand with
the increased mass (in the mass by hand interaction) and longer for the 10
cm movement (in the distance by hand interaction). While we do not want to
dwell on why 10 cm movements appear more complex than 30 cm movement the
overall results are clear in identifying three factors involved in the
organization of bimanual activity; viz., hands, mass (intensity or force-
time), and distance (equilibrium points or length-tension ratios). We
interpret the distance effect as representing the setting of length-tension
ratios because when the hands are making identical movements, there is no
main effect of distance on RT. It is only when the hands must move different distances (i.e., requiring the setting of different length-tension
ratios) that this effect becomes apparent. While it might be tempting to
explain this distance effect as an effect due to differences in required
intensity (the 30 cm movement would require a larger impulse), the fact
that there was no mass by distance interaction seriously challenges the
validity of this interpretation.

The results are clear, then, in indicating three factors underlying the
organization of movement for bimanual activity. The fact that mass and
distance both interact with hands, however, would indicate that these three
factors are not represented by three independent processing stages. The
factor of hands seems to reflect an important stage in movement organization and our results (Table 2) indicate that there is a fundamental asymmetry between the two hands. It can be observed in the distance by hand
interaction that, across conditions, the variability of the left hand RT is
much smaller than that of the right hand (e.g., compare the left hand RT in
the 10-10 condition with the 10-30 condition vs the right hand performance
in the 10-10 condition with the 30-10 condition). We believe this organizational asymmetry to be a pervasive phenomenon not only in bilateral manual
activity but also in unimanual activity and plan to further investigate its
fundamental characteristics.

We now turn to a discussion of movement execution. From Table 1 we can see that, in comparing one-hand MT to two-hand MT, two hands took longer to execute; the 30 cm movement had a longer MT than the 10 cm movement; and added weight to the stylus slowed MT. The first of these findings is inconsistent with the findings of Kelso et al. (in press) although, it must be mentioned that if one examines the individual cell means of the alone vs together conditions (which are averaged over the weight conditions) the effect of going from one hand to two is much less for no weight data. However, this trend was not statistically reliable in that there was no mass by one vs two hands interaction.

The distance and mass effects on MT are directly related to a study by Fitts (1954) where the distance effect agrees with the now known Fitts' law but, unlike his study, the mass of the stylus did affect MT. Shortly, we will provide an interference explanation for why we believe two-hand movements, distance, and mass act to slow MT.

Before doing this however, one more aspect of Table 1 must be discussed. As for RT, single hand movements and two-hand movements resulted in almost identical MTs for left and right hands within any given condition. Thus, when one or two-hands together have identical task requirements, their right and left hand MTs tend to be the same (within any given condition). As in RT, for two-hand movements this can be seen in the top half of Table 2 for both the mass by hand and distance x hand interactions. These data are also consistent with our explanation of MT effects by interference processes.

To fully elucidate the control processes underlying bilateral manual movement, performance of the two hands when performing identical task requirements must be contrasted with conditions where each hand must execute movements under different task requirements. Table 2 presented this comparison and it is important that for MT, there was a mass by hand and a distance by hand interaction, while for CE only the distance by hand interaction was statistically reliable. Consider first the MT effects for the mass by hand interaction. If the condition NW-NW can be considered a control condition, compare the left hand performance to the left hand performance in the NW-W condition. An increase of 17 msec is apparent. Likewise, if one compares the left hand in the W-W condition to the left hand in the W-NW condition an observed 10 msec decrease in MT is observed. One can carry out a similar analysis for the right hand and similar results are obtained — an increase in MT in the first instance and a decrease in MT in the second. Finally, the distance by hand interaction can be broken down in a similar fashion. Again detrimental and facilitation effects are apparent.

The overall result of the above analysis yields the following conclusion. When conditions in which the two hands are required to perform under identical task requirements are taken as control values, then comparing one hand from this condition to the same hand in a condition where the two hands are performing different task requirements demonstrates a detrimental or facilitation effect in MT that is determined by the intensity requirements of the other hand. For example, when comparing the 10-10 condition to the 10-30 condition the left hand is slower in the latter condition because it is paired with a hand that must be moved by a relatively greater impulse. Similarily, comparing the 30-30 condition with the 10-30

condition, the right hand is _faster_ in the latter condition because it is
paired with a hand requiring relatively less intensity. These facilitation
and inhibition effects are consistent for both the mass by hand and distance
by hand interactions in MT. These effects form part of the basis of our
model of two-hand coordination which follows shortly.

Before presenting the model, however, the CE effects in Table 2 also present
some pertinent information regarding our notion of two-hand coordination.
Specifically, the interaction of distance by hand in CE is caused primarily
by the "range-effect" in these data for the 10-30 and 30-10 conditions.
Note that regardless of hand, the 30 cm movement is either undershot or has
a small positive error, while the 10 cm movement is dramatically overshot.
We believe these range-effects to be meaningful and indicative of a control
process quite distinct from the control process that results in MT.

Finally, two other comments about the results presented in Table 2 deserve
mention. First, there is no doubt that when the two hands have different
task requirements, their MTs are dissimilar. This finding is reinforced by
the kinematic analysis presented in Table 3 which shows quite disparate
times to peak for velocity, acceleration and deceleration. We believe
these results support the idea that at least for this type of task, _time_
has no role in the coordination of the two hands. This result is in direct
opposition to Kelso et al. (in press) who conclude from their data that
time is the invariant feature of two-hand coordination. The second point
is that again, like in RT, asymmetries between the hands can be observed in
the MT and CE data and these warrant further attention in future studies.

A model of two-hand coordination. The above results, specifically those of
RT, MT, and CE bear directly on a proposed model of two-hand coordination.

This model is derived from known structural and functional properties of
the nervous system. As reviewed previously, ipsilateral and contralateral
commands may interact at cortical, brain stem and spinal levels (Brinkman
and Kuypers, 1972; Kinsbourne and Hicks, 1978). We have noted these interactions in Figure 1 with respect to the processes involved in movement end
location and movement intensity specifications. Interaction between the
left and right nervous system can occur at: the relatively high levels
where these processes first originate; the brain stem level where movement
commands converge; or, at the spinal level where contralateral and ipsilateral projections interact from both corticospinal and descending brain
stem pathways. In this respect the model is similar to the one proposed by
Preilowski (1975).

The major prediction of the model is that interference in a limb, which
includes both inhibition and facilitation effects, is directly proportional
to the intensity of activity involved in the processes controlling the
contralateral limb. High amounts of activity destined for one limb will
inhibit activity in the contralateral limb, while low amounts of activity
will result in relative facilitation effects of the contralateral limb.

Before detailing the specific inhibition and facilitation effects, a description of the processes relevant to movement organization and execution is in
order. From the RT results noted above, we postulate that the processes
controlling two-hand movements are hemispheric specific with each hand being
controlled primarily by the contralateral hemsiphere. For the task we

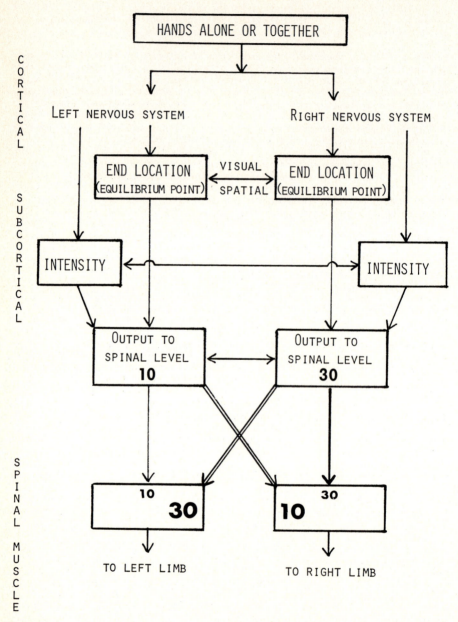

FIGURE 1.   A MODEL OF TWO HAND CO-ORDINATED CONTROL.
            (SEE TEXT FOR EXPLANATION)

investigated, three types of control processes are necessary: first, basic processes involved in the control of hands, which are asymmetrical with respect to performance; second, processes involved in setting equilibrium points (length-tension ratios of agonist and antagonist musculature); and third, processes for establishing the intensity of the intended movement.

We have used the term intensity quite by intention because the data argue strongly that subjects do not use time as a basis for executing movement and the term impulse or force-time production denotes time as a variable. Rather, we view a subject as estimating the required intensity of his movement and then, simply by issuing force commands, supplying the necessary trigger for movement initiation.

This process of intensity specification, however, is preceded by the specification of length-tension ratios to the limbs. In this respect we are in agreement with Turvey (1977) that the setting of length-tension ratios might be seen partly as pretuning effects which occur within the spinal cord before movement begins. The important point about establishing length-tension ratios is that, as Bizzi and his colleagues (1976, in press) have shown, the limb is capable of reaching its end point autonomously once the trigger for movement is supplied.

The importance of the above discussion is the prediction that specifications of intensities and equilibrium points are two independent processes. A subject can set a particular length-tension ratio for a limb, determined by the spatial demands of the task, and then proceed to acquire the spatial target with a wide range of intensities. The end result is that the target will be reached but the kinetics, and hence the kinematics, of the movement will vary dramatically depending on the intensity specification. As mentioned in the previous section we see our MT and CE data as reflecting the intensity and equilibrium point specifications, respectively.

Our model presents a relatively direct prediction about interference in the intensity specification. As Figure 1 illustrates interference can occur at the subcortical level (as represented by the arrows joining the intensity specification processes and the output to spinal level processes) and at the spinal level where ipsilateral and contralateral efferent commands interact. Figure 1 diagrams what happens when "10" units of intensity are specified by the left nervous system for the right limb and "30" units of intensity are specified for the left limb. Because of subcortical or spinal level interactions the left limb has very little inhibition and the right limb has a large amount of inhibition because of the simultaneous activity. This logic can be used to describe why, when the left hand is required to move with high intensity at the same time as a high intensity right hand movement (e.g., W10-W10), it will be inhibited (i.e., lengthened) in MT as compared to when it is paired with a right hand moving with low intensity (e.g., W10-NW10).

This interference in the intensity specification also explains why unimanual activity has faster MTs than bimanual activity. In the former situation there is no contralateral activity and thus the limb moves free from inhibition. However, any contralateral activity, as in two-hand movements, would result in an increase in MT to the limb even though the external task requirements for that limb are identical to the unimanual condition.

The same rationale can be applied to the observed interference effects in the setting of equilibrium points as reflected by CE. However, a rival interpretation, perceptual in nature, can also be advanced. In this latter case, interference would be seen to result from visual-spatial sources and would occur in the actual setting of the equilibrium points. Either interference explanation would predict the present results.

In summary then, the model predicts three basic control processes. The first two, intensity and equilibrium point specifications are modified by the third hand/hemisphere asymmetrical organizational process. The former two processes are seen to be relatively independent with only distance (end point) manipulations affecting length-tension ratio specifications (as reflected by CE) and both distance (how fast or intensely the limb has to travel to the end point) and mass manipulations affecting intensity specifications (as reflected in MT). Further, the model predicts interference effects for both of these processes due to interaction of neural activity at subcortical and spinal levels.

REFERENCE NOTE

1. A more comprehensive report of the entire series of experiments is in preparation (Marteniuk, R.G.; MacKenzie, C.L. and Baba, D.M., in preparation).

REFERENCES

[1] Babinski, J., Sur le role cervelet dans les actes volitionnels necessitant une succession rapide des mouvements (deadococinesie). Review of Neurology, 10 (1902) 1013.

[2] Bizzi, E. and Polit, A., Processes controlling visually evoked movements, Neuropsychologia (in press).

[3] Bizzi, E., Polit, A. and Morasso, P., Mechanisms underlying achievement of final head position, Journal of Neurophysiology, 39 (1976) 435-444.

[4] Brinkman, J. and Kuypers, H.G.J.M., Splitbrain monkeys: Cerebral control of ipsilateral and contralateral arm, hand, and finger movements, Science, 176 (1972) 536-538.

[5] Cohen, L., Interaction between limbs during bimanual voluntary activity, Brain, 93 (1970) 259-272.

[6] Fitts, P.M., The information capacity of the human motor system in controlling the amplitude of movements, Journal of Experimental Psychology, 47 (1954) 381-391.

[7] Hartmann-von Monakow, K., Akert, K. and Künzle, H., Projections of precentral and premotor cortex to the red nucleus and other midbrain areas in Macaca Fascicularis, Experimental Brain Research, 34 (1979) 91-105.

[8] Hausmanowa-Petrusewicz, I., Interaction in simultaneous motor functions, Archives of Neurology and Psychiatry, 81 (1959) 173-187.

[9]   Kelso, J.A.S., Southard, D.L. and Goodman, D., On the coordination of
      two-handed movements, Journal of Experimental Psychology: Human
      Perception and Performance (in press).

[10] Kinsbourne, M. and Hicks, R.E., Functional cerebral space: A model
      for overflow, transfer and interference effects in human performance.
      In: J. Requin (ed.). Attention and Performance VII (New York: Academic
      Press, 1978)

[11] Marteniuk, R.G. and MacKenzie, C.L., Information processing in move-
      ment organization and execution. In: R.S. Nickerson and R.W. Pew
      (eds.) Attention and Performance VIII (New York: Academic Press, in
      press).

[12] Preilowski, B., Bilateral motor interaction: Perceptual-motor perfor-
      mance of partial and complete "split-brain" patients. In: Zülch, K.S.,
      Creutzfeldt, O. and Galbraith, G.C. (eds.) Cerebral Localization
      (Berlin: Springer, 1975) 115-132.

[13] Schmidt, R.A., Zelaznik, H.N. and Frank, J.S., Sources of inaccuracy
      in rapid movement. In: G.E. Stelmach (ed.) Information processing in
      motor control and learning (New York: Academic Press, 1978).

[14] Turvey, M.T., Preliminaries to a theory of action with reference to
      vision. In: R. Shaw and J. Bransford (eds.) Perceiving, acting and
      knowing: Toward an ecological psychology (Hillsdale, N.J.: Erlbaum,
      1977).

[15] Woodworth, R.S. The accuracy of voluntary movement. Psychological
      Review, 3 (1899) (Whole No. 13) 1-114.

Tutorials in Motor Behavior
G.E. Stelmach and J. Requin (eds.)
© *North-Holland Publishing Company, 1980*

11

THE ORGANIZATION OF SIMPLE, SKILLED MOVEMENTS

J.D. Cooke
Department of Physiology
University of Western Ontario
London, Canada

A simple model of the limb is proposed in which
the limb is visualized as a simple damped spring with
mass. 'Movements' in the model are produced by step
changes in spring stiffness. Comparisons are made
between the behaviour of the model and step-tracking
movements made by human subjects. The model provides
adequate qualitative description of these simple limb
movements and provides an explanation for such observations as the linear relation between movement
amplitude and peak velocity seen in humans. Changes
in movement performance produced by the instruction
given to the subject and in some pathological states
can be explained on the basis of the model.

From a comparison of the responses to sudden perturbations it is suggested that the stretch reflexes
act to return the limb as quickly as possible to
its non-perturbed or learned trajectory.

How do we move our limbs from one position to another? In recent years
attention has been particularly directed at the role of the central nervous system in the generation and control of movement. The advent of
single unit recording in the behaving animal has led to detailed studies
of such areas as sensory and motor cortices (10,11,12,19,20,42), cerebellum (45,46,47), basal ganglia (16,17) and parietal cortex (35). Although
studies of this type have deepened our understanding of the central motor
apparatus, it must be acknowledged that we are still not much closer to
being able to describe how the central systems operate or interact in the
generation of simple movements.

One area which has been somewhat neglected by students of motor control
is muscle, the final effector of the system. As Partridge (40) recently
reminded us, "muscle is the final filter through which all motor output
must pass". Partridge also suggested that, in some situations, muscle
may act as something more than a final filter. Rather it may be that the
central nervous system utilizes the mechanical properties of muscles to
more easily accomplish desired movements.

Some experimental evidence for this point of view has come from studies by
Fel'dman (22,23) and by Bizzi and co-workers (2,3,41) on the maintenance
of static limb position. Fel'dman suggested that when the limb is in a
static position a state of equilibrium exists between the forces acting
about the joint (Fig. 1A). Since, if a static position is being maintained, muscle velocity is zero, the force exerted by the opposing muscles
is determined by their length-tension curves (Fig. 1B). Additionally he
suggested that movement to a new position would be accompanied by a shift
in the relevant length-tension curves, by, for example a change in slope.
Such a change in slope is equivalent to a change in the stiffness in the

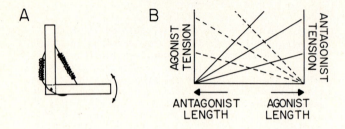

Fig. 1: Representation of a simple model of the
human arm. As indicated in A, movement of the
forearm is considered to be under the control of
two springs representing the opposing muscles
acting about the elbow joint. In B are shown
diagrammatically the length-tension curves of
the opposing muscles. The slope of these lines
indicated muscle stiffness. Note that movement
to a new limb position (change in muscle lengths)
can be produced by altering the stiffness of the
muscles.

muscles. Thus as indicated in Fig. 1A, the muscles might be visualized as
simple springs whose stiffnesses could be altered.

One of the most striking but least recognized characteristics of simple
arm movements made by humans or by well trained primates is their reproducibility or degree of stereotyping. This is illustrated in Fig. 2 in
which average records of movements made during a visual step-tracking task
are shown. One is immediately struck by the low variance in these average
records. This high degree of repeatability of the limb trajectory from
movement to movement is also pointed up by examination of phase plane
plots of the individual movements (Fig. 2B). These representations of the
movement trajectory are obtained by plotting limb velocity (ordinate) as
a function of limb position (abscissa) and are relatively sensitive to
minor variations in limb trajectory. As is seen in Fig. 2B these plots
indicate little variation in limb trajectory in a series of movements.

Although the limb trajectories during performance of well practised movements show little variability, there is considerable variation in the EMG
activity associated with these movements (Fig. 3A). The movements shown
in this figure were associated with a typical pattern of EMG activity first
described by Wacholder and Altenburger (48) and more recently by Hallett
et al. (28). The EMG pattern consists of an initial burst of activity in
the agonist (biceps) termed B1 by Hallett et al. Following this initial

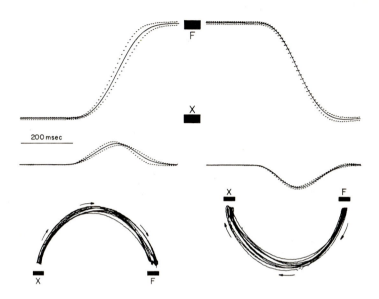

Fig. 2. Step tracking movements performed by a normal human subject.
The top two traces show records of average position and velocity
during performance of flexion (left hand traces) and extension (right
hand traces) movements. The dots around each trace indicate standard deviations. Each trace is the average of 10-15 movements.
The solid bars indicate the target positions. Target center separation is 65 deg and target width 6 deg. Below each velocity record
are shown phase plane plots of the individual movements from which
the averages were obtained. For these plots limb velocity (ordinate)
is plotted as a function of limb position (abscissa) during the
movement. The arrows show the direction of evolution of the plots
during the movements. Note that all movements started with an
initial velocity of zero; the phase planes for the extension
movements have been displaced upwards relative to those for the
flexion movements (DC090579).

burst, the agonist becomes relatively quiescent and activity is seen in
the antagonist (T1). Finally, the agonist again becomes active (B2). As
illustrated in Fig. 3, the variability of the EMG burst magnitudes is high
compared to that of the movement trajectories. Standard deviations of the
burst magnitudes approximate the mean burst magnitudes. In spite of this
variability in the phasic EMG activity there is little variability in the
associated movements. A similar phenomenon has been described in the cat
step cycle (40).

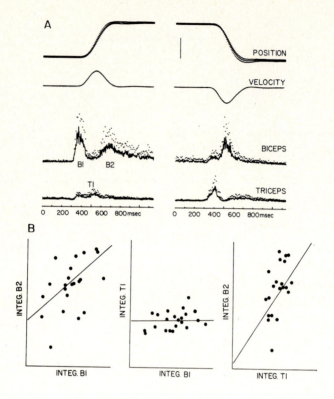

Fig. 3: In A are shown average records from step-tracking movements
by a normal subject. Each trace is the average of 20-25 movements.
An upward deflection of the position trace indiciates flexion of
the forearm. Standard deviations are shown on the position trace
and on the EMG records. The EMG bursts associated with the flexion
movements are identified using the nomenclature of Hallet et al.
(28). In B are shown the interrelation between the integrated EMGs
during bursts associated with the flexion movements in A. The lines
through the points are the best-fit linear regression lines and have
the equations

$$B2 = 270 + 0.90(B1) \quad r = 0.48$$
$$T1 = 307 + 0.01(B1) \quad r = 0.05$$
$$B2 = 544 + 3.84(T1) \quad r = 0.37$$

Now, if movements are generated or controlled primarily by this phasic EMG
activity one would have expected considerable variation in movement trajectories even though the limb could end up at the same final position. One
possible explanation could be that changes in the activity of the agonist

(for example) are compensated for by changed antagonist activity. For
example, if the magnitude of the initial agonist burst (B1) were decreased,
one might expect to see a concomitant decrease in the T1 amplitude. That
such compensatory changes do not occur is indicated in Fig. 3B which shows
correlograms of the integrated EMG components from a large series of movements. The possibility that the movement trajectory is not primarily determined by the associated phasic EMG activity must therefore be considered.

(It must, however, be pointed out that it is slightly naive to consider
only biceps and triceps muscles; other muscles undoubtedly contribute to
these movements. In addition it is possible that varying EMGs in the
prime movers of the forearm may be compensated for or be in response to
alterations in shoulder positioning, etc. An alternate explanation will
be described below).

The suggestion I would like to put forward is an extension of the idea
formulated by Fel'dman. This is that the trajectory of limb movement is
determined to a large extent by simple changes in the limb mechanical properties (13). I would suggest that an adequate model for the generation
of the kinds of movements I have been describing is provided by considering
the limb as a simple second order system. That is, one in which the limb
behaves as if it were a damped spring having mass. Such a model for muscle
has been used for at least half a century, for example by Gasser and Hill
in 1924 (27). The usefulness of the model is attested to by its continued
use (1,37,38,43).

In order to test this hypothesis an analog model of a damped spring with
mass was utilized (13). That is the following equation was modelled

$$m \frac{d^2x}{dt^2} + n \frac{dx}{dt} + kx = F_o$$

Mass (m), viscosity (n) and stiffness (k) were independently variable as
was the 'externally' applied force to the system (F_o). The circuit utilized is shown in Fig. 4C. Movements in the model were produced by a step
change in the slopes of the length-tension curves of the relevant muscles
(Fig. 1B). Note that the model was a lumped model; the two antagonistic
muscles were not modelled separately. In Fig. 4B are shown records of
'movements' obtained from the model which can be compared with those from
a normal human subject in Fig. 4A. Casual inspection reveals little difference between them. Shown in Fig. 4D are phase plane plots of movements
of different amplitudes performed by a human subject and by the model.
The different amplitude movements in the model were obtained by step
changes to different stiffness values from the same initial stiffness.

Recall that movements in the model were generated by step changes in
resting stiffness. How dependent is the movement trajectory on variations
in the final stiffness? That is, we are asking the same question as we
asked about the variability in the EMG records: how much effect on the
actual limb trajectory will random variations in the final stiffness value
have? By considering how springs behave it is obvious that for isotonic
movements the final position (or spring length) will vary with the stiffness. For an ideal spring, F = -kx. Length, x, is thus linearly dependent on k if the net force F, is constant. One would thus expect some

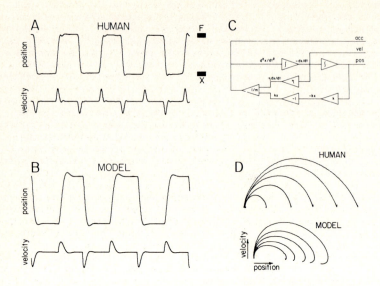

Fig. 4: Movements made by a normal human and by an analog model of
the limb. Shown in C is a simplified circuit diagram of the analog
model of the limb (see text). In A are shown position and velocity
records of movements made by a normal subject during performance of
a visually guided step-tracking task. The target center separation
was 65 deg and the total duration of the trace is 15 sec. In B are
shown analogous traces obtained from the model in which 'movements'
were produced by a step change in the resting spring constant. In D
are shown phase plane plots of movements of different amplitudes
obtained from a normal subject (upper set) and from the model (lower
set). Each phase plane from the subject was derived from the average
of 10-15 movements. Movement amplitudes ranged from 16-80 deg.
Different amplitude movements in the model were produced by step
changes to different final stiffnesses from the same initial stiffness (DC230479, DC090579).

variation in the limb's trajectory associated with the changed movement
amplitude. This indeed can be seen in the phase planes from the human subjects shown in Fig. 2. It should be noted however that the model is a
lumped model; no attempt was made to separately model the antagonistic
muscles. If one considers an ideal spring system, proportional changes in
the stiffness of two springs acting in opposition to each other would result in no change in length of either of the springs. Such changes in
stiffness would tend to counteract each other.

The behaviour of this mechanical model of movement is consistent with another heretofore puzzling aspect of simple movements. It has been found
that there is a linear relationship between peak velocity of movement and
movement amplitude (4,15). Recent experiments in our laboratory (15) have

shown that this relationship holds for step-tracking movement when the
subject is required to vary his motor output over a wide range. In Fig. 5A
are shown velocity-amplitude relationships from experiments in which subjects performed step-tracking movements. Trials were made with the subjects being given the following instructions: a) move as accurately as
possible, b) move as rapidly as possible and c) move in whatever manner you
wish. For this latter instruction no visual target was provided, the subject being free to choose his own movement amplitude. Subjects were cued
to move by an auditory tone. A linear relation between movement peak
velocity and amplitude is seen in each case. Correlation coefficients of
the individual regression lines ranged from 0.85 to 0.98. The effect of
the different instructions, which could produce a doubling of the peak
velocity, is to alter the slope of the relationship; the basic linear
character is unchanged. Is such a linear interrelationship between the
parameters of the movements indicative of the 'organization' of the movements or of the method by which the movements are generated? If so, one
would suggest that all the different movements for Fig. 5A were generated
utilizing some common organization or program. The differences in the
motor output related to the different instructions might have been generated by altering variables in this common motor program.

It should be noted that such relations between movement amplitude and peak
velocity do not imply that movement time is independent of movement amplitude. Preliminary experiments indicate that movement time is directly
dependent on movement amplitude as had been shown for arm movements by
monkeys (5,6,9). The movements described here do not, however, obey Fitts'
Law which describes interrelationships between movement time and movement
amplitude and accuracy. This is presumably due to the lack of a mechanical end-point to these movements in contrast to the movements studied by
Fitts (24,25).

In Fig. 5B are shown similar relations obtained from the model of the limb.
The peak velocity-amplitude relationship is well approximated as a linear
function. The model thus predicts the relationship observed in human subjects. On what is the slope of this relation dependent? The answer to
this comes from considering that movements in the model were generated by
a step change in spring stiffness from some resting or initial value (k_i)
to some final value (k_f). As has been described (Fig. 4C) the amplitude
or final end-point of the movement will depend on the value of k_f. What
of the initial stiffness? As indicated in Fig. 5B, changing the initial
stiffness changes the slope of the peak velocity-amplitude curve for movements in the model: an increased slope is produced by increasing the
resting stiffness. This observation accords with the common experience of
tensing or co-contracting in the expectation of performing a very rapid
movement.

Another observation explainable in terms of this model is the decrease in
movement velocity when external masses are added to the limb. As shown in
Fig. 5C, increasing the mass in the model produces a decrease in the slope
of the peak velocity-amplitude curve. That is, for a given movement amplitude, velocity decreases with increasing mass.

This model of movements generated by relatively simple changes in the limb
mechanical properties may bear on some of the alterations in movement performance seen in pathological states. For example, the hypotonia observed

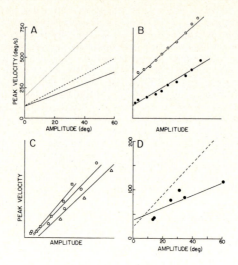

Fig. 5: Velocity-amplitude relations in human subjects and in the
model. In A are shown mean linear regression lines obtained from
movements performed by two subjects. Three instructions were used
during performance of the step tracking movements: fast and accurate - dotted line; accurate - dashed line and voluntary - solid
line (see text) (DC010578, VN020578). In B are shown analogous
curves obtained from the analog model of the limb. Points plotted
as open circles were obtained with a resting spring constant double
that for points plotted as closed circles. In C the effect of
altered mass on the velocity amplitude relation in the model is
shown. The curves were obtained with relative masses of 0.7
(squares), 1.0 (circles) and 1.4 (triangles). In D the velocity-
amplitude relation obtained from a patient with a unilateral
cerebellar lesion is shown. The data was obtained approximately
4 months following the acute onset of unilateral cerebellar dysfunction. Shown for comparison is an average regression line
obtained from data from three normal subjects (dashed line)
(210677).

clinically as a result of cerebellar dysfunction (29) corresponds to a
decrease in the overall resting stiffness in the model. One would thus
expect to observe a decrease in the slope of the peak velocity-amplitude
relations in these patients. Such a decrease has indeed been observed
(7) and is shown in Fig. 5D. It should also be pointed out that the hypermetria commonly seen in patients with cerebellar dysfunction could also
arise from this decrease in resting stiffness. If movement to a given position is 'programmed' or 'learned' in terms of the final stiffness levels,
setting the stiffness to this final value from an initially decreased level will result in an increase in movement amplitude.

The model for simple arm movements as described thus far is qualitatively

adequate. Any such model must, however, be able to describe not only normal operation of the modelled system but must also respond to external
disturbances in the same way as does the modelled system. Comparisons
were therefore made of the behaviour of the model and of normal human subjects in response to brief torque perturbations applied during movement
(13,14). In particular, attention has been paid to the effect of perturbations on the movement trajectory. As has been described (13) and is
illustrated in Fig. 6E, one of the most striking observations with the
human subjects was that the limb trajectory following perturbation was
very similar to the trajectory of the non-perturbed, control movements.
This however did not occur in the model and it thus appeared that the
model was inadequate.

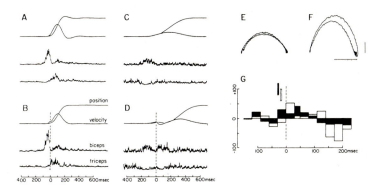

Fig. 6: Effect of sudden perturbations during 'fast' and 'slow'
movements. Shown in A-D are records of limb position and velocity
and of rectified surface biceps and triceps EMGs during performance of step-tracking movements. Each record is the average of
10-15 movements. A and B were obtained from 'fast' movements and
C and D from 'slow' movements. The vertical dashed lines in B
and D indicate the time of onset of a 50 msec perturbation
opposing the flexion movements. The corresponding phase planes
are shown in E (slow movements) and F (fast movements). Note that
following the perturbation in E the limb trajectory closely
resembles the control trajectory whereas in F the control trajectory was not regained following the perturbation. In G the
difference between the biceps EMG during the perturbed and non-
perturbed movements is plotted. EMG traces were aligned at the
onset of the EMG activity preceding movement and integration
performed over discrete bins preceding and following onset of
the perturbation. The solid bars show data from the 'slow' movements and the open bars from the 'fast' movements. The thin
vertical bars indicate movement onset and the vertical dashed
line the perturbation onset. Note that 'reflex' activity is
present in the period 30-80 msec following the perturbation in
the 'slow' but not in the 'fast' movements (A-D VN140379,
E-G RJ040379).

One difference between this simple model and real limbs is that the model does not generate reflex responses to sudden perturbations. As seen in the EMG records in Fig. 6D such responses were indeed evoked by the perturbation in the human subjects. The possibility that reflex responses to sudden limb displacement could be involved with the return to the control trajectory was tested by incorporating a 'pseudo-reflex' into the model. This reflex consisted of a force following the perturbation and in a direction opposite to the perturbation. It was found that the trajectory of the perturbed movements in the model could be made to rematch the control trajectory as closely as desired by appropriate manipulation of the magnitude of the pseudo-reflex (13,14). This then suggested that the degree of rematching of limb trajectories following perturbations depends on the gain of the stretch reflexes.

Little or no reflex response occurs following a perturbation applied during movements where the subject is required to move as rapidly as possible (14,18) (Fig. 6A, D). One would therefore predict that a perturbation applied during such movements would produce a more marked disturbance of movement trajectory which would not return to the control trajectory. Such an effect has indeed been seen and an example is shown in Fig. 6E, F. For the experiment in E, the subject was requested to move 'as accurately as possible' between the target zones. As was described, the trajectory following the perturbation closely matched the control trajectory. For part F of the figure the subject was asked to make rapid movements as indicated by the increased peak velocity of movement in the phase planes. In this case, the movement trajectory following the perturbation did not return to the control trajectory. In G of this figure are shown the differences between the integrated EMGs of the perturbed and non-perturbed movements. In the period from 30-100 msec following the perturbation, activity is seen in the slow movements which is not present in the fast movements. It is in this time period that one would expect any reflex responses to the perturbation to be present (31,32).

As has been clearly stated by Marsden (33) "It is generally accepted that the muscle spindle machinery possesses the properties of a length servo system ... to maintain a constant muscle length". Reflex activity in response to sudden perturbations has thus been seen as a load compensating system attempting to restore muscle length and thereby restore limb position. This view has recently been questioned by Houk (30,37) who has suggested that the stretch reflex acts primarily to linearize the length-tension properties of muscle. The value of this action is that "... the central nervous system probably has access to a model of the system that it controls and ... the model is bound to be simpler if the neuromuscular system behaves in a linear manner" (37). The data presented here and elsewhere (13,14) also suggest that the reflex responses to sudden stretch are not simply involved in length regulation. In agreement with Houk, I would suggest that the CNS has a model of these simple, well learned movements and that on the basis of learning the CNS can predict limb velocities at any limb position during a given movement. The action of the stretch reflexes is to return the limb to some point on this known trajectory so that the CNS can predict the future course of the movement. It must be remembered that in the experiments which have been described the perturbation which was applied was always of the same magnitude but was applied randomly throughout a series of movements. Initial observations indicate that limb trajectory does not return to the control trajectory following the initial application of the perturbation. Thus, in this action of returning the limb to a known state the stretch reflex may be adaptive as has been indicated in other situations (36).

What conclusions can be drawn from the foregoing? First, it appears that many of the characteristics of simple step movements by normal human subjects are explainable if the movements are generated or programmed through changes in the limb mechanical properties. The studies with the model suggest that a step change in limb stiffness would suffice to produce movements similar to those actually observed. It must, however, be emphasized that there are indeed other factors involved in the performance of these simple movements. The question must be raised as to the function of the phasic EMG activity seen in association with movements (cf. Figs. 3A, 6A, C). Current views on the phasic EMG components undoubtedly owe, in great part, to the analysis of Stetson and Bouman (44) who suggested that "The excursion of the limb may be divided into three phases (1) the sudden impulse due to the momentary contraction of the unopposed driving muscles; (2) the free phase, during which the limb swings by its own momentum and has no dynamic connection with the pivot-joint; (3) the arresting phase, during which an outside obstacle, or the contraction of the antagonists stops the movement". At least for 'fast' movements, it has been suggested that the three phase pattern of EMG activity is centrally programmed and only partially under the influence of peripheral events (26,28). Recent studies in our laboratory (8,15) have however indicated the following. First, a burst pattern of EMG activity is seen in 'fast' movements which varies widely in terms of movement amplitude and/or velocity. Secondly, movement amplitude and velocity are poorly and inconsistently related to the magnitudes or durations of the various EMG bursts. Surprisingly, when one looks at these relations in step movements which are made relatively slowly by asking the subject to be 'accurate' in his movements (cf. Figs. 5A, 6C) movement amplitude and velocity are strongly related to the magnitude of the initial burst of agonist activity. Thirdly, in contrast to what was suggested by Hallett et al. (26) it was found that the initial burst of agonist activity could be strongly modified by a perturbation applied preceding the onset of the burst.

In view of the above I would suggest that the phasic drive to alpha motoneurones which is associated with these step movements may subserve different functions under different contexts in which the movements are made. In general their role is to augment or assist the underlying mechanical mechanism for movement generation. Contextual information has been found to be of importance in the generation of cortical or muscular responses to sudden limb perturbation (21). I would suggest that the subject's interpretation of the experimenter's requirements for such things as accuracy, speed, etc. lead to a variable modification of the underlying or base movement by the generation of the phasic input to the muscles.

The author gratefully acknowledges the critical commentary of V. B. Brooks, S. Brown and C. Capaday in the preparation of this manuscript. Studies on cerebellar patients were done in collaboration with J. D. Brown. The author's laboratory is supported by the Medical Research Council of Canada (Grant #MA-6699).

REFERENCES:

[1] Bawa, P. and Stein, R. B., Frequency response of human soleus muscle,
      J. Neurophysiol. 39 (1976) 788-793.
[2] Bizzi, E., Dev, P., Morasso, P. and Polit, A., The effect of load
      disturbances during centrally initiated movements, J. Neurophysiol.
      41 (1978) 542-556.
[3] Bizzi, E., Polit, A. and Morasso, P., Mechanisms underlying achieve-
      ment of final head position, J. Neurophysiol. 39 (1976) 435-444.
[4] Bonisset, S. and Lestienne, F., The organisation of a simple volun-
      tary movement as analysed from its kinematic properties, Brain Res.
      71 (1974) 451-457.
[5] Brooks, V. B., Some examples of programmed limb movements, Brain Res.
      71 (1974) 299-308.
[6] Brooks, V. B., Cooke, J. D. and Thomas, J. S., in: Stein, R. B.,
      Pearson, K. B., Smith, R. S. and Redford, J. B. (eds.), Control of
      Posture and Locomotion (Plenum Press, New York, 1973) 257-272.
[7] Brown, J. D. and Cooke, J. D., Bilateral changes in movement perfor-
      mance following unilateral cerebellar lesions in humans, 8th Ann.
      Meeting, Soc. for Neuroscience (1978) Abstr. 915.
[8] Brown, S. H. C. and Cooke, J. D., Modification of movement-related
      EMG activity by perturbations applied before onset of voluntary human
      arm movements, 9th Ann. Meeting, Soc. for Neuroscience (1979).
[9] Conrad, B. and Brooks, V. B., Effects of dentate cooling on rapid
      alternating arm movements, J. Neurophysiol. 37 (1974) 792-804.
[10] Conrad, B., Matsunami, K., Meyer-Lohmann, J., Wiesendanger, M. and
      Brooks, V. B., Cortical load compensation during voluntary elbow
      movements, Brain Res. 71 (1974) 507-514.
[11] Conrad, B., Wiesendanger, M., Matsunami, K. and Brooks, V. B., Pre-
      central unit activity related to control of arm movements, Exp.
      Brain Res. 29 (1977) 85-95.
[12] Conrad, B., Meyer-Lohmann, J., Matsunami, K. and Brooks, V. B., Pre-
      central unit activity following torque pulse injections into elbow
      movements, Brain Res. 94 (1975) 219-236.
[13] Cooke, J. D., Dependence of human arm movements on limb mechanical
      properties, Brain Res. 165 (1979) 366-369.
[14] Cooke, J. D., The role of stretch reflexes during active movements,
      Brain Res. (1979)(submitted).
[15] Cooke, J. D. and Brown, S. H. C., "Non-guided" limb movements in
      normal humans, Proc. Can. Fed. Biol. Soc., 21 (1978) 90.
[16] de Long, M. R., Activity of pallidal neurons during movement, J.
      Neurophysiol., 34 (1974) 414-427.
[17] de Long, M. and Strick, P. L., Relation of basal ganglia, cerebellum
      and motor cortex units to ramp and ballistic limb movements, Brain
      Res. 71 (1974) 327-335.
[18] Desmedt, J. E. and Godaux, E., Ballistic skilled movements: load
      compensation and patterning of the motor commands, in: Desmedt, J. E.
      (ed.), Cerebral Motor Control in Man: Long Loop Mechanisms 4
      (Karger, Basel, 1978) 21-55.
[19] Evarts, E. V., Relation of pyramidal tract activity to force exerted
      during voluntary movement, J. Neurophysiol. 31 (1968) 14-27.
[20] Evarts, E. V., Activity of pyramidal tract neurons during postural
      fixation, J. Neurophysiol. 39 (1969) 375-385.
[21] Evarts, E. V. and Tanji, J., Gating of motor cortex reflexes by
      prior instruction, Brain Res. 71 (1974) 479-494.

[22] Fel'dman, A. G., Change in the length of the muscle as a consequence
      of a shift in equilibrium in the muscle-load system, Biofizika 19
      (1974) 534-538.
[23] Fel'dman, A. G., Control of the length of the muscle, Biofizika 19
      (1974) 749-753.
[24] Fitts, P. M., The information capacity of the human motor system in
      controlling the amplitude of movement, J. Exp. Psychol. 47 (1954)
      381-391.
[25] Fitts, P. M. and Peterson, S. R., Information capacity of discrete
      motor responses, J. Exp. Psychol. 67 (1964) 103-112.
[26] Garland, H. and Angel, R. W., Spinal and supraspinal factors in
      voluntary movement, Exp. Neurol. 33 (1971) 343-350.
[27] Gasser, H. S. and Hill, A. V., The dynamics of muscular contraction,
      Proc. R. Soc. B. 96 (1924) 398-437.
[28] Hallett, M., Shahani, B. T. and Young, R. R., EMG analysis of stereo-
      typed voluntary movements in man, J. Neurol. Neurosurg. Psychiatry
      38 (1975) 1154-1162.
[29] Holmes, G., Clinical symptoms of cerebellar disease and their inter-
      pretation. The Croonian Lectures I, Lancet 202 (1922) 1177-1182.
[30] Houk, J. C., Regulation of stiffness by skeletomotor reflexes, Annu.
      Rev. Physiol. 41 (1979) 99-114.
[31] Lee, R. G. and Tatton, W. G., Motor responses to sudden limb dis-
      placements in primates with specific CNS lesions and in human pa-
      tients with motor system disorders, Can. J. Neurol. Sci. 2 (1975)
      285-293.
[32] Lee, R. G. and Tatton, W. G., Long loop reflexes in man: clinical
      applications, in: Desmedt, J. E. (ed.), Cerebral Motor Control in
      Man: Long Loop Mechanisms 4 (Karger, Basel, 1978) 320-333.
[33] Marsden, C. D., Servo control, the stretch reflex and movement in
      man, in: Desmedt, J. E. (ed.), New Developments in Electromyography
      and Clinical Neurophysiology 3 (Karger, Basel, 1973) 375-382.
[34] Melvill Jones, G. and Watt, D. G. D., Observations on the control of
      stepping and hopping movements in man, J. Physiol. 219 (1971)
      709-727.
[35] Mountcastle, V. B., Lynch, J. C., Georgopoulos, A., Sakata, H. and
      Acuna, C., Posterior parietal association cortex of the monkey:
      command functions for operations within extrapersonal space,
      J. Neurophysiol. 38 (1975) 871-908.
[36] Nashner, L. M., Adaptive reflexes controlling the human posture,
      Exp. Brain Res. 26 (1976) 59-72.
[37] Nichols, T. R. and Houk, J. C., Improvement in linearity and regu-
      lation of stiffness that results from actions of stretch reflex,
      J. Neurophysiol. 39 (1976) 119-142.
[38] Partridge, L. D., Signal handling characteristics of load-moving
      skeletal muscle, Am. J. Physiol. 210 (1966) 1178-1191.
[39] Partridge, L. D., Interrelationships studied in a semibiological
      "reflex", Am. J. Physiol. 223 (1972) 144-158.
[40] Partridge, L. D., Muscle properties: a problem for the motor phy-
      siologist, in: Talbot, R. E. and Humphrey, D. R. (eds.), Posture
      and movement: Perspective for Integrating Sensory and Motor Re-
      search on the Mammalian Nervous System (Raven Press, N.Y., 1979).
[41] Polit, A. and Bizzi, E., Characteristics of motor programs under-
      lying arm movements in monkeys, J. Neurophysiol. 42 (1979) 183-194.
[42] Porter, R. and Rack, P. M. H., Timing of the responses in the motor
      cortex of monkeys to an unexpected disturbance of finger position,
      Brain Res. 103 (1976) 201-213.

[43]   Rack, P.M.H. and Westbury, D.R., The short range stiffness of active
       mammalian muscle and its effect on mechanical properties, J. Physiol.
       240 (1974) 331-350.
[44]   Stetson, R.H. and Bouman, H.D., The co-ordination of simple skilled
       movements, Arch. Neerland Physiol. 20 (1935) 179-254.
[45]   Thach, W.T., Discharge of cerebellar neurons related to two main-
       tained postures and two prompt movements. I. Nuclear cell output,
       J. Neurophysiol. 33 (1970) 527-536.
[46]   Thach, W.T., Discharge of cerebellar neurons related to two main-
       tained postures and prompt movements. II. Purkinje cell output
       and input, J. Neurophysiol. 33 (1970) 537-547.
[47]   Thack, W.T., Timing of activity in cerebellar dentate nucleus and
       cerebral motor cortex during prompt volitional movement, Brain
       Res. 88 (1975) 233-241.
[48]   Wacholder, K. and Altenburger, H., Beitrage zur Physiologie der
       wurhlichen Bewegung 10. Einzelbewegungen, Pfluegers Arch. 214 (1926)
       1642-1661.

Tutorials in Motor Behavior
G.E. Stelmach and J. Requin (eds.)
© *North-Holland Publishing Company, 1980*

12

ELECTROMYOGRAPHIC RESPONSES TO SUDDEN TORQUES ABOUT THE
ANKLE JOINT IN MAN

Gyan C. Agarwal and Gerlad L. Gottlieb
Department of Physiology
Rush Presbyterian - St. Luke's Medical Center
Chicago, IL 60612
And
College of Engineering
University of Illinois at Chicago Circle
Chicago, IL 60680

ABSTRACT

Measurements of the myotatic reflex in soleus and lateral gastrocnemius
muscles show a latency of about 40 ms and an amplitude which is linearly
and highly correlated with the rate of muscle stretch. The reflex gain
is linearly proportional to the level of tonic voluntary activation and
is proportionately reduced by the tonic contraction of the antagonist.
The anterior tibial muscle behaves similarly except the myotatic reflex
latency is on the order of 80 ms in relaxed foot and the latency decreases
with tonic contraction. The EMG responses in these muscles in the interval beyond that of the myotatic reflex (> 100 ms) depend on the stimulus
parameters, prior instructions, and subject expectation. These post-
myotatic responses are voluntary, triggered reactions and unlike myotatic
reflexes, they are relatively insensitive to prior tonic muscle activity.
Vibration inhibits the myotatic reflex to a degree proportional to the
vibration frequency. The post-myotatic component is not influenced by
vibration. During phasic voluntary flexions of the ankle, prior to and
at the movement's onset, myotatic responses are facilitated but post-
myotatic reactions are not. Both responses are suppressed during the
movement and for some time after its completion. We conclude that phasic
movement is not assisted by effective load-compensating reflex mechanisms.
If the planned movement is in error because of misjudgement or unexpected
perturbation, effective correction requires a new and separate action.

INTRODUCTION

Over an extended period of time and a variety of experimental paradigms
both in animal and human research, it has been recognized that the myotatic
reflex, on its own, is not very effective in regulating limb position
against changing loads. This has prompted many investigators, particularly
in the past ten years, to deal with two resulting questions: What other
functions might the myotatic reflex serve and by what mechanisms is load
compensation finally achieved? Neither question has yet been satisfactorily answered.

The concept of servo-assistance to movement by spinal or supra-spinal
pathways has been extensively looked at. While the evidence for the existence of various closed-loop mechanisms is abundant, the evidence for the
mechanical effectiveness of such loops is not.

In this paper, we will review work performed in our laboratory to characterize the myotatic and post-myotatic responses of the human ankle flexors
and extensors with respect to their dependence upon prior activity, instructions to the subject, and nature of the stimulus. We will not attempt
to review the existing literature which has been done in numerous other
places (3, 4, 5, 8, 9, 13, 17, 19, 20, 21, 22).

METHODS

Sudden changes in torque were applied to dorsiflex or plantarflex the foot
of a subject seated with thigh horizontal, knee flexed about 30 degrees,
and foot strapped to a plate which permitted dorsal-plantar rotation about
an axis through the medial maleolus. Foot angle and torque were sampled
at a rate of 250/sec and rectified, low-pass filtered surface electromyo-
grams (EMGs) from appropriate muscles were sampled at a rate to 500/sec.
These muscles were the ankle extensors soleus (SM) or lateral gastrocnemius
(LG), and the flexor anterior tibial (AT). A schematic of the apparatus
is shown in Figure 1. (For detail, see 1, 11, 12, 13).

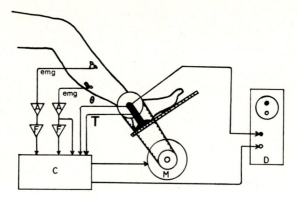

Figure 1. Experimental set-up consisting of a torque motor (M) controlled
by a computer (C). Display Scope (D) provides visual feedback of foot
angle and shows a computer controlled reference position. EMGs from surface electrodes over the soleus or gastrocnemius and anterior tibial
muscles are amplified 1000X (A) before fullwave rectification and filtering
(F). Foot angle (θ) is measured by a continuous potentiometer mounted on
the axis of rotation of the footplate. Torque (T) is measured from a
strain gauge bridge mounted on the arms of the footplate. (From Agarwal
and Gottlieb, 1977).

Measurements of EMG latencies were made by visual inspection of individual
EMG records. The magnitude of the EMG response was determined by averaging
ten records for a particular amplitude of stimulus and experimental conditions and then computing the area under the averaged EMG curve over
visually selected time intervals. Angular rates of ankle rotation were
calculated by digital differentiation of the foot angle data centered
at 20 ms after the application of the torque input.

RESULTS

Figure 2 illustrates how the character of the response changes both with the direction of the applied torque and the instruction to the subject. In Figure 2a a dorsiflexing torque (stretching SM) was applied to the leg at the moment the oscilloscope was triggered. In the top part the subject was instructed to "resist" the torque (proportionately), in the middle to "not react" and at the bottom to "assist" in the direction of the disturbance. In all cases, the torque was a one second long pulse. A strong myotatic reflex is seen in the SM at a latency of about 50 ms irrespective of the nature of the instructions to the subject. The myotatic reflex (MR) in SM frequently has two components, one at 50 ms and the other at 70 ms. The subsequent EMG activity is clearly instruction dependent. In the "resist" paradigm, and only there, we see EMG activity at a latency of about 140 ms which we shall call the "Post-myotatic response" (PMR). In the "do not react" paradigm, no activity follows MR until 250 ms post-stimulus and it is very weak. In the "assist" paradigm, EMG activity appears in the AT approximately 120 ms post-stimulus and is accompanied about 30 ms later by slight SM coactivation.

Figure 2b shows EMG responses to plantarflexing torques (stretching AT) under the same three instructions. There are two noteworthy differences between these AT responses and SM responses in Fig. 2a. First, there is no obvious counterpart to the SM – MR. Second, AT activity at a latency of 100 ms is significantly later than that of SM – MR but significantly shorter than that of the SM – PMR.

Figure 2c shows two cases of torque applied to one leg with the subject instructed to react in the contralateral leg. In the middle, for comparison is a stimulus and ipsilateral response. Irrespective of the direction of stretch of the right joint, the EMG in the left leg SM appears with a latency of about 150 ms.

Myotatic Reflex

Figure 3 shows average angle and EMG responses to different pulse amplitudes of torque delivered with different levels of static bias torques (Fig. 3a). Figure 3b summarizes the relationship between the rate of stretch and the integrated SM EMG response in the time interval from 32 to 100 ms at different levels of biasing torque. The straight lines are the linear regression curves and the slope of these lines may be considered a measure of the gain of myotatic reflex arc. The AT muscle behaves in a similar manner except that the response begins with a latency of about 80 ms which diminishes with voluntary contraction of AT.

From this data, we can draw the following conclusions: Under conditions of constant muscle contraction, the myotatic reflex in both extensor (SM and LG) and flexor (AT) muscles are linearly and highly correlated with the rate of muscle stretch. The reflex gain is linearly proportional to the level of tonic voluntary activation of the agonist and is reduced by tonic contraction of the antagonist. The duration of the myotatic reflex EMG in SM is from 10 to 40 ms, too brief to be a simple response to velocity sensing receptor organ. Either this response is in large measure due to the initial burst of spindle activity that occurs at the start of a ramp stretch, or the motoneuron pool dynamics act as a high-pass filter on afferent inputs (13).

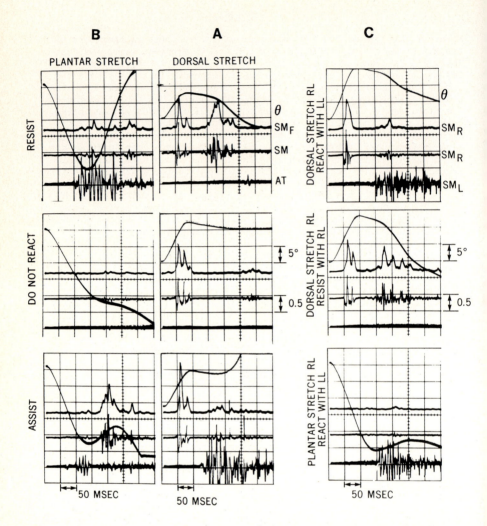

Fig. 2. Angle and EMG responses to forced ankle flexion under different instructions to the subject. a) Dorsiflexion of the foot with the subject instructed to resist (top), do not react (middle) or to assist the motor (bottom). Traces from top to bottom in each photo are foot angle (θ), rectified and filtered SM EMG (SM_F), SM EMG and AT EMG. b) Plantarflexion of the foot. c) Dorsiflexion (top) and plantarflexion (bottom) of right foot with subject instructed to react by contracting left SM. Bottom trace in both photos is left SM EMG (SM_L) while two middle traces show right SM EMG (SM_R). Middle photo shows a response with the subject told to resist with the perturbed foot. Time scale 50 ms, angle scale 5° and EMG scales 0.5 mv.

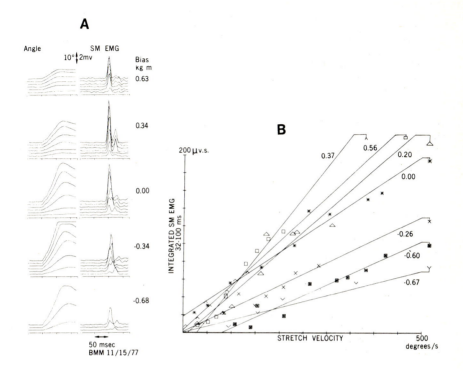

Fig. 3. (A) Angular displacement and rectified, filtered SM EMG following
sudden forced dorsiflexion of the foot. Torque is applied 50 msec after
the start of each record. In this figure as in Figures 4, 6 and 8, each
trace is the average of 10 responses and responses to progressively
stronger torque pulses are plotted from foreground to background. Each
group is for a different level of biasing torque (positive torque requiring plantar contraction to maintain the reference position) shown
at the right. Dorsiflexion is plotted upward. (B) Integrated SM EMG
plotted against the angular velocity of forced dorsiflexion. (Velocity
was measured 16 to 24 msec after torque was applied). The EMG was integrated over the interval 32-100 msec after torque onset. The solid lines
are linear regression curves and the number next to them show the bias
torque (kg.m.) used for those measurements. (From Gottlieb and Agarwal,
1979).

Post-Myotatic Response

Figure 4a shows a set of ensemble average responses to different amplitude of dorsiflexing torques with the three paradigms "resist" (proportionally), "do not react", and "assist". The visual inspection of the EMG response (in the top part) allows us to define the interval of the post-myotatic response which in this case is from 120 to 270 ms. Figure 4b shows the SM EMG post-myotatic responses from a different subject integrated over 136 to 284 ms as a function of stretch velocity at different levels of prior tonic voluntary contraction. The solid lines are linear regression lines.

The amplitude of the SM - PMR is highly and linearly correlated with the rate of forced dorsiflexion at any bias but tonic contraction of agonist or antagonist muscles prior to the onset of a stretching torque has only a slight and usually inhibitory effect on the magnitude of the PMR.

Proportional vs Maximal Response

When the responses to the instruction to react either proportionately (come back to the original position as soon as possible) or to react maximally are compared, we find that the slopes of the MR regression curves are dependent upon prior contraction but not on the instruction. In contrast, the PMR is highly dependent on the instruction while the dependence upon bias torque prior to disturbance is of only modest importance (14).

Post-Myotatic Latency

The latency measurements of the post-myotatic response were made by visual inspection of individual rectified and filtered EMG records with four different instructions. Figure 5 shows the normalized latency histograms. For the data shown in this figure, the mean and standard deviations in msec in the four cases were:

Case Muscle stretch - response	Mean (SD)	n
SM - resist torque	144 (10)	90
SM - assist torque	156 (16)	89
AT - assist torque	140 (12)	89
AT - Contralateral Contraction	151 (16)	90

Similar results were obtained in seven other subjects. The overlap between the histograms is extensive. The student's t - test for the null hypothesis "the mean latency for paradigm X is not different from the mean latency of the soleus post-myotatic response in the resist (proportionally) a dorsiflexing torque paradigm" shows that differences in the means, although small, are statistically significant ($P<0.01$). The simple visual reaction time in the same subject in a step tracking task using the foot pedal is 219 (±39) ms. The mean latencies of the post-myotatic response are all significantly shorter by 60 to 80 ms than those of the simple visual reaction. This absolute difference does not rule out the possibility that our

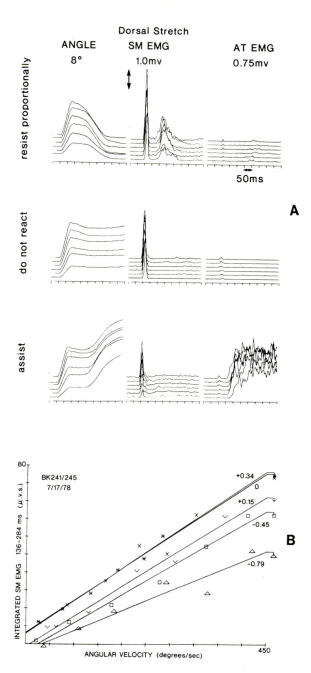

A

B

Fig. 4 (A) Angle and EMG responses to forced dorsiflexion produced by different amplitudes of torque and with different instructions to the subject. Each record is the average of 10 responses. (B) Relationship between SM EMG integrated over an interval of 136 to 284 ms following forced dorsiflexion of the foot. Solid lines are linear regression curves. Number at right are biasing torques (in Kg.m.). Positive bias indicates tonic contraction of SM against torque motor.

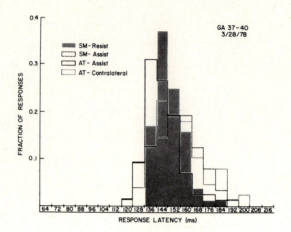

Fig. 5 Histogram of post-myotatic latencies with four
different instructions measured from SM and AT EMGs
following the onset of dorsiflexing (SM - Resist and AT -
Assist) torques. AT - contralateral was measured in left
AT following dorsiflexion of the right foot. Each histogram
was computed from about 90 measurements.

responses are analogous reactions to a different sensory modality.

Stretch-Evoked Response During Phasic Contraction

The effects of voluntary movement were studied by providing the subject
with a moving visual reference (at selected velocities) and instructions
to track it, overcoming any disturbing torque which might occur. The target was driven by a periodic signal with period of 4.1 s and having a constant velocity phase between 0.1 and 1.0 s. Figure 6a shows the angular
displacement and SM EMG following sudden forced dorsiflexion of the foot
induced during phasic voluntary movements. Figure 6b shows the integrated
SM EMG in the interval of the myotatic reflex plotted against the rate of
forced dorsiflexion.

In almost every experiment we found that for "slow" movements the gain of
the myotatic reflex was proportional to the rate of voluntary flexion
(increased by plantarflexion and decreased by dorsiflexion). Faster movements would require stronger contractions and consequently induce a greater
increase (or decrease) in the reflex gain. However, in every subject we
found that at some rate of plantarflexion (varying up to 100 °/s in plantarflexion) the gain began to decrease. Progressively faster plantarflexions
produced further reductions in gain. We were usually unable to evoke MR
with the fastest ballistic movements (12).

In the experiment shown in Figure 6, the disturbance was always applied at
the point when the foot crossed the reference position (zero angle). In a

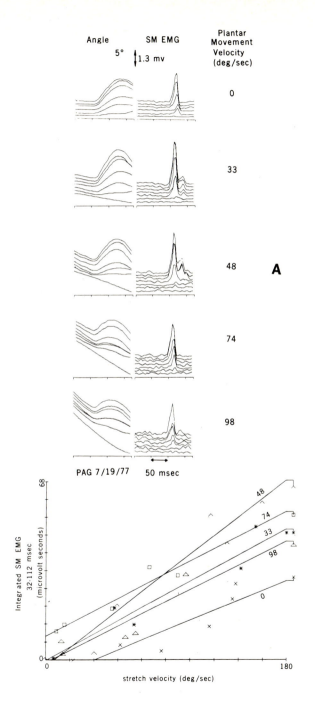

Fig. 6 (A) Angular displacement and rectified, filtered EMGs following sudden forced dorsiflexion of the foot induced during phasic voluntary movements. Numbers at the right show angular velocity of the voluntary movement. Dorsiflexion is plotted upward. (B) Integrated SM EMG plotted versus the rate of forced dorsiflexion of the foot. Solid lines are linear regression curves and adjacent numbers correspond to the angular velocity of voluntary flexion for that set. (From Gottlieb and Agarwal, 1979)

second experiment, the disturbance was applied at various points in a
ballistic, voluntary, plantar contraction. In an interval of about 50 ms
before and after the onset of the EMG of such a ballistic contraction,
there is an increase in the gain of the soleus MR with respect to the
static condition. This is followed by a sudden and total inhibition of the
myotatic reflex and the recovery of the MR occurs after completion of the
movement. This suppression of MR is also observed, but to a lesser degree,
even if actual shortening of the muscle is mechanically prevented by in-
serting a mechanical stop in the foot plate assembly. On the other hand,
the phasic contraction produces a slower and less profound but even more
prolonged reduction in the gain of the post-myotatic response. Figure 7
shows the relative gains of MR and PMR at various points during a ballistic
plantarflexion. Similar results are obtained in the AT muscle during vol
untary dorsiflexions (15).

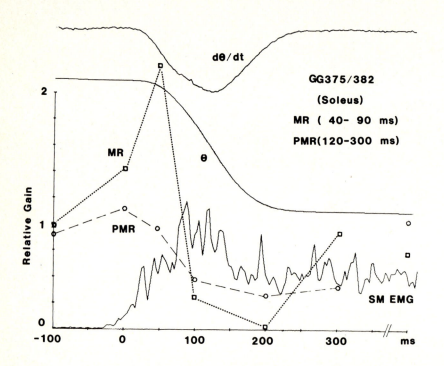

Fig. 7. Relative gain of SM myotatic reflex (MR) and post-myotatic
reaction (PMR) during voluntary plantarflexion. Gain normalized relative
to that found in a relaxed, stationary limb. Average EMG. angle (range of
movement 15°) and angular rate (peak rate about 175 deg/sec) shown on same
time scale. Data points on right without connecting lines show gains in
stationary limb at final joint angle.

Effect of Vibration

Vibration was applied to the achilles tendon at 50, 75, 100, 125, or 150 Hz. Vibration produced a tonic vibration reflex (TVR) contracting the gastrocnemius-soleus muscle. The resulting torque due to the TVR was counterbalanced by applying an appropriate level of bias torque with the motor so that the subject would rest at the reference position with no voluntary effort. Step torques of various amplitudes were applied and the subject was asked to react proportionately to restore the foot to its original position.

Figure 8 shows the averaged response of angular rotation and SM EMG for a subject under vibration free conditions and with 100Hz vibration. In this particular experiment, five runs were made as follows: (a) no vibration with leg relaxed, (b) 100 Hz vibration, (c) 50 Hz vibration, (d) no vibration with contraction against bias torque, and (e) no vibration with leg relaxed (repeated).

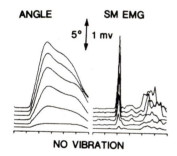

NO VIBRATION

Fig. 8. Angular displacement and rectified, filtered SM EMG following sudden forced dorsiflexion of the foot. Torque is applied 50 ms after the start of each record. The upper group is under no vibration condition and the lower group under 100 Hz soleus tendon vibration condition. Dorsiflexion is plotted upwards.

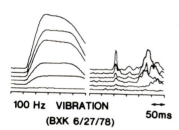

100 Hz VIBRATION
(BXK 6/27/78)   50ms

The integrated SM EMG in the time intervals for myotatic reflex and post-myotatic reactions are shown in Figure 9. Table 1 shows result of the regression analysis for two subjects. The gain of the myotatic reflex is significantly reduced by vibration. The post-myotatic response is not influenced by vibration.

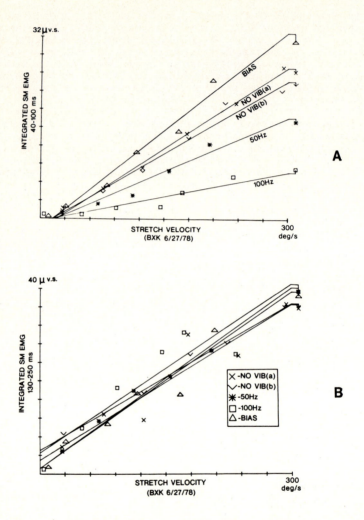

Fig. 9. (A) Integrated SM EMG over the interval of 40-100 ms. The five data sets were no vibration (a) at the start of the experiment, vibration at 50 Hz with TVR counterbalanced, voluntary bias without vibration, and no vibration (b) at the end of the experiment. Results of linear regression analysis are summarized in Table 1. (B) Integrated SM EMG over the interval 130-250 ms.

TABLE 1: Reflex Regression Analysis

Subject	Vibration Frequency	Bias Kg.m.	Myotatic			Post-Myotatic		
			Gain	r	V_T	Gain	r	V_T
GCA	0	0.14	0.267	0.966	16	0.243	0.941	-8
	0	0.05	0.237	0.941	3	0.205	0.981	14
	50	0.06	0.145	0.935	41	0.149	0.924	-78
	100	0.70	0.070	0.999	62	0.190	0.853	-42
	150	0.64	0.019	0.370	-115	0.264	0.942	-15
BXK	0	0.04	0.095	0.998	20	0.111	0.930	-27
	0	-0.12	0.085	0.986	15	0.105	0.966	-49
	50	0.33	0.063	0.974	19	0.129	0.989	-10
	100	0.15	0.029	0.920	13	0.121	0.903	-38
	0	0.30	0.115	0.984	15	0.126	0.955	-10

Gain (μ.V.s./deg/s), velocity threshold V_T (deg/s), and Correlation Coefficient (r) between stretch velocity and integrated SM EMG. The subjects
were instructed to resist to go back to the base line as quickly as possible. The bias is the average value of the torque measured just prior
to the step torque input. When vibration input was applied, the TVR was
counterbalanced by applying appropriate bias torque with the moror to
maintain reference position. The gain corresponds to the slope and the
threshold to the abscissa intercept of the linear regression line.

DISCUSSION

Myotatic Reflex

Sudden dorsiflexion of the ankle joint shows two distinguishable components
in the EMG of the soleus muscle within the first 100 ms (Fig. 2a). In the
40 to 60 ms interval there is a brief and highly synchronous burst giving
rise to the first peak in the rectified, filtered EMG response (Fig. 3a).
It is equivalent to the tendonjerk reflex and can reasonably be attributed
to the monosynaptic response commonly evoked by an achilles tendon tap.
The second component, in the 60 to 80 ms interval (Figs. 2a & 3a) is more
labile, showing less constancy of shape than the first (13). We shall refer to this entire complex as the myotatic reflex.

The integrated SM EMG over the total interval of the myotatic response
(in this case 32 - 100 ms) is linearly related to the velocity of stretch
and the slope of the regression curve depends upon the degree of voluntary
contraction of extensor or flexor muscles about the ankle. A closer inspection of the two components in the myotatic reflex reveals that the
first component (40 to 60 ms) is facilitated by a planter contraction and
inhibited by dorsal contraction and the gain slope is linearly proportional
to the torque bias against which the leg muscles are contracting. The
second component (60 to 80 ms) appears to have a sizable threshold at low
stretch velocities and does not show a significant linear correlation between its gain and the biasing torque. Interpretation of the second component presents a difficult problem and due to its longer latency it likely
represents the summed activity of several reflex arcs involving peripheral
receptors other than Ia alone (13).

The asymmetry between ankle extensors and flexors is quite clear in Fig. 2a
and 2b. In the extensor SM there is no difficulty in distinguishing the
myotatic and post-myotatic response (when present), but in the flexor AT
there is usually only one complex response beginning 80 - 100 ms following
the onset of a plantarflexing torque and continuing for 200 ms or more.

Post-Myotatic Response

The post-myotatic response is evoked, not as a direct consequence of
muscle stretch but by the total kinesthetic input associated with joint
rotation. It can be evoked in different distal leg muscles simply by
properly instructing the subject. Its latency is unaffected by which
muscle is stretched and to which muscle the response is directed (Fig. 5).

Under the paradigm when the subject is instructed to resist a disturbance
and return the foot to its initial position, the magnitude of this response is highly and linearly correlated with the rate at which the foot
was rotated (Fig. 4b). In this respect, this response behaves like a myotatic reflex.

Aside from its greater latency, it differs from the myotatic reflex in that
its magnitude is either unaffected or slightly reduced by prior tonic contraction of either the responding muscle or of its antagonists.

Effects of Voluntary Movements

The very tight coupling between primary spindle afferents and alpha efferents during isometric contraction or slow movement shown by Vallbo (23)
is a convincing evidence of alpha-gamma linkage and that the spinal processes such as the myotatic reflex could provide some degree of load compensation. In Figure 6a, in spite of the muscle shortening that had
occured during slow plantarflexion, both the latency and magnitude of the
myotatic reflex were comparable to those when the foot is initially
stationary. However, in every subject we found that at some rate of
plantarflexion the gain began to decrease (Fig. 6b). Progressively faster
plantarflexion produced further reductions in gain. We are usually
unable to evoke any myotatic reflex with the fastest ballistic movements.

When the disturbance is applied at various times during a repeated phasic
movement, a familiar pattern of myotatic reflex gain modulation is seen

(Fig. 7). The period of reflex facilitation immediately prior to the contraction has been demonstrated long ago for both the tendon jerk and the Hoffmann reflex (11, 18).

The initial increase in gain is likely caused by changes within the anterior horn rather than to changes in spindle sensitivity. This conclusion is drawn from the fact that the gain increase precedes acceleration of spindle discharge from coactivation of alpha and gamma systems. This acceleration occurs only after the appearance of the EMG. The increase in reflex gain may be mediated by presynaptic facilitation of the reflex pathway.

The subsequent suppression of the myotatic gain, beginning as it does during the strong phasic burst of motoneuron activity is in sharp contrast with what is observed during tonic contraction. Activation of the motoneuron pool coupled with seemingly paradoxical myotatic reflex inhibition (Fig. 8) is also a feature of the tonic vibration reflex. The inhibition mechanism there is generally attributed to presynaptic influences on the Ia afferents which may also be the dominant mechanism here (6, 7, 10).

The post-myotatic gain shows little if any facilitation prior to contraction but is clearly reduced during and for an extended period after the phasic movement has been completed. The reduction in gain of PMR may well be related to the diminished influence exerted by the primary afferents during this period which would not only diminish the short latency myotatic reflex but all later responses from higher centers which would normally converge with and re-enforce afferent inputs.

Our finding that both myotatic and post-myotatic compensation is suppressed during phasic movement is not restricted to ballistic movements however. Ballistic movements were associated with the most potent suppression but the phenomenon was clearly in evidence even with the ramp movements at one-tenth their speed. The myotatic reflex also showed progressive reductions in gain which could be related to increasing velocities of movement (Fig. 6b). The conclusion from this is that voluntary movements do not merely lack effective short-latency load-compensating mechanisms; they actively suppress them.

Effects of Vibration

The tonic vibration reflex inhibits the myotatic reflex. This is in contrast to the facilitation of the myotatic reflex by tonic voluntary contraction. The post-myotatic response is not influenced by vibration. Regardless of the mechanisms involved in the suppression of the myotatic component by vibration, the invariance of the post-myotatic response suggest that this response is mediated in part by peripheral afferents other than the Ia afferents.

Recent studies have shown that vibration is not as selective a stimulus for spindle primaries as had been believed from animal studies (6, 16, 17). Even if presynaptic inhibition at Ia terminals is the dominant mechanism for myotatic reflex suppression, it need not necessarily alter the central projections of the muscle afferents to supraspinal centers.

ACKNOWLEDGEMENTS

This work was supported by National Science Foundation Grant ENG – 7608754 and National Institutes of Health Grants NS – 00196 and NS – 12877.

REFERENCES

1.   Agarwal, G.C. and Gottlieb, G.L., Oscillation of the human ankle joint in response to applied sinusoidal torque on the foot. J. Physiol. (Lond.) 288: 151-176, 1977.

2.   Agarwal, G.C. and Gottlieb, G.L. Effect of Vibration on the ankle stretch reflex in man. (manuscript in preparation)

3.   Bizzi, E., Dev P., Morasso, P., and Polit, A. Effect of load disturbance during centrally initiated movements. J. Neurophysiol 41: 542-556, 1978.

4.   Conrad, E., Matsunami, K., Meyer-Lohman, J., Weisendanger, M., and Brooks, V.B. Cortical load compensation during voluntary elbow movements. Brain Res. 71: 507-514, 1974.

5.   Desmedt, J.E. (Editor). Cerebral Motor Control in Man: Long Loop Mechanisms. Prog. Clin. Neurophysiol., vol. 4, Basel: Karger, 1978.

6.   Desmedt, J.E. and Godaux, E. Mechanism of the vibration paradox: Excitory and inhibitory effects of tendon vibration on a single soleus motor units in man. J. Physiol. (Lond.) 285: 197-207, 1978.

7.   Dindar, F. and Verrier, M. Studies on the receptor responsible for vibration induced inhibition of monosynaptic reflexes in man. J. Neurol. Neurosurg. Psychiat. 38: 155-160, 1975.

8.   Evarts, E.V. and Tanji, J. Reflex and intended responses in motor cortex pyramidal tract neurons of monkey. J. Neurophysiol. 39: 1069-1080, 1976.

9.   Evarts, E.V. and Fromm, C. The pyramidal tract as summing point in a closed-loop system in the monkey. In Cerebral Motor Control in Man: Long loop Mechanisms, Prog. Clin. Neurophysiol. 5, edited by J.E. Desmedt, Basel: Karger, 56-78, 1978.

10. Gillies, J.D., Lance, J.W., Neilson, P.D., and Tassinari, C.A. Presynaptic inhibition of the mosynaptic reflex by vibration. J. Physiol. (Lond.) 205: 320-339, 1969.

11. Gottlieb, G.L., Agarwal, G.C., and Stark, L. Interactions between voluntary and postural mechanisms of the human motor system. J. Neurophysiol. 33: 365-381, 1970.

12. Gottlieb, G.L. and Agarwal, G.C. Stretch and Hoffmann reflexes during phasic voluntary contractions of the human soleus muscle. Electroencephalog. Clin. Neurophysiol. 44: 553-561, 1978.

ELECTROMYOGRAPHIC RESPONSES

13. Gottlieb, G.L. and Agarwal, G.C. Response to sudden torques about the ankle in man: Myotatic reflex. J. Neurophysiol. 42: 91-106, 1979.

14. Gottlieb, G.L. and Agarwal, G.C. Response to sudden torques about the ankle in man: 2-Post-myotatic reactions. J. Neurophysiol. (In press)

15. Gottlieb, G.L. and Agarwal, G.C. Response to sudden torques about the ankle in Man: 3-Suppression of stretch-evoked responses during phasic contraction. (Manuscript in preparation)

16. Hendrie, A. and Lee, R.G. Selective effects of vibration on human spinal and long-loop reflexes. Brain Res., 157: 369-375, 1978.

17. Homma, S. (Editor). Understanding the Stretch Reflex. Prog. in Brain Research, vol. 44, Amsterdam: Elsevier, 1976.

18. Kots, Ya. M. The organization of voluntary movement. Plenum Press, New York, 1977.

19. Marsden, C.D., Merton, P.A., and Morton, H.B. Servo action in the human thumb. J. Physiol. (Lond.) 256: 1-44, 1976.

20. Marsden, C.D., Merton, P.A., and Morton, H.B. Stretch reflexes and servo actions in a variety of human muscles. J. Physiol. (Lond.) 259: 5310560, 1976.

21. Melville, Jones, G. and Watt, D.G.D. Observations on the control of stepping and hopping movements in man. J. Physiol. (Lond.) 219: 709-727, 1971.

22. Phillips, C.G. and Porter, R. Corticospinal Neurones. Their Role in Movement. London: Academic Press, 1977.

23. Vallbo, A.B. Muscle spindle afferent discharges from resting and contracting muscles in normal human subjects, In: New Developments in Electromyography and Clinical Neurophysiology, Vol. 3 edited by J.E. Desmedt, Basel: Karger, 251-262, 1973.

Tutorials in Motor Behavior
G.E. Stelmach and J. Requin (eds.)
© *North-Holland Publishing Company, 1980*

13

THE UTILIZATION OF MYOTATIC FEEDBACK
IN MOTOR CONTROL

C.A. Terzuolo, J.R. Dufresne and J.F. Soechting

Laboratory of Neurophysiology
University of Minnesota
Minneapolis, Minnesota

In this paper, we shall take up a few topics which are related
to the functional utility of myotatic feedback, that is, feedback actions originating from muscle receptors and capable of
modifying the motor output to the agonist and antagonist muscles
during different motor tasks. The results of our work on this
subject may be summarized as follows:
1) Such reflex actions behave essentially like a negative velocity feedback during the intentional arrest of fast, ongoing
movements (Soechting,1973; Terzuolo and Viviani, 1974; Viviani
and Terzuolo, 1973).
2) The myotatic feedback can be parameterized in terms of a
negative feedback of position, velocity and acceleration. Such
a parameterization has led to the identification of separate and
independently regulated feedback loops, subserved by different
central anatomical structures (Dufresne et al, 1978; 1979a).
3) The gain in each of these feedback loops depends on the
motor task (Dufresne et al, 1978; 1979b).

INTRODUCTION

When torque perturbations are applied to a limb, changes in limb position
will result from the sum of the externally applied torque and the torque
generated by muscular contraction. The activity of the stretch receptors
in the muscles involved can be expected to reflect these changes in angular
position and its derivatives: velocity and acceleration. The dependence of
Ia afferent activity on these parameters is well established (cf. Matthews,
1972). Since muscle force and angular position are not independent, the activity of Golgi tendon organ afferents will also depend on the same parameters. The extent to which alpha motoneuron output is determined by reflex
activity, that is the extent to which it depends on afferent activity from
stretch receptors, can thus be assessed by a model relating EMG activity
(taken as the output) to angular position and its derivatives (taken as
the input).

Experimentally, pseudo-random sequences of torque pulses were applied at
the elbow joint of normal adult human subjects. The tasks performed by the
subjects were specified not only by the instructions given (e.g. to resist
or not to resist the applied torque) but also by the externally imposed
conditions (such as a constant torque load). Thus the term "operating
point" will be used to specify each experimental condition. EMG activity of
biceps and triceps, forearm angular position and acceleration and the applied torque were recorded. In our results, EMG activity is expressed in

terms of impulse density (when recorded with intramuscular electrodes) or in
terms of the amplitude of full-wave rectified surface recordings.

The model we have chosen is a simple one, namely a linear model with three
feedback terms (position, velocity and acceleration). The time delay for
each of these terms is assumed to be independent. The rationale for this
assumption is as follows: The possibility of multiple feedback pathways
with different time delays is thereby included in the model as well as the
possibility of a central processing of afferent activity analogous to a
mathematical differentiation or integration. In other words, different pathways might use different parameters of the input. The model is arbitrary in
the sense that additional terms, such as derivatives higher than acceleration and nonlinear terms are excluded. However, the restriction of the model
to linear terms will be justified below.

LINEAR MODELS OF REFLEX BEHAVIOR

The extent to which such a model is able to reproduce the observed EMG activity for a typical experiment is shown in Fig. 1. This figure also illustrates the relative contribution by each term of the model. The top trace
shows the average EMG activity of the biceps obtained when the subject was
asked to resist the applied perturbation in the presence of a steady torque
acting to extend the forearm. The torque sequence itself is given at the
bottom of the figure. The estimated contribution to the motor output by
each term is depicted by the traces labeled position, velocity and acceleration. The total feedback, i.e. the sum of the three terms is given by the
trace labeled model.

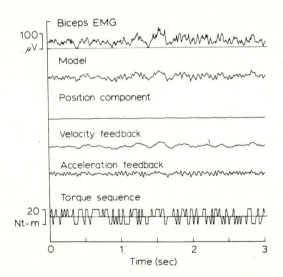

Fig. 1. Fit of a linear feedback model to reflex activity
evoked by torque perturbations. The model is given by:
$$EMG(t) = A\theta(t-\tau_a) + B\dot{\theta}(t-\tau_b) + C\ddot{\theta}(t-\tau_c)$$

The computed EMG fits the experimental data quite well. The least square error (the squared difference between model and EMG) ranged from 25% to 50% of the variance in different experiments. Neither the goodness of the fit nor the coefficients of the feedback terms depended on the structure of the sequence used. Furthermore, a spectral analysis of the error showed it to be uniformly distributed in the frequency domain.

A nonlinear analysis of the experimental data also suggests that the error is mostly due to random noise. Nonlinear models including terms with the square and cube of the velocity and acceleration reduced the error only slightly. By calculating second-order kernels for the impulse response of EMG activity to pulses of torque, we were able to show that the average motor output to pairs of pulses closely approximates the activity obtained by assuming a linear summation of the response to single pulses of torque. This is illustrated in Fig. 2, which shows the average biceps activity and angular velocity and acceleration following two pulses of torque separated by 20 msec. The light trace, labeled linear, is the biceps activity predicted from the average response to a single pulse of torque. The heavier trace shows the extent of nonlinear interaction between pairs of pulses.

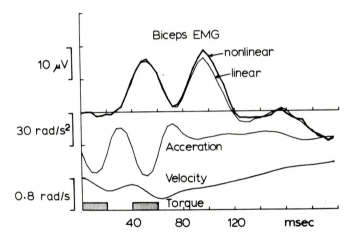

Fig. 2. Impulse response to pairs of torque pulses. The impulse response was calculated by crosscorrelating the pseudo-random torque sequence with biceps EMG activity. Trace labeled linear shows response calculated from the first order kernel, that labeled nonlinear using also the second order kernel.

In contrast to the small improvement in error when nonlinear models were used, a considerable improvement in the fit of the model was obtained when the feedback delays were permitted to be different. The average values for the velocity and acceleration delays were 25 ± 5 msec and 45 ± 6 msec respectively (Dufresne et al, 1979a). The two time delays differ substantially while their standard deviations are quite small. The velocity delay is compatible with segmental reflex mechanisms, being close to the latency of the tendon jerk in man (c.f. Hammond, 1960). The delay for the acceleration feedback is compatible with the involvement of a supraspinal loop. The delay for the position term is much longer (86 $\pm$ 26 msec) and the model is relatively insensitive to its value.

As for the adequacy of the model, we have already mentioned that a spectral analysis of the error and the results of nonlinear modelling suggest that the error is to a large extent random noise. Regarding the specific terms included in the model, the velocity parameter is generally conceded to be prominent in the output of Ia muscle spindle afferents (cf Matthews, 1972). The time delay for the velocity feedback is close to that to be expected for the monosynaptic reflex. The acceleration parameter also contributes substantially to the motor output; the position term is generally negligible. Finally, the dependence of the motor output on the parameters of the movement is not inevitable under our experimental conditions. EMG activity in patients with Parkinsonian rigidity is not well related to the parameters of the movement and the moddelling error increases greatly, despite a brisk reflex response to the perturbation.

VELOCITY AND ACCELERATION FEEDBACK

The bars in the left part of Fig. 3 denote the average values of the coefficients for the velocity and acceleration feedback terms. They represent the average values of results for the biceps muscle from 16 experiments and 7 subjects. These values were obtained when the subjects were instructed to resist the applied perturbation. The mean torque was zero in these experiments.

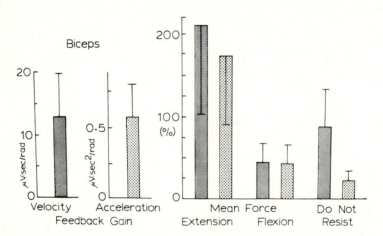

Fig. 3. Gain of the velocity and acceleration feedback at different operating points.

The right hand portion of Fig. 3 shows how the two feedback coefficients vary with the operating point. Their values are expressed as a percentage of the coefficients' values obtained when the subjects were instructed to resist a perturbation having a zero mean torque. The values for the velocity and acceleration feedback coefficients sometimes changed in tandem. For example, they both increased when the biceps was active and opposed a mean

torque tending to extend the forearm and decreased when it acted essentially
as the antagonist (mean torque tending to flex the forearm). At other operating points, a differential change in the values of the coefficients was observed. For example, when the subjects were instructed not to resist the
applied perturbation, the value of the velocity feedback was only slightly
reduced, while that of the acceleration feedback decreased to 24% of the
value obtained when the subjects were instructed to resist the applied perturbation.

Such a differential change in the amount of velocity and acceleration feedback implies an independent regulation of their gain and suggests the existence of separate feedback loops utilizing different feedback parameters.
The significant difference in the value of the time delays for the velocity
and acceleration feedback supports this hypothesis. Note that it is likely
that each of these loops may utilize more than one parameter and conversely
that the time delays of both velocity and acceleration feedback may represent weighted averages of two or more loops. More specifically, if the velocity feedback is provided by the activity of muscle spindle afferents and
segmental reflex mechanisms, position and acceleration feedback at the same
latency should also be present. The model only suggests that acceleration
feedback at longer latencies is dominant.

Regarding the velocity feedback, a contribution by olivo-cerebellar structures must be considered. The experimental evidence for such a contribution
has been provided by a series of studies on the intentional arrest of fast
movements in man and in the squirrel monkey (Soechting et al, 1976; Terzuolo
and Viviani, 1974). These studies indicated that the velocity and acceleration feedback is operational during fast movements which were ballistically
initiated. Under these conditions, the motor output to agonist and antagonist was shown to be causally related to the parameters of the movement both
in man and monkey. Such a coupling between motor output and the velocity of
the movement requires a contribution by cerebellar related activities, since
it was absent in cerebellar patients and markedly reduced in monkeys with
lesions of the cerebellum or inferior olive. Also, single unit recordings
from interpositus and rubral neurons of cats performing the same type of
movement showed that the velocity parameter is represented in the activity
of these neurons during this task (Burton and Onoda, 1978).

Regarding the functional utility of velocity feedback, such a feedback can
effectively damp out externally imposed perturbations and oscillations which
occur during the arrest of fast movements. It is much less useful for an
accurate control of position. Using a simple second order model (consisting
of an inertial mass, viscous damping and a spring) for the mechanical and
reflex properties of the human forearm, we have obtained an estimate for the
viscous time constant on the order of 1.3 to 2.0 seconds when subjects were
instructed not to resist an applied perturbation. When they were asked to
resist, the viscous time constant, according to the model, decreased to 100
to 200 msec. In the former case, the biceps was virtually silent; in the
latter case, its activity was modulated roughly in phase with velocity.

We have hypothesized that the acceleration feedback may involve a transcortical loop (Dufresne et al, 1979a). The hypothesis is based on the following
considerations: 1) The time delay is compatible with such a possibility,
2) the activity of precentral cortical units following torque pulses changes
in a manner appropriate to mediate part of the reflex response to such pulses (Evarts and Tanji, 1976) and 3) the acceleration parameter is represen-

ted in their activity (Conrad et al., 1975). Moreover, when the sensory and cerebellar inflow to the sensory-motor cortex is interrupted by thalamic lesions, the only component of the motor output affected is the one which is correlated with the angular acceleration during ballistically initiated movements (Ranish and Soechting,1976).

The contribution by a transcortical loop to the reflex response to single torque pulses has been the subject of much work and speculation in recent years (cf. Lee and Tatton, 1975). However, Ghez and Shinoda (1978) have shown that the **so called M_2 response which was attributed to a long latency** loop is also obtained in decerebrate and spinalized cats. Thus, evidence for a feedback of acceleration likely to involve a transcortical loop rests solely on the results obtained by modelling and the considerations summarized above.

Assuming this hypothesis to be correct, we may consider the functional utility of such a loop. Phillips (1969) first postulated its existence and attributed to it a focussing action upon muscle spindle feedback while Evarts and Tanji (1974) suggested its function to be a modulation of reflex gain. Finally, Oguztoreli and Stein (1976) called attention to instabilities which are potentially introduced by a loop with a long delay time. Such instabilities would be obviated if the feed back parameter were to be acceleration. Indeed, for frequency components of changes in length below 6 Hz, an acceleration feedback would still lead velocity feedback at the time of their convergence upon α-motoneurons provided that the difference in delay between the two were less than 40 msec. Thus only during the sharpest transients, such as those resulting from a tendon tap, would the velocity feedback be initially dominant.

The appropriateness of an acceleration feedback involving a transcortical loop may be more readily appreciated from the point of view of load compensation and the regulation of muscle force. Note that force and acceleration are mutually related although not equivalent (because of the visco-elastic properties of muscle). In our model we chose acceleration as one of the parameters since it was directly measurable, but we cannot exclude the possibility that force or its derivatives may be a more appropriate parameter.

The afferent source of the acceleration feedback can only be surmised. An acceleration component is present in the linear response of primary endings of muscle spindles to stretch (Poppele and Bowman, 1970). However, if the muscle spindles provided the source for this feedback, their activity would need to be differentiated centrally. Otherwise, the latency of the acceleration and velocity feedback terms would be the same. The involvement of Golgi tendon organ afferents in the acceleration feedback would be another possibility.

The amplitude of the contribution by the acceleration feedback to the motor output ranged from 30% to 120% of that of the velocity feedback in our experiments. This ratio depends on the moment of inertia of the forearm and the motor and the duration of the longest torque pulse in a given sequence, both of these factors influencing the ratio of peak angular acceleration to peak angular velocity. Note that torque pulses produce large accelerations and that the contribution of the acceleration feedback can be expected to be less important under more physiological conditions. Also, given the low-pass

filter characteristics of the transformation between α-motoneuron activity
and muscle tension (cf. Partridge, 1965), the relative contribution of the
acceleration feedback to muscle force is probably even less, although recruitment and/or synchronization of motor units and the potentiation of
twitch tension which occurs for pairs of action potentials at short intervals (Burke et al., 1976; Robles and Soechting, 1979) may compensate for
the drop in gain due to that transformation.

The next topic we wish to address is the possibility of a central regulation of the gain of the velocity and acceleration feedback. First, it
should be noted that a parallel increase or decrease in the value of the
two coefficients may simply reflect a parallel change in the level of α-motoneuron excitability. The increase in the amplitude of the reflex activity
when the muscle is tonically active and called upon to resist a steady
torque (Dufresne et al., 1978; Marsden et al., 1972), which is illustrated
in Fig. 3, can be explained solely on this basis. However, the differential
decrease in the values of the two feedback coefficients observed when the
subjects are instructed not to resist the applied perturbation (Fig. 3)
suggests the possibility of a central regulation of feedback gain independent from the level of α-motoneuron activity.

REFLEX BEHAVIOR DURING INTENTIONAL MOVEMENTS

The variations in the amplitude of reflex activity observed during intentionally generated movements also point to this possibility. Subjects produced sinusoidal movements of the forearm by tracking a sinusoidally modulated signal displayed on an oscilloscope. Figure 4A shows the variation in
the full-wave rectified biceps EMG activity and the forearm angular velocity
during such a tracking movement. The frequency was 1.8 Hz. During some
trials, single extension pulses of torque were applied at different phases
of the movement. The amplitude of the reflex activity evoked by the pulses
of torque was measured and is shown at the bottom of Fig. 4A along with a
sinusoid at the tracking frequency which gave the best fit to the data. The

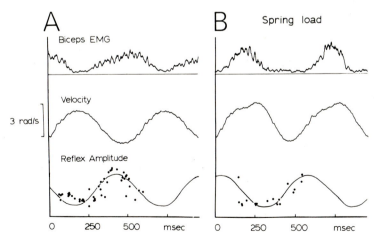

Fig. 4. Variation in reflex amplitude during tracking movements.

modulation of the amplitude of the reflex activity during these cyclic movements was substantial, the largest response being five times as large as the
smallest. Furthermore, changes in reflex amplitude did not coincide with the
intentionally produced modulation of biceps EMG activity. In fact, the
modulation of reflex activity showed a phase lead of $53^{\circ}\pm37^{\circ}$ over the unper-
turbed biceps motor output at a tracking frequency of 1.8 Hz.

These changes in reflex amplitude do not depend on the intentionally generated cyclic motion. This was established by changing the phase between the
intentionally generated motor output and the angular velocity of the forearm by means of a spring load. The results of these experiments are shown
in Fig. 4B. The phase lead of biceps activity over velocity has been reduced
by approximately 80° compared to that obtained in the absence of a spring
load (Fig. 4A). The reflex amplitude is still modulated in an approximately
sinusoidal fashion and leads the intentionally generated biceps EMG activity
by $67^{\circ}\pm30^{\circ}$, which is not significantly different from the phase lead shown
in Fig. 4A.

By applying pseudo-random sequences of torque pulses during such sinusoidal
tracking movements and relating the evoked reflex activity in biceps to the
changes in position, velocity and acceleration produced by these perturbations, we were able to characterize the variations of the coefficients of
the velocity and acceleration terms of the feedback model during such movements (Dufresne et al., 1979b). The results of this modelling study showed
that the gains of the velocity and acceleration feedback both vary. That of
the velocity feedback leads the intentionally generated biceps activity by
$57^{\circ}\pm5^{\circ}$ while that of the acceleration feedback is only $11^{\circ}\pm12^{\circ}$ when a signal varying sinusoidally at 1.8 Hz is tracked. Note that the phase lead ob-
tained for the velocity feedback agrees well with that of the amplitude of
the reflex activity evoked by single pulses of torque and that the changes
in the gain of the velocity and acceleration feedback are not in phase.

The major conclusion from these studies was that the feedback gains are modulated during cyclic intentionally controlled movements, but that this modulation does not depend on the intentionally generated movement (Fig. 4).
If muscle spindle activity were responsible for the observed reflex activity
this conclusion would imply that muscle spindle output should be uncoupled
from the changes in muscle length generated intentionally during the tracking task. The reasoning is as follows: the amplitude of the change in angular velocity produced by the torque pulses did not exceed 40% of the maximum
velocity of the tracking movement. The intentionally generated movement
should therefore be prominently represented in the output of passive muscle
spindle receptors. However, the amplitude of the reflex response sometimes
exceeded the maximum of the intentionally generated motor output and we
found the same modulation of reflex amplitude when there was no movement
prior to an extension torque pulse (the subject was modulating biceps activity by contracting isometrically against a stiff wire, Dufresne et al.,
1979b) as during a tracking movement. Furthermore, muscle spindles become
more sensitive to incremental changes in muscle length at longer lengths
(Poppele, 1973). Therefore, one might expect to find a change in the phase
between reflex and intentional motor output when the phase between intentional velocity and motor output is changed (Fig. 4). All these considerations point to a fusimotor bias on muscle spindles during the tracking
movement.

Muscle spindles of intercostal muscles show evidence of extensive fusimotor biasing during respiration (von Euler, 1966). More recently, it has been found that the activity of primary afferents from muscle spindles can be poorly correlated with changes in muscle length during locomotion (Loeb and Duysens, 1979; Prochazka et al., 1976). If this is also the case under our experimental conditions, as the data suggest, then one may conclude that muscle spindle afferents operate essentially as "error detectors" during movements. That is, their activity would reflect mostly deviations from an anticipated trajectory. This interpretation suggests that γ-static activity, adequate to maintain the muscle spindle's discharge when the muscle is shortening, is task and load dependent and not necessarily rigidly linked to α-motoneuron activity. The timing of γ-activation should take into account the phase difference between intentional motor commands and the resulting motion. Since this phase difference is influenced by the external loading (Fig. 4), a task-dependent modification of the timing of γ-activity relative to α-activity would be required.

ACKNOWLEDGMENTS

This work was supported by USPHS Grants NS-2567 and NS-15018. Computer facilities were made available by Air Force Office of Scientific Research, Grant AFOSR-1221.

REFERENCES

1) Burke, R.E., Rudomin, P. and Zajac, F.E., The effect of activation history on tension production by individual muscle units, Brain Res. 109 (1976) 515-530.
2) Burton, J.E. and Onoda, N., Dependence of the activity of interpositus and red nucleus neurons on sensory input data generated by movement, Brain Res. 152 (1978) 41-63.
3) Conrad, B., Meyer-Lohman, J., Matsunami, K. and Brooks, V.B., Precentral unit activity following torque pulse injections into elbow movements, Brain Res. 94 (1975) 219-236.
4) Dufresne, J.R., Soechting, J.F. and Terzuolo, C.A., The response to pseudo-random torque disturbances of human forearm position, Neuroscience 3 (1978) 1213-1226.
5) Dufresne, J.R., Soechting, J.F. and Terzuolo, C.A., Reflex motor output to torque pulses in man: identification of short and long latency loops with individual feedback parameters, Neuroscience (in press).
6) Dufresne, J.R., Soechting, J.F. and Terzuolo, C.A., Modulation of the myotatic reflex gain in man during intentional movements, submitted.
7) Euler, C. von, Proprioceptive control in respiration, in: Granit, R. (ed.), Muscular Afferents and Motor Control (Almqvist and Wiksell, Stockholm, 1966) 289-322.
8) Evarts, E.V. and Tanji, J., Gating of motor cortex reflexes by prior instruction, Brain Res. 71 (1974) 479-494.
9) Evarts, E.V. and Tanji, J., Reflex and intended responses in motor cortex pyramidal tract neurons of monkey, J. Neurophysiol. 39 (1976) 1069-1080.
10) Ghez, C. and Shinoda, Y., Spinal mechanisms of the functional stretch reflex, Exp. Brain Res. 32 (1978) 55-68.
11) Hammond, P.H., An experimental study of servo action in human muscular control, Proc. 3rd Intern. Conf. Med. Electr. (1960) 190-199.
12) Lee, R.G. and Tatton, W.G., Motor responses to sudden limb displacements in primates with specific CNS lesions and in human patients with motor

system disorders, Can. J. Neurol. 2 (1975) 285–293.

13) Loeb, G.E. and Duysens, J., Activity patterns in individual hindlimb primary and secondary muscle spindle afferents during normal movements in unrestrained cats, J. Neurophysiol. 42 (1979) 420–440.

14) Marsden, C.D., Merton, P.A. and Morton, H.B., Servo action in human voluntary movement, Nature 238 (1972) 140–143.

15) Matthews, P.B.C., Mammalian Muscle Spindles and their Control (Williams and Wilkins, Baltimore, 1972).

16) Oguztoreli, M.N. and Stein, R.B., Effects of multiple reflex pathways on oscillations in neuro-muscular systems, J. Math. Biol. 3 (1976) 87–95.

17) Partridge, L.D., Modification of neural output by muscles: a frequency response study, J. appl. Physiol. 20 (1965) 150–157.

18) Phillips, C.G., Motor apparatus of the baboon's hand, Proc. Roy. Soc. London, Ser. B 173 (1969) 141–174.

19) Poppele, R.E., Systems approach to the study of muscle spindles, in: Stein, R.B., Pearson, K.G., Smith, R.S. and Redford, J.B. (eds.), Control of Posture and Locomotion (Plenum, New York, 1973) 127–146.

20) Poppele, R.E. and Bowman, R.J., Quantitative description of linear behavior of mammalian muscle spindle, J. Neurophysiol. 33 (1970) 59–72.

21) Prochazka, A., Westerman, R.A. and Ziccone, S.P., Discharges of single hindlimb afferents in the freely moving cat, J. Neurophysiol. 39 (1976) 1090–1103.

22) Ranish, N.A. and Soechting, J.F., Studies on the control of some simple motor tasks. Effects of thalamic and red nucleus lesions, Brain Res. 102 (1976) 339–345.

23) Robles, S.S. and Soechting, J.F., Dynamic properties of cat tenuissimus muscle, Biol. cybern. (in press).

24) Soechting, J.F., Modeling of a simple motor task in man: motor output dependence on sensory input, Kybern. 14 (1973) 25–34.

25) Soechting, J.F., Ranish, N.A., Palminteri, R. and Terzuolo, C.A., Changes in a motor pattern following cerebellar and olivary lesions in the squirrel monkey, Brain Res. 105 (1976) 21–44.

26) Terzuolo, C.A., Dufresne, J.R. and Soechting, J.F., Adaptive properties of the myotatic feedback, Prog. in Brain Res. (in press).

27) Terzuolo, C.A. and Viviani, P., Parameters of motion and EMG activities during some simple motor tasks in normal subjects and cerebellar patients, in: Cooper, I.S., Riklan, M. and Snider, R.S. (eds.), The Cerebellum, Epilepsy and Behavior (Plenum, New York, 1974) 173–215.

28) Viviani, P. and Terzuolo, C.A., Modeling of a simple motor task in man: intentional arrest of an ongoing movement, Kybern. 14 (1973) 35–62.

PART III

COORDINATION OF
VISUO-MOTOR MECHANISMS

Tutorials in Motor Behavior
G.E. Stelmach and J. Requin (eds.)
© *North-Holland Publishing Company, 1980*

14

Attention and the Control of Movements

Michael I. Posner and Yoav Cohen[1]

University of Oregon
U. S. A.

During voluntary movements hand and eye are coordinated
under the control of central attentional mechanisms.
Several techniques are reviewed that serve to dissociate
the usually coordinate activity of attention, eye and
hand movements. Discrepancies between central expectancies and visual input produce errors that differentially affect hand and eye. Interference between directed
eye movements and manual probes is used to trace both
the capacity utilization and spatial distribution of
attention during eye movements. Monocular bilateral
stimulation is used to separate endogenous control of
oculomotor responses from pathways subserving centrally
controlled eye movements and consciousness. Taken as
a whole, these techniques provide promising avenues for
understanding the central control of coordinate movements.

One of the most impressive aspects of the study of movement is its coordination. The intention to pick up a cup produces a synchronous coordination of many muscle systems almost entirely without conscious effort. It
is often more difficult to prevent several muscle systems from working
simultaneously than it is to allow them to do so. Talking without accompanying gestures, or movements of the hands with the eyes fixed both seem
more awkward than the coordinated action. Kelso, Southard and Goodman
(1979) have shown the striking degree to which bilateral hand movements
become synchronized independent of the individual difficulties of their
assigned tasks. Similarly, we (Posner, Nissen & Ogden, 1978) reported
that there was no interference between acquiring synchronized eye and hand
movements toward a target over conditions in which the subject was instructed either to move hand alone or eye alone. Indeed, the tendency
suggested that the coordinated movement was more quickly made than those
in which only one organ was involved.

Despite the powerful evidence of coordinated movement of hand and eye,
physiologically separate neural systems underlie their movements. In
addition, some internal system must also serve to exert volitional control
over the movement of hand and eye. We plan to review studies of the
dissociations of the attention, hand and eye systems that seem to be so
effortlessly coordinated in our natural behavior. Our goal in so doing is
the traditional analytic one for scientific research. The very fact that
coordination is so effortless makes it difficult to perceive that complex
systems lie behind each component. Sometimes this becomes apparent only

when injuries produce puzzling dissociations of behavior and attention. We believe that an analytic approach to normal coordination can aid us in understanding both its development and disorders.

Dissociating Hand from Eye

One approach to the study of the coordination of hand and eye movements (Posner, Nissen & Ogden, 1978) involves the degree to which each system is under central control of the subject's expectancies as compared to control by physical stimulus events.

Much of what we know about the eye movement system suggests that movements of the eyes are more powerfully under the control of visual stimuli than are the movements of the hands. To examine this intuition, subjects were given a central cue indicating where in space a stimulus was most likely to occur. Benefits in reaction time that accrued when a stimulus came at the expected position were compared with costs when it did not. Results indicated that both the hand system and the eye system showed significant costs and benefits. Benefits and costs for eye movements were about half as great as for the hand movements. One might interpret this as indicating that the eye was less under the control of the subject's expectancy, at least in the presence of the light, than was the hand.

That this does appear to be the correct interpretation of the data follows from an examination of errors. Between the time of the cue and of the imperative stimulus, subjects showed a tendency to move their eyes in the direction of the cue. Such anticipatory errors never occurred with the hand. Anticipatory hand errors might have been so rare because of requiring the subject to actually move the joy stick from the center position before an error would be recorded. However, Megaw and Armstrong (1973) also report lack of motor anticipatory errors when using an accelerometer to measure the beginning of the hand movement.

The anticipatory errors are markedly different than errors once the imperative visual stimulus actually occurs. Then the errors are largely manual. The hand has a tendency to move in the direction of the expected stimulus irrespective of the place where the stimulus occurs. On 12% of the trials when the subject receives a stimulus in the opposite direction from his expectancy, the hand moved in the wrong direction while the eye moved to the stimulus. This compares with only 2.4% of the time when the eye moved in the wrong direction and only 1.9% when there was a coordinated error. These data indicate that while both hand and eye can be influenced by the subject's intention, the eye is much more influenced by the expectancy prior to the occurrence of the visual stimulus, while the hand is far more influenced once the visual stimulus is presented.

In these original experiments we hoped to find a condition in which the eye would be driven entirely by the visual stimulus so that expectancy would have no effect at all. Such a result would have realized the goal of examining a system under purely reflexive control. No such condition was found.

Recently, Klein (1979) has run an experiment in which, on separate trials within a block, subjects were required either to report the presence of

one stimulus by a manual response (detection) or to move their eyes to
another stimulus. Klein examined costs and benefits in eye movement
reaction time of attending to the position in space from which the eye
movement stimulus was to come.[2] Under these conditions he found that the
eye movement reaction times were the same irrespective of the location of
the subject's focus of attention. Apparently there are conditions where
the eye movement system is almost purely reflexive to the stimulus event.

The sense of reflexive meant here must be carefully qualified. It is true
that subjects can avoid moving their eyes in this situation. The eye movement is not forced by the stimulus against the desire to leave his eyes
fixed. When costs and benefits in eye movement reaction time are found
(Posner, Nissen & Ogden, 1978) it suggests that over and above this general program to allow eye movements attention provides control over the
efficiency of the movement on a given trial.[3] The lack of costs and benefits in Klein's study suggests conditions when this moment to moment control is not present. It seems likely that we will have to distinguish between two more detailed meanings of automatic or reflexive movements.
Some movements are so completely controlled by input that they occur even
when the subject is instructed to prevent them. Another class of movements may be voluntary in this general sense but not require attention for
their programming or release on any given trial once a general instruction
not to resist them has been passed. Apparently it is this latter sense of
automatic that characterizes the eye movement system under some conditions.

One of the disadvantages of comparing eye movements and hand movements
directly is that under almost all conditions eye movements are faster than
hand movements. To show that costs and benefits are minimal for eye movements may simply mean that it is very difficult to effect a movement which
is already so rapid in comparison to one which is somewhat slower.

One way of examining this issue is to find conditions where the eye would
be affected more strongly than the hand. To do this we manipulated the
compatability in a simple reaction time experiment (Posner, Nissen, &
Ogden, 1978). Subjects were required, in one block of trials, to move
their hand or eyes to the left, and in another block of trials to move to
the right. Sometimes the stimulus occurred in the direction of the movement and sometimes in the opposite direction. Results showed that the
compatability manipulation had no effect upon hand movements but a marked
50 msec effect upon eye movements. The visual stimulus has sufficient
power to summon the eye movement system even when the subject is expecting
on every trial to avoid its summons. Klein's data help address this problem because, by making the eye movement relatively rare, he also makes it
relatively long, but in his conditions there are no costs and benefits.

This section provides some evidence that although hand and eye are closely
bound in the movements of everyday life, their underlying systems can be
separated by the relative importance of central expectancy and of external
visual stimuli in their control. In the next section we take a step further and try to separate hand and eye movements from the internal mechanisms that serve as controllers of volitional movements.

Dissociating Covert Attention

Capacity

Posner and Keele (1969) tried to measure the attention demands of movements by adopting the old idea that the capacity required by one task
might be measured by its degree of interference with a secondary task
(Welch, 1898). The primary task in those experiments was a right hand or
arm movement, and the secondary task was a key press by the left hand to
an auditory burst of white noise. A large number of reviews and criticisms of these methods have been presented in the literature (Kerr, 1973;
McLeod, 1978; Posner, 1978). Criticisms have concerned the motor interference that occurs between hand movements and pressing responses (McLeod,
1978) and the possible strategy of subjects to deliberately withold the
motor response in one system until the other was complete (Salmoni,
Sullivan & Starkus, 1976).

The eye movement system seems to be a particularly good one to meet these
criticisms. The movements of the eyes can be quite compatible with a manual response when they are directed at a common target and initiated together. In addition, the eye movement tends to be ballistic and over
rather quickly once initiated so that most of the interference one would
expect to be generated from the initiation of the movement rather than
from its execution. It seems interesting to examine whether desynchron-
izing the timing of the eye and hand movements would produce interference
between them.

In one experiment subjects are fixated on a one degree square in the center
of a cathode ray tube (Posner, in press, for a review of other studies of
this type). At time zero a square stimulus occurs 10 degrees to the left
or right of fixation. In the fixate condition subjects are to ignore this
square, while in the move condition they are to move their eyes to it. On
two thirds of the trials, at varying times, either simultaneously with or
following the occurrence of the square, a single probe dot stimulus
appears either at fixation or at the target event. Two conditions are
compared. In the first condition, subjects are required to maintain fixation and attention at the central fixation point and to ignore the peripheral stimulus. In the second condition, the subjects are to move their
eyes to the peripheral stimulus. They are not given any specific instructions as to their attention. In this experiment the probe stimulus occurs
50% of the time at fixation and 50% of the time at the target. Four subjects were run in this study.

As can be seen from Figure I, subjects show considerable interference between the eye movement and the key press task.[4] Presumably, the task of
rapid generation and execution of eye movements to a peripheral stimulus
is not automatic enough to avoid interference with the secondary task of
pressing the key to a dot. Interference does not seem to arise from the
eye movement itself since that does not occur until 200 msec after peripheral stimulus and interference is present at time zero. Rather, it
arises before the eye movement and is still present at the longest interval studied.

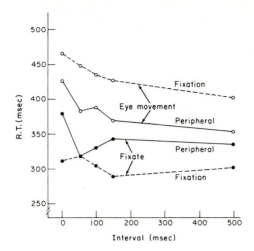

<u>Figure 1</u>:   Reaction time to a manual simple R.T. probe for both eye move-
ment and fixation (control conditions) when probes are presented with
equal likelihood at the original fixation point or at the target for the
eye movement.

Subjects could be deliberately witholding the response until after the
eye movement is complete. This seems unlikely because the interference
remains present even well after the completion of the eye movement.   In
addition, Remington (1978) showed that the generation of an eye movement
increased errors for detection of threshold stimuli.[5]

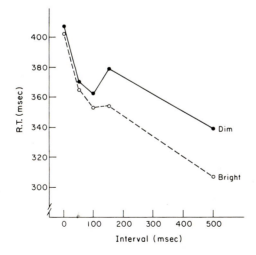

<u>Figure 2</u>:   Reaction time to perform a simple manual key press for bright
and dim probe stimuli presented at varying delays after the command to
move the eyes.

A striking result of our experiments is that the effects do not depend upon the stimulus events being of low intensity. Figure 2 displays the results of a study (twelve subjects run for three days) in which the intensity of the probe dot varies over a sufficient range to produce about 40
msec difference in reaction time under fixate conditions. Intensity variations uniformly lead to improvements in reaction time in a large variety
of compatible and incompatible stimulus situations including eye movements
(Nissen, 1977). As shown in Figure 2, the manual response to the more intense stimulus seems to show a greater interference from the dual task
than it does to the less intense stimulus. Since subjects can perform
synchronous eye and hand movements without interference, it appears that
the committing of the subject to force an eye movement to the peripheral
stimulus tends to interfere with some aspects of the detection of the
dot stimulus.

Direction

We wish to stress a second and newer dimension of the probe data. Not
only do the probes show us something about the capacity invested in the
eye movement, but they also give us some information about the direction
of attention.

Figure I compares the reaction time to fixation and target probes when the
subject is both fixated and maintains attention at the center with when he
needs to move his eyes to the edge. There is a large advantage to the
center condition when fixation is maintained and a large advantage to the
target position in the movement condition. The relative advantage for the
target is greater at 50-100 msec than at zero. Although in this experiment there is no significant interaction between target location and interval, in other experiments (Posner, in press) there is a significant interaction in the direction of a greater relative advantage at the target
after 50-100 msec than at zero. The tendency of a stimulus at the target
to be facilitated 50-100 msec after the command for an eye movement is
similar to the time course of enhancement of cellular activity at collicular levels (Wurtz & Mohler , 1976). The peripheral stimulus summoning
the eyes to the target appears to produce an attention shift well before
the eyes begin to move. Elsewhere (Posner, in press) the evidence for
this proposition is reviewed in more detail.

These studies suggest the use of the probe reaction time method to examine
both the capacity required by the movement and the direction of attention
during its course. Presumably, similar changes in the direction of attention could be found during movements of other types.

                    Internal and External Eye Movement Control

Physiological Systems

So far we have been examining hand, eye and attention as though they were
each unified systems functioning in a single way. This is far from the
full story. The eye muscles are connected by a variety of pathways to
various structures in the brain. Potential cortical control may be exercised from frontal eye fields, motor systems, occipital lobe, parietal
lobe and inferotemporal cortex. Single cell studies show selective

enhancement to the target of eye movements before the eyes begin to move at parietal lobe and collicular sites (Robinson, Goldberg & Stanton, 1978; Wurtz & Mohler, 1976). Studies of event related potentials suggest that both parietal and frontal eyefields are active during repeated saccadic movements (Kurtzburg & Vaughn, 1977). Frontal eyefields also seem to be involved in increases in cerebral blood flow during certain types of saccadic movements. On the other hand, single cell studies have not suggested the frontal eyefields play a causative role in the eye movement chain. Retinal to collicular pathways in the cat seem to take torturous routes through the corpus collosum before descending to the colliculi of the opposite side (Antonini, Berlucchi, & Sprague, 1978).

Functional Systems

If one ignores the complex physiology of eye movement control and examines the function of saccades, there is also considerable complexity. Our eyes often move in the dark or idly about the visual field without a clear intention. Our eyes may be drawn to stimulus events such as rapid motion or bright stimuli in the periphery, sometimes without intention. Given a task such as reading or viewing a picture, eye movements may seem directed and controlled by a plan of examination of the stimulus object.

We view saccadic movements as being controlled by three complex functional systems. The first has the function of moving the eyes to a peripheral target with a minimal of central control. It may use retinal pathways that reach midbrain structures either directly or via cortical loops. A second system of external control would involve striate cortex, parietal lobe and other structures leading to conscious detection of the stimulus that may in turn lead to a centrally mediated decision to move the eye. A third functional system is responsible for moving the eyes in the absence of any stimulus, entirely through endogenous control. This may involve frontal systems, parietal lobe, and perhaps other sources of stimulus control from higher centers. These systems must be interrelated since, as we have discussed previously, even with a peripheral stimulus, eye movements can either be influenced by central expectancies (Posner, Nissen & Ogden, 1978) or not (Klein, 1979).

Is it possible to separate the control systems underlying these functions? If it is, one could determine which characteristics of stimulus events (e.g. form, color, and intensity) have their actions upon pathways moving the eyes exogenously and which are mediated by internal control mechanisms from higher centers. The traditional physiological way of examining such things is through lesions; excising structures in one pathway and examining their effects (Sprague, 1966). This work has certainly confirmed some of the complex interrelationships between midbrain and cortical structures in controlling the eye movement system. For example, Sprague (1966) showed that, in the cat, total loss of contralateral eye movements following unilateral removal of the occipital temporal neocortex is restored after subsequent removal of the superior colliculus contralateral to the cortical lesion. Presumably, this effect is mediated by the inhibitory connections between the two superior colliculi involved in the coordination of conjugate movements.

Stimulation of the superior colliculus produces eye movements in the direction opposite the stimulated colliculus. While it is known that cat
retinal to collicular pathways are predominantly crossed, it is not clear
what roles both superior colliculi and higher centers cause in generating
the movements. Moreover, the dominance of contralateral to ipsilateral
pathways in retinal to collicular connections found in the cat are not so
strongly shown in either the monkey or the human (Kaufman, 1974).

Peripheral Control

Ignoring the difficulty of tracing the exact wiring, one can examine the
logic of control of externally driven eye movements. Contralateral control of movement systems is a basic feature of mammalian neurophysiology.
The eyes move in conjugate fashion and the midbrain centers involved in
their control seem to be connected by inhibitory pathways. These make it
reasonable to suppose information arising from the left eye would be dominant in moving the eyes in a leftward direction, while information arising from the right eye would be dominant for moving the eyes in a rightward direction. The direct pathways for information from the left eye to
reach the right half of the brain come from the nasal hemiretina. Thus
one might suppose that information from the temporal visual field of each
eye would be dominant in moving the eye in the direction of that eye.
According to this line of reasoning, as far as eye movement control is
concerned, stimuli arising from the left side of space would operate directly through the left eye, while those arising from the right side of
space would do the reverse. Accordingly, information that falls on the
temporal hemiretina of both sides would not have direct input to the eye
movement system. This information should lead to changes in accommodation
or to head movements. In summary, this hypothetical organization suggests
that for externally driven eye movements the temporal visual field of each
eye should be dominant.

To test this idea we decided to compare eye movements when both eyes were
open with eye movements following the occlusion of the left and right eye.
The subject was instructed to move his eyes in the direction that felt
most comfortable on any given trial and to move as quickly as possible to
the occurrence of the stimulus. Stimuli were clear bright dots occurring
10 degrees to the left or right of fixation. A block consisted of 36
trials. On 12 of these trials a dot came on in the center of the screen
and the subject was to press a key as quickly as possible. The center
dots were used in this experiment simply to make sure that fixation was
maintained in the center of the screen. For 6 trials the dot on one side
of the screen preceded the dot on the other by 150 msec and on 6 trials by
500 msec. The left and right dot led equally often and this was randomized. On the remaining 12 trials both dots came on simultaneously. The
subject's head was lightly held in a chin rest and they were instructed to
maintain careful fixation in the center of the screen. EOG was used to
monitor their eye positions. Subjects were instructed to remain fixated
in whatever direction they moved first. Twelve subjects were run in four
blocks. The first and last block involved two eyes open (binocular), the
middle blocks involved left or right eye open (monocular) and the other
occluded by an eye patch.

Almost without exception subjects moved their eyes in the direction of the first stimulus to occur in the 150 and 500 msec delay conditions. That is, they easily fell into a rhythm of moving the eyes in the direction of the one which came on earliest, provided there was a long interval between the two stimulus events.

Critical to our analysis are those occasions when the dot occurred simultaneously on the two sides. Over the four blocks this involved 24 events in the binocular condition and 12 events with each monocular condition. The median number of movements in each direction was calculated for each subject. These are given in terms of percentages of movements in each direction for the simultaneous trial in the first row of Figure 3.

% Movement Direction

Visual Condition

	2 eye		Left		Right	
Movement →	L	R	L	R	L	R
Simultaneous (12)	50	50	80	20	22	78
Central (14)	48	52	48	52	50	50
Auditory (12)	41	59	55	45	54	46

Figure 3: Percentage of eye movements in the leftward and rightward direction as a function of the type of stimulus conditions and the viewing conditions (see text). ( )=number of subjects

There is no overall bias of direction in the binocular condition. Although many subjects showed strong biases in one direction or another, these averaged out. However, in the monocular condition there was a very strong tendency to move in the direction of the open eye. These tendencies were symmetric between the two eyes and this pattern was shown by nearly every subject in the experiment.

These data appear to be confirmation of the notion that the temporal visual field controls the tendency for eye movements in each direction. One alternative interpretation is that the directional preferences in the monocular condition had nothing to do with the external stimuli but were motor preferences induced by wearing the patch. Some subjects suggested that it was difficult to move their eyes across their nose.

Central Control

Two experiments were performed to test this idea. In one experiment the central dot which had been used previously to occasion a manual movement was now used as a command to move the eyes in either direction. The

remainder of the trials used 500 msec between the two dots. Thus on 24
of 36 trials in each block, the subjects were clearly moving to the first
external dot. On the remaining 12 trials the subjects received a single
central dot and this was used as a cue to move their eyes in one direction
or another, whichever seemed most comfortable.

With the 500 msec conditions, the subjects uniformly moved their eyes in
the direction of the dot that arrived first. The crucial data from the
central dot cue are shown in the second line of Figure 3. Clearly no
biases are introduced in this condition. One might believe that on central cue trials subjects would move their eyes either in the same direction
as the last movement or to alternate directions. No evidence of consistent strategies of this type was found.

As a further check of possible motor bias, the central cue was replaced by
a binaural auditory stimulus. This guaranteed that even if there were
imperfections in the fixation point, no lateralized visual information
could be controlling the eye movement on the crucial trials. These data
are shown in terms of percentage of movements in different directions in
the last row of Figure 3. These results seem to rule out any motor bias
as an explanation of the asymmetries found in the simultaneous visual
conditions.

Conscious Judgements

It has been reported that temporal order judgements (TOJ)(Rutschmann, 1973)
and reaction times (Woodworth, 1938) show biases in favor of the temporal
over the nasal visual field. Some experiments are confounded because only
the right eye is used and the differences could be due to the fact that
the right eye's temporal field goes to the left hemisphere (Efron, 1963).
Moreover, these effects are quite small, usually about 10 to 20 msec.
Nonetheless, one explanation for our data might be that input information
from the temporal visual field simply arrives faster at internal centers
than information from the nasal visual field, and this leads to eye movement preferences because the subject perceives the temporal dot first.

To test this idea we decided to obtain temporal order judgements from all
subjects who had appeared in our experiment. Following the eye movement
condition we ran subjects with the same visual stimuli used in the eye
movement studies.   Intervals of either 0, 10, 30 or 60 msec between dots
were used. As before, subjects received four blocks of 36 trials, the
first and last having both eyes open and the two center blocks in counterbalanced order allowing vision with either the left or right eye. Within
each block of trials a single center dot occurred 12 times, with two peripheral dots occurring 24 times, six at each of the four intertrial intervals. The left and right dot led equally often. The subjects were instructed to report which dot came on first. When the center dot alone came
on, they were to report center.

The results for the left eye and right eye conditions are shown in Figure
4. There are in these data small biases in the direction that one might
expect from an advantage for the temporal field in the seeing eye. For
example, with the left eye, when the stimuli occurred simultaneously

subjects were likely to report the left leading about 53% of the time while with the right eye open they reported it only 39% of the time.

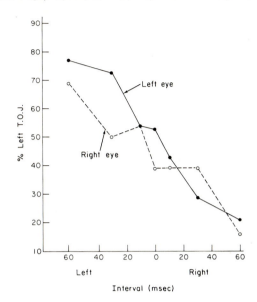

Figure 4: Percentage of judgements that the left stimulus led the right as a function of the interval between stimuli and the eye with which the stimulus was viewed.

The overall data do not show as good performance as one might expect from TOJ data because the stimuli are relatively far apart. When uninstructed to look for temporal order judgements, most subjects do not notice differences in timing but feel the stimuli come on simultaneously. When instructed to make some temporal order judgements, they do reasonably well. Clearly the time between the stimuli is more important in determining the subject's judgement than which eye is being used.

In order to compare TOJ with eye movements directly, the next experiment involved the use of the same temporal conditions as the TOJ experiment but required the subjects to make eye movements. A total of 26 subjects were run in this experiment. All the subjects were run in them prior to having participated in any TOJ blocks. Experiments were run as before, in four 36 trial blocks. Within each block 12 trials were center stimuli to which the subject pressed a key and the remainder involved presentation of stimuli to the left and right of fixation, either simultaneously or with one leading by 10, 30, or 60 msec. Six trials within each block occurred at each temporal condition. Subjects were merely instructed to move their eyes in whatever direction seemed most natural on that trial.

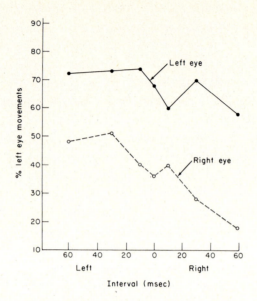

Figure 5: Percentage of leftward eye movements as a function of the interval between stimuli and the eye which viewed the stimulus event.

The results are shown in Figure 5. There is little difference in the percentage of left movements as the time interval is varied from 60 msec lead to 60 msec right lead. The results are mainly affected by the eye which is open. When the left eye is open, the subjects move left approximately 70% of the time, almost irrespective of the temporal order of the stimuli.

Conclusions

These experiments provide support for the hypothesis that externally driven eye movements are controlled from the temporal field of the ipsilateral eye. The eye movement system appears to be relatively insensitive to small differences in temporal order of the input. If this view is correct, we seem to have a method for separating those features of the input information that serve to drive eye movements and those features that lead to conscious discrimination.

For example, one would expect movement size and degree of distance from the fovea to have large effects upon the eye movement system (Singer, Zihl & Poppel, 1977), while shape, priming and time differences might have more effect on conscious judgement. A possible alternative to this view might be that the same information is being used to drive eye movements and for conscious TOJ judgements, but the fact that the TOJ judgements are unhurried produces a higher level of accuracy and less dependence upon the eye of input. This possibility will have to be explored in further experiments.

A motivation for proposing separation of information between eye movement control and conscious attention in the human subject arises from experiments with neurological patients. In the case of occipital scatoma, it has been reported (Perenin & Jeannerod, 1978; Poppel, Held & Frost, 1973; Weiskrantz, Warrington, Sanders & Marshall, 1974) that stimuli of which the subject is unaware in a conscious sense still may be used as input to orienting mechanisms such as eye movements. On the other hand, in the case of the syndrome called visual neglect (Heilman & Watson, 1977), the ability to make unilateral discriminations is preserved but there is difficulty in orienting toward one side in conditions where simultaneous stimulation occurs.

Our data raises some interesting possibilities about the visual neglect syndrome. If visual neglect resulting from right parietal lesions has stronger effects upon endogenous control of the eye movement system than upon exogenous control, one might expect difficulty in spontaneous orienting of the eyes to stimuli arising on the left side of space, but less interference in the control of eye movements by exogenous stimuli. Consider conditions in which there was a powerful peripheral tendency to move the eyes in the neglected (leftward) direction. According to our data with normals, such conditions would occur with left monocular presentations. If simultaneous stimuli were presented to the left eye under these conditions, there should be a tendency for the eyes to move to the left, but information from the left visual field is going to the right hemisphere which is the damaged one. Would subjects then have difficulty in reporting the stimulus to which they had oriented or would the neglect be broken? This experiment might aid us in coming to understand more fully the neglect syndrome. Similar studies in normals, with masked stimulus input, could aid in a basic understanding of the degree of independence between motor commands producing orienting with the eyes and pattern recognition. Finally, by keeping the eyes fixed and allowing orienting by attention, similar studies could clarify the relationship of covert orienting and pattern recognition.

Summary

We began this paper by noting the beautiful coordination in daily life between hand and eye and attention. It has been argued that the emphasis in psychology ought to be exclusively on the coordination of behavior of these systems and how this coordination is manifest in much skilled activity (Neisser, 1976). No doubt there is considerable reason for such an approach, and psychologists should be studying the skills of daily life. At the other extreme, it is also argued that the psychological analysis of the functional control of hand, eye and attention via behavioral experiments is not sufficiently analytic. Only animal experimentation involving single cell recording, lesions, or histochemical technique can trace the detailed pathways of control of these systems. Undoubtedly the work on single cell recording in alert organisms has provided new models.

The sheer complexity of the interconnections between neural systems (Mountcastle, 1978) indicates the importance of the kind of analysis of functional systems that we have been exploring. Evidence of the close

connection between results of studies involving movement, attention and
visual perception (Posner, in press) encourages us that basic principles
of neural functioning are emerging from work at this level. The ability
to make principled ties between normal and pathological functioning in
syndromes such as visual neglect, apraxia and dyslexia argue for the utility of the approach. New methods for the on-line analysis of neural systems in the human being, such as regional blood flow (Risberg, in press)
and metabolic activity (Raichle, Welch, Grubb, Higgins, Ter-Pogossian &
Larson, 1978) may provide us with new tools for the coordination of temporal and spatial dynamics of internal processes. It seems that the future
for the study of the internal control mechanisms of attention and movement
in humans is promising.

Reference Notes

1. This research was supported by NSF Grant BNS7618907-A02 to the Univer-
    sity of Oregon. The authors are grateful to Joelle Presson for
    suggesting the work in the third section, based upon her review of
    collicular control of eye movements in cats. Many of the ideas for
    the section on direction of visual attention have been developed
    jointly with Mary Jo Nissen. Charles R. R. Snyder and Tom Stoffregen
    were very helpful in the collection and analysis of these data.

2. Klein insured that attention had been shifted to a particular location
    by measuring simple R.T. to probes that occurred there in comparison
    with unexpected locations. The presence of attention as measured by
    the probe method did not influence eye movement latency. Klein also
    considered the possibility that attention to a spatial location would
    only be effective for an expected event, but this explanation is not
    consistent with evidence we have obtained showing enhancement from
    spatial selection of letter-digit classifications (Posner, Snyder &
    Davidson, in press).

3. For a somewhat similar idea of reflex control, see Klein (1979).

4. Although the experiment described here and illustrated in Figure I
    involved only four subjects, in its main outlines and results it was
    identical to many other experiments described in Posner (in press).
    However, it is the only one that contained both a fixation control and
    equally probable probes at fixation and target in the same experiment.
    The main effects are highly consistent across subjects and statisti-
    cally significant. Since the experiments were conducted mainly for the
    study of spatial attention rather than capacity measurement, they do
    not include all the time delays and controls that might be desireable.
    Further experiments could work to eliminate possible strategies of with-
    holding the manual response and substituting manual responses whose
    direction is identical to the eye movement. Certainly the results of
    Figure I provide sufficient evidence that large and consistent probe
    effects can be obtained.

5. Salmoni et al (1976) present convincing U-shaped data from arm move-
    ment studies. Their results are clearly against an explanation of the
    probe interference effects based upon a strategy of delay until com-
    pletion of the motor response.

References

Antonini, A., Berlucchi, G. & Sprague, J. M.   Indirect, across-the-midline
    retinotectal projections and representation of ipsilateral visual
    field in superior colliculus of the cat. Journal of Neurophysiology,
    1978, 41, 285-304.
Efron, R. The effect of handedness on the perception of simultaneity and
    temporal order. Brain, 1963, 86, 261-284.
Heilman, K. M., & Watson, R. T. Mechanisms underlying the unilateral neg-
    lect syndrome. In E. A. Weinstein & R. P. Friedland (Eds.), Hemi-
    inattention and hemisphere specialization. New York: Raven Press, 1977.
Kaufman, L. Sight and Mind: an introduction to visual perception. New
    York: Oxford University Press, 1974.
Kelso, J. A., Southard, D. L., & Goodman, D. On the coordination of two-
    handed movements. Journal of Experimental Psychology: Human Percep-
    tion and Performance, 1979, 5.
Kerr, B. Processing demands during mental operations. Memory & Cognition,
    1973, 1, 401-412.
Klein, R. Does oculomotor readiness mediate cognitive control of visual
    attention? Attention and Performance VIII. Hillsdale, N. J.:
    Lawrence Erlbaum Associates, 1979.
Kurtzburg, D., & Vaughn, H. G., Jr. Electrophysiological observations on
    the visuomotor system and visual neurosensorium. In J. E. Desmedt
    (Ed.), Visual evoked potentials in man: new developments. Oxford:
    Clarendon, 1977, 314-331.
McLeod, P. D. Does probe R.T. measure central processing demand?
    Quarterly Journal of Experimental Psychology,
Megaw, E.D., & Armstrong, W. Individual and simultaneous tracking of a
    step input by the horizontal saccadic eye movement and manual control
    systems. Journal of Experimental Psychology, 1973, 100, 18-28.
Mountcastle, V. B. An organizing principle for cerebral function: the unit
    module and the distributed system. In G. M. Edelman & V. B. Mount-
    castle (Eds.), The Mindful Brain. Cambridge, Mass.: MIT Press, 1978.
Neisser, U. Cognition and Reality. San Francisco: Freeman, 1976.
Nissen, M. J. Stimulus intensity and information processing. Perception
    and Psychophysics, 1977, 22, 338-352.
Perenin, M. T., & Jeannerod, M. Visual function within the hemianopic
    field following early cerebral hemidecortication in man. I. Spatial
    localization. Neuropsychologia, 1978, 16, 1-13.
Poppel, E., Held, R., & Frost, D. Residual visual functions after brain
    wounds involving the central visual pathways in man. Nature, 1973,
    243, 295-296.
Posner, M. I. Chronometric explorations of mind. Hillsdale, N.J.:
    Lawrence Erlbaum Associates, 1978.
Posner, M. I. Orienting of attention. Sir Frederic Bartlett Lecture.
    Quarterly Journal of Experimental Psychology, in press.

Posner, M. I., & Keele, S. W. Attention demands of movements. <u>Proceed-ings of the 17th Congress of Applied Psychology</u>. Amsterdam: Zeitlinger, 1969.

Posner, M. I., Nissen, M. J., & Ogden, W. Attended and unattended pro-cessing modes: the role of set for spatial location. In H. L. Pick & I. J. Saltzman (Eds.), <u>Modes of perceiving and processing informa-tion</u>. Hillsdale, N.J.: Lawrence Erlbaum Associates, 1978.

Posner, M. I., Snyder, C. R. R., & Davidson, B. J. Attention and the de-tection of signals. <u>Journal of Experimental Psychology: General</u>, in press.

Raichle, M. E., Welch, M. J., Grubb, R. L. Jr., Higgins, C. S., Ter-Pogossian, M. M., & Larson, K. B. Measurement of regional substrate utilization rates by emission tomography. <u>Science</u>, 1978, <u>199</u>, 986-7.

Remington, R. Visual attention, detection and the control of saccadic eye movements. Unpublished doctoral dissertation, University of Oregon, 1978.

Risberg, J. Regional cerebral blood flow measurements by 133 Xe-inhala-tion: methodology and applications in neuropsychology and psychiatry. <u>Brain and Language</u>, 1978, in press.

Robinson, D. L., Goldberg, M. E., & Stanton, G. B. Parietal association cortex in the primate: sensory mechanisms and behavioral modulations. <u>Journal of Neurophysiology</u>, 1978, <u>41</u>, 910-932.

Rutschmann, R. Visual perception of temporal order. In S. Kornblum (Ed.) <u>Attention and Performance IV</u>. New York: Academic Press, 1973.

Salmoni, A. W., Sullivan, S. J., & Starkus, J. L. The attention demands of movements: a critique of the probe technique. <u>Journal of Motor Behavior</u>, 1976, <u>8</u>, 161-169.

Singer, W., Zihl, J., & Poppel, E. Subcortical control of visual thresh-olds in humans: evidence for modality specific and retinotopically organized mechanisms of selective attention. <u>Experimental Brain Research</u>, 1977, <u>29</u>, 173-190.

Sprague, J. M. Interaction of cortex and superior colliculus in mediation of visually-guided behavior in the cat. <u>Science</u>, 1966, <u>153</u>, 1544-47.

Weiskrantz, L., Warrington, E. K., Sanders, M. D., & Marshall, J. Visual capacity in the hemianopic field following a restricted occipital ablation. <u>Brain</u>, 1974, <u>97</u>, 709-728.

Welch, J. On the measurement of mental activity through muscular activity and the determination of a constant of attention. <u>American Journal of Physiology</u>, 1898, <u>I</u>, 288-306.

Woodworth, R. S. <u>Experimental Psychology</u>. New York: Holt, 1938.

Wurtz, R. H., & Mohler, C. W. Organization of monkey superior colliculus: enhanced visual response of superficial layer cells. <u>Journal of Neurophysiology</u>, 1976, <u>39</u>, 745-765.

Tutorials in Motor Behavior
G.E. Stelmach and J. Requin (eds.)
© *North-Holland Publishing Company, 1980*

15

THE MULTICHANNELING OF VISUAL CUES AND
THE ORGANIZATION OF A VISUALLY GUIDED RESPONSE

J. Paillard

C.N.R.S., Institut de Neurophysiologie & Psychophysiologie,
31, ch. J. Aiguier, 13274 Marseille Cedex 2, France

A two-component model has been proposed for the regulative visual feed-back involved in guiding and correcting the trajectory of an on-going pointing movement. A stroboscopic procedure has been used to study the respective roles of "position" cues, mainly processed by central vision, and of "movement" cues, processed by peripheral vision, in the organization of a visually-guided response.
1) Evidence has been obtained from a developmental study of visuo-motor pointing in children to show that the slowing down of movement speed, which allows time for the closed feedback loop to operate, has to be incorporated in the feedforward component of pointing and that this incorporation is the result of a long-term process occurring between age 6 and 11.
2) Further evidence has been obtained for the separate and additive contribution of both "movement" and "positional" channels to the directional recalibration of pointing after prismatic displacement. Self-generated movement cues are exclusively encoded by peripheral vision whereas positional cues, related to the changing position of the actively or passively moving arm, are mainly processed by central vision.
3) A selective long-term deprivation of the "movement channel" from birth does not preclude the development of visuo-motor coordination in the kitten, as long as stroboscopic illumination at a fixed frequency is used. In contrast, the use of a random flashing light during rearing leads to a significant impairment of the visual guidance of the forelimb without impairing the visually guided locomotion of the kitten.

INTRODUCTION

The wide distribution of visual afferents throughout the central nervous system is now well documented, both anatomically and physiologically. Several distinct pathways convey retinal information to a number of distinct brain areas which are retinotopically organized and arranged in somewhat distorted maps (see Cowey, 1979). These pathways differ from each other by such characteristics as the diameter of impinging fibers, the arrangement of their receptive fields or the encoding of some characteristic features of the visual stimulus. The way in which the patterning of such input information, which converges onto central maps, is coded in order to allow some control system to release a behaviourally significant and organized motor output (Arbib, 1980) is a matter for speculation at the present time. Clearly, visuomotor mechanisms must be described in terms of elementary behavioural units before we can gain further insights into the functional significance of the multichanneling and multimapping of visual information in the brain.

The now classical view of "two visual systems" (Ingle, 1967 ; Trevarthen, 1968 ; Schneider, 1969) offered a conceptual basis for the hypothesis that

"shape" and "location" cues are conveyed by two separate channels: the
retino-geniculo-striate pathway that projects to the striate cortex where
the central part of the retina (capable of high resolution) is mainly
represented; the retino-tectal pathway that projects to the collicular
structures where the peripheral retina provides the major projection. The
distinction between central or "focal" vision devoted to the analysis of
the shape of objects, as opposed to peripheral or "ambient" vision dealing
with spatial relationships (Trevarthen, 1968), has now found wide acceptance. It seems to constitute, however, an oversimplified view, as will be
shown in a study of the visuo-motor mechanisms underlying a pointing task,
to be described in detail later.

In this task, the role of visuo-motor mechanisms is to match the final
position of a moving limb with the position of a target located in visual
space. The paradigm of pointing has been widely used as a convenient model
for the study of visuo-motor control. This task minimizes the contribution
of both visual and tactile "shape channels" and places the major emphasis
on locating and positioning processes (Paillard, 1971). It permits a clear
distinction between the triggered and the guided components of the pointing
movement. The visual requirements of these two components may therefore be
specified experimentally (Paillard and Beaubaton, 1978).

This presentation focusses mainly on the sensory requirements for the visual guidance of an on-going pointing movement. A two-component model of
regulative visual feedback for guided pointing has been proposed (Paillard,
1979). It stems from experimental evidence obtained in our laboratory during the past few years, both in man (Conti and Beaubaton, 1976 : Brouchon-
Viton and Jordan, 1978) and split-brain monkey (Beaubaton et al., 1979)
performing a visual pointing task (see a review of this work by Paillard,
1979).

It has been established that central and peripheral vision may each have a
characteristic distribution in the visual guidance of movement. Two kinds
of error signal for guiding and correcting the trajectory of the hand toward the target are provided through separate visual channels. Central
vision, highly sensitive to position cues, subserves the error-detecting
mechanism involved in the late phase of adjustment of pointing. It encodes
the rate of change of position of the moving hand relative to the stationary target and allows corrective feedback to operate for an accurate homing
in of the hand on the target. This will be referred to as the "positional
channel".

At the same time, the visual axis remains fixed with respect to the target,
by the mechanism of foveal grasp, during the whole course of the movement.
Control of the direction of the trajectory of the hand, relative to the
stabilized orientation of the visual axis, is thus possible and relies on
movement and directional cues provided essentially by peripheral vision.
This channel will be referred to as the "movement channel". Such a model
is supported by both psychophysical and neurophysiological data that have
established the existence of two basic mechanisms underlying movement perception (Grüsser and Grüsser-Cornehls, 1973 ; Bonnet, 1977).

A new set of experiments was designed, based on the following postulates.

Visual and proprioceptive information about target location trigger a central programming unit which generates, on the basis of past experience, a set of instructions for an executive effector unit. The latter activates a given pattern of muscular activity with the prescribed force required to trigger pointing in the right direction and at the appropriate distance. A ballistic movement is then released which approximates the correct trajectory both in direction and amplitude. The final homing in on the target is further refined by closed-loop feedback mechanisms. It is assumed that visual information about the on-going movement operates through two distinct central loops: one is for "immediate" correction of the trajectory which we shall refer to as the "error-correcting" loop; the other operates even after the movement is completed to tune more accurately the instruction set for the next activation of the programme, and will be referred to as the "adaptive" loop.

The question of how the "movement" and the "positional" visual channels may contribute to either of these two loops has been addressed by three groups of studies carried out in our laboratory, whose main findings will be summarized below.

EXPERIMENTAL STUDIES

I - Evidence for a long-term process of interaction between programming and feedback control systems   in the development of visuomotor pointing in children.

The progressive improvement in reaching during the first years of life has always been a major topic of interest in neurological and psychological studies. Until recently, however, the main focus was the "shape" channel of visuomotor control, serving the preshaping of the hand-grip. The progressive differentiation of a precision grip from the primitive grasping reaction has been described in great detail. In contrast, relatively little attention has been paid to the "transport phase" of reaching. It is now attracting more interest, specially since the pioneering work of Held and Hein (1963) that established the distinction between a visually "elicited" or "triggered" extension of the forelimb and the visually "guided" placing of the forepaw in the visual-placing reaction of the kitten. The former belongs to the genetically inbuilt movement repertoire of the animal. The latter requires for its development a certain amount of exposure to patterned stimulation under conditions of self-produced movement. These two patterns probably correspond to the two components of the pointing response in man.

However, despite the numerous studies devoted to early reaching in the human infant (see an extensive review by Hay, 1979), the distinction between the ballistic, visually triggered part of reaching and the visually guided component has not been adequately studied. Bower and Wishart (1972) studied reaching in the young infant using a technique of light extinction during the movement. They showed that accurate reaching could be observed, in this "open-loop" condition, in infants of 20 weeks and concluded that a non-guided, "ballistic-type" reaching is possible for this age group. Moreover, Bower claims (1974) that in very young infants 40% of attempts to hit an object-target are successful by the age of two weeks and that direct reach-

ing could be triggered even in neonates a few days old. These findings
have spread the idea that some inbuilt eye-hand coordination is available
to the very young infant and that further progress depends on increasing
control by improvement of visual guidance.

McDonnel (1975) was the first to seek for direct evidence of visual guidance in young infants. He filmed reaching movements in infants wearing
30-diopter prisms, whose ages varied from 4 to 10 months. The analysis of
reach trajectories indicated that the infant switched (at about midcourse)
from a miss-path, directed toward the virtual position of the target, to a
hit-path consistently as the hand moved across the line of gaze fixation.
This corresponded with stimulation of the central field of vision and seems
to indicate that visual feedback operates in central vision to correct the
trajectory.

In our laboratory, Laurette Hay (1978a) has studied children of 4 to 11
years of age. The subject's right arm was outstretched and supported by a
metallic cradle which could swing in the horizontal plane when the arm
moved. His limb was hidden by a black horizontal screen. Seventy-two
normal, right-handed children were divided into eight groups of nine subjects each. Ten normal, right-handed adults, were also tested. All groups
were balanced with equal numbers of males and females. Three small red
lights, positioned at angular intervals of 20° in front of the subjects,
could be lit successively in random order. Accuracy of pointing in the
open-loop condition was then measured.

Surprisingly, the accuracy scores of children were not significantly different from those of the adults, except for those of the 7, 8 and 9 year
old groups (see Fig. 1A). The accuracy was least between ages 6 and 7,
with a progressive improvement appearing between 7 and 10 years. This
unexpected outcome may be related to a change of strategy with age. The
open-loop procedure does not trouble young children: the accuracy of
pointing toward the target is comparatively good. These results fit the
hypothesis that young children use a primitive ballistic mode of reaching
whose accuracy is unexpectedly good. They also suggest that at the age of
7 visual feedback is increasingly used, allowing a temporary reduction of
the importance of the "feedforward programme".

This newly-acquired control mechanism would then allow a greater tolerance
in the ballistic programme without affecting the final accuracy of performance. This increasing tolerance would, in turn, leave room for further
improvement in the use of the hand. At this stage, when the guiding system becomes dominant over the ballistic one, the open-loop situation is
highly disorganizing for the child. Only after several more years do the
two mechanisms of feedforward and feedback interact harmoniously.

In a second set of experiments, Laurette Hay (1978b) filmed pointing movements in four groups of children, 5, 7, 9 and 11 years old. The curves
obtained (see Fig. 1B) have been classified into three types:

Type I - Sigmoidal-type curves with high initial acceleration and high
final deceleration. These are characteristic of age 5 thus confirming the
brusque ballistic mode of reaching that precludes any possibility of feed-

back control. The frequency of this kind of curve drops abruptly from age 5 onward and disappears almost completely by age 9.

Type II - Sigmoidal-type curves with smooth final deceleration. Curves of this type, relatively rare at age 5 increase in frequency with age, becoming dominant at age 11. They are characteristic of the adult mode of reaching where peripheral feedback control cues are harmoniously coordinated with central programming.

Type III - Non-sigmoidal step-wise and ramp-like curves. These are practically absent at age 5, maximal at age 7, but still present at age 11 in spite of the predominance of type II curves. They are evidence of the dominance of feedback control over central programming at age 7.

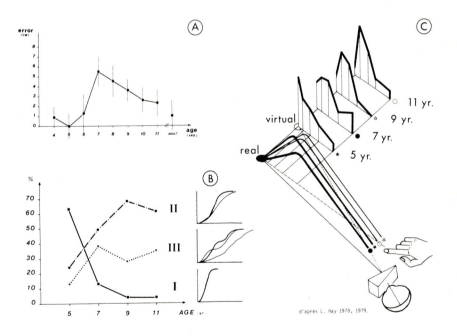

Figure 1 - (A) mean relative error of pointing as a function of age (N = 215 ; Ss = 9, for each group) ; (B) percentage of different movement patterns (I, II, III) (N = 304 : Ss = 19, for each group) in an open-loop pointing task as a function of age ; (C) histogram of the final correction levels of the hand trajectories (N = 72 ; Ss = 12, for each group) in a pointing task with prismatic vision. (See comments in the text by L. Hay, 1978a and 1979).

In a third set of experiments, L. Hay (1978c) used the McDonnel procedure
i.e. prismatic displacement of the visual field, together with an analysis
of the filmed trajectories of the movement. 48 children, in four age
groups (5, 7, 9 and 11 years) were asked to reach toward a light target
with the finger tip while wearing prisms. The virtual position of the
target was displaced 17° from the real position. The children moved their
hands toward the virtual position of the target until they were able to
detect visually the "miss-path" of their trajectory. They then switched
to a "hit-path" in the direction of the real position of the target. This
change in direction probably reflects the moment at which visual feedback
comes into play. The time of occurrence varied systematically with age
(see Fig. 1C). Results showed that, at the age of 5, most of the changes
in trajectory occurred at the end of the movement. The children almost
"hit" the virtual target before correcting toward the real one. The mean
trajectory for each age group is schematically represented in Fig. 1C.
This figure also gives, for each group, the frequency distribution of the
distance at which the trajectory changed direction, as a percentage of the
total distance covered between the starting point and the target.

At age 5, an asymmetrical distribution can be noted of which the mode
corresponded to class 0%. That is, correction of the trajectory occurred
only when the total distance to the virtual target had been covered by the
hand. The correction occurred significantly earlier at age 7, whereas
intermediate values were observed at age 9 and 11.

These data confirm the hypothesis put forward by Laurette Hay in the light
of her preceding results. She points out that the stereotype of ballistic
reaching, observed before 6 years of age, could be interpreted in terms of
an immaturity of the braking control movement. She refers to earlier
studies by Andre Rey (1968) with children of the same age group. Rey
showed that the balanced modulation between the contraction of agonist and
antagonist muscles undergoes a progressive development which is only completed at about 12 years of age.

Feedback implies time to operate. Visual feedback supposedly requires at
least 160 to 190 msec (Keele and Posner, 1968). Deceleration is therefore
necessary, specially when the hand enters the zone of central vision,
allowing feedback that corrects position to intervene optimally during the
terminal part of the trajectory. As rightly pointed out by L. Hay (1979),
the problem of the relationship between feedback function and motor programming, which has always been a focus of controversy with regard to the
acquisition of motor skills in the adult, is particularly relevant for the
ontogenetic development of skill. It does not, however, call for an
"either-or" solution. We are faced with a process of interaction between
the feedforward and the feedback mechanisms rather than with a simple
mechanism of servo-assistance giving flexibility to a rigidly pre-arranged
programming system. This point of view has recently been reappraised by
Glencross (1977).

II - Further evidence for the separate and additive contribution of both
     "movement" and "positional" channels to the adaptive recalibration
     of programmed reaching after prismatic displacement.

Pointing behaviour constitutes the overall motor output that is involved
in visuo-motor adaptation following prismatic displacement of the visual
field. The functional segmentation of the whole performance into subunits
allows the analysis of their respective contribution to the overall adap-
tative process, in an additive, supplementary or mutually exclusive mode
of interaction (Paillard, 1979).

Recent evidence from our laboratory (Brouchon-Viton and Jordan, 1978)
shows that, in humans, central and peripheral vision may contribute differently and additively to the overall process of prismatic adaptation.
The two-component model of regulative visual feedback, proposed for the
visuo-motor guidance of body-centered limb movement (Paillard, 1979),
stresses that the "positional" system of central vision and the "kinetic
proprioceptive" system of peripheral vision make separate contributions to
the control process that programmes reaching movements.

Let us briefly recall the paradigm of the prism-adaptation studies. The
subject is exposed to an optical displacement of the visual field. After
experimentally-controlled visual exposure that requires the visuo-motor
control loop to operate (closed loop condition), the effects of visually
directed movements on the feedforward programmed component are examined in
open-loop conditions. The difference between pre- and post-exposure performance in the open-loop condition is taken as a measure of the extent to
which the control processes have contributed to an adaptive change in the
feedforward instruction set that releases a new and appropriate pattern of
motor output. Here again, as in the developmental condition studied above,
it is the ability of feedback information to remodel durably the programming system that is the main focus of inquiry. The emphasis, however, is
clearly placed on the directional component of the programme.

Further experiments, as yet unpublished, by Brouchon-Viton and Jordan will
be briefly reported here in a preliminary form. They used a stroboscopic
procedure (3, 5 c/sec.) that is presumed to suppress movement cues and
therefore to deprive the "movement" channel of its appropriate information.
In so doing, they intended to disclose the specific contribution that each
of the two visual channels makes to the adaptive process taking place at
the level of the central generator.

The procedure has been systematically applied to the same four basic exposure conditions as in the earlier experiment: normal whole-field vision,
vision restricted to either the central or the peripheral visual fields,
and vision of the moving hand occluded by an opaque screen. The exposure
conditions, as in the first experiment, used either the "terminal feedback" procedure (pointing at a stationary target) or the "free-moving"
procedure of Held.

As summarized in figure 2, the results confirm strikingly that the filtering of "position" and "movement" cues into two separate channels is a
function of central and peripheral vision respectively. Peripheral vision
is highly "strobe-sensitive", i.e. it becomes inoperative in stroboscopic
lighting, whereas the "positional" channel of central vision is not affected. It is worth noting that in this study, adaptation was scored, as a

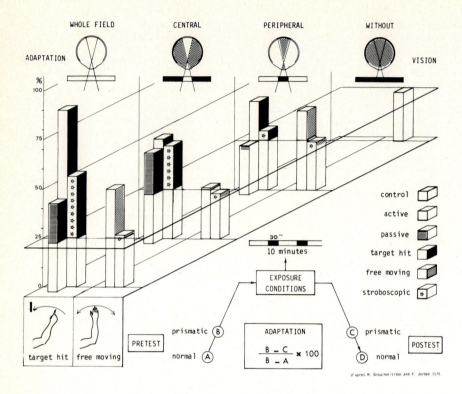

Figure 2 - Percentage of adaptation to a prismatic displacement of the visual field (eleven degrees) following 10' exposure (distributed in 10 packs of 1' each separated by 30" rest in dark) as a function of: (1) four modalities of restriction of the visual field by means of a mechanical occluder (central vision was restricted to a conic angle of 8°), (2) two modalities of movement: either actively hitting a target (lateral-black) or actively free-moving over a non-structured background (lateral-obliquely striped). The former was additionally tested in passive conditions (front-horizontally striped), (3) two conditions of illumination: normal or stroboscopic at 3 c/sec. (front-stars). The horizontal plan corresponds to the control level of adaptation (25%) obtained when the moving-arm is concealed from view by an opaque screen. Mean results from 8 subjects. (See comments in the text, M. Brouchon-Viton and P. Jordan (1978) and unpublished results (1979)).

percentage of the apparent displacement. The latter was measured by comparing the open-loop performance in pre-exposure tests, under both normal and prismatic conditions. This procedure eliminated the small, but systematic error (1 to 3 degrees) observed in visually directed pointing, the origin of which remains obscure (Foley, 1975). This correction explains the unusually high scores of adaptation percentage obtained in this experiment as compared with those quoted in the literature in which the expected displacement is given by the physical characteristics of the prism.

Finally, and most importantly, the data obtained by this new set of experiments by Brouchon-Viton and Jordan, show clearly, at least as far as the adaptive control operation is concerned, that the "movement" channel is only tuned for processing information resulting from self-induced arm movement. Information resulting from passive arm movement is simply not taken into account. The percentage of adaptation then drops to the control level (25%) obtained in the condition in which vision of the moving arm was occluded. In contrast, the contribution of the "positional" channel to the adaptive process does not depend on the type of movement, whether active or passive.

III - A selective long-term deprivation of the "movement" channel from birth does not preclude the development of visuomotor coordination in kittens.

As shown in the previous section, the "movement" channel of the peripheral retina uses only self-generated visual information to recalibrate the reaching programme. Held and Hein (1963), have stressed the crucial importance of self-produced visual reafferences in the early development of visuo-motor coordination and in the later ability to accommodate to changing environmental conditions. Comparing both sets of results, we should logically infer that Held and Hein's kittens were essentially using the "movement" visual channel. We may then predict that a selective deprivation of the "movement" channel, during the first month of life, should have a dramatic effect on the further development of visuo-motor mechanisms. This hypothesis is, fortunately, a testable one; it prompted the experiments of Amblard and Crémieux who investigated the visually guided behaviour of cats reared for a minimum of 12 months from birth in a stroboscopically illuminated environment that deprived them of any continuous direct visual experience of movement.

These workers had already studied the behavioural effects of this kind of visual deprivation on kittens reared in light flashing at 2 c/sec. Visual guidance was tested using a conditioned reaching response for a target-lever with the forelimb. Animals tested at varying ages, from 12 to 21 months, showed surprisingly little or no significant deficit as compared with control animals. They achieved direct hits, suggesting that the control system is programmed for ballistic reaching. Misdirected trajectories were corrected in the terminal phase, as with control animals, giving grounds for supposing that the error-correcting mechanism still operates in "strobe-reared" cats. (Crémieux and Amblard, 1978).

Assuming that the findings of Brouchon-Viton and Jordan are valid for the cat, we are led to conclude that the "positional" visual channel, the functioning of which is not affected by stroboscopic illumination, is perfectly adequate for organizing the development of successful visually guided behaviour and compensating for the lack of use of the "movement" channel. Finally, the question arises as to the mechanisms that enable compensation to occur.

A new set of experiments has been performed by Amblard and Crémieux, (1979) stemming from the basic idea that the periodic sampling of visual information, permitted by stroboscopic illumination, may provide the system with important information that allows the position of a moving object to be predicted. This would require the computation of an instantaneous velocity signal from the relative distance between two successive positions. To test this hypothesis, Amblard and Crémieux included a third group of five more kittens reared in light flashing at random frequencies from 0,5 to 3,5 c/sec. (for details see Amblard and Cremieux, 1979). Figure 3 summarizes the main results of this study.

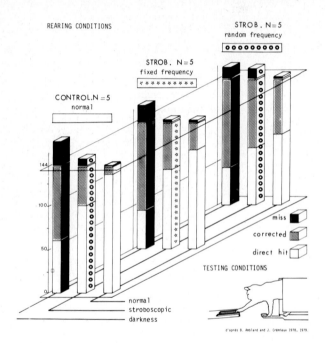

Figure 3 - Accuracy of reaching to a target-lever expressed in number of trials scored as miss (front-black), corrected (front-obliquely striped) or direct hit (front-white) as a function of: (1) three rearing conditions: normal light (control), strobe-light at fixed frequency (2 c/sec.) or at random frequency (from 0,5 to 3,5 c/sec.) (2) three testing conditions: normal light (lateral-white), strobe-light either at fixed (lateral-stars) or random frequency (lateral-black circled stars) ; darkness (lateral-black). 5 kittens in each group, 144 rewarded trials for each column. (See comments in the text, Crémieux and Amblard 1978, Amblard and Crémieux 1979).

As in the previous experiment, the animals were first tested at ages varying from twelve to twenty-one months. They had to reach and press a lever-target under three conditions of illumination : darkness, stroboscopic and normal light.

The results confirmed that long exposure to stroboscopic light at a fixed frequency did not prevent cats from successfully carrying out visually guided behaviour. In contrast, cats reared in randomly flashing light showed a strikingly significant impairment.

A slight but statistically insignificant difference was observed in normal light between control animals and cats "strobe-reared" at a fixed frequency, in favour of the control cats. We might speculate that there was some impairment of the peripheral vision mechanism in the "strobe-reared" cats whereas this mechanism allowed for efficient guided reaching by control animals in most trials. More data are clearly required to elucidate this question. In the meantime, it is perhaps worth noting that a comparable difference had already been observed in the prismatic experiments cited above.

A further finding of interest was that "random strobe-cats", who did not perform significantly better in stroboscopic light than in darkness, showed a slight improvement in performance when allowed to reach for the target in normal light. This raises the question as to whether there is any possibility of progressive recovery when deprived cats return to normal light conditions.

As far as we can tell, on the basis of data from one "random strobe-cat" who has now been living in normal light for two months, the specific impairment of visual placing with the forepaw may be permanent.

From this observation, which needs to be extended and confirmed, we could tentatively suggest that if visual information is restricted from birth to randomly distributed packs (as in the condition of stroboscopic illumination at random frequencies), then there may be a permanent impairment of a basic mechanism used by the positional error - correcting system for the guidance of visually-directed movement.

The surprising fact, however, is that such animals behave quite appropriately in their visual environment, avoiding obstacles, jumping, and walking on a beam without any apparent difficulty. The impairment of visually-guided reaching can then only be disclosed by using relatively sophisticated experimental procedures.

DISCUSSION

Most important for the analysis of neuronal mechanisms underlying visuo-
motor control is the understanding of how the control system selects, dis-
patches and finally exploits visual information for the production of
behaviourally significant motor output. To that end, we have focussed on
two experimentally separable input channels and proceeded to analyse their
respective contribution to the control of simple visuo-motor pointing. In
this context, the results, that have been reported here, call for some
general and specific comments.

1 - The concept of a two-step organization of reaching, one concerned with
ballistic open-loop control, and the other dealing with closed-loop feedback regulation is now widely accepted. In addition, our experimental
analysis of the pointing task strengthens the view that visual channels for
movement and position cues may both feed two different types of control
loop. The first deals with error-correcting mechanisms and allows the
ballistic approximation of the pointing programme to be refined so as to
achieve accuracy. The second feeds some adaptive process that results in a
temporary or more durable change of the instruction-set. This change
allows the executive unit to reshape its efferent output in order to facilitate the specific timing and pre-tuning requirements of the feedback loop
to operate. Pre-tuning means here that appropriate input channels are
selected according to their specific relevance for the on-going operation.

The question of the presumed neural counterpart of such a conceptual model
is then raised. It can only be treated summarily here. Increasing knowledge of cerebellar function reinforces the view that this structure
intervenes in the initiation and control of movement (Massion and Sasaki,
1979). Thus, it becomes a privileged target for the investigation of the
neuro-physiological substrate of the formal model described above. Eccles
(1967) expressed the view that the main function of the cerebellum has to
be envisaged as that of a "closed-loop" system of which the error-correcting capacity operates only after movement has been initiated and during
its ongoing activity. Furthermore, Llinas (1970) accepted the idea that
the cerebellum could also function in an open-loop manner with regard to
its feeding by peripheral afferent input: "As a particular pattern of
motor action is organized by the central control system and sent toward
the final common path, the cerebellum could, almost simultaneously, be
correcting supraspinal errors that had not yet been integrated into motion
but that were already included in the descending motor triggering signals".
Such an open-loop system is likely to be employed in all motor behaviour
involving rapid movement like reaching, because the closed-loop turnover
time due to transmission delays, would not allow the control system to make
the appropriate correction at a sufficient speed. This could explain the
two step organization of reaching movement: one devoted to ballistic open-
loop control which approximates the correct trajectory of transport under
the regulation of the cerebellum, the other dealing with the closed-loop
feedback regulation which refines the final homing in of the limb on the
place of the target.

This last operation requires time and then an appropriate decrease of speed of movement, which is indeed observed. Therefore, the slowing down of movement speed, which depends on the activity of the antagonist musculature, has to be programmed at the right time. It is likely to be included later in the prescriptions of the triggered programme of reaching. Llinas did not rule out the possibility that the cerebellum could assume both open and closed-loop regulation.

This is consistent with recent findings using reversible exclusion (by cooling) of the dentate and interpositus nuclei which distribute cerebellar efferents to the motor cortex. Reversible exclusion of the dentate nucleus in monkey (Papio papio) has been shown to reduce dramatically the movement time of pointing to a visual target, while increasing the latency of the response (Beaubaton et al., 1978), thus leading to brusque reaching movements very like those described by Hay in younger children (4 to 6 years). On the other hand, Strick (1979) states that the response of interpositus neurons during the task could often be related to parameters of the afferent input generated by limb displacement. In contrast, the response of dentate neurons was profoundly influenced by the motor set of the animal and their phasic discharges were related to events taking place prior to the initiation of movement.

This distinction is indeed very appealing in terms of the dissociation made between the feedback and the feedforward loops. It is then tempting to envisage dentate and interpositus nuclei as the two main output pathways of the cerebellum for the feedforward planning of the movement and for the feedback regulation of its execution respectively. The planning process has so far yielded few neurophysiological experiments but the "initiation" process is now beginning to be subjected to experimental attack. We may refer here to the recent suggestion (Wiesendanger et al., 1979) that the cortico-ponto-cerebellar loop that connects associative areas with the motor cortex could be suitable for the triggering of ballistic programmed movement, in view of its high transmission speed.

On the other hand, the "error-correcting" feedback loop has always been a major topic for experimental investigation and for the modelling of cerebellar function. Let us note in relation to the studies described here that the "stopping" function of movement and speed control appears to be of the utmost importance in allowing the feedback loop to operate. In fact, braking is one of the most disrupted mechanisms in the neocerebellar syndrome. MacKay and Murphy (1979) have recently obtained interesting new data on the role of a proprioceptive transcortical loop in this braking function and established the role of the cerebellum in its control. In their view, "the cerebellum has not to be considered as a serial component of proprioceptive control loops but as a metasystem which adjusts gain and phase relationships of the primary motor loops so that they operate appropriately in varying circumstances". This view suggests a way in which the "adaptive control process" may operate.

Moreover, attention has recently been paid to the role of the striatal loop in visuo-motor mechanisms. Interesting results have been obtained by Flowers (1976) who used a pointing task to compare the performance of patients with Parkinsonism and with intention tremor, in open- and closed-loop conditions. He showed that Parkinsonism disrupts the triggered ballistic part of a pointing movement in open-loop whereas visual guidance (presumably through the "positional channel") still operates in closed-loop conditions so that accuracy of pointing is achieved but with much slower movements. In general terms, the reverse situation seems to characterize the performance of the "cerebellar" patients.

2 - The interpretation of Hay's developmental study directly depends on the model described above. As shown, her results speak against a strict central programming interpretation of movement initiation and control (Keele, 1968). Rather they provide strong support for the idea that both levels of the control system interact, in a cooperative non-hierarchical manner, for the developmental organization of visuo-motor pointing. They also show that the progressive improvement of coordination between the feedforward and the feedback components of the control system develops by reciprocal tuning of their complementary roles. Every reduction in the capacity of the feedforward instruction to approximate the correct trajectory needs to be compensated by an increasing capacity of the feedback mechanism to make the appropriate corrections. Depending on the accuracy requirement of the task, closer approximation of the triggered programme provided by the adaptive loop may require the feedback control to operate a much finer range of error detection, so that further improvement of feedback may occur (Hay, 1979). This could account to some extent for the fact that the developmental process, whose neural counterpart remains as yet unknown, takes such a long time.

3 - Problems arise with the attempt to relate Hay's conclusions to those derived from similar studies on reaching carried out with much younger infants during the very first weeks or months of life. For instance McDonnel (1975) claimed, quite rightly, that the decline in prism trajectory errors observed between four and nine months of age reflects the increasing control of visual feedback mechanisms over the primitive ballistic mode of reaching. This reflects a widely-held interpretation of the development of reaching in infants. Laurette Hay, for her part, describes a ballistic mode of pointing which is characteristic of four, five and six year-old children and, on the basis of filmed curves of pointing, she concludes that the further improvement of pointing observed in older children should also be explained by the increasing control of visual feedback mechanisms over central programming.

There are alternative interpretations of the data from these two studies. First, there may be a two-stage process in the development of reaching. If so, a complete reconsideration of current theory is enforced. Second, and more plausibly, a functional interactive process between the feedforward and feedback mechanisms - as postulated by L. Hay for the age range she studied - operates from birth during the whole course of development. The latter hypothesis requires further investigation within the framework of the model presented above. The "state space model" of Raibert (1978) could also be of interest.

Further studies should pay more attention to the segmentation of the functional components of reaching (see Paillard, 1979), in order to assess their respective contribution to the development of overall performance. New experimental procedures are required, such as the use of stroboscopic illumination which allows the selective exclusion of the "movement channel" so that its presumed contribution to the directional guidance of movement and to the processing of self-generated visual information can be assessed. Experiments must be designed so as to allow the two loops of the control system to be separately evaluated; and a clearer distinction has to be made between the coding components of direction and distance within the pointing programme.

4 - There is little to add to the convincing evidence provided by the studies of Brouchon-Viton and Jordan on the distinctive roles of peripheral and central vision in the recalibration of the directional pointing component after prismatic displacement of the visual field. They confirm that stroboscopic procedures offer a powerful tool to exclude functionally the "movement channel" and to bring stationary positional cues into prominence. The clear demonstration that the "movement channel" (which operates in peripheral vision) is tuned to accept visual information originating from self-induced movement and rejects that generated by passive movement is of considerable theoretical interest and could well have a bearing on practical problems of remedial treatment. The complementary demonstration that the "positional channel" (which operates in central vision) also processes both kinds of visual information, whether generated by active or passive movement, is also important.

Their data may lead to a reconsideration of the mechanisms underlying the adaptive processes that are involved in the recalibration of pointing after prismatic displacement. They may possibly generate new neurophysiological studies to trace the central distribution of the specific signals conveyed by the two channels to nervous structures supposedly involved in their further processing. Furthermore, they are likely to contribute to the clarification of some of the conflicting issues that have obscured the field for the last two decades. Many acute questions remain unanswered. For example, the surprisingly large amount of adaptation (25%) that is observed following exposure conditions, in which vision of the moving arm is occluded, deserves further investigation.

It clearly establishes the contribution of a third component to the process of short-term adaptation. The remarkably stable "control level", observed in all experimental conditions, argues for its permanent contribution, in addition to that of the two other components. Its origin is unknown but various suggestions have been put forward, including a change in the registered position of the eye relative to the head. Cognitive mechanisms have also to be taken into account. The fact that this third component does not directly involve visual cues associated with vision of the moving arm during exposure does not mean that visual information is not in fact involved. A contribution from muscular or articular proprioception is also probable in conjunction with information about the visual frame of reference that is available to the subject during the exposure condition (Conti and Beaubaton, 1979).

5 - The surprisingly good performance of the "strobe-reared" kittens of
Amblard and Crémieux seems, at first sight, to require a complete reconsideration of current views. Indeed, the findings of these authors
contradict the conclusion of Held and Hein that self-induced movement is
a necessary condition for the development of visuo-motor behaviour. Yet,
as was deduced from the "prism" experiments, the necessity of self-
generated movement is limited to the activation of the visual "movement"
channel. Therefore, when this channel is excluded by stroboscopic procedures (as in the studies of Amblard and Crémieux) and prominence is given
to the activation of the "positional" channel, we can expect that
passively-induced, as well as actively-induced movement will provide
information that is functionally useful for adaptation.

As far as we know, no experiments have been carried out either in kitten
or in monkey, to establish that vision of the passively moved limb would
exclude the eventual possibility of that limb being visually-guided. In
fact, the original definition of the role played by active movement in the
acquisition of visually guided placing was a direct extrapolation to kitten
of results obtained by Held and Freedman (1963) on man. They imply the
necessity of visual feedback from self-induced movement to regain accurate
reaching following prismatic displacement of the visual field. This
specific point has been a matter of dispute for many years. The work of
Brouchon-Viton and Jordan has, however, considerably clarified the problem:
the "free-moving" exposure conditions, used by Held and Freedman, lead to
a dominant activation of the "movement channel" and then to a clear
dependence on self-generated visual feedback whereas the "terminal feedback" exposure conditions, used by Howard (1963), give prominence to the
activation of the "positional channel", activated by self-generated as
well as by passively-generated visual feedback from the moving limb.

Until now, there has been no serious argument against the validity of
extrapolating these findings to the cat, except perhaps a possible difference in the visual equipment of the two species. Indeed, the "strobe-
reared" kittens behave as predicted by the model derived from our
"prismatic" experiments. The "positional channel" is well able to provide
the adaptive control system with appropriate information for the acquisition of visually guided reaching. The model predicts, furthermore, that,
for kittens reared in a normally structured visual environment, visual
feedback from self-generated movement is not a necessary condition for
the acquisition of visuo-motor guidance mechanisms.

The question as to whether the two channels interact, in a cooperative or
antagonistic way, during normal vision (MacKay and MacKay, 1976) and
specifically in visuo-motor guidance, remains. The results from prismatic
experiments, however, support the view that the two channels simply add or
subtract their effects depending on the experimental conditions, without
any clear evidence of interaction.

6 - The significant impairment of performance observed in "random strobe-
reared" cats raises new problems. Because there is neurophysiological
evidence that specific visual neurons afferented through the "movement
channel" directly code a velocity signal (Grüsser and Grüsser-Cornehls,

1973) and psychophysical evidence that both systems allow movement perception, then it is reasonable to consider that the "positional channel"
may also be able to compute such a signal. Indeed, a velocity signal
might be necessary for the error-correcting system to guide the movement.
The "movement channel" seems to be directly fed by a velocity signal whereas the "positional channel" is fed primarily by position cues. These cues
are eventually processed for the evaluation of relative distance (see
Bonnet, 1977). Clearly, the time that has elapsed between two successive
positions has to be taken into account for a final computation of the
velocity dimension.

Our strobe-reared cats were submitted to neurophysiological investigations
in order to study the effects of the rearing condition at the neuronal
level. These suggest that the "strobe cats" might have lost permanently
their capacity for velocity and directionality detection at the cortical
level (Orban et al., 1978). and also at the collicular level (Flandrin
et al., 1976). We could then infer that "strobe-cats", deprived of their
velocity detectors, nevertheless learn to predict the next position by
using the stable delay between each flash as a fixed time-constant. This
would enable further computation of the velocity signal required by the
error-detecting mechanism. As for the "random-frequency" condition, the
irregular time base would either prevent any prediction or enable a meantime base to be computed that would nevertheless be too imprecise to be
useful. Alternative hypotheses need to be explored.

7 - Another striking outcome of these experiments was that the overall
gross behaviour of "random strobe" cats appeared normal. There are several
possible interpretations. The most interesting one being that the impairment of "random strobe" cats is specific to their reaching abilities whereas their visually guided locomotor activities remain unimpaired.

The distinction between two different control systems for visually guided
movement could be in favor of this interpretation. One system is devoted
to visually guided locomotion, the other specifically deals with the visual
guidance of limb movement, each involving differently localized brain areas.
Such a distinction is well established by both developmental and neurological studies. The developmental studies of Held and Hein (1963) show that
both control systems for locomotion and visual placing of the limb may
serially interact in their respective functional development in kitten.
The development of the first being a prerequisite for the development of
the second. These control systems may be differentially affected by the
rearing conditions in our experiments.

Another plausible explanation is that accurate guidance of visual placing
obviously requires the "positional system" to detect precise error-signals,
either to allow the feedback loop to generate a final adjustment or to
allow the feedforward loop to tune a more accurate reaching programme. As
far as the gross locomotor behaviour of the animal is concerned such precise error signals are not necessary; it would therefore be less affected.

8 - Recent experimental studies of Hyvarinen's group (1974) and of
Mouncastle's laboratory (1975) support the idea that associative parietal
areas (specially areas 7 and 5) are involved in the specific organization

of visuo-proprioceptive guidance of limb movement toward a visual target.

This set of studies recently provided a new impetus for studies of the
neurological syndrome of "optic ataxia" associated with parietal lesions
(Rondot et al., 1977). The most obvious component of this defect is
inaccurate reaching, essentially due to a defect of visual guidance.
Indeed the directional component of the triggered movement is generally
correct. In addition, movements which do not require visual guidance, such
as those directed to the body, are not impaired. Moreover visually oriented locomotion remains unaffected (Damasio and Benton, 1979). These observations support the idea that these cortical areas play a specific role in
the information processing that allows the error-correcting feedback loop
to operate in visual guidance. The information required obviously includes
error signals of the type we assume to be conveyed by the "positional
channel".

Further research must determine whether "identified neurons" in these
regions - "tracking" neurons those responding to change of relative
position or "projection" neurons - are afferented by the "positional
channel", as defined in this study.

Moreover, it is not yet known whether movement cues from peripheral vision
project to these parietal areas. This point specifically merits further
investigation. The fact that the so-called "projection neurons" require
for their activity, both eye gazing at a stationary target and limb actively moving towards the target clearly invokes the properties of the signals
that are presumed to be carried by the "movement channel". The channel
probably projects mainly onto the collicular visual map. Its interrelation
with cortical visual maps and with the parietal association area is well-
documented anatomically.

9 - Finally, when considering the endeavour of the neurosciences to understand motor control mechanisms, it has to be admitted that an impressive
amount of new and systematic data has been collected, especially during the
past decade. Nevertheless, the gap between analyses at the level of micro-
structure and micro-mechanism and the study of the motor output of the
overall control system in a behaviourally significant context is far from
being filled (Arbib, 1980). To bridge that gap, formal tools - both
theoretical and experimental - are badly needed. Here, the study of
visuo-motor mechanisms offers an important opportunity for fruitful collaboration between neurophysiological, behavioural and theoretical approaches.
It is therefore our conviction that further progress with behavioural
studies and theoretical analyses of biological control systems could be
soundly based on the study of reaching as a functional unit of motor
control.

ACKNOWLEDGEMENTS

B. Amblard, D. Beaubaton, M. Brouchon-Viton, J. Crémieux, L. Hay have
greatly contributed to the subject matter of this paper. I would like
to thank them also for their help in its preparation. I am grateful to
J. Guiton and J. McPherson for helping with the translation and M. Fabre
for expert secretarial assistance.

The work was supported by Grants INSERM ATP 80-79-112.

REFERENCES

(1)   Amblard, B. and Crémieux, J., Visually guided reaching in the kitten
      reared in fixed or random frequency stroboscopic light, Neurosc. Lett.
      (1979) (in press).
(2)   Arbib, M. A., Perceptual structures and distributed motor control, in:
      Brooks V. B. (ed.), Handbook of Physiology, vol. III, Motor control
      (Bethesda, Maryland, American Physiol. Soc., in press, to be published
      in 1980).
(3)   Beaubaton, D., Trouche, E., Amato, G. and Grangetto, A., Dentate
      cooling in monkeys performing a visuo-motor task, Neurosc. Lett., 8
      (1978) 225-229.
(4)   Beaubaton, D., Grangetto, A. and Paillard, J., Contribution of posi-
      tional and movement cues to visuo-motor reaching in split-brain monkey,
      in: Steele-Rusell, I., Van Hoff, M. W. and Berlucchi, G. (eds.), Struc-
      ture and function of cerebellar commissures (London, The Macmillan
      Press, 1979).
(5)   Bonnet, C., Visual motion detection models : feature and frequency
      filters, Perception, 6 (1977) 491-500.
(6)   Bower, T. G. R., Aspects of development in infancy (San Francisco,
      Freeman, 1974).
(7)   Bower, T. G. R. and Wishart, J. G., The effects of motor skills on
      object permanence, Cognition, 1 (1972) 165-172.
(8)   Brandt, T., Dichgans, J. and Koenig, E., Differential effects of
      central versus peripheral vision on egocentric and exocentric motion
      perception, Exp. Brain Res., 16 (1973) 476-491.
(9)   Brouchon-Viton, M. and Jordan, P., Relevant cues in visuo-motor rear-
      rangement, Neurosc. Lett., supp. 1 (1978) S386.
(10) Bruner, J. S. and Koslowski, B., Visually preadapted constituents of
      manipulating action, Perception, 1 (1972) 3-14.
(11) Conti, P. and Beaubaton, D., Role of structure visual field and visual
      reafference in accuracy of pointing movements, Percept. and Motor
      Skills (1979) (in press).
(12) Conti, P. and Beaubaton, D., Utilisation des informations visuelles
      dans le contrôle du movement : étude de la précision des pointages
      chez l'homme, Travail Humain, 39 (1976) 19-32.
(13) Cowey, A., Cortical maps and visual perception. The Grindley memorial
      lecture, Quart. J. exp. Psychol., 31 (1979) 1-17.
(14) Crémieux, J. and Amblard, B., Effects of visual movement deprivation
      on a visuo-motor task in cat, Neurosc. Lett., supp. 1 (1978) S387.
(15) Damasio, A. R. and Benton, A. L., Impairment of hand movements under
      visual guidance, Neurol., 29 (1979) 170-178.

(16) Eccles, J. C., Circuits in the cerebellar control of movement, Proc. Nat. Ac. Sc. USA, 58 (1967) 336-343.

(17) Flandrin, J. M., Kennedy H. and Amblard, B., Effects of stroboscopic rearing on the binocularity and directionality of cat superior colliculus neurons, Brain Res., 101 (1976) 576-581.

(18) Flowers, K. A., Visual "closed-loop" and "open-loop" characteristics of voluntary movement in patients with parkinsonism and intention tremor, Brain, 99 (1976) 269-310.

(19) Foley, J. M., Error in visually directed manual pointing, Percept. and Psychophys., 17 (1975) 69-74.

(20) Gibson, J. J., The senses considered as perceptual systems (Boston : Houghton Mifflin, 1966).

(21) Glencross, D. J., Control of skilled movements, Psychol. Bull., 84 (1977) 14-19.

(22) Grüsser, O. J. and Grüsser-Cornehls, V., Neuronal mechanisms of visual movement. Perception and some psychophysical and behavioral correlations, in: Jung, R. (ed.), Handbook of sensory physiology, vol. VII/Central processing of visual information (1973).

(23) Hay, L., Accuracy of children on an open-loop pointing task, Percept and Motor Skills, 47 (1978a) 1079-1082.

(24) Hay, L., Hand movement toward a target, in children, Neurosc. Lett., supp. 1 (1978b) S113.

(25) Hay, L., Visual guidance of movement with displaced vision in children Brain Res., 32 (1978c) R18-R19.

(26) Hay, L., Spatial-temporal analysis of movements in children : motor programs versus feedback in the development of reaching, J. Motor Behav. (1979) (in press).

(27) Hay, L., Le mouvement dirigé vers un objectif visuel, chez l'adulte et chez l'enfant, Année Psychol. (1980) (in press).

(28) Held, R. and Freedman, S. J., Plasticity in human sensory motor control, Science, 142 (1969) 445-462.

(29) Held, R. and Hein, A., Movement-produced stimulation in the development of visually guided behavior, J. comp. physiol. Psychol., 56 (1963) 872-876.

(30) Howard, I. P., Displacing the optical array, in: Freedman, S. J. (ed.) The Neurophysiology of spatially oriented behavior (Homewood, Ill., Dorsey Press, 1963).

(31) Hyvarinen, J. and Poranen, A., Function of the parietal associative area 7 as revealed from cellular discharges in alert monkeys, Brain, 97 (1974) 673-692.

(32) Ingle, D., Two visual mechanisms underlying the behavior of fish, Psychol. Forsch., 31 (1967) 44-51.

(33) Keele, S. W., Movement control in skilled performance, Psychol. Bull., 70 (1968) 387-403.

(34) Keele, S. W. and Posner, M. I., Processing of visual feedback in rapid movements, J. exp. Psychol., 77 (1968) 155-158.

(35) Llinas, R., Neuronal operations in cerebellar transactions, in: Schmidt, F. O. (ed.), The Neurosciences, Second Study Program, chap. 39 (N.Y. Rockeffer Univ. Press, 1970).

(36) MacKay, D. M. and MacKay, V., Antagonism between visual channels for pattern and movement, Nature, 263 (1976) 312-314.

(37) MacKay, W. A. and Murphy, J. T., Cerebellar influence on proprioceptive control loops, in: Massion, J. and Sasaki, K. (eds.), Cerebello-cerebellar interactions (Amsterdam, Elsevier/North Holland Biomed. Press, 1979).

(38) Massion, J., and Sasaki, K. (eds.), Cerebello-cerebellar inter-actions (Amsterdam, Elsevier/North Holland Biomed. Press, 1979).

(39) McDonnel, P. M., The development of visually guided reaching, Percept and Psychophys., 18 (1975) 181-185.

(40) Mountcastle, V. B., Lynch, J. C., Georgopoulos, A., Sakata, H. and Acuna, C., Posterior parietal association cortex of the monkey : command functions for operations within extrapersonal space, J. Neurophys., 38 (1975) 871-908.

(41) Orban, G. A., Kennedy, H., Maes, H. and Amblard, B., Cats reared in stroboscopic illumination : velocity characteristics of area 18 neurons, Arch. ital. Biol., 116 (1978) 413-419.

(42) Paillard, J., Les déterminants moteurs de l'organisation de l'espace, Cahiers de Psychol., 4 (1971) 261-316.

(43) Paillard, J., The contribution of peripheral and central vision to visually guided reaching, in: Ingle, D. J., Mansfield, D. J. W. and Goodale, M. A. (eds.), Advances in the analysis of visual behavior (Cambridge, Mass., MIT Press, 1979, in press).

(44) Paillard, L. and Beaubaton, D., De la coordination visuomotrice à l'organisation de la saisie manuelle, in: Hécaen, H. and Jeannerod, M. (eds.), Du contrôle moteur à la coordination du geste (Paris, Masson, 1978).

(45) Raibert, M. H., A model for sensorimotor control and learning, Biol. Cybernetics, 29 (1978) 29-36.

(46) Rey, A., Le freinage volontaire du mouvement graphique chez l'enfant, in: Epreuves d'intelligence pratique et de psychomotricité (Neuchatel et Niestlé, 1968).

(47) Rondot, P., De Recondo, J. and Ribadeau, C., Visuomotor ataxia, Brain, 100 (1977) 355-376.

(48) Schneider, G. E., Two visual systems, Science, 163 (1969) 895-902.

(49) Strick, P. L., Control of peripheral input to the dentate nucleus by motor preparation, in: Massion, J. and Sasaki, K. (eds.), Cerebello-cerebellar interaction (Amsterdam, Elsevier/North Holland Biomed. Press, 1979).

(50) Trevarthen, C. B., Two mechanisms of vision in primates, Psychol. Forsch., 31 (1968) 299-337.

(51) Wiesendanger, M., Ruegg, D. G. and Wiesendanger, R., The corticopon-tine system in primates : anatomical and functional consideration, in: Massion, J. and Sasaki, K. (eds.) (Amsterdam, Elsevier/North Holland Biomed. Press, 1979).

Tutorials in Motor Behavior
G.E. Stelmach and J. Requin (eds.)
© *North-Holland Publishing Company, 1980*

16

VISUO-MOTOR COORDINATION IN SPACE-TIME

David N. Lee
Department of Psychology
University of Edinburgh
Edinburgh, Scotland

Activity takes place in a space-time world.   It therefore
requires spatio-temporal information for its guidance.   Where
does this information come from?   Since activity involves
movement relative to the environment it generates a constantly
changing optic array at the eye--a spatio-temporal optic flow
field.   This paper sets out to examine the cooperative relationship between vision and action--how the optic flow field yields
spatio-temporal information for guiding activity and how activity
makes that information available.   The central thesis is that
the visual system and the motor system are functionally inseparable: they are components of a unified perceptuo-motor system,
which is itself a component of the organism-environment system.

INTRODUCTION

"Henceforth space by itself, and time by itself, are doomed to
fade away into mere shadows, and only a kind of union of the two
will preserve an independent reality."
                                        H. Minkowski, 1908

Though Minkowski was addressing a meeting of physicists in the early days
of Relativity Theory, his words are equally germane for students of motor
control. For actions are performed in a space-time world and controlling
activity means directing it through "points" in space-time.   Running to
intercept a cross-ball at soccer or playing a tennis shot are clear
examples of skills requiring getting both to the right place and at the
right time.   Furthermore, it makes no sense, if the player happens to
miss the ball, to attempt to attribute this either to an error in spatial
judgment or to a timing error, for success could have been achieved by
getting either to the same place at a different time or to a different
place at the same time--or, indeed, to a different place at a different
time.   The error is a spatio-temporal one.   Similarly, even such
apparently purely spatial tasks as reaching for a stationary object or
hitting a golf ball are spatio-temporal skills.   While there is no
external time constraint as there is in hitting a moving ball, nonetheless
the act has to be organised in space-time; the act is a dynamical process
requiring the appropriate modulation of muscular forces both in the right
place and at the right time.

Controlling activity in the environment clearly requires perceptual
information about the dynamic relationship of the organism to the
environment.   The information required is not simply exteroceptive, about
the spatial structure of the environment and the motions of objects, nor

is it simply proprioceptive, about the positions, orientations and movements of the limbs relative to the body.   It is what has been termed
exproprioceptive information (Lee, 1978), a union of exteroceptive and
proprioceptive information, namely information about the position,
orientation and movement of the body or part of the body relative to the
environment.

This paper sets out to explore how vision affords exproprioceptive
information and how that information might be used in controlling activity.
We start by examining what information is available to the eye.

THE OPTIC FLOW FIELD

Whenever the head is moving, however slightly, relative to the environment
the pattern of light at the eye is constantly changing.   This time-
varying pattern or optic flow field is the normal stimulus for vision.
J. J. Gibson (1950 & 1958) was the first to tackle the problem of
determining the information available in the optic flow field for
controlling activity.   The following outline analysis owes much to his
insights (for more details see Lee, 1974 & 1976).

The environment consists of material substances bounded by surfaces.   It
is by means of the light reflected from surfaces that visual perception is
possible.   Now a surface does not reflect light uniformly, unless it is
mirror-like.   It contains facets, patches of differing pigmentation and
so on.   In short, a surface may be considered to be densely covered with
texture elements which reflect light differently from their neighbours.
Thus the light reflected from the surfaces in the environment forms a
densely structured optic array at a point of observation.   The optic
array may be thought of as a bundle of narrow cones of light with their
apices at the point of observation, each cone having as its base a
distinct environmental texture element and thus being optically differentiable from its neighbours in terms of the intensity and/or spectral
composition of the light it contains.

At each point of observation there is a unique optic array.   It is the
passage of the eye through successive points of observation that gives
rise to the optic flow field at the eye.   A convenient way of describing
the optic flow field is in terms of its interception with a projection
surface.   For the purpose of analysis, it is immaterial the projection
surface we choose since the description of the optic flow field in terms
of its projection on one surface can be uniquely transformed into a
description for any other surface.   For clarity of exposition, we will
here consider the projection of the optic flow field onto a plane surface
behind the point of observation, like the image plane of a camera, and
confine our attention to the analysis of the rectilinear optic flow field
i.e., that which results when the eye is moving along a straight path
through the environment.   (For an analysis of the curvilinear optic
flow field see, e.g., Lee & Lishman, 1977).

It is easier to explain, and equivalent geometrically, if we consider the
eye stationary and the environment moving.   Figure 1 shows the
environment moving with velocity V towards the eye in a direction
perpendicular to the projection plane (the schematic retina).   P and G
denote any two environmental texture elements, G being on the ground.

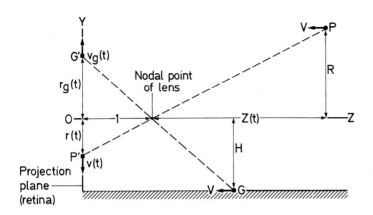

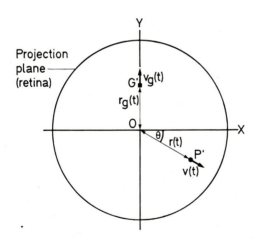

Figure 1 Showing how rectilinear movement of the point of observation
relative to the environment generates an optic flow field. The schematic
eye is considered to be stationary and the environment moving towards it
with velocity V in the direction Z to O. P and G denote texture elements
on surfaces in the environment, G being on the ground surface. Light
reflected from the moving environmental texture elements passes through the
nodal point of the lens giving rise to the moving optic texture elements
P' and G' on the "retina". The densely textured environment gives rise to
a densely textured optic flow field wherein all optic texture elements move
outwards along radial flow lines emanating from O. How the optic flow
filed affords information about the environment and about an animal's movement relative to it is explained in the text. (Modified from Lee, 1974)

Corresponding to P and G are the optic texture elements P' and G'.   It is clear that whatever the layout of surfaces in the environment the optic flow field has the invariant property that all optic texture elements move outwards along radial flow lines emanating from the centre O of the "retina".   (With backward movement of the observer, the optic flow is inwards towards O.)

It has been shown mathematically (Lee, 1974) that the existence of a rectilinear optic flow field at the eye specifies that the eye is moving along a straight path through the environment; i.e., the flow field could not have been generated in any other way (except by artifice).   In other words, there is visually available exproprioceptive information about the organism's movement relative to the environment.   That this is potent information has been demonstrated experimentally.   The human subjects' visible surroundings--a floorless "swinging room" suspended from a high ceiling--were moved in such a way as to produce optic flow fields at their eyes corresponding to forward and backward or sideways movement of themselves.   The experiments showed that vision affords the most sensitive exproprioceptive information about body sway for controlling standing balance, both in toddlers (Lee & Aronson, 1974) and in adults (Lee & Lishman, 1975), and that when a person has conflicting visual and non-visual exproprioceptive information about the direction in which he or she is walking or being passively moved, the conflict is normally dominated by vision (Lishman & Lee, 1973).

Let us now turn to a more detailed analysis of the optic flow field to determine the information it contains about the layout of the surfaces in the environment and about the moving organism's dynamic relationship to those surfaces.   Returning to Figure 1, the position of an environmental texture element P relative to the eye may be defined by the distance coordinates $Z(t)$ and R together with the angle between the OZP and OZX planes.   This angle is specified in the optic flow field by the angular coordinate ϑ of the optic texture element P'.   But are the distance coordinates $Z(t)$ and R optically specified?   From similar triangles

$$Z(t)/R = 1/r(t) \qquad\qquad (1)$$

This equation is an expression of the well-known problem of the missing depth dimension which arises when the visual stimulus is treated as an image, a time-independent spatial structure.   The problem is that the position of an optic texture element specifies only the direction in which an environmental texture element lies, not its distance away.   This problem of the missing depth dimension has puzzled theorists for a century or more and has lead to the view that there must be embodied in the visual system quite detailed "assumptions" about what is being viewed for three-dimensional perception to be possible, or else that depth perception requires binocular vision.   However, if we examine the spatio-temporal structure of the optic flow field we find that the depth dimension is not in fact missing.   Differentiating equation (1) with respect to time we obtain

$$R/V = r(t)^2/v(t) \qquad\qquad (2)$$

where $V = -dZ(t)/dt$ is the velocity of the eye relative to the environment and $v(t) = dr(t)/dt$ is the velocity of the optic texture element P'.

Eliminating R between equations (1) and (2)

$$Z(t)/V = r(t)/v(t) \qquad\qquad (3)$$

These equations (2) and (3) mean that the distance coordinates (R,Z(t)) of all visible environmental texture elements are optically specified in terms of the organism's velocity.

Equation (3) is particularly informative. It states that the time remaining before the eye will be level with the texture element P (assuming the current velocity V were maintained) is directly specified by the value of the optic variable $r(t)/v(t)$. In particular, if there is a frontal plane surface ahead, then the value of the optic variable specifies the time-to-contact with the surface; in this case the value of the optic variable will be the same for all points on the surface and equal to the inverse of the rate of dilation of the optic image of the surface (Lee, 1976). In the following sections we will examine how the optic variable specifying time-to-contact under constant approach velocity affords information for controlling various activities, including those where the approach velocity is not in fact constant. Since the optic variable appears to be a particularly informative one we will give it its own symbol $\tau(t)$.

CATCHING AND HITTING

Catching a ball requires not only getting the hand to a place where the ball will be and appropriately orienting it but also starting to close the fingers before the ball reaches the hand. Alderson et al (1974) in a high speed cine analysis of one-handed catching of tennis balls projected from about 6m found that the fine orientation of the hand started about 150-200ms before the ball contacted the palm and the grasp started 32-50ms before and ended about 10ms after contact. Taking into account the time taken for the ball to pass from the outstretched finger tips to the palm (ca 16ms) and the velocity with which the ball would rebound from the palm of the hand (ca 2.5ms^{-1}) they calculated that the error margin for the timing of the grasp was from about 16ms before to less than 30ms after the optimum time. In successful catches their subjects initiated their grasps within about $\pm$ 14ms of the optimum time.

Such precise timing of the grasp must be based on equally precise predictive visual information about the time of arrival of the ball at the hand. It seems likely that the catcher uses the directly available visual information about time-to-contact discussed above. This information would have to be available an adequate time before contact so that the preparatory orienting of the hand leading on to the start of the grasp can be accurately timed. Sharp and Whiting's (1974 & 1975) experiments indicate that the critical time for the information to be available to the eye is when the time-to-contact is about 300ms. The subjects' view of the tennis ball, projected from about 7m, was limited by turning on and off the room lights. In their 1974 study where they used exposure periods of 20-160ms, one-handed catching performance was best (about 50%) when the ball was visible for at least 40ms when about 300ms from contact with the hand. Longer exposure periods up to 160ms spanning the 300ms time-to-contact point had no significant effect on performance. In their 1975 study they found that catching performance increased to about 85%

when the ball was visible for 240ms up to the 300ms time-to-contact point. This longer exposure would allow time for the subject to foveate the ball, thus making available more precise visual information about time-to-contact.

Why should there apparently be an optimum time-to-contact of about 300ms when the catcher needs to see the ball?   It is reasonable to suppose that the decrement in performance when the ball is only seen when less than 300ms away is due to there being inadequate time to properly program and execute the reaching and catching movement.   But why should earlier (i.e., longer) time-to-contact information be not so effective?   Consider again the catching task.   The performer has to reach out, orient the hand and start the grasping action, this whole movement having to be accurately timed to occupy the time-to-contact interval.   In principle, there are two temporal degrees of freedom which the performer has to control: when to initiate the movement and its duration.   An efficient solution to the visuo-motor problem would be, with practice, to standardise the duration of the movement thereby reducing the problem to that of initiating the movement at a specific time-to-contact.   In a study of a similar skill involving moving a slider in a frontal plane to hit a target directly approaching at a constant speed, Schmidt (1969) found that subjects tended to keep their movement durations constant, achieving a mean absolute timing error of 20-30ms (about the same as found by Alderson et al (1974) in ball catching).   In a later related study, Schmidt and MacCabe (1976) found that movement time became more consistent with practice.

Hitting a ball similarly involves precise timing, and again there is evidence that performers tend with practice to develop a standard movement duration.   Tyldesley and Whiting (1975) found that for expert and intermediate table-tennis players the durations of their forehand drive shots were consistent to within about $\pm$4ms, whereas novices showed no such consistency.   In a film analysis of baseball batters, Hubbard and Seng (1954; see also an analysis by Fitch and Turvey, 1977) found that the batters tended to synchronize the start of their step forward with the release of the ball from the pitcher's hand, adjusted the duration of the step to the speed of the ball and kept the duration of their swings constant.   The timing of the initiation of the swing appears to be based on time-to-contact information picked up during the 500ms or so that the ball is in flight.

The visuo-motor skill of intercepting a moving object appears to start developing at an early age.   Hofsten and Lindhagen (1979) found, for example, that 18 week old infants could reach out and catch an object moving across in front of them at $0.3ms^{-1}$.   Their results indicated that by the time infants have mastered reaching for stationary objects they can also catch moving ones, suggesting that there is a basic human capacity to coordinate behaviour with external events.

PLUNGE DIVING

The prey-catching behaviour of the gannet (Sula bassana) is a beautiful example of finely timed activity.   This large seabird (length about 0.9m wing-span 1.70m) hovers over the water at heights up to about 30m.   When it sights its prey it plummets down with wings half open, presumably to give it some steerage, and then just before hitting the water it starts to

fold its wings so that its body is streamlined for entering the water.
Given that from a height of 30m it will hit the water at about $25ms^{-1}$
or 55 miles h^{-1}, it clearly has to time the folding of its wings very
precisley to avoid possible fatal injury.   It normally catches its fish
on its way back up to the surface.

How does the gannet time the folding of its wings preparatory to entering
the water?   A recent film analysis of ten plunge dives indicated that the
birds do not allow themselves much of a safety margin.   The mean time
before hitting the water when they started to fold their wings was about
310ms (S.D 90ms, range 200-440ms) and the mean time taken to fold their
wings was about 400ms (S.D 80ms, range 240-520ms).   Only two of the birds
had their wings completely folded when they hit the water, but they all
had before they were submerged.   Given the range of heights from which
the birds were diving (about 4 - 12m) and hence the range of falling times
(about 900-1550ms) it is infeasible that the dive is simply a stereotyped
act with the wings being programmed to fold an invariant time after the
start of the dive.

The timing of the wing folding clearly appears to be under visual guidance.
What type of visual information might the birds be using?   While it is
theoretically conceivable that the bird might visually determine its
hovering height, from this compute how long it will take to reach the
water and then pre-program the timing of its wing folding, this does not
seem very likely if only because the vicissitudes of the wind could easily
set its predictions much awry.   It seems most probable that the bird
determines when to fold its wings on the basis of visual information
picked up during its dive.

The film analysis indicated that the birds based their judgments on
information about their time away from the water rather than their
distance away, which makes sense in view of their varying speeds of
contact with the water.   For example, in a 12m dive the bird started
to fold its wings when it was about 5.5m above the water whereas in a
4m dive the wing folding started at a height of about 2.3m, but the times
away from the water when wing folding started were quite similar (400ms
and 320ms respectively).   It is interesting to note, however, that the
wing folding started earlier with the higher dive.   This general tendency
shown in the film data suggests the type of temporal information the birds
might be using.

For the bird to compute its actual time-to-contact with the water when
diving would be a complex task requiring information about its current
speed and distance away from the water and its acceleration.   There is,
however, a simple heuristic that the bird could use, which is to initiate
its wing folding when the optic variable τ (the inverse of the rate of
dilation of the image of the water) reaches a certain margin value τ_m.
As was shown in Section 2, the value of τ specifies the time-to-contact
with the water if the current speed were to be maintained.   It does not
therefore specify the gannet's actual time-to-contact with the water, since
the bird is accelerating.   However, as we will show, it does constitute
adequate information for timing wing folding.   Furthermore, using this
information would result in wing folding starting sooner before hitting
the water the higher the dive, which is what the film data indicated.

Suppose the gannet starts diving from a height h_0 at time $t = 0$. Then at time t later its velocity v and its height h above the water will be

$$v = gt$$

$$h = h_0 - 0.5gt^2$$

where g is the gravitational acceleration. Thus the optic variable will attain the margin value τ_m at time t_m where

$$\tau_m = h/v = (h_0 - 0.5gt_m^2)/gt_m$$

i.e. $$t_m = \sqrt{\tau_m^2 + 2h_0/g} - \tau_m \qquad (4)$$

Now the bird's total falling time will be $\sqrt{2h_0/g}$ and so at time t_m, when $\tau = \tau_m$, its actual time-to-contact t_c with the water will be, from equation (4)

$$t_c = \sqrt{2h_0/g} - t_m$$

$$= \tau_m + \sqrt{2h_0/g} - \sqrt{\tau_m^2 + 2h_0/g} \qquad (5)$$

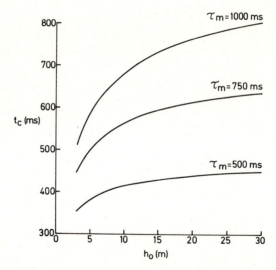

Figure 2

A graphical representation of this equation is given in Figure 2. The curves show how following the simple heuristic strategy of initiating wing folding when the value of the optic variable τ reaches a margin value τ_m would result in the wing folding starting at a longer time t_c before contact the higher the height h_0 of the dive, thus allowing a higher margin for error the greater the risk of injury. It would, of course, take the bird a certain response time to register that the margin value had been

reached and to start the act of folding its wings.   To allow for this,
the values of t_c shown in Figure 2 would need to be lowered by this
response time. Thus, for example, with a response time of 150ms and using
a margin value τ_m of 750ms, the time-to-contact where the wings would
start to fold would be 300ms from a dive height of 3m and 480ms from 30m.

RUNNING AND JUMPING

The importance of vision for movement control is particularly evident when
one is walking or running through the normal cluttered environment.   The
motor program generating the coordinated pattern of locomotor movements
has to be continually adjusted on the basis of visual and other sensory
information in order to meet the demands of the terrain--adjusting to
varying compliance of the ground, negotiating steps, securing adequate
footing, leaping over obstacles and so on.

Consider a person running over a level stretch of ground.   As Bernstein
(1967) has shown, the coordinated pattern of limb movements is normally
cyclicly very regular.   In particular, the swing-through phase of each
leg is accurately timed so that the foot strikes the ground in the right
way, normally just in front of the hips.   Now there are three components
to the swing-through time: the first flight time (between the foot leaving
the ground and the other foot striking it), the ground-contact time of the
other foot and the second flight time.   The flight times will be determined
by the vertical component of the launch velocity, which in turn will be
determined by the strength of the thrust force applied to the ground and
the compliance of the ground.   For example, the same thrust applied to
more compliant ground will result in a shorter flight time and hence
require a shorter swing-through time.   Thus in running over ground of
irregular compliance, the temporal patterns of muscular forces controlling
the swing-through and the thrusts on the ground have to be finely
coordinated and adjusted to the terrain.   The same is true when running
over undulating ground.   Here the flight times will vary with the
undulations; stepping into a dip, for instance, will result in a larger
flight time, requiring lengthening the swing-through time.

These examples illustrate some of the subtleties of locomotor control in
which everyday experience suggests that vision plays a major regulatory
role.   For instance, running over undulating ground in the dark is a
jarring experience, whereas in the light it is normally quite smooth.
Another example is stepping off a kerb that one has not noticed.   This
brings us to another aspect of locomotor control, namely the shock-
absorber action of the leg muscles.   When the foot strikes the ground
there is a sudden passive stretching force applied to the muscles which
has to be adequately resisted to avoid jarring the skeletal structure.
Melvill Jones and Watt (1971) have shown that this is achieved, at least
in part, by tensioning the gastrocnemius muscle some 140ms before
contacting the ground.   That vision is essential for the programming of
such preparatory activity is indicated by the study of Freedman et al
(1976) on stepping down (e.m.g recording from the triceps surae) and that
of Dietz and Noth (1978) on falling on one's hands against an inclined
board (e.m.g recording from the triceps brachii).   In both studies,
preparatory muscular activity timed to cushion the landing occurred only
when the subjects were allowed normal vision.

In running over uneven ground the timing of the swing-through and the
preparatory shock-absorber action of the leg could be based on the visual
information about time-to-contact discussed above.   To be sure, a runner
is in a different situation to a diving gannet;   the runner needs information about time-to-contact of the foot with the ground whereas for the
bird it is time-to-contact of the head with the water that matters.
However, it can be shown that the type of heuristic strategy proposed
above for the gannet would also work in timing landing on the feet.   It
will be remembered that following the strategy would result in preparatory
activity being initiated sooner before contact the higher the fall.   This
was observed in the film data on the gannet and is also evidenced in
Greenwood and Hopkin's (1976, Fig. 5) data on the preparatory tensioning
of the soleus muscle of a person's leg during sudden drops from different
heights.

Let us now consider another locomotor control problem, that of securing
adequate footing.   Running over stepping stones is a good example.
The person not only has to appropriately adjust the lengths of his strides
but also has to land on each successive stone in just the right way else
he will not be able to propel himself to the next stone.   For example,
if he is running down a straight line of stones and then has to veer to
the right down another line, he has to land on the corner stone with his
centre of gravity to the right of his foot.   If the stones afford only
narrow footing, this means that he has to prepare for the veer by
launching himself off in the right direction from the stone before the
corner one.   In other words he has to plan at least two strides ahead.
In a recent study involving such a set-up (small blocks of wood screwed
to the laboratory floor), it was found that subjects often started
preparing their veers by shifting their centres of gravity when they were
about two strides from the corner stone, and that if they were prevented
from seeing which way they had to veer until after they were about 150ms
away from landing on the stone before the corner one then they could not
veer successfully.

Running over stepping stones brings to light the problem of distance and
size perception which so far we have discussed rather little.   In Section
2 it was shown that there is available in the optic flow field at the eye
information about the _relative_ sizes and distances of surfaces in the
environment, scaled in terms of the animal's velocity.   However, what
an animal needs is information that is relevant to controlling its
activity--e.g., that a hurdle is a certain fraction of its own height, so
many strides away and so on.   That is, it needs _body-scaled_ spatial
information about its environment.   Let us consider two ways that body-
scaled information might be obtained from the optic flow field.

Consider an animal running straight over a level stretch of ground.
Suppose at a particular time t its speed is V.   One bodily yard-stick it
could use is the height H of its eye above the ground, which will be more
or less constant.   Referring to Figure 1, H is the R-coordinate of any
texture element on the ground over which the animal's eye will pass.
Therefore, applying equation (2), Section 2, to the ground texture element
G depicted in Figure 1

$$H/V = r_g(t)^2/v_g(t) \qquad\qquad\qquad (6)$$

and eliminating V between equations (2), (3) and (6)

$$R/H = r(t)^2 v_g(t)/r_g(t)^2 v(t) \tag{7}$$

$$Z(t)/H = r(t)v_g(t)/r_g(t)^2 v(t) \tag{8}$$

In other words there is a particular relation between the optic flow from the line of ground ahead and the optic flow from other environmental texture elements which specifies the current distances away and the sizes of surfaces and objects in the environment in units of the animal's eye height.

Another potential bodily yard-stick is stride length. Suppose that at time t an animal's stride length is L and the duration of its strides is t_s. Then for any environmental texture element P (see Figure 1) we have

$$Z(t-t_s) - Z(t) = L \tag{9}$$

Thus from equation (3), and noting that $r(t)/v(t) = \tau(t)$, viz. the "time-to-contact" optic variable,

$$\left[Z(t-t_s) - Z(t)\right]/V = L/V = \tau(t-t_s) - \tau(t) \tag{10}$$

and so eliminating V between equations (2), (3) and (10)

$$R/L = r(t)\tau(t)/\left[\tau(t-t_s) - \tau(t)\right] = r(t)\tau(t)/t_s \tag{11}$$

$$Z(t)/L = \tau(t)/\left[\tau(t-t_s) - \tau(t)\right] = \tau(t)/t_s \tag{12}$$

i.e., the current distances away and the sizes of surfaces and objects in the environment are optically specified in units of the animal's stride length.

As an example of the combined use of visual body-scaled spatial and temporal information, consider a horse jumping a fence. The horse needs body-scaled information about the height of the fence in order to determine how hard to thrust from the ground and time-to-contact information to determine when to jump. (It may be said that it has to judge where to leap from, but the proper place depends on its speed whereas the proper time does not.) For the horse to achieve an optimally efficient jump where at its zenith it is just above the top of the fence, the energy that it needs to put into its leg thrust is essentially proportional to the height h that it has to raise its centre of gravity and the time-to-contact when it should start its jump is proportional to $\sqrt{h}$.

Another example is the long jump run-up. The athlete not only has to strike a narrow take-off board when running at maximum speed but also has to strike the board in the right posture for take-off, for while it is the horizontal momentum developed during the run-up that carries the athlete forward in the jump, it is the vertical take-off velocity that determines the duration of the jump and hence its length for a given run-up speed. Clearly, the last few strides to the board are critical in setting up the right posture for a powerful vertical thrust at take-off. Now a skilled athlete can, after sprinting 40m, strike the take-off board with a standard error of about 10cm. How is such accuracy achieved? Since no adjustments to the stride pattern are normally apparent, many coaches and athletes believe that it is all a matter of developing a standard run-up. However, a recent film analysis of athletes showed that their run-ups were nowhere near as standard as they thought (Lee, Lishman & Thomson, 1977). The standard errors of their footfall positions increased considerably down the track, reaching a peak of 35cm for one Olympic athlete (see Fig.3)

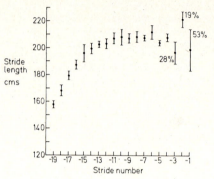

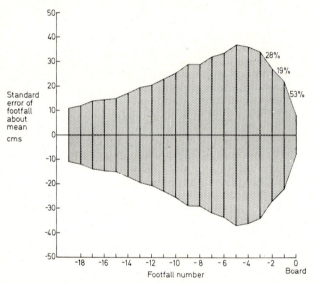

Figure 3. Visual guidance in the long jump. Performance of an Olympic athlete over six jumps with a 40m, 21-stride run-up. (1) Means and standard deviations (SDs) of stride lengths for the last 19 strides to the take-off board. Note how high the SD is over the last three visually adjusted strides. (2) The SDs of successive footfall positions down the track. Note how the SD progressively increases up to a peak of 35cm and then suddenly drops to about 8cm over the last three strides. The percentages shown are estimates of the proportion of the total adjustment made on each stride, derived from linear regression analyses. (Modified from Lee, Lishman & Thomson, 1977)

Over the last three strides, however, the standard error decreased
dramatically to about 8cm at the take-off board, the length of each stride
being highly correlated with the athlete's distance from the board.

The athletes were clearly visually adjusting their last three strides to
zero-in on the take-off board. Furthermore, since the total duration of
these three strides was only about 0.7s, it is likely that they were
programming these strides as a unit. What visual information could the
athletes have been using? One possibility is information about time to
reach the board (specified by the value of the optic variable τ for the
board), for the task of zeroing-in on the board may be conceived of as
programming the durations of the forthcoming strides so as to just fill
the time remaining to reach the board. This temporal conception of the
task is probably more appropriate than a spatial one (i.e., programming
stride lengths), since, as was pointed out above, a runner has direct
control over the duration of his strides by how hard he thrusts vertically
on the ground, whereas the length of his strides are a function also of
his speed of travel.

DRIVING

The central theme of this paper has been that activity takes place in a
space-time world, that controlling activity means directing it through
"points" in space-time and that this requires perceptual spatio-temporal
information. By considering a variety of skills it has been attempted
to show that no matter how purely spatial a skill might appear, temporal
information is always required and could indeed substitute, in part at
least, for spatial information. To conclude, let us consider another
common skill, stopping a vehicle at an obstacle. This skill is a
particularly interesting one for it appears to require neither spatial
information as such nor temporal information as such but some kind of
dimensionless union of the two.

In order to stop at an obstacle a driver not only has to start braking
soon enough but he also has to adjust his deceleration to an adequate
level during the stop in order to avoid running out of braking power.
In other words, the driver can get himself into a "crash state" (his
speed too high in relation to his distance from the obstacle) well before
he actually hits the obstacle. To avoid getting into a crash state while
he is braking the driver clearly needs some kind of visual information
about his dynamic relationship to the obstacle so that he can appropriately
adjust his braking. It might seem that he needs three types of information; his distance from the obstacle, his speed and his deceleration.
However it turns out that none of this information as such is necessary.

Suppose that at a time t the driver is a distance $Z(t)$ from the obstacle,
his instantaneous velocity is $V(t)$ and he is braking at a deceleration D.
Then his deceleration D is adequate if and only if the distance it will
take him to stop with that deceleration is less than or equal to his
current distance from the obstacle, i.e., if and only if

$$V(t)^2/2D \leqslant Z(t)$$

or $$Z(t)D/V(t)^2 \geqslant 0.5 \qquad (13)$$

Now $Z(t)/V(t)$ is specified by the value of the optic variable $\tau(t)$ for the obstacle (see equation (3)), i.e.,

$$Z(t)/V(t) = \tau(t) \tag{14}$$

and differentiating this equation with respect to time we obtain

$$Z(t)D/V(t)^2 = 1 + d\tau(t)/dt \tag{15}$$

Hence, from equations (13) and (15), the value of the time derivative of the optic variable $\tau(t)$ specifies whether the driver's current deceleration is adequate or not.   It is adequate if and only if

$$d\tau(t)/dt \geqslant -0.5 \tag{16}$$

A safe braking strategy would therefore consist in the driver adjusting his braking so that $d\tau(t)/dt$ remained at a safe value.   The deceleration profiles produced by this hypothetical braking strategy (Lee, 1976) in fact matched quite closely those of test drivers recorded by Spurr (1969), the only data on visually controlled braking found in the literature.

It will be noted that the information used in this strategy is not spatio-temporal in any conventional sense: the time derivative of the "time-to-contact" optic variable τ is a dimensionless quantity. Nonetheless this dimensionless optic variable affords information for controlling a space-time activity.   Perhaps this was the kind of thing Minkowski was hinting at.

References

(1) Alderson, G. J. K. Sully, D. J. and Sully, H. G.,   An operational analysis of a one-handed catching task using high speed photography, Journal of Motor Behavior, 6 (1974) 217-226.
(2) Bernstein, N., The Co-ordination and Regulation of Movements (Pergamon Press, Oxford, 1967).
(3) Dietz, V. and Noth, J., Pre-inervation and stretch responses of triceps bracchii in man falling with and without visual control, Brain Research, 142 (1978) 576-579.
(4) Fitch, H. L. and Turvey, M. T., On the control of activity: some remarks from an ecological point of view, in: Landers, D. M. and Christina, R. W. (eds), Psychology of Motor Behavior and Sport-1977, (Human Kinetics Publishers, Champaign, Illinois, 1977).
(5) Freedman, W., Wannstedt, G. and Herman, R., EMG patterns and forces developed during step-down, American Journal of Physical Medicine, 55 (1976) 275-290.
(6) Gibson, J. J., The Perception of the Visual World,(Houghton Mifflin, Boston, 1950).
(7) Gibson, J. J., Visually controlled locomotion and visual orientation in animals, British Journal of Psychology, 49 (1958) 182-194.
(8) Greenwood, R. and Hopkins, A., Muscle responses during sudden falls in man, Journal of Physiology, 254 (1976) 507-518.
(9) Hofsten, C. von and Lindhagen, K., Observations on the development of reaching for moving objects, Journal of Experimental Child Psychology, in press.

(10) Hubbard, A. W. and Seng, C. N., Visual movements of batters, Research Quarterly, 25 (1954) 42-57.

(11) Lee, D. N., Visual information during locomotion, in: McLeod, R. and Pick, H. (eds), Perception: Essays in Honor of J. J. Gibson (Cornell University Press, Ithaca, 1974).

(12) Lee, D. N., A theory of visual control of braking based on information about time to collision, Perception, 5 (1976) 437-459.

(13) Lee, D. N., The functions of vision, in: Pick, H. and Salzmann, E. (eds) Modes of Perceiving and Processing Information,(Erlbaum Associates, Hillsdale, 1978).

(14) Lee, D. N. and Aronson, E., Visual proprioceptive control of standing in human infants, Perception and Psychophysics, 15 (1974) 529-532.

(15) Lee, D. N. and Lishman, J. R., Visual proprioceptive control of stance, Journal of Human Movement Studies, 1 (1975) 87-95.

(16) Lee, D. N. and Lishman, J. R., Visual control of locomotion, Scandanavian Journal of Psychology, 18 (1977) 224-230.

(17) Lee, D. N., Lishman, J. R. and Thomson, J., Visual guidance in the long jump, Athletics Coach, 11 (1977) 26-30 and 12, 17-23.

(18) Lishman, J. R. and Lee, D. N., The autonomy of visual kinaesthesis, Perception, 2 (1973) 287-294.

(19) Melvill Jones, G. and Watt, D. G. D., Observations on the control of stepping and hopping movements in man, Journal of Physiology, 219 (1971) 709-727.

(20) Minkowski, H., Space and Time, Address delivered at the 80th Assembly of German Natural Scientists and Physicians, Cologne, 21 September (1908).

(21) Schmidt, R. A., Movement time as a determiner of timing accuracy, Journal of Experimental Psychology, 79 (1969) 43-47.

(22) Schmidt, R. A. and McCabe, J. F., Motor program utilization over extended practice, Journal of Human Movement Studies, 2 (1976) 239-247.

(23) Sharp, R. H. and Whiting, H. T. A., Exposure and occluded duration effects in a ball-catching skill, Journal of Motor Behavior, 6 (1974) 139-147.

(24) Sharp, R. H. and Whiting, H. T. A., Information-processing and eye movement behaviour in a ball-catching skill, Journal of Human Movement Studies, 1 (1975) 124-131.

(25) Spurr, R. T., Subjective aspects of braking, Automobile Engineer, 59 (1969) 58-61.

(26) Tyldesley, D. A. and Whiting, H. T. A., Operational timing, Journal of Human Movement Studies, 1 (1975) 172-177.

Tutorials in Motor Behavior
G.E. Stelmach and J. Requin (eds.)
© *North-Holland Publishing Company, 1980*

17

DO OCULOMOTOR SIGNALS CONTRIBUTE
IN EYE-HAND COORDINATION ?

M. Jeannerod, C. Prablanc and M.T. Perenin
Laboratoire de Neuropsychologie Expérimentale
INSERM U 94   69500 - BRON - FRANCE

The question as to whether signals related to eye position
and/or movements can be used in directing the hand at a
visual target was raised. Apparently conflicting data were
obtained from Ss with paralysis of extrinsic ocular muscles
where the final hand position seemed to be influenced by
an exaggerated oculomotor output, and from normal Ss
where the final hand position appeared to be unrelated to
oculomotor signals. It is thought that these extra-retinal
signals only contribute minimally in eye-hand coordination
and that their contribution may become apparent in situations
where the available cues for directing the hand at a visual
goal are reduced.

Position of gaze axis in space has been claimed to represent a major cue
for the organization of behaviour directed at extrapersonal space. Hence,
gaze fixation on a given object would determine the visual direction of
that object with respect to body axis, and would produce a signal for the
guidance of corresponding reaching movements of the hand.

Since the relationship of retinal coordinates to body axis does not hold
constant, due to head and eye movements, the retinal locus where the
object projects cannot by itself be the source of information about its
egocentric localization. The retinal map can only contribute to a central
map where eye-re-head and head-re-body positions (the sum of which is gaze
position) are taken into account.

Eye-re-head position depends on the occurence of eye movements, which match
coordinates on the peripheral retina determined by selective attention.
Goal-directed eye-movements[*] thus imply the occurence of two types of
central signals. Retinal signals are drawn from the process of foveation,
involving nullification of the retinal "error", and fulfillment of the
perceptual hypothesis or goal. Extra-retinal signals are represented by
neuronal events related to the displacement and/or the position of the eyes,
whatever their origin may be (see below).

Arguments for a central monitoring of extra-retinal signals related to eye-
movements, and for their contribution to a central representation of extrapersonal visual space, can be tracked in the literature as early as
Charles Bell (1823). This author (quoted by Wade, 1978) had noticed that

---

[*] Eye and hand reaching movements are considered herein as the expression
of visually goal-directed behaviour, i.e. a behaviour where the goal is
transformed into a set of commands for specific action in space.

visual after-images seem to move with the eyes in spite of beeing stationary on the retina. Hence, Bell thought that "... vision in its extended
sense is a compound operation, the idea of position of an object having
relation to the activity of the muscles". If we move the eyes by the voluntary muscles... we shall have the notion of place or relation raised in
the mind".

The origin and the nature of these extra-retinal signals have been, and
still are, the object of a one-century controversy among philosophers and
neuroscientists (see Jones, 1972), mostly due to the fact that no direct
experimental evidence as to their existence can be found in the literature
However, many indirect observations are available, particularly those
related to the effect of paralysis (experimental or pathological) of
extrinsic eye muscles on hand reaching behaviour.

We have recently observed 4 patients with a complete paralysis of either
the VIth or the IIId nerve in one eye (Perenin et al., 1977). Patients
were tested for pointing by hand at visual targets appearing in their
peripheral visual field, including on the side of the paralysis. The normal
eye was occluded, the head was fixed and the view of the arm was prevented.
In addition, movements of the normal eye (under cover) were recorded.

When targets appeared in the area of the visual field corresponding to the
paralysis, the hand was pointed far more distally from the midline than
the actual position of the target. For example, for a target presented at
a retinal locus corresponding to 30 degrees from the fovea, the hand would
reach a point in space corresponding to 50 degrees from the fovea, or more
(fig. 1a). This effect, classically known by ophtalmologists as "past-
pointing" has sometimes been used as a clinical sign to determine which
muscle is paralyzed. Indeed, targets presented in the other half-field of
the same eye (i.e. corresponding to non-paralyzed muscles) elicited pointing movements correctly directed at the actual location of the target.

An explanation for this phenomenon can be found by observing the output of
the oculomotor system (as from the movements of the normal, covered eye) in
response to targets presented at the paralyzed eye. As demonstrated in fig.
1b, saccades of the normal eye clearly over-reached target position. This
effect is likely to be due to the impossibility for the paralyzed eye to
foveate the target : the retinal error cannot be nullified by the saccades,
and the oculomotor system behaves as if it were constantly reafferented by
a positive feedback loop (Young and Stark, 1963). For the present purpose,
however, the important point is the close correspondence between an exaggerated oculomotor output and past-pointing, when the subject attempts to
reach for targets in the direction of the paralysis. This is in fact what
would be predicted if the subject would rely upon a monitoring of the oculomotor output to direct his hand in visual space. Indeed, by asking one of
our patients to keep his gaze fixated at the midline and not to try to
foveate the targets (in other words, to use purely retinal cues rather than
extra-retinal signals) we observed that the hand pointings became correctly
directed at the actual target location (fig. 1a).

Experiments were undertaken in normal subjects in order to determine the
respective contributions of retinal cues, foveation and extra-retinal signals in eye-hand coordination. Subjects with the head fixed were presented
with targets appearing randomly at different locations within their

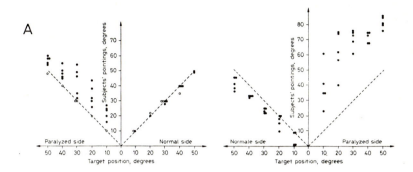

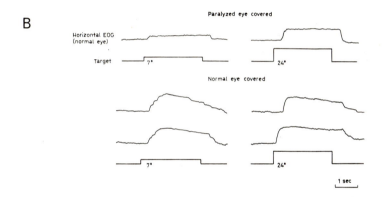

Fig. 1 Relationship of hand pointing errors to exaggerated oculomotor output in subjects with paralysis of extrinsic ocular muscles.
A : Past-pointing is clearly observed in two patients with a paralysis of the left external rectus, and of the left internal rectus, respectively. In the patient displayed on the right side of the figure, filled circles represent pointing trials with free eye movements. Open circles represent trials where the subject has been required not to move the eyes.
B : Eye movements recordings from the normal eye during pointing trials in a patient with a paralysis of the left internal rectus (same patient as in A, left part of the figure).
Upward deflections correspond to saccades directed to the right.

peripheral visual field, along the horizontal meridian. The required task was to point rapidly by hand at the location of these targets. Correction of possible residual errors after completion of the movement was not allowed. The view of the hand could be either allowed (closed loop situation) or prevented (open loop situation). Regardless the status of the eye-hand loop (open or closed) three experimental conditions were used. In condition 1, the target jumped from the midline position at which the subject was

fixating his gaze to a given position within the peripheral visual field.
The subject automatically tracked the target by eye and fixated his gaze at
the new target position. In condition 2, the target jumped to a given position in the peripheral field but disappeared at the onset of the saccade
directed to it. In condition 3, the target located at the midline position
remained on during the trial, while another target appeared within the peripheral field. The subject was required to keep his gaze fixated at the midline target (fig. 2).

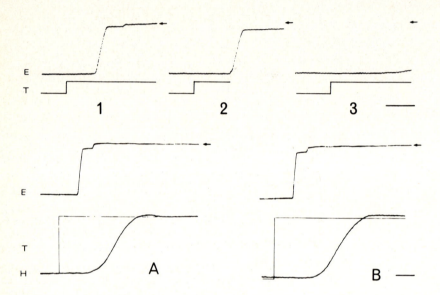

Fig. 2 Aspect of the oculomotor output in the three experimental conditions
used in normal subjects.
Upper row : E : eye position as recorded with the EOG technique. T : target
events. Time calibration : 250 msec.
Condition 1 : the target jumps from midline to a position within the peripheral visual field (in this case, 30 degrees to the right). Note saccadic
change in eye position, followed by a secondary "correction" saccade.
Arrow on the right of the record indicates the location of the target.
Condition 2 : the target jumps and is cut off at the onset of the corresponding saccade. Note lack of secondary saccade, which results in undershooting
with respect to target location. Condition 3 : the subject is required to
keep his gaze fixated at midline when the target jumps.
Lower row : Display of the eye-hand sequence obtained in condition 1, in the
closed-loop situation (A) and in the open-loop situation (B).
E : eye position. T : target position. H : hand position. In this particular
case, hand position has been recorded continuously by having the subject
keeping his hand in contact with the recording surface during his movement.
Note the difference in delay between movement of the eye and movement of
the hand. Time calibration 250 msec.

Eye and hand positions were recorded. Accuracy of eye and hand positions with respect to target position was automatically measured and averaged by a computer.

Baseline values of accuracy can be obtained from condition 1, with the eye-hand loop closed. Except for the fact that the head was fixed, this condition is quite similar to the normal situation for reaching. Errors were limited to a few millimeters and their amplitude was not influenced by the eccentricity of the target (fig. 3).

Limiting the available cues related to gaze position in space (as in conditions 2 and 3) decreased the absolute accuracy of hand pointings. Condition 2 with the eye-hand loop closed selectively impaired the possibility to foveate the target at the end of the saccade. In this condition, saccades appeared to be correctly oriented in the direction where the target has disappeared, but constantly fell short with respect to its exact position. This undershooting (by a few degrees) can be related to the non-occurence of the secondary saccade following a saccade directed at a target in the peripheral visual field (Prablanc and Jeannerod, 1975). The amplitude of absolute errors for the hand increased in condition 2, an effect which was influenced by the eccentricity of the targets (fig. 3). No particular trend could be observed for the direction of these errors, i.e., the hand could undershoot as well as overshoot target position. Hence, it is clear that no relationship could be established with the direction of errors made by the eye.

In condition 3 with the eye-hand loop closed, the absence of target oriented saccades was verified on the records. Hence, not only was the foveation of the peripheral target prevented, but also the occurence of an extra-retinal signal. Hand pointings, directed on the basis of peripheral retinal cues only, appeared to be unprecise, particularly for the more eccentric targets. Absolute errors, however, were constantly smaller in this condition than in condition 2 (fig. 3). This can be explained by the possibility, which may exist in condition 3 but not in condition 2, to compare visually the respective retinal positions of the hand and of the target at the end of the movement. This information can be a source for mechanisms optimizing the trajectory of the hand at the target.

Other visual cues, however, independent from the occurence of eye movements seem to be far more important in ensuring the accuracy of hand position. Indeed, in our experiment, opening the eye-hand loop resulted in all three conditions in a severe deterioration of the precision of reaching. In condition 1, for instance, though foveation was achieved and though extra-retinal signals were presumably available, the hand nevertheless missed the target by a large amount (with a constant trend toward undershooting). In addition, precision was comparatively less deteriorated in condition 3 where no eye movements were performed (fig. 3).

At first inspection our results from the experiments with normal subjects do not support a role of eye-movement and/or position related signals in guiding the hand at a visual target. In the closed-loop situation, precision of reaching is deteriorated by the lack of foveation (condition 2) as well as by the absence of eye movement (condition 3). A common factor to both conditions is the impossibility to make the fine visual adjustment of hand position with respect to target location. This factor would be

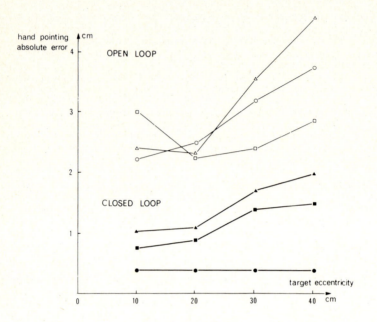

Fig. 3   Pointing errors in normal subjects.
Circles : condition 1, triangles : condition 2, squares : condition 3 (see
fig. 2). Filled symbols : closed loop situation. Open symbols : open-loop
situation. Subjects (N = 8) point with their right hand at targets
appearing in their right normal hemifield.

sufficient to explain the observed effects, i.e., the increased scatter of
hand final positions and the further deterioration of precision for larger
eccentricities of the targets (see Brown et al., 1938). The greater increase in absolute error of the hand when the subject is shifted from the closed-loop to the open-loop situation might be due to the suppression of an
additional factor related to the view of the hand prior to or during the
reaching movement. Prablanc et al. (in preparation) have shown that the
possibility to see the hand prior to the movement (the eye-hand loop being
thus open at the onset of the hand movement) restores a better precision.

However, an attempt can be made at reconciling the results obtained from
patients with paralysis of extraocular muscles, which favor a role of extra-
retinal signals in eye-hand coordination, with those from normal subjects,
which don't. It should be reminded that both the amplitude and the nature
of reaching errors are different in the two experiments. In the experiment
with normal subjects in the open-loop situation, the error typically represents some 10 per cent of the target eccentricity and results in a constant
but slight undershooting of the hand with respect to the target. In the experiment with "paralyzed" subjects, the error can amount as much as 40% of

target eccentricity, though it results in a strong overshooting of the hand.

A plausible hypothesis would be the following. Extra-retinal signals would contribute only to a small extent to the overall precision of the hand, and would add up to other cues, as mentioned above. In the open-loop situation where these cues are no longer available, the scatter of final hand positions would thus represent the net contribution of extra-retinal signals. In subjects with paralyzed extra-ocular muscles, where the extra-retinal signals can be thought to be grossly exaggerated, the scatter of final hand positions is massively displaced in the direction of overshooting, which makes its relationship to eye position to become more apparent.

This explanation, however, probably holds true only for a limited number of situations, i.e., those where the subject's head is held fixed. In normal behaviour with head free, it can reasonably be assumed that the head-eye system behaves as a unit, the eye-re-head position being maintained constantly null by the vestibulo-ocular reflex. Signals related to static head position could thus automatically ensure the referencing of the retinal map to body coordinates. In that case, a monitoring of the eye position in the orbit (e.g. through inflow information) or of the oculomotor output (e.g. through outflow information) would both become un-necessary. It remains to be demonstrated whether availability of head position cues in experimental situations similar as ours would result in a better precision of reaching at a visual target by hand. There are some indications that this might be the case (Marteniuk, 1978).

References

N.S. Brown, E.B. Knauft and G. Rosenbaum : The accuracy of positionning reactions as a function of their direction and extent, Amer. J. Psychol. 61 (1948) 167-182.
E.G. Jones : The development of the 'muscular sense' concept during the nineteenth century and the work of H. Charlton Bastian, J. Hist. Med. all. Sci. 27 (1972) 298-311.
R.G. Marteniuk : The role of eye and head positions in slow movement execution, in : Stelmach, G.E. (ed.), Information Processing in motor learning and control (Academic Press, New York, 1978, pp. 267-288).
M.T. Perenin, M. Jeannerod and C. Prablanc : Spatial localization with paralyzed eye muscles, Ophtalmologica, 175 (1977) 206-214.
C. Prablanc and M. Jeannerod : Corrective saccades : dependence on retinal reafferent signals, Vision Research, 15 (1975) 465-469.
N.J. Wade : Sir Charles Bell on visual direction, Perception, 7 (1978) 359-362.
L.R. Young and L. Stark : Variable feedback experiments testing a sampled-data model for eye tracking movement, IEEE Trans. Human Factors in electronics, HFE4 (1963) 38-51.

Tutorials in Motor Behavior
G.E. Stelmach and J. Requin (eds.)
© North-Holland Publishing Company, 1980

18

EYE AND HEAD FIXATION MOVEMENTS:
THEIR COORDINATION AND CONTROL

A.Roucoux[*] and M.Crommelinck
Laboratoire de Neurophysiologie
University of Louvain
Brussels, Belgium

INTRODUCTION

Most displacements of the visual axis are realized, at least in higher mammals, by synchronous and coordinated eye and head rotations. The way motor orders are adequately distributed to the eye and head motor centers and how the two movements are subsequently coordinated is presently still unclear. Our aim here is to sketch a model of this motor control and coordination, based on observations made in the alert cat.

Some insight in the mechanism of eye-head coordination in the monkey has been gained recently thanks to Bizzi and his collaborators (Bizzi et al., 1972; Morasso et al., 1973). They demonstrated that, in the monkey trained to fixate visual targets, gaze shifts are accomplished by combined eye and head movements. The sum of the amplitudes of eye and head rotations matches the target eccentricity. If the head is prevented from moving, the eye alone realizes the correct fixation. The adaptation of the eye saccade amplitude to the importance of the head movement is mainly done by the vestibulo-ocular reflex (V.O.R.), the slow phase of which is added to the saccadic command (Dichgans et al., 1973). In other words, the displacement of the visual axis in space is identical, whether the head moves or does not. Only the eye saccade amplitude needs to be accurately coded: the head movement, if present, being automatically taken into account by the V.O.R. Another important consequence is that the amplitude of every gaze shift made with a single eye saccade is limited to the maximal excursion of the eye within the orbit: the rôle of the head movement is indeed not to increase the amplitude of the total gaze shift, but to prevent the eye from reaching too eccentric positions. This is crucial and implies that a monkey, whose oculomotor range (O.M.R.) is limited to about 40 deg from central eye position, is incapable of executing a gaze shift larger than 40 deg, by means of single saccade, even if he moves his head. The consequences would still be more drastic for animals such as the cat whose O.M.R. has a radius of only 25 deg. There is not doubt that the natural repertoire of eye and head movements of these animals contains a large number of successive gaze shifts of small amplitude. However, our observations revealed that alert cats spontaneously and not infrequently shift their gaze by 60 deg and more, with a single saccade. It also appears from Barnes'

---

[*]Chargé de Recherche FNRS, Belgium

data (1979) that man behaves similarly. As a consequence, the mode of eye-
head coordination described above is certainly not the only one utilized
by higher mammals.

    In connection with these considerations, the presently accepted model
of visual target acquisition control is the "foveation hypothesis", put
forward by Schiller and Stryker (1972) and Robinson (1972). This theory postulates that the command of eye fixation saccades finds its origin in the
superior colliculus (S.C.). The superficial layers of this structure contain a map of the visual field retinotopically organized. In parallel, the
deep layers are specifically connected to the brainstem eye motor centers
in such a way that a neuron, or a small group of neurons, discharging at a
particular site in these layers triggers a well-defined eye saccade. The
organization is such that the "motor map" in the deep layers matches the
sensory retinotopic map of the upper layers. Thus, any visual target, within the reach of the eye, can trigger a fixation reflex which will bring
the visual axis in its direction. The fixation saccade is said to be retinotopically coded. This model, developed from data collected in the monkey,
does not take head movements into account. In this animal indeed, the S.C.
does not seem to be implicated in the control of head movements (Robinson
and Jarvis, 1974; Stryker and Schiller, 1975). The origin of the command
of the head movement accompanying most fixation saccades is thus unknown.
In the cat, however, S.C. is definitely involved in the control of head movement (Straschill and Schick, 1977; Roucoux et al., in prep.). We have been
able to show that cat's S.C. possesses a double organization (Roucoux and
Crommelinck, 1976; Crommelinck et al., 1977). In its anterior part, which
receives the projection of the central 25 deg of the visual field, the deep
layers retinotopically control eye saccades, in a way similar to the monkey.
In the posterior part, corresponding to the periphery of the visual field
(>25 deg), lower layers directly control head movements. The mode of eye-
head coordination is different in both cases. These two strategies have also been observed in the spontaneously behaving cat.

METHODS AND RESULTS

    Our observations were made on alert cats, free to move their head.
Eye and head movements were measured with the coil in magnetic field technique. The main advantage of the method, besides a lack of drift and a
great accuracy of calibration, is a complete absence of mechanical interference with the head movements. S.C. was stimulated with cathodal pulses
delivered through metallic microelectrodes, with typical intensities of
10 uA. In all the figures, gaze (G) is the position of the line of sight in
space, head (H) is the head position in space and eye (E) is the eye orientation in the orbit, obtained by subtracting H from G. In each case, horizontal and vertical components were recorded.
    In fig.1, cat's right S.C. is shown, as viewed dorsally with, super-
imposed, the retinotopic map of the upper layers.
On this map, two zones are delimited, according to the properties of the
eye and head movements evoked there by electrical stimulation of deep
layers. In the anterior zone, evoked eye saccades are retinotopic i.e.
their amplitude and direction are only determined by the position of the
stimulating electrode with respect to the map.

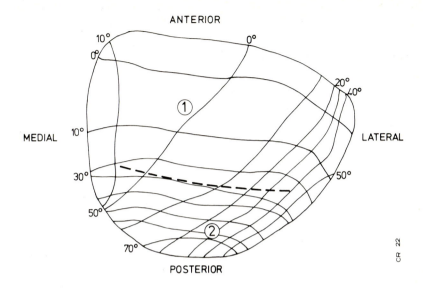

Fig.1.: Dorsal view of right S.C. with the retinotopic map.
The thick broken line delimits the two functional zones.

Saccades illustrated in fig.2 were evoked at the site marked 1 on the map.
Their amplitude was about 6 deg and they were almost horizontal.
      In the posterior zone, saccades are goal-directed (fig 4,A) i.e.
their amplitude and direction depend on the orientation of the eye when the
stimulus is applied, so as to bring the eye to a "goal" in the orbit. The
eccentricity of the goals, for all stimulated sites, is between 8 and 15
deg and thus, does not fit the retinotopic map which covers, in this zone,
the periphery of the visual field. The goal is a fixed position in the orbit and thus, goal-directed saccades are coded with respect to the head
frame of reference. A third collicular zone has also been identified but
will not be discussed here (Guitton et al.,in prep.). Interestingly, the
border between the two zones described (25 to 30 deg on the retinotopic
map) corresponds to the extent of cat's O.M.R. (25 deg from the central
eye position).
      Fig.2,C illustrates the combined eye and head movements evoked in si-
te 1. This site of stimulation is rostral and the evoked saccade, small
(6 deg). A brief stimulation train (100 ms) evoked only one saccade and
no head movement. A longer train (200 ms) evoked a succession of 2 saccades
accompanied by a small and slow head rotation. Similarly a 800 ms pulse
train triggered a succession of six saccades and a larger head movement.
The onset of the head movement followed the first saccade. We could demonstrate that the head began to move as soon as the eye left a central zone
in the orbit (Roucoux et al., 1979). It appears that the head is not triggered by the collicular stimulus itself, but rather, by the change of eye
position in the orbit. The fact that saccades evoked by a long stimulus
were repeated till the current was switched off is another indication that

these saccades are retinotopic: the central stimulation simulates a retinal error the saccade attempts to annul repeatedly without success, the
visual feedback loop is indeed open.

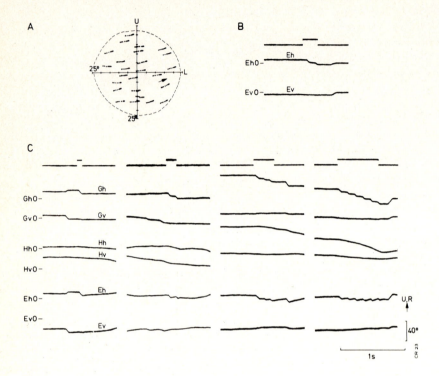

Fig.2: Eye and head movements evoked in anterior zone of right S.C.
(site 1 on fig 1). In A: head fixed, 100 ms stimulation train. Evoked
saccades were displayed in X-Y mode. Z input was modulated with 1 ms
pulses, 400 Hz, during saccades to give an idea of velocity. The dotted contour is the limit of the O.M.R. The arrow shows the direction
of the saccades. U:up, L:left, for the cat. In B: head fixed, 300 ms
stimulation. Succession of identical saccades. In C: head free. Gaze,
head and eye movements evoked by 100, 200, 400 and 800 ms trains.
v:vertical; h:horizontal.

If one compares, as illustrated in fig.3, the gaze displacement evoked
at a particular site in this zone, when the head is fixed and free to rotate, one can estimate the eventual participation of the head movement to the
total gaze shift. In this case, as for all the movements evoked in this anterior collicular zone, gaze shifts were identical, head being fixed or
free. This means that the V.O.R. compensatory slow phase is constantly added to the saccadic command, and that its gain is equal to unity (fig.3,C).

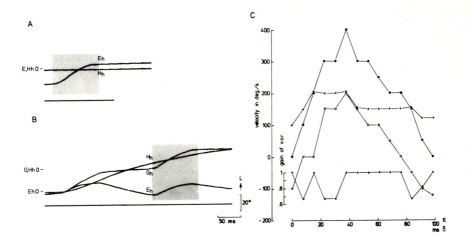

Fig.3. A:Head fixed; 150 ms stimulus train (black bar). Horizontal
saccade evoked in anterior zone (ampl.:25 deg). B:Head free; 800 ms
train. C:Velocity of eye and head within the time interval delimited by the stippled areas in A and B. ●:Eye in orbit, head fixed;
O:Eye in orbit, head free; ＋:Head in space; ▲:Velocity gain of
V.O.R. computed as follows: $\dfrac{\dot{\text{E}}\text{ head fixed} - \dot{\text{E}}\text{ head free}}{\dot{\text{H}}}$

Negative velocities correspond to compensatory eye movements.

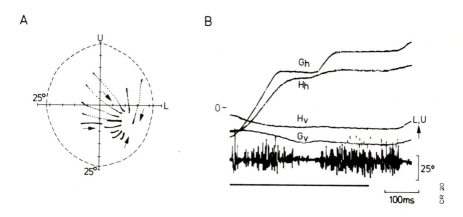

Fig.4.: Eye and head movements evoked in posterior zone of right
S.C. (site 2 in fig.1). In A: head fixed, 400 ms stimulus train.
In B: head free, 400 ms train; EMG activity recorded in left bi-
venter cervicis muscle.

Fig.4 illustrates combined eye and head movements evoked in the posterior zone. In A, are shown the goal-directed saccades evoked with head
fixed. The goal is 12 deg away from the center of the O.M.R., below the
horizontal. Fig.4 B shows the combined eye and head movements evoked at
this site. The eye saccade remains goal-directed. It is accompanied by a
large and fast head movement the onset of which is simultaneous to the beginning of the saccade. The amplitude and direction of the head saccade
correspond to the retinotopic map in the overlaying superficial layers
(65 deg amplitude). The stimulus being rather long in this case, the head
movement tends to be repeated (the phenomenon is comparable to the "stair-
case" of eye saccades in the anterior zone). This quite clearly appears on
the E.M.G. recording from the neck muscles contralateral to the stimulated
S.C. The very short and constant E.M.G. latency (7-10ms) after stimulus
onset is also remarkable. This strongly suggests that head movement is directly controlled by this collicular zone. The largest head saccade we
could evoke had about 70 deg.

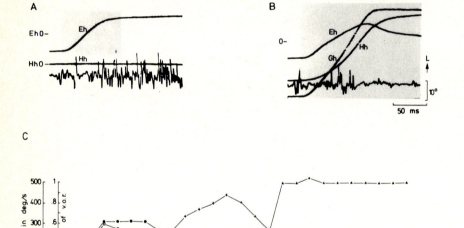

Fig.5. A:Head fixed; 400 ms stimulus train. Horizontal saccade
evoked in posterior zone. B:Head free; 400 ms stimulus train.
EMG as in fig.4. C:Velocity of eye and head and V.O.R. gain as
in fig.3.

initial position of the eye in the orbit: the head only starts to move
when the eye leaves its central position in the orbit. The coordination
of the combined eye and head movement is realized by a constant addition
of the V.O.R. slow phase to the saccadic eye command. The net result is
that gaze shift is identical, whether the head is moving or not. The anterior part of the S.C. is directly implicated in the control of the eye saccade alone.

     b) if the target lies more than 25 deg away from the center of the vi-
sual field, a saccadic head movement of adequate amplitude is programmed.
Synchronously, and in the same head coordinate system, a motor command is
sent to the eye which, for its part, makes a goal-directed saccade. The
V.O.R. slow phase signal is not added to the eye saccade. On the contrary,
an anticompensatory movement or quick phase soon replaces the first saccade in order to adapt the eye velocity to actual head velocity. This quick
phase ceases and is replaced by the slow phase as soon as gaze is on target (Roucoux et al., in prep.). The contribution of the head movement to
the total gaze shift is thus important. The posterior part of the S.C.
directly controls the head saccade.
In the monkey, only the first strategy has been observed (Bizzi et al.,
1972) but in man, it appears that two modes of eye-head coordination also
exist (Barnes, 1979), dependent on target eccentricity.

REFERENCES

Barnes, G.R., Vestibulo-ocular function during coordinated head and eye
movements to acquire visual targets, J. Physiol. (London) 287 (1979)
127-147.

Bizzi, E., Kalil, R.E., Morasso, P. and Tagliasco, V., Central programming
and peripheral feedback during eye-head coordination in monkeys, Bibl.
ophtal. 82 (1972) 220-232.

Crommelinck, M., Guitton, D. and Roucoux, A., Retinotopic versus spatial
coding of saccades: clues obtained by stimulating deep layers of cat's
superior colliculus, in: Baker, R. and Berthoz, A. (eds.) "Control of gaze
by brainstem neurons". (Elsevier North-Holland Biomedical Press, Amsterdam,
1977) pp. 425-435.

Dichgans, J., Bizzi, E., Morasso, P. and Tagliasco, V., Mechanisms underlying recovery of eye-head coordination following bilateral labyrinthecto-
my in monkeys, Exp. Brain Res. 18 (1973) 548-562.

Guitton, D., Roucoux, A. and Crommelinck, M., Eye movements evoked by stimulation of the superior colliculus in the alert, head restrained cat:
a reinvestigation, in preparation.

Morasso, P., Bizzi, E. and Dichgans, J., Adjustment of saccade characteristics during head movements, Exp. Brain Res. 16 (1973) 492-500.

Robinson, D.A., Eye movements evoked by collicular stimulation in the alert
monkey, Vision Res. 12 (1972) 1795-1808.

Robinson, D.L. and Jarvis, C.D., Superior colliculus neurons studied during head and eye movements of the behaving monkey, J. Neurophysiol. 37 (1974) 533-540.

Roucoux, A. and Crommelinck, M., Eye movements evoked by superior colliculus stimulation in the alert cat, Brain Research, 106 (1976) 349-363.

Roucoux, A., Crommelinck, M. and Meulders, M., Visual fixation: a collicular reflex?, Progress in Brain Research, 1979, in press.

Roucoux, A., Guitton, D. and Crommelinck, M., Eye and head movements evoked by stimulation of superior colliculus in the alert cat, in preparation.

Schiller, P.H. and Stryker, M., Single unit recording and stimulation in superior colliculus of the alert rhesus monkey, J. Neurophysiol. 35 (1972) 915-924.

Straschill, M. and Schick, F., Discharges of superior colliculus neurons during head and eye movements of the alert cat, Exp. Brain Res. 27 (1977) 131-141.

Stryker, M.P. and Schiller, P.H., Eye and head movements evoked by electrical stimulation of monkey superior colliculus, Exp. Brain Res. 23 (1975) 103-112.

Tutorials in Motor Behavior
G.E. Stelmach and J. Requin (eds.)
© North-Holland Publishing Company, 1980

19

DENTATE AND PALLIDAL CONTROL OF A GOAL-DIRECTED MOVEMENT IN MONKEYS

D. Beaubaton, E. Trouche and G. Amato[*]
CNRS - Institut de Neurophysiologie &
Psychophysiologie - 31, ch. J. Aiguier
13274 Marseille Cedex 2, France

Both human pathology and experimental studies have shown that lesions of the basal ganglia or cerebellum produce severe disturbances of motor activity. Anatomical convergence from the basal ganglia and cerebellum, via a thalamic relay, to the motor cortex suggest an analogous role for these two central loops. The present study was aimed at investigating some aspects of the functional role of both systems in a goal-directed movement. Baboons were trained to point at a visual target. The latency of the response (reaction time, RT), the speed of execution (movement time, MT) and the terminal spatial accuracy were recorded. The cerebellar dentate nucleus or the globus pallidus were temporarily blocked by cooling or permanently inactivated by electrolytic lesions. Increased reaction time, changes in movement time and impairment of accuracy were observed after dentate inactivation. Decreased reaction time and modifications of speed and accuracy of responses were noted after pallidal inactivation. Complementary influences of dentate nucleus and pallidum on the thalamo-cortical pathway, or on alternative subcortical systems, are discussed with regard to their role in the triggering and execution of limb movements in primates.

INTRODUCTION

Programming, initiation and execution of a movement represent different stages of motor organization subserved by sequentially ordered functional operations. Visual reaching may be considered as an example of this type of behavioural sequence in which localization and identification processes provide the necessary parameters of the elaboration and triggering of limb movement. It is generally assumed that the ballistic trajectory of the hand towards a target does not require retroactive correction although the terminal adjustment is dependant on sensory feedback (cf. Paillard & Beaubaton, 1976). The complexity of such functional operations may explain the difficulties encountered by neurophysiological approaches to this behaviour. The problem is however to determine which nervous structures are involved and what their respective roles are in the different phases of visuo-motor coordination.

---

[*] CNR-NATO post-doctoral fellow - Instituto di Fisiologia Umana, Palermo, Italia.

In the present study the performances of monkeys executing a visuo-motor
pointing task were tested. The subjects were experimentally deprived of
the control normally exerted by the neocerebellar dentate nucleus or the
globus pallidus. The choice of these structures has been made in consideration of their functional importance as revealed by many clinical, anatomical, and physiological data.

Recent investigations have stressed the major role of the cerebellum in
the spatio-temporal organization of movement (Evarts & Thach, 1969 ;
Massion, 1973 ; Brooks, 1979), thus confirming classical data on motor dysfunction following cerebellar damage. From anatomical and physiological
considerations (Evarts & Thach, 1969 ; Allen & Tsukahara, 1974 ; Chan
Palay, 1977 ; Wiesendanger et al., 1979) it must be noted that the neocerebellum receives inputs from different cerebral cortical areas and sends
back efferents to the motor cortex, through the ventro-lateral nucleus
of the thalamus. One of the main points of the present discussion concerns
the link between the association cortex and the neocerebellum. This connection, sometimes overestimated, seems not to be well developed in the
monkey (Sasaki, 1979), whereas the connections between the primary sensory
areas and motor cortex on the one hand, and pontine nuclei on the other
are well developed (Wiesendanger et al., 1979). Certainly the close reciprocal connections between the neocerebellum and the forelimb area of the
motor cortex in primates suggest that the lateral cerebellar cortex and
its associated dentate nucleus may be critical centers for the organization of limb movement. Another currently discussed point is related to
the link between the cerebellar nuclei and subcortical centers. Electrophysiological (Bantli & Bloedel, 1976) investigations have demonstrated a
pathway from the cerebellum to the spinal cord via the brain-stem. Recent
microstimulation experiments (Schultz et al., 1979) suggest that this
pathway may mediate a postural function of the lateral cerebellum. Cortical, or subcortical, cerebellar relationships could be responsible for
the elaboration of some movement parameters and/or modulation of cerebral
motor outflow. Within this framework, the data obtained by Brooks and
his collaborators (see Brooks, 1979) by reversible cooling of cerebellar
nuclei in rhesus monkeys, emphasize the role of these structures in the
initiation and control of elbow movement. The importance of the dentate
nucleus in a pointing movement performed by baboons have also been demonstrated (Beaubaton et al., 1978 ; Trouche et al., 1979).

With respect to the basal ganglia, human pathology and experimental
studies in animals classically consider this system as critical in motor
control. Disturbances of motor activity and posture following basal ganglia lesions are well known (Martin, 1967 ; Denny-Brown & Yanagisawa,
1976). However, extrapyramidal diseases show different and sometimes opposite symptoms, akinesis versus hyperkinesis for instance. Attempts have
been made to consider these disorders as expressing a single motor dysfunction. According to Kornhuber's hypothesis (1971) the disturbances
would be explained by deficiency of a special generator responsible for
ramp movements. DeLong's electrophysiological data (1979) support this
view, at least for the putamen. On the other hand, the observation of
Parkinson's disease and experimental lesions in animals led Denny-Brown
& Yanagisawa (1976) to consider the principal motor disorders as resulting
from an incorrect preparation of a "postural set" which is normally necessary for the initiation of movements.

A systematic analysis of the relationships between motor impairment and cerebellar damage is rendered difficult by the fact that the basal ganglia include a series of nuclei which have complex anatomical and physiological characteristics. As stated by Teuber (1976) "we need detailed experimental analyses of the ways in which behavior is altered after fractional basal ganglia lesions". In the present study the purpose was more specifically to investigate the role of the internal segment of the pallidum within the basal ganglia system. This nucleus represents one of the principal outputs of the corpus striatum, itself supplied by cortical motor areas and mainly projecting back to the motor cortex, through the ventro-lateral nuclear complex of the thalamus. Moreover, projections from the internal pallidal segment to the midbrain tegmentum have been described (Nauta & Mehler, 1966). This stresses the fact that, as for the cerebellum, in addition to thalamo-cortical pathways, descending influences upon the spinal cord may exist. From a functional point of view, electrophysiological studies (Delong, 1972 ; Neafsey et al., 1978) and cooling experiments (Hore et al., 1977 ; Amato et al., 1978 ; Trouche et al., 1979) suggest a role of the pallidum in the initiation and execution of a motor act. However the exact importance of this structure in the organization of visuo-motor performance remains to be elucidated.

The analogy between these two main central loops, involving on the one hand the cerebellum and on the other the basal ganglia, has been pointed out by several authors. Reciprocal anatomical connections with the motor cortex were stressed as well as the convergence of both systems at thalamic levels (Kemp & Powell, 1971 ; Allen & Tsukahara, 1974). According for instance to Kemp & Powell (1971), the cerebellar cortex would be essentially equivalent to the neostriatum and the cerebellar nuclei to the globus pallidus ; moreover they suggest that the projection of the dentate nucleus and the globus pallidus on the midbrain also represent equivalent pathways, both ultimately influencing the spinal cord. It could be therefore that the two systems are engaged in feed-forward or feedback mechanisms assisting commands issued from the primary motor cortex (Denny-Brown, 1976) or that they act in parallel to set up patterns of thalamo-cortical output necessary for the appropriate activation of cortico-spinal neurons (Evarts & Thach, 1969). The involvement of basal ganglia and cerebellum in some aspects of movement planning seems now to be assured. The question is to know precisely in which processes they are specifically concerned. The functional model proposed by Kornhüber (1971) postulates the existence of special function generators elaborating spatio-temporal kinetic patterns. In this model, the cerebellum would control the patterning of ballistic movements and the basal ganglia that of ramp movements. The possibility remains that the cerebellum and the basal ganglia act, more or less in synergy, to specify some movement parameters, to select the appropriate programme, or to organize the postural adjustments underlying the motor response.

The present experiments were aimed at investigating the roles of the internal pallidal segment and the cerebellar dentate nucleus in the different phases of a learned goal-directed movement. The inactivation of these nervous structures has been performed in baboons trained to execute a visuo-motor pointing task. The effects of reversible cooling or permanent lesions were studied by analyzing the initiation, the speed, and the accuracy of the movements.

METHODS

The investigations were carried out on eight baboons (Papio papio) maintained in a cage specially designed to standardize the working posture. The
head of the animal was partially restrained by sliding panels in order to
ensure a correct position facing the experimental device. The cage was
located in front of a panel on the lower part of which a lever was positioned. The monkey was trained to press the lever, and to hold it pressed
until a luminous spot appeared on the panel, after a variable and unpredictable interval. On the appearance of the visual signal, the subject had to
release the lever and to touch the target with its index finger. The position of the target was randomly varied at each trial. The reward was directly fed into the mouth. Initiation, speed and accuracy of this pointing
response are analyzed in various spatio-temporal parameters. Reaction-time
(RT) was defined as the time between onset of the signal and release of the
lever ; movement time (MT) as that between release of the lever and contact
on the panel. The first contact of the finger with the surface of the panel
automatically provided the rectangular coordinates of the pointing response.
Spatial error (E) was given by the distance between the target and the position of the finger. The programmed sequences were controlled on-line by
a micro-processor system which also recorded the data and carried out the
statistical treatment.

In four monkeys reversible blockade of the nervous structure was obtained
by cooling the nucleus, according to the method designed and described by
Benita and Condé (1972). After electrophysiological recording, a unilateral
chronic cryoprobe was stereotaxically implanted either in the external lateral part of the dentate nucleus, ipsilateral to the operant hand, or in
the internal part of the pallidum, contralateral to the operant hand. In
this latter case an oblique trajectory was chosen in order to avoid lesions
of the internal capsule. The blocking temperature of 0° C at the tip of the
probe was applied during sets of 30 trials (about 5 min), in a random way
within the sessions to avoid effects linked to habituation. The data collected during cooling sets were statistically compared with the performance
observed in non-cooling blocks of trials.

In four other monkeys, permanent electrolytic lesions were made either in
the dentate nucleus or in the internal pallidal segment. Sessions carried
out before inactivation of the structures, in a period of stabilized performance, served as controls. They were statistically compared with post-
operative sessions performed within 15 days of operation. Histological
controls have shown an exact localization either of the electrolytic lesions
or of the implanted cryoprobes.

RESULTS

1. Reaction times

The RTs obtained in the eight subjects are represented in Fig.1. Data collected from lesioned animals refer to about 500 trials for each pre- or
post-operative period. For monkeys with reversible cooling, results concern
about 300 trials, collected during 10 successive sessions. In each case the
performances observed under control conditions are compared with those obtained during reversible or permanent inactivation of the nervous structures.

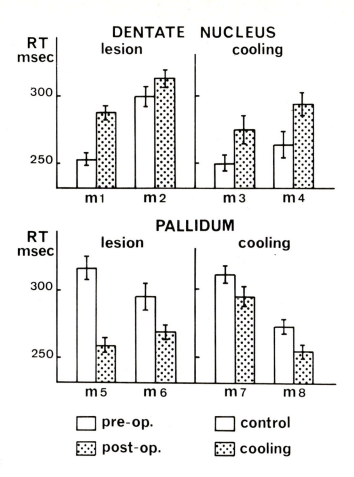

Figure 1. Mean reaction times (RT) with their confidence limits (p = .05) for eight monkeys with either a lesion (left part) or cooling (right part) of the dentate nucleus or pallidum. The pre-operative or control data (white histograms) are compared with the post-operative or cooling one (dotted histograms).

These results provide evidence that the RT increases during cooling of the dentate nucleus or after dentatotomy (Tab. 1). In all cases initiation of the visually triggered response is delayed. Contrarily, the data shows a decrease of RT after permanent or temporary inactivation of the internal pallidal segment (Tab. 2). In the four subjects non-functioning of the pallidum results in early triggering of the motor response. In the whole population, the differences tested by Student's test are statistically significant, except in subject 2 (Tab. 1).

Table 1 - DENTATE NUCLEUS

			REACTION TIME (msec)	MOVEMENT TIME (msec)	ERROR (mm)
LESION					
	Monkey 1	Pre-op	252.7	249.8	11.6
		Post-op	285.2*	268.7*	24.1*
	Monkey 2	Pre-op	300.1	165.0	8.3
		Post-op	313.9	182.0*	22.6*
COOLING					
	Monkey 3	Control	250.7	171.3	14.6
		Cooling	274.7*	137.1*	36.6*
	Monkey 4	Control	262.9	193.5	5.5
		Cooling	292.7*	221.7*	15.1*

Table 2 - PALLIDUM

			REACTION TIME (msec)	MOVEMENT TIME (msec)	ERROR (mm)
LESION					
	Monkey 5	Pre-op	313.9	231.9	2.4
		Post-op	257.5*	253.4*	10.9*
	Monkey 6	Pre-op	294.0	206.6	6.5
		Post-op	268.1*	221.5*	14.9*
COOLING					
	Monkey 7	Control	311.2	225.8	5.1
		Cooling	294.9*	239.8*	10.1*
	Monkey 8	Control	272.9	230.6	7.0
		Cooling	255.6*	241.4	9.5*

* significant difference between the pre-operative and post-operative periods or the control and cooling trials (Student's test, $p < .05$).

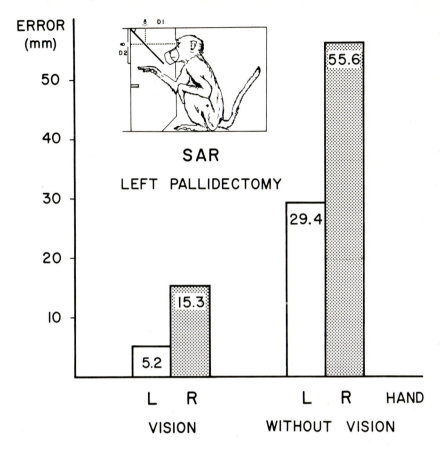

Figure 2. Mean pointing errors observed in one monkey with a left pallidal
         lesion. The left (L) and right (R) hands are either compared in
         normal visual conditions or while preventing vision of the moving
         limb.

2. Speed and accuracy

The speed of execution as revealed by MTs and the terminal pointing accuracy estimated from spatial errors are given in Tab. 1 for dentate inactivation. The analysis of MTs indicates a velocity impairment during dentate cooling or after dendatotomy. In the four animals, significant changes in MT occur. The effect generally consists in a MT lenghtening,
however an opposite effect can also be observed (see Tab. 1). The accuracy
of pointing responses was significantly impaired without control by the
dentate nucleus. The spatial errors increased (Tab. 1) and a complementary
analysis showed that these errors are characterized by hypermetric and
systematic directional misreaction.

Results of MT and accuracy during pallidal cooling or after pallidectomy
are given in Tab. 2. The deficit resulting from pallidal inactivation
consists in the increase of MTs and the inaccuracy of pointing responses.
The animals deprived of the internal pallidal segment show disturbances in
the execution of goal-directed movement ; however it must be noted that
this effect is rather slight compared to that observed for the dentate
nucleus. The comparison of both methods, cooling vs. electrolytic lesion,
suggests that the strongest effects, for the pallidum, were obtained in
monkeys with electrolytic lesions. Such a relationship, probably due to a
difference in volume of inactivated nervous tissue, is not found with the
dentate nucleus.

Finally, in one subject (Fig. 2) the pointing errors were observed in both
hands, contralateral and ipsilateral to the injuried pallidum in the normal condition and compared with a visual "open-loop" situation. In the
latter case an inclined mirror was placed in the experimental apparatus
and reflected the visual targets while preventing vision of the moving
limb. The data clearly show that the hand contralateral to the inactivated
structure is impaired. However a greater difference can be noted between
both hands when the monkey has no possibility of using visual cues to
correct the ongoing movement.

DISCUSSION

The overall data obtained in the present experiments demonstrate that
reversible or permanent inactivation of the dentate nucleus or pallidum
results in significant impairment of a visuo-motor pointing response.
Changes in reaction times, movement times and spatial accuracy were observed. They are in agreement with the hypothesis that these nervous structures participate in the initiation and execution of a goal-directed
movement.

Movement initiation

The importance of the cerebellum in initiating motor activity was first
proposed by Holmes (1917), who described delayed movement onset in patients
with cerebellar lesions. Electrophysiological studies revealed the respective roles of different cerebellar structures by showing that the first
changes in unitary activity, preceding the discharge of pyramidal tract
neurons, are in the dentate nucleus. Thus experimental inactivation of
structures including the dentate nucleus, may result in lengthening the
latency of a movement. The increase of RT observed in this study after
dentate cooling or dentatotomy is consistent with a possible leading role
of the neocerebellum in motor initiation. This result is also in agreement
with other data obtained in rather different conditions (Meyer-Lohman et
al., 1977 ; Lamarre et al., 1978). Combining cooling and recording methods,
Meyer-Lohman et al. (1977) observed an increase in RT during inactivation
of the dentate nucleus, accompanied by a delay in discharge of precentral
units. Such a delay would not be due to a decrease in tonic background
activity, i.e. a disfacilitation effect on motor cortex. The possibility
of a phasic movement instruction transmitted from the cerebellar nuclei to
the motor area of the cortex is indicated.   This hypothesis is discussed
by Massion & Sasaki (1979) according to whom the question arises as to
whether the cerebellum participates in the programming of a motor response
or in the fast triggering of movement elaborated elsewhere. The role of the
association cortex in motor commands has been extensively investigated

(see Leinonen, this volume). In this context the connections between association and motor cortex on the one hand, and motor cortex and cerebellum
on the other, must be reconsidered. Wiesendanger et al. (1979) hypothesized a major role of the pontine nuclei, integrating motor and sensory
cortical activities and capable of triggering a programme in response to
a peripheral signal. Triggered fast movements would therefore be dependant
on the ponto-cerebellar system, including the dentate nucleus. A possible
role of the thalamo-cortical pathway in movement initiation can not be
ruled out either, since it has been shown in cats that ventrolateral thalamic cooling increases the RT (Benita et al., 1979). Finally, increase in
RT may also be explained by cerebellar influences on motoneurons via subcortical routes (Meyer-Lohman et al., 1977). An involvement of cerebellar
nuclei in postural adjustment has been suggested by Massion (1973). Microstimulation of the dentate nucleus in monkeys (Schultz et al., 1979) demonstrates a control of flexor muscles mediated by brain-stem structures.
This mechanism could play an important functional role in postural adaptation underlying movement initiation.

Difficulty in initiation of voluntary movements is a characteristic feature of Parkinson's disease (cf. Denny-Brown, 1966). But the exact role of
the different structures of this system in motor initiation has not yet
been established. Delong's neurophysiological studies (1972) have indicated that neurons in the pallidum discharge prior to a limb response, pre-
ponderently, but not exclusively, in relation to slow movement. Early
activation of movement related units in the globus pallidus has also been
observed in cats by Neafsey et al. (1978). This early activity (more than
500 ms before the response) is suggested by the authors as evidence of the
implication of the pallidum in a "set system". The neural substrate of the
motor preparation would include the basal ganglia, the thalamic VL and
the medial motor cortex in the cat. However, as discussed by Requin (1979),
it seems difficult to correlate such an early activity with preparatory
adjustments specifically related to the characteristics of the intended
movement.

In our experiments the contrasting effects on RT resulting from the inactivation of the dentate nucleus or pallidum suggest differential roles of
both systems in reponse triggering or motor preparation. It is known that
efferent fibers from basal ganglia and cerebellum both project to the VL,
but generate differents discharge patterns in the thalamo-cortical projections, which differently engage output cells of the motor cortex (Purpura,
1976). Recently an inhibitory monosynaptic effect on VL has been demonstrated (Uno & Yoshida, 1975). Therefore the decreased RT after pallidal
inactivation could be explained by a disinhibitory effect. In this context,
it would be within the interneuronal ventro-lateral network that complementary pallidal and cerebellar influences determine an integrated activity able to trigger a motor response in the cortico-spinal pathway. An
alternative and interesting hypothesis has been put forward by Moll &
Kuypers (1977), who claimed that suppression of the indirect pallidal control of descending brainstem pathways could result in the disinhibition
of subcortical centers responsible for the steering of the arm to a visual
target.

Movement execution

The cerebellar syndrome is mainly characterized by hypotonia, muscular

asynergia and tremor. It has been known for a long time that hypotonia
results from the suppression of a tonic facilitatory effect on motor structures. Lesions of cerebellar nuclei, made by Gilman (1970) in monkeys,
induced a marked depression of the gamma system. However it must be noted
that a few cortical motor cells seem to be depressed during dentate cooling
(Meyer Lohman et al., 1977). Therefore, hypotonia can certainly not be
considered as the only explanation for cerebellar dyskinesia.

An important component of movement disorders after cerebellar lesions is
due to muscular asynergia. Indeed, the velocity impairment described in
our experiments could result from an abnormal timing of agonistic-antago-
nistic sequences. The movement time probably reflects delayed and wrongly
time-linked muscular activities. Part of the MT changes are also certainly
dependant on terminal oscillations. Such oscillations have been compared by
Ruch (1951) to those of a servomechanism system deprived of feedback
control. Difficulties in the termination of movement are obvious in cerebellar disease and as stressed by Massion & Sasaki (1979), braking is markedly
impaired in the neocerebellar syndrome. The dentate nucleus would be an
important link in a central system elaborating a braking program. Incorrect
programming of the deceleration phase could even result, as sometimes
observed in our experiments, in MTs shortening.

The inaccuracy of pointing responses as well as the direction of systematic
errors suggest that the spatial deficit depends on an impairment of speed
and cessation of movement. This could explain hypermetric responses in
this type of task. But directional error seems to be dependant on a specific spatial deficit. Muscular dyssynergia may result in errors of reaching.
It has been suggested that the dentate nucleus controls the proximal musculature (Rispal-Padel, 1979), which is involved in such goal-directed movement. Moreover incorrect control, after dentate inactivation, of a specific
flexor or extensor group can induce a systematic spatial deviation. It
remains to be elucidated whether spatial errors result from a strictly
muscular dyssynergia or rather from a deficit of sensory integration. In the
case, for instance, of an impairment of visual localization, the existence
of direct control exerted by the dentate nucleus on the oculo-motor system
must be taken into account (Chan Palay, 1977).

Clinical and experimental data suggest the importance of the pallidum in
motor and postural mechanisms (Martin, 1967 ; DeLong,1972). Surprisingly
no evident motor deficits have been reported after unilateral lesions of
this structure. The disturbances however appear when animals have no visual
information about arm position (Hore et al., 1977). Quantitative analysis
of movement duration and fine terminal accuracy show evidence, in our pointing task, of increased MTs and a slight, but significant, spatial error.
Of course, these impairments might be due to alteration of preparatory processes. The shortening of RT, during pallidal inactivation, could explain
an incomplete computation of the motor response parameters. At the present
stage of analysis this interpretation must be considered as hypothetical.
In fact direct intervention of the pallidum in the execution phase of a
motor act cannot be ruled out. Once more, descending influences of the
striatum on the spinal cord (Kemp & Powell, 1971) may be responsible for
the sequential distribution of muscular tone or the coordination of limb
muscular activity. According to Kornhüber's theory the possibility still
remains of a deficit selectively affecting the terminal, visually controlled, ramp phase of the pointing movement. Finally, the intervention of the

basal ganglia in the integration of proprioceptive intputs (Martin, 1967) must be considered. In agreement with results obtained by Hore et al. (1977), data are presented in this paper which show that, after pallidectomy, preventing vision of the moving limb increases pointing errors. The spatial deficit would be, at least in part, compensated when the monkey is able to use visual cues in order to correct the ongoing movement. Aggravation of ataxia in visual "open-loop" conditions is, according to Ruch (1951), characteristic of the lack of visual compensation for missing proprioceptive information. The role normally played by proprioceptive inputs in basal ganglia function could differentiate this system from the neocerebellum which is more specifically involved in internal feedback.

The heuristic value of the generally proposed analogy between neocerebellar and strio-pallidal systems can by no means be ruled out. However the complexity of their intervention in motor control, as suggested by the data presented, needs further detailed investigation. In addition to corticopetal influences, the exact functional role of the connections with brainstem structures must be clarified. Moreover, progress in this field certainly depends on an accurate investigation of posturo-kinetic relationships and of course on a systematic analysis of the various parameters defining visuo-motor behavior.

AKNOWLEDGMENTS

The authors wish to thank A. Grangetto and E. Legallet for their valuable technical assistance, R. Massarino for the mechanical work on the testing equipment, G. Poveda for training the monkeys, and A. Zenatti for the adaptation of computer systems. This work was supported by INSERM Grant 29.76.61.

REFERENCES

(1) G.I. Allen and N. Tsukahara: Cerebro-cerebellar communication systems, Physiol. Rev. 54 (1974) 957-1006
(2) G. Amato, E. Trouche, D. Beaubaton and A. Grangetto: The role of the internal pallidal segment on the initiation of a goal directed movement, Neurosc. Letters 9 (1978) 159-163
(3) H. Bantli and J.R. Bloedel: Characteristics of the output from the dentate nucleus of the spinal neurons via pathways which do not involve the primary sensorimotor cortex, Exp. Brain Res. 25 (1976) 199-220.
(4) D. Beaubaton, E. Trouche, G. Amato and A. Grangetto: Dentate cooling in monkeys performing a visuo-motor pointing task, Neurosc. Letters 8 (1978) 225-229.
(5) M. Benita and Condé H: Effects of local cooling upon conduction and synaptic transmission, Brain Res. 36 (1972) 133-151.
(6) M. Benita, H. Condé, J.F. Dormont and A. Schied: Effects of cooling the thalamic ventrolateral nucleus of cats on a reation time task, Exp. Brain Res. 34 (1979) 435-452.
(7) V.B. Brooks: Control of intented limb movement by the lateral and intermediate cerebellum, in: Asanuma, H. and Wilson, V.J. (eds.), Integration in the nervous system (Igaku-Shoin, Tokyo, New-York, 1979).
(8) V. Chan Palay: Cerebellar dentate nucleus (Springer-Verlag, Berlin, 1977).
(9) M.R. DeLong: Activity of basal ganglia neurons during movement, Brain Res. 40 (1972) 127-135.

(10) D. Denny-Brown and N. Yanagisawa: The role of the basal ganglia in
     the initiation of movement, in: Yahr M.D. (ed.), The basal ganglia
     (Raven Press, New-York, 1976).
(11) E.V. Evarts and W.T. Thach: Motor mechanisms of the CNS : cerebro-
     cerebellar interrelations, Ann. Rev. Physiol. 31 (1969) 451-498.
(12) S. Gilman: The nature of cerebellar dyssynergia, in: Williams D.
     (ed.), Modern Trends in Neurology (Butterworths, London, 1970).
(13) G. Holmes: The symptoms of acute cerebellar injuries due to gunshot
     injuries, Brain 40 (1917) 461-535.
(14) J. Hore,J. Meyer Lohmann and V.D. Brooks: Basal ganglia cooling
     disables learned arm movements of monkeys in the absence of visual
     guidance, Science 195 (1977) 584-586.
(15) J.M. Kemp and T.P.S. Powell: The connexions of the striatum and globus
     pallidus : synthesis and speculation, Phil. Tran. R. Soc. Lond. B.
     262 (1971) 441-452.
(16) H.M. Kornhüber: Motor function of the cerebellum and basal ganglia :
     the cerebello-cortical saccadic (ballistic) clock, the cerebello-
     nuclear hold regulator, and the basal ganglia ramp (voluntary speed
     smooth movement) generator, Kybernetik 8 (1971) 157-162.
(17) Y. Lamarre, B. Bioulac and B. Jacks: Activity of precentral neurones
     in conscious monkeys : effects of deafferentiation and cerebellar a-
     blation, J. Physiol. Paris 74 (1978) 253-264.
(18) J.P. Martin: The basal ganglia and posture (Pitman Medial, London,
     1967).
(19) J. Massion: Intervention des voies cérébello-corticales et cortico-
     cérébelleuses dans l'organisation et la régulation du mouvement,
     J. Physiol. Paris 67 (1973) 117A-170A.
(20) J. Massion and K. Sasaki: Cerebro-cerebellar interaction : solved
     and unsolved problems, in: Massion J. and Sasaki K. (eds.), Cerebro-
     cerebellar interactions (Developments in Neuroscience, Elsevier,
     Amsterdam, 1979).
(21) J. Meyer-Lohmann, J. Hore and V.B. Brooks: Cerebellar participation
     in generation of prompt arm movements, J. Neurophysiol. 40 (1977)
     1038-1050.
(22) L. Moll and H.G.J.M. Kuypers: Premotor cortical ablations in monkeys :
     contralateral changes in visually reaching behavior, Science 198
     (1977) 317-319.
(23) W.J.H. Nauta and W.R. Mehler: Projections of the lentiform nucleus in
     the monkey, Brain Res. 1 (1966) 3-42.
(24) E.J. Neafsey, C.D. Hull and N.A. Buchwald: Preparation for movement
     in the cat : II : Unit activity in the basal ganglia and thalamus,
     Electroenceph. clin. Neurophysiol. 44 (1978) 714-723.
(25) J. Paillard and D. Beaubaton: Triggered and guided components of
     visual reaching. Their dissociation in split-brain studies, in:
     Shahani M. (ed.), The motor system : Neurophysiology and muscle
     mechanisms (Elsevier, Amsterdam, 1976).
(26) D.P. Purpura: Physiological organization of the basal ganglia, in:
     Yahr M.D. (ed.), The basal ganglia (Raven Press, New-York, 1976).
(27) J. Requin: La préparation à l'activité motrice:vers une convergence
     des problématiques psychologique et neurobiologique, in: Requin J.
     (ed.), Anticipation et Comportement (Edition du CNRS, Paris, 1979).
(28) L. Rispal-Padel: Functional characteristics of the cerebello-thalamo-
     cortical pathway in the cat, in: Massion J. and Sasaki K. (eds.),
     Cerebro-cerebellar interaction (Development in Neuroscience   Elsevier,
     Amsterdam, 1979).

(29) T.C. Ruch: Motor system, in: Stevens S.S. (ed.), Handbook of experi-
     mental Psychology (John Wiley & Sons, INC. New-York, London, 1951).
(30) K. Sasaki: Cerebro-cerebellar interconnections in cats and monkeys,
     in: Massion J. and Sasaki K. (eds.), Cerebro-cerebellar interactions
     (Developments in Neuroscience, Elsevier, Amsterdam, 1979).
(31) W. Schultz, E.B. Montgomery and R. Marini: Proximal limb movements in
     response to microstimulation of primate dentate and interpositus
     nuclei mediated by brain-stem structures, Brain 102 (1979) 127-146.
(32) H.L. Teuber: Complex functions of basal ganglia, in: Yahr M.D. (ed.),
     The basal ganglia (Raven Press, New York, 1976).
(33) E. Trouche, G. Amato, D. Beaubaton, E. Legallet and A. Zenatti:
     The role of the internal pallidal segment on the execution of a goal
     directed movement, Brain Res. (1979) (in press).
(34) E. Trouche, D. Beaubaton, G. Amato and A. Grangetto: Impairments and
     recovery of the spatial and temporal components of a visuo-motor
     pointing movement after unilateral destruction of the dentate nucleus
     in the baboon, Appl. Neurophysiol. 42 (1979) 248-254.
(35) M. Uno and M. Yoshida: Monosynaptic inhibition of thalamic neurons
     produced by stimulation of the pallidal nucleus in cat, Brain Res.
     99 (1975) 377-380.
(36) M. Wiesendanger, D.G. Ruegg and Wiesendanger R.: The corticopontine
     system in primates : anatomical and functional considerations, in:
     Massion J. and Sasaki K. (eds.), Cerebro-cerebellar interactions
     (Developments in Neuroscience, Elsevier, Amsterdam, 1979).

PART IV

STAGE ANALYSIS AND
RESPONSE PREPARATION

Tutorials in Motor Behavior
G.E. Stelmach and J. Requin (eds.)
© *North-Holland Publishing Company, 1980*

20

STAGE ANALYSIS OF REACTION PROCESSES

A.F. Sanders
Institute for Perception TNO, Soesterberg, The Netherlands

In this paper some methodological issues and empirical results
are discussed on stage analysis of reaction processes by means
of the additive factor method. The methodological problems
center around: (1) the basic logic, (2) the reaction process
as a single dimension, (3) the statistical decision, and (4)
the notion of serial and independent stages.

The discussion of experimental results is limited to those of
the standard choice reaction task. The data tentatively suggest the operation of six stages. There are conflicting results with regard to the effects of relative S-R frequency and
foreperiod duration, which are discussed in some detail. It is
concluded that, hitherto, a moderate optimism about the applicability of the additive factor method to choice reaction processes is justified.

INTRODUCTION

One of the oldest hypotheses of Experimental Psychology is that a reaction
time (RT) is composed of the sum of a finite number of processing times,
each of which is consumed by a processing stage involved in the translation
of a signal into a response. The demands on all stages are supposedly reflected in the RT, from the arrival of the signal until a response is emit-
ted. In this way RT differs from "percentage correct" where one is concerned with the extent to which something goes wrong somewhere during processing. It will not be surprising that the main aim of studying RT has been
to establish internal stages, unobservable by themselves, through manipulation of tasks or task variables. This was the intent of the classical
investigators (Donders 1868, Exner 1873, Wundt 1903), as well as of more
recent researchers (Smith 1968, Welford 1968, 1971, Sternberg 1969). If
the hope of establishing stages in this way is abandoned, as occurred in
the first half of this century, the popularity of RT measurement declines
sharply. As Woodworth (1938) wrote: "Since we cannot break up the reaction
into successive acts and obtain the time of each act, of what use is the
reaction time?" (p. 83).

This was an expression of disbelief in the usefulness of the major classical approach towards fractination of RT, referred to as Donders' *subtraction method* (Donders, 1868; see also Pachella, 1974). This method suggested
that the time taken by a stage might be estimated through stage deletion.
If one task comprised *n* stages and another *n-1* stages, the duration of the
deleted stage can be obtained by simple subtraction of the times taken by
the reactions in the two tasks. The problem is, of course, that this proce-

dure requires *a priori* postulates concerning which stages play a role, while the objective is actually to infer stages. The problem of *a priori* statements concerning stages in tasks was already clear from the research in Wundt's laboratory (e.g. Berger, 1888). The validity of the assumed stage deletion proved difficult to test. In 1895 the subtraction method was seriously questioned by Külpe who correctly argued that changing from one to another task is likely to imply more than merely deleting a stage. It might as well imply a completely different processing structure. This criticism was in line with the theoretical frameworks dominating the first half of the century. Hence the discussion of RT was absent in the later edition of *Experimental Psychology* (Woodworth and Schlosberg, 1954), as well as in other texts appearing at that time.

The rise of cognitively-oriented theory brought a renewed interest in the study of reaction processes which was immediately accompanied by a fresh look into the possibilities of stage analysis. In the 1950's and 1960's this was usually a matter of describing the effects of experimental variables in terms of some general model. It was recognized that there were time-consuming afferent and efferent processes as separate components, while the remaining processes were summarized in a single explanatory principle. As such the information channel (Broadbent, 1958) and a probabilistic decision principle (Edwards, 1966; Laming, 1968), have served as general models of RT. The idea that a reaction process might consist of several central processing stages - each requiring its own process model - gained ground towards the end of the 1960's. Thus, Welford (1968) discussed several lines of evidence suggesting that identification of a signal and choice of a response constitute separate processing stages. On the basis of some experiments on S-R compatibility, Sanders (1967) argued that a compatible response to a signal is an immediate and unavoidable stage with a further translation process to produce the incompatible response. Smith (1968) distinguished *preprocessing*, *identification*, *response choice* and *response execution*. However, Sternberg's (1969) paper on the additive factor method (AFM) as a tool for "discovering processing stages" has been undoubtedly the main impetus for the present interest in stage analysis of reaction processes.

The basic logic of this method is well known. If two variables have a main effect on RT, while their effects do not interact, two different processing stages are likely to be involved. The rationale is that the effect of the one variable does not appear to depend on the state of the other. Alternatively, if the effects interact, the variables are likely to affect at least one common processing stage, since the size of the effect of the one variable depends on the state of the other. In this way an attempt is made to *infer* processing stages from experimental data and in this respect the AFM and the subtraction method are basically different. Yet, both methods also share assumptions. In short they concern the very hypothesis that RT does indeed consist of the sum of a series of independent processing durations[1], successive in nature, and *of equal output* across levels of experimental variables. Hence, a basic element of Külpe's objection remains relevant: Does a change in the level of an experimental variable merely change the processing duration of the stages underlying that variable? Or does it affect the total structure of the reaction process? Note that there are influential modern theories that are quite sympathetic towards answering the last question positively in terms of reallocation of capacity from a common pool (Moray, 1967) or changes in the investment of effort (Kahneman, 1973) when the conditions in a reaction task are varied.

Thus, in spite of its present popularity, a stage analysis of reaction processes is not self-evident. The concept of a stage remains a hypothesis,
the usefulness of which should be proven as well as its possible range of
application. With this in mind, a review of some recent studies using the
AFM as its main tool - empirical as well as theoretical - will be presented. In addition, some comments will be given on the usefulness of RT measurement *per se*. There are various question marks in the recent literature
that should not remain unnoticed. For example, Pachella (1974) concluded
his well known tutorial by saying that "much more must become known about
the general strategies used by the subjects in the generation of reaction
times before a high degree of confidence can be had about interpreting
these measures in subtle substantive controversies" (p. 80). This is still
mildly stated in comparison to Wickelgren's (1977) polemic plea for complexity substituting RT measurement by speed-accuracy functions. The question is obviously to what extent traditional measurement provides an adequate basis for stage analysis.

METHODOLOGICAL ISSUES

Since Sternberg's publication, various doubts about the AFM have been expressed. They concern the *basic logic*, the reaction process as a *single
dimension*, the *statistical decision* (accepting the null hypothesis), the
notion of *seriality and independence* and, finally, the question of *precision of measurement*.

a) *The basic logic*: In his original formulation Sternberg (1969) observed
that "one can imagine exceptions to both of these rules" (p.282), i.e. the
connection between additive effects and separate stages on the one hand and
between interactions and a common processing stage on the other hand. Prinz
(1972) put this more strongly and argued that the deduction 'if variables
affect different processing stages, then their effects on RT add' cannot be
logically reversed into 'If two variables have additive effects they affect
different processing stages'. For example, as Sternberg noted, variables
might happen to affect the same stage additively. *Mutatis mutandis* the
same can be said with regard to interactions. Here the most obvious coun-
terexample is met when the assumption of identical stage output is violated. In that case the effects of variables may interact which should not
be interpreted as an effect on a common stage.

These problems require that the results of any single experiment should be
regarded with great caution. Thus, additive effects might be tentatively
interpreted in terms of different stages but further tests should be undertaken. For example, if a third variable interacts with both or with neither variables, the effects of which are additive, then additivity by coincidence might be suspected. In the case of true additivity, the additive
effect should be robust in the sense that it should remain additive, irre-
----
[1] It is not uncommon to obtain experimental results that show additive
mean reaction times, while the variances interact. Although this means a
violation of the assumption of stochastic independence, it can be argued
that this is due to shortcomings in experimental control - e.g. sequential
effects in a block of trials (Kornblum, 1973) - rather than to a real stochastic dependence. Note also that differences in variance between conditions actually violate the assumptions of the ANOVA! Fortunately the outcomes of the ANOVA are not very sensitive to differences in variance. In
the following the main emphasis will be on effects on means.

spective of interactions of either variable with a third one. The idea is
that if the processing demands on one stage are increased, this should in
principle not affect the processes at another stage. If examples of this
type can be found (see p.336 for one instance), direct evidence is obtained
against the possibility of additivity by coincidence.

Observed non-significant interactions will sometimes require the Bayesian
principle of deferring judgment. It is often useful in such cases to repeat the experiment with larger differences between factor levels in order
to get more sizeable main effects. When additive effects are found over a
sizeable range of factor levels, it is less likely that an interaction is
obscured. On the other hand, it should be noted that when in a given study
the main effect of a variable on RT is small, an interaction with another
variable may be obscured because of a lack of "operating space". On still
other occasions the occurrence of an interaction or of additivity may be
determined by the range of factor levels for other reasons. For example,
it is known that "auditory pitch discrimination" and "auditory stimulus intensity" affect common processes in the basilar membrane in the inner ear.
High intensity decreases discriminability, except when very large differences in pitch are used. In a pilot study I have recently observed that
the RT reducing effect of higher stimulus intensity is indeed less if the
difference in pitch is smaller. It was also possible to avoid this interaction, however, by choosing the pitches in the "low" discriminability condition sufficiently far apart so as to eliminate the interfering effect of
the higher intensity. The "normal" case seems to be an interaction, but
there is an area which is not sufficiently sensitive for this relation to
show up. Alternatively there may also be cases in which the "normal" effects are additive while an interaction is only found when extreme factor
levels are studied. I will return to this point later on(p.336). It will
be argued that such instances may provide interesting indications about the
processes taking place in a stage.

Another issue is that the application of the AFM is limited to those variables, the effects of which can be reasonably expected to affect processing
durations rather than stage structure or stage output. For example, variation in type of reaction task - e.g. simple, selective or choice - does
not represent a task variable but a comparison between different tasks.
This can be useful, but the results of such experiments should not be interpreted by way of the AFM. Other examples are signal modality and physical vs. name identity. This last example is particularly interesting
since the identity paradigm has been very fruitful (Posner, 1978). This
illustrates that there are various alternative routes for studying information flow, the results of which should eventually converge with those
using the AFM.

These examples are clear cases in which a change of condition implies a
change in stage structure or output. In other cases the situation may be
less clear. Mutually conflicting interactive and additive relations may
be indicative of a change in output. Yet, an interpretation in terms of
output change rather than processing duration is an escape explanation when
not based upon a clear argument. It constitutes an emergency-brake for the
AFM that should not be needed too often.

b) *The reaction process as a single serial dimension*: A strong implication
of the AFM is that a reaction process is one-dimensional in the sense that
the output of a stage cannot serve as input for more than one next stage.

Even if the activity of a second dimension were completely aspecific, as for example assumed for arousal mechanisms, there would be dependencies between stages. Again, as Prinz (1972) has argued, an interaction between the effects of two variables might not be directly related to a selective influence on a certain stage, but rather to supraordinate monitoring of the information flow. In particular, the effects of 'strategical variables', like stressors, instructions, time-on-task etc. could belong to that category.

It is almost certain that the information flow is multi-dimensional, even within the limited range of the reaction process. Thus, in the following a set of studies is described (p.338), the data of which are most readily understood when assuming a second dimension. Yet, this does not necessarily render the AFM invalid. As long as there is a consistent pattern of deviating results, the one-dimensional scheme can be used as a frame of reference for interpreting when and how a second dimension operates.

With regard to supraordinate monitoring of the information flow there are two main possibilities. First, it could be that the monitoring process increases or decreases the general rate of processing or brings about a reallocation of resources. That would imply interactive relations between strategical variables and most other variables affecting RT. Alternatively, a strategical variable may have a highly selective effect on a certain stage. In that case that stage may be either directly affected or indirectly through a monitoring process. The AFM cannot decide but selective effects would be certainly more interesting from its point of view.

A final word concerning the serial nature of processing. This should not be taken to imply that stages are passive unless busy processing. For example certain operations within stages may occur prior to the arrival of a signal, although the extent to which presetting is possible may differ between stages.

c) *Accepting the null hypothesis*: An objection that has been repeatedly raised concerns the fact that when deciding that two variables have additive effects, the null hypothesis is accepted. This is vital, since the occurrence of additivity is the major, although not the only, means for distinguishing between processing stages. Yet, this problem may not prove to be that serious. There are various recent studies warning against the traditional prejudice against the null hypothesis (e.g. Greenwald, 1975; Rouanet, 1978) and suggesting procedures for a more balanced attitude by considering a null-range rather than a null-point hypothesis. Trivial deviations from the null point should still be considered as in line with the null hypothesis and lead to the acceptance of the null hypothesis by considering the probability that a treatment effect is within the null-range. A problem is that standard significance tests for a null-point hypothesis are not very adequate for testing a null-range hypothesis, although this problem may be less urgent with small samples as commonly used in RT studies.

d) *Effects of violations of seriality and independence*: Taylor (1976) has described an extended class of processing stages which have the property that they can be linearly dependent in the sense that successive stages may overlap in time or that an increase in time required for one stage may have the effect of decreasing the time required by a subsequent stage. As Taylor argues, the main consequence of this relaxation of the assumptions is

that additive effects cannot be interpreted. The case in point is that interactions can be easily disguised by variations in overlap. It follows
that only the structures of interactive patterns can provide a picture of
the stages involved in a given process.

The possibility of temporal overlap between stages has also been considered
by Stanovich and Pachella (1977). They have suggested that temporal overlap may be often inferred from *underadditive* interactions. Their argument
is that when two variables have the effect of increasing the processing duration of a certain stage, the interaction should usually be overadditive.
The increase in processing demands due to the manipulation of the one variable should be magnified when manipulation of another variable also implies an increase in processing demands on the same stage. This is indeed
observed in many experiments. Underadditivity, on the other hand, means
that the one increase in processing demands can be partly compensated by
another increase. According to Stanovich and Pachella (1977), a parsimo-
neous solution for underadditivity is that the two variables affect different processing stages, the durations of which overlap under the most difficult conditions. In particular when the durations are relatively long,
there might be the possibility of sending information from the one stage to
the next before processing in the first stage has actually been completed.
Upon completion, the remaining information is also passed on, but in the
mean time the next stage has already started processing the earlier acquired information. Hence, there is a gain in total reaction time that becomes
apparent in an underadditive relation. The arguments of Taylor and Stanovich and Pachella have the common element of disguise due to the possibility of overlapping stage durations. Taylor emphasizes that additive effects
may in fact be disguised overadditive interactions. Stanovich and Pachella
argue that underadditive interactions may be disguised additive effects.
However, given overlapping processing durations, underadditive interactions
could also be disguised overadditive interactions. It all depends on the
degree of overlap. Therefore, if one accepts overlapping stages, underadditive as well as additive effects should share the fate of being uninter-
pretable. However, when considering the issue of serial vs. overlapping
stages, it is important to realize what is actually meant by a stage. It
is worth repeating Sternberg's (1969) remark that "the additive factor
method cannot distinguish processes but only processing stages" (p. 309).
The processing stage is an operational and not a theoretical concept. An
extreme consequence is that "it represents a shorthand for conceptualizing
the effects of experimental variables" (Pachella, 1974: p. 57). In itself
this would be meaningful as a convenient way of documenting empirical relations, but the hope is obviously that a stage corresponds to a functionally independent *set* of *processes*. Thus, there may be two parallel processes which both must be completed before the next stage can begin. Two
variables "that influenced these processes separately would interact negatively and both processes would be identified as a single stage (Sternberg,
1969: p. 288). This argues against Stanovich and Pachella's (1977) suggestion that overadditivity is the normal way in which a stage is affected
by two variables. This may be only valid if both variables affect the same
process, but not if they affect different processes within the same stage.
The underadditivity of the effects of pitch discriminability and auditory
stimulus intensity (p. 333) is a good example.

Thus, within a stage processes may overlap, occur in parallel, or be interconnected through feedback loops, but between stages they do not. This is
the very *hypothesis* of the AFM. "Overlapping stages" would mean that sets

of processes overlap, which ideally should be identified as a single stage.
Hence the problem of additivity by coincidence and of disguised interactions due to variations in overlap are basically concerned with the same
issue. Of course, there remains the question of whether serial stages exist and whether they correspond to intuitively interesting aspects of information processing. If all processes would overlap and be interconnected
through feedback loops one would find one stage encompassing the complete
reaction process (Broadbent, 1979, note). The answer is a matter of empirical study. If a coherent picture emerges the enterprise will be eventually successful. If the data turn out to be conflicting or unreliable
the idea will ultimately fail.

e) *AFM and speed-accuracy trade-off*: A final issue, that is not basically
related to the AFM as such, but yet quite relevant to the practice of experimentation, concerns the issue of speed-accuracy trade-off. It has been
emphasized repeatedly in recent years that RT and accuracy are intimately
related. Hence, traditional RT measurement should be abandoned in favour
of measuring complete speed-accuracy functions (Pachella, 1974; Ollman,
1977; Wickelgren, 1977). Variations in speed-accuracy criteria, both within and between blocks of trials on the same condition, but also between
subjects, obviously have a negative effect on the precision of measurement.
Moreover, since the additive factor method only deals with times, a neglect
of error rates can lead to serious misinterpretations. For example, when
faced with increased processing demands, subjects may choose to keep processing times constant at the cost of more errors. When only RT is taken
into account, the misleading conclusion would be reached that the increase
had no effect on information flow. A complication is that, under some circumstances, a change in error rate may remain unnoticed or appear little
dramatical, since a considerable shift in criterion may be accompanied by
only slight increases in errors (Pachella, 1974).

It is of course theoretically possible to base the AFM upon the outcomes of
speed-accuracy functions. In this way the analysis can be carried out on
RT obtained at various constant-accuracy levels. In practice this under-
taking is only feasible when only a very few factors and corresponding factor levels are involved to keep the amount of measurement within practical
limits. Note that the increased amount of measures on the same subjects,
as required when measuring complete speed-accuracy functions in multi-fac-
tor experiments, is not easily reconciled with the principle of limiting
repeated measurements on the same subjects (Poulton, 1974). Moreover, it
may be questioned whether this procedure is really desirable, since it can
be the major effect of some experimental variables to evoke a shift in
speed-accuracy trade-off.

For example, Harm and Lappin (1973) observed in a speed-accuracy trade-off
study that the effect of relative S-R frequency on RT could be completely
ascribed to changes in speed-accuracy. Being set towards the more frequent
S-R combination results in more errors when the less frequent one occurs.
If one corrects for speed-accuracy changes the effect of relative S-R frequency disappears. This would mean, however, that the effect of a relevant
RT variable is artificially annihillated.´

It is not this type of variable-induced shift one wants to control but
rather unsystematic shifts occurring within as well as between blocks of
the same condition and both within and between subjects. Faced with this
problem, the best one may do is to maintain RT measurement as the primary

procedure, but to standardize procedures as much as possible. This means foremost that data should be usually obtained from well practiced subjects. A possible criterion for "well practiced" might be that the standard deviation in a block of trials should not exceed 10-15 percent of the mean (Cocholle, 1940). Another criterion is that means of blocks of trials on the same condition, but obtained at different sessions should be within the limits of the standard error criterion. During practice sessions these limits on variability should be clearly expressed to the subjects through knowledge of results. In this way variations in strategy within experimental conditions can be strongly limited. If accuracy is emphasized at the same time a fair approximation of the "ideal point" on the trade-off curve may be obtained. Subjects who cannot comply with these rules should be excluded from participation.

I would like to plea for this type of RT experiment as a generally agreed procedure. Too many papers in the literature report experimental data based upon only a few practice trials. In addition to the RT studies, speed-accuracy experiments are relevant for various reasons. First, to study the speed-accuracy issue for its own sake. Second, to determine strategical effects of experimental variables, and third, to check certain interesting cases of additivity or interactions on eventual extra contributions of speed-accuracy shifts.

ANALYSIS OF SOME EXPERIMENTAL RESULTS

1. *Additive effects in the choice reaction process*: The discussion will be limited to standard choice reaction processes in the sense of Posner's (1964) information conservation. Thus there is always a set of possible imperative signals, each element of which has an exclusive connection to one element of a set of responses (e.g. key-pressing, vocal naming and pointing). Usually the presentation of an imperative signal is preceded by a warning signal. Some experimental results are summarized in Table 1.

Table 1

Summary of additive and interactive effects of choice reaction variables.

Additive effects:
Signal quality x *S-R compatibility*: Sternberg (1969), Shwartz *et al.* (1977) Frowein and Sanders (1978), Sanders (1979).
Signal contrast x *S-R compatibility*: Shwartz *et al.* (1977), Sanders (1977).
Signal contrast x *signal discriminability*: Pachella and Fisher (1969), Shwartz *et al.* (1977).
Signal contrast x *signal quality*: Frowein (note 2), Sanders and Akerboom (Table 3).
Signal contrast x *word frequency*: Becker and Killion (1977).
Signal quality x *word frequency*: Stanners *et al.* (1975).
Signal discriminability x *S-R compatibility*: Fisher and Pachella (1969), Shwartz *et al.* (1977)
S-R compatibility x *Instructed muscle tension*: Sanders (1979).
Signal quality x *Instructed muscle tension*: Sanders (1979).
S-R compatibility x *Response specificity*: Sanders (1970).

Interactive effect:
Signal quality x *Movement frequency* x *Movement Predictability*: Wertheim (1979).
Stimulus contrast x *S-R compatibility*: Stanovich and Pachella (1977).
Stimulus contrast x *Meaningfulness*: Miller and Pachella (1976).

Priming x *Word frequency*: Becker and Killion (1977).
Priming x *Signal quality*: Meyer *et al*. (1975).
Priming x *Signal contrast*: Becker and Killion (1977).

This is obviously a very rough summary that bypasses issues like definition
of the variables and actual levels investigated. For example, *Signal-Response compatibility* is an ill-defined variable. It refers to the degree
of natural or overlearned relations between signals and responses. Naming
of familiar verbal materials, pointing responses to lights and immediate
tactual responses are common examples of high S-R compatibility (Leonard,
1959; Brainard *et al*., 1962; Fitts *et al*., 1963) but the weakness of the
variable is that there is no clear underlying continuum relating to 'natu-
ralness'. The implication is that comparisons between studies on S-R compatibility are often difficult since the operational meaning of 'compatible' and 'incompatible' varies across experiments. The only possible comparison is *post-hoc* in terms of the size of the effect on RT. There are
similar problems with some of the other variables listed in Table 1. *Signal quality* is sometimes varied by superimposing visual noise by way of
either a checkerboard pattern (Sternberg, 1969), random visual noise (Frowein and Sanders, 1978), or a random dot pattern (Frowein, note 2). However, on other occasions signal quality has been defined in terms of stimulus contrast (Stanovich and Pachella, 1977). *Signal discriminability* is
distinguished from signal quality in that the similarity between the signals themselves is varied. Again this has been operationalized in various
ways; for example by varying the degree of similarity between the capital
letters 'A' and 'H' (Shwartz *et al*., 1977) or between the spacing of possible horizontal bar positions (Pachella and Fisher, 1969). *Muscle tension*
has been manipulated (Sanders, 1979) by instructions to either relax or be
optimally tense during the warning interval preceding the presentation of
a signal. The problem is here - as with most other instruction variables -
that there is not always adequate control with regard to obeying the instruction. Simultaneous EMG-recordings of the involved muscles provide a
fair control for the relaxed condition, but in the tense condition it is
unknown whether the observed muscle activity is actually optimal. It is
also virtually impossible to distinguish further factor levels between
'tense' and 'relaxed'.

Response specificity is used here as a label, indicating the extent to
which responses have a common element. In an experiment by Sanders (1970),
vocal responses started either with a common or a specific phoneme (e.g.
ses or *sas* vs. *es* or *as* as responses to a visually presented E or A). One
may imagine variation of response specificity with pointing responses (i.e.
the extent to which the movements have a common vector), but to my knowledge this has not been investigated. The final two variables of Table 1 -
Movement frequency and *predictability* - are concerned with movements of the
signal environment (Wertheim, 1979). Subjects followed a moving white dot
in which a reaction signal was presented. The frequency of the moving dot
was defined in the usual way as the number of cycles per second. In the
predictable condition the dot described a circular path. In the unpredict-
ible condition this was changed at random intervals to a path of a congruent circle, tangential to the original one at the point of change.

Interpretation of the additive effects of Table 1 leads roughly to six
stages in the standard choice reaction task, an intuitive sequence and la-
belling of which is presented in Table 2.

Table 2

Suggested stages on the basis of typical additive effects.

Stage	Typical additive variables
Preprocessing	Signal contrast
Feature extraction	Signal quality
Identification	Signal discriminability, word frequency
Response choice	S-R compatibility
Response programming	Response Specificity
Motor Adjustment	Instructed Muscle Tension

The most clearly established additive relation is between S-R compatibility and signal quality since it has been repeatedly observed in different settings. Thus, Sternberg (1969) used naming responses as did Shwartz *et al.*, (1977), while Frowein and Sanders (1978) and Sanders (1979) used pointing responses to lights. As argued, a recurrent additive effect in different settings reduces the probability of additivity by coincidence. Sternberg (1969) has proposed that a signal may be 'cleaned up' by a feature extraction process, the outcome of which is used as a stimulus for response choice. When using relatively unpracticed subjects, an interaction between signal quality and S-R compatibility has been found, (Rabbitt, 1967) which disappears at a later stage of testing (Biederman and Kaplan, 1970). Sternberg (1969) has suggested that unpracticed subjects may fail to complete the 'cleaning up' which would change the stage *output*.

As shown in Table 1, there are also some studies suggesting additive relations between the effects of stimulus contrast and S-R compatibility (Sanders, 1977; Shwartz *et al.*, 1977), but Stanovich and Pachella (1977) have found an underadditive interaction, the effect of contrast reduction being less in the incompatible than in the compatible condition. Although these conflicting results require further study, a curious difference may be noted between the data of Stanovich and Pachella and those of the other studies. The intensity effect in the last experiments ranged from 25-40 msec which reasonably agrees with what is usually found for supra-threshold signals differing by some two log units (e.g. Sanders, 1971). Stanovich and Pachella, on the other hand, observed effects between 100 and 200 ms which leads one to suspect that their low contrast condition was near-threshold. If this were true, one might wonder whether the bright and dim conditions had identical stage outputs. An underadditive interaction might be expected if in the dim condition the response choice stage received a distorted signal. In particular the more compatible S-R relation would suffer from a distorted input since the 'natural' signal-response relation is affected. It is usually found that minor deviations from optimal compatibility have a relatively large effect on RT. This could also explain the underadditive relation between signal contrast and 'meaningfulness' (Miller and Pachella, 1976). In the high-meaningfulness condition the digits 1-8 were used while pseudo letters were presented in the low meaningfulness condition.

As mentioned, variation in signal contrast is sometimes set equal to variation in signal quality. To test the validity of this assumption two experiments were carried out, attempting to manipulate these variables independently. Frowein (note 2) presented digits in dot patterns. In the degraded condition more dots were added in random positions on the background. Simone Akerboom and I used tilted dotted lines, pointing either to the right or to the left, the quality of which was manipulated in the same way. The intensity level was either 3,7 cd/m^2 or 0,09 cd/m^2 on a 0,5 cd/m^2 background. Sixteen subjects were tested in a within-subjects design. In both studies additive effects of contrast and signal quality were found (see Table 3). Thus, a more peripheral and a more central feature extraction stage may be involved. Note that a "normal size effect" of contrast was observed. Eriksen and Schultz (1977) found the effects of signal quality and *retinal locus* to interact, while an interaction between effects of stimulus contrast and retinal locus is a classical finding. As Eriksen and Schultz (1978) suggest, the effect of retinal locus may be attributed to neural transmission time from the retina to the higher processing centers as well as to stimulus analysis at the higher processing centers.

Table 3

Mean RT and accuracy (log odds) as related to *signal contrast* and *signal quality*.

Signal quality	Signal contrast		
	Bright	Dim	Diff.
Degraded	469 (1.19)	497 (1.20)	28
Undegraded	387 (1.30)	414 (1.33)	27
Diff.	82	83	

Evidence for a third 'perceptual' stage can be derived from work of Fisher and Pachella (1969) and of Shwartz *et al.* (1977) who found additive effects of signal discriminability, signal quality and S-R compatibility. Similarly, Meyer *et al.* (1975) reported additive effects of signal contrast and word frequency. The effect of this last variable might be located as well in the identification stage. Prior priming of the signal had the effect of reducing the size of the word frequency effect while the effect of priming has also been found to interact with that of signal contrast (Becker and Killion, 1977). With prior priming a variation in signal contrast had less effect. Thus, priming may have the double effect of preactivating the signal (identification stage) and lowering the criterion set for the extent of preprocessing. Conversely, Miller and Pachella (1976) found an underadditive interaction between stimulus contrast and 'meaningfulness' of verbal stimuli, but this result was again accompanied by the earlier discussed extreme effect of stimulus contrast.

The evidence for the 'motor' stages in Table 2 seems more tentative than for the perceptual ones since they are based upon very limited evidence and, moreover, not all relations have been tested. Thus a study on the relation between the effects of instructed muscle tension and response specificity is still in preparation. There is also an obvious need to study the relations with the effects of motor variables, as distinguished in the motor literature (Klapp, 1977; Kerr, 1978; Marteniuk and MacKenzie, 1979). There exists a considerable amount of research on the effects of movement variables on RT, but so far the questions have been largely restricted to which movement variables have any effect on RT at all. Following the Fitts-tradition, there has been the suspicion that these effects are negligible (Fitts and Peterson, 1964), but more recent research has revealed a variety of effects, the size of which depends on the movement variable under investigation. Thus *resisted force* and *reversals* during the movement appear to have at best very slight effects on RT. The same is observed for precision (i.e. target width) except when the movement takes very little time to complete (Klapp, 1977). On the other hand, systematic effects on RT have been found for variables like *instructed velocity*, *pauses* within a response (e.g. Klapp and Erwin, 1976) and number of successive responses in one trial (Sternberg *et al.*, 1978). The very few studies, employing the AFM (Rosenbaum, 1979; Sternberg *et al.*, 1978; Klapp, 1977) have been most concerned with mutual relations between specific motor parameters. So far no attempts have been made to tie the motor variables to those of the standard choice reaction paradigm. Hence very little can be said except that the two motor stages, as distinguished in Table 2 may correspond to an abstract programming stage and one in which specific muscle commands are realized (Klapp, 1977; Kerr, 1978).

For didactic reasons a discussion of the effects of three more highly important variables has been postponed. Some of their relations are summarized in Table 4.

Table 4

Summary of additive and interactive effects of relative S-R frequency, Nu. Alternatives and Foreperiod duration.

Additive effects

Relative S-R frequency x *Signal contrast*: Miller and Pachella (1973); Miller and Pachella (1976)
Relative S-R frequency x *Foreperiod duration*: Holender and Bertelson (1975)
Foreperiod duration x *Stimulus quality*: Frowein and Sanders (1978); Wertheim (1979)
Foreperiod duration x *Signal contrast*: Raab *et al.* (1961); Sanders (1977)
Foreperiod duration x *S-R compatibility*: Posner *et al.* (1973); Sanders (1977); Frowein and Sanders (1978)
Foreperiod duration x *Nu Alternatives*: Alegria and Bertelson (1970)
Foreperiod duration x *Movement predictability*: Wertheim (1979)
Foreperiod duration x *Movement frequency*: Wertheim (1979)

Interactive effects

Relative S-R frequency x *S-R compatibility*: Fitts *et al.* (1963); Sanders (1970); Theios (1975)
Relative S-R frequency x *Response specificity*: Sanders (1970)
Relative S-R frequency x *Foreperiod duration*: Bertelson and Barzeele (1965)
Relative S-R frequency x *Foreperiod duration* x *Instructed muscle tension*: Sanders (1979)
Relative S-R frequency x *Stimulus contrast*: Miller and Pachella (1973); Stanovich and Pachella (1977)
Foreperiod duration x *Auditory signal contrast*: Sanders and Wertheim (1973) Sanders (1975)
Foreperiod duration x *Auditory signal contrast* x *S-R compatibility*: Sanders and Andriessen (1978)
Foreperiod duration x *Movement velocity*: Wertheim (1979)
Foreperiod duration x *S-R compatibility*: Broadbent and Gregory (1965)
Nu. Alternatives x *S-R compatibility*: Brainard *et al.* (1962); Fitts *et al.* (1963); Broadbent and Gregory (1965)
Nu. Alternatives x *Signal quality*: Sternberg (1969)

---

2. *Relative S-R frequency*: It has been well established that the effect of relative S-R frequency interacts with that of S-R compatibility (Fitts *et al.*, 1963; Broadbent and Gregory, 1965; Sanders, 1970). Theios (1975) even failed to find any residual effect of relative S-R frequency in a highly compatible naming task and has suggested therefore that the effect of this

variable is exclusively related to the response choice stage. Yet this
finding deviates from the usual result that a small but stable effect remains in a highly compatible situation (e.g. Mowbray, 1960; Stone and Call-
away, 1964). Sanders (1970) has observed in a naming task that the size of
this residual effect depends on whether the response starts with a common
or a specific phoneme, suggesting that response programming is affected by
relative S-R frequency. In the case of a common phoneme *and* high S-R compatibility, no effect of relative S-R frequency was left, while a consistent effect remained when the phonemes were specific. Finally, Sanders
(1979) found a second order interaction between the effects of instructed
muscle tension, relative S-R frequency and foreperiod duration, suggesting
also an effect of relative S-R frequency on the motor adjustment stage.

Hence, the locus of relative S-R frequency seems to be predominantly in the
later stages of information processing. There remains the question whether
relative S-R frequency also affects processing stages at the perceptual
side. This is related to the extent to which one may selectively be set
towards either perceiving a signal and/or responding. It may be noted that
in the 1960's this question was approached by an information-reduction
paradigm in which infrequent signals could correspond to either an infrequent or a frequent response. The reasoning was that if an *'infrequent
signal-frequent response'* combination would render reaction times similar
to those in a *'frequent signal-frequent response'* combination this would be
evidence for a response locus of the effect. Conversely, if results similar to the *'infrequent signal-infrequent response'* combination were obtained, this would argue for a perceptual locus (LaBerge and Tweedy, 1964; Bertelson and Tisseyre,1965). From a point of view of the AFM, this paradigm
is not satisfactory since the dichotomy 'perceptual vs. response' is too
simple. Thus, the frequent response given to an infrequent signal might be
inhibited by the fact that this response is usually given to the frequent
signal.

The relation between the effect of relative S-R frequency and the 'percep-
tion-oriented' stages has been mainly studied by Pachella and coworkers.
Thus Miller and Pachella (1973) found an interaction between relative S-R
frequency and signal contrast in a digit-naming task, which was subsequently confirmed by Stanovich and Pachella (1977, exp. 1). It should be noted,
however, that the interaction was only found at very small probability values ($p = 0.025-0.07$). There, a relatively long RT appears in the dim condition while the effects look roughly additive at larger probabilities
(> 0.07). As said earlier, the studies by Pachella and coworkers on signal
contrast are also characterized by unusually large contrast effects. Therefore the interaction may be a special case rather than a common rule.

Earlier I have suggested that, in order to ensure efficient coding, activated internal codes of the digits may be needed when the items are badly
visible. When the items are more clearly visible their encoding may be
automatically triggered whatever the state of preactivation. Thus it could
be that very improbable items out of a relatively large set (Stanovich and
Pachella used 8 alternatives) remain inactivated and therefore require a
longer encoding time when badly visible. This would mean that relative S-R
frequency can affect the identification stage, but only in extreme cases.
A similar suggestion has been made by Lupker and Theios (1975) to explain
some deviations from the predictions of the Falmagne (1965) model for two-
choice reaction time.

What complicates the picture, however, is that Stanovich and Pachella (1977, exp. 2 and 3) found additive effects of signal contrast and relative S-R frequency for the whole range of frequencies when the digits were not named but when keypressing reactions were required. This result requires the additional speculation that no preactivation occurs in the identification stage when the responses differ from the signals. As discussed on p. 340 the underadditive interaction between signal contrast and S-R compatibility, found in the same experiments could be due to a distorted input to the response choice stage in the case of very dim contrasts and no preactivated traces.

It is only fair to mention that Stanovich and Pachella interpret their results by assuming temporally overlapping stages of stimulus identification and response choice. Prior to these stages there is a feature analysis stage, the output of which is sent to both the identification and response choice stages. Feature analysis and identification have a feedback relation so that the result of the identification stage may finally be passed on to response choice processes. Whether or not such occurs depends on the duration of the response choice process. If short, as with highly compatible S-R relations, identification may outlast response choice, in which case the last stage may get hardly involved. Identification is affected by signal contrast as well as by relative S-R frequency so that an interaction between these variables is expected when identification is the dominant process, not when response choice is dominant as with low S-R compatibility. The underadditive signal contrast x S-R compatibility interaction is due to the temporal overlap of one stage - identification - which is affected by signal contrast and another stage - response choice - which is not.

The disadvantages of accepting overlapping stages have been discussed on p. 336. Therefore, the complex alternative interpretation of the results in terms of changing output was developed. It should be realized, though, that this means pulling the emergency break, which may be only acceptable if Stanovich and Pachella's results represent an extreme case.

3. *Number of Alternatives*: Originally this variable and relative S-R frequency were supposed to both reflect the information load of the choice reaction task (Hyman, 1953). Indeed the variables are confounded, except if relative S-R frequency is taken as frequency imbalance vs. equiprobability Defined in this way the locus of the effect of the number of alternatives seems more towards the input stages, witness the observed interaction with the effect of signal quality, and not towards the motor stages. Thus additive effects of the number of alternatives and of foreperiod duration have been found (Alegria and Bertelson, 1970). As argued, relative S-R frequency is certainly affecting the motor stages while the effect on the perceptual ones is still dubious. Yet both variables have a pronounced common locus in the response-choice stage.

4. *Foreperiod duration*: Inspection of Table 4 suggests a far from homogeneous picture of relations between the effect of foreperiod duration and other variables. Additive as well as interactive effects have been obtained with signal contrast, with relative S-R frequency and with S-R compatibility. Are the phenomena relating to foreperiod duration basically unreliable in the sense of repeated additivity by coincidence? This would clearly undermine the credibility of the AFM. Is there, alternatively, some reasonable explanation behind the divergent findings? This last hypo-

thesis will be defended by the following. It will imply a violation of the
axiom of single-dimensional processing, but in an interesting and intuitively reasonable way. The basic ingredients for the argument can also be
found in Sanders (1977, 1979). They will be briefly summarized and completed with more recent evidence. The starting point is that additive effects of foreperiod duration and signal contrast are typically found with
visual and with auditory signals, when intensities do not exceed 60 dBA.
However, the effect of foreperiod duration is reduced when louder (> 70
dBA) auditory signals are employed and probably also when tactual signals
are used (Broadbent and Gregory, 1965; Sanders, 1975). Yet the reduced effect of foreperiod duration does not always appear. It is mainly observed
with simple or selective reactions but with choice reactions it is usually
weak or absent except in the case of extremely high S-R compatibility
(Sanders, 1977; Sanders and Andriessen, 1978). The relation with type of
task (simple vs. choice) stemmed from different experiments, but the effects have been recently replicated in our laboratory in one study where
two-choice as well as simple reactions were used (see Table 5).

Table 5

Mean RT as related to *Type of task* (simple versus two-choice), *Type of signal* (visual, auditory 35 dBA, auditory 85 dBA) and *Foreperiod duration*
(2 secs, 20-40 secs).

| | Type of task | | | | | |
| | simple reaction | | | two-choice reaction | | |
Foreperiod duration: Type of signal	2 secs	20-40 secs	*Diff*	2 secs	20-40 secs	*Diff*
Visual	213	283	*70*	335	460	*125*
Auditory (35 dBA)	185	265	*80*	306	445	*139*
Auditory (85 dBA)	160	205	*45*	284	410	*126*

Summary: Two groups of 8 subjects each were tested after an intensive
practice period. One group performed the simple and the other the choice
task. The other variables were within subjects. The visual signal was
either a horizontal or a vertical line pattern (only horizontal in the simple task). The auditory signal was either 500 or 3000 Hz (only 3000 in
the simple task). Keypressing responses were used. 20% catch trials were
given in the simple task but only in the 2 secs foreperiod duration conditions. This may explain the significant Type of task x Foreperiod duration interaction (F = 7.67, Df 1,14) (see also Table 6). All main effects were significant and also Type of signal x Foreperiod duration (F =
7.92, Df 2,28) and Type of task x Type of signal x Foreperiod duration
(F = 3.48, Df 2,28). *As expected, the effect of Foreperiod duration is
reduced in the case of a loud auditory signal and a simple reaction task.*

Hence, the interaction with signal contrast and with S-R compatibility is
limited to the special conditions where either tactual or loud auditory
signals are used and - as far as choice reactions are concerned - where
extremely high compatibility relations are involved. In the other conditions their effects are largely additive to that of foreperiod duration.

When limiting the discussion to this last set of conditions there is no
evidence that foreperiod duration affects either any of the perceptual

stages or the response choice stage. Instead, the foreperiod duration may
mainly affect the motor adjustment stage. External evidence for this suggestion stems from recent developments in research on cortical correlates
of the reaction process (e.g. Gaillard, 1978). The slow negative wave in
the EEG is related to foreperiod duration and is mainly found in the deri-
vation from the motor cortex. Behavioral evidence comes from an interaction between foreperiod duration and instructed muscle tension, the effect
of foreperiod duration being more pronounced in the tense condition (Sanders, 1979). In addition from a second order interaction between the effects of instructed muscle tension, foreperiod duration and relative S-R
frequency. The effects of the last two variables interacted in the tense,
but not in the relaxed condition. This result may reconcile the conflicting findings on the relation between the effects of relative S-R frequency
and foreperiod duration, which sometimes have been found to interact (Bertelson and Barzeele, 1965) and to add on other occasions (Holender and Bertelson, 1975).

A motor locus of the foreperiod effect is not necessarily contradicted by
the finding that foreperiod duration affects d' in a visual signal detection task (Klein and Kerr, 1974). Quite possibly, preparatory activity for
detecting a signal consists largely of motor adjustments. The interaction
between the effects of foreperiod duration and movement velocity in Wertheim's (1979) ocular pursuit task (see also p. 433) is also not inconsistent with this picture. The motor requirements involved in visual tracking
of moving objects may prevent optimal motor adjustment needed for a fast
response to the signal.

5. *Immediate Arousal*: The results showing interactive effects of auditory
signal contrast, S-R compatibility and foreperiod duration can be considered as a well documented violation of the single-dimensional processing assumption. Any attempt to interpret these data in a single-dimensional
scheme leads to inconsistencies. As an alternative, it has been suggested
that when a signal exceeds a certain 'intensity level' it exerts an immediate arousing effect along with its effect on signal preprocessing (Sanders, 1977). Tactual signals are supposed to be arousing at a low level of
intensity. Auditory signals exert the effect at the intensity level of 70
dB and higher, while a quite high level of visual stimulation is needed to
produce immediate arousal. Immediate arousal would directly affect the motor adjustment stage by reducing the distance to the 'motor action limit'
(Näätänen and Merisalo, 1977) in particular if this distance is more sizeable as is presumably the case with a longer foreperiod duration. The immediate arousing effect carries the obvious danger that errors are made
when some sort of choice is involved, since the central computational
stages of identification and response choice are bypassed. Indeed, Sanders
and Wertheim (1973) observed a considerable increase in errors in conditions where immediate arousal is supposed to exert an effect. Consequently,
it may not be surprising that, as the load on the central processing stages
increases, the effect of immediate arousal is inhibited. This accounts for
the second order interaction between the effects of S-R compatibility,
foreperiod duration and auditory signal intensity as observed by Sanders
and Andriessen (1978). There a reduction of the effect of foreperiod duration was only found when auditory signal intensity was high *and* when the
S-R relations were optimally compatible. It would be obviously misleading
to interpret this result by assuming that the three variables directly affect a common stage. Another instance of suppression of immediate arousal
may be in some recent data from v.d. Molen and Keuss (1979) who found that,

as auditory signal intensity increased, RT decreased in a simple reaction task, levelled off at a constant value in a selective reaction task and in-creased - after an initial decrease - in a two-choice reaction task. In principle, similar effects of immediate arousal should occur when an im-perative visual signal is accompanied by an accessory auditory stimulus (e.g. Nickerson, 1972). Some recent results from our laboratory are pres-ented in Table 6. Indeed, the effects of either a loud auditory signal (Table 5) or an accessory stimulus (Table 6) appear to be quite comparable.

Table 6

Mean RT and error percentages as related to *Foreperiod duration* (2 secs, 20-40 secs), *Type of task* (simple vs. two-choice), and *Type of signal* (with or without a 70 dBA 1200 Hz accessory auditory stimulus).

	Type of task					
	simple reactions			two-choice reaction		
Foreperiod duration:	2 secs	20-40 secs	*Diff*	2 secs	20-40 secs	*Diff*
Type of signal						
with Accessory	184	253	*69*	323	431	*108*
	(11.3)	(18.3)		(5.9)	(7.5)	
without Accessory	191	307	*116*	321	443	*122*
	(1.3)	(0.0)		(5.4)	(8.2)	

Summary: These data are from 8 subjects in a within-subjects design, who were thoroughly practiced prior to running the experimental conditions. The imperative signal was either a horizontal or a vertical line pattern (only a vertical in the simple task). Keypressing responses were used. In all simple conditions 30% catch trials were inserted. A second order Foreperiod duration x Type of task x Type of signal interaction was found (F = 14.1, Df 1,7). In contrast to Table 5 the first order Foreperiod du-ration x Type of task was not significant, which may be due to the use of catch trials in all simple conditions.

From the hypothesis that immediate arousal affects the motor adjustment stage it also follows that the effect of an accessory stimulus should in-teract with that of instructed muscle tension in a simple reaction task but not in a choice reaction task. This is indeed observed (Table 7). Thus, these results taken together constitute a fairly homogeneous picture.

Table 7

Mean RT and accuracy (log odds) as related to *Type of task* (selective vs. choice reaction), *Type of signal* (with or without a 80 dBA 1200 Hz acces-sory auditory stimulus) and *Instructed muscle tension* (tense vs. relaxed).

		selective reaction			choice reaction		
	Muscle tension:	tense	relaxed	*Diff*	tense	relaxed	*Diff*
	Type of signal						
Mean	with Accessory	286	302	*16*	324	361	*37*
RT	without Accessory	294	324	*30*	334	370	*36*
log	with Accessory	.36[+]	.45[+]	*0.09*	1.03	.99	*-0.04*
odds	without Accessory	.59[+]	.84[+]	*0.25*	1.03	1.05	*0.02*

+ Based upon errors of commission vs. correctly withheld responses.

Summary: 12 subjects were tested in a within-subjects design. The imperative signal was either a horizontal or a vertical line pattern. In the
choice reaction task the response consisted of moving the right index
finger from a home button to either one of two target buttons located at
the left and right of the home button. In the selective task a movement to
the right target button was required in the case of the horizontal pattern
and no response had to be given in the case of the vertical pattern. Prior
to the experimental sessions subjects were thoroughly practiced and taught
how to relax by EMG feedback. 6 subjects first completed all selective
conditions followed by the choice conditions, while this order was reversed
for the other subjects. The RT data suggest that the accessory stimulus
reduces the effect of muscle relaxation in the selective, but not in the
choice reaction task although this was not substantiated by a significant
second order interaction. This interaction was significant (F = 7.93, Df
1,5) for the group receiving the selective-choice order, but not for the
choice-selective order, which may be interpreted as an asymmetric transfer
effect (Poulton, 1974). The accuracy data confirm that the accessory stimulus hardly affected log odds in the choice task but did so in the selective task. Moreover, the relaxed conditions were more affected than the
tense conditions (F = 4.77, Df 1,10), which is in line with the idea that
relaxation causes a greater distance from the motor-action limit, which is
reduced by the accessory stimulus.

It is reasonable that variables as signal intensity and foreperiod duration
are troublesome for a single-dimensional processing model since they are
the variables that are most commonly linked to arousal. "Stimulus intensity is always mentioned as important in eliciting an orientation reaction
and time uncertainty is often considered as a mere functional factor, with
reference to the measurement of alertness" (Sanders, 1977, p. 20).

DISCUSSION

The results reviewed in the previous section are all concerned with the
traditional choice reaction process. Limitations in space prevent a treatment of the application of the AFM to the related area of memory search and
binary classification tasks (Sternberg, 1969, 1975). The choice reaction
literature has also not been fully covered. Interesting phenomena like in
repetitions vs. alternations (Kornblum, 1973), the presence vs. absence of
an irrelevant cue (e.g. Simon *et al.*, 1976) and mixed compatibility tasks
(e.g. Duncan, 1978) have suffered a total neglect. Thus the review is restricted, but within its limits the question about the applicability of the
AFM should be raised. Is it possible to reach an interim conclusion about
its prospects? For the moment I would assert that a moderate optimism is
justified that at least for limited sets of problems the method will work.
In any case it seems advisable to extend the database as outlined in the
previous section.

When so doing the AFM will gain credibility if not too many 'new' stages
are discovered in the choice reaction process. Sanders (1977) discussed
three processing stages, while Table 2 lists six stages. However, the number of stages should be finite, in particular since a stage is conceived of
as a *set* of processes rather than a single process. The discovery of many
more stages would be worrying and raise questions about additivity by coincidence or biases towards additivity. Hence as remarked on p. 333 the
main emphasis should be on extension of the present evidence. A good example of extension is in Wertheim's (1979) result that effects of foreper-

iod duration and signal degradation remain additive in the ocular pursuit task, some variables of which interact with signal degradation and others with foreperiod duration. A strategy of extension will also stimulate a search for new variables in choice reaction tasks which, in turn, will extend the scope of the paradigm. An example of such a 'new' variable is instructed muscle tension, which was investigated with the explicit idea of extending evidence (Sanders, 1979).

In discussing some of the experimental evidence the emergency brake was pulled twice with regard to the effects of relative signal frequency and of foreperiod duration. Does the explicit violation of the single-dimensionality assumption, as inferred from the effects of foreperiod duration, invalidate the AFM? As argued on p. 346 it does not. It rather suggest that under certain conditions a different stage structure becomes active, the basic elements of which remain embedded in the original one. The interpretation of some of the effects of signal contrast and relative signal frequency is more troublesome. It remains to be proven that the results of Pachella and coworkers are exceptions. If so, they remain valuable with regard to what is going on in the perceptual stages. Note also that the Pachella results are likely to refer to a basic issue in the analysis of information flow. Usually naming of a familiar visual pattern, say a digit or an object, is considered as the end product of identification. When a compatible naming response is required, the response program corresponds directly to the identified name. The idea is that the relation between visual pattern and name is overlearned to the extent that no response choice is involved. But what about the case when this relation is weakened, say by using pseudoletters as signals so that naming is not 'automatically' achieved? Is there an extended identification process or is a pattern passed on to the response selection stage which subsequently finds the correct name? These questions are basically unanswered but should be kept in mind when interpreting effects of choice RT.

Another issue concerning relative SR frequency as well as foreperiod duration is that both belong to the 'state' variables. Their effect is largely determined prior to the arrival of the signal and presumably consists of presetting certain stages during the foreperiod rather than of 'computing' during processing the signal. This means that their effect is strongly determined by motivation and instruction. It disappears largely or altogether with a heavy emphasis on accuracy (Harm and Lappin, 1973; Posner *et al.*, 1973). The same was recently found in our laboratory with regard to the effect of instructed muscle tension. The dependence on motivation and instruction implies that their effects will tend to be more variable than those of the computational variables. The second order interaction between relative S-R frequency, foreperiod duration and instructed muscle tension may be viewed in this way. In itself it is interesting that the AFM suggests that the 'state' variables are motor rather than perceptual variables. Motivational variables appear more related to action than to perception.

Two final points remain. The first concerns the divergence between stage analysis and the pooled capacity conception. At this time the general trend favors the first approach. The effects as reviewed are too specific to allow conceptions in terms of changing resource allocation. This is also underlined by various recent studies on the effects of hypnotic and stimulant drugs and of dual task load on choice reaction time (Frowein, note 2,3; Whitaker, 1979). The effects observed in those studies are highly selective and do not suggest a single supraordinate monitoring principle that reallocates resources or slows down or speeds up the reaction process in general. Rather, the effects are related to specific aspects of processing. This does not mean that supraordinate principles are excluded, but that their activity is embedded in and limited by existing structural conditions. Yet the contra-position between pooled capacity and processing stage conceptions may be too extreme. The possibility of hybrid models, such as proposed by Kantowitz and Knight (1976), should be pursued further.

The last point concerns the analysis of processes within stages. It is obvious that following a tentative outline by way of the AFM, the development of stage-specific process models is the next step. Although the AFM itself has nothing to say on this issue it still may provide two relevant entries. The first is that an attempt is made to specify the variables which are affecting a certain stage. For example in thinking about a process model for response choice it would be wise to concentrate on the combined effects of S-R compatibility, number of alternatives and relative signal frequency. Perhaps some emphasis should be on S-R compatibility, since the other variables affect various stages, while - at least to the present knowledge - the main effect of S-R compatibility is on response choice.

A second entry is in the interpretation of interesting deviations: If two variables are additive within a certain range but interact under extreme conditions - perhaps as in Stanovich and Pachella (1977) - interesting deductions about processing with a stage may follow (see p. 336). Obviously, however, the major contribution for process models should come from investigation of the variables *per se* (e.g. Duncan, 1978). The ultimate aims are in that direction. The AFM may at best serve as an heuristic tool in serving that aim.

ACKNOWLEDGEMENT

This research was supported by Grant 15-26-08 from the Netherlands Foundation for the Advancement of Basic Research (ZWO). The cooperation of Mr. W. Spijkers in the experimental studies is gratefully acknowledged.

Reference notes

Broadbent, D.E. (1979). The maltheser cross: a new simple model for human memory. Paper to the 21ste Tagung experimentell arbeitenden Psychologen, Heidelberg, April 1979.
Frowein, H.W. (1979). Stimulus contrast and quality and the locus of the effect of barbiturate on choice reaction time. Report in preparation.
Frowein, H.W. (1979). Effects of amphetamine on response selection and response execution process in choice reaction tasks. IZF report 1979-8

References

|1| J. Alegria and P. Bertelson (1970). Time uncertainty number of alternatives and particular signal-response pair as determinants of CRT. In: A.F. Sanders (Ed.) Attention and Performance 3 36-44 (Acta Psychologica, 30).
|2| C.A. Becker and T.H. Killion (1977). Interaction of visual and cognitive effects in word recognition. Journal of Experimental Psychology:

Human Perception and Performance 3 389-401.
|3| P. Bertelson and J. Barzeele (1965). Interaction of time uncertainty
    and relative signal frequency in determining choice reaction time.
    Journal of Experimental Psychology 70 448-451.
|4| P. Bertelson and F. Tisseyre (1966). Choice reaction time as a function
    of stimulus versus response relative frequency of occurrence, Nature
    212 1069-1070.
|5| G.O. Berger (1886). Ueber den Einfluss der Reizstärke auf die Dauer
    einfacher psychischer Vorgänge mit besonderer Rücksicht auf Lichtreize,
    Philosophische Studien 3 38-93.
|6| I. Biederman and R. Kaplan (1970). Stimulus discriminability and sti-
    mulus response compatibility: Evidence for independent effects on
    choice reaction time, Journal of Experimental Psychology 86 434-439.
|7| R.W. Brainard, T.S. Irby, P.M. Fitts and E.A. Alluisi (1962). Some
    variables influencing the rate of gain of information, Journal of Ex-
    perimental Psychology 63 105-110.
|8| D.E. Broadbent (1958). Perception and Communication, London, Pergamon.
|9| D.E. Broadbent and M. Gregory (1965). On the interaction of S-R compa-
    tibility with other variables affecting reaction time, British Journal
    of Psychology 56 61-67.
|10|R. Cocholle (1940). Variations des temps de réaction auditifs en
    fonction de l'intensité à diverses fréquences, L'Année Psychologique
    41 5-124
|11|F.C. Donders (1868). Die Schnelligkeit psychischer Prozesse, Archive
    für Anatomie und Physiologie 657-681.
|12|J. Duncan (1978). Response selection in spatial choice reaction:
    Further evidence against associative models, Quarterly Journal of
    Experimental Psychology 30 429-440.
|13|W. Edwards (1966). Optimal strategies for seeking information: models
    for statistics, choice reaction times and human information processing,
    Journal of Mathematical Psychology 2 312-319.
|14|C.W. Eriksen and D.W. Schultz (1977). Retinal locus and acuity in
    visual information processing, Bulletin of the Psychonomic Society 9
    81-84.
|15|C.W. Eriksen and D.W. Schultz (1978). Temporal factors in visual infor-
    mation processing: A tutorial review. In: J. Requin (Ed.) Attention and
    Performance 7 3-23. Erlbaum, Hillsdale N.J.
|16|S. Exner (1873). Experimentelle Untersuchung der einfachsten psychi-
    schen Prozesse, Pflügers Archiv für die gesammte Physiologie 7 601-660.
|17|J.C. Falmagne (1965). Stochastic models for choice reaction time with
    application to experimental results, Journal of Mathematical Psychology
    2 77-123.
|18|P.M. Fitts, J.R. Peterson and G. Wolfe (1963). Cognitive aspects of in-
    formation processing. II. Adjustments to stimulus redundancy, Journal
    of Experimental Psychology 65 423-432.
|19|P.M. Fitts and J.R. Peterson (1964). Information capacity of discrete
    motor responses, Journal of Experimental Psychology 67 103-112.
|20|H.W. Frowein and A.F. Sanders (1978). Effects of visual stimulus de-
    gradation, S-R compatibility, and foreperiod duration on choice reac-
    tion time and movement time, Bulletin of the Psychonomic Society 12
    106-108.
|21|A.W.K. Gaillard (1978). Slow brain potentials preceding task perform-
    ance, Academische Pers, Amsterdam.
|22|A.G. Greenwald (1975). Consequences of prejudice against the null
    hypothesis, Psychological Bulletin 82 1-20.
|23|O.J. Harm and J.S. Lappin (1973). Probability, compatibility, speed and

accuracy, Journal of Experimental Psychology 100 416-418.
|24| D. Holender and P. Bertelson (1975). Selective preparation and time uncertainty, Acta Psychologica 39 193-203.
|25| R. Hyman (1953). Stimulus information as a determinant of reaction time, Journal of Experimental Psychology 45 188-196.
|26| D. Kahneman (1973). Attention and Effort, Englewood Cliffs, N.J.
|27| B.H. Kantowitz and J.L. Knight (1976). Testing tapping time sharing II: Auditory secondary task, Acta Psychologica 40 343-362.
|28| B. Kerr (1978). Task factors that influence selection and preparation for voluntary movements. In: G.E. Stelmach (Ed.), Information Processing in Motor Control and Learning. Academic Press N.Y.
|29| S.T. Klapp (1977). Response programming as assessed by reaction time does not establish commands for particular muscles, Journal of Motor Behavior 9 301-312.
|30| S.T. Klapp and C.I. Erwin (1975). Relation between programming time and duration of the response being programmed, Journal of Experimental Psychology: Human Perception and Performance 2 591-598.
|31| R.M. Klein and B. Kerr (1974). Visual signal detection and the locus of the foreperiod effects, Memory and Cognition 2 431-435.
|32| S. Kornblum (1973). Sequential effects in choice reaction time: A tutorial review. In: S. Kornblum (Ed.) Attention and Performance 4 259-289.
|33| O. Külpe (1895). Outlines of Psychology, MacMillan, N.Y.
|34| D. LaBerge and J.R. Tweedy (1964). Presentation probability and choice time, Journal of Experimental Psychology 68 477-481.
|35| D.R.J. Laming (1968). Information theory of choice reaction times, Academic Press, N.Y.
|36| A. Leonard (1959). Tactual choice reactions, Quarterly Journal of Experimental Psychology 11 76-83.
|37| S.J. Lupker and J. Theios (1975). Tests of two classes of models for choice reaction times, Journal of Experimental Psychology: Human Perception and Performance 104 137-146.
|38| R.G. Marteniuk and C.L. McKenzie (1979). Information processing in movement organization and execution. In: R.S. Nickerson (Ed.) Attention and Performance 8 Erlbaum, Hillsdale, N.J. in press.
|39| D.E. Meyer, R.W. Schvaneveldt and M.G. Ruddy (1975). Loci of contextual effects on visual word-recognition. In: P.M.A. Rabbitt and S. Dornic (Eds.) Attention and Performance 5 98-118, Academic Press London.
|40| J.D. Miller and R.G. Pachella (1973). Locus of the stimulus probability effect, Journal of Experimental Psychology 101 227-231.
|41| J.D. Miller and R.G. Pachella (1976). Encoding processes in memory scanning tasks, Memory and Cognition 4 501-506.
|42| M.W. v.d. Molen and P.J.G. Keuss (1979). The relationship between reaction time and intensity in discrete auditory tasks, Quarterly Journal of Experimental Psychology 31 95-102.
|43| N. Moray (1967). Where is capacity limited? A survey and a model. In: A.F. Sanders (Ed.) Attention and Performance 1 84-92 (Acta Psychologica 27).
|44| G.H. Mowbray (1960). Choice reaction times for skilled responses, Quarterly Journal of Experimental Psychology 12 193-203.
|45| R. Näätänen and A. Merisalo (1977). Expectancy and preparation in simple reaction time. In: S. Dornic (Ed.) Attention and Performance 6 115-139 Erlbaum Hillsdale, N.J.
|46| R.S. Nickerson (1973). Intersensory facilitation of reaction time: Energy summation or preparation enhancement? Psychological Review 80 489-509.

|47|R.T. Ollman (1977). Choice reaction time and the problem of distinguish-
   ing task effects from strategy effects. In: S. Dornic (Ed.) Attention
   and Performance 6 99-113 Erlbaum Hillsdale, N.J.
|48|R.G. Pachella (1974). The interpretation of reaction time in informa-
   tion processing. In: B. Kantowitz (Ed.) Tutorials in performance and
   cognition, Erlbaum Hillsdale, N.J.
|49|R.G. Pachella and D.F. Fisher (1969). Effect of stimulus degradation
   and stimulus similarity on the trade-off between speed and accuracy in
   absolute judgments, Journal of Experimental Psychology 81 7-9.
|50|M.I. Posner (1964). Information reduction in the analysis of sequential
   tasks, Psychological review 7f 491-504.
|51|M.I. Posner (1978). Chronometric explorations of mind, Erlbaum
   Hillsdale, N.J.
|52|M.I. Posner, R. Klein, J. Summers and S. Buggie (1973). On the selec-
   tion of signals, Memory and Cognition 1 2-12.
|53|M.I. Posner and R.M. Klein (1973). On the functions of consciousness.
   In: S. Kornblum (Ed.) Attention and Performance 4 21-37 Academic Press,
   New York.
|54|E.C. Poulton (1973). Unwanted range effects from using within-subjects
   experimental designs, Psychological Bulletin 80 113-121.
|55|W. Prinz (1972). Reaktionszeit - Fraktionierung durch Varianzanalyse?
   Archiv für Psychologie 124 240-252.
|56|D. Raab, E. Fehrer and M. Hershenson (1961). Visual reaction time and
   the Broca-Sulzer phenomenon, Journal of Experimental Psychology 61
   193-199.
|57|P.M.A. Rabbitt (1967). Signal discriminability, S-R compatibility and
   choice reaction time, Psychonomic Science 7 419-420.
|58|D.A. Rosenbaum (1979). Human movement initiation: selection of arm,
   direction and extent, Journal of Experimental Psychology: General, in
   press.
|59|H. Rouanet, D. Lepine and D. Holender (1978). Model acceptability and
   the use of Bayes-fiducial methods for validating models. In: J. Requin
   (Ed.) Attention and Performance 7 687-701.
|60|A.F. Sanders (1967). Some aspects of reaction processes. In:
   A.F. Sanders (Ed.) Attention and Performance 1 115-130 (Acta Psychologica 27).
|61|A.F. Sanders (1970). Some variables affecting the relation between
   relative signal frequency and CRT. In: A.F. Sanders (Ed.) Attention
   and Performance 3 45-55 (Acta Psychologica 33).
|62|A.F. Sanders (1971). Psychologie der Informations Verarbeitung, Huber,
   Berlin.
|63|A.F. Sanders (1975). The foreperiod effect revisited, Quarterly Journal
   of Experimental Psychology 27 591-598.
|64|A.F. Sanders (1977). Structural and functional aspects of the reaction
   process. In: S. Dornic (Ed.) Attention and Performance 6 3-25 Erlbaum,
   Hillsdale, N.J.
|65|A.F. Sanders (1979). Some effects of instructed muscle tension on
   choice reaction and movement time. In: R.S. Nickerson (Ed.) Attention
   and Performance 8 Erlbaum, Hillsdale, N.J. in press.
|66|A.F. Sanders and J.E.B. Andriessen (1978). A suppressing effect of re-
   sponse selection on immediate arousal in a choice reaction task, Acta
   Psychologica 42 181-186.
|67|A.F. Sanders and A.H. Wertheim (1973). The relation between physical
   stimulus properties and the effect of foreperiod duration on reaction
   time, Quarterly Journal of Experimental Psychology 25 201-206.
|68|J.R. Simon, E. Acosta, S.P. Mewaldt and C.R. Speidel (1976). The effect

of an irrelevant directional cue on choice reaction time: Duration of
the phenomenon and its relation to stages of processing, Perception and
Psychophysics 19 16-22.

|69| S.P. Shwartz, J.R. Pomerantz and H.E. Egeth (1977). State and process
limitations in information processing: An additive factor analysis,
Journal of Experimental Psychology: Human Perception and Performance 3
402-410.

|70| E.E. Smith (1968). Choice reaction time: an analysis of the major
theoretical positions, Psychological Bulletin 69 77-110.

|71| R.F. Stanners, J.E. Jastrzembski and A. Westbrook (1975). Frequency and
visual quality in a word - non word classification task, Journal of
Verbal Learning and Verbal Behavior 14 259-264.

|72| K.E. Stanovich and R.G. Pachella (1977). Encoding, stimulus-response
compatibility, and stages of processing, Journal of Experimental Psychology: Human Perception and Performance 3 411-421.

|73| S. Sternberg (1969). The discovery of processing stages: Extensions of
Donders' method. In: W.G. Koster (Ed.) Attention and Performance 2
276-315, Acta Psychologica 30.

|74| S. Sternberg (1975). Memory scanning: new findings and current contro-
versies, Quarterly Journal of Experimental Psychology 27 1-32.

|75| S. Sternberg, S. Monsell, R.L. Knoll and C.E. Wright (1978). The laten-
cy and duration of rapid movement sequences: comparisons of speech and
and typewriting. In: G.E. Stelmach (Ed.) Information processing in
motor control and learning, Academic Press.

|76| G.L. Stone and E. Callaway (1964). Effects of stimulus probability on
reaction time in a number-naming task, Quarterly Journal of Experimental Psychology 16 47-55.

|77| D.A. Taylor (1976). Stage analysis of reaction time, Psychological
Bulletin 83 161-191.

|78| J. Theios (1975). The components of response latency in simple human
information processing tasks. In: P.M.A. Rabbitt and S. Dornic (Eds.)
Attention and Performance 5 418-440 Academic Press, London.

|79| A.T. Welford (1968). Fundamentals of skill, Pergamon Press, London.

|80| A.T. Welford (1971). What is the basis of choice reaction time?
Ergonomics 14 679-693.

|81| L. Whitaker (1979). Dual-task interference as a function of cognitive
processing load, Acta Psychologica 43 71-84.

|82| W.A. Wickelgren (1977). Speed-accuracy trade-off and information pro-
cessing dynamics, Acta Psychologica 41 67-85.

|83| A.H. Wertheim (1979). Information processed in ocular pursuit, Thesis
Academische Pers, Amsterdam.

|84| A.H. Wertheim (1979). Information processing mechanisms involved in
ocular pursuit. This volume.

|85| R.S. Woodworth (1938). Experimental Psychology, Holt, N.Y.

|86| R.S. Woodworth and Schlosberg (1954). Experimental Psychology
Methuen & Co. New York.

|87| W. Wundt (1896). Grundriss der Psychologie, Englemann, Leipzig.

Tutorials in Motor Behavior
G.E. Stelmach and J. Requin (eds.)
© *North-Holland Publishing Company, 1980*

21

THE UBIQUITOUS ROLE OF PREPARATION

Robert Gottsdanker
Department of Psychology
University of California
Santa Barbara, California

A preparation-theory hypothesis of the psychological
refractory period was supported by a step function relating RT (reaction time) to ISI (intersignal interval) for
constant ISIs with adequate controls. The contribution
of probability effects was demonstrated with varied ISIs.
Preparation theory proposes that RT is an inverse function
of available preparation capacity, which is apportionable
but which may be shared. Equations derived from preparation models for the effect of number of alternatives,
both equally and unequally probable, fit existing data
reasonably well. Experiments on the aged support the
distinction between preparatory ability and its control.

I was introduced to the potency of preparation when I accidentally
found that RT (reaction time) to a signal is lengthened by knowledge that
there will be another signal for response in a half second. (Gottsdanker,
Broadbent, & Van Sant, 1963.) Later I found that my discovery of "holding
back" had been preceded by publication of the same effect by Fraisse (1957)
and by Slater-Hamel (1958). In his report of a subsequent experiment on
the effect conducted in my laboratory, Salthouse (1970), using the framework of a shared capacity theory of human performance, introduced the term
"allocation of preparation." I was doubtful about that idea and wanted to
get back to my studies of PRP (psychological refractory period).

If preparation were of as little importance in an RT experiment as I
and others had thought we could dispense with warning signals, or their
equivalent, and even with instructions. Yet, preparation seldom figures
in explanations advanced for the effects found in RT experiments. In the
years following psychology's awareness of information theory a number of
RT relations to uncertainty were investigated in which preparation might
have been considered but typically was not. Alternative uncertainty was
described by Hick (1952) and by Hyman (1953) as showing a logarithmic
relation to RT in accordance with information theory. Time uncertainty,
objective and subjective, was described by Klemmer (1956, 1957) to have a
similar relation to RT. However, Gordon (1967) found a relation with
event-occurrence uncertainty (proportion of catch trials) which does not
fit a logarithmic relationship. Previously, Drazin (1961) varying both
time and event-occurrence uncertainty obtained rather different results
than Klemmer and interpreted them in terms of preparation, or to be exact,

This research was supported by grants to the University of California
from the National Institute on Mental Health (MH 10447) and the National
Institute on Aging (1 R01 AG00011).

readiness. I followed this work with a demonstration that with objective
time uncertainty, RT at the initial portion of the range is actually
<u>increased</u> by good timekeeping; the subject is unwilling to prepare with low
momentary probability because he knows "what time it is" not because he does
not (Gottsdanker, 1970). This finding has been corroborated and extended by
Buckholz and Wilberg (1975).

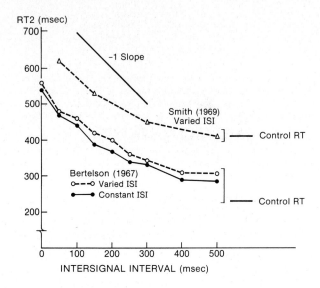

Figure 1. Typical findings on RT2 as a function of ISI.

    Typical findings of experiments on PRP are shown in Figure 1; with a
pair of closely successive signals for response, RT2 (to the second signal)
is long. As ISI is lengthened there is a smooth, exponential-like decrease
in the value of RT2. The classic explanation advanced is quite different
from that for the uncertainty effects previously mentioned but similar in
having its origin in communication theory, that of intermittent processing
because of a single channel limitation. In Figure 2, the paradigm of the
experiment is shown and also the basis for the single-channel theory
(Welford, 1952). In the control procedure, there is simply a warning signal
(W) and a signal for response (S). In the critical procedure the signal for
response (S2) is briefly preceded by another signal for response (S1). The
observation is that RT2 is longer than control RT. The reason cited is that
there is an enforced delay in the processing of S2 until the processing of
S1 has been completed. Of course if ISI is longer than RT1, RT2 will equal
control RT. Thus, when ISI is shorter than RT1:

$$RT2 = RTN + RT1 - ISI \qquad\qquad (Equation\ 1)$$

Here, RTN stands for normal RT, such as control RT.

    Since there have now been a very large number of experiments on PRP,
virtually all of which have yielded the general shape of the functions
shown in Figure 1, the foregoing formulation has been accepted in a general
way. There have been controversies over the amount of initial slope, with

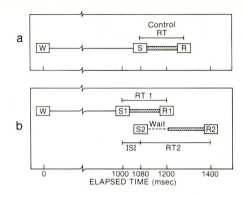

Figure 2. Paradigm and single-channel account of PRP. The time
values here would be: Control RT and RT1 = 200 msec; ISI = 80
msec; RT2 = 320 msec.

a minus 1 slope--shown in Figure 1--supporting intermittent processing
(Welford, 1952) and a shallower slope supporting shared processing
(Bertelson, 1967). There has also been controversy concerning the length of
time the curve descends, as indicative of the processing operations
included in the PRP: to identify it with RT1 (the whole time S1 is being
processed), to exclude that part of the time devoted to peripheral operations but to add central recovery time (Davis, 1957), or to include the
monitoring of proprioceptive feedback from the first response (Welford,
1968, p. 109). However, there is fairly general agreement that the lengthening of RT2 results from some kind of <u>interference</u> from S1-R1 processing.
As can be seen in Figure 2 and Equation 1, interference models are concerned only with events that start with S1. No difference is considered to
exist in the state of the subject before the occurrence of S1.

    The few voices raised against this neglect have not gained a very
attentive audience. John (1964) states quite clearly (although in
reference to studies without overt RT1) that the comparison of control RT
and RT2 is questionable since it assumes that preparatory set is the same
on the two tasks and, "Unfortunately no such assumption seems valid since
in the simple RT situation the subject is set for only one type of signal
whereas in the two signal situation the subject is set for two types of
signals which follow each other in random intervals." (p. 88). Near the
beginning of research on PRP Poulton (1950) advanced a preparation hypothesis that applied to both constant ISI procedures (insufficient time to
get ready) and varied ISI procedures (insufficient time to get ready plus
low initial expectancy). This entire hypothesis has been incorrectly
labeled the expectancy theory. It has thus been "eliminated" (Broadbent,
1971, p. 309) with the chief evidence coming from experiments that the PR
(psychological refractoriness) effect is found using constant ISIs with
choice reactions.

    Recently I made a direct test of the hypothesis that when the subject
knows which signal will be presented first he is initially unprepared for
the second signal (Gottsdanker, 1979).   What was done was to use a
constant ISI of 100 msec but to omit S1 on a small proportion of trials.
It was hypothesized that RT2 would be lengthened over its normal control

value on those trials. This result was obtained. It was concluded that
the basic reason for lengthening of RT2 in PRP experiments is that the
subject is unprepared to respond to S2 because of preparation for S1-R1.
It was argued that the term <u>unprepared period</u> was more accurate than PRP.

Still, it is possible that the lengthening of RT on probe trials does
not reflect what happens on regular trials on which S1 occurs. Perhaps the
effect is due to the subject's surprise that S1 did not occur. An experiment was needed in which surprise was not a factor. Results from a
previous study (Gottsdanker, 1975) provided a lead. In this study it was
found that after the subject had been in a state of low preparation because
of low event-occurrence probability, a presignal that event probability had
been raised on an isolated trial was entirely without effect up to a duration of 200 msec but completely effective for durations of 300 msec or
longer. In a PRP experiment if the occurrence of S1 allows the subject to
begin preparing for S2-R2, there should thus be an RT2 function that does
not fall for ISIs up to 200 msec and then falls suddenly to normal RT
values for longer ISIs. This would appear to be a bad prediction since,
as is seen clearly in Figure 1, RT2 descends gradually.

However, almost all previous studies were subject to a number of
artifacts that would tend to produce a gradual decline in RT2. This point
will be considered more fully in the discussion of the experiment about to
be described. Fortunately, I had on hand data from an experiment that
avoided these artifacts. I had not written about this experiment previously because it had made no sense to me as I was in an "interference"
frame of mind during those years (Way and Gottsdanker, 1968). Here then,
is the experiment that should have been done last but which was done first.

The Experiment on PRP

<u>Method</u>

   <u>Tasks</u>. In the double task, which was the main experimental condition,
the subject used his left hand to move a short lever either toward himself
or away from himself--depending on which half of the top surface became
lighted--and released a switch held closed with his right thumb if a tone
was sounded.

   The control single tasks were simply the two parts of the double
task, the visual choice task and the auditory key-release task. A block
of trials was composed entirely of one type of task: double, visual, or
auditory.

   In the double task the ISI between the visual and auditory signals had
one of 6 values: 50, 100, 150, 250, 450, or 850 msec. In the Constant
Procedure a given subject was tested at only one of these ISIs. The tone
occurred randomly on half of the trials. In the Varied Procedure ISI was
randomly varied among the 6 values within each block of trials. Again,
there was no auditory signal on half the trials at random. Thus, for
the Varied Procedure there were effectively 6 values of ISI ranging from
50 to 850 msec and also an "infinitely long" value of ISI.

   Each trial started with the flash of a red warning light located just
above the base of the response lever. The visual-choice stimulus came on
after a constant warning interval of 1 sec. This was also the case for
the single visual control task. Single auditory control task trials were
the same for each subject as those in his double-choice task except there
was no preceding visual signal.

Subjects. Forty-two right-handed male college students were used as subjects in the experiments. They ranged from 18 to 23 years of age. Each was paid $20 for 10 hours of participation.

On Day 1 of the experiment they were tested on the two single tasks for assignment to one of the 6 constant ISI groups or to the varied ISI group. Matching was used to equate means and standard deviations on both single tasks.

Conduct of Experiment. Testing was done over 10 daily sessions of about 45 minutes each. On Days 2-10 there were 6 35-trial blocks, all on the same task. The interval between the starts of adjacent trials was 6 sec. A 1 minute rest was provided between adjacent blocks.

The subject was informed of his RT on each of the first 5 trials of a block. Thereafter, shortest and longest times were reported to him at the completion of a block. Only the last 30 trials of a block were used for data analysis. The data for this experiment were those obtained in the second week of testing: Days 6 through 10, by which time performances were fairly well stabilized. On Day 6 the auditory task was given and on Day 9 the visual; on Days 7, 8, and 10 the double task was given. Technical details of programming and recording have been described previously (Gottsdanker, 1969b).

Results. Over-all mean values of individual mean RTs to auditory signals are shown in Figure 3 for the 6 Constant Procedure groups and for the Varied Procedure group. Trials are not included in which an error occurred. With the exception of those trials and the few on which there was a malfunction of the equipment each double-task RT2 to the auditory signal in the Constant Procedure is based on 270 responses for each subject, on the average. Control RTs to the auditory signal are based on approximately 90 trials for each Constant Procedure subject. The corresponding numbers of trials for each Varied Procedure subject are 45 and 15.

Constant Procedure. It is seen in Figure 3 that for the Constant Procedure, RT2 was very similar for ISIs 50, 100 and 150 msec and that the values for longer intervals are appreciably shorter. Further, the near equality for RT2 over the 50 to 150 msec ISIs are based upon substantially the same percentages of error. In fact, the 254 msec value for the 150 msec ISI is coupled with a slightly higher error percentage than is the 241 msec value for the 50 msec ISI. The prediction of a step-function would appear to be strongly supported. There is a little problem in that the control RTs to the auditory signal differed among the 6 groups. However, when the results are examined in terms of the amount of lengthening over the control values in Figure 1 (upper dark bars) it is seen even more clearly that the lengthening of RT2 followed a step function. There was essentially a 70 msec lengthening for the short intervals and no lengthening for the longer intervals.

Three analyses of variance of RT2 support the foregoing conclusions. The analysis over all 6 intervals, using control auditory RT as the covariate shows a significant effect of ISI, $F (5, 29) = 7.93$, $p = .0001$. However, the separate analysis for the 3 shortest intervals shows an insignificant effect of ISI, $F (2, 14) = 0.16$, $p = .8538$. Also, the separate analysis for the 3 longest intervals shows no significant effect of ISI, $F (2, 14) = 2.14$, $p = .1546$.

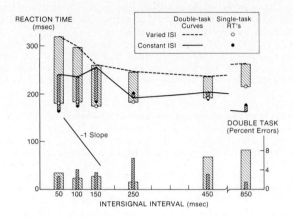

Figure 3. RT2 and percent errors (anticipations and false alarms).
The narrow darker bars represent the Constant Procedure and the
wider lighter bars the Varied Procedure. Bars in the top half of
the figure show the difference between double-task and single-
task RT. Bars in the bottom half show percent error.

Varied Procedure. It is seen in Figure 3 that RT2 gradually descended
from a peak of 319 msec and reached a low of 236 msec at the 450 msec ISI
followed by a rise to 262 msec at the 850 msec ISI. The initial slope is
not underestimated because of differential error rate since the percentage
of errors was higher for the 50 msec ISI than for the next three succeeding
ISIs. Errors again tended to increase after that point. There is some
inequality in single-task control RT among the different ISIs. However,
when the results are plotted in terms of the lengthening over the control
values in Figure 3 (light bars), the account remains the same. Also, it
is important to note that unlike the curve for constant ISIs, this curve
remains considerably above baseline, never becoming closer than 45 msec to
the control value. That is, there was lengthening of RT2 at all intervals.

The analysis over all 6 intervals, using control auditory RT2 as the
covariate shows a significant effect for ISI, F (5, 24) = 3.88, p = .0102.
The greatest change, of course, took place over the 3 shortest ISIs. For
each of the 6 subjects, RT2 was longer than control RT at each of the 3
longest ISIs. Any further statistical test seems unnecessary to substan-
tiate the continued PR effect.

Reaction Time to Visual Signals. It may be argued that the curves of
Figure 3 do not give an appropriate test of the single-channel hypothesis,
Equation 1; RT1 may vary between ISIs. There is a problem in applying
Equation 1 to present data as the occurrence of S2-R2 shortened RT1 as
has been described previously (Gottsdanker, 1969b). This effect was
greatest at the 50 msec ISI. However, even using RT1 values on trials
with S2 gives little comfort to the single channel hypothesis. It is predicted for the Constant Procedure that RT2 would be reduced from 348 to 294
msec between the 50 and 150 msec ISIs. In fact there was an increase
from 241 to 256 msec. The fit is not quite so bad for the Varied Procedure:
predicted 363 to 274 msec against obtained 319 to 260 msec. Of course the
Varied Procedure was greatly influenced by momentary probability.

Discussion of Results. The step function obtained for the Constant Procedure is markedly different than the smooth curves shown in Figure 1 that are typical of findings on PRP. Smith (1969) found no important differences between Constant and Varied Procedure. Why should these new findings be accepted? My argument is that relatively peripheral effects abound in PRP research (e.g. Way and Gottsdanker, 1968) and these weaken as ISI lengthen, tending to produce a smooth curve. There are no comparable artifacts which would tend to produce a step function. Hence, all that is needed to support the preparation hypothesis is the obtaining of a step function reliably in one experiment. As a matter of fact I did obtain something close to a step function in an earlier experiment (Gottsdanker and Way, 1966) but was thoroughly confused by it. RT2 was the same for ISIs of 50 and 100 msec. Specifically, the Bertelson (1967) and Smith (1969) experiments used in Figure 1 suffered from the same peripheral effect. Visual signals were used for both S1 and S2 with a horizontal displacement of from 8 to 12 degrees. The subject knew which signal would occur first and was presumably fixating in that direction. At the onset of S1, visual acuity for S2, which was in the parafoveal field was undoubtedly poor. In the Bertelson study—and presumably in the Smith study—the stimulus lights remained on until the next trial. As ISIs lengthened there must have been a shift during ISI in both visual attention and direction of regard.

In the present study a great deal of effort went into reducing the effect of factors that lie outside the PRP paradigm. Artifactual interference effects were minimized by difference in signals, responses, and task structure. Use of an auditory S2 eliminated problems of stimulus interference, and direction of visual attention. Moreover, subjects were well practiced and tested on only one condition to reduce carryover effects.

A hierarchical model of how preparation theory operates in the Constant Procedure is shown in Figure 4. The top level is essential for interpretable performance in any RT study. Responses will be made according to instructions and made quickly only with the cooperation of the subject. Primary determinants of Willingness to respond as directed are the social context and the subject's expectation of a signal for response. The next level, Preparation Control, refers to the translation of instructions, given the subject's state of knowledge, into a plan. Here, the subject, knowing which signal will occur first, will allocate as much preparation as possible to the S1-R1 task. Allocation of preparation as depicted by Kahneman (1973, p. 15) more generally for mental effort is never quite exclusive; there is always some spare capacity (perhaps for emergencies). The plan also includes a shifting of preparation as soon as S1 does occur. The third level shows the quantitative allocation of preparation at each moment of time. Finally, the actual signals and responses are shown at the bottom level.

With the occurrence of the warning signal, W, the Willingness Determinants initiate Preparation Control so that most capacity is allocated to S1-R1. There is thus a short RT1 when S1 occurs. At that instant the reallocation of preparation to S2-RT, which will require between 200 and 250 msec begins. However, if S2 occurs before there has been time to reallocate preparation, the response must be made on the basis of "spare" preparation. Since preparation is attained suddenly, there will be the same low level of preparation up to an ISI of about 250 msec. However, if S2 occurs at any time after reallocation of preparation, there will be a rapid response based on the new high level.

In the Varied Procedure RT2 show the continuous initial decline which
is typical of PRP results. The large differences between procedures at the
two shortest ISIs might be due to differences in momentary probability of
signal occurrence; e.g. at the 50 msec ISI, 1/2 for the Constant Procedure
and 1/12 for the Varied Procedure. Still, the means are almost identical
at the 150 msec ISI, even though the momentary probability difference
remains large; 1/2 as compared with 1/10. There is obviously an effect of
probability change in the Varied Procedure responsible for the decline of
the curve. Another puzzling aspect of the Varied Procedure data is the
persistence of a PR effect at 850 msec. Perhaps the best lesson to be
learned from the present results is that varied procedures introduce
probability effects on willingness to prepare but not in any well understood
way.

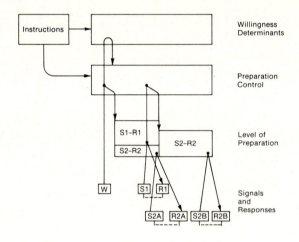

Figure 4. Preparation model of PRP with the Constant Procedure.
Dashed lines indicate RT1, RT2 for short ISI (left), and RT2 for
long ISI.

A somewhat tentative model illustrating the operation of the preparation theory for the Varied Procedure is shown in Figure 5. What is added to
the Constant Procedure model is the effect of signal probability on the
subject's willingness to prepare. Thus, the occurrence of S1 coincides with
low momentary probability of a signal and preparation is initially set low.
As time passes without occurrence of S2, its momentary probability
increases bringing about heightened preparation for S2-R2. Finally, the
decreasing probability that a signal will occur on the trial overcomes
increased momentary probability so that willingness is again reduced with a
consequent reduction in level of preparation.

Supporting evidence for the preparation theory of psychological
refractoriness are found in the results of the study by Elithorn and
Lawrence (1955). In that study, the subject did not know in advance which
signal would occur first, or consequently which response would be required.
A varied procedure was used. As might have been expected, RT eventually
became shorter as ISI increased. However, with practice, two of the three
subjects had the same level of RT2 up through the ISI of 250 msec.

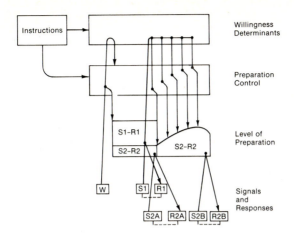

Figure 5. Preparation model of PRP with the Varied Procedure.
Dashed lines indicate RT1, RT2 for short ISI (left), and RT2 for
long ISI.

Experiments in which no response is required to S1 would appear to
provide evidence against the preparation theory (e.g. Fraisse, 1957, Davis,
1959). However, preparation has been shown to be important in such experiments. PR has been found only in experiments arranged so that there is a
high level of preparation for the signal for response. Where time
uncertainty is great (and preparation low) the lengthening of RT by a preceding irrelevant signal has not been found (Bertelson and Tisseyre, 1969;
Davis and Green, 1969; John, 1964). When there is a high level of preparation it is apparently disrupted by the extraneous signal; without a high
level of preparation there can be no disruption. In any event, the
increase of RT in such studies is far less than that found when a response
is required to S1.

Preparation Theory and Choice Reaction Time

As is well known, choice RT is longer than simple RT. Also, in
choice RT, higher values are generally found as the number of alternatives
is increased. In a wide variety of circumstances the increase appears to
be related logarithmically to the number of alternatives. This relation
is generally known as Hick's law although I would prefer to honor Hyman's
early contribution and use the term, the Hick-Hyman law.

Theories to account for the number-of-alternatives effect have been
divided by Welford into two classes, serial classification models and
simultaneous scanning models. He notes (1968, p. 77): "One possibly
significant point is that the simultaneous models have been
conceived as a means of handling identification of signal, whereas the
successive models seem more applicable to choice of response: perhaps
this is where their principal application lies." Identification of signal
would seem to be excluded as a primary consideration--except if signals
are deliberately made confusable--by my experiment (1969a), in which the
same set of signals gave a sizeable difference between simple and choice

RT for button pressing and directional movement but not for unidirectional step tracking. Hick (1952), in explaining the logarithmic relation proposed a serial classification model in which a series of decisions is made, each of which halves the number of alternatives. This approach has been greatly developed in recent years by Welford (1975). However, Welford (1968, p. 79) had also proposed a neurological scanning model that "makes the subject's task in selecting a response essentially similar to that of discrimination between different signals."

What is to be proposed here is a model that flows from preparation theory. We may note some striking parallels between certain findings on PRP and on number of alternatives. In unidirectional step tracking, I found that S2 exerted its initial effects without any PRP delay (Gottsdanker, 1973) even though the response was typically inadequate. Megaw (1972) had also noted that he found no PR delay in a unidirectional step tracking task and refers to his unpublished doctoral thesis. To parallel these findings, I found only a 9 msec difference in unidirectional step tracking between a simple and a choice response (Gottsdanker, 1969a). Megaw (1972) found negligible difference in unidirectional step tracking between 2 and 4 alternatives in one experiment and between 3 and 5 alternatives in another experiment. These two sets of findings would appear to be bridged by the concept of preparation. There can be common preparation if responses differ only in amplitude modulation. In the PR experiment, being prepared for S1 allows preparation for S2. In the unidirectional step tracking being prepared for one alternative allows preparation for the others as well. This consideration would seem to rule out Welford's neurological scanning model in which RT should be lengthened by similarity of responses. Even more compelling evidence that RT is reduced by similarity of responses has been presented recently by McCauley (1979). The subject's task was to move the forefinger from a home key to the alternative light that had been turned off. Shorter RTs were found as the angular separation between alternatives was reduced.

Another parallel between PRP and number-of-alternatives findings has to do with the effect of practice. Anyone who has witnessed a subject's first few practice trials in a PRP experiment is acquainted with the extremely high values of RT2 that are found--often higher than will fit any formulation. Gottsdanker and Stelmach (1971) found that the PR effect was reduced to less than half its initial amount by extended practice. If the same processing of S1 were taking place early and late in training, there should be the same lengthening of RT2. Similarly, Mowbray and Rhoads (1959) and Mowbray (1960) have shown the number-of-alternatives curve to flatten with extended practice. How is it possible for the successive binary decisions to become so much faster? Welford (1968, p. 87) suggests a qualitative difference in the way in which a choice with a number of alternatives is made early and late in practice from "a series of sub-decisions to a single decision..." Such a change means essentially going outside of the explanatory models. Of course it remains to be seen whether a preparation-theory model can handle learning in a more satisfactory way.

I should first like to demonstrate that a preparation model can fit number-of-alternatives data at least as well as a logarithmic equation. What is being proposed is simply that the subject is able to apportion his preparation before the signal occurs. The assumption is that RT is shorter as more preparation is available, the same assumption as in the models for PRP. The other assumption is that there can be preparation in common for two or more responses. This assumption seems justified by the finding that choice RT is shortened by the similarity of responses (Gottsdanker, 1969; McCauley, 1979; Megaw, 1972). A very simple model applying preparation theory to choice RT is shown in Figure 6. In a and b the proportion of common capacity for preparation is .25. The difference is that in a there is more specific capacity per alternative than in b, because it is divided between two alternatives rather than among four. In c, there are again 4 alternatives but each has more capacity than those in b since the common capacity is .75 of the total. There would thus be a shallower slope of RT against number of alternatives for the situation represented by c. The "diodes" show the one-way transfer of preparation capacity.

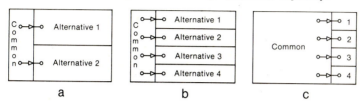

Figure 6. Model of allocation of preparation capacity. (See text)

In Figure 7 there is shown the data of Hick (1952) and Hyman (1953, as brought together by Welford, 1968, p. 68). Logarithmic spacing is used for the number of alternatives and the best-fitting straight lines are drawn. The open circles show the predictions of the preparation model, setting the portion of common capacity at .20. The equation for RT to an alternative i of n equally-probable alternatives is derived as follows, with P_i representing the proportion of preparation capacity allocated to an alternative, c representing proportion of common capacity, and RT' representing RT with full available capacity.

According to the major assumption,

$$RT_i = RT' \ \frac{1}{P_i} \qquad\qquad \text{(Equation 2)}$$

For n equally-probable alternatives,

$$P_i = c + \frac{1}{n} (1-c) \qquad\qquad \text{(Equation 3)}$$

Consequently,

$$RT_i = RT' \ \frac{n}{c(n-1)+1} \qquad\qquad \text{(Equation 4)}$$

Hick's data seem at least as well fitted by Equation 4, with RT' = 150 msec, as by the straight-line logarithmic function. It is noteworthy that there is almost perfect fit to 2 and 10 choices. The main problem in finding any fit to Hyman's data is that the function appears markedly sigmoid. Even so, the preparation model with RT' = 220 msec provides at least as good a fit as the logarithmic equation. Actually, the preparation model is better fitted by the logarithmic equation than are Hyman's data! It is realized that Welford's use of log (n+1) tends to fit many sets of data better than does log n. However, there is a strong ad hoc aspect to such a revision even though it is justified as the inclusion of temporal uncertainty. Perhaps a way of testing that idea would be to eliminate time uncertainty as can be done using the transit-signal method (Gottsdanker, 1970a) in which the subject knows exactly when the signal will occur, i.e. at the instant of transit of a moving target past a fixed line. In that case log n should fit the data better than log (n+1).

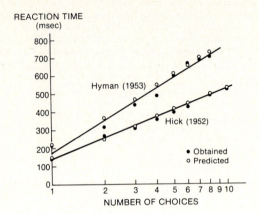

Figure 7. Data of Hick (1952) and Hyman (1953), closed circles, fitted by logarithmic functions, straight lines, and by preparation-theory equations, open circles.

However, it is difficult to see how any logarithmic function can encompass results that are obtained for RT to individual choices when probabilities are different. With the preparation model this would imply a larger portion of preparation capacity for the more probable choice. Using probability as the direct indicator of proportion of preparation capacity allocated to an alternative i leads the general version of Equation 3 as follows, with p_i representing the probability of occurrence of alternative i:

$$P_i = c + p_i(1-c) \qquad\qquad \text{(Equation 5)}$$

Substituting in Equation 1,

$$RT_i = RT' \frac{1}{c + p_i(1-c)} \qquad\qquad \text{(Equation 6)}$$

Finally,

$$\overline{RT}_{i=\overline{1,n}} = RT' \sum_{i=1}^{n} P_i \frac{1}{c + p_i(1-c)} \qquad\qquad \text{(Equation 7)}$$

Figure 8 compares the fit to the data of Kaufman and Levy (1966) of logarithmic functions and Equation 6 for both an equally probable condi- tion and an unequally probable condition. For the equal probability condition, there were either 2, 4, 6, or 8 choices. For the unequal probability condition there were always two choices but with the following sets of probabilities for the two alternatives: .90 and .10, .80 and .20, .70 and .30, .60 and .40. The obtained mean RTs for the equal probability condition are shown in the shaded area and for the unequal probability condition they are outside that area. It can be seen that the data of the equal probability condition can be fitted fairly well by a straight line,

indicative of a logarithmic relation. However, an extension of this line
passes considerably above the low information (high probability) means
found with the unequal condition. Moreover the high information (low
probability) means of the unequal condition lie considerably above the
values for the equal probability condition. This is not just a matter of
there being another logarithmic function for the unequal probability
condition. An extension to the left of the line fitting the high-informa-
tion means is seen to pass far above the low-information means.

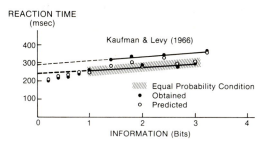

Figure 8. Data of Kaufman and Levy (1966), closed circles, fitted
by logarithmic functions, straight lines, and by preparation-
theory equations, open circles.

        A rather better fit is found using the preparation model. The equal
probability points are satisfactorily fitted by using a value of .60 for c.
An encouraging rather than a really close fit to the unequal probability
points is found by setting c to .50. In both cases RT' is set at 200 msec.

        Perhaps it will be necessary to increase the complexity of the model
somewhat to reflect important variables that affect choice RT. Some
suggestions are shown in the augmented model in Figure 9. Already discussed is the representation of differential probability by proportion of
area. The unused area at the top corresponds to the spare capacity shown
for S2-R2 in the PRP experiment. I have argued that increasing the number
of alternatives in the first task (see Smith, 1969) reduces preparation
available for the second task (Gottsdanker, 1979). The area to the
right indicates that level of alertness may be increased to give more
capacity for all of the alternatives. The shaded control indicates that the
process of control itself takes away from capacity similarly to a computer
program. In this vein, it would be expected that use of low-compatibility
signal-response pairs would result in more capacity being occupied by
control functions. The effect would be to bring about a steeper rise of RT
with number of choices, as has been found in the literature (Brainard et al,
1962). The effect of learning should be just the opposite. Less control
relative to individual alternatives should be required, which would expand
the common capacity. Such a change would be in line with a recurrent idea
on perceptual-motor learning to be constituted of increasingly larger units
(e.g. Welford, 1968, pp. 192-196). Perhaps there is also a reduction in the
absolute size of the segregated areas. The model allows testing of such
hypotheses simply by computing the relevant areas.

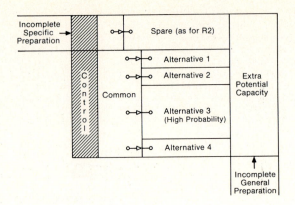

Figure 9. Augmented model of allocation of preparation capacity.
(See foregoing text).

Control of Preparation

The models shown in Figures 7 and 9 do not include representations of
Instructions, Willingness Determinants, or Control of Preparation as in
Figure 4 and 5. It is to be understood that they are part of the model.
Instructions and Willingness Determinants actually represent "outside
influences" and the only real purpose for including them is so that we will
not forget about them. However, it is a fair question of whether we need
be concerned with a level of Preparation Control above Preparation itself.
A series of experiments on aging shows that effects occur that must be
assigned to abilities at such a level.

A "cross-over" effect has been observed for elderly subjects as it has
long been for schizophrenics (Houston, Shakow, & Riggs, 1937). That is, at
short preparatory intervals a constant procedure gives lower values of RT
than does a varied procedure, but at somewhat longer intervals the difference is reversed (Botwinick, Brinley, & Robbin, 1959). Young subjects may
show such a tendency but not in so marked a degree. The interpretation has
been that the young but not the old are capable of maintaining a state of
preparation. However, Loveless and Sanford (1974) showed that half of that
conclusion was questionable. Using the measure of contingent negative
variation (CNV) they found that young subjects do not, in fact, maintain a
high level of preparation throughout the preparatory interval; they peak
their preparation for the appropriate instant. Old subjects do not use
that strategy. In recent work, not yet published, I have found that there
is no difference between young and old subjects in maintaining preparation.
This was done by using a constant probability of signal occurrence following
its first possible occurrence. Thus, there is no deficiency of the old in
executing a plan. The deficiency previously found must be assigned to the
ability to plan or control preparation.

Conclusions

I believe that a start has been made toward a quantitative preparation
theory of RT. Some success has been achieved in bringing into the same
framework the following effects: holding back, event-occurrence uncertainty,

time uncertainty, psychological refractoriness in its various forms, and
alternative uncertainty with equally and unequally probable alternatives.
At the present time explanations for these effects have been various with
little hope for reconciliation. Suggestions are given of possible effects
of learning and these are open to empirical investigations. Also, some
guidance has been given of the locus of deviant or non-optimal RT performance.

A more restricted conception of the RT task has been introduced than
that which is prevalent. It is meant to refer to situations in which discrimination among, judgment of, or search for stimuli is minimal. I suspect that the latency laws concerning clearly differentiable signals are
quite different from those in which decisions are important. This is
entirely in the spirit of the originator of the term reaction time, Sigmund
Exner (Woodworth, 1938, p. 305) who regarded the responses as "prepared
reflexes." The distinction Norman and Bobrow (1975) make between data-
limited and resource-limited processes is germane here. The present theory
is concerned entirely with the latter. Specifically, it proposes for preparation a linear performance-resource function in the resource limited area.
In this connection it should further be noted that Shaw (1978) has presented
a mathematical capacity allocation model for reaction time. However, its
application is to tasks such as visual search with the capacity being used
for display processing.

Preparation has been considered here in a molar, undifferentiated way.
This is not in the least to disparage the efforts of those who are investigating selective aspects of preparation, notably Thomas (1974). It is my
personal belief that the rough outlines should be established before the
details are filled in. Also, there is not even a suggestion of the processes
through which increased preparation shortens RT. A conspicuous omission is
any treatment of errors. That remains to be worked out. Finally, this is
far from a general theory of human performance, as RT occupies but a small
corner of that area in respect to our typical and important activities. I
hope that it will be possible before long to integrate ideas concerning RT
with those on serial performance, such as are being developed by Shaffer
(1976).

References

Bertelson, P. The refractory period of choice reactions with regular and
    irregular interstimulus intervals. Acta Psychologica, 1967, 27, 45–56.
Bertelson, P., & Tisseyre, F. The time-course of preparation: Confirmatory
    results with visual and auditory warning signals. In W. G. Koster
    (Ed.) Attention and Performance II. North Holland Publishing Company:
    Amsterdam, 1969.
Botwinick, J., Brinley, J. F., & Robbin, J. S. Maintaining set in relation
    to motivation and age. Journal of Applied Psychology, 1959, 72,
    585–588.
Brainard, R. W., Irby, T. S., Fitts, P. M., & Alluisi, E. A. Some variables
    influencing the rate of gain of information. Journal of Experimental
    Psychology, 1962, 63, 105–110.
Broadbent, D. E. Decision and Stress. London: Academic Press, 1971.
Buckolz, E., & Wilberg, R. A priori probability effects on simple reaction
    time. Journal of Motor Behavior, 1975, 7, 73–80.
Davis, R. The human operator as a single channel information system.
    Quarterly Journal of Experimental Psychology, 1957, 9, 119–129.

Davis, R., & Green, F.   Intersensory differences in the effect of warning
    signals on reaction time.   In W. G. Koster (Ed.), Attention and
    Performance II.   North Holland Publishing Company: Amsterdam, 1969.
Drazin, D. H.   Effects of foreperiod, foreperiod variability, and probabil-
    ity of stimulus occurrence on simple reaction time.   Journal of
    Experimental Psychology, 1961, 62, 43-50.
Elithorn, A., & Lawrence, C.   Central inhibition--some refractory observa-
    tions.   Quarterly Journal of Experimental Psychology, 1955, 7, 116-127.
Fraisse, P.   La période réfractaire psychologique.   Année Psychologique,
    1957, 57, 315-328.
Gordon, I.   Stimulus probability and simple reaction time.   Nature, 1967,
    215, 895-896.
Gottsdanker, R.   Choice reaction time and the nature of the choice response.
    Psychonomic Science, 1969a, 14, 257-258.
Gottsdanker, R.   Interacting responses to crowded signals.   In W. G. Koster
    (Ed.), Attention and Performance II.   North Holland Publishing
    Company: Amsterdam, 1969b.
Gottsdanker, R. A transit-signal methodology for studying reaction time.
    Behavior Research Methods and Instrumentation, 1970a, 2, 6-8.
Gottsdanker, R.   Uncertainty,timekeeping, and simple reaction time.
    Journal of Motor Behavior, 1970b, 2, 245-260.
Gottsdanker, R.   Psychological refractoriness and the organization of step-
    tracking responses.   Perception and Psychophysics, 1973, 14, 60-70.
Gottsdanker, R.   The attaining and maintaining of preparation.   In P.
    Rabbitt and S. Dornic (Eds.), Attention and Performance V.   Academic
    Press: New York, 1975.
Gottsdanker, R.   A psychological refractory period or an unprepared period?
    Journal of Experimental Psychology: Human Perception and Performance,
    1979, 5, 208-215.
Gottsdanker, R., Broadbent, L., & Van Sant, C.   Reaction time to single
    and to first signals.   Journal of Experimental Psychology, 1963, 66,
    163-167.
Gottsdanker, R., & Stelmach, G. E.   The persistence of psychological
    refractoriness.   Journal of Motor Behavior, 1971, 3, 301-312.
Gottsdanker, R., & Way, T. C.   Varied and constant intersignal intervals
    in psychological refractoriness.   Journal of Experimental Psychology,
    1966, 72,792-804.
Hick, W. E.   On the rate of gain of information.   Quarterly Journal of
    Experimental Psychology, 1952, 4, 11-26.
Houston, P. E, Shakow, D., & Riggs, L. A.   Studies of motor function in
    schizophrenia: II.   Reaction time.   Journal of General Psychology,
    1937, 16, 39-82.
John, I. D.   The role of extraneous stimuli in responsiveness to signal.
    Refractoriness or facilitation?   Australian Journal of Psychology,
    1964, 16, 87-96.
Kahneman, D.   Attention and Effort.   Englewood Cliffs, New Jersey:
    Prentice-Hall, 1973.
Klemmer, E. T.   Time uncertainty in simple reaction time.   Journal of
    Experimental Psychology, 1956, 51, 179-184.
Klemmer, E. T. Simple reaction time as a function of time uncertainty.
    Journal of Experimental Psychology, 1957, 54, 195-200.
Loveless, N. E., & Sanford, A.J.   Effects of age on the contingent negative
    variation and preparation set in a reaction-time task.   Journal of
    Gerontology, 1974, 29, 52-63.
McCauley, M. E.   Spatial response options and the latency of movement
    initiation.   Unpublished doctoral dissertation, University of
    California, Santa Barbara, 1979.

Megaw, E. D. Direction and extent uncertainty in step-input tracking.
    Journal of Motor Behavior, 1972, 2, 171-186.
Mowbray, G. H. Choice reaction times for skilled responses. Quarterly
    Journal of Experimental Psychology, 1960, 12, 193-202.
Mowbray, G. H., & Rhoades, M. V. On the reduction of choice reaction times
    with practice. Quarterly Journal of Experimental Psychology, 1959,
    11, 16-23.
Norman, D. A., & Bobrow, D. G. On data-limited and resource-limited processes.
    Cognitive Psychology, 1975, 7, 44-64.
Poulton, E. C. Perceptual anticipation and reaction time. Quarterly
    Journal of Experimental Psychology, 1950, 2, 99-112.
Salthouse, T. Human performance as a function of future demands.
    Perceptual and Motor Skills, 1970, 30, 327-336.
Shaffer, L. H. Intention and performance. Psychological Review, 1976, 83,
    375-393.
Shaw, M. L. A capacity allocation model for reaction time. Journal of
    Experimental Psychology: Human Perception and Performance. 1978, 4,
    586-598.
Slater-Hamel, A. T. Psychological refractory period in simple paired
    responses. Research Quarterly, 1958, 29, 468-481.
Smith, M. C. The effect of varying information on the psychological
    refractory period. In W. G. Koster (Ed.), Attention and Performance
    II. North Holland Publishing Company: Amsterdam, 1969.
Thomas, E. A. C. The selectivity of preparation. Psychological Review,
    1974, 81, 442-464.
Way, T. C., & Gottsdanker, R. Psychological refractoriness with varying
    differences between tasks. Journal of Experimental Psychology, 1968,
    78, 38-45.
Welford, A. T. The "psychological refractory period" and timing of high
    speed performance--a review and a theory. British Journal of
    Psychology, 1952, 43, 2-19.
Welford, A. T. Fundamentals of Skill. London: Methuen, 1968.
Welford, A. T. Display layout, strategy and reaction time: tests of a
    model. In P. Rabbitt & S. Dornic (Eds.), Attention and Performance V.
    Academic Press: New York, 1975.

Tutorials in Motor Behavior
G.E. Stelmach and J. Requin (eds.)
© North-Holland Publishing Company, 1980

22

TOWARD A PSYCHOBIOLOGY OF PREPARATION FOR ACTION

Jean Requin

Département de Psychobiologie expérimentale, Institut de
Neurophysiologie et psychophysiologie du C.N.R.S., Marseille, France

In this paper some experimental findings, which provide evidence
that the efficiency of processing systems involved in the elaboration of motor activity could be enhanced by presetting processes,
are reviewed. Referring to the central hypothesis that preparation is not a stage in a process, but rather a change in the
functional state of a processing system, selection of data is
based upon few operational criterions, namely optionality and
predictive value for performance, making it possible to identify
a phenomenon as a preparatory one. Using psychological and
neurophysiological approaches, these data are ordered according
to the emerging statement that current conceptions in both fields
converge toward a three-stage serial model of motor organization.
Action project definition or response determination, motor program specification or building and movement execution, thus formed
three successive operations, which could be specifically facilitated by relatively independent preparatory adjustments. This
parallel requires the close combination of psychological and
neurobiological methods to study preparatory processes for
action in a psychobiological perspective.

INTRODUCTION

The concept of preparation, as well as the related notions of presetting,
pretuning or preprogrammation, is increasingly used in the analysis of behavior to give a meaning to a number of covert or open activities that seem
to have no intrinsic finality, and that can be only understood by reference
to the subsequent element of behavior they announce and sometimes pre-
figure. Especially significant in this way is the recent success encountered by the notion of feedforward, which formalized the idea that the
functional state of a still inactive processing system is modified in advance by the output of an earlier processing stage. In spite of the well-
recognized heuristic value of the concept of preparation, already emphasized thirty years ago by Poulton (1950) when he noted that expectations
about the near future form the main determinants of the actual behavior of
a living organism, it remains, however, impossible to propose a satisfactory current definition of preparation outside of precise, but limited,
theoretical frameworks. In addition to the notion of "extrinsic finality"
suggested above, some of the elements entering such a general but operational definition, making it possible to identify a process as preparatory,
could be nevertheless offered (cf. Requin, in press). One must especially
emphasize that preparation probably refers to "optional" rather than to
"necessary" processes; in other words, that performance is only more or
less facilitated by preparation but that the initiation and achievement of

an action remains possible even for an unprepared subject. This idea could be formalized within the framework of current models of information processing where hypothetical constructs as preparation, attention or activation have not been included as structural elements, or processing stages, but as functional states of processing systems, a distinction recently stressed again by Garner (in press). Preparation cannot be thus considered as an early and necessary stage in a serial model of sensorimotor activity, but as a modification, set in advance, of the processing efficiency of the various systems responsible for the successive operations underlying this activity. In this way, preparation appears as a decisive determinant of the functional plasticity of specialized processing systems. As a direct implication of this conception, the main operational criterion to identify a phenomenon as being preparatory is probably to show that manipulation of factors expected to control preparatory adjustments results in covariations of performance level. This notion of a predictive value for performance misses its sense when preparation is conceived as a stage included in a fixed sequence of operations, or in statistical terms when a time dependence between processes does not enable valid information to be drawn from a correlation analysis of the behavioral changes controlled by these processes.

These elements of definition would also stress the proximity of concepts of preparation and of attention, especially when the latter refers to the selective processing of information relevant to organizing behavior at a given time. What must be probably emphasized here is that the coexistence of both concepts was mainly related to a tradition where "attention" was preferably used when input selection was concerned and "preparation" when output selection was concerned. However, the recent conceptual evolution in these fields of research, made selective filtering or modulating effects in information processing models intervene later and later, first from peripheral sensory systems, then to memory access, storage or retrieval, and last to motor processing stages. The maintenance of two concepts which cover very similar phenomena and underlying mechanisms is now probably useless. In any case, this could explain that sixty years after Woodrow (1914), attention and motricity appear again as related fields (see, for instance, Klein, 1976 and Posner, 1975).

Lastly, preparation is currently considered as presenting a double dimension, or, even, as covering two different kinds of processes (cf. Holender, in press; Requin, 1978). The first one refers to the so-called "short-term" unspecific preparatory adjustments related to subject's expectancy about the time when he will have to do something, mainly studied in paradigms where subject's time uncertainty is controlled. The second one refers to the so-called "long-term" specific preparatory adjustment related to subject's expectancy about characteristics of the task he will have to perform, mainly studies in paradigms where subject's event uncertainty is controlled. Of course, the former analysed elsewhere in this volume (see Gottsdanker and Sanders) will not be considered here. On the other hand, my aid is obviously not to propose an exhaustive synthesis of experimental findings collected about specific preparatory processes to motor activity, but rather to show that data provided by psychological and neurobiological approaches are increasingly coherent. Such a tendency mainly results from an emerging convergence between conceptions proposed by psychologists and by neurobiologists about the structural and functional organization of motor activity.

THE ISOMORPHIC RELATION BETWEEN MODELS OF MOTOR SYSTEMS

As it was recently stressed again by Posner (1978), serial models of information processing originate from the dependency of early experimental psychology on the well-established physiological theories, such as the 'reflex
arc' model of nervous functioning was at the end of the last century.
After having been ostracized by the somewhat coercive behavioristic viewpoint, they were reactivated when principles of communication theory were
applied to biological functioning. Moreover, Sternberg (1969) gave them
the last impulse when he developed, a century after Donders, both the
theoretical statements and the methodological implications involved in considering sensorimotor activity as a series of independent serially-
organized processing stages, thus starting up the lasting success of the
so-called "additive factor method" (see Sanders, in this volume).

In spite of the number of methodological issues it raises (cf. Holender,
1975; Pachella, 1974; Sanders, in this volume), the experimental strategy
resulting from Sternberg's development of chronometric methods was and remains most fruitful. In recent reviews by Sanders (1977; in this volume),
their efficiency is well illustrated. The additive and interactive effects
upon RT of factors related to the stimulus, the response and the SR code
characteristics cannot be accounted for by a simple three-stage model of
reaction processes derived from the initial 'reflex arc' schemata, for
instance stimulus coding, decision making and response output processes.
These results force one to subdivide the sensorimotor sequence more finely.
Along this line, Sander's suggestion of three "motor" stages meets the
reaction process model proposed by Theios (1975), where motor activity develops through three serial operations, namely, response determination,
response program selection and response output. In the former, the response
associated to the identified stimulus would be retrieved in the stimulus-
response coding system, and though its span depends upon the individual
coding system, it remains necessarily limited. Indeed, each significant
environmental change cannot call for an exhaustive register of motor
strategies corresponding to the unrestricted context diversity in which
the same finality can be reached. Thus, the stock of available "responses"
must be conceived in terms of "holistic" goals for an action not specified
enough to allow motor planning. This motor programming stage supposes that
the selection of kinetic formula adapted to the action project be permanently adjusted to changes occurring in the surroundings and therefore controlled by sensory inputs. The latter will go on through the next process-
sing stage, when both the chronology and the amount of muscle activation
underlying movement performance are determined by the precise and yet flexible structure of the motor program. Of course, it is not our aim to develop issues about the nature of processes which take place within each
stage; this has been thoroughly done elsewhere in this book. What we wish
to emphasize is the neurobiological data supporting such a view of motor
organization.

The recent use of single unit recording methods in relatively free-moving
animals contributed to orienting neurobiological interest, primarily focussing on mechanisms underlying the biomechanics of movement outside of
any behavioral context, toward the function of motor systems according to
the finality of the behavioral sequence in which action takes place. Such
an evolution, or even a "revolution" as stressed by Brooks (1978), partly
answers the concerns and criticisms expressed some years ago by Granit (1973)

when he noted "if one merely persists in demonstrating that site A inhibits or excites sites B, C or D, neglecting the teleological questions of
what purpose all of it serves and how it responds to variations of demand,
then, in the end, one will be in possession of a body of knowledge, to be
sure, but knowledge likely to become merely an amorphous conglomerate of
well-documented facts".

In this rapidly developing perspective of a behavioral neurophysiology, a
structural and functional organization of motor systems, which presents
some analogy to the serial processing stage models of psychologists, is
progressively emerging. A privileged axis would be formed by a) a first
stage, starting in the association cortical areas and ending in the neocerebellum, responsible for the action "project" definition, b) a second
stage, starting in the neocerebellum and ending in the precentral motor
cortex, where the motor program is selected and build, c) a third stage,
starting in the motor cortex and ended by motoneuron activation, accounting for movement execution. Such an organization emerges from the converging arguments developed in a number of review papers, as those from Allen
and Tsukahara (1974), Brooks (1975, 1977), Brooks and Stoney (1971), Deecke,
Grözinger and Kornhuber (1976), Evarts and Thach (1969), Kemp and Powell
(1971), Kornhuber (1974). An explicit summary of this model was proposed
by Thach (1975) when he wrote, "a command for movement occurs in cerebral
association cortex and then sequentially feeds through pons, dentate,
VA-VL thalamus, and motor cortex, gaining specifications at each stage".

The hypothesis that the association cortex could intervene in the earliest
stages of motor activity was primarily suggested by its privileged connections with the cerebellum (Evarts and Thach, 1969) and by the motor deficits
which follow injuries of these structures. For instance, it is well known
that lesions of the parietal cortex could be followed by an impairment of
visual or visuomanual exploration of the motor proximal space, even by
some difficulties associated with "ideomotoric" apraxia (cf. Hecaen, 1978),
while lesions of the prefrontal lobe disturb the timing, especially the
sequencing, of motor action (cf. Teuber, 1972). Recent microphysiological
studies (Mountcastle, 1976; Mountcastle, Lynch, Georgopoulos, Sacata and
Acuna, 1975; Hyvarinen, 1977; Hyvarinen and Poranen, 1974) confirmed that
these cortical areas have to be qualified as "association" ones, not only
since various inputs converge on them but mainly because they could be considered as some kind of interface between sensory information and related
motor activity. For example, the activity of a number of parietal neurons
is triggered by visual inputs, but only when visual stimuli must be fixed
or tracked to obtain some reinforcement, or when they form a target for
visual or manual reaching. These findings support the conclusion proposed
by Hyvarinen (1977) that the functional role of the posterior parietal
areas would be "to convey sensory information from surrounding space to the
structures of motor planning". These motor planning structures would thus
receive a permanently up-dated picture of the sensory context, to which
specifications of the action project must be obviously adjusted. Such a
coincidence would be the main condition for the triggering of an holistic
"command function" of the parietal structures, only underlying the "intentional" dimension of the action engaged to reach biologically significant
goals, the responsibility for details of motor programming being assumed by
a later processing stage (Mountcastle, 1976). While such speculation was
not proposed for prefrontal areas, one can suggest that these latter structures could play a similar role in temporal information. Some equivalent
of the parietal "command function" could be found in Teuber's hypothesis

(1972) of "corollary discharges" originating from the frontal cortex to preset posterior cortical structures to receive sensory consequences of action. Information conveyed by this feedforward mechanism is probably also useful for planning motor activity. The functional complexity of association in cortical areas seems to be thus related to the close over-lapping of an integrative function for sensory inputs and of a "command function". The congruence of both would start the motor program building stage. It is tempting to propose that such a functional organization makes association cortical areas the possible locus of the Stimulus-Response coding process conceived as the determination of the adequate response among the register of associations progressively built between perceptual and action schemata.

The second segment of the motor system organization accords a privileged role to the neocerebellum, the efferents of which increase in the precentral motor cortex as teleokinetic motricity in primates development. While the role of the cerebellum in the control of posture, equilibrium, and in the assistance of movement execution is well-known, its intervention in motor programming is a relatively recent proposal. A more sophisticated conception along this same line was suggested by Kornhuber (1974). He argued, from the impairment in movement timing which follows injuries to the neocerebellar cortex and from the regular cytoarchitectonics of these structures which makes them especially amenable to the temporal coding of neuronal messages, that the cerebellum plays a role of "motor function generator" responsible for programming speed movements and coordinating movement sequences. Microphysiological studies of Purkinje cells in the cerebellar cortex (Thach, 1970), as well as neurons in dentate and interposate nuclei (Thach, 1975), have shown increased activity preceding movement initiation and were related to movement parameters. Moreover, there is an isomorphism between activity patterns observed in the cerebellum and motor cortex, but the former intervene before the latter; the same conclusion about the timing of processes was drawn from dentate cooling experiments (Brooks, 1975, 1977). This set of recent results partially contradict, on the other hand, the previously suggested opposition between roles played by the cerebellum and basal ganglia respectively, these latter structures being often considered in the involvement of slow movement programming (Kemp and Powell, 1971; DeLong, 1972; Deecke et al., 1976). An alternative hypothesis would be to accord an extended role in action planning to the neocerebellum, while the basal ganglia would only accompany motor activities set up to assist movement execution, thus explaining their privileged intervention when movements, slowly executed, imply a "closed-loop" control. In the same way, the puzzling presence of a thalamic relay in the cerebellocortical pathway, the activity of which precedes precentral neuron discharge (Evarts, 1971; Joffroy and Lamarre, 1974; Strick, 1976) is now interpreted less as a filtering gate of information transmission to motor cortex than as a programming structure for complex muscular synergies including postural substrate of movement performance (Massion, 1976). This adds to the idea that motor specifications controlling precentral activity result from a progressive building in a series of structures, possibly modulated at each step by sensory inputs. However, the precise coding of movement parameters (i.e., extent, direction, force and speed) in the activity patterns which lead to the motor cortex, remains largely, unknown (Brooks and Stoney, 1971; Paillard, 1976).

Following this complex programming process, the activation of the precentral cortical areas is classically considered as initiating the movement
execution stage. Of course, the increasing knowledge accumulated about
the structural organization of direct and indirect corticospinal connections constitutes the obvious basis for the involvement of these systems
in movement control (cf. Kuypers, 1973; Massion, 1978). However, when one
considers both structure and function, the idea of a clear cut distinction
between programming and execution processes seems somewhat flimsy. First,
the problem set up by the precise role played by precentral neuron
"colonies" either responsible for muscle activation, through innervation
of one spinal motorneuron pool, or for movement control, the activity of
several motoneuron pools, remains still partially unsolved. Furthermore,
one must emphasize the autonomy of the motor cortex, the subcortical
structures included in corticospinal pathways, as well as spinal motor
structures, in modulating programs they have to execute and, also in partially ensuring this programming process itself. Lastly, the motor cortex
is, in fact, a sensorimotor cortex, reached by almost all sensory inputs,
organized somatotopically such that each specialized neuron pool forms an
input/output functional unit explaining the so-called "cortical reflexes"
whose intervention in movement control has recently been emphasized (see
Desmedt, 1978). Microphysiological studies of motor cortex activity,
initiated by Evarts (1964), have confirmed this functional complexity of the
corticospinal system, for instance by rejecting the hypothesis of a fixed
specialization of precentral neurons, according to the body side involved and
to the agonistic vs antagonistic role played by muscle in movement performance (Evarts, 1969). Along the same line, it is difficult to point out
the clear relationship between neuronal activity and the intensive movement
parameters, extent, force, and velocity (Fromm and Evarts, 1976; Evarts,
1968), which stresses that the corticospinal system contributes to the adjustment of movement specifications, instead of acting as a "command register", or as "hardware", passively executing orders received from motor programming structures. A similar conclusion could be drawn if one considers
the interrelated roles played at the spinal terminal level by the alpha/
gamma motoneuron organization and by interneuron networks in mediating cortical commands (cf. Miles and Evarts, 1979).

As a concluding remark, we must underline that the hypothesis of three
serially organized segments in motor systems appears likely at a macroscopic
level only and becomes challenging as soon as the precise functioning of
nervous structures included in each segment is considered. Of course, the
same remark would be suitable for the three-processing stage model proposed
by psychologists. A thorough analysis of what happens within each stage
would require the introduction of overlapping and simultaneously conducted
operations. The point in developing such an idea of isomorphism in structural models of sensorimotor activity is to raise the question of preparation for action in analogous (and somewhat reductionistic) terms for both
psychological and neurobiological approaches. This could be done by setting
up a relationship between processing stages and neuronal systems on one hand,
and between processes and nervous mechanisms on the other hand. Some of the
main experimental facts collected in the field of preparation will now be
ordered according to this guideline.

PREPARATORY ADJUSTMENTS FOR RESPONSE DETERMINATION

According to a serial model of sensorimotor activity, the first process that could be accelerated by preparation is the memory search of the adequate response after the stimulus has been identified. The possibility of a functional presetting of the systems responsible for such a process is supported by an analysis of the results observed in choice-RT paradigms. In this situation the subject is faced with "event uncertainty" based upon the use of different SR associations considered as discriminable but unpredictable events. Hence, the nature of the physical differences between stimuli and biomechanical differences between responses, which partly condition the durations of the perceptual identification process and of the motor programming process must be considered. What is important here, is to look at the RT effects of the amount of information given to the subject on a trial, that is, the identity of the SR association one has to process when the objective probability is manipulated. It is well-known that, in such conditions, RT for a given SR association increases as its frequency ov occurrence decreases, either when the number of equiprobable SR alternatives (Hick, 1952; Crossman, 1953; Hyman, 1953) or when the relative frequency of this SR association within a constant set of alternatives (Bertleson and Barzeele, 1965; Falmagne, 1965; Fitts, Peterson and Wolpe, 1963; Hyman, 1953) is varied. Two kinds of problems are raised by this probability effect on RT. The first one concerns the locus of this effect, which refers to the perceptual vs motor side of the reaction process, since stimulus and response probabilities were most often varied simultaneously in these paradigms. The second one concerns its timing, in other words, the legitimacy of interpretating the probability effect as a pre-stimulus, or preparatory one, rather than as a post-stimulus one.

By using experimental procedures where relative frequencies of stimuli and responses were varied independently, LaBerge and Tweedy (1964) and Bertelson and Tisseyre (1966) initiated an active field of investigation aimed at teasing out the locus of probability effects in processing stages. The first set of experiments emphasized the role of stimulus frequency (Bertelson and Tisseyre, 1966; Hawkins and Friedin, 1972; Hawkins and Hosking, 1969; Hinrich and Krains, 1970; LaBerge, Tweedy and Ricker, 1967; Orenstein 1970), while, in another series of experiments, manipulations of response frequency also resulted in RT variations (Biederman and Zachary, 1970; Blackman, 1972; Hawkins, Snippel, Presson, McKay and Todd, 1974; Hinrich and Craft, 1971; LaBerge, Legrand and Hobie, 1969). Moreover, the analysis of sequential effects confirmed that response probability could intervene in in choice RT. Others have shown that RT is generally shorter when the response is partial-ly or totally identical to the preceding one in a series of trials (Bertelson, 1965; Kornblum, 1973; Rabbitt, 1965; Smith, Chase and Smith, 1973). Attempts to more precisely locate the impact of probability effects in response processing stages well illustrate the cross-checking strategy borrowed from Sternberg's additive factor method. The interacting effects on RT observed when SR frequency and compatibility were varied together suggest that the same stage is affected by both factors; since SR compatibility is considered as directly reflecting the availability of a response in memory, one can therefore conclude that an increase in SR probability improves RT by speeding up the response determination process. Such kinds of interactions were observed by manipulating either the SR relative frequency among a fixed set of SR alternatives (Fitts et al., 1963; Sander, 1970; Theios, 1975) or the number of equiprobable SR alternatives (Brainard, Irby, Fitts and Alluisi, 1962; Morin and Forrin, 1965;

Theios, 1975). For instance, the frequency effect generally observed when the subject has to press buttons with his fingers on visually-presented letters according to a conventional but unexperienced code, decreases or even disappears when responses are formed by the familiar verbal naming of stimuli. Moreover, the interaction of SR compatibility and frequency of stimuli associated with the same response was also observed (Hawkins et al. 1974; Spector and Lyons, 1976). Similarly, this interpretation can be used for the decreased disappearance of the frequency effect with long practice (Mowbray and Rhodes, 1959), a factor which can also be considered as increasing SR compatibility. As a concluding remark, one must emphasize the historical evolution of this problem: While originally considered as intervening upon early stages of information processing, the frequency effect was progressively explained by a modulation of motor processes, namely operations underlying response determination.

Until recently, the mechanisms proposed to explain RT variations resulting from changes in SR probability were thought to act after stimulus presentation (see, for example, Smith, 1968). The improvement of RT when the number of SR alternatives decreases was generally related to a shortening of the memory search process to identify the signal and to discover the correct response. Such an explanation supposes in fact, that this memory scanning, either exhaustive or self-terminated, is limited to SR alternatives used in the task. These SR alternatives form a subset arbitrarily extracted from a more extensive register. This implies a preselection of the strategy used in memory search process, based upon information the subject draws from instructions as Bartz (1971) demonstrated in his one-trial RT experiments, and/or from practice of experimental conditions. Further, the improvement of RT when the SR-relative frequency is increased or when the value of a speed response for a given signal is enhanced by using a differential payoff (see for example, Holender, 1975), was generally related to a lowering of criterions used to identify the corresponding response, making the latter more available in memory. Such an hypothesis also supposes that decision thresholds in the response identification process are differentially predetermined according to the subject's representation of the SR frequency distribution or to the values attributed to the different responses.

The preselection of the strategy in the memory scanning process and the predetermination of decision criterions that end this process could be thus considered as two kinds of preparatory adjustments reducing the duration of the first stage of reaction processing, namely response determination. The gap between such conclusions, issued from experimental psychology, and those, issued from neuropsychology and neurobiology, give some evidence for a presetting of the nervous structures possibly responsible for the earliest stage of motor activity, still remains large.

Nevertheless, in spite of the polymorphism and versatility of motor systems following lesions of cortical associative areas, clinical observations suggest that these structures are the locus of functional presetting facilitating motor initiation. It is well known that frontal lesions often result in a complex deficit in the ability to anticipate the consequences of action, as emphasized by Teuber (1964): "the patient is not altogether devoid of capacity to anticipate a course of events, but cannot picture himself in relation to those events as a potential agent". On the other hand, pathological or traumatic injuries of prefrontal and parietal lobes are sometimes followed by subtle troubles of "volitional" aspects of motor activity, which cannot be classified as apraxia; such "motor neglects" are characterized by akinetic symptoms. Patients, without any clear motor deficit, hesitate to spontaneously use a limb and, when they do, they initiate and execute movements very slowly (Castaigne, Laplane and Degos, 1972). Of course, it is very difficult to interpret this kind of phenomenon in the framework of the processing stage model we proposed, without any complementary information that could provide a more precise examination of these patients in standardized experimental conditions. The hypothesis we suggested is that these troubles could result from a specific impairment of preparatory processes facilitating the holistic "command function" attributed by Mountcastle to the cortical associative areas, especially the parietal.

Microphysiological experiments in animals recently provided some evidence for the involvement of cortical associative areas in a preselection process of the sensorimotor "material" used in the later stages where the motor program is built. The sustained or progressively increasing cell activity recorded by Kubota, Iwamato and Susuki (1974) and Susuki (1977) in the frontal cortex during the response delay of a conditioning paradigm is relevant to the hypothesis that these structures process memorized information related to the timing of expected events, which is certainly necessary to plan motor activity. Suggestive also are the data from Hyvarinen's experiments (1977), showing that the reactivity of some neurons of the posterior parietal area to different inputs can be differentially modulated according to the environmental demand. For instance, the reactivity of a unit, normally activated by both tactile and visual inputs, decreases for tactile stimuli when a significant event, that is, a target for a reaching movement of the monkey, is visually presented. Such a phenomenon presents a good model for a presetting process resulting in a preselection of information necessary to update the internal representation of the sensory context in which a future action will be performed. Insofar as it is also fould for "command" neurons, this kind of anticipatory modulation could be interpreted as an index of the predetermination process of a specific "action project", which would be the earliest stage of motor activity.

Lastly, the distribution of slow negative shifts recorded as cerebral potentials over the scalp developing almost 1 sec before a spontaneously performed movement must be noted (cf. Deecke et al., 1976). The amplitude of this so-called "readiness potential" is maximal on the parietal area, which certainly indicates an early functional involvement of these structures, clearly dissociable from the "motor potential" which is related to the precentral cortex activity timelocked to the execution phase of the movement. Recent studies partially support the hypothesis that neuronal mechanisms underlying the "readiness potential" have a predictive value for the characteristics of the subsequent response. First, the amplitude of this slow negative shift during the last 150 msec preceding movement initiation is related to the speed of response performance (Deecke et al., 1976). Second, its parietal component is sensitive to the direction, extension vs flexion, of the movement (Deecke, Eisinger and Kornhuber, 1978). Lastly, a slight hemispheric asymmetry of the "readiness potential", the amplitude of which is greater on the contralateral cortex to the active limb, was observed by Kutas and Donchin (1977). By recording central nervous structures during stereotaxic surgery in humans, Ganglberger, Haider, Groll-Knapp and Schmid (1978) have recently shown that the activity of spread pools of parietal and prefrontal neurons is modified when a signal warning the subject about a motor performance is given. Speculating about the meaning of these "ideatoric" potentials, the authors suggest that they could "reflect the activity of command-centers for voluntary movement". Taking into account the conditions in which they were observed, these phenomena probably give the best evidence for a preparatory setting of the associative cortical structures involved in motor action.

PREPARATORY ADJUSTMENTS FOR MOTOR PROGRAM SELECTION

Since psychologists' interests were mainly focussed on stimulus detection, coding, and identification processes, investigations aimed at examining a functional presetting of the systems responsible for the operations underlying motor program building are recent and still rare. Data in this field were collected in choice-RT paradigms where "event-uncertainty" does not only result from using a number of SR alternatives, but since number is fixed, it also refers to information given to the subject about the biomechanical properties of the different possible motor responses. Of course, responses cannot be so simple as pressing or releasing buttons but have to be more complex (for instance, in pointing tasks where spatial parameters of movements can be controlled). In turn, this response complexity introduces the difficult methodological problem of the possibility of a trade-off between speed in movement initiation and precision in target reaching. This makes inferences from RT measurements questionable when RT and movement time covary. An ideal situation from which to interpret data is therefore reaching when controlled variations in response factors result in selection effects on RT.

The general framework guiding this line of experimentation, based upon some kind of isomorphism between response organization, motor program and preparatory set, can be stated as follows. In an RT task with a response alternative, preparation for performing one movement supposes the presetting of motor systems responsible for planning a given muscular synergy. Such a presetting may disturb the simultaneous building of the motor program necessary to perform the other movement, if the latter involves a very different muscular strategy. If one supposes that the subject tries to set up a pattern of preparatory adjustments facilitating the elaboration of both motor programs, the level of preparation reached for the movement that will be really performed must be lowered, and therefore is RT lengthened, as the differences between the two motor programs increase. Predictions would be the same in the case where the subject takes the risk of preparing only one movement and must, in half the trials, execute the other one in an inadequate state of preparation. In an appropriate paradigm, RT can therefore be considered as an index of the "compatibility" of preparatory adjustments corresponding to different motor programs.

By manipulating biomechanical parameters of reaching movements in tracking or pointing tasks, Ells (1973), Gibbs (1965), Griew (1968), Kerr (1978), Megaw (1972), and Semjen (1970) have shown that choice-RT depends upon direction uncertainty. This effect was not found when extent uncertainty was varied (Gottsdanker, 1969; Lagasse and Hayes, 1973; Megaw, 1972; Megaw and Armstrong, 1973). Fiori, Semjen and Requin (1974) and Semjen and Requin (1976) have found that RT increases as the course of movements starting from the origin become more divergent. Because RT and movement time covary when the mean distance of both targets increases, the results observed when movement extent was manipulated were not so clear. Nevertheless, the slight, but significant, RT lengthening when the "contrast" between movement extents increases can be explained by a progressive "incompatibility" of prepara-

tory adjustments to the selection of elements in the motor program determining movement extent. A part of the data recently collected by
Rosenbaum (in press) supports this hypothesis. When the subject is instructed to prepare a response, the RT increase observed as the imperative
signal calls for another response depends upon the "dimension" in which the
prepared movement and the performed movement differ. RT increases are organized according to a hierarchical ordering of limb used, then of movement
direction, and finally of movement extent. We have proposed the same
notion of a hierarchy in preparatory processes, isomorphous to the hierarchy in programing processes. One can explain that a progressive increase
of the time constraints in planning complex muscular synergies could lead
the subject to successively renounce the preselecting of different elements
of the motor program, according to an "urgency" order where movement extent
is always sacrificed to movement direction (Semjen, Requin and Fiori, 1979).

Other data from Rosenbaum's experiments greatly contribute toward the clarification of the organization of preparatory adjustments to motor program
elaboration. In a choice-RT paradigm, RT improvement observed when the
warning signal partially informs the subject about some characteristics of
the movement response can be related to the time gain which results from a
pre-selection of program elements that define movement parameters. Moreover,
when the warning signal provides combined information about several movement parameters, RT could be analyzed using the additive factor method.
For instance, in a pointing task where the warning signal informs the subject of the response parameters (side of the body, active limb, movement
direction, and movement extent) the preselection of the corresponding elements of the program appears as an independent, serially organized operation which is preferentially performed in this order. Using a similar
method, Stelmach and Bonnet (unpublished data) found the same results for
rotation movements of the foot around the ankle axis. RT improvement is
greater when the warning signal provides information about movement direction than when advance information given to the subject concerns movement
extent. Furthermore, these effects are additive, confirming that preselection processes of the elements used for motor program specification are
serially and hierarchically organized.

At this point, one can question the necessity of using the concept of preselection rather than that of selection, or, in other words, of interpreting the data summarized above in terms of preparation rather than in terms
of programming. One could, in fact, consider that the time profit observed
when the warning signal provides advance information about response movement properties means merely that movement programming is performed during
the preparatory period. This interpretation supposes that a processing
stage (that is, a structural element in the serial model of sensorimotor
activity) takes place partially before the response signal occurs. However,
such a conception would make the concept of preparation useless and can be
challenged in two ways. Firstly, one must admit that since the subject has
to wait for the imperative signal to appear, a processing stage could end
before the immediate start of the next. This means that the result of the
first processing stage is stored in order to be available later on. In
other words the functional state of the systems to be involved in processing
information - here, the motor program register - is modified before this
process starts; that is what I call preparation. Secondly, one must question the possibility that the elements of the motor program, which, for example, determine movement extent, could be selected and ready for use without any knowledge of movement direction or limb involvement. Hence, one is

more likely to accept the idea that processes triggered by the warning signal on the one hand and by the imperative signal on the other, are different in nature. The so-called preparatory processes could be defined as
preselection among a register of kinetic modules conceptualized as a
matrix for which the entries would correspond to the different movement dimensions. This makes the elements necessary to plan the motor activity individually unitilizable and more available. The second process would
underlie the motor program spcification itself, by extracting a set of elements from memory and by integrating them according to the action project.
This process could be conceived as somewhat analogous to the building of a
computer program by introducing, in the machine, a set of elementary subrou-
tines in a defined order.

Results from neurophysiological investigations support the hypothesis that
modifications of neuronal activity, which implicate preparatory processes
possible intervening to facilitate the programming of movement parameters,
are mainly observed at the level of the cerebello-cortical pathways. It
has already been noted that such a presetting process specifically related
to biomechanical aspects of movement cannot be found by recording unitary
neuronal activity as well as integrated activity of large pools of neurons
in cortical associative areas. Their role seems to be devoted to a "holistic" definition of the action project in terms of goals. Based on the isolated observation of Evarts and Tanji (1974) a set of experiments were
conducted unsuccessfully to find evidence that spinal motor structures are
functionally preset according to the biomechanical parameters of the movement performed (Requin, Bonnet and Semjen, 1977). These negative results
emphasize, of course, the meaning of microphysiological data recently collected by investigating the activity of nervous structures included in the
cerebello-cortical circuits. This method, used at first by Hammond (1956)
and popularized by Evarts (1973) is as follows. The monkey holds a handle
joined to a lever, which can rotate horizontally around the elbow axis. A
visually presented warning signal first informs the animal about the forearm movement (extension for pushing or flexion for pulling) it will have
to perform. After a preparatory period, a sudden externally controlled rotation of the lever, either away from or toward the animal, serves as an
imperative signal triggering the previously instructed response. Since
somatotopic organization of sensory and motor representations overlap in a
number of cortical and subcortical structures, this perturbation of the
lever position, by stretching either the muscle performing the movement
response or the antagonistic muscle, triggers a "reflex" response from the
neurons in some way involved in the control of these muscles. Therefore,
the state of reactivity of central neurons functionally related to muscle
action can be compared when the monkey was previously instructed   to activate or not to activate, this muscle to perform the response. With this
method, Strick (1976, 1977) has shown that the   reactivity of neurons in
the dendate nucleus, which forms the first relay for information transmission from the neocerebellum to the motor cortex, is differentially modulated according to instructions given to the animal by the warning signal.
Neuronal activity, triggered by stretching the muscle, is greater when this
muscle will be involved than when it will not be involved in the movement.
Moreover, a decrease in neuronal discharge frequency is sometimes observed
when the stretched muscle is antagonistic to movement performance. Such a
presetting of structures considered to be mainly responsible for motor
planning certainly shows some of the nervous mechanisms underlying preparatory adjustments to motor program specification. While the data were not

collected in standardized conditions, they show that neuronal activity recorded in the thalamic ventrolateral nucleus, which forms the second step of the cerebello-cortical pathway, is often modified several hundred milliseconds before the movement starts (Joffroy and Lamarre, 1974 ; Hull and Buchwald, 1977; Neafsey, Hull and Buchwald, 1978 b).

The position of the precentral cortex (the terminal for pathways respon- sible for motor programming and the origin of corticospinal command path- ways) in nervous organization would justify elaboration here. Such data show that a presetting of the motor cortex neurons is specifically related to movement properties, but since the data were often collected in conditions making a comparison possible with similar phenomena observed at the level of spinal structures, they will be described within the framework of preparation for movement performance. They could be added as well to re- sults supporting the conclusion that as soon as a subject is engaged in a goal-directed activity, a functional reorganization of systems responsible for motor programming starts. Preselection of the different elements of the program which will determine movement parameters probably takes place through relatively separable sequentially organized processes. However, it remains difficult to resolve the distribution and hierarchy of the roles that the different nervous structures involved in motor programming play in these processes.

PREPARATORY ADJUSTMENTS FOR MOVEMENT PERFORMANCE

Study of preparatory adjustments intervening to facilitate movement execu- tion cannot be considered only within the three stage model of motor activi- ty. Performing a movement obviously cannot be restricted to the coordinated activation of the few muscles necessary to correctly displace a part of the skeleton in order to reach the goal assigned to action. Firstly, the physi- cal condition in which this action is performed necessitates some supplemen- mentary operations conducted simultaneously in order to set these condi- tions or, more often, to change them according to the new constraints issued for the movement. Second, except for ballistic movements (the para- meters of which are determined by motor programs), motor activity is per- formed by taking into account sensory information, especially from proprio- ception. This is necessary for an adequate guidance of teleokinetic move- ments. Preparation to perform a movement is therefore not only involved in processes intervening directly to preset systems responsible for the pro- grammed muscular activation, but can also be expressed through a reorgani- zation of the postural substrate and a modulation of motor control mechanism efficiency.

Of course, it is not possible here to examine thoroughly processes underly- ing the reorganization of the postural substrate, obtained by activating a number of muscles which are not directly involved in reaching the goal. They especially collaborate to ensure body equilibrium, by continuously adapting the skeleton configuration to changes in forces generated from on- going movement, and to steady the skeleton area subjected to such forces by blocking joints. One must emphasize that the analysis of the timing of neuromuscular activities underlying movement and posture shows that such a reorganization of the postural substrate, by anticipating consequences of movement performance, can obviously be identified as a preparatory process. It probably forms a part of a more extended class of "motor sets", the most spectacular examples of these being the fixed ritual of motor activities which precede a number of athletic motions. Lastly, one must note that

these postural preparatory adjustments can also be viewed as programmed
motor activities and thus as possibly being facilitated by preparation.
For instance, Hull and Buchwald (1977) have shown in the pallidum that neuronal activities broadly preceding movement initiation could express a presetting of nervous structures included in the indirect corticospinal pathways and considered to be mainly involved in postural maintenance.

A number of contributions in this volume are devoted to the analysis of
the various control mechanisms which intervene to guide movement execution
(see also Hecaen and Jeannerod, 1978). Obviously, they cannot be summarized
here, but, in the context of preparation, it is important to mention the
recent accumulation of experimental data showing that the sensitivity of
sensory receptors directly or indirectly solicited duing movement performance, as well as the efficiency of feedback mechanisms acting upon motor
systems, could be modulated by pretuning processes according to information
the subject has about the characteristics of his future action. The resulting changes in the gain of regulation loops intervening in motor control
thus form a second class of preparatory adjustments acting through feedforward mechanisms which make it possible to anticipate the sensory consequences of motion. They partly justify Semjen's suggestion (1978) to
extend the notion of programming to processes underlying sensory control of
motor activity, thus breaking the traditional conceptual opposition between
programmed "open-loop" and controlled "closed-loop" movements.

The statement of preparatory adjustments which directly modulate the
functioning of systems responsible for movement performance itself eludes
to the efficiency of the chronometric methods used by psychologists. Of
course, RT is not an appropriate measurement of events which follow response
initiation. However, a condition in which the starting point of the movement is operationally defined, generally from a time mark, leads one to
suppose that part of the processes underlying movement execution is included
in the classical RT measurement. Some attempts were thus conducted to subdivide RT, by referring to time marks provided either by the first discharge
of motor cortex neurons (Granit, 1973) or by the beginning of electromyographic activity (Botwinick and Thompson, 1966; Weiss, 1965), in "premotor"
(or central) time and "motor" (or peripheral) time. The latter, which can
be considered as measuring only a part of the duration of the movement execution process, was generally unchanged when factors known to affect RT were
varied. On the other hand, movement time measurement, as it was already
noted, does not appear to be a reliable method for analyzing operations
which take place during the movement execution stage, because of the difficulty in interpreting results when RT and movement time covary. While movement time is generally longer in choice-RT conditions than in simple-RT,
the general tendency for the duration of the movement execution phase is to
remain unchanged when subject's uncertainty about response parameters are
manipulated (for example, Guiard and Requin, 1973 ; Fiori et al., 1974 ;
Rosenbaum, in press). These limitations in chronometric methods point out
that preparatory modulations of the functional state of the systems responsible for movement performance are mainly provided by neurophysiological investigation.

Methods for investigating unitary neuronal activity in free-moving animals,
which was described above, was at first used by Evarts (1973) and by Evarts
and Tanji (1974, 1976). They demonstrated a functional presetting of the
precentral motor cortex neurons by giving advance information to monkeys
about the direction of the movement response. Repercussions about the con-

clusions of these experiments were so strong and enduring that it is useful to examine carefully data supporting such findings. In a first set of experiments (Evarts and Tanji, 1974), it was shown that the spontaneous activity of a number of pyramidal cells in the motor cortex was differentially modified after the warning signal was presented. This kind of conditioned neuronal activity during the preparatory period was found again by Tanji and Taniguchi (1979) and by Neafsey, Hull and Buchwald (1978 a) in the motor cortex of the cat. Moreover, the passive displacement of the forearm, resulting from a perturbation of the handle position, triggered, in some cortical neurons, (after a 20 msec latency) a "reflex" response. The amplitude of this response depended upon the instructions given by the warning signal. An increase in discharge frequency was observed when the cell was later involved in motoneuronal activation. A decrease was sometimes observed for neurons controlling spinal structures activating muscles antagonistic to the instructed movement. Unfortunately, such presetting of cortical motor structures was not clearly found again in the following experiments (Evarts and Tanji, 1976). The short-latency response was no longer sensitive to advance information, while such a property was found for a later response. However, the 40 or 50 msec latency of this second response makes the interpretation of the instruction effect as a presetting prosess, resulting from the warning signal, questionable. One can suggest that it expresses merely the beginning of the movement execution process triggered by the lever perturbation which also served as an imperative signal.

While studies devised to show preparatory processes at the level of spinal motor structures are among the oldest and most numerous ones, the results obtained in this field are not the most convincing. The examination of spinal excitability changes in human subjects by soliciting either the monosynaptic reflex pathway (Requin, 1969; Requin et al., 1977) or the polysynaptic pathways (Bonnet and Requin, 1972), has revealed, during the preparatory period of RT tasks, a preselection of motoneurons involved in the response execution process. However, this presetting is expressed by a relative decrease of reflex amplitude, whose predictive value for performance level remains very weak (Requin and Paillard, 1970). Moreover, this depression of reflex pathway reactivity is not closely related to controlled changes of the biomechanical parameters, especially direction and force, of the intended movement (Requin et al., 1977). These last findings were recently confirmed by a method, previously designed by Hammond (1956), where a muscular overload formed at once the reflexogenic mechanical stimulus and the imperative signal. The amplitude of the monosynaptic stretch reflex so triggered did not depend upon advance information given to the subject about the direction of the movement, the performance of which either increased or reduced muscular load (Crago, Houk and Hasan, 1976; Evarts and Granit, 1976). This is contrary to the somewhat premature conclusion that Evarts and Tanji (1974) drew from an unrepeated observation on one monkey.

Despite these rather disappointing data, it remains difficult to conclude that preparatory adjustments, centrally set up,have no effect at the spinal level. One can, in fact, suspect the reflexogenic method of not being reliable for the investigation of motoneuronal excitability changes. There is now some converging experimental evidence that the efficiency of the reflexogenic stimulation, in soliciting a response from motoneurons is affected during the preparatory period by an inhibitory phenomenon spreading to all the spinal structures more or less involved in motor activity. However, since preparation can be also considered as a period when the intended movement is actively postponed, this inhibitory phenomenon would remain understandable within the same framework. Its functional meaning would be thus related to the necessity, at that time, of protecting motoneurons against disturbing influences, especially those of peripheral origin, which could trigger a premature activation (Requin et al., 1977). Moreover, the unverified hypothesis that this inhibition exerts itself through a presynaptic mechanism (Bonnet and Requin, 1972) would make the information given equivocal by testing monosynaptic reflexes, since their amplituaes would result from the mixed variations of the presynaptic inhibition and of the motoneuronal excitability. For instance, it must be remembered that in RT tasks electromyography has generally shown an increase in the tonic motoneuronal activity during the preparatory period especially in the muscles to be involved in the response movement (cf. Requin, 1965; Requin et al., 1977). On the other hand, in spite of this depression of the spinal reflex pathway reactivity, it was found that short RTs were generally preceded during preparation by larger reflex responses (Requin and Paillard, 1970). While of weak statistical significance, this covariation is concordant with our initial hypothesis that preparation is expressed through an increase of the excitability of spinal motor structures involved in movement performance, thus making a speeding-up of their activation by central command explainable.

Recent experiments have contributed to the hypothesis that the presetting of motoneurons can be masked by a protective presynaptic block, which would be especially effective in the classical condition where the subject is required to be relaxed set up for investigating spinal reflexes. When, on the contrary, the general level of spinal reactivity is artificially increased, for instance by activating midbrain reticular formation just before reflex testing, the preparatory changes in excitability of motoneuron pools mainly involved in performing the response appear to depend upon movement parameters (Bonnet, Requin and Semjen, 1977, in press). Our interpretation of these results, that the presynaptic masking block was reduced in these conditions, could be also relevant to the isolated observation of Evarts and Tanji (1974) quoted above. The amplitude of the stretch reflex triggered in the monkey's biceps by a lever displacement "away" was greater when the intended movement was a forearm flexion. An excitability increase of motoneurons controlling biceps activation was thus triggered when the animal was informed in advance that this muscle would be involved in movement performance. Task conditions probably explain that in this case the inhibitory influences exerting themselves upon spinal structures are reduced. Since the monkey is asked to actively hold and steady a lever, the maintaining of this posture during the preparatory period supposes a high tonic muscular activity, a prerequisite for powerful activating proprioceptive feedback.

Obtained with the same methods as we used, results recently provided by Brunia and Vuister (in press) introduce a new aspect to the problem of spinal presetting, by stressing a possible interaction between the time course and the predictive value for performance level of preparatory changes in spinal excitability. With a preparatory period of 4 sec duration (although this duration did not exceed 2 sec in the studies already mentioned) these authors observed, after a 1 sec depression period following the warning signal, a progressive increase of reflex reactivity until the imperative signal, the slope of which appeared slightly dependent upon movement parameters. Thus it seems as if the warning signal triggers a fixed change course of spinal excitability that the imperative signal would interrupt, according to the preparatory period duration arbitrarily chosen, at a time more or less responsible for bringing out the functional meaning of the processes that this spinal excitability change expresses. These data, subject to confirmation, present a problem somewhat analogous to that raised by recent studies showing that the "contingent" negative variation of the cortical potential, classically considered as loosely re- lated to performance level (cf. Gaillard, 1978; Tecce, 1972), would present such a non-specific property during the first two seconds of the prepara- tory period only. When preparation continues, a second phase, which seems to depend upon task characteristics and which is sometimes associated with the readiness potential, develops (cf. Rohrbaugh, Syndulko and Lindsley, 1976; Lang, Ohman and Simons, 1978). The hypothetical proposal of Papakos- topoulos and Cooper (1973), that a close relationship between cortical and spinal events exists is, however, questionable for two reasons. First, the possibility of modulating the time course of cortical and spinal reac- tivity changes which follow the warning signal, by varying the time con- straints of the task or changes "urgency" of readiness, would not support the hypothesis of a fixed course of these presetting processes (cf. Macar, 1976; Semjen, Bonnet and Requin, 1973). Second, it is surprising that 2 sec would be necessary for these processes to appear preparatory or related in some way to the intended movement parameters, though it was well demon- strated that a state of specific preparation can be reached after only some hundred milliseconds (Holender, in press; Requin, 1978).

Lastly, since researchers' interest focussed mainly on monosynaptic reflex responses, the opportunity offered by later responses (involving more com- plex pathways) to investigate presetting processes in motor structures was disregarded for a long time. Hammond (1956) observed, by stretching a muscle already tensed, an electromyographic response of 50 to 70 msec latency. The amplitude of this latency was dependent upon the movement the subject had to perform when the overload occurred; either a relaxation or an activation of the stretched muscle. A phenomenon apparently involving nervous pathways different from the monosynaptic circuit therefore appeared to be modulated by advance information about movement direction. That could mean either that such an indirect access to motoneurons avoids, at least in part, the presynaptic block, or that structures preset by prepara- tory processes are included in the involved pathways. Unfortunately, the neurophysiological mechanisms underlying these late responses, either a transcortical loop of primary fusorial afferents or an intraspinal loop of other types of proprioceptive afferents, remains largely unknown (cf. Desmedt, 1978). In the same way, their functional significance is now discussed. They are considered sometimes as late reflex responses (Bonnet and Requin, in press), sometimes as automatic "compensatory" responses to muscular overload (Melvin Jones and Watt, 1971; Evarts and Tanji, 1974; Marsden, Merton and Morton, 1973), and sometimes as very early "voluntary" responses triggered at the supraspinal level by speed proprioceptive affer- ents (Crago et al., 1976; Evarts and Granit, 1976; Hufschmidt, Killinov and Linke, 1977). Of course, answers that future experiments could provide to these unsolved questions will be probably crucial in clearing up the re- maining uncertainty in the interpretation of data collected by reflexologic methods. In any case, the current, but often implicit, idea that prepara- tory adjustments for movement performance are shown through a total reorganization of the spinal terminal, which would extend presetting pro-

cesses evident at the earlier stages of motor planning, must however be
considered a very likely, but still unconfirmed, hypothesis.

CONCLUSIONS

From this overview of two sets of results, provided by experimental psychology on one hand and by neurophysiology on the other hand, three main
conclusions emerge. First, as soon as a subject becomes involved in a behavioral sequence ended by a motor act, an adaptive functional reorganization of the systems responsible for successive stages of action project
definition, motor programming and movement execution, is set up. Such a
preset, secondly, does not result from unspecific processes which could
facilitate any motor activity. Based upon information about the specific
aspects of the action and of the context in which it will develop, this
presetting takes into account, according to the processing level to which
it applies, the characteristics of the goal given to action, the specifications of the motor program to be followed to reach this goal and the resulting requirements for the effectors and their control systems to define
and to maintain the biomechanical parameters of the intended movement.
Lastly, presetting processes which intervene to modulate the successive
operations underlying motor activity would be serially and hierarchically
organized, in the way that some of the corresponding elements in the action
project, in the motor program and in the movement biomechanics, appear to
be privileged and preselected by priority.

This last point stresses that the presetting processes underlying specific
preparatory effects seem themselves to result from a planned and coordinated
action. It seems therefore, as if a central processor integrates information necessary to control and order a series of adjusting operations in
order that a set of processing systems be adapted to a specific task. Of
course, the question raised by the structural and functional properties of
this central processor leads to speculation. One likely hypothesis would
be to reactualize and to specify Penfield's (1954) conception of the role
played by a "centrencephalic" system formed by all the reticular structures
of the central nervous system. One must note that these structures were
considered for a long time, but from results of experiments conducted on
animals outside of any behavioral context, as only involving an unspecific
regulation of the activity level of specialized neuronal pools, and before
their "multispecific" abilities were recognized. Such an omnipotence would
be, of course, the main property required for a command and control center.
This hypothesis is, however, an explicit criticism of the current idea (now
revived by the development of neuropsychological studies) that the cerebral
cortex has a pre-eminent role. It should be noted, though, that the high
specialization of cortical structures opposes, nevertheless, such a directional function.

The attempt which was made to order experimental data indicating the role
of preparatory adjustments in motor activity was mainly based upon an
emerging isomorphism between the current conceptions of motor processing in
both fields of psychology and neurobiology. Of course, at each stage of
the three-stage model (which seems to optimally integrate these conceptions),
there is no experimental confirmation that what is termed preparation or
presetting by psychologists and neurophysiologists refers to the same functional processes. Such an identification is only supported by some converg-
int opinions issued from two different approaches which still remain some-

what detached. It could be suggested, however, that this gap can now be bridged, as has recently been proposed by Mountcastle (1976). He noted that "it is now possible to combine in one experiment the methods and concepts of each to yield a deeper insight into the brain mechanisms that govern behavior than is possible with either alone". Applied to the problem of specific preparation for action, this optimistic psychobiological perspective would lead us to consider the paralleling of quite different data as a set of testable hypotheses. The experiments suggested can only be briefly described. For instance, a first hypothesis proposed that the earlier stage of action project definition (representing a "holistic" determination of an adapted response to environmental change) is processed by the associative cortex, which then sends to the neocerebellum something like a "command" underlying the "volitional" aspect of action and the set of sensorimotor material necessary to motor program building. It would therefore be interesting to analyze the unitary or integrated activity of these associative structures, expecially the posterior parietal area, in experimental paradigms capable of examining the preparatory adjustments expected to act upon the response determination processing stage. Of course, choice-RT tasks, where probabilities for the different responses to be performed are controlled, would be the most suitable. In the same way, it is very likely that the motor program is progressively specified in a nervous circuit starting in the neocerebellum and ending in the precentral motor cortex . Therefore, it would be logical to attempt to examine especially with microphysiological techniques, a presetting of these structures when the subject's uncertainty about response movement parameters is manipulated. Experimental procedures designed by Rosenbaum (in press), where information given to the subject about characteristics of his or her intended movement is controlled, as well as the binary choice-RT tasks set up by Fiori et al. (1974), where the biomechanical differences between the two possible movements are varied, would be the suitable paradigms to employ. Lastly, one can object that experiments aimed at observing presetting processes at the level of the corticospinal terminal (which undoubtedly accounts for movement execution) did not provide the expected results, although they were conducted along the line of the psychobiological approach we proposed. It was emphasized that a questionable choice of the physiological cues, in addition to the unexpected difficulties in the interpretation of data collected, could explain the disappointment in this field of research. It must be added, nevertheless, that possibly still not enough attention was paid to the likely hypothesis that preparatory processes intervening at this last stage of motor activity are expressed more through an anticipatory tuning of systems which assist movement execution than via a presetting of motor structures directly involved in effector control.

Reference Note

Stelmach, G. E. and Bonnet, M. The Hoffman reflex in a preceiving paradigm. Unpublished data, C.N.R.S., Marseille, France, 1977.

References

(1) Allen, G. G. and Tjukahara, N. Cerebro-cerebellar communication system, Physiol. Rev., 54, (1974), 957-1006.

(2) Bartz, A.E., Reaction time as a function of stimulus uncertainty on a single trial, Percept. Psychophys., 9, (1971), 95-96.

(3) Bertelson, P., Serial choice reaction-time as a function of response versus signal-and-response repetition, Nature, 206, (1965), 217-218.

(4) Bertelson, P., & Barzeele, J., Interaction of time uncertainty and relative signal frequency in determining choice reaction time, J. exper. Psychol., 70, (1965), 448-451.

(5) Bertelson, P., & Tisseyre, F., Choice reaction time as a function of stimulus versus response relative frequency of occurrence, Nature, 212, (1966), 1069-1070.

(6) Biederman, I., & Zachary, R.A., Stimulus versus response probability effects in choice reaction time, Percept. Psychophys., 7, (1970), 189-192.

(7) Blackman, A.R., Influence of stimulus and response probability on decision and movement latency in a discrete choice reaction task, J. exper. Psychol., 92, (1972), 128-133.

(8) Bonnet, M., & Requin, J., Variations des réflexes polysynaptiques cutanés au cours de la période préparatoire au TR simple chez l'homme, Psychol. Fr., 17, (1972), 165-174.

(9) Bonnet, M., & Requin, J., Evolution des réponses musculaires à la surcharge pendant la période préparatoire à un mouvement orienté, Proc. intern. Congr. phys. Educ., Québec, in press.

(10) Bonnet, M., Requin, J., & Semjen, A., Intervention d'influences réticulaires dans une réorganisation des structures motrices spinales pendant la préparation au mouvement, in Requin J. (ed.), Anticipation et Comportement, (Editions du C.N.R.S., Paris, in press).

(11) Bonnet, M., Requin, J., & Semjen, A., The patterning of reticulospinal influences during preparation to motor program execution, Proc. intern. Congr. physiol. Sci. (Paris, 1977).

(12) Botwinick, J., & Thompson, L.W., Premotor and motor components of reaction time, J. exper. Psychol., 71, (1966), 9-15.

(13) Brainard, R.W., Irby, T.S., Fitts, P.M., & Alluisi, E.A., Some variables influencing the rate of gain of information, J. exper. Psychol., 63, (1962), 105-110.

(14) Brooks, V.B., Roles of cerebellum and basal ganglia in initiation and control of movements, Can. J. neurol. Sci., 2, (1975), 265-277.

(15) Brooks, V.B., The role of cerebellum in initiation and control of movement. Proc. XXVIIth intern. Congr. physiol. Sci. (Paris, 1977).

(16) Brooks, V.B., "Concluding remarks", in Massion J., Paillard J. et Wiesendanger M. (eds.) : Pyramidal micro-connexions and motor control (Paris, J. Physiol., 1978).

(17) Brooks, V.B., & Stoney, S.D., Motor mechanisms : the role of the pyramidal system in motor control. Ann. Rev. Physiol., 33, (1971), 337-392.

(19) Brunia, C.H.M., & Vuister, F.M., Spinal reflexes as indicator of motor preparation in man, Physiol. Psychol., in press.

(20) Castaigne, P., Laplane, D., & Degos, J.D., Trois cas de négligence motrice par lésion frontale pré-rolandique, Rev. neurol., 126, (1972), 5-15.

(21) Crago, P.E., Houk, J.C., & Hasan, A., Regulatory actions of human stretch reflex, J. Neurophysiol., 39, (1976), 925-936.

(22) Crossman, E.R., Entropy and choice time : the effect of frequency un-
     balance on choice response, Quart. J. exper. Psychol., 5, (1953), 41-
     51.
(23) Deecke, L., Grözinger, B., & Kornhuber, H.H., Voluntary finger move-
     ment in man : cerebral potentials and theory, Biol. Cybernetics, 23,
     (1976), 99-119.
(24) Deecke, L., Eisinger, H., & Kornhuber, H.H., Comparison of cerebral
     potentials preceding voluntary flexion and extension movement in man,
     Neurosci. Letters (North Holland, Amsterdam, 1978, suppl. n° 1).
(25) De Long, M.R., Putamen : activity of single units during slow and
     rapid arm movements, Science, 179, (1972), 1240-1242.
(26) Desmedt, J.E. (ed.), Cerebral motor control in man : long loop mecha-
     nisms (Karger, Basel, 1978).
(27) Ells, J.G., Analysis of temporal and attentional aspects of movement
     control, J. exper. Psychol., 99, (1973), 10-21.
(28) Evarts, E.V., Temporal patterns of discharge of pyramidal tract neu-
     rons during sleep and waking in the monkey, J. Neurophysiol., 27,
     (1964), 152-171.
(29) Evarts, E.V., Relation of pyramidal tract activity to force exerted
     during voluntary movement, J. Neurophysiol., 31, (1968), 14-27.
(30) Evarts, E.V., Activity of pyramidal tract neurons during postural
     fixation, J. Neurophysiol., 32, (1969), 375-385.
(31) Evarts, E.V., Activity of thalamic and cortical neurons in relation to
     learned movement in the monkey. Intern. J. Neurol., 8, (1971), 321-
     326.
(32) Evarts, E.V., Motor cortex reflexes associated with learned movements,
     Science, 179, (1973), 501-503.
(33) Evarts, E.V., & Granit, R., Relations of reflexes and intended move-
     ments, in Homma S. (ed.), Understanding the stretch reflex (Karger,
     Basel, 1976).
(34) Evarts, E.V., & Tanji, J., Gating of motor cortex reflexes by prior
     instruction. Brain Res., 71, (1974), 479-494.
(35) Evarts, E.V., & Tanji, J. Reflex and intended responses in motor cortex
     pyramidal tract neurons of the monkey, J. Neurophysiol., 39, (1976),
     1069-1080.
(36) Evarts, E.V., & Thach, W.T., Motor mechanism of the CNS : cerebro cere-
     bellar interrelations, Ann. Rev. Physiol., 31, (1969), 451-498.
(37) Falmagne, J.C., Stochastic models for choice reaction time with appli-
     cations to experimental results, J. math. Psychol., 2, (1965), 77-124.
(38) Fiori, N., Semjen, A., & Requin, J., Analyse chronométrique du pattern
     préparatoire à un mouvement spatialement orienté, Le Travail humain,
     37, (1974), 229-248.
(39) Fitts, P.M., Peterson, J.R., & Wolpe, G., Cognitive aspects of informa-
     tion processing : II. Adjustments to stimulus redundancy, J. exper.
     Psychol., 65, (1963), 423-432.
(40) Fromm, C., & Evarts, E.V., Motor cortex discharge associated with pre-
     cisely controlled fine movements, Proc. Sixth an. Meeting Soc. Neuro-
     sci. (Toronto, 1976).
(41) Gaillard, A., Slow brain potentials preceding task performance. Ph.D.
     thesis (Amsterdam, 1978).
(42) Ganglberger, J.A., Haider, M., Groll-Knapp, E., & Schmid, H., Movement-
     related cortical and subcortical potentials in the human brain, Neuro-
     sci. Letters (North-Holland, Amsterdam, 1978, suppl. n° 1).
(43) Garner, W.R., "Association lecture", in Nickerson R.S. (ed.), Attention
     and Performance VIII (Lawrence Erlbaum Assoc., Hillsdale, in press).

(44) Gibbs, C.G., Probability learning in step-input tracking, Brit. J. Psychol., 56, (1965), 233-242.
(45) Gottsdanker, R., Choice reaction time and the nature of the choice response, Psychon. Sci., 14, (1969), 257-258.
(46) Granit, R., Demand and accomplishment in voluntary movement, in Stein R.B., Pearson K.G., Smith R.S. and Redford J.B. (eds.), Control of posture and locomotion (Plenum Press, New York, 1973).
(47) Griew, S., Information gain in tasks involving different stimulus-response relationships, Nature, 182, (1968), 1819.
(48) Guiard, Y., & Requin, J., Effects of preparatory period on a reaction time followed by a pointing movement either guided or not, Percept. motor Skills, 37, (1973), 980-982.
(49) Hammond, P.H., The influence of prior instruction to the subject on an apparently involuntary neuromuscular response, J. Physiol., 132, (1956), 17.
(50) Hawkins, H.L., & Friedin, B.D., The relative frequency effect and S-R compatibility, Psychon. Sci., 28, (1972), 329-330.
(51) Hawkins, H.L., & Hosking, K., Stimulus probability as a determinant of discrete choice reaction time, J. exper. Psychol., 82, (1969), 435-440.
(52) Hawkins, H.L.n Snippel, K., Presson, J., MacKay, S., & Todd, D., Retrieval bias and the response relative frequency effect in choice reaction time, J. exper. Psychol., 102, (1974), 910-912.
(53) Hecaen, H., Les apraxies idéomotrices. Essai de dissociation, in Hecaen H. and Jeannerod M., Du contrôle moteur à l'organisation du geste (Masson, Paris, 1978).
(54) Hecaen, H., & Jeannerod, M. (eds.), Du contrôle moteur à l'organisation du geste (Masson, Paris, 1978).
(55) Hick, W.E., On the rate of gain of information, Quart. J. exper. Psychol., 4, (1952), 11-26.
(56) Hinrich, J.V., & Craft, J.L., Verbal expectancy and probability in two-choice reaction time, J. exper. Psychol., 88, (1971), 367-371.
(57) Hinrich, J.V., & Krains, P.L., Expectancy in choice reaction time : anticipation of stimulus or response ? J. exper. Psychol., 85, (1970), 330-334.
(58) Holender, D., Contribution expérimentale à l'étude des propriétés temporelles des ajustements préparatoires. Ph. D. thesis (Université libre de Bruxelles, 1975).
(59) Holender, D., Le concept de préparation à réagir dans le traitement de l'information, in Requin J. (ed.), Anticipation et Comportement (Editions du C.N.R.S., Paris, in press).
(60) Hufschmidt, H.J., Killinor, M., & Linke, D., Short reaction times. Proc. XXVIIth intern. Congr. physiol. Sci. (Paris, 1977).
(61) Hull, C.D., & Buchwald, N.A., Importance of the basal ganglia in the regulation of response and cognitive set, Proc. XXVIIth intern. Congr. physiol. Sci. (Paris, 1977).
(62) Hyman, R., Stimulus information as determinant of reaction time, J. exper. Psychol., 45, (1953), 188-196.
(63) Hyvarinen, J., Function of parietal associative area 7, Proc. XXVIIth intern. Congr. physiol. Sci. (Paris, 1977).
(64) Hyvarinen, J., & Poranen, A., Function of the parietal associative area 7 as revealed from cellular discharges in alert monkeys, Brain, 97, (1974), 673-692.
(65) Joffroy, A.J., & Lamarre, Y., High cell activity in the ventral lateral thalamus of the unanesthetized monkey. Exper. Neurol., 42, (1974), 1-16.

(66) Kemp, J.M., & Powell, J.P.S., The connections of the striatum and glo-
     bus pallidus : synthesis and speculation, Phil. trans. Roy. Soc.,
     London, B, 262, (1971), 441-457.
(67) Kerr, B., Decisions about movement direction and extent, J. Human
     Movement Stud., 3, (1976), 199-213.
(68) Klein, R.M., Attention and movement, in Stelmach G.E. (ed.), Motor
     Control (Academic Press, New-York, 1976).
(69) Kornblum, S., Sequential effects in choice reaction time : a tutorial
     review, in Kornblum S. (ed.), Attention and Performance IV (Academic
     Press, New-York, 1973).
(70) Kornhuber, H.H., Cerebral cortex, cerebellum and basal ganglia : an
     introduction to their motor functions, in Schmitt F.O. and Worden G.
     (eds.), The Neurosciences, third study program (M.I.T. Press,
     Cambridge, 1974).
(71) Kubota, K., Iwamato, T., & Susuki, H., Visuokinetic activities of pri-
     mate prefrontal neurons during delayed-response performance, J. Neuro-
     physiol., 37, (1974), 1197-1212.
(72) Kutas, M., & Donchin, E., The effects of handedness, of responding
     hand and of response force on the controlateral dominance of the
     readiness potential, in Desmedt J. (ed.), Attention, voluntary con-
     traction and event-related cerebral potential (Bruxelles, 1977).
(73) Kuypers, H.G.J.M., The anatomical organization of the descending path-
     ways and their contribution to motor control expecially in primates,
     in Desmedt J. (ed.), New development in electromyography and clinical
     Neurophysiology (Karger, Basel, 1973).
(74) LaBerge, D., & Tweedy, J.R., Presentation probability and choice time,
     J. exper. Psychol., 68, (1964), 477-481.
(75) LaBerge, D., Legrand, R., & Hobbie, R.K., Functional identification of
     perceptual and response biases in choice reaction time, J. exper.
     Psychol., 79, 295-299.
(76) LaBerge, D., Tweedy, J.R., & Richer, J., Selective attention : incenti-
     ve variables and choice time, Psychon. Sci., 8, (1967), 341-342.
(77) Lagasse, P.P., & Hayes, C.C., Premotor and motor reaction time as a
     function of movement extent, J. Motor Behav., 5, (1973), 25-32.
(78) Lang, P.J., Ohman, A., & Simons, R.F., The psychophysiology of antici-
     pation, in Requin J. (ed.), Attention and Performance VII (Lawrence
     Erlbaum Assoc., Hillsdale, 1978).
(79) Macar, F., Signification des variations contingentes négatives dans
     la dimension temporelle du comportement. L'Année psychol., 77, (1976),
     439-474.
(80) Marsden, C.D., Merton, P.A., & Morton, H.B., Latency measurements com-
     patible with a cortical pathway for the stretch reflex in man, J.
     Physiol., 230, (1973), 58P-59P.
(81) Massion, J., The thalamus in the motor system, Appl. Neurophysiol.,
     39, (1976), 222-238.
(82) Massion, J., Le système pyramidal : données récentes, in Hecaen H. et
     Jeannerod M. (eds.), Du contrôle moteur à l'organisation du geste
     (Masson, Paris, 1978).
(83) Megaw, E.D., Direction and extent uncertainty in step-input tracking,
     J. motor Behav., 3, (1972), 171-186.
(84) Megaw, E.D., & Armstrong, W., Individual and simultaneous tracking of
     a step input by the horizontal saccadic eye movement and manual con-
     trol systems, J. exper. Psychol., 100, (1973), 18-28.
(85) Melvil Jones, G., & Watt, D.G.D., Observation on the control of step-
     ping and hopping movements in man, J. Physiol., 219, (1971), 709-727.

(86) Miles, F.A., & Evarts, E.V., Concepts of motor organization, Ann. Rev. Psychol., 30, (1979), 327-362.
(87) Morin, R.E., & Forrin, B., Information processing : choice reaction times of first and third-grade students for two types of associations, Child Develop., 36, (1965), 713-720.
(88) Mountcastle, V.B., The word around us : neural command functions for selective attention, Neural Sci. Res. Bull., 16, (1976), suppl. n°2.
(89) Mountcastle, V.B., Lynch, J.C., Georgopoulos, A., Sakata, H., & Acuna, C., Posterior parietal association cortex of the monkey : command functions for operations within extrapersonal space, J. Neurophysiol., 38, (1975), 871-908.
(90) Mowbray, G.H., & Rhoades, M.V., On the reduction of choice reaction times with practice, Quart. J. exper. Psychol., 11, (1959), 16-23.
(91) Neafsey, E.J., Hull, C.D., & Buchwald, N.A., Preparation for movement in the cat. I. Unit activity in the cerebral cortex, EEG clin. Neurophysiol., 44, (1978 a), 706-713.
(92) Neafsey, E.J., Hull, C.D., & Buchwald, N.A., Preparation for movement in the cat. II. Unit activity in the basal ganglia and thalamus, EEG clin. Neurophysiol., 44, (1978 b), 714-723.
(93) Orenstein, H.B., Reaction time as a function of perceptual bias, response bias, and stimulus discriminability, J. exper. Psychol., 86, (1970), 38-42.
(94) Pachella, R.G., The interpretation of reaction time in information processing research, in Kantowitz B. (ed.), Human Information Processing (Lawrence Erlbaum Assoc., Hillsdale, 1974).
(95) Paillard, J., Le codage nerveux des commandes motrices. Rev. EEG et Neurophysiol., 6, (1976), 453-472.
(96) Papakostopoulos, D., & Cooper, R., The contingent negative variation and the excitability of the spinal monosynaptic reflex, J. Neurol. Neurosurg. Psychiatr., 36, (1973), 1003-1010.
(97) Penfield, W., Studies of the cerebral cortex of man. A review and an interpretation, in Delafresnaye J.F. (ed.), Brain mechanism and consciousness (Blackwell, Oxford, 1954).
(98) Posner, M.I., Psychobiology of attention, in Gazzaniga, M.S. and Blackemore C. (eds.), Handbook of Psychobiology (Academic Press, New-York, 1975).
(99) Posner, M.I., Chronometric explorations of mind (Lawrence Erlbaum Assoc., Hillsdale, 1978).
(100) Poulton, E.C., Perceptual anticipation and reaction time. Quart. J. exper. Psychol., 2, (1950), 99-112.
(101) Rabbitt, P.M.A., Response facilitation on repetition of a limb movement, Brit. J. Psychol., 56, (1965), 303-304.
(102) Requin, J., Quelques problèmes théoriques et méthodologiques posés par l'étude psychologique de l'attitude préparatoire à l'action, Cah. de Psychol., 8, (1965), 101-113.
(103) Requin, J., Some data on neurophysiological processes involved in the preparatory motor activity to reaction time performance, in W.G. Koster (ed.), Attention and Performance II (North Holland, Amsterdam, 1969).
(104) Requin, J.,Spécificité des ajustements préparatoires à l'exécution du programme moteur, in Hecaen H. et Jeannerod M. (eds.), Du contrôle moteur à l'organisation du geste (Masson, Paris, 1978).
(105) Requin, J.,La préparation à l'activité motrice : vers une convergence des problématiques psychologique et neurophysiologique, in Requin J. (ed.), Anticipation et Comportement (Editions du CNRS, Paris, in press).

(106) Requin, J.,& Paillard, J., Depression of spinal monosynaptic reflexes
       as a specific aspect of preparatory motor set in visual reaction
       time, in Visual information processing and control of motor activity.
       (Bulg. Acad. Sci., Sofia, 1970).
(107) Requin, J., Bonnet, M.,& Semjen, A., Is there a specificity in the
       supraspinal control of motor structures during preparation ? in
       Dornic, S. (ed.), Attention and Performance VI.(Lawrence Erlbaum
       Assoc., Hillsdale, 1977).
(108) Rohrbaugh, J.W., Syndulko, K.,& Lindsley, D.B., Brain wave components
       of the contingent negative variation in humans, Science, 191, (1976),
       1055-1057.
(109) Rosenbaum, D., Human movement initiation : specification of arm,
       direction and extent, J. exper. Psychol. : General, in press.
(110) Sanders, A.F., Some variables affecting the relation between relative
       stimulus frequency and choice reaction time, in Sanders, A.F. (ed.),
       Attention and Performance III,(North Holland,Amsterdam, 1970).
(111) Sanders, A.F., Structural and functional aspects of the reaction
       process, in Dornic, S. (ed.), Attention and Performance VI. (Lawrence
       Erlbaum Assoc., Hillsdale, 1977).
(112) Semjen, A., Phase organization of amplitude regulated movements :
       the "action threshold" of movement, the programming of its direction
       and amplitude, Magyar Pszichol. Szemle, 28, (1970), 355-369 (in hun-
       garian).
(113) Semjen, A., From motor learning to sensori motor skill acquisition,
       J. human Movement Stud., 3, (1978), 182-191.
(114) Semjen, A., & Requin, J., Movement amplitude, pointing accuracy and
       choice reaction time, Percept. Motor Skills, 43, (1976), 807-812.
(115) Semjen, A., Bonnet, M., & Requin, J., Relation between the time-course
       of Hoffmann-reflexes and the foreperiod duration in a reaction time
       task, Physiol. Beh., 10, (1973), 1041-1050.
(116) Semjen, A., Requin, J., & Fiori, N., The interactive effect of fore-
       period duration and response-movement characteristics upon choice-
       reaction time in a pointing task, J. Human Movement Stud., 4, (1978),
       108-118.
(117) Smith, E.E., Choice reaction time : an analysis of the major theoreti-
       cal positions, Psychol. Bull., 69, (1968), 77-110.
(118) Smith, E.E., Chase, W.G., & Smith, P.G., Stimulus and response repeti-
       tion effects in retrieval from short-term memory : trace decay and
       memory search, J. exper. Psychol., 98, (1973), 413-422.
(119) Spector, A., & Lyons, R.D., The locus of stimulus probability effect
       in choice reaction time, Bull. Psychon. Sci., 7, (1976), 519-521.
(120) Sternberg, S., The discovery of processing stages : extensions of
       Donder's method, in Koster, W.G. (ed.), Attention and Performance II
       (North-Holland, Amsterdam, 1969).
(121) Strick, P.L., Activity of ventrolateral thalamic neurons during arm
       movement. J. Neurophysiol., 39, (1976), 1032-1044.
(122) Strick, P.L., Peripheral input to the dentate nucleus : control by
       motor preparation, Proc. XXVIIth Intern. Congress Physiol. Sci.,
       Paris (1977).
(123) Susuki, H., Modification of visual message in the prefrontal cortex.
       Proc. XXVIIth Intern. Congress of Physiol. Sci., Paris, (1977).
(124) Tanji, J., & Taniguchi, K., Activity of slowly conducting pyramidal
       tract neurons in a trained motor task, in Massion, J., Paillard, J.
       and Wiesendanger, M. (eds.), Pyramidal micro-connections and motor
       control, (J. Physiol., Paris, 1979).

(125) Tecce, J.J., Contingent negative variation (CNV) and psychological
       processes in man, Psychol. Bull., 77, (1972), 73-113.
(126) Teuber, H.L., The riddle of frontal lobe function in man, in Warren,
       J.M. and Akert, K. (eds.), The frontal granular cortex and behavior,
       (Mc Graw Hill, New-York, 1964).
(127) Teuber, H.L., Unity and diversity of frontal lobe functions, Acta
       Neurobiol. Exper., 32, (1972), 615-656.
(128) Thach, W.T., Discharge of cerebellar neurons related to two maintened
       postures and two prompt movements. I. Nuclear cell output, J. Neuro-
       physiol., 33, (1970), 527-536.
(129) Thach, W.T., Timing of activity in cerebellar dentate nucleus and
       cerebral motor cortex during prompt volitional movement, Brain Res.,
       88, (1975), 233-241.
(130) Theios, J.,The components of response latency in simple human infor-
       mation processing tasks, in Rabbitt, P., Dornic, S. (eds.), Attention
       and Performance V,(Academic Press, London, 1975).
(131) Weiss, A.D., The locus of reaction time change with set, motivation
       and age, J. Gerontol., 20, (1965), 60-64.
(132) Woodrow, H., The measurement of attention. Psychol. Monogr., 17,
       (1914), whole n°76.

Tutorials in Motor Behavior
G.E. Stelmach and J. Requin (eds.)
© *North-Holland Publishing Company, 1980*

23

MOTOR PREPARATION, RECORDED ON
THE CORTICAL AND SPINAL LEVEL

C.H.M. Brunia

Tilburg University
Department of Psychology
Physiological Psychology Section
Tilburg, The Netherlands

EEG and Hoffmann reflexes were recorded during
the four sec foreperiod of two reaction time
experiments. Subjects responded with a plantar
flexion of either their right or left foot.
Preceding right foot movements larger CNV amplitudes
were found over the right hemisphere. With left foot
movements amplitudes also were larger over the right
hemisphere, but the difference in amplitude between
both hemispheres was much smaller than with right
foot responses. The time course of changes in reflex
amplitudes gave no indication of a selective element
in the preparatory process. A hypothesis is presented
about the relation between changes on the cortical
and spinal level during motor preparation.

INTRODUCTION

Motor preparation can be studied during fixed foreperiod
reaction time (RT) experiments. A warning signal S1 indicates
the arrival of an imperative stimulus S2, upon which a subject
has to respond as quickly as possible. The shortening of the
mean RT during such a paradigm implies an earlier discharge of
pyramidal tract neurones (PTN's) in the cortex and of spinal
motoneurones, innervating the muscles involved in the response.
Although in man it is not possible to make direct recordings of
the excitability changes of neurones both on the cortical and
spinal level, at least an estimation of such changes on both
levels can be made.

Changes in dendritic activity of cortical cells are the basis
of the Electroencephalogram (EEG). More specifically related to
motor preparation is the recording of the Bereitschaftspotential
(BP) and the Contingent Negative Variation (CNV). The BP is a
slow wave preceding a voluntary movement, which can be
demonstrated by averaging the EEG backwards from the moment the
movement is made (Kornhuber and Deecke (1965); Vaughan (1974)).
The original work of Walter, Cooper,Aldridge, McCallum and
Winter (1964) showed the development of a slow wave, when using
a foreperiod of one sec. This so called CNV has been related to
different psychological constructs (Tecce (1972)); motor preparation has been stressed by Low, Border, Frost and Kellaway
(1966). Recently, it has become clear that, using a foreperiod

of several sec, two components can be distinguished (Loveless
and Sanford (1974); Rohrbaugh, Syndulko and Lindsley (1976))
that differ in latency and topography.The first is more
pronounced in the frontal area and is related to the warning
properties of S1 (Loveless (1977)). The second is mainly
present in the central and parietal area. Its amplitude is
larger with shorter RT's (Rohrbaugh et al.(1976); Gaillard
(1977)). Several authors (Rohrbaugh et al. (1976); Gaillard
(1978)) point to the similarity of the second wave and the BP.
Although Deecke, Grözinger and Kornhuber (1976) stress the
differences in paradigm used in CNV and BP studies, further
evidence for a common physiological substrate of both slow
waves is presented recently by Grünewald, Grünewald-Zuberbier,
Netz, Hömberger and Sander (1979). In nearly all CNV and BP
studies hand and finger movements have been investigated.
Because in our institute motor preparation is studied on the
spinal level with foot movements, a CNV experiment was done in
which subjects also had to respond with either their right or
left foot. A fixed foreperiod of four sec was used. Reflex data
from an earlier study (Brunia and Vuister, in press) will be
presented as well, to compare physiological changes on the
cortical and spinal level within the same experimental
paradigm.

Changes in excitability of spinal motoneurones before a
movement can be estimated by means of monosynaptic reflexes
(Gerilovsky and Tsekov (1975); Requin (1969); Requin, Bonnet
and Semjen (1977)). A change in amplitude indicates a shift in
the output of the motoneurone pool and is consequently an index
of fluctuations in (1) motoneurone excitability and (2) presynaptic inhibition of the Ia fibres, which conduct the
afferent volley to the motoneurone pool. The study will be
limited to the recording of the amplitudes of reflexes evoked
via the motoneurone pool involved in a standard movement and
the contralateral homologous pool. The movement to be investigated is a plantar flexion of the foot, for which the calf
muscles have to contract. Monosynaptic Hoffmann (H) reflexes
are evoked in these muscles by electrical stimulation of the
Ia afferent fibres of the tibial nerve in the popliteal fossa.

In the study to be presented H reflexes have been evoked
simultaneously in both legs at different moments of the foreperiod. The response had to be given by one leg. This provides
the opportunity to study the time course of changes in the
output of motoneurone pools, involved and not involved in the
response. Up to now only foreperiods of one sec have been
investigated (Gerilovsky and Tsekov (1975); Mitchie, Clarke,
Sinden and Glue (1975); Requin (1969); Requin et al. (1977);
Semjen, Bonnet and Requin (1973)). In a study of Papakostopoulos
and Cooper (1973) a two sec foreperiod has been used, but
subjects had to respond with their left hand, hence the calf
muscles were not involved in the response.

MATERIAL AND METHODS

Experiment I (CNV)

20 Right handed and footed subjects, 18-27 years of age and
of both sexes took part in this experiment. They were seated
in an electrically shielded, sound proof room. Their legs
rested upon a holder, with a microswitch under the right and
left foot plate. A Lab 8E computer was used for stimulus
presentation. S1 was an auditory stimulus (2900 Hz, 75 dB, 50
msec) which was followed by a visual stimulus S2 (red LED
display, 9.6 cm^2, 100 msec). Each session consisted of two
conditions, in which a plantar flexion of either the left or
right foot had to be given in blocks of 52 trials. The Inter
Trial Interval (ITI) varied randomly from 16.4 to 22.4 sec in
steps of two sec. Reaction times were measured by the Lab 8E
computer. The response had to be given within 400 msec. If
subjects reacted too late, a buzzer sounded. Such trials were
discarded from the analysis. Non polarizable Beckman Ag-AgCl
electrodes were affixed to the subject's scalp, at F_3, F_4, C_3,
C_4, P_3 and P_4, according to the 10-20 system. Linked mastoids
served as reference. Inter electrode impedance was less than
3000 Ohm. Electrodes above and below the left eye were used
for vertical eye movement and blink potential recording. EEG
signals were amplified by modified Beckman amplifiers (time
constant 30 sec, -3 dB point at 30 Hz). Both EEG and EOG
signals were recorded on magnetic tape (Hewlett Packard 3968 A,
bandwidth 0-312 Hz) and on paper. Trials were discarded from
analysis if blinks were present between one sec before S1 and
one sec after S2, and in case subjects reacted too early or
too late. Subjects ought to have 30 successfull trials in order
to be accepted. One sec before S1 a symmetrical calibration
pulse of 60 microvolt (peak-peak) was superimposed on the EEG
and EOG signals. This pulse was used for normalizing the CNV
amplitudes. EEG data were analyzed by a PDP 11/10 computer from
one sec before S1 until one sec after S2. Sample frequency was
82.5 points per sec. The CNV data recorded during the foreperiod preceding the 10 most rapid and the 10 slowest reaction
times per subject were analyzed separately. The baseline was
determined over a period of one sec, preceding S1.Thirty trials
per subject were used to calculate the individual grand avera-
ges.For statistical analysis the amplitude was measured at eight
measuring points: 3.25, 3, 2.75, 2.5, 0.8, 0.55, 0.3 and 0.05
sec before the presentation of S2. The values of these amplitudes were calculated per trial by averaging five sample points.

Statistical analysis

Analyses of variance (Anova's) with a two factor design:
"left/right hemisphere" and "measuring points" with repeated
measurements were carried out on the data of the whole experiment per response side for the two frontal, the two central and
the two parietal derivations separately. Similar anova's were
carried out on the data of the early and late wave apart. Moreover, anova's were carried out on the CNV's recorded at each
electrode position, the factors being "right/left foot" and
"measuring points".

Experiment II (H reflexes)

40 subjects,for the greater part ambidexters, 18-32 years of
age and of both sexes, took part in this experiment. They were
seated comfortably in a specially devised chair with supports
for head, arms and legs. The feet were carefully fixed to a
footpedal, which could not be moved on the non-involved side.
On the involved side a plantar flexion could be made with the
distal half of the footpedal. Two conditions were run. Half of
the subjects made the movement on the right side, the other
half on the left side.

Constant current square waves of one msec were applied trans-
cutaneously to the tibial nerve in the popliteal fossa in order
to evoke the H reflexes. A Simon electrode was used, the anode
being placed proximal of the knee. At the beginning of the
experiment the current strength was adjusted so that a small
direct motor response was visible. H reflex amplitudes were
about 50% of the maximum value. For each subject it was tried
as much as possible to obtain equal reflex amplitudes in both
legs. Reflexes were recorded by means of Ag-AgCl electrodes,
attached to the skin above the triceps surae muscle, four cm
apart. Peak to peak amplitudes were measured on line by a Lab
8E computer. Presentation of a tone as S1, of a light as S2
and triggering of the stimulation equipment was done by the
computer.

Each foreperiod of four sec was followed by an ITI of 16 sec.
Reflexes were evoked in a random order, 10 times at each of
13 different measuring points during the foreperiod: at 100,
200, 300, 500, 1000, 1500, 2000, 2500, 3000, 3500, 3700, 3800
and 3900 msec after S1. During each ITI a reflex was evoked at
random between six and ten sec after the RS. For each subject
means and standard deviations were calculated per ISI measuring
point. The ITI data per subject were taken together and
considered one point. The values of the 13 different measuring
points were expressed as a percentage of the mean ITI level.

Statistical analysis

The data of the involved leg from both conditions (right or
left response) were taken together, as were those from the
non-involved leg. An anova with a two factor design: "involvedness" and "measuring points" with repeated measurements was
carried out on the scores of experiment II.

TABLE I

ANOVA's ON CNV AT THREE DIFFERENT SITES OF BOTH HEMISPHERES: FRONTAL CENTRAL AND PARIETAL.LEFT-RIGHT HEMISPHERE DIFFERENCES AND MEASURING POINTS ARE TESTED.

RESPONSE: RIGHT FOOT		FRONTAL $(F_3$ vs. $F_4)$	CENTRAL $(C_3$ vs. $C_4)$	PARIETAL $(P_3$ vs. $P_4)$
	df	F	F	F
left-right hemisphere	1,285	20.8^{xxx}	61.7^{xxxx}	30.51^{xxxx}
measuring points	7,285	2.79^{xx}	13.2^{xxxx}	19.85^{xxxx}
left-right hemisphere X measuring points	7,285	0.19	0.64	0.35

RESPONSE: LEFT FOOT		FRONTAL $(F_3$ vs. $F_4)$	CENTRAL $(C_3$ vs. $C_4)$	PARIETAL $(P_3$ vs. $P_4)$
	df	F	F	F
left right hemisphere	1,285	1.64	10.10^{xx}	10.34^{xx}
measuring points	7,285	5.60^{xxxx}	7.07^{xxxx}	22.35^{xxxx}
left-right hemisphere X measuring points	7,285	0.02	0.12	0.17

^{x} $p < .05$ ^{xx} $p < .01$ ^{xxx} $p < .001$ ^{xxxx} $p < .0001$

RESULTS

Experiment 1

- Between S1 and S2 two components are present. The early slow wave has its largest amplitude in the frontal area at about 800 msec after S1, the late wave in the central area just before the presentation of S2 (Fig. 1). The main effect measuring points (Table I) indicates a change over time of the CNV amplitudes, which of course is related to the presence of the two components. For both left and right foot responses, this effect is most pronounced in the frontal early wave (Table II). For the late wave it is significant over the central and parietal cortex with right foot responses (Table III).
- The main effect "left-right hemisphere" is significant for right foot responses in the three cortical areas. The largest F values are found in the central and parietal derivations. This holds for the entire curve and for the slow and late components separately (Table I, II and III). With left foot movements a similar effect is found, but only in the central and parietal areas. It has to be noted that the F values found with left foot movements are much smaller than with the corresponding right foot movements (Table I, II and III). Larger amplitudes are found above the ipsilateral hemisphere with right foot responses. With left foot responses differences are less well pronounced, but they also are larger above the right hemisphere in the central and parietal area (Figs. 1, 2 and 3).
- Faster responses are preceded by larger late wave amplitudes. This result is more pronounced with right foot than with left foot responses.
- The main effect "left-right foot" is significant at F_4 and C_4

(Table IV). This implies larger amplitudes over the right
hemisphere preceding right foot movements (Fig. 6). The
same figure shows slightly larger amplitudes over the left
hemisphere with left foot movements, especially in the
late wave. Although this effect is not significant (Table IV),
it has to be kept in mind that per component only four
measuring points were used for calculations.

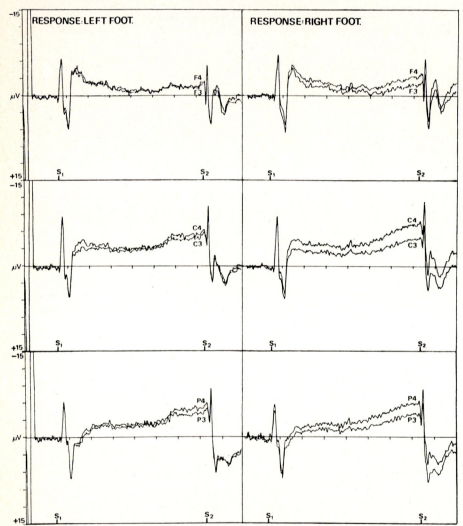

Fig. 1. Grand averages of CNV, recorded during a four sec foreperiod.
Three electrode positions per hemisphere: F3, F4, C3, C4, P3 and
P4. Number of subjects: 20. Response: left or right foot.

TABLE II

ANOVA's ON CNV EARLY WAVE: AT THREE DIFFERENT SITES OF BOTH HEMISPHERES: FRONTAL, CENTRAL AND PARIETAL.LEFT-RIGHT HEMISPHERE DIFFERENCES AND MEASURING POINTS ARE TESTED.

RESPONSE: RIGHT FOOT		Frontal (F$_3$ vs. F$_4$)	Central (C$_3$ vs. C$_4$)	Parietal (P$_3$ vs. P$_4$)
	df	F	F	F
left-right hemisphere	1,133	14.378^{xxx}	33.076^{xxxx}	16.603^{xxx}
measuring points	3,133	11.194^{xxx}	2.405	1.630
left-right hemisphere X measuring points	3,133	0.171	0.194	0.059

RESPONSE: LEFT FOOT		Frontal (F$_3$ vs. F$_4$)	Central (C$_3$ vs. C$_4$)	Parietal (P$_3$ vs. P$_4$)
	df	F	F	F
left-right hemisphere	1,133	2.09	9.105^{xx}	5.735^{x}
measuring points	3,133	14.744^{xxxx}	3.122^{x}	7.012^{xxx}
left-right hemisphere X measuring points	3,133	0.021	0.438	0.141

^{x} $p < .05$ ^{xx} $p < .01$ ^{xxx} $p < .001$ ^{xxxx} $p < .0001$

TABLE III

ANOVA's ON CNV LATE WAVE AT THREE DIFFERENT SITES OF BOTH HEMISPHERES: FRONTAL, CENTRAL AND PARIETAL.LEFT-RIGHT HEMISPHERE DIFFERENCES AND MEASURING POINTS ARE TESTED.

RESPONSE: RIGHT FOOT		Frontal (F$_3$ vs. F$_4$)	Central (C$_3$ vs. C$_4$)	Parietal (P$_3$ vs. P$_4$)
	df	F	F	F
left-right hemisphere	1,133	28.653^{xxxx}	76.200^{xxxx}	42.542^{xxxx}
measuring points	3,133	2.430	5.440^{xx}	5.599^{xx}
left-right hemisphere X measuring points	3,133	0.042	0.083	0.115

RESPONSE: LEFT FOOT		Frontal (F$_3$ vs. F$_4$)	Central (C$_3$ vs. C$_4$)	Parietal (P$_3$ vs. P$_4$)
	df	F	F	F
left-right hemisphere	1,133	1.034	7.285^{xx}	13.887^{xxx}
measuring points	3,133	0.687	0.128	0.284
left-right hemisphere X measuring points	3,133	0.030	0.031	0.127

^{x} $p < .05$ ^{xx} $p < .01$ ^{xxx} $p < .001$ ^{xxxx} $p < .0001$

TABLE IV

ANOVA's ON CNV AT SIX DIFFERENT ELECTRODE POSITIONS: F_3, F_4, C_3, C_4, P_3 AND P_4.
LEFT-RIGHT FOOT DIFFERENCES AND MEASURING POINTS ARE TESTED.

	df	F_3 F	F_4 F	C_3 F	C_4 F	P_3 F	P_4 F
TOTAL CURVE							
left-right foot	1.285	0.002	6.104^x	2.610	4.370^x	2.899	0.390
measuring points	7.285	2.100	2.009	5.189^{xxxx}	7.184^{xxxx}	11.629^{xxxx}	18.644^{xxxx}
left-right foot X measuring points	7.285	0.303	0.582	0.239	0.600	0.339	0.407
EARLY WAVE							
left-right foot	1.133	0.198	0.747	1.775	0.575	2.269	0.019
measuring points	3.133	4.459^{xx}	5.525^{xx}	0.545	2.201	2.376	1.576
left-right foot X measuring points	3.133	0.384	0.165	0.193	0.304	0.654	0.761
LATE WAVE							
left-right foot	1.133	0.109	8.123^{xx}	1.229	5.967^x	1.315	0.525
measuring points	3.133	0.047	0.094	0.639	0.680	0.470	1.109
left-right foot X measuring points	3.133	0.376	0.559	0.401	0.599	0.337	0.412

x $p < .05$ xx $p < .01$ xxx $p < .001$ xxxx $p < .0001$

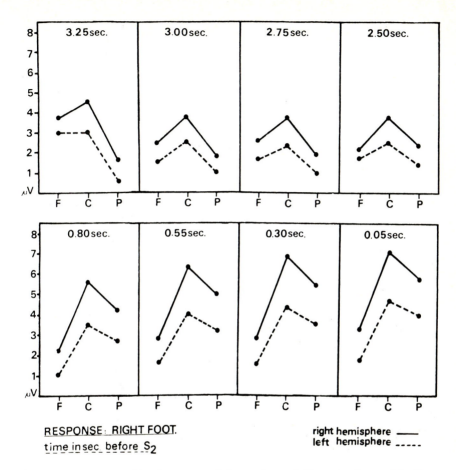

RESPONSE: RIGHT FOOT.

time in sec before S₂

right hemisphere _____
left hemisphere _ _ _ _ _

Fig. 2. Mean CNV amplitudes, recorded at three different sites of both
hemispheres. F: frontal, C: central, P: parietal electode
positions. Amplitudes were measured at eight points during a
four sec foreperiod: 3.25, 3, 2.75, 2.50, 0.80, 0.55, 0.30 and
0.05 sec before S2. Number of subjects: 20. Response: right foot.

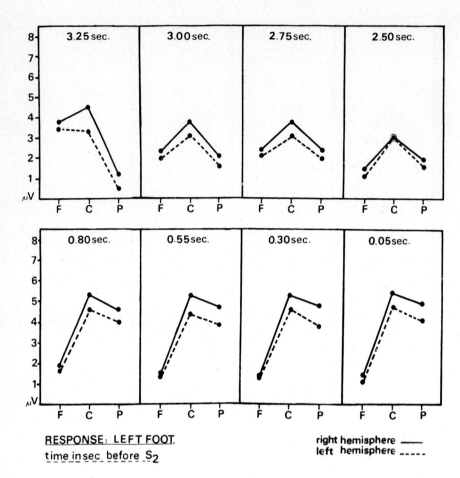

Fig. 3. Mean CNV amplitudes, recorded at three different sites of both hemispheres. F: frontal, C: central, P: parietal electrode positions. Amplitudes were measured at eight points during a four sec foreperiod: 3.25, 3, 2.75, 2.50, 0.80, 0.55, 0.30 and 0.05 sec before S2. Number of subjects: 20. Response: left foot.

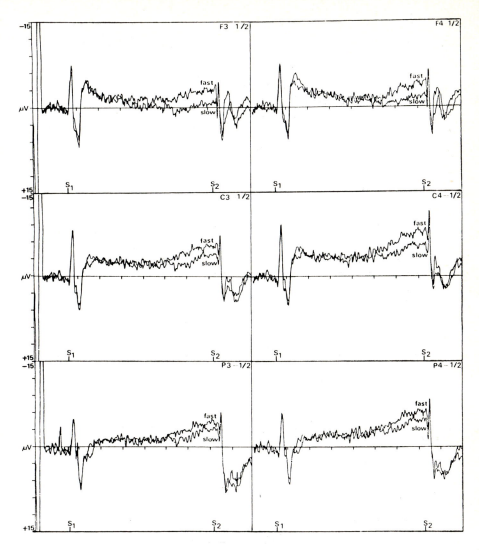

RESPONSE: RIGHT FOOT.

Fig. 4. Grand averages of CNV, preceding the 10 most rapid and the 10 slowest reaction times per subject. Six electrode positions. Number of subjects: 20. Response: right foot.

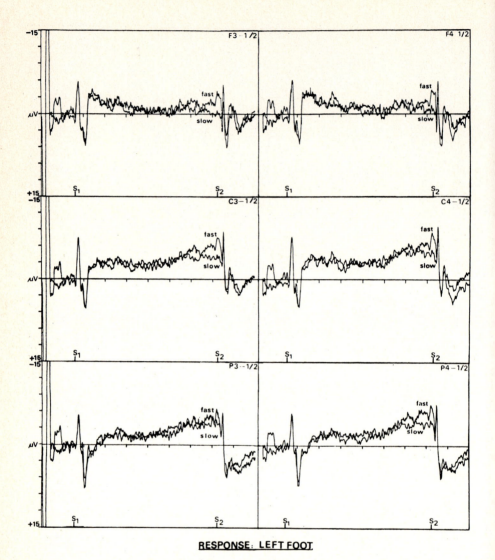

RESPONSE: LEFT FOOT

Fig. 5. Grand averages of CNV, preceding the 10 most rapid and the 10 slowest reaction times per subject. Six electrode positions. Number of subjects: 20. Response: left foot.

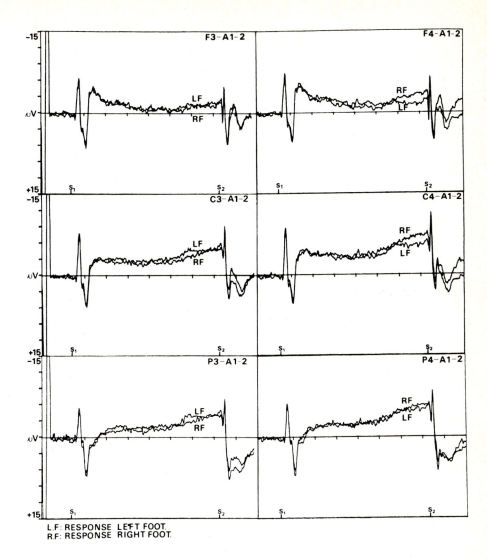

L.F: RESPONSE LEFT FOOT.
R.F: RESPONSE RIGHT FOOT.

Fig. 6. CNV recordings at six different electrode positions showing larger late wave amplitudes, preceding ipsilateral movements. Number of subjects: 20. Only F_4 and C_4 differences are significant (see Table IV).

Experiment 2

- H reflexes of involved and non involved muscles are during
  the ISI larger than during the ITI (Fig. 7).
  The main effect "involvedness" is not significant. This
  points to a lack of difference in the time course of H
  reflex amplitudes in both legs. The main effect "measuring
  points" indicates systematic changes in the reflex amplitudes over time. This is especially important during the
  last three sec of the ISI (Table V).
- At 200 msec after S1 amplitudes are larger than at 1000 msec.
  Amplitudes have their lowest values at 1000 msec, the
  difference between 200 msec and 1000 msec being significant.
  The same holds for the difference between 1000 and 3900 msec
  (Table VI).
- A significant trend to larger amplitudes is present from
  1000 to 3900 msec (Page test: p $<$ .001).

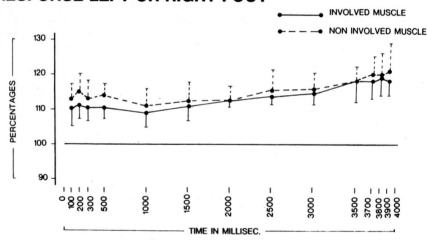

Fig. 7. Mean amplitudes of H reflexes, evoked at 13 different measuring
points of an ISI of four sec. Reflexes recorded during the ITI
were taken as control (100%). Vertical lines indicate 95% level
of confidence. Number of subjects: 40. Note that involved and non-
involved muscles show the same change over time.

TABLE V

ANOVA's ON HOFFMANN REFLEX AMPLITUDES DURING 4 SEC ISI.

	ISI (4 sec)		first sec of ISI		last sec of ISI	
	df	F	df	F	df	F
involvedness	1,39	1.570	1,39	2.896	1,39	1.223
measuring points	12,468	10.400[xxxx]	4,156	0.920	8,312	12.352[xxxx]
involvedness X measuring points	12.468	0.556	4,156	0.095	8,312	0.793

[x] $p < .05$ [xx] $p < .01$ [xxx] $p < .001$ [xxxx] $p < .0001$

TABLE VI

WILCOXON MATCHED PAIRS SIGNED RANKS TEST ON H REFLEX AMPLITUDES.

INVOLVED MUSCLE		z	p	NON INVOLVED MUSCLE		z	p
200 msec	1000 msec	2.11	$<.02$	200 msec	1000 msec	2.14	$<.02$
1000 msec	3900 msec	4.29	$<.0001$	1000 msec	3900 msec	4.93	$<.0001$

DISCUSSION

The presence of two slow waves in a 4 sec foreperiod (Fig. 1)
is in agreement with the data of Weerts and Lang (1973),
Loveless and Sanford (1974), Klorman and Bentsen (1975),
Rohrbaugh et al. (1976), Gaillard (1977, 1978) and Grünewald
et al. (1979).
Rohrbaugh et al. (1976) found larger late wave amplitudes, when
their subjects gave faster responses with their finger. Our
results show a similar relation between late wave amplitudes and
the speed of foot movement. Therefore it seems very likely that
the late wave amplitude represents at least the physiological
substrate of the velocity aspect of the preparatory process.
The findings of Kutas and Donchin (1974, 1977) and of Kristeva
and Becker (1978) indicate that BPs are related to muscular
effort. If the CNV late wave and the BP would be based on the
same physiological substrate, this would indicate that several
aspects of motor preparation are represented in the slow waves,
preceding the response. Therefore it seems necessary to investigate whether or not a more detailed and better specified relation between several aspects of the motor preparation process
and different aspects of slow waves might be found.
With right foot responses larger amplitudes are recorded in
the ipsilateral hemisphere. This corroborates the results of
an earlier study in which CNV late wave amplitudes at C_4 were
larger than at C_3, preceding a plantar flexion of the right
foot (Brunia and Vingerhoets, in preparation). Our present data
show that the difference concerns not only the central, but
the frontal and parietal area as well. Moreover, CNV amplitudes
are larger over the right hemisphere with right than with left
foot responses (Fig. 7, Table IV). Over the left hemisphere
slightly larger amplitudes with left foot responses are found.
To explain this rather puzzling result, it is necessary to keep
in mind that the projection area of the limb is situated in the
depth along the fissura longitudinalis. It might be suggested
that the dipole field is oriented in such a way that its activity is more easily recorded above the opposite hemisphere. This
would imply that the larger amplitudes at C_4 in fact reflect
the activity in the left hemisphere, preceding the right foot
response. The problem remains why with left foot responses also
larger amplitudes are found above the right hemisphere (Fig. 1).
Presumably, dominance plays a role as well. All our subjects
were right handed and footed. This implies that making a right
foot response two factors could play a role: the activation of
the left hemisphere (moto)neurones and the dominance factor.
Dominance might be related to a more or less constant activation
of the apical dendrites of a group of PTN's. If one agrees
that with foot movements both factors more easily are recorded
above the right hemisphere, this could explain the large
difference in amplitude between the right and left hemisphere,
preceding a right foot movement. With left foot movements the
two factors might oppose each other. Because our subjects were
right footed the dominance factor might be the strongest, thus
explaining the slightly larger amplitudes recorded above the
right hemisphere. Further experiments with left footed subjects
will be carried out in order to test this interpretation.

About the changes on the spinal level several points should be
stressed. The larger H reflex amplitudes during the foreperiod
point to an increase of the excitability of the alpha motoneurones or a decrease of presynaptic inhibition. This change is
not constant during the foreperiod. An early increase in H reflex amplitudes takes place 100-200 msec after S1, followed by
a relative decrease, which after 1000 msec is succeeded by a
new systematic increase with a maximal value just before S2.

Davis and Beaton (1968) found that the early increase is related to stimulus parameters of S1. Recent data from our laboratory (Brunia and Haagh, in preparation) suggest that the early
increase also is related to the probability of the presentation
of S2.

The relative decrease until 1000 msec also has been reported by
Requin et al. (1977) during a foreperiod of one sec. These
authors interpreted the decrease as a specific element of the
preparatory process, because it was much more pronounced in
the involved than in the non-involved leg. It could be explained
by a presynaptic inhibitory process, which might prevent the
motoneurone pool from being influenced by too large a disturbing peripheral inflow. Although a similar tendency is present
in our data, with smaller amplitudes in the involved leg during
the first sec, the main effect "involvedness" is not significant. Moreover, amplitudes do not fall below the ITI level,
thus casting doubt upon a real inhibition. However, comparing
electromyographic activity and reflex data, Brunia and
Vingerhoets (in preparation) point to the possibility that
presynaptic inhibition of the Ia afferent fibres might be present on the involved side, combined with a postsynaptic facilitation.

The second systematic increase seems to be related to the
arrival of S2. Perhaps, this effect is comparable to the
systematic increase in amplitude of the late CNV wave. Accepting this as a working hypothesis, it should be investigated
if larger H reflex amplitudes before S2 are correlated with
shorter reaction times. However, it must be taken into account
that Semjen et al. (1973) were not able to find a systematic
relation between H reflex amplitudes and reaction time during
an ISI of one sec.

H reflex amplitudes in involved and non involved muscles did
not show a different change over time. This implies that no
indication of a specific preparatory process on the spinal
level was found. In recent experiments in our laboratory,
Brunia and Haagh found a sharp increase of tendon reflex
amplitudes after S2 and before the onset of the EMG. This increase was much more pronounced in the involved leg. However,
this selective activation of the motoneuron pool, involved in
the response, presumably is already an expression of the
execution of the movement, in stead of its preparation.

Coming to a comparison of the physiological changes on the
cortical and the spinal level, we have tried to indicate the

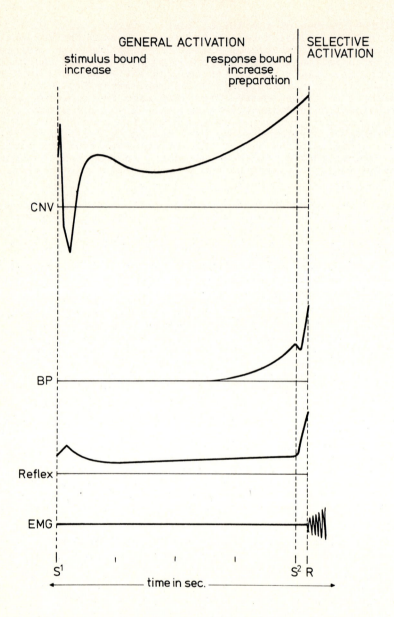

GENERAL ACTIVATION

stimulus bound
increase

response bound
increase
preparation

SELECTIVE
ACTIVATION

CNV

BP

Reflex

EMG

S¹

time in sec.

S² R

Fig. 8. A proposed model of the relations between physiological
changes on the cortical and spinal level (see text).

possible relation between these changes in Fig. 7. The model is
provisional, but several experiments can be carried out to test
its usefulness. It is supposed that at the onset of the foreperiod physiological changes are more related to the processing
of information, given with the warning stimulus, whereas at the
end a relation to motor preparation is more important. Although
the late wave amplitude indicates a larger involvedness of the
contralateral hemisphere, this effect is so generalized over the
cortex, that we, tentatively, characterize it as generalized
activation. It is obvious that different processes take place in
the mean time. The term "generalized activation" is used to
stress the contrast with the "selective activation" of a well
described group of PTN's on the cortical and of alpha motoneurones on the spinal level. The following presuppositions are
implied:
- The evoked potential on S1 and the early CNV wave are related
  to the stimulus properties of S1. The same holds for the early
  increase of the H reflex amplitudes on the spinal level, which
  might be related to similar processes as is the N2 of the
  evoked potential.
- The DC shift in the EEG, which is present during the four sec
  ISI might be related to the larger reflex amplitudes, found
  during the same period.
- The CNV late wave might be identical to the BP. Deecke,
  Becker, Grözinger and Kriebel (1976) have done an interesting
  experiment, in which a voluntary button press started 1.5 sec
  after a tone, upon which their subjects had to press the same
  button as quickly as possible. This provided the possibility
  to compare the potential distribution of the BP, preceding
  the first button press and of the CNV, between button press
  and tone. Although the authors found a different distribution
  for both slow waves, this experiment should be repeated with
  a four sec interval, because only in that case the CNV late
  wave develops very clearly.
- The wide spread slow waves during the foreperiod reflect a
  rather generalized cortical activity. Before the movement is
  going to be made, this activity has to be focussed on the
  PTN's in the motor cortex, from where the spinal motoneurones
  are to be fired. The model supposes a relation between the
  motor potential of Kornhuber and Deecke and the final increase
  in H reflex amplitudes which is present after S2 and before
  the movement.

Because the proposed relation between the different physiological changes both on the cortical and spinal level needs further
evidence, experiments will be carried out to test its validity.

REFERENCES

(1) Brunia, C.H.M. and Vuister, F.M., Spinal reflexes as indi-
     cator of motor preparation in man, Physiological Psychology
     (to appear).
(2) Davis, C.M. and Beaton, R.D., Facilitation and adaptation
     of the human quadriceps stretch reflex produced by auditory
     stimulation, Journal of Comparative and Physiological Psy-
     chology,66 (1968) 483-487.
(3) Deecke, L., Becker, W., Grözinger, B and Kriebel, J., CNV-
     Bereitschaftspotential relationships, in: McCallum, W.C.
     and Knott, J.R. (eds.), The responsive brain (J. Wright and
     Sons Ltd., Bristol, 1976) 214-216.
(4) Deecke, L., Grözinger, B. and Kornhuber, H.H., Voluntary
     finger movement in man: Cerebral potentials and theory,
     Biological Cybernetics, 23 (1976) 99-119.
(5) Gaillard, A.W.K., The late CNV wave: preparation versus
     expectancy, Psychophysiology, 14 (1977) 563-568.
(6) Gaillard, A.W.K., Slow brain potentials preceding task
     performance, Institute for Perception TNO, Soesterberg
     (1978).
(7) Gerilovsky, L. and Tsekov, T., Changes in the excitability
     of the segmental apparatus for reciprocal inhibition of
     agonist during a fixed waiting period, Agressology, 16
     (1975) 233-236.
(8) Grünewald, G., Grünewald-Zuberbier, E., Netz, J., Hömberg,
     V. and Sander, G., Relationships between the late component
     of the contingent negative variation and the Bereitschafts-
     potential, Electroencephalography and Clinical Neurophysio-
     logy, 46 (1979) 538-545.
(9) Klorman, R. and Bentsen, E., Effects of warning signal dura-
     tion on the early and late components of the contingent
     negative variation, Biological Psychology, 3 (1975) 263-
     275.
(10) Kornhuber, H.H. and Deecke, L., Hirnpotentialänderungen bei
     Willkürbewegungen und passiven Bewegungen des Menschen:
     Bereitschaftspotential und reafferente Potentiale, Archiv
     für die gesammte Physiologie, 284 (1965) 1-17.
(11) Kristeva, R. and Becker, W., Cerebral potentials preceding
     voluntary isometric force deployements of varying amplitudes,
     Pflügers Archiv für die gesammte Physiologie, 373 (suppl.)
     (1965) 74.
(12) Kutas, M. and Donchin, E., Studies of squeezing: handedness,
     responding hand, response force and asymmetry of readiness
     potential, Science, 186 (1974) 545-548.
(13) Kutas, M. and Donchin, E., The effect of handedness, of res-
     ponding hand and of response force on the contralateral
     dominance of the readiness potential, in: Desmedt, J.E.
     (ed.), Attention, voluntary contraction and event related
     cerebral potentials (Karger, Basel, 1977) 189-210.
(14) Loveless, N.E., Event related brain potentials in selective
     response, Biolobical Psychology, 5 (1977) 135-149.
(15) Loveless, N.E. and Sanford, A.L., Slow potential correlates
     of preparatory set, Biological Psychology, 1 (1974) 303-314.

(16) Mitchie, P.T., Clarke, A.M., Sinden, J.D. and Glue, L.C.T., Lateral facilitation of Hoffmann reflexes prior to voluntary movement in a choice reaction time task, Applied Neurophysiologie, 38 (1975) 191-196.

(17) Papakostopoulos, D. and Cooper, R., The contingent negative variation and the excitability of the spinal monosynaptic reflex, Journal of Neurology, Neurosurgery and Psychiatry, 6 (1973) 1003-1010.

(18) Requin, J., Some data of neurophysiological processes involved in the preparatory motor activity to reaction time performance, in: Koster, W.G. (ed.), Attention and Performance II (North Holland Publishing Company, Amsterdan, 1969) 358-368.

(19) Requin, J., Bonnet, M. and Semjen, A., Is there a specificity in the supraspinal control of motor structures during preparation?, in: Dornic, S.(ed.), Attention and Performance VI (Lawrence Erlbaum Ass. Inc., Hillsdale, 1977) 139-174.

(20) Rohrbaugh, J.W., Syndulko, K. and Lindsley, D.B., Brain wave components of the contingent negative variation, Science, 191 (1976) 1055-1057.

(21) Semjen, A., Bonnet, M. and Requin, J., Relation of the time course of Hoffmann reflexes and the foreperiod duration in a reaction time task, Physiology and Behavior, 10 (1973) 1041-1050.

(22) Tecce, J.J., Contingent negative variation (CNV) and psychological processes in man, Psychological Bulletin, 77 (1972) 73-108.

(23) Vaughan, H.G., The analysis of scalp recorded brain potentials, in: Thompson, R. and Patterson, M.M. (eds.), Bioelectric recording techniques. Part B. Electroencephalography and human brain potentials (Academic Press, New York, 1974) 158-209.

(24) Walter, W.G., Cooper, R., Aldridge, V.J., McCallum, W.C. and Winter, A.C., Contingent negative variation: an electrical sign of sensory-motor association and expectancy in the human brain, Nature, 203 (1964) 380-384.

(25) Weerts, T.C. and Lang, P.J., The effect of eye fixation and stimulus and response location on the contingent negative variation (CNV), Biological Psychology, 2 (1973) 1-19.

Tutorials in Motor Behavior
G.E. Stelmach and J. Requin (eds.)
© *North-Holland Publishing Company, 1980*

24

INTERFERENCE
BETWEEN A VOCAL AND A MANUAL RESPONSE
TO THE SAME STIMULUS

Daniel Holender

Département de Psychobiologie expérimentale
Institut de Neurophysiologie et Psychophysiologie
du C.N.R.S., Marseille, France

Three experiments were reported in which subjects were
instructed to make both a naming and a key-pressing response to a single stimulus which was a letter. Compared
with single tasks in which each response was performed
alone, it was found that, in the dual-task, there was no
slowing down of the manual response but the naming response was considerably delayed. The same pattern of results was also observed in a task requiring to synchronize both responses. Finally, instructions to give full
priority to the naming response resulted in a severe impairment of the two response latencies. The results were
discussed in the framework of Theios' (1973) model.

I. INTRODUCTION

The background for the present study has to be found in the information processing model proposed by Theios in 1973 to account for a large variety of results obtained with reaction time tasks . One of the purpose of
that model was to explain the difference between key-pressing and naming
responses to alpha-numerical stimuli in situations involving a one-to-one
stimulus-response mapping. When key-pressing responses are required, reaction time (RT) is an increasing function of the number of equally likely
stimulus alternatives or, with a constant number of stimulus alternatives,
RT is a decreasing function of the increasing presentation probabilities of
the stimulus alternatives. When naming responses are required, RT is generally not affected by either the number of stimulus alternatives or by the
relative stimulus frequency. Though this last proposition is certainly an
overgeneralization, Theios (1973) is not the only one to use the difference between naming and key-pressing responses to alpha-numerical stimuli to
infer that different information processing mechanisms should be used in
each case (e.g. Keele, 1973; Sanders, 1967).
Theios argued that, since the whole naming process is unaffected by
either the number of stimuli or stimulus frequency, whereas key-pressing
responses are strongly affected, it implies that the effect of those variables has to be located at the level of response determination and selection but not at all at the level of stimulus identification. Identification
of the stimulus is carried out by a parallel search into long term memory.
For overlearned responses such as naming of letters or digits, response
determination presumably requires only a small transformation of the iden-

tification code, which is also unaffected by the number of stimulus alternatives or by their relative frequencies of occurrence. Newly learned stimulus-response associations such as key-pressing for letters or digits can
be retrieved either by a slow parallel long term memory search or by a fast
serial scanning of a limited capacity short term buffer into which some of
the stimulus-response associations are **temporarily stored. Serial self ter-**
minating scanning, and the number and position of the stimulus-response associations included into the buffer are responsible for the effects of stimulus set size as well as the effects of the frequency of occurrence of the
stimuli.

The Theios'further assumption that the long term memory response retrieval
and the short term scanning can be carried out in parallel was at the origin of the present work. If this assumption is correct, there is at least
the possibility for two simultaneous RT tasks, each involving only one of
the two different processing mechanisms, to be carried out simultaneously
without interference. The first experiment was designed to test the more
restrictive hypothesis that a naming and a key-pressing response to the same stimulus, which was a letter, can be performed concurrently without impairment, that is with no increase in the latency of each response in the
dual-task relative to their latency when performed in isolation.

A non rejection of the hypothesis of no interference between the vocal
and manual responses would constitute a further argument in favor of the assumption that both kind of responses are mediated by different mechanisms.
A rejection of that hypothesis would be compatible with two different interpretations. The first is that both responses share some stages of processing
so that they are not mediated by independent mechanisms.The second is that
mechanisms are in fact independent but that they compete for a common limited processing capacity. It should be stressed that the fact that naming
responses are unaffected by the number or the frequency of the stimuli does
not imply no capacity demand at all, but rather that the same amount of
capacity is necessary whatever the level of these variables. Since the problem of mechanism independence is orthogonal to the question of capacity
independence, one cannot chose between the two interpretations on the basis
of the data alone. A reappraisal of the arguments favouring the independent
mechanism model would be welcome at this point.

There is no doubt that manual response latencies are influenced by set
size and by stimulus frequency. On the other hand, Theios' contention that
naming responses are not affected at all by those variables has to be considered with caution. Evidence for the contrary can be found in the literature.

It is not always true that set size exerts no effect at all on naming
alpha-numerical stimuli. Letters and digits are to be considered as ordered
sets of elements. Following Fitts and Switzer (1962) a familiar subset consists of consecutive elements taken from the beginning of the natural ordered set. Compared with an eight-choice naming condition, Fitts and Switzer
(1962) observed faster RT for a two-choice condition using a familiar subset but no advantage when an unfamiliar subset was used. A strong effect of
the number of alternative stimuli was also found by Hawkins and Underhill
(1971) with 2, 4 and 8 - choice tasks using the familiar subsets : A,B;A,B,
C,D; and A,B,...,H. With unfamiliar subsets, subjects (Ss) behave as if elements from the entire set might be presented so that, except for the slight
effect found by Forrin and Morin (1966), naming latencies are generally unaffected by stimulus set size (Brainard, Irby, Fitts & Alluisi, 1962; Morin,
Konick, Troxell & McPherson, 1965; Mowbray, 1960; Theios, 1973).

When observed, set size effects on naming responses are generally weak and cannot be considered as very damaging for Theios'model. The problem of stimulus relative frequency is more serious. This time, the absence of effect has to be considered as the exception and reliable strong effects as the rule. Aside from Theios (1973,1975), most of the studies have shown relative frequency effects on naming latencies (Fitts, Peterson & Wolpe, 1963; Hawkins & Underhill, 1971; Krinchik, 1974; Miller & Pachella, 1973). A study by Sanders (1970) gave a possible clue to the understanding of those discrepant results. With the letter E more frequent than the letters A, I and O, Sanders (1970) observed a strong frequency effect when Ss were required to respond by saying ES, AS, IS, and OS and no frequency effect with the responses SES, SAS, SIS and SOS. Sanders (1970) speculated that this frequency effect reflected a verbal motor preparatory adjustment. Preparation would mean preshaping of the vocal tract in order to be ready to pronounce a particular response. That this would logically be possible only when the responses begin with different phonemes is actually suported by Sanders' (1970) results. In each of the above mentioned studies showing an effect of stimulus frequency on naming responses, the effect could have been achieved by motor preparation. On the other hand, Theios' (1973,1975) use of the digits four and five as stimuli prevented the use of motor preparation and no frequency effect was observed.

The assumption that, with naming responses, the relative frequency effect is to be located at the level of response execution rather than at the level of response retrieval is of critical importance for the acceptance of the model proposed by Theios (1973) in the form outlined above. This assumption will be further documented in Experiment 1.

II. EXPERIMENT 1

The main aim of Experiment 1 was to test the hypothesis that naming and key-pressing in response to a letter could be carried out simultaneously without interference, that is without increase in the RT for each response in the dual-task relative to their RT when performed in isolation. The second aim of Experiment I was to know whether stimulus frequency effects on the vocal response would be observed with letters beginning by the same phoneme, so that no motor preparation would possibly take place.

1. Method

Ss were eight students from the Université Libre de Bruxelles. They were given one training and four one-hour experimental sessions each comprising three different four-choice tasks. In the vocal single task, Ss were required to name the presented letter; in the manual single task, Ss had to press the key assigned to the presented letter; in the dual-task, Ss performed both the vocal and the manual responses to the same stimulus. Each task was performed with two different blocks of trials. The first block consisted of a random sequence of 20 stimuli with equal frequencies of occurrence of each of the four letters. The second block consisted of 64 trials with unequal frequencies of the letters. There were four different letter frequency assignments each of which was used during one experimental session. The four frequency assignments were respectively for the letters L, N, R, and S : .50/.125/.125/.25, .25/.125/.125/.50, .125/.25/.50/.125 and .125/.50/.25/.125.

The letters L, N, R and S were chosen as stimuli because, when pronounced in French, they all begin with the same phoneme.This was assumed to be
a sufficient condition to avoid different triggering delays of the voice-
key and to preclude verbal motor preparation (Sanders, 1970).

The stimuli were displayed on a Nixie indicator located, at eye level,
at a distance of approximately 80 cm from the seated S. The response keys
for the manual responses consisted of four vertical strips of steel resting on microswitches. Their tips were flush with the distal edge of a
weakly inclined board on which S rested his hands and forearms. From left
to right, the keys respectively corresponded to the letters L, N, R,and S
and were respectively activated by the left middle, left index, right index, and right middle fingers. The verbal response activated a microphone
located in the center of the response board, approximately 30 cm from the
mouth of the S.

An interval of ten sec separated each successive presentation of a new
stimulus as a function of a preprogramed random sequence. One second before
the letter onset, a small neon bulb, located above the Nixie, was flashed
for half a second in order to provide a warning signal.

In the single tasks, Ss were required to react as fast as possible
while keeping a high accuracy level. Ss were encouraged to do so by rewarding each fast response by a monetary bonus and by deleting the equivalent
of two fast responses for each error. For each single tasks, the mean RT
in the training session was used as a cutoff for judging fast responses.
Ss were given knowledge of their gain after each block.

In the dual-task, Ss were told that the criterions for fast responses
remained the same as in the single tasks. They were instructed to try to
go as fast for each response in the dual-task as for the corresponding responses in the single tasks. Ss were given no trial by trial information
about their performance. After each block, Ss were only informed about
their gain but not about the way it was attained.

2. Results and Discussion

Figure 1 shows the mean RT, averaged over Ss and sessions, for the vocal and the manual responses in the single and in the dual-task as a function of relative stimulus frequency. The data were submitted to various a-
nalysis of variance and to subsequent post-hoc comparisons when necessary.
Since the results generally speak for themselves, no detailed report of
the analysis will be given. A level of .05 was required for statistical
significance.

In the single tasks, the vocal RT is always faster than the manual
one. There is a slight effect of stimulus relative frequency for the vocal
response and a strong effect for the manual one leading to the usual interaction between relative frequency and response mode. Subsequent post-hoc
Duncan comparisons carried out on the naming latencies showed the .50 response to be significantly faster than the two other ones as well as faster
than the control condition. No other difference was significant.

In the dual-task, the vocal RT is slower than the manual one by an
amount of time that is constant over the different stimulus frequencies.
As a consequence, there is no more interaction between relative frequency
and response mode. As can be seen in Figure 1, both the absolute level of
performance and the relative frequency effect are exactly the same for the
manual response either performed alone or concurrently with the vocal one.
The dependence of the naming latency upon the key-pressing latency not only holds at the level of the mean RT but also at the level of the whole RT

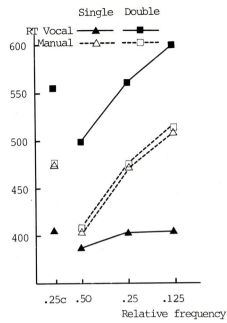

Figure 1. Mean RT for the vocal and the manual responses in the single and in the dual tasks as a function of relative frequency of occurrence of the stimuli. .25c stands for the control condition with equally likely stimuli.

distribution. Within each block of trials, the Bravet-Pearson correlation coefficient between the manual and the vocal latencies was very high, ranging from .74 to .88 with a mean of .83.

Like in Theios (1973,1975), the possibility to use a strategy of verbal motor preparation was probably preclude in the present experiment since each response began with the same phoneme. Nevertheless, contrary to Theios (1973,1975), the naming response was still slightly affected by stimulus relative frequency. It is important to note that this effect differs from the one observed with key-pressing response in at least two ways : i. only the most frequent response is concerned, ii. even in that case, the effect is much more weaker than with manual responses. In my opinion, a reasonable conclusion is that the present results cannot be considered as strong arguments against the assumption that naming and key-pressing responses to letters are mediated by different processing mechanisms.

The assumption that a naming and a key-pressing response to a letter could be carried out concurrently without interference is not supported by the results of Experiment 1. There seems to be some stage or stages of analysis, necessary subsequent to stimulus identification which is common for both responses, that cannot be carried out in parallel. In view of that limitation, it is surprising that both responses were not impaired. Instead, the dual-task exerts a detrimental effect on the vocal response only, without any decrement in the manual performance. Whatever the reasons for which Ss are so consistently giving priority to the manual response, it is clear from the results that the vocal response cannot be released before a minimum delay after manual response initiation has ellapsed. It is not possible to know which stage (stages) of the key-pressing response is (are) responsible for the delay in the naming response. All the operations after stimulus identification are possible candidates. On the other hand, one can spe-

culate that the only operation that is prevented to occur is vocal response
initiation. This assumption is supported by the fact that response determination and selection are assumed to be achieved by a small transformation
of the identification code. Moreover, the whole naming process is normally
carried out faster than the key-pressing one, as it is clearly the case in
the single tasks.

There is another way to interpret the results of Experiment 1. Namely,
the results are compatible with the hypothesis that Ss make a grouped response to the stimulus. Since the vocal response is normally faster than
the manual one, it means that Ss have to delay the vocal response in order
to synchronize it with the manual one. The fact that the responses are actually not simultaneous does not refute that hypothesis because we do not
know what Ss are eventually trying to synchronize. Since both responses result from partially different processes and are executed by different effectors, it could well be that a successful covert synchronization of two
events still leads to asynchroneous overt responses.

Since both interpretations of the delay in the naming responses predicts a high correlation between the RT for the two responses, which is indeed the case in Experiment 1, it is not possible to chose between them on
the basis of the observed results.

III. EXPERIMENT 2

The first purpose of Experiment 2 was to know whether it is possible to
choose between the two interpretations proposed above by asking Ss either
to realize a double performance or a synchronization of the responses in
the dual-task. The second aim of this experiment was to study what happens
if Ss are required to give priority to the vocal response instead of the
spontaneous manual priority they showed in Experiment 1.

1. Method

The main characteristics of the procedure were the same as in Experiment 1. The frequency bias was suppressed and Ss were only tested with four-
choice tasks with equally likely alternatives. A basic experimental unit
consisted of three blocks of 40 trials, one of which was used for the single
manual task, the other for the single verbal task, and the last one for the
dual-task. This unit was repeated twice in each of two sessions. The first
unit was considered as practice and discarded from the analysis except that
the mean RT in the single tasks provided cutoffs to judge for fast responses during the rest of the experiment.

Three groups of six Ss each were tested. Groups differed only by the
way Ss were instructed to perform the dual-task. Here are the instructions
for each group :

Group 1 : Ss were given the same dual RT task and the same instructions
as in Experiment 1. They were required to go as fast for each response in
the dual-task as for the corresponding responses in the single tasks. They
were rewarded accordingly.

Group 2 : Ss were required to synchronize both responses. They were
told that the main aim of the task was to keep the interval between the two
responses at a minimum. A bonus was given each time the two responses were
separated by less than 40 msec. Ss were not informed about that criterion.
Ss were also asked not to respond to slowly but this was a secondary goal

for which they were not rewarded. Ss were given no trial by trial information about their performance, they were only told their total gain after
the block was completed.

Group 3 : Ss were instructed to give full priority to the vocal response while doing their best for the manual one. They were rewarded only
for naming responses faster than the mean RT in the single naming task.
Fast key-pressing responses were not rewarded at all.

2. Results and Discussion

The mean RT for correct responses are shown in Figure 2. For the single tasks, which were the same in each condition, the three groups display
very similar performances. This is true both at the absolute level and for
the average 80 to 90 msec advantage of the naming response over the key-
pressing one.

As can be seen in the left panel of Figure 2, the results of the dual
RT task are very similar to the one observed in Experiment 1. The manual
mean RT is not affected at all by the concurrent vocal response whereas the
vocal response is significantly slower than the manual one. Though the delay is smaller than with the control trials in Experiment 1 (45 vs.83 msec),
it is clear that the naming response has to wait for the completion of the
key-pressing one in order to be elicited. This is confirmed by the fact
that, again, there is a high correlation between the RT for the two responses (r = .79 on the average accross Ss).

Except for a slight increase in the manual RT, which is not astoni-
shing since speed was not emphasized in that condition, Ss in the synchro-

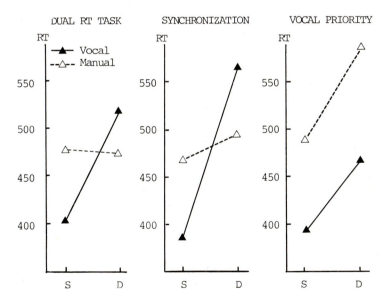

Figure 2. Mean RT for the vocal and the manual responses as a
function of the type of task (S: single task, D: dual-task) in
each condition of Experiment 2

nization task behave much like the ones in the dual RT task. As can be seen
in the central panel of Figure 2, the failure to synchronize the responses
give place to a delayed vocal response very similar to the one observed in
group 1, except that the delay was somewhat bigger in group 2 (69 msec)
than in group 1 (45 msec). The correlation between the two RT is still higher, but not significantly so, than in group 1. The average of the individual correlation coefficients is .90.

Though Ss in group 3 gave their vocal response before the manual one,
they were unable to fulfil the requirement to go as fast as in the single
vocal task. The right panel of Figure 2 indicates that, when Ss are urged
to behave in a way different from the one they spontaneously adopt, performances of both responses, instead of naming performance only, are severely
impaired. There was only one S who was able to perform the task almost perfectly. His vocal response was only 20 msec slower in the dual-task relative to the single task, but his manual response was now 320 msec slower than
when performed alone. For that S, it seems that the verbal response processing prevented all manual information processing beyond stimulus identification to take place. Although, at a superficial level, the results of that
S look like a mirror image of the results observed in the other groups,there
is an important difference : that is, RT for both responses are not correlated (r = -.14). On the average, the correlation between the RT is much
smaller in this condition (r =   .38) than in the other ones.

The most puzzling observation in Experiment 2 is that, aside from some
differences too small to be taken into account, Ss seems to behave in a very similar manner under two different instructions. Namely, the results of
the dual RT task are almost the same as the results of the synchronization
task. One possible explanation lies in the fact that Ss in the synchronization task were also required to go fast. Even if that requirement was clearly defined as secondary, it could have contributed to reduce the difference
between the results of group 1 and group 2. One of the motivation for the
third experiment was to test this latter hypothesis.

IV. EXPERIMENT 3

The main purpose of Experiment 3 was to study the synchronization performance in a situation that was not possibly contaminated by RT task requirements. In order to do that, Ss were never submitted to an RT task and
speed of responses was never stressed. Ss were only required to synchronize
the naming and the key-pressing responses any time they want after stimulus
presentation. The second aim of Experiment 2 was to study whether the particular letters used so far have any influence on the observed effects. In addition to L, N, R and S, Ss were also tested with B, D, P and T.

1. Method

Eight Ss, different from the one used in the other experiments, were
tested during two 45-minutes sessions. Compared with the synchronization
condition of Experiment 2, two procedural differences were introduced :
single RT tasks were performed and blocked rather than random presentations
of each letter were used. In addition of the letters L, N, R and S that
were used during one of the two sessions, the letters B, D, P and T were
used during the other session. From left to right, the manual response as-

signements for B,D,P and T was the same as for L, N, R and S. Instructions and payoff were the same as in the synchronization condition of Experiment 2 except that Ss were allowed to make their responses any time they wanted after stimulus onset.

2. Results and Discussion

Table 1 shows the differences between the latencies of the vocal and the manual response for each letter. For the set composed of the letters L, N, R and S, the usual 70 msec delay is observed. This delay is significantly increased with the set including the letters B, D, P and T being 102 msec on the average. The faster S made his first response after a delay of approximately 300 msec whereas the slowest S waited for more than one sec. But the delay in the vocal response was independent of the synchronization latency.

L	N	R	S	MEAN
56	76	83	66	70
B	D	P	T	
91	112	94	109	102

Table 1. Mean difference (in msec): vocal response latency minus manual response latency. Letters in the same column were responded with the same finger

The main result of this experiment is that, like Ss in Experiment 2, Ss experiencing no time pressure at all make their naming response 70 msec later than the manual one. The assumption that speed requirements might have played a role in the naming response delay observed in the synchronization condition of Experiment 2 is therefore clearly ruled out.

It is interesting to note that the delay in the naming response is not independent of the phonological aspects of the response. This might give some clues about the events Ss try to synchronize. This follows from the fact that the time at which the energy necessary to activate the voice-key become available is not independent of the utterance. For responses starting with a vowel sound, this energy is present from the very beginning of the utterance. On the contrary, for responses starting by a stop consonant, that is by a closure of the vocal tract, there is probably no useful energy before the voicing that follows the explosion. The observation of a greater delay for responses starting by a stop consonant than by a vowel sound (see Table 1) can therefore be used to infer that it is the beginning of the vocal response that Ss try to synchronize with some unknown part of the manual response. Would the responses have been pronounced by native speakers of English, the same argument could have been used to predict a greater delay for unvoiced than for voiced stop consonants. But no such prediction would hold for French speakers because the Voice onset Time is probably close to 0 msec rather than to 30 msec like in English. As a matter of fact, no difference between the voiced and unvoiced responses was observed. Finally, I have no ready explanation for the observation that, for responses starting with a stop consonant, the delay depends on the place of articulation, being greater with bilabial than with dental responses.

     As was pointed out in the introduction, Theios' (1973) contention that
naming and key-pressing responses to alpha-numerical stimuli are fully different in nature is perhaps a little exaggerated. The reason is that naming
responses are sometimes influenced by stimulus set size as well as stimulus
relative frequency. Though the importance of the former effect has been
dismissed, the fact that naming responses are sometimes affected by stimulus relative frequency to the same extent as key-pressing responses casts
some doubts about the assumption of independent processing mechanisms. But,
only studies allowing for vocal motor preparation display naming relative
frequency effects (Fitts, Peterson, & Wolpe, 1963, Hawkins & Underhill,1971,
Krinchik, 1974, Miller & Pachella, 1973). When motor preparation is preclu-
ded, either no effect is observed (Theios, 1973, 1975), or, as in the present Experiment 1, a weak effect, qualitatively different from the one affecting key-pressing responses, is obtained. These results are consistent
with the hypothesis that, for naming, relative frequency effects have to be
located at the stages of response initiation and execution rather than at
the stages of response determination and selection. To conclude,I am inclined to think that there is no strong evidence against the assumption that
naming and key-pressing responses are processed by different mechanisms.
     With regard to the main purpose of the reported studies, the hypothe-
sis that naming and key-pressing responses to letters can be carried out
in parallel is not supported by the results. Dual RT tasks show at least
their vocal performance impaired. By accepting the assumption of independent mechanisms for the verbal and manual response, one is left with only
one interpretation of the results. That is, at least part of the stages
involved in each processing competes for a common limited processing capacity pool. But, this interpretation relies upon the assumption that Ss are
actually emphasizing speed for the two responses as they are required to do.
In this regard, the fact that Ss behave in a similar manner in the dual RT
task and in the synchronization task is troublesome. This, together with
the very high correlation between the two RT, is consistent with the idea
that Ss are grouping the two responses while performing the dual RT task.
Since the vocal latency is shorter than the manual latency when the responses are performed alone, deliberate grouping of the responses should necessarily entail an increase in the vocal RT, but no increase in the manual
one. If this is indeed the case, nothing could be said about an hypothetical sharing of a limited processing capacity between the two responses unless one demonstrates that the grouping strategy itself is to be considered
as a consequence of capacity limitation. Of great consideration for that
matter are the results of the vocal priority condition of Experiment 2. Ss
were unable to do the task as required. Ss gave their vocal response prior
to the manual response but at the cost of severe decrements in the two latencies relative to the latencies in the single tasks. This demonstrates
two things. The first is that most part of the manual response processing
cannot be carried out concurrently with the naming processing. The second
is that half the dual RT task instructions are impossible to fulfil. In
view of these limitations, the grouping strategy appears to be the best
possible compromise that allows for a partial fulfilment of the dual RT
task instructions while keeping the global performance impairment at a minimum. As a matter of fact, Ss were able to execute the manual response
without performance decrement relative to the manual single task.
     In summary : the results reported here are consistent with the follo-
wing assumptions : i. Naming and key-pressing responses to letters are me-

diated by independent processors, ii. when used together, these processors compete for a common processing capacity pool, and iii. the grouping of the responses is a consequence of processing capacity limitation.

This work has been partially carried out at the Université Libre de Bruxelles while the author was supported as "Aspirant" by the Belgian "Fonds National de la Recherche Scientifique". The author's address : Laboratoire de Psychologie Expérimentale, 117, av.Adolphe Buyl,1050 Bruxelles,Belgium.

REFERENCES

Brainard, R.W., Irby, T.S., Fitts, P.M., & Alluisi, E.A. Some variables influencing the rate of gain of information. *Journal of Experimental Psychology*, 1962, *63*, 105-110.

Fitts, P.M., & Switzer, G. Cognitive aspects of information processing : I. The familiarity of S-R sets and subsets. *Journal of Experimental Psychology*, 1962, *63*, 321-329.

Forrin, B., & Morin, R.E. Effect of contextual associations upon selective reaction time in a numeral-naming task. *Journal of Experimental Psychology*, 1966, *71*, 40-46.

Hawkins, H.L., & Underhill, J.R. S-R compatibility and the relative frequency effect in choice reaction time. *Journal of Experimental Psychology*, 1971, *91*, 280-286.

Keele, S.W. *Attention and Human Performance*. Pacific Palisades, California: Goodyear, 1973.

Krinchik, E. Probability in choice reaction time tasks. *Perception & Psychophysics*, 1974, *15*, 131-144.

Miller, J.O., & Pachella, R.G. Locus of the stimulus probability effect. *Journal of Experimental Psychology*, 1973, *101*, 227-231.

Morin, R.E., Konick, A., Troxell, N., & McPherson, S. Information and reaction time for "naming" responses. *Journal of Experimental Psychology*, 1965, *70*, 309-314.

Mowbray, G.H. Choice reaction times for skilled responses. *Quarterly Journal of Experimental Psychology*, 1960, *12*, 193-202.

Sanders, A.F. Some aspects of reaction processes. In A.F. Sanders (Ed.), *Attention and Performance I, Acta Psychologica*, 1967, *27*, 115-130.

Sanders, A.F. Some variables affecting the relation between relative stimulus frequency and choice reaction time. In A.F. Sanders (Ed.), *Attention and Performance III, Acta Psychologica*, 1970, *33*, 45-55.

Theios, J. Reaction time measurements in the study of memory processes : Theory and data. In G.H. Bower (Ed.), *The Psychology of Learning and Motivation : Advances in research and Theory*, Vol. 7. New York : Academic Press, 1973.

Theios, J. The components of response latency in simple human information processing tasks. In P.M.A. Rabbitt, & S. Dornic (Eds.), *Attention and Performance V*, London : Academic Press, 1975.

Tutorials in Motor Behavior
G.E. Stelmach and J. Requin (eds.)
© *North-Holland Publishing Company, 1980*

25

INFORMATION PROCESSING MECHANISMS
INVOLVED IN OCULAR PURSUIT[*]

Alexander H. Wertheim
Institute for Perception TNO
Soesterberg, The Netherlands

Subjects reacted manually to visual stimuli presented in
a moving target, followed with the eyes. Independent variables were the predictability, the velocity and the frequency of target movement as well as the time uncertainty
with which the stimuli appeared in the moving target. The
reaction time data showed that the effects of target velocity and time uncertainty interacted. The effects of the
other target movement parameters were additive with that
of time uncertainty. This suggests that target velocity
affects a stage of information processing related to preparatory motor processes. All target movement parameters
also affect one or more perceptual stages. In terms of
Kahneman's effort theory the results seem to suggest that
an ocular pursuit task becomes more difficult when target
velocity is increased, but not when the frequency of target movement increases or when its predictability is reduced.

In research on pursuit tracking it is usually observed that performance deteriorates as target velocity increases. If a target describes a repetitive
pattern, an increase in frequency has a similar effect. Tracking performance is also known to be impaired when the predictability of a movement
pattern is reduced. The effects of these target movement parameters are
usually described in the terminology of control-theory. However, concepts
such as gain-loss or phase-lag of the tracking response do not add to the
knowledge about information processing mechanisms involved in tracking performance, or about the specific effects which frequency, predictability or
velocity may have on such mechanisms.

In this paper an approach is presented which enables the investigation of
such mechanisms and of their relation to target movement parameters. The
experiments concern an ocular pursuit task, but the approach can be extended to any kind of tracking task. Instead of analysing the effects of target
movement parameters on tracking *per se*, performance is studied on a reaction task (secondary task), performed concurrently with an ocular pursuit
task (main task). The model underlying the experiments is based on the

---

[*] Part of this research has been supported by a grant from the Praeventie-
fonds.

additive factor method (Sternberg, 1969) which is discussed in some detail
in this volume by Sanders. Here it suffices to mention that if manipulation
of a certain target movement variable affects reaction time on the secondary task and if this effect interacts with that of another reaction time
variable, then it follows that both variables affect a common information
processing stage.

In the present research the uncertainty about the timing of a stimulus in
the secondary reaction task was varied. According to Sanders (1979; see
also this volume) time uncertainty affects a motor adjustment stage, sensitive to variations in preparatory state.

Interactions between the effects of time uncertainty and target movement
parameters can also be interpreted in terms of a rather different theoretical frame of reference associated with Kahneman's effort theory (Kahneman,
1973). There experimental effects are not interpreted in terms of information processing stages but in terms of capacity requirements and task
difficulty. According to this theory, man has a limited (although not fixed) amount of capacity (to be understood as a kind of activating energy)
available for performing any task. It requires the investment of effort to
use a certain amount of this capacity for purposes of task performance. If
a task becomes more difficult it means that more capacity is required and
more effort must be invested. If there is not sufficient capacity available performance deteriorates. The theory also assumes that the total a-
mount of capacity available can never be used completely. There always remains a certain amount of spare capacity available for other purposes, such
as performing a secondary task. However, spare capacity is always reduced
when a task becomes more difficult. Since performance on a secondary task
also requires capacity, performance on a difficult secondary task will
suffer more from a reduction of spare capacity than performance on an easy
secondary task. Hence if the effect of a main task variable is to change
main task difficulty, the performance difference between an easy and a
difficult secondary task will also be affected by that variable. In the
absence of such an effect the main task variable cannot be said to affect
the capacity requirements of the main task (or the amount of effort to be
invested) and thus does not affect main task difficulty. (See for a more
detailed discussion of this issue Kantowitz and Knight, 1978.)

The literature on reaction time indicates that time uncertainty can be
associated with task difficulty because time uncertainty is associated with
alertness or attention (Posner, 1975), concepts which are used by Kahneman
as synonyms for capacity.

In summary, the experiments reported here investigated whether the frequency, the velocity and the predictability of a moving target to be followed
with the eyes, have effects on performance on a secondary reaction time
task, which interact with the effects of time uncertainty. If so, then
such target movement parameters can be associated with a stage of preparatory motor adjustment in the information processing sequence. Another interpretation of such an interaction would be that the target movement parameters involved affect the capacity requirements (and thus the difficulty)
of ocular pursuit.

METHOD

In most research on tracking, target movement frequency, velocity and predictability have been confounded in experimental designs. If, for example,
the frequency of a sinusoidal target movement is increased, its velocity
also increases. Often unpredictable target movements are created by combining several sinusoidal movements of different amplitudes and frequencies,
or by varying the amplitude of a given sinusoidal movement. This means
that such unpredictable target movements differ from simple sinusoidal
(predictable) target movements in many respects, including frequency and
velocity.

Another problem is that sinusoidal target movements in one dimension (e.g.
horizontal or vertical) - a type of target movement often used in pursuit
tracking tasks - involve variable velocities and accelarations: velocity
is maximal half way through the movement and zero at the turning points.

The investigation of the specific effects of frequency, velocity and predictability requires independent manipulation of each of these parameters.
In addition velocity and frequency should remain constant during the whole
of an experimental session.

In the present research these requirements are met by using two-dimensional
target movements. The target moved in a circular pattern with a given constant velocity and frequency. The velocity of the target could be manipulated by changing the amplitude of the circular pattern. This type of movement will be termed a *predictable* movement condition (PC).

In an *unpredictable* movement condition (UC) the target also moved along a
circular path, identical to the one used in a PC. However, after a period
of random duration - but shorter than one cycle - the target started to
move along the path of a congruent circle, tangential to the first one at
that point. This process was subsequently repeated. The resulting movement pattern consisted of a target which continuously switched at random
intervals from one circular pattern to another (with restrictions to prevent excessive visual angles). Since the movement pattern in an UC consisted of the same basic circular patterns as the ones used in a PC the
frequency and velocity of a target movement could be made equal in both
conditions.

The target consisted of a bright circular spot (7 cm diameter) projected
on a large screen with the help of a mirror system which could make the
target move over the screen (see Wertheim 1979 for a more detailed description). The visual reaction stimulus consisted of a black asterisk which
could be projected in the center of the moving target. Subjects (seated
at 200 cm from the screen) were required to follow the moving target with
their eyes and, in addition, to react to the presentation of a stimulus in
the moving target by pushing a reaction button. As a warning signal the
target was colored red for a period of .35 sec. Reaction times were measured by a PDP-8 computer.

Horizontal eye-movements were recorded on paper during the experiment
(using two Ag-AgCl electrodes at the outer canthi of the eyes) in order to
check whether subjects followed the instructions. This was shown by the
occurrence of smooth pursuit eye-movements.

EXPERIMENT 1

Reaction times were measured in two tracking conditions differing in frequency, velocity and predictability. If no interaction is observed between the effects of time uncertainty and tracking conditions this would suggest that none of the target movement parameters affects a stage of information processing related to preparatory motor processes. In terms of the theory of Kahneman this would suggest that the parameters do not affect the capacity requirements of the ocular pursuit task.

In the PC, frequency was .5 Hz and velocity was 30 cm/sec. Hence the amplitude of the circular pattern was 19 cm. In the UC, frequency was 1 Hz and velocity 40.8 cm/sec. Thus the amplitude of the basic circles was 13 cm. Seven subjects received two blocks of 100 stimuli each, in both tracking conditions. In one block stimuli arrived after warning intervals ranging between .5 and 2.5 sec. In the other block stimuli were associated with constant 1.5 sec. warning intervals. The conditions were presented in balanced order.

The results are shown in Fig. 1. The main effects of tracking condition and time uncertainty were significant ($F = 109$; $df = 1,6$; $p < .01$ and $F = 27.7$; $df = 1,6$; $p < .01$). In addition a significant interaction between time uncertainty and tracking condition was observed ($F = 11.6$; $df = 1,6$; $p < .02$). This indicates that at least one of the three target movement

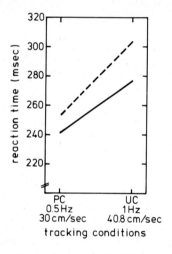

Fig. 1. Reaction time as a function of tracking condition with constant and variable warning intervals (exp. 1). Solid lines: constant warning intervals Dashed lines: variable warning intervals

parameters affects an information processing stage related to preparatory motor activity or somehow affects the capacity requirements of the ocular pursuit task.

In a first attempt to determine which target movement parameter is responsible for the interaction the experiment was replicated with tracking conditions of equal velocity.

EXPERIMENT 2

In this experiment target velocity in both tracking conditions was made
equal (40.8 cm/sec) but frequency remained 1 Hz in the UC and .5 Hz in the
PC. (Amplitude was 13 cm in the UC and 26 cm in the PC.) Twelve subjects
participated in three sessions. In each session two blocks were presented
consisting of five runs of 20 reactions each. In one block stimuli were
associated with constant warning intervals and in the other with variable
ones.

Fig. 2 shows again a significant main effect of tracking condition ($F =$
32,3; df = 1,11; $p < .01$) and of time uncertainty ($F = 107$; df = 1,11;
$p < .01$).

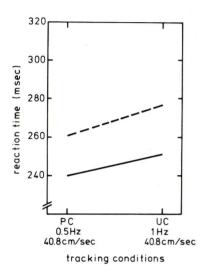

Fig. 2. Reaction time as a function of
tracking conditions of equal velocity
with constant and variable warning
intervals (exp. 2).
Solid lines: constant warning intervals
Dashed lines: variable warning intervals

However, the interaction between the effect of time uncertainty and that of
tracking condition has disappeared ($F = 1.68$; df = 1,11; $p < .25$). Apparently the interaction observed in exp. 1 cannot be ascribed to the differences in frequency or predictability because these differences were also
present in exp. 2 where no interaction was observed. Therefore the interaction must stem from the velocity differences between the two tracking
conditions. Hence either the effect of velocity interacts with that of
time uncertainty or the combined effects of velocity with frequency or predictability (or with both) interact with the effect of time uncertainty.
The next experiment was designed to test these hypotheses.

EXPERIMENT 3

In this experiment frequency, velocity and predictability were manipulated
orthogonally in the experimental design. Table 1 illustrates the design
and shows the amplitudes used to produce the same two levels of velocity
at each of the two frequencies used in both predictable and unpredictable
conditions.

438   A.H. WERTHEIM

Table 1

Experimental conditions used in experiment 3

Predictability	Predictable (PC)				Unpredictable (UC)			
Frequency (Hz)	.4		1.2		.4		1.2	
Velocity (cm/sec)	34	68	34	68	34	68	34	68
Amplitude (cm)	27	54	9	18	27	54	9	18

The foreperiod effect was increased by using either short or long variable warning intervals (ranging between 1.3 and 1.6 sec, and between 2 and 6 sec, respectively). This was done to increase the difference in the amount of spare capacity needed during performance on the easy and difficult reaction tasks. In terms of Kahneman's theory this ensures a more pronounced effect of variations in main task difficulty on the difference in reaction time between the two levels of the reaction task. Twelve subjects participated. In each of the conditions they received four blocks of fifteen stimuli; two blocks with short and two blocks with long warning intervals.

The results showed significant main effects of velocity (F = 71; df = 1,11; p < .01), frequency (F = 108; df = 1,11; p < .01), predictability (F = 169; df = 1,11; p < .01) and time uncertainty (F = 678; df = 1,11; p < .01).

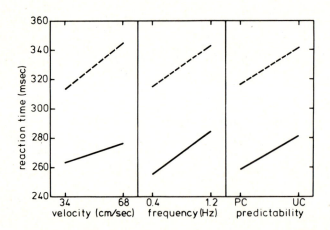

Fig. 3. Reaction time as a function of target movement velocity, frequency and predictability with short and long variable warning intervals.
Solid lines: short variable warning intervals
Dashed lines: long variable warning intervals

In addition the effect of velocity interacted with that of time uncertainty (F = 28.4, df = 1,11; p < .01) while those of frequency and predictability did not (F < 1). There was no statistical evidence of any other interaction with the effect of time uncertainty. However, the effects of frequency and predictability interacted significantly with each other (F = 38,3; df = 1,11; p < .01) and so did those of velocity and frequency (F = 7.5; df = 1,11; p < .02). In addition a slight trend towards an interaction between velocity and predictability was observed (F = 3.2; df = 1,11; p < .10).

It should be noted that in the present research velocity was manipulated by changing the amplitudes of the basic circles from which the target movement patterns in both predictable and unpredictable conditions were constructed. Hence it should be investigated whether the influence of velocity on the effects of time uncertainty should not be ascribed to amplitude manipulations. Table 2 shows the reaction time differences between conditions with short and long warning intervals for each of the amplitudes.

Table 2

Mean reaction time as a function of frequency, velocity and amplitude

Movement parameters			Mean reaction times		
Frequency (Hz)	Velocity (cm/sec)	Amplitude (cm)	Short warning intervals	Long warning intervals	Difference
1.2	34	9	274	325	51
1.2	68	18	294	367	73
.4	34	27	251	301	50
.4	68	54	258	328	70

This table clearly shows that amplitude does not affect the foreperiod effect in any systematic way.

DISCUSSION

Taken together the results indicate that target velocity and time uncertainty are variables affecting a common processing stage, presumably a stage related to preparatory motor processes. Neither frequency nor predictability appear to affect this stage. The interactions between the effects of velocity and frequency, between those of frequency and predictability and the trend towards an interaction between the effects of velocity and predictability may indicate that velocity, frequency and predictability all affect one other stage. This suggestion is supported by other experiments (Wertheim, 1979) in which a higher order interaction between the effects of the three movement parameters was observed as well as an interaction between the effects of stimulus degradation and those of frequency and predictability (and probably also velocity). Hence this common stage is most likely a perceptual stage, not related to motor processes.

With respect to the theory of Kahneman one might say that velocity of the target is the main determinant of the difficulty of an ocular pursuit task because only velocity interacts with time uncertainty. It should be realised however, that such an assertion rests solely on the assumption that time uncertainty affects task difficulty. As mentioned earlier this assumption is derived from a theoretical argument associating time uncertainty with alertness (Posner, 1975) and from the association between alertness and

capacity (Kahneman, 1973). The assumption should be seriously questioned
if time uncertainty has no effects interacting with those of other variables that either relate to alertness or, for other reasons, can be associated with capacity. If so, either time uncertainty cannot be associated
with task difficulty or Kahneman's theory should be revised, in particular
the important premise that the difficulty of a task reflects its capacity
requirements.

It is interesting to note that in the literature describing the operations
of the oculomotor system, target velocity also appears to be a crucial factor. The oculomotor smooth pursuit system can be conceptualised as a closed loop feedback system in which visual input serves as feedback. It is
generally assumed that this system acts as a velocity servo, which means
that those aspects of the visual input which do function as feedback signals are velocity coded (see for a recent discussion of this issue, Miles
and Evarts, 1979). The fact that velocity is the only movement parameter
which affects a stage preparatory to motor activity fits in rather nicely
with this assumption.

References

|1| D. Kahneman: Attention and Effort, Prentice Hall, New York 1973.
|2| B.H. Kantowitz and J.L. Knight: When is an easy task difficult and
    vice versa? Acta Psychologica, 1978 42 163-170.
|3| F.A. Miles and E.V. Evarts: Concepts of motor organization, Annual
    Review of Psychology, 1979 30 327-362.
|4| M.I. Posner: Psychobiology of Attention. In: Handbook of Psychobiolo-
    gy, M.S. Gazzaniga and C. Blakemore (Eds.) Academic Press, New York
    1975.
|5| A.F. Sanders: Some effects of instructed muscle tension on choice
    reaction time and movement time. In: Attention and Performance VIII,
    R.S. Nickerson (Ed.) Erlbaum, Hillsdale 1979 (in press).
|6| A.F. Sanders: Stage analysis of reaction processes, This volume.
|7| S. Sternberg: The discovery of processing stages: extensions of
    Donders' method, Acta Psychologica, 1969 30 (Attention and Performance
    II) 276-315.
|8| A.H. Wertheim: Information processed in ocular pursuit, Monograph of
    the Institute of Perception, Soesterberg, The Netherlands 1979.

PART V

TIMING AND SEQUENCING
OF ACTION

Tutorials in Motor Behavior
G.E. Stelmach and J. Requin (eds.)
© *North-Holland Publishing Company, 1980*

26

ANALYSING PIANO PERFORMANCE:
A STUDY OF CONCERT PIANISTS*

L.H. Shaffer
Department of Psychology
University of Exeter
Exeter, Devon

A theory of motor programming is presented within
which one can consider fluency, expressiveness and
flexibility as basic properties of skilled performance. It is emphasized that these are emergent
properties of skill, absent or poorly represented
in unskilled performance. Hence it is argued that
motor programming is best studied looking at the
performance of skilled exponents. A method of
recording piano performance directly onto a computer
is described, together with results obtained from
such recordings of concert pianists. These bear
on the hierarchic structure of timing, expressive
freedom of timing and its reproducibility in
successive performances.

INTRODUCTION

The basic idea of motor programming is that a sequence of movements can be
coordinated in advance of their execution to form a single complex action.
An extension of this idea is that a large-scale performance may be organized as a sequence of superordinate actions; another extension is that the
principle of coordination may apply recursively, so that a motor program
constructs an intended performance as a hierarchy of units. Early
discussions of planned coordination can be found in Bryan & Harter (1899),
writing on receiving and transmitting morse, and in Book (1908) on typing.
The evidence was obtained by observing trainees over months of practice,
but derives mainly from their verbal reports. I shall show that more convincing evidence of motor programming was obtained in the 1930s, yet the
first major theoretical account of this mode of control came much later
with the seminal paper on serial order by Lashley (1951).

Following Lashley we should consider three basic functions of a motor program. First, that it can confer fluency on a movement sequence so that
the sequence unfolds at a fast rate, achieving its goals accurately and
with an economy of movement. Second, it can confer expressiveness, so
that the sequence acquires definite rhythms of timing and intensity, and
in dancing or gymnastics it may take on a quality of gracefulness. Third,
it has a generative flexibility and so can produce a performance appropriate
to its context for an indefinitely large variety of contexts. Clearly the
properties served by these functions will be fully manifest only in highly

---

*This research is supported by the SSRC.

developed skills: unskilled performance may show the rudiments of one or
other of these properties, while the unlearned, genetically programmed
actions found in animals are usually stereotyped or show limited flexibility.
Thus, if our aim is to understand the mechanisms of motor programming this
is best served by studying skilled performance, observing and interpreting
unskilled performance as approximations to, or simpler forms of this. The
study of language acquisition provides a good precedent for this argument.

Psychology like the physical sciences tries to design experiments so as to
observe a phenomenon in its simplest forms. As Newell (1973) and others
have pointed out, these methods are likely to be successful in proportion
to our ability to satisfy two conditions: that we can provide a good
description of the phenomenon in its natural manifestations, and that we
have a well established theory to guide us in producing the simplifications
that leave invariant the psychological properties of interest. But these
conditions are seldom met in the study of skill and many of the theoretical
concepts derived from research using laboratory tasks may have little
relevance to skilled performance, because the relation of laboratory to
real tasks is often tenuous and the time-scale of practice in the laboratory
is of a different order from that required to master real skills. It need
not, of course, devalue conventional laboratory research if its domain is
defined as mainly that of unskilled performance.

In current research on motor programming there appear to be two distinct
disciplines, both influenced in different ways by Lashley. One of these
examines performance on laboratory tasks involving single movements or
short movement sequences; it tends to adopt Lashley's concern with physiological explanation and to contrast a concept of motor program with a
cybernetic concept of feedback (Stelmach, 1976). Related to it is the work
on tracking, influenced more directly by Craik (1948), concerned with the
role of prediction in performance and with the information theoretic concept of limited channel capacity (Pew, 1974; Poulton, 1957). The other
discipline is dominated by the study of speech, an activity in which most
people reach a fairly high level of skill, and it seeks to develop
Lashley's speculations on the cognitive component of skill, regarding motor
programming as basically a cognitive activity and making free use of the
ideas of generative grammar (Clark & Clark, 1977). If my analysis is
correct there is no conflict between these disciplines; one is studying
relatively unskilled and the other skilled performance.

A difficulty arises only in attempting to extrapolate concepts from one
discipline to the other and this may not be symmetrical. Enough is known
about skilled performance (Shaffer, 1976) to suggest that the principles
of cybernetic and information theory can be adapted only to restricted
aspects of skill, but there is a better prospect that cognitive theory can
be utilized to describe unskilled performance. To prepare a case for this,
here is a brief sketch of skill acquisition:

In learning a new skill performance may take the form of a concatenation of
movements, one triggering the next, with continual tests against the stimulus input for the correctness or adequacy of each movement. Gradually,
and perhaps erratically with practice concatenation is replaced by program
control, such that superordinate elements come to represent and are able to
generate movement sequences. Eventually these elements may in turn be
generated by abstract procedures, so that in the fully mastered skill motor

programming becomes a cognitive exercise in problem solving on a continuous
input.

THEORETICAL FRAMEWORK

The main purpose of this paper is to survey recent research on piano performance, but it will be easier to interpret the findings if I first develop
a theoretical framework of motor programming. It is applicable to a wide
range of skills including speaking, typing, writing, drawing, dancing, as
well as playing music.

An extended skilled action starts with a plan that provides a set of goals
and gives an overall structure to the performance. A general description
of plans was given by Miller, Galanter & Pribram (1960); Clark & Clark
(1977) describe plans for language discourse and Sloboda (1979) and Shaffer
(1979) describe plans for playing music. A plan is an abstract homomorphism
of the performance, representing its essential structure. It does not
represent all the details of performance but allows these to be generated
or accessed as they are needed in the execution.

The plan is executed in a continually renewing succession of higher-order
units by a motor program, which may construct one or more intermediate
representations leading to output, adding the details necessary to specify
the movement sequence. This idea of using a hierarchy of abstract representations to construct performance from an intention is analogous to recent
proposals in artificial intelligence for programs that solve problems
(Sacerdoti, 1974). The motivations for constructing such programs are that
they enable more flexible problem solving and they produce solutions more
rapidly than programs that consider all the possible domain of information
in a single abstract space. Both these properties, speed and flexibility,
are relevant to skilled performance.

A prerequisite of motor programming is that an intended output can be
represented as a sequence of higher-order units. Such a representation is
compact and can be combined with the specifications of expressive features
that range over large segments of the performance. Because these units are
abstract they allow different derivations of motor command strings, so that
the commands are appropriate to their context. If the translation procedures called by the motor program can access in parallel the set of commands
coded in a single unit, then the rapid availability of the command information enables the high speeds observed in skilled performance (Shaffer,
1973).

The evidence from speech and typing suggests that motor programs in these
skills maintain at least two intermediate levels of representation of output (Fromkin, 1973; Garrett, 1975; Shaffer, 1973, 1976). The first of
these, generated from the input, represents the movement sequence as a
string of elements, marked in terms of higher-order units, together with a
marking of expressive features such as rhythm and intensity: I call this
the structural string. Each element in this string designates a motor
command and so the string can be used to generate a command string which
now specifies all the details of movement for a sequence of movements.
Again it is possible that translation from designating element to command
is context-sensitive, so that further flexibility of output can be introduced at this level in the program. This stage of translation is in any

case not a trivial one for it brings into the command string procedural information acquired through long practice of the skill. For instance, in piano playing the abstract instruction to play a particular note with a certain intensity and quality of legato must be translated into a motor command assigning a particular finger to go to a specific target location in keyboard space with an appropriate postural adjustment of hand and arm, and an acceleration of the finger to achieve the desired intensity and quality of key-stroke.

A motor command is a set of target specifications governing a complex movement. These are specifications of location in space, force and manner of movement. I shall conjecture that the motor program, as I conceive it, plays no further part in movement execution but relinquishes control to a peripheral computer in the cerebellar-spinal system. This system has built up and refined through years of practice the computational procedures for translating target commands into muscle contractions. I shall further conjecture that the major role of proprioceptive feedback, which elsewhere features so prominently in the discussion of movement control, is in constructing and maintaining the precision of these computations. The role may be as important in maintenance as in the original construction, for with disuse of a skill the movements lose some of their accuracy and economy. Similarly, with the loss of external feedback the specification of target may become degraded, as in the speech of people who become deaf.

The structural string in a motor program can represent the timing of movements as an abstract schedule. To translate this into action in real time the program must have access to some form of clock and must contain a timing mechanism which can activate motor commands at appropriate moments in time according to the schedule. In the study of musical performance this component takes on great prominence.

EARLIER RESEARCH ON MUSIC PERFORMANCE

There has indeed been little earlier research on playing music that is relevant to the discussion. This may not reflect lack of interest or temerity: until laboratory computers and suitable transducers became available it was difficult to obtain data on performance in a reasonably assimilable form, and we are still learning how to exploit the new technologies.

Some research on piano performance was carried out in the 1930s in Seashore's laboratory in Iowa (Seashore, 1938). By attaching balsa wood fins to the hammers inside the piano he was able to obtain a photographic record on continuously moving film of the hammer movements, giving him an analogue record of the timing and intensity of striking each key. He and his associates used this method to record the performances of concert pianists playing Beethoven and Chopin. Analyses of the data showed that these pianists used considerable rubato - variation in tempo - in the timing of notes, bars and phrases. Yet in a repeat performance of the piece these variations were reproduced with remarkable consistency and this provides the first major demonstration, alluded to earlier, of program control in skilled performance. There is no question that the variation was a planned use of expression and did not reflect merely variation of difficulty in the music, for Seashore showed that when asked the pianists could play the same music with quite good metrical timing.

Given this promising start two, more recent studies of keyboard performance
are disappointing in their scope. Povel (1977) used filtering techniques
to extract from gramophone recordings the note times of performances by
three harpsichordists of the first Prelude of Bach's 48 Preludes and Fugues.
This has a recurring rhythm in each bar (measure) and Povel averaged the
durations of corresponding notes over all bars, for each performer, to
obtain a timing profile for the bar. He showed that notes with the same
time value were played with different durations over the bar; also that the
three players produced different timing profiles. This is trivial since it
is understood in music that the performer is allowed expressive freedom of
timing, albeit to a degree that has varied in different periods of music.
Povel, however, outlines a more ambitious program, which is to study how
expressive features of timing are used for aesthetic effect.

Michon is associated with the study of timing through his work on repetitive
tapping (Michon, 1967). More recently (Michon, 1974) he obtained performances by music students of numerous repeats of the short theme and
variations in Satie's Vexations. He too used filtering techniques to get
his data from sound recordings on tape. Putting the timing data into a
factor analysis he obtained a result that certain groups of notes tended
to covary in duration as a function of the overall speed of performance.
This raises the intriguing possibility that rhythm in performance may not
be invariant with speed, but the method of analysis was too indirect to
allow this as a firm conclusion. It is of interest because one learns to
play a complex rhythmic figure by playing it slowly, counting the beats,
and gradually speeding the performance. If the rhythm changes with speed
is the effect perceived, by player or listener, or is it a failure of
motor programming? Eric Clarke, in Exeter, is currently investigating this
problem.

CURRENT RESEARCH ON PIANO PERFORMANCE

The research to be described is related most directly to that carried out
by Seashore and his associates and to my earlier work on typing. The work
on typing made use of a keyboard interfaced to a PDP-12 computer so that
typing output could be timed and then analysed by the computer. The
results on skilled typing are contained in a series of papers covering
different aspects of motor programming in this activity (Shaffer, 1973,
1975a & b, 1978). A further paper (Shaffer, 1976) reviewed some of this
work and considered the possibility of a general theory of motor programming covering typing, speech, playing music and other skills.

The apparatus to study piano playing, like that of Seashore, obtained direct
recordings from the action of the piano, but instead of an analogue record
the data are stored digitally in the computer. When a piano key is struck
it actuates a hammer, throwing it against a string, and also releases a
damper from that string allowing it to sound. When the key is released
the hammer falls from an intermediate to its resting position and the
damper returns to the string, stopping its sound. Using a pair of photocells for each hammer we can detect the onset of key movement, the moment
the hammer hits the string and the moment of key release. From the time
difference of hammer transit past the two photocells we can infer its
speed of movement and so reconstruct the intensity of activation, which
will be related to the dynamic, or loudness, of the sound produced (Shaffer,
1979). With further sensors for the foot pedals we can thus detect all the

activity at the interface of pianist and keyboard. What we do not have,
but which could be obtained from a filmic record, is information about
body movements and the assignment of fingering in a performance.

The activation of a photocell produces a brief signal that is fed to a
special circuit, which detects all such signals at any moment in time and
encodes these into 12-bit words, holds them in a buffer store and feeds
them into the computer. On receipt by the computer a word is assigned a
clock time and stored. Timing accuracy is of the order of a microsecond -
an accuracy needed not for the occurrence of events but for the estimation
of intensity.

Following a recording session the stored data are printed out as a listing
showing, for each note played, the time the string was struck, the time the
key was released, the derived time that the note was played, and the transit
time of the hammer between the photocells - inversely related to intensity.
This listing is then annotated to indicate the part, or voice, in which
each note occurs, the playing of notes in a simultaneous chord, the presence
of notated rests in the music, and the location of bar boundaries. When
the annotation is fed back into the computer a new listing is obtained
which now divides the performance into successive bars, separates the
notes for each voice and indicates chordal groups of notes. The derived
information about notes is now musically more meaningful. Note duration
is given as the time before it is replaced by the next note in the same
voice; note quality is given as the extent of overlap of these two notes,
such that legatissimo is positive overlap, legato is zero overlap and
staccato is negative overlap (i.e. the notes are discrete); note intensity
is estimated as the inverse of transit time.

The piano is a Bechstein grand maintained to a standard suitable for concert performance. The electronics introduced into the instrument in no
way affect its action or its sound. The pianists are mostly professional
musicians and some are internationally known concert pianists. The
penalty of studying the best pianists I can find is that I cannot always
choose in advance what they should play: often I have to discuss with
them which among the pieces they have recently practiced will be of use in
the research. In the remaining time I shall survey some of the results
obtained so far and indicate some of the data I have still to analyse. A
fuller account of the results will be published elsewhere.

The first performances I shall report were also the first ones obtained.
The pianist, Peter O'Brien, who is a very good sight-reader of music,
agreed to play spontaneously a piece directly from the score, without
preparation. The piece is a fugue from Bach's '48': it has four voices,
i.e. four melodic lines in counterpoint, and it lasts about 1½ minutes.
The pianist claimed he had not played this piece for many years.

On request he played the Fugue twice at its proper speed and once more
very slowly. In the last he had difficulty maintaining the rhythmic
pulse of the music and gradually drifted to a faster speed. Playing keyboard counterpoint raises a number of interesting points. The player is
required to achieve a tonal separation of the voices so that they can be
heard individually, and ideally it should sound as though four musicians
are playing, collaborating with each other but having some degree of
independence. So far on this point I have only looked at note intensities

in the slow performance. The graphs for the four voices show that there
was indeed a tonal separation, the voices with higher pitch being played
with greater intensity. This is not the most subtle way to play the
Fugue and with more practice on the piece he would doubtless have introduced more interplay of dominance between the voices. Certainly, at a
point in the music where two voices take a rest he anticipated this by
raising the intensity in the other voices.

Baroque music should be played at a fairly even tempo with moderate use of
accentual rubato. In the first two performances there was an acceleration
in the opening bars and a slowing in the closing bars; in between there
was a fluctuation in speed such that the duration of a four-bar phrase
ranged between 4.85 and 5.15 seconds. A hierarchic analysis of variance
was carried out on the central portion, identifying the durations of 15
phrases (P), 60 bars (B), 120 minim (half-note) beats (M) and 240 crotchet
(quarter-note) half beats (C). There were separate analyses for the two
performances and another comparing them. For hierarchic variables the
error term was taken as the variance at the next lower level. It is
instructive to look at the variance table:

Source	df	Performance 1 MS	F	Performance 2 MS	F	Both Perform MS	F
P	14	656.9	3.68	354.3	1.74	912.4	2.84
B/P	45	178.5	0.88	203.7	0.87	321.3	1.10
M/B/P	60	202.5	0.72	234.5	0.66	293.3	0.60
C/M/B/P	120	280.8		354.4		487.1	3.19
Replication,R	1					264	1.73
R X P	14					98.9	1.62
R X B/P	45					60.9	0.45
R X M/B/P	60					134.6	0.88
R X C/M/B/P	120					152.7	

Note that in the individual analyses the F ratios for bars-within-phrases
(B/P) and minims-within-bars (M/B/P) are less than 1, while in the comparison analysis the interactions of these terms with performance are less
than 1. Some of these ratios would be significant if referred to the left
tail of the F distribution, but it is a nice Catch-22 situation that if an
effect is significant in this tail then the independence assumption of the
test has been violated and, therefore, significance cannot be tested.
This will have to be rectified mathematically but the F ratio still provides a heuristic index of sequential constraint among the time intervals:
a ratio less than one indicates less variation in the timing of a unit
than one should expect from the error term. In hierarchic ratios it
indicates negative autocorrelation at one level induced by constraint on
timing at the level above; positive autocorrelation or, of course, genuine
differences in the timing of higher-level units will induce F ratios
greater than 1 (and we have to examine covariance to decide between these).

Thus, the pulse of the music seems to have been carried at the level of the
beat or the bar, or was perhaps hierarchically applied at both. We cannot

yet decide between these but we can note that within a performance the beat seemed to show the most constraint. Across performances, however, it is the bar that shows the smallest interaction with performance and this indicates that much of the detailed variation in bar timing was reproduced in the two performances, showing it to be systematic variation.

A similar inference of structural constraint can be made from the residual error terms. In the separate analyses this term is crotchets-within-minims (C/M/B/P) and in the joint analysis it is the interaction of this with performance. The latter is much smaller, showing that much of what appears as random variation in a performance is replicated across performances and hence is systematic. Taking the error term in the general analysis as an estimate of unclassifiable variation we obtain a standard deviation of 12.4 milliseconds for a mean crotchet duration of 312 ms. The ratio of these gives us a coefficient of variation of 4 per cent. The best subject observed by Michon (1967) in a task of regular tapping achieved a coefficient value of 3.2 per cent when the sequence was corrected for temporal drift. Seen from this viewpoint the precision in the piano playing is quite impressive, given the complexity of the music and that the performances were unprepared.

The score for the Fugue was on two pages of music. At the top of the second page all four voices move upwards in pitch and to accommodate this the bass stave, in this edition, changes, for a couple of bars, to a treble stave, thus requiring a translation of all the notes. In his first performance the pianist was briefly thrown by this translation and for about one and a half bars he made a series of note errors, two in the right hand and five in the left. What is important is that the errors were all harmonically acceptable and show that the pianist had established the harmonic structure at this point in the music and could improvise within this; also that in this interval the rhythm did not falter and the crotchet times showed no greater variation than elsewhere. All one notices in the sound recording is that he attempted (uncharacteristically) to alter one note in the left hand, which was actually correct but did not fit into his improvisation, and this produced an out of time note in that voice only. In playing music, maintaining the rhythm is of paramount importance and the result emphasizes a point made by Lashley (1951), that skilled movement is constructed on a rhythmic matrix.

The structure in musical performance, in timing, intensity and quality of touch, is beyond question, for one can hear this in any concert or recorded performance. What is interesting is the accuracy with which a performance can be reproduced and the implication this has for a theory of motor programming. If the pianist had not played the Fugue for many years we have to suppose either that he had a permanent storage of a plan containing a large number of very precise specifications, or that he was able to generate the motor program from his general knowledge of piano playing, building or reconstructing an interpretive plan as he went along. He would suppose the latter and he claims to have a poor memory for music, making him reliant on sight-reading: he also claims, and I hope to test this, that he usually improvises the fingering and may do it differently on successive performances.

In support of the generative concept I have a recording of a session in which another pianist, John Bryden, practiced at the piano a piece he had

not played or heard before, a Bagatelle by Beethoven. I have yet to
analyse this but one thing is clear from the recording session. With only
a quick glance through the music as preparation he was able to play it
straight through at sight, giving a fluent and musically acceptable performance at the proper speed, without error. All the information required
to construct the motor program was already available to him. What
occupied him for the rest of the session, leading to a more polished
performance, were matters of interpretation and details of shaping a
phrase, or giving the right prominence to one of the voices in the music.

Still on the theme of replication we can look next at recordings of John
Sloboda. He is a psychologist and also an excellent pianist, who came to
do an experiment of his own in my laboratory. In exchange for the
facilities he gave me performances of Bach, Mozart and Bartok, as well as
multiple performances of two of the miniature pieces he had written for
his experiment. These were melodies for the right hand only, the first
being a single three-bar phrase and the second having two four-bar
phrases. He played the first piece 5 times, the second piece 5 times, and
then the first piece another 5 times (actually 6 because he miscounted).

Given the rhythmic structure of the first piece it was only possible to
identify throughout the phrase the timing of bars and half-bars, i.e. the
accented beats. In a hierarchic analysis of variance the main effect of
bar duration had an F ratio of 0.48 (df = 2,3) and the interaction of bar
duration with performance had an F ratio of 0.67 (df = 18,27). Thus again
we see the consistent constraint of bar duration on its sub-intervals.
The residual error had a standard deviation of 11.1 ms and the mean
duration of half-bars was 900 ms, hence the coefficient of variation was
1 per cent. There was a slight but progressive drift towards faster
speeds across all the performances, but considering the 10 performances
in 2 groups of 5, the interaction of bar duration with group had an F
ratio of 0.32 (df = 2, 3), showing very close resemblances between the
groups even though performances of the other piece had intervened.

In the second piece the timing of bars, beats and half-beats were
identified in the first three bars of each phrase, the fourth bar containing a single note. In a hierarchic analysis of variance only phrase
duration showed constraint as a main effect, but the interaction of
performance with bars-within-phrases had an F ratio of 0.45 (df = 15,48)
and the interaction of performance with beats-within-bars had an F ratio
of 0.63 (df = 48,72), suggesting two levels of constraint on timing. The
standard deviation of residual error was 6.08 ms and mean half-beat
duration was 217 ms, giving a coefficient of variation of 2.8 per cent.
Performing an analysis of variance on note intensities to remove main
effects led to an estimated coefficient of variation of 6 per cent.

Despite the simplicity of the pieces they were played with rubato,
accurately reproduced across performances as the analyses show. An
attempt has been made to find prominence rules that will generate these
variations in timing (cf Sundberg & Lindblom, 1976). One basic rule
seems to apply recursively to different levels and it needs supplementing
by a context-sensitive rule at each level. The rule assigns greater
timing prominence to the beginning and end of a unit structure, and in
fact it would apply at the level of the whole set of performances, since
the very first performance started slowly and the very last (redundant)

performance ended slowly relative to the others. This exercise has
parallels in current work on the prosodies of speech (e.g. Lindblom, 1975;
Cutler & Isard, 1979).

Another feature of interest in Sloboda's performances is that although
nothing was specified he allowed exactly a bar's rest between the
successive performances. Michon (1976) following Fraisse has argued and
shown experimentally that unfilled pauses between significant events,
having no intrinsic structure are subjectively indeterminate in length.
Again this does not generalize to skilled performance: if he wishes the
skilled performer can time such pauses very accurately.

The last piece of evidence on replication is in some ways the most
impressive. It comes from performances by Margaret Gulley of the opening
pages of a Schubert sonata she was preparing for recital. In the character
of the music there was much greater variation of timing, both gradual and
sudden throughout the music, together with larger and more dramatic
changes in intensity, than had been observed earlier. The slowest bar took
more than twice as long as the fastest. Nevertheless, there was the same
degree of accuracy of reproduction in two successive performances as was
obtained by the others. Before discussing the significance of this it is
necessary to enter a reservation on reproduction. Concert pianists do
not usually attempt to plan performances in such detail that every aspect
of a performance is precisely fixed. They believe it important to leave
the details of expression to the mood of the moment and they expect to
adjust these to the acoustics of the piano and the hall. Giving me such
similar performances was perhaps a response to a slightly unusual situation.
Indeed, although the similarities of the Schubert performances were
statistically convincing the second differed systematically from the
first in the stronger accenting of a certain recurrent chord and, at one
point, in a progressively slower buildup to this chord. (I have since
heard Margaret Gulley give a different interpretation of the sonata in
recital and have new recordings to analyse of the opening pages).

Again, analyses of variance on different parts of these performances
showed hierarchic constraints, as indexed by the small F ratios, on the
timing of different units in the performance. So often do these small F
ratios turn up their significance cannot be in doubt. I have also been
able to look at the level of constraint depending upon the resemblance of
rhythm in the two hands.

What is the timing mechanism for these performances and what is represented
in the plan that enables such accurate reproduction of performance? I
have suggested that the structural representation in the motor program,
derived from the plan, contains an abstract timing schedule for movements
which is realized against an internal clock. The schedule may contain a
separate entry for each note but it is more likely that a timing pattern
is allocated to a group of notes containing a rhythmic figure. This is
how one learns to identify and play rhythms. More important, particularly
in the context of the Schubert performances, is how the timing is
modulated when there is a large amount of rubato. The variation could be
introduced into the schedule, but this is unlikely on two grounds. First,
it implies a large amount of computation in constructing the schedule
and, second, it denies the flexibility of expression from one performance
to another. I have data to analyse on multiple performances in which the

pianist has been asked to change the mood, in particular performances by
John Lill playing Beethoven and John Sloboda playing Mozart. Seashore,
also, showed that the pianist could on request leave out the rubato.

I suggest as an alternative that expressive features are marked abstractly
in the structural string, which take prominence indices that can change
from one occasion to another, as can decisions to translate prominence
into rubato or intensity. In the case of timing variation the easiest way
to implement this is to deform the output of the internal clock. In this
way a schedule for a metrical performance can be put through a gamut of
expressive changes with no new computation, and if the prominence indices
are left unchanged the expression will be reproduced.

Bearing on this conjecture are results on the performance of a Chopin
Study by Penelope Blackie. The Study is a sustained exercise in playing
different rhythms in each hand. Twice in each bar there is a rhythmic
figure in which the right hand plays three even notes while the left hand
plays four, known as the cross-rhythm of three against four. The pianist
had no difficulty playing this cross-rhythm and managed to combine this
with even greater rubato than was observed in the Schubert. She even
seemed able to let one hand play off the beat in relation to the other.
Playing or singing off the beat is a feature of jazz music and bel canto
opera singing, but in piano playing the performer plays both the off-beat
voice and its accompaniment. Mozart described playing in this way, but
in the classical style of playing the left hand kept a fairly metrical
pulse: combining rubato in both hands with a 'singing' voice in the
melody is a product of the romantic style.

Even though the pianist has an international reputation, I have to con-
vince the sceptic that the freedom in her performance is not merely making
the best of a motor incoordination. Graphs of the timing of individual
notes in each hand show that the rubato was structured recursively within
bars and four-bar phrases, and follows the rule described earlier. When
she chose she could play several bars at a stretch with perfectly even
timing; and having slowed at the end of a phrase she could return very
precisely to the tempo that preceded it. Graphs of note by note intensity
show that the right hand, carrying the melody, played with consistently
more weight than the left; also that both gradual and sudden changes in
intensity could be made independently by each hand. If the graphs of
timing and intensity are superimposed it is clear that these two variables
were independent of each other (Shaffer, 1979).

The focus of interest, however, is on the production of different rhythms
in each hand and the coordination of timing between them. A set of graphs
was drawn, one for each bar, plotting the actual timing of notes on the
X axis and their metrical timing for the same bar duration on the Y axis.
The coordinate intersections gave separate curves for each hand showing
a deformation of timing within the bar (in a metrical performance these
curves would lie on the diagonal through zero). If the hands were playing
the same rubato then even though they played their notes at different
times they should produce similar deformation curves, in which case the
best inference is that their timing was generated by a common underlying
clock. In many of the graphs the overlay of the two curves was almost
exact, but in other graphs the differences were quite large and these
were associated with asynchronies of the two hands at the beginning or end

of the bar.

The distributions of asynchrony for the first and third beats in each bar, i.e. the beats initiating a rhythmic figure of three against four, had a marked skew towards shorter times but long right tails. For the first beat the largest asynchrony was 150 ms and the median was 45 ms; for the third beat these figures were 90 ms and 25 ms, showing that there was more constraint in the middle than at the beginning of the bar. The amount of skew suggests that these were mixed distributions, showing a range from controlled synchrony to a 'singing' of one hand away from the other.

Since discrepancies between deformation curves for each hand were assoc-iated with beat asynchrony, new graphs were constructed on the intervals in which the hands moved out of and returned to synchrony. This time only the deformation curve for the left hand was drawn and this was used to generate from metrical assignments on the Y axis the predicted times for notes in the right hand. This led to sets of difference scores between predicted and observed note times and these now showed a simple pattern. Asynchrony was often initiated and resolved at a beat boundary, a delayed entry of the last note of a bar in one hand being compensated by a delayed entry of the first note of the next bar in the other hand. Sometimes the asynchrony was sustained for one or more bars, still being introduced and resolved at a bar boundary. In the asynchronous interval the notes in the right hand kept a proper division of the beat against the deformed time scale defined by the left hand. It is as though the movement commands for one hand were held in a delay line relative to the other hand, but both hands were playing their respective divisions of the beat against the time scale of an elastic clock.

Thus I conclude that the clock underlying skilled performance represents time continuously, so that small adjustments of timing are possible, and that it can be programmed to generate its output at a varying rate accord-ing to parameter values contained in the structural representation of motor output.

Conclusion

The last study indicates some of the dimensions in which an accomplished pianist can maintain independence between the two hands, and to these I could add the differences of legato touch and the logistics of hand and finger movement. I have also ignored the details of pedalling that were recorded in the performance. This and the other studies emphasize the precision with which a musician can realize a sustained and complex motor intention. A theory of motor programming should be able to describe skills at this level.

References

(1) W.F. Book: The Psychology of Skill. Missoula: Montana Press, 1908.
(2) W.L. Bryan and N. Harter: Studies on the telegraphic language.
    Psychological Review, 1899, 6, 345-375.
(3) H.H. Clark and E.V. Clark: Psychology and Language. New York:
    Harcourt Brace Jovanovich, 1977.
(4) K.J.W. Craik: Man as an element in a control system. British Journal
    of Psychology, 1948, 38, 142-148.

(5) A. Cutler and S.D. Isard: The production of prosody. In B. Butterworth
    (Ed.), Language Production. New York: Academic Press, 1979 (to appear).
(6) V.A. Fromkin (Ed.): Speech Errors as Linguistic Evidence. The Hague:
    Mouton, 1973.
(7) M.F. Garrett: The analysis of sentence production. In G. Bower (Ed.),
    The Psychology of Learning and Motivation, Vol. 9. New York:
    Academic Press, 1975.
(8) K.S. Lashley: The problem of serial order in behavior. In
    L. Jeffress (Ed.), Cerebral Mechanisms in Behavior. New York: Wiley,
    1951.
(9) B.E.F. Lindblom: Some temporal regularities of spoken Swedish. In
    G. Fant and M. Tatham (Eds.), Auditory Analysis and Perception of
    Speech. London: Academic Press, 1975.
(10) J.A. Michon: Timing in Temporal Tracking. Soesterberg, The Netherlands:
    Institute for Perception RVO-TNO, 1967.
(11) J.A. Michon: Programs and 'programs' for sequential patterns in motor
    behavior. Brain Research, 1974, 71, 413-424.
(12) J.A. Michon: Holes in the fabric of subjective time. Heymans Bulletin
    Psychologische Instituten R.U. Groningen, NR:76-HB-218EX, 1976.
(13) G.A. Miller, E. Galanter and K.H. Pribram: Plans and the Structure of
    Behavior. New York: Holt, 1960.
(14) A. Newell: You can't play 20 questions with nature and win. In
    W. Chase (Ed.), Visual Information Processing, New York: Academic
    Press, 1973.
(15) R.W. Pew: Human perceptual-motor performance. In B. Kantowitz (Ed.),
    Human Information Processing. Hillsdale, N.J.: Erlbaum, 1974.
(16) E.C. Poulton: On prediction in skilled movements. Psychological
    Bulletin, 1957, 54, 467-478.
(17) D-J. Povel: Temporal structure of performed music. Acta Psychologica,
    1977, 41, 309-320.
(18) E.D. Sacerdoti: Planning in a hierarchy of abstraction spaces.
    Artificial Intelligence, 1974, 5, 115-135.
(19) C.E. Seashore: Psychology of Music. New York: McGraw-Hill, 1938.
(20) L.H. Shaffer: Latency mechanisms in transcription. In S. Kornblum
    (Ed.), Attention and Performance IV. New York: Academic Press, 1973.
(21) L.H. Shaffer: Control processes in typing. Quarterly Journal of
    Experimental Psychology, 1975, 27, 419-432 (a).
(22) L.H. Shaffer: Multiple attention in continuous verbal tasks. In
    P. Rabbitt and S. Dornic (Eds.), Attention and Performance V.
    New York: Academic Press, 1975 (b).
(23) L.H. Shaffer: Intention and Performance. Psychological Review, 1976,
    83, 375-393.
(24) L.H. Shaffer: Timing in the motor programming of typing. Quarterly
    Journal of Experimental Psychology, 1978, 30, 333-345.
(25) L.H. Shaffer: Performance of a Chopin Study: a cognitive analysis,
    1979 (to appear).
(26) J.A. Sloboda: Music performance. In D. Deutsch (Ed.), Psychology of
    Music. New York: Academic Press, 1979 (to appear).
(27) G.E. Stelmach (Ed.): Motor Control. New York: Academic Press, 1976.
(28) J. Sundberg and B. Lindblom: Generative theories in language and
    music description. Cognition, 1976, 4, 99-122.

Tutorials in Motor Behavior
G.E. Stelmach and J. Requin (eds.)
© *North-Holland Publishing Company, 1980*

27

EXECUTION-TIME MOVEMENT CONTROL

David J. Ostry
Department of Psychology
McGill University
Montreal, Que.

The dynamic modification of motor programs is examined
in a study where typists copy words and non-words in
immediate and delayed response conditions. A
comparison of the immediate and delayed conditions
allows an evaluation of the extent to which movements
are organized before their execution. Differences are
found between words and non-words and between faster
and slower typists. But there are also marked
similarities and in no case does the benefit of
preparation extend beyond the first three or four
characters in a word. The findings are interpreted
as showing that motor processing is not completed
before the start of a movement and properties of
real-time organization are discussed.

INTRODUCTION

Almost everyone agrees that movements must be organized prior to their
execution. There must be decisions about target locations, about angles,
velocities and joint torques, about muscular activation patterns, and
postural adjustment (Saltzman, in press) and the decisions must be
coordinated over a set of movements. In general, this is what we mean
when we say that movements are programmed.

With the concept of programming we make the assumption that action is
organized prior to its execution. We assume that organization precedes
action and in the most general form of the programming view we assume
only this and make no further assumptions about how long before action
the organization needs to occur. In this general sense programming
could occur as naturally during a movement as it does in the latent
period prior to its onset.

While most of us probably agree that this is a reasonable way to
characterize programming, the fact of the matter is the concept of
programming has been bound up almost exclusively with only part of this
process, with the more restricted notion of motionless preparation or
preprogramming. The association was originally formed for quite
legitimate and sensible reasons, as part of the "central" theorists' need
to demonstrate movement control in the absence of peripheral feedback.
And while most theorists no longer intend that the term programming apply
only in the restricted sense of motionless preparation, programming
continues to be evaluated as if all movements were structured before any

action was possible.

There are two related problems in allowing motionless preparation to serve
as a model for central motor control. To begin with, it encourages the
use of principles of discrete movement as a basis for all motor theory,
thus producing a rather unnatural picture of motor function and probably
an unnecessary reduction as well. Further, it tolerates the assumption
that the structuring of movement can be understood in entirety in terms of
the motor processing that precedes the onset of action. The idea that
movements are structured and then executed is at best correct for only
certain types of movement. This is not to say that movements are not
centrally controlled but rather that not all central control occurs before
movement begins. Complex, continuous action would not be possible unless
central control were exercised both during a movement as well as during
its preparation.

The evidence presented here is based on the performance of a complex serial
skill--typewriting. The emphasis is not on typewriting itself; we assume
it is representative of many skills that involve complex motor coordination.
The typewriting studies point to the existence of execution-time processing.
They enable the identification of certain of its properties and suggest its
relation to prestructured sequences. But let us consider first the
principles of real-time organization.

The notion of execution-time movement control is in itself very general.
It provides a framework that allows motor control to begin in a latent
period prior to movement, to continue into execution and to remain of the
same character throughout. It recognizes that certain computations such
as postural adjustment or trajectory planning occur more frequently prior
to movement than during its ongoing control and that other computations
such as effector deployment or intermuscular coordination occur while the
limbs are actually in motion. While different computations occur at
different points in time and at different levels in a movement hierarchy,
a fact common to all of them is that the principles of motor processing
are not altered in the transition from motionless preparation to actual
movement. The same cannot be said of models based on prestructured motor
sequences.

The preprogramming concept is like a compiled language computer program
where movements are structured, capacity is allocated and high level macro
or conceptual code is translated prior to movement into a form that can
be implemented without modification at run-time. Such prestructuring
involves the reduction of a multi-level motor representation to a single
level run-time code which of necessity is written in the language of the
muscles. The consequence of theoretical importance is that once the
translation is effected then the program codes and their sequence are not
dynamically modifiable. Rather, once compiled they are executed directly
without further reference to higher level planning structures and without
substantial sensitivity even to low level execution-time contingencies.

Some actions may be organized in this manner, but overall, this is an
unnecessarily narrow view of what a program is and how it functions.
Consider some very general similarities in the principles of program
organization in motor systems and computers. A program is an
organization of basic procedures that are represented at several levels

of a processing hierarchy. There are many types of programs and one way
in which they differ is in terms of the point at which the final
translation to output code occurs. Some programs like the compiled
language computer program effect the translation in its entirety prior
to their execution. They trade flexibility for replicability and speed
of execution and where they appear in motor systems it is usually the
result of biological constraints on the complexity of nervous system
computation. Other programs such as production systems or table driven
computer programs remain modifiable even at run-time but do so at the cost
of substantially increasing the complexity of the program and its
management. If a program is to support continuous real-time movement
control, it must be modifiable at several levels in real-time and this
will be achieved only if the ultimate translation to low-level code is not
effected any sooner than is absolutely necessary.

A main difference between the notions of execution-time and prestructured
movement control lies in the levels of the processing structure at which
the program is modifiable at run-time. All programs or at least all
processing sequences are modifiable to some degree at execution. In the
least flexible cases such as the compiled language program or its
prestructured motor equivalent relatively few computations are modifiable
after the translation to output code and the modifications that can occur
affect at best only the order of computations within an otherwise fixed
structure. Once a program has been compiled a set of sequenced operations
is defined in a code that can directly control the effectors. The
processing sequence in such a program can be modified by the data or its
operating environment, but only in accordance with those options that are
provided for in the compiled code. So, for example, the processing
sequence in a compiled language computer program is modifiable in the
sense that the program can branch on the outcome of an operation and
subsequently follow a different processing sequence or it can execute a
calculation some number of times specified by the data, again modifying the
exact sequence of calculations in accordance with specific conditions in
the data. But with the exception of those contingencies that were
specified when the program was constructed, the processing sequence is
insensitive to other variations in the data.

This does not mean that modification in prestructured sequences has to be
restricted to the lowest levels in the hierarchy. This may be true in the
case of the motor systems of insects where adaptability is restricted to
properties of surfaces such as compliance or friction and to air-flow in
the case of flight. But there is no reason why more elaborate
prestructured systems could not achieve complex sequencing changes such as
those necessary for the modification of frame of reference or for obstacles,
or simply for changes in load or torque. However, even this degree of
flexibility will not eliminate the fact that prestructured systems are
basically constrained since the programs themselves are not modifiable
during movement. Whether a system is hardwired or simply programmed prior
to action, it will be sensitive during on-going movement only to those
variations that have been accounted for and worked out in detail before
the action begins.

In real-time systems the programs themselves must be dynamically
modifiable and probably at several levels of the representation. The
system must be able to amend plans during movement, to bring about arbitrary

change in direction and to abort ongoing movements altogether. It must be able to produce relatively precise changes in timing among many sets of muscles in separate limbs and to compensate dynamically for subtle or even gross postural change, for undershoots or overshoots, for incorrect damping or inaccurate timing. To achieve such flexibility the final translation to output code must not occur any sooner than is actually necessary to maintain the fluency of the movement. And this, of course, is a principle difference between real-time and prestructured systems.

The capacity for the dynamic modification of motor representations implicates feedback in an account of central motor function. A real-time system would not exist without information about its operating environment. But the need for sensory information does not require of a system that it function as an automaton, driven strictly on the basis of sensory feedback. Quite to the contrary, if a system is to be sensitive to the consequences of its actions it must of course be able to utilize feedback at many levels of the representation and must have central control mechanisms whose models and programs can be modified while the limbs are in motion, both as a result of variations in its own behavior and that of the environment.

On the basis of the data presented below it will be argued that in a real-time system dynamic flexibility is achieved by more or less minimizing the number and complexity of movements over which control at execution is extended at any given time. In this context the concept of a motor output span will be introduced, a number of responses that can be organized together as an output grouping either in preparation for or during a movement. A relatively restricted span of control will be shown to function in real-time and to account for the complex serial coordinations in typewriting. Before turning to that evidence we will consider certain limitations on the notion of programming as a characterization of motor processing.

We have thus far considered some general principles that are shared by motor programs and programs that are used in computing devices. We have seen that the level and timing of program modification is a basis on which we can distinguish real-time and prestructured views of movement control. However, in two important respects programs in computers are very unlike what we would expect of programs in a motor system.

The first of these problems concerns the exactness of the relation among the levels of the processing structure; the second concerns the independence of the individual instructions. Consider the simplest case. When a compiled language computer program is to be executed a translation program reduces the original multi-level representation to a single uniform code, which in the case of motor systems would be used to drive the muscles. The task is accomplished by what is essentially a one to one mapping process where every operation that is represented at higher levels in the processing structure is simply worked out in greater detail at the lower levels through a series of identity preserving re-write rules.

Several writers have argued against this sort of formulation because they felt that the relation among the levels in a motor hierarchy was less rigidly defined than would for instance be the case if we were to model motor processing on analogy to computer programs (e.g., Greene, 1972).The spirit of their proposals is that the levels in motor processing be viewed more like those of a corporate hierarchy where the flow of control is achieved by instructions of a very general sort and where each level in the hierarchy maintains virtually independent control over the details of its internal operations and the means by which its goals are achieved. With this reformulation the rigid mapping rules implied by a strict interpretation of the term programming could be eliminated in favour of a system in which the subsystems in a multi-leveled structure address similar problems but in different ways and communicate by passing only that information which is necessary for incorporation in another level's autonomous function.

A second and somewhat related problem with the notion of programming is that in the final analysis each instruction in a real program is executed almost independently of the others. This is almost certainly not the case in motor systems. Skill in any complex movement is not simply the activation of a preestablished representation one movement at a time but the ability to establish and modify the timing of effectors at output, to adjust the timing and trajectory of each relative to the others in such a way as to achieve coordinated movement.

The studies of typewriting performance that are reported here were conducted in my laboratory by Steven Hartwell. In addition to providing evidence for real-time processing in a complex skill, they enable to estimation of its extent, that is, they allow us to specify the number of responses that can be organized together during movement, a motor output span, or span of ongoing control and they additionally provide evidence regarding changes in real-time structure as a function of level of skill. In these experiments typists copy either single words or random letter strings. In all cases performance is assessed in terms of initial latencies and inter-response times for correctly typed words. The variable of interest is the pattern of inter-response times over successive characters as a function of word length.

II. Experiment

The organization of motor processing should be reflected in the latency to initiate a complex movement and in the timing of the actual response. If all movements in a typewriting response were structured before any of them were executed, the time needed for preparation would increase with the complexity of the sequence being programmed and presumably with word length measured in characters. The pattern of inter-response times would be indifferent to all features of the preparation process but would nevertheless reflect the unity of the program. If, on the other hand, motor processing were achieved entirely at execution, the latency to initiate an action would be independent of differences in the complexity of the response. The latency to the first character would be independent of the number of characters to be executed, and more important, inter-response times would be sensitive to the nature of the ongoing motor processing. It should be clear from their pattern that the coordination of movements does not extend over the entire output sequence and it should be possible to estimate the extent or span of ongoing motor control.

Method

An IBM 2741 terminal, interfaced to a PDP-11/34 was used for testing. A Tektronix video screen displayed the test items in upper case and

generated audio signals for response initiation. All response times were
measured with one msec accuracy. Twelve students whose typing speeds
ranged from 33 to 88 wpm on prose served as subjects. All followed
standard finger-key assignments.

The stimuli,which were either words or non-words, were presented one at a
time in either an immediate or a delayed response condition. A separate
block of trials was devoted to each of the four conditions (word immediate,
word delayed, non-word immediate, non-word delayed) with the order of
blocks balanced over subjects by means of a Williams square. In the
immediate response conditions each test item was accompanied at presentation
by an auditory signal to respond. In the delayed conditions, the response
signal lagged the stimulus item by one second.

Typists were instructed to begin preparing their response when an item
appeared on the screen and to begin typing as soon as they could after the
auditory signal, while maintaining as low an error rate as possible. The
time from the response signal to the first key press and the time intervals
between successive key strokes were recorded. Each subject provided median
inter-response times, based on a complete set of correctly typed items, at
each character position and all word lengths in each of the four conditions.

The stimulus set varied in length from three to seven characters and in
total there were 64 items tested at each word length. The set of word
stimuli was selected to balance for hand movements and for word and digraph
frequencies. At each word length all possible patterns of hand alternation
and repetition were tested. There are four such patterns at word length
3, eight at length 4, 16 at length 5, etc. Complete sets of 64 items were
obtained by testing each movement sequence a number of times, with
different words used for each test of a particular pattern. The
proportion of high frequency words was equal at all word lengths. High
frequency digraphs occurred equally often at all character positions and
at all word lengths. No item required the repetition of the same finger
for two successive keys.

The set of non-words was constructed by taking the keyboard mirror image
of each of the characters in every test word. Kwh corresponded to dog,
and qiwqsi to people. Thus word and non-word conditions were exactly
balanced for hand movements except that one was the mirror image of the
other. In cases where the corresponding key on the opposite hand was a
non-alphabetic character, the nearest appropriate key was substituted
while observing the restriction that no two successive characters were to
be typed with the same finger of a single hand.

The order of presentation of items was separately randomized for each
subject in each of the four blocks. Items that were typed incorrectly
were replaced at random in the stimulus file and re-presented later in
the block.

Results

Two analyses of the data evaluated differences in performance with
increasing word length. One tested initial latencies, the other inter-
response times excluding the initial latency. Error rates were obtained
for each subject; they ranged from .06 to .10, with an average of .07, but

there was no relation between average typing speed and the observed error
rates ($\underline{r}$=-.03). Error rates also varied over the four conditions, averaging .06, .07, .08, .08 for word immediate, word delayed, non-word immediate,
and non-word delayed, respectively.

Initial Latency Analyses

The initial latencies were evaluated as a function word length in
characters. They were considerably longer than inter-response times and
increased modestly with differences in word length. The values obtained
for slope estimates were 2.8, 3.8. 6.7, and 3.8 msec per character for
conditions word immediate, word delayed, non-word immediate and non-word
delayed, with $\underline{r}^2$=.39, .90, .33, .61, respectively.

Over all, initial latencies were greater for non-words than for words (651
vs. 514 msec) ($\underline{F}$(1,11) 111.24, $\underline{p}$<.01) and for immediate than for delayed
responses (787 vs. 378 msec) ($\underline{F}$(1,11) 94.61,$\underline{p}$<.01). These factors interacted ($\underline{F}$(1,11) 5.21,$\underline{p}$<.05), such that the difference between words and
non-words was greater in the immediate response condition than in the de-
layed condition (184 vs. 88 msec).

Inter-Response Time Analyses

Inter-response times were partitioned with respect to word length, and
separate analyses were conducted for the word and non-word conditions. For
the purposes of these analyses, the subjects were divided into two groups
on the basis of their average inter-response times. The overall average
for the faster group was 148 msec per character and for the slower group,
236 msec per character.

The patterns of inter-response times are shown in Figures 1 (words) and
2 (non-words) for each word length separately. Each panel displays the
latency profiles of the two groups of typists in both the immediate and
delayed response conditions. There were differences associated with response delay and typing skill, but there were also marked similarities
across conditions. In general, the initial latency was followed by a re-
latively short interval from character $\underline{1}$ to $\underline{2}$. Performance slowed in the
interval from character $\underline{2}$ to $\underline{3}$ and again from character $\underline{3}$ to $\underline{4}$ and then
progressively speeded up as fewer characters remained in the word. The
duration of the longest latency increased with word length. And for words
five characters or longer the final inter-response time was essentially
independent of the number of characters that had been copied.

Except at word lengths $\underline{3}$ and $\underline{4}$, the pattern of short latencies at the beginning and the end of the word and slower performance in the middle was
obtained for all typists in both groups and at all word lengths as well.
At the two shorter word lengths performance began rapidly and progressively
slowed towards the end of the word. Similar patterns have also been obtained by Sternberg, Monsell, Knoll, and Wright (1978) for non-words in a
delayed response condition and by Shaffer and Hardwick (1970) for both
words and non-words in continuous text.

<u>Words</u>. Response timing for words differed as a function of skill. Both
the slowing towards mid-word and the speeding at the end of the word were
less pronounced for faster typists. The two groups also responded somewhat differently to the opportunity for sequence preparation afforded by
the response delay. Slower typists seemed to take some advantage of the
delay interval to prepare their response, as indicated by their more rapid

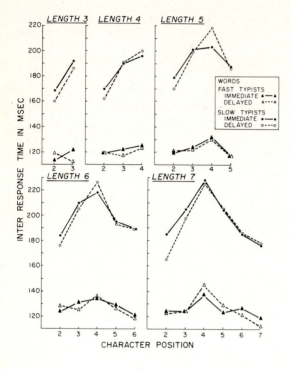

Figure 1

Mean inter-response
times in msec for
words, with initial
latencies excluded.
The individual data
points give the
inter-response time
for the interval
preceding the
specified character.
Standard errors
(averaged over the
five word lengths)
were 2.16 and 3.18
msec for faster and
slower typists
respectively.

performance over the first character positions in the delayed condition.
There was no indication of this for faster typists, whose latency profiles
for the immediate and delayed conditions were essentially identical.
However, even in the case of the slower group, preparation during the
response delay extended at best to the first two characters in a word.

ANOVA tested for differences in performance as a function of response delay
for each word length individually. With initial latencies excluded from
the analysis, faster typists were not found to benefit from the delay
interval, though overall differences in inter-response times were themselves
reliable at all word lengths but <u>6</u>, showing that the timing of performance
had changed over word length. At length <u>3</u> there was some indication that
the delay interval was being used for response preparation. The typical
pattern of slowing over the early character positions was obtained in the
immediate response condition but changed to a monotonically decreasing
function when the response delay was added ($\underline{F}(1,5)=10.67,\underline{p}<.05$).

Slower typists produced somewhat different latency profiles in the two response conditions; their performance was more rapid over the first character positions with a delayed response. However the differences observed for slower typists were reliable by Tukey contrasts only at word length $\underline{7}$, and even there, only at the first and second letter positions ($q=5.62$, $\underline{p} < .05$ at character position $\underline{2}$). But, like faster typists, overall differences in inter-response times were themselves reliable at all

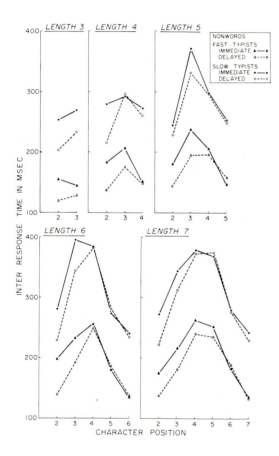

Figure 2

Mean inter-response times in msec for non-words, with initial latencies excluded. Standard errors (averaged over the five non-word lengths) were 5.24 and 8.42 msec for faster and slower typists respectively.

word lengths, indicating a change in performance over the length of a word.

Non-words. A different pattern emerges from an analysis of the non-word data. Overall, performance was much slower than when typists copied words. Here again the two groups differed as a function of skill. The slowing at mid-word was greatly accentuated in the slower group and the delay interval now favoured the faster group of typists.

Slower typists' performance in the delayed condition was more rapid than in the immediate. But the difference extended only to the second letter position and in one case to the third (q=6.67, $\underline{p}$ < .05; q=6.24, $\underline{p}$ < .05; q=9.62, $\underline{p}$ < .01 for word lengths 4, 5, and 7 at character position 2 and q=5.96, $\underline{p}$ < .05 for word length 7 at character position 3). At word length 6 the advantage to the delayed condition was not reliable by post-hoc tests (q=4.88).

The faster typists were likewise more rapid in the delayed condition but the advantage of the response delay extended further in the word than was the case with slower typists. Differences between immediate and delayed response conditions were reliable at both the second and third letter positions at word lengths 4, 5, 6, and 7 for the faster group (q=8.47, $\underline{p}$ < .01; q=7.33, $\underline{p}$ < .01; q=7.54, $\underline{p}$ < .01; q=7.69, $\underline{p}$ < .01 for differences at letter position 2 at word lengths 4 through 7 and q=5.52, $\underline{p}$ < .05; q=8.32, $\underline{p}$ < .01; q=5.24, $\underline{p}$ < .05; q=7.28, $\underline{p}$ < .01 for differences at letter position 3, again at word lengths 4 through 7). While varying degrees of sequence preparation were thus recorded for fast and slow typists in both word and non-word conditions, the differences attributable to the response delay never extended beyond the peak of the latency function in the middle of the word.

Discussion

In the introduction I outlined very generally the features that would be necessary if a system were to support real-time behavior. I concentrated on a multi-level processing structure whose models and programs could be dynamically updated. I also argued that a reasonable way to achieve modifiability at execution would be to restrict the number of responses that get organized together and during this organization, to maintain distinct and separate representations at each of the processing levels for as long as possible. We can now consider how the performance of typists bears on this account of organization and modifiability of motor processing.

The pattern of typewriting performance suggests that motor structuring is not completed until well into execution. We have seen that typists copy in bursts that do not correspond in any simple way to a unitary response program and this probably indicates that all movements are not organized together at any one time. The motor organization of one response burst probably begins in the latent period prior to movement. But as control is only exercised over a few characters at a time the continuity of action must be provided for during movement.

The regular pattern of speeding and slowing suggests that typewriting responses are not executed independently. Several real-time processes could generate such a pattern but for the present I want to concentrate on one of these, a system where actions are organized in small output groupings and where the timing of each response is adjusted relative to the others. We can think of this small set of movements that are organized

together as a motor output span. With longer words we can see that perhaps the first three or four characters are organized as a group, as are
the three or four from mid-word to the end.

The temporal pattern of the initial grouping seems to reflect the regular
use of a less than optimal timing strategy. Speed at the second letter
position seems to be gained at the cost of a progressive loss of speed
over the next several characters and this pattern persists until very high
typing speeds are achieved (Ostry, 1978). The performance of the entire
output grouping bears the mark of the particular strategy that is adopted.
And there is no reason to assume that the strategy will guarantee the
smooth execution of one instruction after another as for example a literal
interpretation of the programming analogy might expect.

The speeding from mid-word is probably what we would assume to be the
characteristic temporal pattern of a rationally organized output group.
The first response in the set are executed slowly, much in the same way
as spoken words are at times produced slowly and hesitantly as an individual begins to speak. Then, as better coordination is achieved within
the sequence, successive responses can be executed both more rapidly
and with greater ease. Skill in typewriting as in speech production is
evident in the ability to assemble responses efficiently at relatively
high speeds in real-time. It is the ability to maintain phrasing through
changes in timing and effector trajectory and to plan the course of subsequent movements without undue hesitation.

There are relatively few constraints on the temporal pattern of output
though two in particular are worthy of consideration. One is a restriction on the use of those timing and trajectory combinations that will
not enable sufficiently accurate performance. Strategies that emphasize
maximum speed or fail to account adequately for reactive forces will
generally fall into this category. The second restriction results from
the composition of the individual motor span. Membership in a particular
output group is at least in part established on the basis of non-local
considerations such as the stress pattern, the syllable structure, the
rhythm of the movement, or possibly to optimize the motor advantage afforded by automatized sequences such as spacing. It is probably only in the
absence of these higher level grouping strategies that the particular motor
span will be as large as its limit.

The non-local input to the establishment of a motor grouping should not be
taken to imply a unidirectional translation. Nor should the use of the
term span prompt a picture of a single level processor that is the final
link in a serial output chain. To achieve coordinated movement, the output group must at very least encompass sufficient processing power to
effect changes in timing and velocities, in postural adjustment, muscle
torque, and movement trajectory, and all in real-time. The cooperative
adjustment of timings and trajectories will require the capacity for dynamic reorganization at several levels of the processing structure. And
such a mechanism would function optimally if the translation to output
were effected no sooner than necessary to maintain coordination within
the output group. Higher level planning and decision processes are also
probably capable of real-time intervention but the specific processes that
cooperate in this type of control and the exact nature of their interaction are yet largely unspecified.

Consider next what takes place when typists are given an enforced delay in which to organize their response. We find of course that the extent to which they benefit from the delay depends on their typewriting skill and on the composition of the material. But we also find that the delay in itself does not eliminate the modulated timing pattern. If the timing effects had been due to either incomplete perceptual analysis or to insufficient opportunity for the organization of the motor response, then the extended delay should have produced uniformity of timing or some other marked change in the temporal pattern. The very persistence of grouped timing seems to force the conclusion that the organization of movement is ordinarily associated with on-going behavior.

By examining the ways in which faster and slower typists use the response delay we find that preparation prior to movement is more a strategy employed by the operator than an inviolable basis of motor organization. If prestructuring were the basis of movement control we should probably expect more of it for skilled than for non-skilled individuals. We should surely expect evidence of it when words are used as stimuli and we should likewise expect it to be evident first at the shortest word lengths. We do find evidence of prestructuring in the case of non-words and more of it for skilled than for non-skilled typists. But we also find quite the opposite when we examine the timing patterns of words and in fact if any consistent advantage at all is detected it is found at longer rather than at shorter word lengths and for non-skilled rather than skilled typists. The lack of consistency makes it difficult to argue that prestructuring is anything more than a strategy for motor timing.

Acknowledgments

This work was supported by the National Sciences and Engineering Research Council of Canada grant A7053.

References

[1] Greene, P.H., Problems of organization of motor systems. In R. Rosen & F. Snell (Eds.). Progress in theoretical biology (Vol. 2) New York: Academic Press, 1972.

[2] Ostry, D.J., Organization in real-time. Paper presented at the Psychonomics Society, San Antonio, Texas, November, 1978.

[3] Saltzman, E. Levels of sensorimotor representation. Journal of Mathematical Psychology, in press.

[4] Shaffer, L.H., & Hardwick, J. The basis of transcription skill. Journal of Experimental Psychology, 1970, 84, 424-440.

[5] Sternberg, S., Monsell, S., Knoll, R.L., & Wright, C.E. The latency and duration of rapid movement sequences: Comparisons of speech and typewriting. In G.E. Stelmach (Ed.), Information processing in motor control and learning. New York: Academic Press, 1978.

Tutorials in Motor Behavior
G.E. Stelmach and J. Requin (eds.)
© *North-Holland Publishing Company, 1980*

28

THE LONG AND SHORT OF TIMING IN RESPONSE SEQUENCES[1]

Alan M. Wing

Medical Research Council Applied Psychology Unit,
15, Chaucer Road, Cambridge, CB2 2EF, England.

This chapter is concerned with psychological processes underlying the timing of sequences of discrete motor responses. The continuation paradigm for the study of repetitive responding is described and a two-process model of the variation observed in self-paced interresponse intervals is reviewed. The model ascribes departures from periodic responding to the imprecision of a hypothetical timekeeper and to temporal "noise" in the execution of motor responses triggered by the timekeeper. Studies that throw light on the component processes of the model are discussed. The relevance of the model to the coordination of different phases of movement and to rhythm is shown.

1.   Introduction.

For coordinated movement the appropriate muscle or muscle group must be chosen, the degree of activity in terms of motor unit recruitment and firing rate must be selected, and the times of onset and offset of activity need to be specified. These have been referred to as the spatial, quantitative and temporal aspects of motor control (DeLong, 1971). This chapter takes as its topic the nature of temporal control and focuses on variability in timing in sequences of responses. With the aim of minimising the information processing demands imposed by the spatial and quantitative aspects of motor control, the tasks used in its study are usually based on simple repetitive movements. Nonetheless I hope those with interests in complex skills will bear with me since I believe the theoretical framework and the methods of analysis that I discuss are appropriate to the timing of movement in skills in general.

2.   The continuation paradigm.

Nearly a hundred years ago L.T.Stevens (1886) developed what has proved to be a very powerful technique for studying the timing of interresponse intervals (IRIs). On each trial a metronome was set to give a fixed-interval beat. Subjects were instructed to synchronize Morse key-tap responses with the metronome clicks. When the IRI of interest was established, the experimenter stopped the metronome and started a smoked-drum kymograph that recorded times of responses. Without pause, subjects continued to reproduce the same

interval repeatedly for another minute or so.   These
continuation IRIs were the data of interest.   The
synchronization phase of each trial existed only to provide
experimental control over response rate.   A schematic
representation of the paradigm is given in Figure 1.

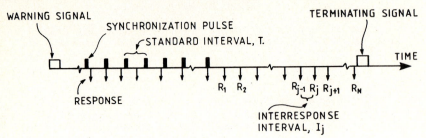

FIGURE 1. The continuation paradigm.

   Though it was not the main focus of his work, Stevens
commented that there was a remarkable manner of variation in
the IRIs produced by subjects when tapping without the aid of
the metronome.   He stated that there was a rapid alternation or
zig-zag in the length of immediately successive IRIs and he
attributed this to a correction process.   Specifically he
assumed that any discrepancy between an IRI just produced and
the remembered standard is used, with sign reversed, as a basis
for adjusting the next IRI.   As sources for the discrepancy
Stevens hinted at a distinction between peripheral and central
sources of variation in timing.   He wrote "the hand (or perhaps
the will during the interval) cannot be accurately true" to the
standard[2].   In the next section I review a model in which the
execution of the hand movement may be identified with one
process and the controlled delay introduced by the "will" may
be identified with another, separate process.   Assuming delays
in each process are liable to independent variation, I show how
the model predicts a degree of alternation in the length of
successive IRIs without recourse to a correction process.   In
the fourth and fifth sections of the chapter I consider the
nature of the two processes in more detail.

3.   The two-process model for response timing.

   The model for self-paced responding shown in Figure 2
(Wing, 1973;   Wing and Kristofferson, 1973) recognises that
departures from periodic responding may arise from imprecision
in a hypothetical timekeeper and from temporal "noise" in the
execution of responses triggered by the timekeeper.   At time
intervals C the timekeeper emits pulses each of which initiates
a motor response.   A motor output delay D intervenes between
the initiation and occurrence of the overt response R.   Each
IRI is the sum of a timekeeper interval plus the difference in
motor delays associated with the responses that initiate and
terminate the IRI:

$$I_j = C_j + D_j - D_{j-1}$$

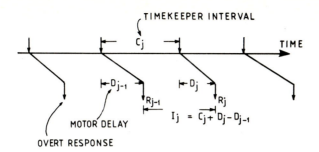

FIGURE 2. The two-process model for response timing.

Even if no active correction process is assumed, this model predicts statistical dependence among IRIs. Specifically, the model predicts that in a sequence of responses successive IRIs will be negatively correlated. To show this we write the covariance between pairs of IRIs in terms of the component delays:

$$\text{cov}(I_j I_{j-k}) = \text{cov}\{(C_j + D_j - D_{j-1})(C_{j-k} + D_{j-k} - D_{j-k-1})\}.$$

By the distributive property of covariances and assuming independence of timekeeper intervals and motor delays, so that terms involving the covariance of C with D are zero:

$$\text{cov}(I_j I_{j-k}) = \text{cov}(C_j C_{j-k}) + \text{cov}(D_j D_{j-k}) + \text{cov}(D_{j-1} D_{j-k-1})$$
$$- \text{cov}(D_j D_{j-k-1}) - \text{cov}(D_{j-1} D_{j-k}).$$

If it is assumed that the timekeeper intervals and motor delays are sequences of independent random variables, the terms $\text{cov}(C_j C_{j-k})$, $\text{cov}(D_j D_{j-k})$ are zero for all j,k except k=0.

When k is zero, we have the covariance of the random variable with itself which is the variance. Thus:

$$\text{cov}(I_j I_j) = \text{var}(I) = \text{var}(C) + 2\text{var}(D)$$

$$\text{cov}(I_j I_{j-1}) = -\text{var}(D)$$

$$\text{cov}(I_j I_{j-k}) = 0, \qquad k>1.$$

The correlation between adjacent IRIs is obtained by dividing $\text{cov}(I_j I_{j-1})$ by $\text{cov}(I_j I_j)$. Thus:

$$\text{cor}(I_j I_{j-1}) = -1/\{2 + \text{var}(C)/\text{var}(D)\}.$$

IRIs that don't share a response as common boundary (ie IRIs separated by one or more intervening IRIs) are uncorrelated. The negative sign of the correlation between adjacent IRIs means that if an IRI is by chance shorter than

average, the next one will tend to be longer than average and
vice versa. Successive IRIs will alternate about the average
more often than would be expected in a purely random sequence.
This is in qualitative agreement with Stevens' data although
our interpretation is very different from his. The magnitude
of the negative correlation is a function of the relative
variances of timekeeper intervals and of motor delays. In the
case of a completely periodic timekeeper (which would imply
that any IRI variance is entirely due to motor variance) the
correlation is minus one half. The other limiting value of
zero is approached as motor variance becomes much smaller than
timekeeper variance.

Correlation data from four subjects, run in a continuation
paradigm very similar to that of Stevens, may be found in Wing
and Kristofferson (1973, Experiment A). We tested the
correlation prediction for adjacent IRIs using the lag one
autocorrelation, $p_I(1)$. This is equivalent to $\mathrm{cor}(I_j I_{j-1})$ taken

over all j since the sequences of self-paced IRIs are samples
from a stationary process under the model[3]. For IRIs between
180 and 400 msec, averaged estimates of lag one autocorrelation
were significantly less than zero and lay between -.15 and
-.30. This is within the range predicted by the two-process
model.

The two expressions for var(I) and $\mathrm{cov}(I_j I_{j-1})$ involve just

two unknowns. They can thus be rearranged to give expressions
for the variance of timekeeper intervals and motor delays:

$$\mathrm{var}(C) = \mathrm{var}(I) + 2\mathrm{cov}(I_j I_{j-1})$$

$$\mathrm{var}(D) = -\mathrm{cov}(I_j I_{j-1})$$

Our estimates of timekeeper variance averaged over the four
subjects ranged from a low value of 19 msec2 (for IRIs of 180
msec) upto 67 msec2 (for IRIs of 350 msec). Corresponding
estimates of motor variance were 17 and 24 msec2 respectively.
The shorter IRIs are probably more characteristic of the
response intervals occurring in commonly used motor skills.
For motor skills in general therefore it would seem reasonable
to suppose that motor variance is at least as important as
timekeeper variance in determining the statistical properties
of the IRIs.

3.1 Correction of timing errors.

Stevens suggested that when an IRI differs from the
remembered standard the target for the next interval is set at
a value deviating from the standard by the same amount but with
opposite sign. Such corrections would keep responses in phase
with an external pacing stimulus for example during
synchronisation (see the discussion of the ideal linear
predictor in section 5; also Fraisse and Voillaume, 1971;
Voillaume, 1971). However, there is no requirement to persist
with such corrections during self-paced responding when the
external pacing stimulus has been discontinued.

I have run an experiment, based on the continuation
paradigm, that was designed to examine the corrections, if any,
that people make to IRI timing errors (Wing, 1977a).
Finger-tap responses were defined by contact of the index
finger with a touch-plate. On each trial the standard interval
was 350, 500 or 650 msec. Subjects wore earphones and after
every response there was a brief auditory pulse that appeared
to be simultaneous with the response. On a randomly selected
response in the self-paced phase a small perturbation was
applied to the normal delay between response and auditory
pulse, (see Figure 3). Since no feedback paths are specified
in the two-process model, we might expect no effect of this

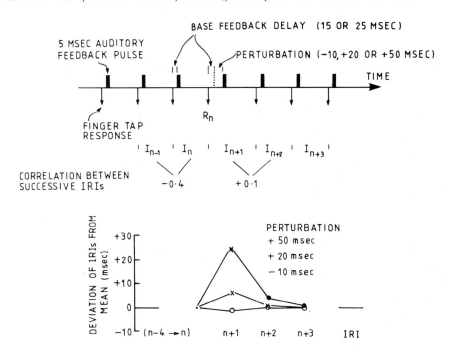

FIGURE 3. Perturbation of auditory feedback delay. (Average
          data from 3 subjects, 8 sessions of 72 trials.)

manipulation of feedback delay. In fact, though not as large
as the perturbation, effects in the direction of the
perturbation were observed on the mean of the next one or two
IRIs.

    In terms of intervals between feedback pulses, a change in
length of one interval (caused by the experimenter) resulted in
a change in length of the same sign in the next interval or
intervals. Stevens' interpretation of the alternation of
successive intervals that would lead us to predict a change of
opposite sign to the perturbation is therefore not supported.
Nonetheless the result indicates a role for feedback monitoring

processes in response timing. Although feedback is not treated
further in the present chapter (but see Wing, 1977a) it should
be noted that to the extent that subjects do make corrections
of the sort observed in this experiment there will be a
reduction of any negative correlation between successive IRIs.
The data of this experiment show a positive correlation between
IRIs after the perturbation (see Figure 3). This indicates
that the effects of correction processes can swamp the
two-process model prediction under certain circumstances.

4. Motor delays.

     In my presentation of the two-process model I defined the
motor delay as the time taken by response execution. Suppose
response execution may be decomposed into a set of functionally
distinct stages that are accessible to experimental
observation. Intervals could then be defined between
"responses" that represent activity at any particular stage.
The variances of such IRIs would reflect the variance of the
timekeeper and the variance of the truncated motor delay from
the timekeeper upto that stage. The covariance of adjacent
IRIs would provide an estimate of the variance of this
truncated motor delay[4]. If one could place a recording device
prior to all the stages that comprise the motor delay, motor
variance would be zero and adjacent intervals between responses
would be uncorrelated. The presence of correlation between
adjacent IRIs serves as an indicator of presence of motor
variance. It could therefore be used to demonstrate that a
particular observation point is within the set of stages that
comprise the motor delay[5].
     As an example of this point we will consider pilot data
that I collected to examine the possibility that motor variance
is entirely due to variability in the parameters of the
movement trajectory preceding the overt response. I recorded
the emg of the long flexors of the index finger simultaneously
with overt finger-tap responses. I ran myself through ten
sequences of approximately 20 responses with average IRI of 363
msec. The average delay from onset of flexor emg to the overt
tap was 55 msec. I found that the lag one autocorrelation of
intervals between overt responses was -.23, while that for
intervals defined between onsets of flexor emg activity was
-.10. We thus tentatively conclude that motor delays are
defined prior to muscle activity onset and that motor variance
is not just due to variation in the movement following muscle
activity onset[6]. As a more general point we might also note
that this technique allows one to determine the relative
contribution to motor variance of different sources of temporal
"noise".
     Different combinations of muscle and limb differ in their
mechanical characteristics and possibly in the prior
organisation required to effect coordinated movement. Any
particular combination is likely to have a characteristic
distribution of motor delays. An experiment is described in
Wing (1977b) in which finger-tap responses at intervals of 400
msec were made by four groups of ten subjects. Each group used
a different movement to bring the index finger into contact

with a touch-plate. The left side of Figure 4 shows the
estimated variances of timekeeper intervals and of motor delays

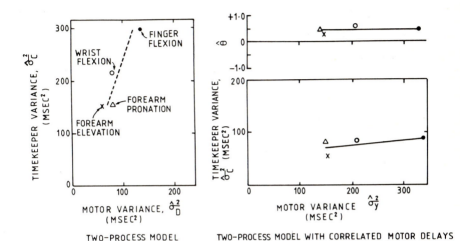

FIGURE 4. Effect of type of movement. (Average data from
         10 subjects per group, 10 trials per subject.)

for movements that involved raising and lowering the forearm
from the elbow, rotating the forearm, raising and lowering the
hand from the wrist, or raising and lowering the index finger.
Contrary to what one would expect, the nature of the movement
appears to have had more of an effect on timekeeper variance
than on motor variance.
    In section 3 we noted that although the two-process model
predicts negative covariance between adjacent IRIs, IRIs
separated by at least one interval should be uncorrelated.
However in this experiment I found that covariances of IRIs
separated by one or more IRIs were reliably less than zero.
Although these results might be taken as evidence against the
two-process model, another possibility is that they arise as a
consequence of violations in the assumptions of statistical
independence of timekeeper intervals or of motor delays.
Taking the latter view, I have shown (Wing, 1977b, 1979a) that
the form of the autocovariance function was consistent with a
three-parameter development of the original two-process model.
The additional parameter θ reflects a correlation between
successive motor delays.
    The lower right of Figure 4 shows revised estimates of the

variances as a result of fitting the three-parameter model. It
will be observed that the estimates of timekeeper interval
variance are now little affected by the type of response.
Estimates of θ, shown in the upper right of the figure, are
positive. While this result raises the question of what causes
the correlation between successive response delays it also
points to the importance of checking whether correlations
between intervals at lags greater than one are zero. If they
are not, one or more of the statistical independence
assumptions embodied in the basic two-process model may have
been violated.

4.1 Coordination of different phases of movement.

        Repetitive finger tapping involves more than just flexion
of the finger. A prerequisite for flexion is that the finger
be elevated as a result of extensor action. What controls the
timing of this second phase of the movement cycle? Figure 5
contrasts two possible extremes. In Model I, the two phases of

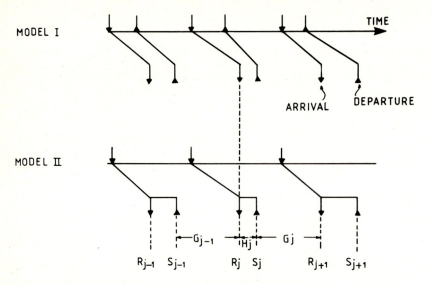

FIGURE 5. Timing of two phases of movement.

the activity R,S are handled independently of each other. In
Model II it is assumed that the occurrence of one phase of the
movement R serves as a "trigger" for the other phase S. The
timekeeper initiates a compound response of finger flexion and
extension.
        The two models differ in their predictions for the
covariance of intervals between successive phases of the
activity. H is the time the finger is in contact with the
plate between R and following S. G is the time the finger is
out of contact with the plate from departure S until the
subsequent arrival R. For Model I the crosscovariances at lag

one (between H and preceding G) and at lag zero (between H and following G) are negative. Their magnitudes are given by the variance of the delay from the timekeeper to the intervening boundary event (R and S respectively). In Model II the crosscovariance at lag one is zero and at lag zero is negative with magnitude equal to the variance of the response delay upto R plus the variance of the delay from R to S. Data from 40 subjects who produced finger-tapping responses with mean IRI of 400 msec and mean contact time H of 93 msec yielded crosscovariances at lags zero and one that were reliably less than zero, (Wing, 1979b). Thus the evidence favours Model I and we conclude the two phases of movement are initiated independently. Departure from the touch-plate is not triggered by the preceding arrival.

From the experimenter's point of view the continuation paradigm involves one repeated response. But it appears that the subject has to take account not of one compound response, but two differentiated responses. This may be of fundamental importance to understanding the breakdown of coordination. When repetitive skills are performed at high rates, "blocking" or temporary pauses in output can occur. If a single timekeeper controls timing perhaps we should treat blocking as the chance reversal of order of the two phases of movement with respect to their central initiations. This would be more likely to occur if timekeeper intervals are short with respect to the range of motor delays.

An alternative interpretation of blocking arises if we suppose two separate timekeepers operating in parallel are responsible for the two phases of movement. With separate timekeepers, blocking could occur if a slight difference in rate leads to an unchecked and progressive discrepancy in their relative phase. This latter hypothesis seems consistent with Glencross' (1974) observations of hand cranking of a wheel as fast as possible. He noted that each occurrence of blocking was preceded by progressive slippage in the relative timing of the different phases of movement in the activity[7].

4.2 Simultaneous responses.

In the preceding section we rejected the idea that arrival and departure are treated as a compound response to be triggered by the timekeeper at a single point in time. However there are some activities for which it is reasonable to imagine that two responses are triggered "as one". Consider the case of occulomotor control. When the eyes are moved to bear on a target, a step change in the background firing rates of the agonist and antagonist muscles determines the final resting position of each eye, (Bahill and Stark, 1979). However the driving force that causes the rapid flick (saccade) of the eyes to the new position is a brief, pulsed change in level of activity of the agonist and antagonist muscles. Mismatches between the saccade termination point and the position determined by the step change do occur. The result is then a slow, glissadic movement to the final resting position after the saccade.

For subjects with normal vision, Bahill and Stark report

that glissades usually arise in errors of duration of the pulse
rather than in errors of amplitude. Moreover, they observe
that glissades are usually monocular, that is they involve one
or other eye but not both eyes together. Suppose we recognise
two distinct components to motor delays involved in executing
simultaneous eye movements. Some operations, such as the
specification of pulse duration to achieve a given angular
extent of movement, may be shared by both eyes. However,
delays such as those in the peripheral nervous system and the
musculature will be specific to each eye. If duration errors
are mostly monocular it implies that variance in the timing of
eye movements is introduced by the motor delays coming after
response execution processes common to both eyes. We will now
consider a possible analogue in finger tapping.

     In the case of hand and arm movements we know there is
some variance in the interval between "simultaneous" left and
right movements, (Bartlett and White, 1965; Nakamura,
Taniguchi and Oshima, 1975; Rosenbaum and Patashnik, 1978).
For a task involving repetitive simultaneous tapping of left
and right index fingers we might construct the following
account of timing variability. A timekeeper initiates compound
left-with-right responses at intervals with mean equal to the
required IRI. We assume there are variable motor delays
following initiation and prior to the occurrence of the left
and right responses. Motor delays for left and for right
responses may each be divided into two components. We assume
the earlier part of each delay is introduced by a process, or
processes, common to both responses. The remaining part of
each delay we assume arises in processes specific to the left
or right response. If we now consider IRIs defined by left
responses, the covariance of adjacent IRIs will be equal to
minus the variance of the motor delay, that is minus the sum of
the variance of the common component and the variance of the
delay specific to the left response. Similarly, the covariance
of adjacent IRIs defined by the right reponse will be minus the
sum of the common delay variance and the variance of the delay
specific to the right response. The covariances of intervals
between left and right responses will be given by the variances
of the specific delays for left and right responses (without
the contribution of the common delay variance). Thus the
variance of the common delay could in principle be estimated.
One could argue this common component of the motor delay is
especially interesting since it represents an early and perhaps
more cognitive aspect of the execution of responses.

5.   Timekeeper intervals.

     I mentioned earlier that the synchronisation phase of the
continuation paradigm was included as a device to provide
experimental control over response rate. Indeed the efficacy
of this procedure or, to be precise, the ability of subjects to
match and maintain the standard interval is one reason for
talking in terms of a timekeeper. The form of the relation
between the variance and mean of intervals produced by the
timekeeper is of theoretical interest.
     In certain psychophysical studies, duration discrimination

performance has indicated a linear relation between the
stimulus interval and the variance of the perceived interval,
(Creelman, 1962; Abel, 1972). Such a linear relation is
consistent with a stochastic count basis for the "internal
clock" in which elapsed time is judged in relation to how many
of a pool of neural events fire in that time. If the times of
occurrence of the events are random, the count obtained for any
given interval will follow a Poisson distribution with mean
equal to the variance. Although the perceptual data are not
unequivocal about the form of the relation between the inferred
mean and variance (for example see Getty, 1977) it would be
interesting if the timing of responses were also consistent
with a stochastic process interpretation of the timekeeper[8].
Is a timekeeper interval produced by waiting until the number
of neural events since the beginning of the interval reaches a
predetermined count? The greater the count the longer will be
the associated time interval on average and the greater will be
the variance.

Data on the relation between mean IRI and timekeeper
variance are shown in Figure 6. These data, based on averages

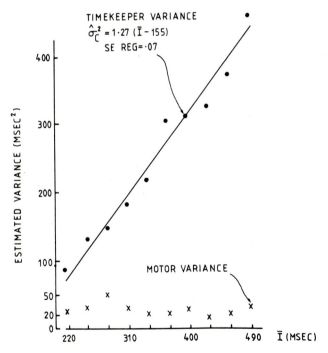

FIGURE 6. Effect of IRI. (Average data from 4 subjects,
50 trials at each IRI.)

over four practised subjects, were collected in a continuation
paradigm in which the standard interval was selected at random
for each trial from ten values in the range 220-490 msec (Wing,

1973, Experiment 2). In support of my earlier point about
adjustability of the timekeeper note the proximity of mean IRI
to the standard interval markers along the horizontal axis.
The regression line shows that timekeeper variance is linearly
related to the mean IRI. Although each subject's data was
well-described by a linear function there were large individual
differences in the slope. I have also observed considerable
differences in slope in different experiments. For example,
slopes reported by Wing and Kristofferson (1973) for IRIs in
the range 180 to 350 msec were one fifth of that shown in
Figure 6. In the stochastic model of the timekeeper, slope
changes can be interpreted as differences in the average rate
of occurrence of the underlying neural events; the greater the
slope the lower the rate.

Changes in the slope of linear functions relating IRI
variance to the mean as a function of experimental condition
have been reported by Rosenbaum and Patashnik (1978, see also
this volume). Their task involved the speeded production of a
left- followed by a right-finger response with target IRIs of
from 0 to 1050 msec. Two conditions that differed in the
required precision of timing were run; under "stringent"
requirements the slope of IRI variance versus mean was halved
relative to a "relaxed" condition. Reaction time was some 20%
greater for the stringent condition. In accounting for these
results Rosenbaum and Patashnik proposed that an internal
timekeeper is set on the occurrence of the imperative signal
and that more precise settings in the stringent condition,
based on less variable or shorter average intervals between
"ticks" (equivalent to our neural events), require more time.

Experiments that bear further on adjustment of the
timekeeper may be found in Michon (1967). He studied the
ability of people to make abrupt changes in IRI in the context
of "temporal tracking", that is matching IRIs to a sequence of
standard , "stimulus" intervals. At random points in the
sequence, the standard interval was increased by 8, 16, or 32%
of the base interval of 600, 1200, or 2400 msec. The response
of an "ideal linear predictor" to the step change in pulse rate
would be two-fold. One interval after the step occurred it
would set the timekeeper to the new standard interval corrected
by the mismatch (lead) of pulse and response due to the step
change. On the next interval it would set the timekeeper
interval at the new standard interval. The nature of
departures of the averaged data of five subjects from this
model led Michon to propose two modifications to the ideal
linear predictor as an account of human performance. These
took the form of two parameters in the transfer function
relating input (the stimulus intervals) to output (the IRIs).
An attenuation factor was needed because subjects failed to
introduce a sufficient first increment in the timekeeper
interval. A damping factor was introduced because subjects
failed to reduce the timekeeper interval sufficiently on the
second (and later) adjustments.

Although Michon's results do not allow us to assess the
separate contributions of processes responsible for perception
(of the change in stimulus interval) and production (of the new
interval between responses), they do suggest that resetting the

timekeeper to change IRIs may not be a simple process.   In that case one might ask how skills with frequent controlled adjustments of IRI are accomplished.   For example, how are different time-values between notes achieved in music performance?   In the next section we consider an alternative to continual adjustment of a single timekeeper that might underlie the production of rhythm.

5.1 Rhythm.

In the continuation paradigm the subject responds once with every synchronising pulse.   Suppose pulses are systematically omitted so that three out of every four pulses are silent.   The subject could now be required to tap at the same rate as before and only every fourth response would coincide with an audible pulse.   In effect the subject would be asked to subdivide the synchronisation measure into four parts much as a bar of music is subdivided into four equal beats in 4/4 time.   What happens to self-paced responding under such circumstances?   Does the requirement of handling successive responses differently during synchronisation result in a restructuring of the underlying timing mechanism?   Figure 7 shows two models treated by Vorberg and Hambuch (1978) for

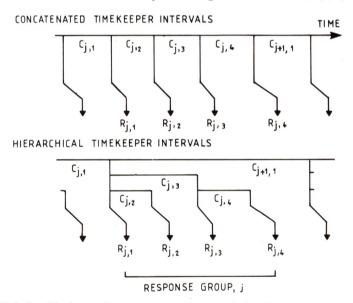

FIGURE 7. Timing of responses grouped in fours.

this situation.   In both models there is a repeating cycle of four intervals under timekeeper control, the termination of each interval giving rise to an overt response after a motor delay.   In the upper model the timekeeper intervals are concatenated in serial fashion.   The lower model represents a hierarchy with timekeeper intervals at three levels.   At the

highest level is an interval responsible for the onset of
groups of four responses. At the next level down the group is
subdivided by an interval leading to the third response in the
group. The two halves of the group are further subdivided at
the lowest level by timekeeper intervals culminating in the
first and fourth responses in the group. An important feature
of the hierarchical model is that irregularities occurring in
timekeeper intervals at lower levels of a group will not affect
the overall duration of the group.

Assuming equal variance of motor delays, Vorberg and
Hambuch showed that the variance-covariance structure of the
IRIs can be used to distinguish between these two models or
indeed between hybrids having an incomplete hierarchical
structure. They ran an experiment with three subjects
responding at rates of 2 or 3 responses per second with
grouping of 2, 3 or 4 responses on any given trial. The
results failed to support models having hierarchical
organisation of the timekeeper intervals. They found that the
variance of the sum of r IRIs was the same whether r (the
number of responses per group) was chosen within or across the
boundary of a group. This result is consistent with the
concatenated timekeeper interval model. It is evidence against
models that contain any element of hierarchical timekeepers
because any interval, other than the one defined on the group
boundary or "stressed" response, would include variances of the
timekeeper intervals at lower levels in the hierarchy as well
as the variance of the highest level.

Could Vorberg and Hambuch's result be due to a failure of
the modified synchronisation procedure to induce grouping?
They found there were reliable differences in mean between IRIs
within supposed groups. Thus their autocovariance functions,
computed without regard to these mean differences, showed
significant positive peaks at lags equal to the number of
responses to be grouped under a given experimental condition.
The modified synchronisation procedure may thus be said to have
had a grouping effect. However the nature of the differences
in mean IRI suggest it may be premature to apply the rejection
of the hierarchic model to timing of rhythmic groups in motor
skills in general or in music performance in particular (for
example see Shaffer, this volume). Vorberg and Hambuch found
only small differences in mean IRI between successive responses
in a group. Suppose these grouping effects were due to
differences in motor delays and not in timekeeper intervals.
For example, a subject might make the first response in each
group with increased velocity to give it "emphasis". This
could give a small reduction in the average motor delay and so
shorten the IRI (at the same time lengthening the subsequent
IRI). The hierarchic model may only apply if successive IRIs
differ to an extent that cannot be met by one timekeeper
operating with a single repeated interval (or four concatenated
timekeepers operating with the same interval).

6. Conclusions.

In the work that I have reviewed in this chapter, the
tasks have been defined to the subjects in terms of the timing

of their responses. The use of very simple responses probably minimised other aspects of movement coordination and this may also have encouraged subjects to focus their attention on the timing of their responses. Nonetheless there are data that suggest the relevance of the two-process model even where timing is not an explicit part of the skill.

Shaffer (1978) has reported negative correlations between adjacent IRIs in typewriting which he interpreted in terms of the two-process model. Elsewhere, (Wing, 1978) I have considered the two-process model in the context of timing movements in handwriting. The correlations I found between the durations of successive movements (defined for the letters n,w,m between local maxima and minima of letter height) were not all negative. I speculated this was due to conversion of spatial targets for movement to a specification involving timing of muscle responses. Kozhevnikov and Chistovich (1965) have observed negative correlations between the durations of successive phonemes (and between the durations of successive syllables) in spoken utterances. They also interpreted the correlations in terms of variance in the delay associated with the boundary articulatory event superimposed on intervals generated by the underlying speech programme. Wright (1974) has attempted to infer underlying timing structures in speech using differences in correlations between intervals separated by different articulatory events, (but see the critique by Ohala and Lyberg, 1976).

In contrast to simple repetitive responding, successive responses in these skills are qualitatively dissimilar. It is thus reasonable to ask whether the responses are differentiated in their temporal structure. In our treatment of the two-process model, extensions that allowed hierarchical relations among response delays or timekeeper intervals were considered for situations where responses may be differentiated. While there is as yet no firm evidence in their favour, I consider these developments particularly relevant to the frequently raised issue of overall rate control. In some skills, such as musical performance or speech, changes in response rate may be introduced by the performer as an expressive feature (see chapters by Shaffer and by McNeilage in this volume). However it is commonly observed that rate changes are not scaled equally over the durations of all types of responses. In speech, for example, vowels are shortened less than would be expected at high speech rates. This observation suggests there may be several timekeepers having a degree of autonomy in their rate settings. Yet they would clearly need to be constrained relative to one another in their operation. Hierarchical arrangements would seem to be appropriate for this purpose. This may not be true of the kind of rate changes observed in typing or handwriting (for example see Viviani and Terzuolo's chapter in this volume). In these cases changes in "response" intervals are uniformly scaled over all the different responses and this could be achieved by a change in rate of a single underlying timekeeper.

Finally, I would like to make a methodological point. At first glance one might be tempted to characterise the research summarised in this chapter as being no more than an

investigation of the temporal aspect of movement control.   But
I would like to emphasize the importance I attach to the
general approach. Successive performances of what passes for
the same action are rarely, if ever, alike. Moreover, many
would say that what characterises skilled performance is the
reduced level of variability. Yet in the study of motor
behaviour the emphasis is so often on average levels of
performance. Perhaps with this chapter I have shown the
potential power of explicit consideration of "noise" in
building up an understanding of the nature of motor control.

References.

Abel, S.M. Discrimination of temporal gaps. Journal of the
  Acoustical Society of America, 1972, 52, 519-524.
Bahill, A.T. & Stark, L. The trajectories of saccadic eye
  movements. Scientific American, 1979, 240, 85-93.
Bartlett, N.R. & White, C.T. Synchronization error in attempts
  to move the hands simultaneously. Perceptual and Motor Skills,
  1965, 20, 933-937.
Creelman, C.D. Human discrimination of auditory duration.
  Journal of the Acoustical Society of America, 1962, 34,
  582-593.
DeLong, M. Central patterning of movement. Neurosciences
  Research Program Bulletin, 1971, 9, 10-30.
Fraisse, P. & Voillaume, C. Les reperes du sujet dans la
  synchronisation et dans la pseudo-synchronisation. Annee
  Psychologique, 1971, 71, 359-369.
Getty, D.J. Discrimination of short temporal intervals: A
  comparison of two models. Perception & Psychophysics, 1975,
  18, 1-8.
Glencross, D.J. Pauses in a repetitive speed skill. Perceptual
  and Motor Skills, 1974, 38, 246.
Kozhevnikov, V.A. & Chistovich, L.A. Speech: Articulation and
  Perception. U.S. Dept of Commerce Joint Publication Research
  Service No 30543, 1965.
Meijers, L.M.M. & Eijkman, E.G.J. The motor system in simple
  reaction time experiments. Acta Psychologica, 1974, 38,
  367-377.
Michon, J.A. Timing in Temporal Tracking. Soesterberg, The
  Netherlands: Institute for Perception RVO-TNO, 1967.
Nakamura, R., Taniguchi, R. & Oshima, Y. Synchronization error
  in bilateral simultaneous flexion of elbows. Percpetual and
  Motor Skills, 1975, 40, 527-532.
Ohala, J.J. & Lyberg, B. Comments on "Temporal interactions
  within a phrase". Journal of the Acoustical Society of
  America, 1976, 59, 990-992.
Rosenbaum, D.A. Patashnik, O. Time to time in the human motor
  system. In R.S. Nickerson (Ed) Attention and Performance VIII.
  Hillsdale, NJ: L. Erlbaum Associates, 1979, in press.
Schmidt, R.A. Proprioception and the timing of motor responses.
  Psychological Bulletin, 1971, 76, 383-393.
Shaffer, L.H. Timing in the motor programming of typing.
  Quarterly Journal of Experimental Psychology, 1978, 30,
  333-345.

Stevens, L.T. On the time sense, Mind, 1886, 11, 393-404.
Voillaume, C. Modeles pour l'etude de la regulation des
mouvements cadences. Annee Psychologique, 1971, 71, 347-358.
Vorberg, D. Problems in the study of reponse timing: Comments
on Reece's (1976) 'A model of temporal tracking'. Acta
Psychologica, 1978, 42, 67-77.
Vorberg, D. & Hambuch, R. On the temporal control of rhythmic
performance. In J. Requin (Ed.) Attention and Performance VII.
Hillsdale, NJ: L Erlbaum Associates, 1978.
Wing, A.M. & Kristofferson, A.B. Response delays and the timing
of discrete motor responses. Perception & Psychophysics, 1973,
14, 5-12.
Wing, A.M. The timing of interresponse intervals by human
subjects. PhD Thesis, McMaster University, Hamilton, Ont,
Canada. 1973.
Wing, A.M. (a) Perturbations of auditory feedback delay and the
timing of movement. Journal of Experimental Psychology: Human
Perception and Performance, 1977, 3, 175-186.
Wing, A.M. (b) Effects of type of movement on the temporal
precision of response sequences. British Journal of
Mathematical and Statistical Psychology, 1977, 30, 60-72.
Wing, A.M. Response timing in handwriting. In G.E. Stelmach
(Ed.) Information Processing in Motor Control and Learning.
New York: Academic Press, 1978.
Wing, A.M. (a) A note on the estimation of the autocovariance
function in the analysis of timing of repetitive responses.
British Journal of Mathematical and Statistical Psychology,
1979, 32, 143-145.
Wing, A.M. (b) Timing of movement phases of a repeated
response. Journal of Motor Behavior, 1979, in press.
Wright, T.W. Temporal interactions within a phrase and sentence
context. Journal of the Acoustical Society, 1974, 56,
1258-1265.

Footnotes.

1. I thank H.Buxton, G.Hitch, E.Hunt, J.Long, D.Rosenbaum and
   D.Vorberg for critical comments on an earlier version of
   this chapter.
2. Stevens did not assume the remembered standard was
   necessarily invariant. In noting the presence on some
   trials of long-term or slow-wave fluctuation in IRIs he
   suggested its origin was different from the alternation of
   successive intervals. He attributed the long-term
   fluctuation to "rhythmic variation of the standard carried
   in the mind".
3. A commonly used estimator of autocovariance is

$$G_I(k) = \sum_{j=k+1}^{N} (I_j - \bar{I})(I_{j-k} - \bar{I})/(N - k)$$

where

$$\bar{I} = \sum_{j=1}^{N} I_j / N$$

As Vorberg (1978) has pointed out, this estimator is only assymptotically unbiased as N becomes large. The nature of the bias depends on the theoretical autocovariance function. Thus Vorberg suggests testing particular timing models in terms of predicted autocovariance functions that include terms for the bias associated with a particular value of N. In the case of the basic two-process model with N in the region of 20, the "biased" prediction becomes slightly less than zero at lags greater than one, (Wing, 1979a).

4. Meijers and Eijkman (1974) have shown how the time at which a muscle contracts could have less variance than the time of onset of activity in pyramidal tract neurons that originally gave rise to the contraction. Their argument is statistical and is based on temporal summation of activity over tens of parallel channels from the central nervous system all with independent firing characteristics. To the extent such mechanisms operate in our functional model and reduce the variance of later stages relative to earlier stages in the motor delay, the covariance of IRIs defined on a greater number of stages in the motor delay (ie more peripheral) need not be greater than IRIs defined on earlier stages.

5. The converse does not follow. Zero correlation between successive IRIs indicates there is no motor delay variance. This does not necessarily imply there is no motor delay.

6. A possible component of motor variance is variability of measurement error. Suppose the recording device is unreliable in detecting the response as soon as it occurs, perhaps because the sampling rate is too low. If the error in registration is independent of the motor delay, the registration delay variance will sum with the subject's motor variance. In the case of the emg data, measurement resolution was limited to 5 msec. If the resulting measurement error is assumed to be a random variable uniformly distributed about the true event time, the error variance contributes about 5% to the negative lag one autocorrelation of the intervals defined on flexor emg onset.

7. Two separate timekeepers operating at the same rate with no adjustment of phase over a period of n cycles would give a linear increase in variance of, for example, the interval H. Depending on the form of the distribution of H and given the mean of H, a probability of obtaining a negative value for H could be computed. Such a negative value would indicate a reversal of arrival and departure, likely to result in blocking. However this would be preceded by systematic increase in variance rather than by a progressive change in the mean of H.

8. Time perception and the timing of movement need not be based on timekeepers with similar characteristics. Some theories proposed as the basis of timing of movement are specific to movement. For example, it has been suggested that proprioceptive feedback arising from a movement completed earlier in a sequence (or memory trace of that feedback) may serve as a cue for initiation of the next response, (Schmidt, 1971).

Tutorials in Motor Behavior
G.E. Stelmach and J. Requin (eds.)
© North-Holland Publishing Company, 1980

29

A Mental Clock Setting Process Revealed by Reaction Times*

David A. Rosenbaum and Oren Patashnik
Bell Laboratories
Murray Hill, New Jersey 07974

To study the preparation of timing for forthcoming movements we require subjects to produce specified time intervals between two responses and also to minimize the simple reaction time (RT) for the first response. RTs are longer when a specified interval must be produced than when no second response is required, and RTs increase as target intervals decrease from 1050 to 50 msec. We reject the hypothesis that these effects are due to "competition" between the two responses, to processing of visual feedback about the intervals, or to a process of adjusting the covariance of the motor delays for the two responses. We argue that the effects can be attributed to a mental clock setting process whose duration is predicted by an analogue of Fitts' Law. That the clock setting process is not used exclusively for timing overt movements is shown in an additional experiment. We infer from the latter result that a central clock is used to time motor and perceptual events. We infer from the applicability of Fitts' Law to mental clock setting that processes of movement *preparation* bear an isomorphic relation to processes of movement *execution*, although the former are much faster than the latter.

I. Introduction

In this paper we describe a series of experiments on how people control time delays between successive movements. The work reported here extends work that we have reported elsewhere (Rosenbaum & Patashnik, in press), and focuses on the *preparation* of movement timing. We believe that the study of movement timing preparation may help shed light on some issues of long-standing concern in the motor control research area. One such issue is whether motor programs are used to control movement timing when proprioceptive feedback is available (Adams, 1977; Cauraugh & Christina, 1978; Kelso, 1978). If one can show that the delay between two movements is prepared before the first movement is executed, even if there is enough time to use proprioceptive feedback from the first movement to time the onset of the second movement, it can be concluded that motor programs are used when proprioceptive feedback is available. Another issue that may benefit from the study of movement timing preparation is the nature of motor programming. If one can discover how the characteristics of timing preparation are related to the temporal characteristics of subsequent movements, it may then be possible to develop detailed models of the programs used for timing control.

The experimental procedure we have used to study the preparation of movement timing is shown in Figure 1. In each session the subject's task is to produce one specified time interval between two responses (key presses made with the left and right index fingers). The specified intervals range from 0 to 1050 msec. On each trial we give feedback to help the subject produce an approximation to the specified interval. The feedback takes the form of a vertical line on a CRT screen. The line points up if the produced interval is too long and down if the produced interval is too short; the length of the line shows how large the proportional error is. (More details about the feedback are given in Rosenbaum & Patashnik, in press.) Besides producing the specified interval, the subject is also required to make the first response as quickly as possible after the onset of the reaction signal, that is, to minimize the reaction time (RT). The length of a horizontal line on the

* We thank Ronald L. Knoll, Judith F. Kroll, David L. Noreen, and Saul Sternberg for suggestions, and Gwen O. Salyer for assistance with data collection. This paper was formatted with a Bell Laboratories computer phototypesetting system.

screen shows the subject how long the RT is. Our working assumption is that the length of the RT reflects the duration of timing preparation.

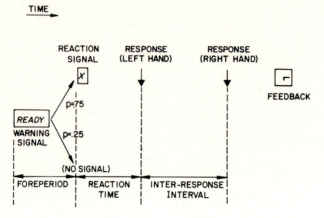

Fig. 1. Overview of the experimental procedure. "Catch trials" were used 25% of the time to discourage anticipation responses.

Figure 2 shows the results of our first experiment. Here three right-handed women who had had extensive practice in the interval production task participated in eight one hour sessions each. In each session one interval was tested in eleven blocks of 60 trials, with the first block for practice. As is seen in the left panel of Figure 2, mean RTs declined as target intervals increased, for target intervals greater than or equal to 50 msec. The RT curve dropped at 0 msec, and the subjects said that this condition seemed qualitatively different from the rest in the way the interresponse intervals were controlled.[1] An aspect of the RT data that we find particularly interesting is that for every subject RTs were longer when two responses had to be made (regardless of the required interval) than when only one response had to be made — — in the condition we call "infinity" (∞). The panel on the right gives an indication of how precisely the intervals were produced. For all three subjects mean produced intervals were within a few msec of their corresponding target values, and mean interval variances increased linearly with interval means.

How can these results be interpreted? One of the first models we developed is shown in Figure 3. We call it an *alarm clock* model. The model says that after the reaction signal is detected, an internal alarm clock is set to tick n times. Once the value of n has been set to the subject's satisfaction, the ticking process is begun and the first response is executed after a motor delay, d_1. After the nth tick has occurred, an "alarm" goes off, as it were, and response 2 is executed after a motor delay, d_2. The linearly increasing variance function is explained by saying that variance accumulates with each delay between successive ticks of the clock. The model says that delays between clock ticks fluctuate randomly about a mean and that successive intertick delays are stochastically independent (see Wing & Kristofferson, 1973). With this type of model, the RT data shown in Figure 2 can be explained by saying that it takes less time to set the clock as the value of n increases. This could come about if the clock's setting returned to some large value of n after each usage, or if there were fewer possible settings as n increased.

In the next section of this paper we will consider some alternatives to the *alarm clock* model which we have tested and rejected. Then, in Section III, we will show that the *alarm clock* model, as described above, fails to explain two of the major results that we obtained in testing alternatives to the *alarm clock* model. A revised and more specific *alarm clock* model will then be described. In Section IV, we will address the question of whether the clock setting process is unique to the timing of movements. We will show that it is not. Finally, in Section V, we will review the main results of our experiments and consider some of their theoretical implications.

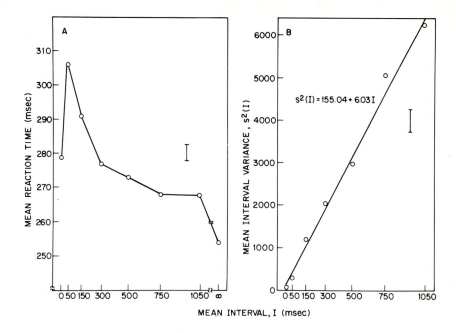

Fig. 2. Results of the first experiment, averaged over the three subjects. The values on the abscissa designate the target intervals, and the plotted points, each of which represents a mean of about 1300 observatons, are plotted above the corresponding mean obtained intervals. Errors of responding on catch trials, responding before the reaction signal was presented, or responding first with the right finger when nonzero intervals were required occurred altogether on less than 2% of the trials in each of the eight conditions. (A) Mean RTs and estimate of standard error ($\pm$SE). The three subjects had similar functions: The mean RT function for the 2-response conditions accounts for 93.7%, 98.4%, and 96.9% of the variance of mean RTs for corresponding conditions for the three subjects, respectively. (B) Mean interval variances, fitted linear function, and estimate of $\pm$SE. Linear regression accounts for 98.9% of the variance of mean variances, which is not significantly surpassed by fitting a quadratic function to the same points. Slopes (in msec) and zero-intercepts (in $msec^2$) of fitted linear functions for the three subjects are 8.64 and 141.44, 2.57 and 39.80, and 6.87 and 273.90, respectively. Estimates of $\pm$SE here and in all other figures are based on mean squares from fits of mean functions to individual subject data.

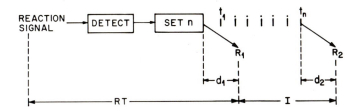

Fig. 3. An *alarm clock* model for performance in the interval production task.

II. Alternatives to Clock Setting

A. Response Competition

One alternative to the clock setting model says that the RT effect we obtained is due to competition between the two responses, where the amount of competition, and hence the RT, increases as the delay between responses decreases (up to values near 0 msec). (For discussions of competition between responses in RT experiments, see Rosenbaum, in press, and Sternberg, Monsell, Knoll, & Wright, 1978.) The *response competition* hypothesis allows that the delay between triggering of response 1 and response 2 may be controlled by a clock, but it says that any clock setting activity that occurs during the RT takes a negligible or constant amount of time.

According to the *response competition* hypothesis, the RT should depend on the interresponse interval but not on the variability of interresponse intervals. We tested this prediction in an experiment whose results are shown in Figure 4. In one condition we had subjects attempt to produce the same intervals as in the first experiment, with the same accuracy requirements as we had used in the first experiment; we called this the "stringent" condition. In another condition — — the "relaxed" condition — — we had the same subjects attempt to produce the same mean intervals, but now they were allowed to have much higher interval variances. To get the subjects to do this, we simply reduced the scale of the vertical feedback line so that in most cases subjects could only tell if the intervals they produced were too long or too short.

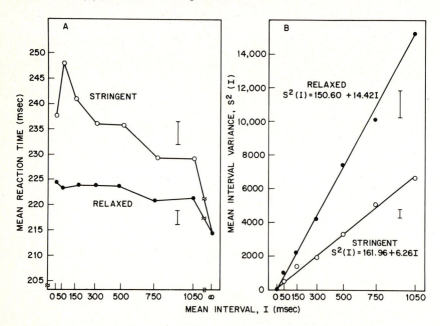

Fig. 4. Results of the second experiment. Details of the procedure and results can be found in Rosenbaum and Patashnik (in press).

As is seen in the right panel of Figure 4, interval variances were higher in the *relaxed* condition than in the *stringent* condition, but interval means in the *relaxed* and *stringent* conditions were close to one another and also close to the target values. As is seen in the left panel of Figure 4, the pattern of mean RTs in the *stringent* condition was like the pattern of mean RTs in the first experiment (although the range of RTs was smaller here with this different group of subjects). In the *relaxed* condition mean RTs were significantly shorter than in the *stringent* condition, and the effect of target interval (including the reduction of mean RTs for the 0 msec target) was virtually eliminated;

an analysis of variance showed that the interaction between target interval and degree of required precision was statistically significant.

The results from the *relaxed* condition argue strongly against the *response competition* hypothesis, which predicted that mean RTs should depend on mean interresponse intervals. In general, the data from this experiment indicate that mean *RTs* depend critically on the precision with which interresponse intervals must be produced.

B. Some Response Competition and/or Visual Feedback Processing

We cannot rule out the possibility that in the above experiment there was some effect of response competition on RT, because mean RTs were longer when two responses had to be made than when only one response had to be made. To determine whether there was some effect on RTs of merely having to make a second response, we conducted the following experiment. Subjects were told to respond as quickly as possible with the left index finger when the reaction signal appeared (as in the previous experiments) and then to respond with the right index finger *any time later*. We told the subjects that the second response was necessary merely "to turn on the feedback signal." In the control condition of this experiment no second response was required. Our aim was to find out whether the RT for the first of two responses could be as small as the RT for just one response when there was no pressure to produce a specific interresponse interval.

In this experiment we also wanted to check on the possibility that RTs were longer for two responses than for one because of the need to study the vertical line that gave feedback about the interresponse intervals. To test this hypothesis in the new experiment, we presented a vertical line in the 2-response condition and told subjects that when the vertical line pointed up they should prepare to respond normally in the next trial, but when the vertical line pointed down they should refrain from responding in the next trial, even though the reaction signal would appear. This made it necessary for subjects to attend to the vertical line after making the second response.

After trials in which the vertical line pointed up, the following events occurred. On 75% of the trials both the warning signal and reaction signal appeared, and after the second response was made the vertical line again pointed up with 75% probability. On the remaining 25% of the trials (following trials with an upward-pointing line), after the warning signal appeared no reaction signal was presented. In these catch trials no vertical line appeared, but the subject was instructed to get ready to respond on the next trial.

The vertical line had a fixed length approximately equal to its mean length in the second experiment reported here. We made it clear to the subjects that the behavior of the vertical line did not depend in any way on the interresponse intervals. There were four subjects, all of whom had been in one or more of our previous experiments. After practicing the 2-response task for 1 hr, each subject returned the next day for a 1 hr session consisting of five 2-response blocks followed by five 1-response blocks, or the opposite. Each block had 25 trials, and the first block in each half of the second session was for practice. Catch trials occurred on 25% of the trials in the 1-response condition.

For every subject, errors of responding before or in the absence of a reaction signal occurred on less than 2% of the trials in both the 1-response and 2-response conditions. In the entire experiment there were only three errors of failing to respond correctly to the vertical line. The remaining discussion will be concerned with errorless trials only.

Table 1 shows the main results of the experiment. Even though in earlier experiments each of the subjects had produced longer RTs for the first of two responses than for just one response, here mean RTs were the same when just one response had to be made and when the first response could be followed any time later by the second response. This result implies that it was not simply the need to make a second response that lengthened RTs. (This conclusion is supported by the fact that the mean produced intervals were generally within the range that was required before. Moreover, the produced intervals had higher variances than were found earlier for intervals with comparable means.) A second conclusion we reach with the present experiment is that the need to attend to the vertical feedback line did not cause RTs to be longer in the 2-response conditions than in the 1-response condition of our earlier experiments, although we cannot rule out the possibility that earlier there was some effect of having to study the *length* of the line. Notwithstanding the latter possibility, our main conclusion is that in the previous experiments RTs were lengthened by a process responsible for precisely controlling the interresponse intervals.[2]

Table 1

Mean Reaction Time (RT) and Interval (I)
When 1 or 2 Responses Were Required

| Subject | Number of Required Responses | | | | | |
| | 1 | | 2 | | | |
	RT	sd	RT	sd	I	sd
1	201.5	27.8	200.4	26.5	384.6	92.6
2	199.8	18.9	200.6	21.3	1059.4	149.4
3	201.8	26.4	200.1	21.2	943.6	186.9
4	202.3	23.8	202.4	23.7	326.7	187.0
Mean	201.3	24.2	200.8	23.1	678.5	153.9

C. Response Delay Covariance

Is there any kind of process other than a clock setting process that could affect the precision of interresponse intervals and also lengthen RTs? One possibility is that during the RT the subject sets the covariance between the motor delays for the two responses (d_1 and d_2), possibly by adjusting muscle tensions in the two arms. The rationale for this *response delay covariance* model is that as $cov(d_1, d_2)$ increases, $var(I)$ will decrease. Therefore, it is to the subject's advantage to maximize $cov(d_1, d_2)$. Suppose, however, that it takes time during the RT to set $cov(d_1, d_2)$ for a forthcoming response sequence, such that the time needed to set $cov(d_1, d_2)$ increases with the level of $cov(d_1, d_2)$ that is actually achieved. If we assume that the RT effects obtained in the first two experiments reflected differences in the time spent setting $cov(d_1, d_2)$, and did not reflect differences in the time spent setting a clock that may have been used to control the delay between the triggering of response 1 and response 2, the *response delay covariance* model predicts that $cov(d_1, d_2)$ should increase as mean RT increases.

We tested this prediction as follows. Suppose the following two relations hold:

$$RT = P + d_1$$
$$I = C + d_2 - d_1 \, , \tag{1}$$

where P is a random variable representing the time to prepare a forthcoming interresponse interval I (that is, P includes the time to detect the reaction signal, set $cov(d_1, d_2)$, and carry out all other aspects of preparation that precede response 1), and C is a random variable representing the total duration of clock ticking. The covariance of RT and I, $cov(RT, I)$, is then

$$cov(RT, I) = cov(P, C) + cov(P, d_2) - cov(P, d_1) + \\ cov(d_1, C) + cov(d_1, d_2) - cov(d_1, d_1) \, . \tag{2}$$

If we assume that all the random variables in (2) are independent except d_1 and d_2, and also that $cov(d_1, d_2)$ is independent of mean d_2, we have

$$cov(RT, I) = cov(d_1, d_2) - cov(d_1, d_1) \\ = cov(d_1, d_2) - var(d_1) \, . \tag{3}$$

For the *stringent* condition of the second experiment, where mean RTs decreased to an asymptote as mean interresponse intervals increased (to approximately 1050 msec), the prediction of the *response delay covariance* model is that as mean interresponse intervals increase, $cov(d_1, d_2)$ should approach 0, so that $cov(RT, I)$ should approach $-var(d_1)$ as an asymptote. Of course, we cannot independently measure $-var(d_1)$, so the specific prediction stated above cannot be tested. Nevertheless, we can see whether $cov(RT, I)$ approaches an asymptote less than 0, where this asymptote is assumed to approximate $-var(d_1)$.

Figure 5 shows $cov(RT, I)$ in the *stringent* condition of the second experiment. As is seen in the figure, $cov(RT, I)$ remained fairly constant at about -56 msec^2 in the 50-1050 msec range. The slope of the best-fitting straight line for these points was only .005, and did not differ significantly from zero. The flatness of this curve contradicts the prediction of the *response delay covariance* model. Since the mean $cov(RT, I)$ in the 50-1050 msec interval range was negative, the simplest explanation of the data seems to be that $cov(d_1,d_2)$ in this range was approximately zero, in which case $cov(RT, I) \cong -var(d_1)$. One reason why this seems like a reasonable explanation is that Wing and Kristofferson (1973) and Vorberg and Hambuch (1978) obtained estimates of response delay variance quite close to 56 msec^2.

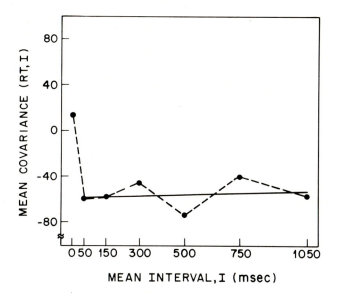

Fig. 5. Mean $cov(RT,I)$, averaged over the three subjects, in the *stringent* condition of the second experiment. For the 0 msec target condition, algebraic values of *I* were used to compute $cov(RT,I)$; that is, intervals where the right finger led the left were considered negative. The resulting estimate of $cov(RT,I)$ did not differ significantly from zero. (When absolute values of *I* were used, the estimate of $cov(RT,I)$ did not differ significantly from zero or from the estimate obtained with algebraic values.) For the nonzero conditions, slopes (in msec) and mean covariances (in msec^2) were .01 and -72.06 -.003 and -21.86, and .008 and -74.81 for the three subjects, respectively.

If we examine $cov(RT,I)$ for the *relaxed* condition of the second experiment, we find similar effects to those described above. In the *relaxed* condition, the slope of the best-fitting straight line for values of $cov(RT,I)$ in the 50-1050 msec interval range was .001 (not significantly different from zero), and mean $cov(RT,I)$ was -60 msec^2. The fact that mean $cov(RT,I)$ in the *relaxed* condition was close to (and not significantly different from) mean $cov(RT,I)$ in the *stringent* condition violates the prediction of the *response delay covariance* model that $cov(RT,I)$ should depend on RT.

For the first experiment, the slope of the best-fitting straight line for values of $cov(RT,I)$ in the 50-1050 msec range was only -.008 (not significantly different from 0), and mean $cov(RT,I)$ in this range was -51 msec^{-2}. The flatness of this slope, like the flatness of the slope in the *stringent* condition of the first experiment, militates against the *response delay covariance* model.

(It is interesting to note that $cov(RT,I)$ for $I = 0$ was markedly different from the other values. This finding appears to support subjects' introspective reports that the simultaneous response condition was qualitatively different from the other conditions.)

III. Clock Setting Models

So far we have explained why we do not favor a simple *response competition* model or a simple *response delay covariance* model. Now we turn to the kind of model we favor — — an *alarm clock* model.

Earlier, we proposed one kind of *alarm clock* model which we can now reject. This model said that the time required to set the alarm clock during the RT decreased as the desired set time (i.e., the desired value of *n*) increased. We can now reject this model because in the *relaxed* condition of the second experiment we found mean RTs to be essentially unrelated to interval means, and also because the second experiment showed that interval *precision* was the key determinant of mean RTs.

What other kind of *alarm* clock model can be considered then? As a way of addressing this question, let us consider how a mental clock setting process might differ from the process of setting an external clock, say, the alarm clock in one's bedroom. In setting a conventional bedroom alarm clock, once the clock has been set it can be made to go off at its set time on future occasions without being reset. For example, if such an alarm clock is set to go off at 6 o'clock one morning, all that has to be done to make the alarm clock go off at 6 o'clock some later morning is to turn on the alarm system the preceding night; the alarm clock does not have to be reset. Now if all that was involved in reusing a mental alarm clock was reactivating the alarm system, one would not expect the time required to start the clock to depend on the clock setting.

Suppose that unlike the bedroom alarm clock the mental alarm clock stores its previous set times, but it does so imperfectly (see the left panel of Figure 6.) Suppose that after the alarm clock has been used in an experimental trial its setting drifts randomly so that at the start of the next experimental trial the setting is some expected amplitude, A, away from the clock's target setting, T_I, for desired interval I. (We will assume that A is the same for all values of I.) As a result of this random drift, before the clock can be used again for the production of interval I the clock's "pointer" must be moved back through A, that is, the clock must be reset at T_I.

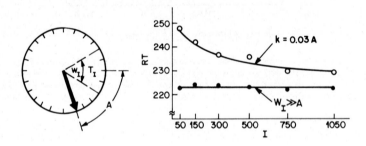

Fig. 6. Schematic diagram of a clock whose "pointer" drifts randomly over an expected amplitude A after being positioned within a window of size W_I around a target setting T_I [left panel]. Obtained RTs (empty and filled points for the *stringent* and *relaxed* conditions of the second experiment, respectively) and RTs predicted by applying Fitts' Law to mental clock setting [right panel].

Now, we found that RTs are affected by the precision of produced intervals. This fact leads us to suggest that the subject places a "tolerance window" of size W_I around the target setting for I. W_I is important for two reasons. First, if we assume that the clock does not have to be reset if the pointer is within the window, then as W_I decreases, the likelihood of having to reset the clock will increase. Second, if we assume that W_I defines the range of settings to which the pointer can be returned before the clock is reused, the precision required to return the pointer to within the window will increase as W_I decreases.

We assume that W_I depends both on the size of I and on the subject's motivation for precision. The nature of these dependencies can be established as follows. Let the random variable N be the number of clock ticks between the triggering of response 1 and 2. Let the time between ticks $i - 1$ and i ($1 \leqslant i \leqslant n$) be a random variable X_i, where the random variables X_i are independent of N and identically distributed as a random variable X with finite mean and variance. The interresponse interval, I, is

$$I = X_1 + \cdots + X_N + D , \tag{4}$$

where D is a random variable representing the difference between response delays d_1 and d_2, and where X_i, N, and D are mutually independent. Using the expression for the variance of a random sum (Parzen, 1962, p. 56), we have

$$Var \ (I) = E(N) \ Var \ (X) + Var \ (N) \ E^2(X) + Var \ (D) . \tag{5}$$

Recalling that we found $Var(I)$ to be linearly related to $E(I)$, and noting that

$$E(N) = \frac{E(I) - E(D)}{E(X)} , \tag{6}$$

we have

$$Var(N) = \frac{\alpha + \beta E(I) - Var(D) - \left[\dfrac{E(I) - E(D)}{E(X)}\right] Var(X)}{E^2(X)} . \tag{7}$$

As stringency and I are varied, all the terms in (7) are assumed to be constants except for $Var \ (N)$ and $E(I)$. Therefore, we can rewrite (7) as

$$Var \ (N) = c_1 + c_2 E(I) , \tag{8}$$

where c_1 and c_2 are constants. In view of the fact that a qualitatively different kind of timing control seemed to be used in the 0 msec condition and in the other 2-response conditions, it seems reasonable to assume that for $E(I) = 0$, $Var(N) = 0$, in which case we can set $c_1 = 0$. We also assume that when there are n clock ticks the clock is initially set at n (i.e., that there is perfect correspondence between the number of ticks that are set and that occur). We can now characterize the range of clock settings used in repeated attempts to produce a desired interval I by the standard deviation of clock settings,

$$W_I = k\sqrt{E(I)} , \tag{9}$$

where $k = \sqrt{c_2}$.

With the above assumptions, we can liken the process of setting a mental alarm clock to the process of positioning a clock pointer to a setting within W_I. In order to characterize how the time required for such repositioning could depend on W_I, let us turn briefly to studies of *overt* positioning movements, in particular to manual positioning movements.

When the hand must be moved to a target of width W over a distance A, the movement time is found to be a linearly increasing function of $\log_2(2A/W)$. This relationship is known as Fitts' Law (1954). We will now show that mean RTs in our interval production task can be accounted for with the following analogue of Fitts' Law:

$$RT_I = \begin{cases} a, & \text{for } W_I \gg A \\ a + b \ \log_2 \dfrac{2A}{W_I}, & \text{otherwise.} \end{cases} \tag{10}$$

Here a represents the time to make a response to the reaction signal when the clock does not have to be reset (i.e., when the clock pointer is already within W_I), and b represents the time per bit of information transmitted, where the number of bits is given by $\log_2(2A/W_I)$.

When W_I is very large relative to A (i.e., $W \gg A$), and if the clock pointer is initially set near T_I, the pointer will rarely drift outside of W_I. Consequently, the number of occasions on which the pointer will have to be repositioned to a setting within W_I will approach zero as W_I increases. In the *relaxed* condition of the second experiment, where theoretically W_I was very large relative to A, mean RTs were roughly constant across changes in I. Thus, we can set a equal to the mean RT in the *relaxed* condition[3].

In the *stringent* condition of the second experiment, where W_I theoretically was much smaller than in the *relaxed* condition, there would have been many more occasions on which the clock pointer had to be repositioned to within W_I. For the *stringent* condition, therefore, we must describe how repositioning times would vary across changes in I. To do so, we turn to the second line of (10). We note first that the second line of (10) can be rewritten as

$$RT_I = a + b(1 + log_2 A - log_2 k - \frac{1}{2} log_2 E(I)) .$$ (11)

The observed range of mean RTs in the *stringent* condition can then be expressed as the difference between RT_{1050} and RT_{50}, which is

$$RT_{50} - RT_{1050} = 17\,msec = \frac{b}{2}(log_2 1050 - log_2 50) .$$ (12)

(The obtained mean intervals in the 1050 and 50 msec conditions were so close to their corresponding target values that we use the target values here and in all other computations involving $E(I)$.) The value of b can then be estimated as 7.74 msec/bit (or 129 bit/sec). In order for RT_{1050} to equal 230 msec (the observed value of RT_{1050} in the *stringent* condition), we must make

$$b(1 + log_2 A - log_2 k - \frac{1}{2} log_2 1050) = 230 - 222\,msec .$$ (13)

Thus,

$$(1 + log_2 A - log_2 k) = 6.05\ bit ,$$ (14)

in which case $k = .03\ A$. We can now predict RTs for the remaining intervals, and those predicted RTs are contained in the upper curve in the right panel of Figure 6. The predicted RTs account for 97.4% of the variance among mean RTs in the *stringent* condition.

With our application of Fitts' Law we can account for interval variance data as well as mean RT data. By making use of Eqs. (6) and (8), we can rewrite Eq. (5) as

$$Var(I) = E(I)[c_3 + k^2 c_4] + c_5 ,$$ (15)

where c_3, c_4, and c_5 are constants. We have assumed that k--the factor that determines how large W_I is in relation to $E(I)$--was much larger in the *relaxed* condition than in the *stringent* condition of the second experiment. Thus, according to (15), the slope of the interval variance function should be larger in the *relaxed* condition than in the *stringent* condition, and the zero-intercepts of the two functions should be equal. This is essentially what we found (see Fig. 4B).

It should also be noted that the assumptions and results concerning $cov(RT,I)$, presented in Section IIC, are consistent with the Fitts' Law model. (According to the model, the time to prepare any particular interval whose corresponding target setting is within W_I should be no different, on the average, than the time to prepare any other such interval having the same target setting. Thus, the model assumes $cov(P,C)=0$, which is necessary for the covariance results to be consistent with the model.)

Because of the success of the Fitts' Law model, we believe that the model is a reasonable way of conceptualizing preparation in the interval production task. Later, we will consider the possible implications of this development for interpretations of Fitts' Law and for an understanding of the relation between the preparation and execution of movements.

IV. Centrality of Clock Setting

We turn now to the issue of whether the clock setting process is used exclusively for timing delays between overt movements. It is also possible that the clock setting process is used for timing delays between movements and stimuli or delays between two (or more) stimuli.

We investigated whether the clock setting process is used for timing the delay between a movement and stimulus by conducting the following experiment. As before, on 75% of the trials a reaction signal appeared and the subject was required to respond as quickly as possible with the left index finger. This response defined the start of the subject's interval, as was the case in the earlier experiments. Now, however, the end of the interval was defined by the onset of a brief burst of vibration applied to the tip of the subject's right index finger. The vibration was delivered with a Bimorph bender (Vernitron No. 60572) for 20 msec at 200 Hz. In each session there were several different delays between the response and stimulus which were distributed around a single target interval. The subject's task on each trial was to say whether the presented delay was longer or shorter than the target interval.

For each target interval we presented six equally spaced response-stimulus intervals, using the method of constant stimuli. The mean of these six test intervals was equal to the target interval, the range was approximately equal to 98% of the mean range of produced intervals for the corresponding target interval in the *stringent* condition of the second experiment, and the test intervals closest to the target interval were presented three times more often than the test intervals farthest from the target interval and one and a half times more often than the test intervals at the middle distance from the target interval. Each of the three subjects was permitted to take as long as needed to give her verbal time judgment. Feedback took the same form as in the earlier experiments except that the word "Right" or "Wrong" was added to the display. There were five blocks of 48 trials each in every session, with the first block for practice.

The results are shown in Figure 7. As is seen in Panel A, mean RTs decreased with target intervals and mean RTs were longer when time judgments were necessary than when subjects simply made one response. As before, mean variances increased approximately linearly with intervals; the slope and zero-intercept of the linear function fitted to the mean variance points were comparable to what we found in the 2-response experiments.

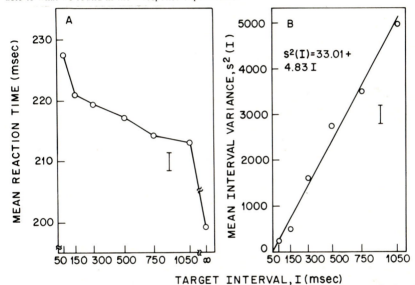

Fig. 7. Results of the time judgment experiment, averaged over the three subjects. Each point represents a mean of about 430 observations. Errors of responding on catch trials or responding before the reaction signal was presented occurred altogether on less than 2% of the trials in each of the seven conditions. (A) Mean RTs and estimate of ±SE. For all subjects mean RTs were shortest in the ∞ (no judgment) condition. The mean RT function in the judgment conditions was quite representative of all subjects, as is shown by the fact that the mean function accounts for 99.1%, 92.7%, and 98.5% of the variance of mean RTs for the three subjects, respectively. (B) Mean variances (averaged over the three subjects) of the psychophysical functions for each target condition, fitted linear function, and estimate of ±SE. The method used to estimate variances comes from Woodworth and Schlosberg (1954, pp 204-210). Linear regression accounts for 98.8% of the variance of mean variances, which is not significantly surpassed by fitting a quadratic function to the same points. Slopes (in msec) and zero-intercepts (in msec^2) of fitted linear functions for individual subjects are 3.61 and 28.54, 5.15 and 43.89, and 5.71 and 26.73, respectively.

These results add weight to our conclusion that the main RT effects obtained in our earlier experiments were not due to response competition or adjustment of response delay covariance, since in the present experiment there was no overt second response. The main conclusion we can reach with the present experiment is that the clock setting process used for interresponse intervals is also used for timing delays between movements and stimuli. (One could imagine that in the time judgment task the mental alarm clock was set to go off near the target time so that time judgments could be made by judging the order of detection of the alarm and vibration.)

V. Conclusion

The main results of this study can be summarized as follows. First, we have shown that the time to make the first of two responses depends on the required precision of the interresponse interval and does not merely depend on there being a second response or on the requirement to make use of visual feedback. Second, we have shown that this RT effect does not derive from a process of adjusting the covariance of motor delays for the two responses. Third, we have shown that our RT results can be explained by a clock setting process whose duration is predicted by an analogue of Fitts' Law. Fourth, we have shown that the clock setting process is not used exclusively for the timing of overt movements.

What are the theoretical implications of these findings? One implication concerns the use of proprioceptive feedback in movement timing. Many interresponse intervals that we required were long enough for proprioceptive feedback from the first response to be available to control the onset time of the second response. Yet even for such long interresponse intervals, we found that RTs were longer than when no specific interresponse interval had to be made. This result leads us to believe that the availability of proprioceptive feedback does not eliminate the need (or at least the tendency) for motor preprogramming.

A second implication of our study concerns the application of Fitts' Law to the hypothesized clock setting process. To our knowledge, the present study is only the second to use Fitts' Law to account for RT data. The first such study was by Fitts and Peterson (1964). The fact that Fitts' Law can be applied to RT data as well as movement time data (see Langolf, Chaffin, & Foulke, 1977, and Schmidt, Zelaznick, & Frank, 1978), implies that Fitts' Law may be a very general description of the relation between speed and precision in human performance.

We would like to go a step further, however, and propose that the applicability of Fitts' Law to RT data as well as movement time data (for the motion of a hand to a target) suggests that processes of movement *preparation* bear an isomorphic relation to processes of movement *execution*[4]. One of the identifiable differences between the two kinds of processes, however, is that preparatory processes occur much more rapidly than execution processes. That this is so is implied by the fact that estimates of information transmission rates $(1/b)$ for RTs are much higher than for movement times: Fitts and Peterson's estimate of $1/b$ for RTs was 185 bit/sec and our estimates of $1/b$ for RTs have ranged from 57.6 to 137 bit/sec in the experiments reported here. By contrast, estimates of $1/b$ for movement times are usually around 10 bit/sec (see Langolf et al. and Schmidt et al.). Why are information transmission rates higher for preparatory processes than for execution processes? Perhaps by having rapid preparation processes, it becomes possible for the actor to make decisions effectively about which of the indefinitely large set of possible movements he or she should perform at any given time.

The final implication of our study that we mention here is drawn from our last experiment, where we showed that the clock setting process is not used exclusively for controlling time intervals between movements. In 1961 Hirsch and Sherrick concluded from a series of experiments on temporal-order judgments that the human nervous system possesses a central clock that is linked to different afferent modalities. Our last experiment suggests that this clock (or some clock) may be linked both to afferent and efferent modalities, thereby making it a truly central clock in the central nervous system.

FOOTNOTES

1. In the 0 msec condition subjects were permitted to respond with the right finger before the left, and *RT* was defined by the latency of the first response. The RT drop in the 0 msec condition was not attributable to fast RTs when the right finger led the left (which was permitted only in this condition), because right-first RTs were only 3 msec longer on the average than left-first RTs.

2. After completing this experiment, we informally retested two of the subjects in the 1-response condition and in the standard interval production task. In the latter condition we required each subject to produce the same mean interval as she had produced in the experiment, but with reduced interval variance. For both subjects the RT difference between the 2-response and 1-response condition reappeared, indicating that practice had not eliminated the RT difference.

3. The reason why we do not set *a* equal to the mean *RT* in the ∞ condition is that the clock is presumably not used in this condition. Consequently, there is no need to check whether the clock pointer is outside W_l, and there is no need to activate the clock once it has been set. Either or both of these processes could inflate *a*. These considerations imply that in the experiment reported in Section IIB, the clock either was not used in the 2-response condition or, if the clock was used, the position of the pointer was almost never checked to see if the clock needed to be reset *and* activation of the clock took a negligible amount of time.

4. This idea is reminiscent of the idea that preparation of a movement is mediated by an "anticipatory response image" (e.g., Greenwald, 1970, Kelso & Wallace, 1978) which is thought to bear some *structural* similarity to the movement.

REFERENCES

[1] Adams, J. A. Feedback theory of how joint receptors regulate the timing and positioning of a limb. Psychol Rev. 84 (1977) 504-523.

[2] Cauraugh, J. H. and Christina, R. W. Proprioceptive feedback as a mediator in interlimb timing. J Motor Behav. 10 (1978) 239-244.

[3] Fitts, P. M. The information capacity of the human motor system in controlling the amplitude of movement. J Exp Psychol. 47 (1954) 381-391.

[4] Fitts, P. M. and Peterson, J. R. Information capacity of discrete motor responses. J. Exp. Psychol. 67 (1964) 103-112.

[5] Greenwald, A. G. Sensory feedback mechanisms in performance control: With special reference to the ideo-motor mechanism. Psychol Rev. 77 (1970) 73-99.

[6] Hirsch, I. J. and Sherrick, C. E., Jr. Perceived order in different sense modalities. J Exp Psychol. 62 (1961) 423-432.

[7] Kelso, J. A. S. Joint receptors do not provide a satisfactory basis for motor timing and positioning. Psychol Rev. 85 (1978) 474-481.

[8] Kelso, J. A. S. and Wallace, S. A. Conscious mechanisms in movement, in Stelmach, G. E. (ed), Information Processing in Motor Control and Learning (Academic Press, New York, 1978).

[9] Langolf, G. D., Chaffin, D. B., and Foulke, J. A. An investigation of Fitts' Law using a wide range of movement amplitudes. J Motor Behav. 8 (1976) 113-128.

[10] Parzen, E. Stochastic Processes (Holden-Day, San Francisco, 1962).

[11] Rosenbaum, D. A. Human movement initiation: Specification of arm, direction, and extent. J Exp Psychol: Gen. In press.

[12] Rosenbaum, D. A. and Patashnik, O. Time to time in the human motor system, in Nickerson, R. S. (ed.), Attention and Performance VIII (Erlbaum, Hillsdale, New Jersey, In press).

[13] Schmidt, R. A., Zelaznick, H. N., and Frank, J. S. Sources of inaccuracy in rapid movement, in Stelmach, G. E. (ed.), Information Processing in Motor Control and Learning (Academic Press, New York, 1978).

[14] Sternberg, S., Monsell, S., Knoll, R. L., and Wright, C. E. The latency and duration of rapid movement sequences: Comparisons of speech and typewriting, in Stelmach, G. E. (ed.), Information Processing in Motor Control and Learning (Academic Press, New York, 1978).

[15] Vorberg, D. and Hambuch, R. On the temporal control of rhythmic performance, in Requin, J. (ed.), Attention and Performance VII (Erlbaum, Hillsdale, New Jersey, 1978).

[16] Wing, A. and Kristofferson, A. B. Response delays and the timing of discrete motor responses. Percept & Psychophys. 14 (1973) 5-12.

[17] Woodworth, R. S. and Schlosberg, H. Experimental Psychology (Holt, Rinehart and Winston, New York, 1954).

Tutorials in Motor Behavior
G.E. Stelmach and J. Requin (eds.)
© *North-Holland Publishing Company, 1980*

30

THE SPEED-ACCURACY PARADOX IN MOVEMENT CONTROL:
ERRORS OF TIME AND SPACE

K. M. Newell
Institute for Child Behavior and Development
University of Illinois at Urbana-Champaign

It is suggested that a paradox exists in the speed-
accuracy trade-off phenomenon in the control of
movements constrained by requirements of both time
and space. Namely, that increased movement velocity
engenders the dual and opposing effects of increasing spatial error but decreasing timing error. This
paradox is demonstrated in an experiment which independently manipulated movement time and velocity
in a discrete aiming movement task. Explanations
for, and the practical implications of this paradox
are discussed.

INTRODUCTION

The phenomenon of speed accuracy trade-offs is one of the most reliable and
pervasive relationships which has been established between movement parameters. Since Woodworth's (1899) seminal work on this issue, the finding
that increased movement velocity leads to greater movement error has been
replicated in a variety of tasks over many experimental conditions. This
paper offers a caveat to the general speed-accuracy trade-off notion by
demonstrating the paradox that exists when both spatial and timing errors
are employed as dependent variables.

Almost without exception, investigations of speed-accuracy trade-offs involve some kind of spatial measure as the dependent variable. For example,
in choice reaction time (RT) studies there is a point where significant decreases in RT can only be achieved through an increase in error as reflected
in pressing the wrong key (e.g., Fitts, 1966; Pew, 1969). Similarly, in
discrete aiming tasks, increases in movement velocity or decreases in movement time (MT) can only be achieved with an increase in movement error, as
reflected in either percentage of target misses or actual distance error
from the designated target (e.g., Schmidt, Zelaznik & Frank, 1978). These
increases in movement spatial error, however, only occur when the movement
velocity is above a certain level, a fact that is often overlooked (see top
half of Figure 1).

In contrast, timing error decreases as movement velocity increases (Newell,
Hoshizaki, Carlton & Halbert, 1979a) and this reduction of timing error, as
measured by AE/MT%, is a logarithmic function of average velocity (Newell,
Carlton, Carlton & Halbert, 1979b). Timing error decreases at higher average velocities principally through a reduction of variable error rather

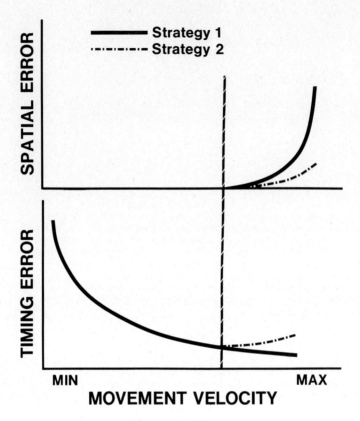

Figure 1. Hypothetical functions for spatial and timing errors as a func-
          tion of movement velocity.

than any shifts in constant error. The decline in timing error is essentially independent of MT although MT's which are on the order of a RT or less
tend to generate a timing error function with higher intercept values,
particularly at low movement velocities. The effect that movement velocity has upon timing performance has been masked in previous studies because movement velocity and MT have not been manipulated independently. In
summary, our findings reveal a curvilinear decrease in timing error with
increases in the average velocity of movement up to about 95% of the maximum velocity that can be generated for a given amplitude. A hypothetical
function of these findings is depicted in the bottom half of figure 1.

Our earlier experiments on timing error were all generated from movements
which were constrained by a unidimensional trackway which leaves open the
possibility that our findings are peculiar to that task. In particular, it
may be that the timing error function only occurs when the spatial demands
of the task are minimized, or when timing error is a direct reflection of
spatial error as in unidimensional timing tasks. On the other hand, it
could be that the spatial and timing error functions demonstrated previous-

ly can operate simultaneously in a two or three dimensional task (see Figure 1). That is, if one moves at a velocity which is on the lower side of the cut-off point at which spatial errors begin, increased movement velocity could facilitate the timing of the response without causing any increase in movement error. On the upper side of the movement velocity cut-off point typical speed-accuracy trade-offs would occur although the exact function would vary according to the instructional set. If the emphasis of the task is the reduction of timing error then increased movement velocity could decrease timing error but result in dramatic increases in spatial error (Figure 1, strategy 1). If one attempts to compensate by moving slower, then a leveling off or increase in timing error would occur together with a reduction in spatial error (Figure 1, strategy 2). The cut-off point on the velocity continuum at which spatial errors start to occur would be a function of the spatial error constraints of the task together with the average movement velocity. In other words, the smaller the target or effective bandwidth of error tolerated the lower the velocity at which spatial errors are generated.

The above description suggests that a paradox may exist in speed-accuracy trade-offs when both time and space are criterion independent measures. The experiment reported investigates this paradox using a Fitt's Law (Fitts & Peterson, 1964) discrete aiming movement paradigm over a range of average velocities using various MT-distance combinations. The basic thrust of the experiment was to determine if increased movement velocity leads to increases and decreases in spatial and temporal movement errors, respectively. An additional concern was the interactive effects of MT and velocity in determining both spatial and temporal errors.

METHOD

Subjects

The subjects were eight right-handed volunteers from the University of Illinois.

Apparatus

A 16 x 72 cm rectangular aluminum plate provided the base for a circular copper target and a copper starting pad on which to rest the stylus at the start position. The target disk was 7 mm in diameter. The location of the copper starting pad could be changed to accommodate any movement distance. Adjacent to the target disk was a twenty-eight volt incandescent red light which was used as the warning signal.

MT and the error rate for missing the target were recorded. MT was the time period from the release of the stylus from the start pad until the stylus contacted the target disk or the surrounding aluminum plate. Error rate was the ratio (%) of the number of target misses to the number of trials analyzed. These measures were recorded via a digital interface unit which also determined the random foreperiod (1-2-3-4 sec) used for each trial.

Procedures

All testing was conducted in a soundproof laboratory test room. The sub-

ject sat with the apparatus placed on a table in front of him so that the
target was directly in front of the mid-point of the body. The start point
was placed to the right of the target at the appropriate distance so that
the subject always moved the stylus from right to left.

Before each trial, the subject held the stylus in his right hand on the
start position and awaited the auditory warning signal as a precursor to
the onset of the starting light. The subject was instructed to move the
stylus from the start position and hit the target in a time as close as
possible to the designated MT. The subject was instructed that the emphasis of the task was MT even at the expense of missing the target spatially.
A clock provided the subject with knowledge of results of the MT immediately at the end of each movement. Subjects performed a trial about every 5
seconds.

Experimental Design

Subjects performed 80 trials at each MT-distance combination. Different
distances were examined at each of 3 MTs (200, 300, 400 msec). The distances used at the 3 MTs were: 200 msec MT, 1/2, 1, 2, 4, 8 and 16 cm; 300
msec MT, 3/4, 1 1/2, 3, 6, 12 and 24 cm; and 400 msec MT, 1, 2, 4, 8, 16
and 32 cm. All the distances within a MT were performed at one sitting.
Order of the MTs over days and distances within MT were randomly determined. Only the data from the last 50 trials (Trials 31-80) were utilized in
the analyses.

RESULTS

Spatial Error

The % of target misses as a function of MT and average velocity are depicted in Figure 2. An analysis of variance revealed that only the velocity
factor was significant, $F (5,35) = 5.74$, $p < .01$. In other words, % target misses tended to follow movement velocity independently of MT. Figure
2 shows, however, that there was a trend for error rate to be reduced in
the 400 msec MT at the highest average velocity. This was to be expected
given that 80 cm/sec is a lower %'of the maximum velocity that can be generated in a 400 msec movement than it is in a 200 msec movement.

Timing Error

Table 1 shows the mean timing errors as a function of average movement
velocity. Important to the outcome of this experiment was the condition
that subjects moved with a MT around the criterion MT and that there be no
differences in constant error (CE) over the average velocities. Analysis
of CE revealed that the main effects of MT, $F (2,14) = 2.50$, $p > .05$, and
velocity, $F (5,35) = 1.21$, $p > .05$, together with their interaction ($F < 1$)
were non significant. Thus, subjects generally moved in a time either
side of the criterion MT at each respective movement condition.

Analysis of absolute error (AE) and variable error (VE) showed that the main
effects of velocity and MT together with their interaction were significant.
These were for AE and VE respectively, MT, $F (2,14) = 14.58$ and 6.48, $p <
.01$, velocity, $F (5,35) = 11.56$ and 4.63, $p < .01$, and their interaction,
$F (10,70) = 2.26$ and 2.56, $p < .05$. As would be expected with a range

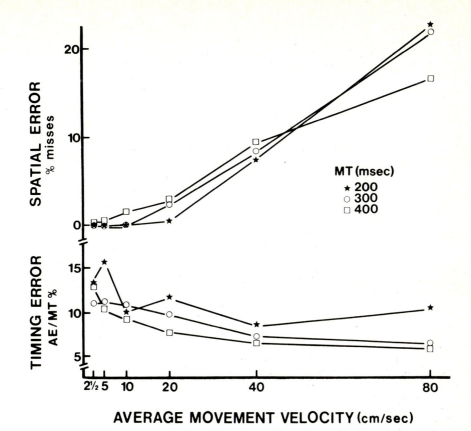

Figure 2.   Spatial and timing errors as a function of MT and velocity

effect both AE and VE increased with longer MTs. Increased movement velocity generally decreased both AE and VE. One exception was in the 200 msec
80 cm/sec condition where an increment in both AE and VE occurred relative
to the 40 cm/sec condition for that MT. This increase in error seems to
have been due to the fact that subjects slowed their responses somewhat as
reflected by a small elevation of CE.

Perhaps the most meaningful assessment of timing error as a function of MT
can be advanced on the basis of AE/MT expressed as a percentage (AE/MT%).
Figure 2 shows AE/MT% as a function of MT and average velocity. The main
effects of MT, F (2,14) = 9.80, p < .01 and velocity, F (5,35) = 9.70,
p < .01 were significant. Post-hoc analysis through the Newman-Keuls procedure indicated that AE/MT% at the 200 msec MT (M = 11.83) was significantly higher (p < .01) than both the 300 msec MT (M = 9.45) and 400 msec
MT (M = 8.99). Post-hoc analysis showed that the slow velocity conditions
of 2 1/2 and 5 cm/sec produced significantly (p < .05) greater error than
all other velocity conditions and that the 40 and 80 cm/sec velocity condi-

tions generated significantly less error than the 20 cm/sec condition.

In summary, timing error tends to decrease as average movement velocity increases, and this function is consistent over a range of MTs. Movements
with a duration on the order of a RT or less tend to generate proportionally greater timing error than movements with longer durations.

Table 1

Movement Timing Errors (msec) as a
Function of Movement Velocity (cm/sec)

Movement Error	Average Movement Velocity					
	2.5	5	10	20	40	80
CE	2.06	5.09	2.89	9.11	3.93	7.99
AE	37.59	36.03	29.98	28.03	22.04	22.32
VE	3181.83	2377.44	1614.11	1487.99	957.22	1212.10
AE/MT%	12.58	12.64	10.10	9.81	7.52	7.91

DISCUSSION

The results from this rather simple experiment demonstrate quite clearly the
paradox of the speed-accuracy trade-off phenomenon in the control of movements. Namely, that increased movement velocity generates increments in
spatial error but decrements in timing error. The error functions for the
spatial and temporal parameters essentially follow those shown previously
for both spatial (e.g., Schmidt, et al., 1978) and timing (e.g., Newell,
et al., 1979a) errors when each has been considered independently. It
appears, however, that increased movement velocity produces relatively
smaller gains in timing performance at the expense of somewhat larger
losses in spatial performance.

There was no interaction between the effects of MT and velocity upon either
the spatial or timing errors. This was surprising, particularly for spatial errors since it might be expected that fewer errors would occur at the
highest velocity condition for the 400 msec MT than the 200 msec MT. This
is because the velocity for the 400 msec MT is a smaller percentage of the
maximum velocity that could be generated in comparison to a MT of shorter
duration. Figure 2 suggests, however, that differences in spatial error
between movement times would have occurred had higher movement velocities
been utilized (Schmidt, et al., 1978). For timing error, the 200 msec MT
condition produced significantly greater error proportionally than the
larger MT's. This finding is consistent with our previous work (Newell,
et al., 1979b) and suggests that the availability of feedback principally
lowers the intercept of the error function over velocity rather than fundamentally changing the characteristics of the timing error function.

Why has this paradox not been revealed previously in speed-accuracy trade-
offs in the control of movements? Several potential reasons are apparent
most of which are methodological in origin. First, there have been no
systematic attempts to measure spatial and temporal errors simultaneously,

and where both parameters have been recorded, little regard has been given
to the temporal error. Second, most studies of speed-accuracy trade-offs
in discrete aiming tasks have insisted that subjects move as fast as possible with a certain error rate, rather than have subjects attempt to aim for
a target in a certain MT (e.g., Fitts & Peterson, 1964). Third, previous
research, in large part as a consequence of the above two points, has rarely required subjects to move with a velocity which is on the left hand side
of the hypothetical cut off point where spatial errors above a set tolerance begin to occur (see Figure 1). Fourth, most timing error studies have
been conducted on a unidimensional trackway which results in spatial errors
(which are rarely measured) being a direct function of the MT-distance requirements of the task. Considering the above points collectively, it is
not surprising, therefore, that the extant research has led to the generally accepted notion that increased movement velocity leads to increments in
performance error, rather than the more accurate statement that higher movement velocities lead to the dual and opposing effects of increments in
spatial error and decrements in timing error.

Over the years a number of explanations have been advanced to explain speed-
accuracy trade-offs (c.f., Schmidt, et al., 1978). Given that the explanations principally relate to spatial errors it seems pertinent to ascertain
which of these theoretical accounts can also logically relate to timing
error. Before pursuing explanations for the paradox in speed-accuracy
trade-offs in movement control it must be recognized that the relative contribution of central and peripheral mechanisms to the phenomenon will vary
according to the task demands. For example, MT would be a fundamental variable determining the degree of contribution of both proprioceptive (e.g.,
Adams, 1977) and visual (Keele & Posner, 1968) feedback information to movement control. Similarly, the impulse required to initiate the response
could well be a factor determining the variability of the response output.
These illustrations should be sufficient to indicate that the relative contribution of central and peripheral factors to movement control rests on a
dynamic rather than static relationship.

One centralist explanation recently advanced to explain Fitts' (1954) law
and the speed-accuracy trade-off in general is that increased movement
velocity or force output leads to greater "noise" in the force and time
production mechanisms (Schmidt, et al., 1978). This increase "noise" in
the response system leads to greater variability in response output and as
a consequence spatial error around the to-be-aimed-for target. Given that
increased "noise" is seen to occur in the force-time mechanisms one would
expect that increases in the size of the impulse would also lead to decrements in timing performance. The current experiment, together with the
earlier ones in the series (Newell, et al., 1979a; Newell, et al., 1979b),
clearly indicates that this is not the case. Indeed, the opposite result
occurs with larger response impulses leading to smaller timing errors. This
consistent finding casts doubt on the validity of "noise" as a concomitant
of increases in impulse generated, even if it is to be an account of spatial
error.

The current findings for timing error as a function of movement velocity
seem to invite an explanation which is completely opposite to the impulse
variability argument generated by Schmidt, et al., (1978). One hypothesis
which is in line with the current findings for temporal error is that proposed by Basmajian (1977) who suggested that movements are controlled

through the inhibition of muscle fibers not involved in the movement.
Given that slow movement velocities of a constant mass require smaller impulses for response initiation it would seem that proportionally more motor
units would have to be inhibited. On this view, greater emphasis on the inhibitory aspects of motor unit recruitment might increase the complexity of
the response and processing required to initiate the response. Some support for the latter viewpoint is already available in that RTs for the initiation of a single motor unit response are found to be longer than that
required to generate an overt key press (Kimm & Sutton, 1973). Additionally, we have recently shown that initiation times tend to decrease systematically as a function of increases in average movement velocity (Newell,
et al., 1979a; Hoshizaki & Newell, 1979). Thus Basmajian's (1977) theoretical notions are compatible with the timing error function but have still
not been directly examined due to the fact that few EMG studies have been
conducted on this issue in a dynamic movement context. An additional concern is how such an impulse argument produces differential effects on timing and spatial errors.

It is possible that different explanations need to be sought to account for
the opposite effects of movement velocity on timing and spatial errors.
Our current bias is toward outflow explanations given that the velocity
effect for both timing and spatial errors operates in movements of very
short duration. This does not eliminate the role of feedback in movement
control but short duration movements probably confine it to a role of making the response more like the one intended, rather than inducing any overt
error correction that are typically found in movements of longer duration.
The fundamental cause of spatial errors could be mechanical in that similar
spatial deviations from some intended initial movement trajectory lead to
greater spatial error from a larger response impulse. This is a typical
outcome of increased velocity of movements engaged in the projection of an
object. The degree of error correction will depend upon the deviation from
the intended path and the time available to bring about an amendment of
the response.

Feedback theory has traditionally been invoked to explain speed-accuracy
trade-offs in movement error. Visual feedback clearly facilitates both
spatial accuracy and timing of discrete movements when the MTs are in the
order of a RT or longer (Keele & Posner, 1968). Similarly, proprioceptive feedback has been shown to facilitate timing of discrete responses (e.g.,
Ellis, Schmidt & Wade, 1968) although interestingly, little effect has been
demonstrated on spatial error (e.g., Fitts, 1954; Schmidt, et al., 1978).
It is clear then, that visual and proprioceptive feedback contributes to
the minimization of performance error when these processes can and need to
be invoked to bring about movement control. Performance error still occurs,
however, in movements with discrete corrections. The spatial error seems
to be a function of the distance travelled during the last error correction
(Howarth, Beggs & Bowden, 1971) and yet again the reverse appears to be the
case for timing error.

In summary, feedback explanations do not seem to be able to account for the
speed-accuracy paradox in movement control with respect to spatial and timing errors. The most appealing approach to this paradox would seem to stem
from some combination of outflow and mechanical processes with the realization that feedback will augment response control in varying degrees according to the task demands and skill level of the performance. Thus, we re-

main in the somewhat frustrating position of apparently having a phenomenon in search of a concise and viable explanation.

Finally, the practical implications of the paradox in speed-accuracy trade-offs should not go without comment. Obviously, the appropriate point on the velocity continuum (see Figure 1) at which to operate will vary according to the task and the costs and pay-offs associated with errors of space and time. It would, however, seem most efficient to minimize temporal error given a certain level of tolerance for spatial error. In short, when both time and space are criterion response parameters one would want to function as close as possible to the left hand side of the cut off point established for the task. Only in this way will effective utilization be made of the relationship that exists between parameters in speed-accuracy trade-offs, and specifically the finding that increased movement velocity engenders the dual and opposing effect of increasing spatial error but decreasing timing error.

FOOTNOTE

I would like to thank Les Carlton for help in conducting the experiment.

REFERENCES

|1| Woodworth, R. S., The accuracy of voluntary movement, Psychological Review Monograph Supplement. 3(1899) No. 13.

|2| Fitts, P. M., Cognitive aspects of information processing: III, Set for speed vs. accuracy, Journal of Experimental Psychology. 71 (1966) 849-857.

|3| Pew, R. W., The speed-accuracy operating characteristic, Acta Psychologica. 30 (1969) 16-26.

|4| Schmidt, R. A., Zelaznik, H. N., and Frank, J. S., Sources of inaccuracy in rapid movement, in: Stelmach, G. E. (Ed.), Information Processing in Motor Control and Learning. (Academic Press, New York, 1978).

|5| Newell, K. M., Hoshizaki, L. E. F., Carlton, M. J., and Halbert, J. A. Movement time and velocity as determinants of movement timing accuracy, Journal of Motor Behavior. 11 (1979a) 49-58.

|6| Newell, K. M., Carlton, M. J., Carlton, L. G., and Halbert, J. A., Movement velocity as a factor in movement timing accuracy, Manuscript submitted for publication, 1979b.

|7| Fitts, P. M., and Peterson, J. R., Information capacity of discrete motor responses, Journal of Experimental Psychology. 67 (1964) 103-112.

|8| Adams, J. A., Feedback theory of how joint receptors regulate the timing and positioning of a limb, Psychological Review. 48 (1977) 504-523.

|9| Keele, S. W., and Posner, M. I., Processing of visual feedback in
      rapid movements, Journal of Experimental Psychology. 77 (1968) 155-
      158.

|10| Fitts, P. M., The information capacity of the human motor system in
      controlling the amplitude of movement, Journal of Experimental Psy-
      chology. 47 (1954) 381-391.

|11| Basmajian, J. V., Motor learning and control: A working hypothesis,
      Archives of Physical Medicine and Rehabilitation. 58 (1977) 38-40.

|12| Kimm, J., and Sutton, D., Foreperiod effects on human single motor
      unit reaction times, Physiology and Behavior. 10 (1973) 539-542.

|13| Hoshizaki, L. E. F., and Newell, K. M., On the relative contribution
      of movement time, aplitude and velocity to response initiation, Manu-
      script submitted for publication, 1979.

|14| Ellis, M. J., Schmidt, R. A., and Wade, M. G., Proprioception vari-
      ables as determinants of lapsed-time estimation, Ergonomics. 11
      (1968) 557-586.

|15| Howarth, C. I., Beggs, W. D. A., and Bowden, J. M., The relationship
      between the speed and accuracy of movement aimed at a target, Acta
      Psychologica. 35 (1971) 207-218.

Tutorials in Motor Behavior
G.E. Stelmach and J. Requin (eds.)
© *North-Holland Publishing Company, 1980*

31

THE ROLE OF THE
MOVEMENT STRUCTURE IN
ANTICIPATORY TIMING

D.A. Tyldesley
Interfakulteit Lichamelijke Opvoeding
Vrije Universiteit
Amsterdam, Nederland

The proprioceptive input hypothesis is difficult
to generalize to movement components of everyday
skills which are frequently complete in less than
200 msec.. A series of discrete linear movement
timing experiments is described which provides
little support for proprioceptive mediation in
timing. Superior explanations of the data are
found in terms of program control, the influence
of instructions and the structure of the movement
itself. Studies of a biphasic ball-striking task
indicate that trained subjects use spatially-
consistent movement patterns to reduce temporal
uncertainty in both closed and open environments.
Timing is viewed as an 'action-oriented' process
wherein information is extracted from the display
to match the 'run-times' of pre-planned movement
structures.

INTRODUCTION

Studies of motor timing have remained closely related to cognitive
theories of time perception. As a consequence, timing is usually seen as an
input-steered, sometimes conscious, process and the movement structure and
its integration into the timed interval are ignored. This article points
out that, in normality, the process of timing always includes a substantial
movement of the same limb as the anticipatory response. Its integration
into the estimated interval and prediction of its duration are essential in
the prior planning of complex movement sequences.

MOVEMENT TIMING

Of the various factors which constitute the cognitive representation of a
planned movement, the time structure is one of the most likely to be predetermined. Conrad's (1955) early definition of timing as being the
creation of the most favourable conditions for response, focussed clearly
upon the planned nature of timing but gave no indication of the means by
which this analysis-by-synthesis was carried out. Since then, various
experiments have provided evidence that certain aspects of temporal
patterning (such as rhythmicity) are pre-written into the motor program
(Summers,1975). Glencross (1973) noted proportional time consistencies in
movement components when subjects cranked a handle at different speeds.

Furthermore, the fraction of the total cycle time represented by the
same component in different subjects remained roughly constant. Similarly,
Armstrong (1970) found that the relative timing of different components
of a lever movement remained constant although the total time for the
pattern varied. These results suggest that while overall speed is a
parameter which can vary between trials, the relative timing is an
integral part of the program itself.

Despite this demonstration of the importance of output features, theories
of timing in motor skill have directed attention mainly at the <u>perceptual</u>
anticipatory elements of the task. It is possible that this preoccupation
with input factors is related to (a) the traditional elimination of
movement time from reaction time studies and (b) the growth of current
theories out of concepts of experiential time.

THEORIES OF TIME EXPERIENCE

Researchers ascribe either to a pulse counter or information storage
approach when considering time experience. The former 'passive' metaphor
sees time as a dimension of the real world, perceived by some counter
mechanism linked to a timebase, and typical of this approach are the
mathematical models of Treisman (1963) and in more recent years Abel
(1972) and Kinchla (1972). The latter 'active' metaphor holds that
time does not exist independently of events and perception of time is
seen as a subjective reconstruction based upon the quantity of stored
information during the estimated interval (Vroon, 1970).

Unfortunately, these theories of time experience do not contribute to an
understanding of how everyday actions are 'timed'. The processes by
which we judge the time available to cross the road in the face of
oncoming traffic, are not elucidated by studies of duration experience,
and Vroon (1970) clearly separates time perception and the 'faultless
timing of motor activities'.

THEORIES OF MOVEMENT TIMING

Timing is usually defined in perceptual terms with either exteroceptive
or interoceptive cues performing a timebase function which mediates an
anticipatory judgement. Responses as a whole coincide more or less
accurately with an external event. The process of timing is seen as
predominantly an input/central operation, based on the perception of a
cue series, the predictable features of which are more accurately
utilized after a period of practice under similar conditions. This
input-oriented approach is typified by the experimental work of Bartlett
and Bartlett (1959), Treisman (1963) and Christina (1970, 1971).

A combination of factors led, in the late sixties and early seventies to
a hypothesis which suggested that the root of timing behaviour lay in
mechanisms concerned with movement production. The proprioceptive feedback
(PFB) was postulated as a source of regular cues which, when learned,
could mediate temporal anticipation. More specifically, the proprioceptive
input hypothesis holds that PFB from an early portion of a response can
help time the initiation of later responses or response components
(Christina, 1976). A number of testable predictions arise from this and
experiments have been established to examine whether the degree and type

of PFB affects the movement timing.

Typically, these experiments require subjects, without preview, to use a discrete left arm movement to time a right hand finger response. Two amplitudes of the left arm movement are assumed to generate low and high levels of PFB respectively and the implication is, that increased movement distance increases the number of 'discriminable response categories' which can enhance timing in the opposite hand. Timed intervals are invariably of an order of magnitude of 1.5 to 2.0 seconds.

In general   , results for absolute error tend to show a gradually increasing superiority of the high feedback group over trial blocks with subsequent support for the hypothesis. There is no doubt that the hypothesis, as it stands, is adequately tested but the generalisation from such experiments is limited. Given a situation devoid of normal cues (e.g. vision) and given instead a movement to aid anticipation, then it is not surprising that superior results are obtained in a high feedback group. The evidence that links timing directly with proprio-ceptive feedback under normal conditions, is not strong. Furthermore, the intervals investigated were unrealistically long in the motor context. A two second movement over ten inches means a slow average velocity which would normally be avoided by some strategy of moving quickly to the general area of the target and then 'homing-in' on time.

Other points may be added which limit the interpretation of these data:
1. The instructions bias subjects to a strategy wherein conscious attention is paid to PFB. The establishment of idiosyncratic timing strategies is suppressed.
2. Knowledge of the form of movement-generated information suggests that it is unlikely to be a timebase which is available to the central processes during short duration movements (Higgins and Angel, 1970) and unlikely to be sufficiently consistent from trial to trial (Smith, 1969).
3. In general, support for the input hypothesis is derived on an absolute error basis without consideration of whether the timing improvements noted were in the accuracy or consistency. The movements may, in a purely output fashion, have contributed to timing consistency.

The PFB timing paradigm is thus limited and fails to consider ecologically valid timing operations. As Neisser (1976) warns:

>   Experimental arrangements that eliminate the continuities of the
>   ordinary environment may provide insights into certain processing
>   mechanisms, but the relevance of these insights to normal perceptual
>   activity is far from clear.

A series of experiments is described which examine the anticipatory timing of short and long duration movements both with and without preview. These experiements are conducted using discrete linear movements and also fine-grained analysis of a ball-striking task on predictable and unpredictable trajectories.

EXPERIMENT 1

This experiment replicated some of the major features of the PFB/timing paradigm. A 'movement' and a 'no-movement' group were both required to

operatively define one of a range of relatively long time intervals
(between 500 and 2000 msec.). The movement group filled the interval
with a 10 inch movement while the control group attempted to delimit the
interval with some form of mental activity. Estimates were made in the
absence of visual and auditory information and the movement group were
not specifically instructed to use the movement to aid their timing.
The control group were allowed to make no movements which could aid
estimation and thus, overt counting was not available. The results of
this experiment are summarised in figure 1:

FIGURE 1   Mean variable error and constant error as a function of
           estimated interval and movement condition

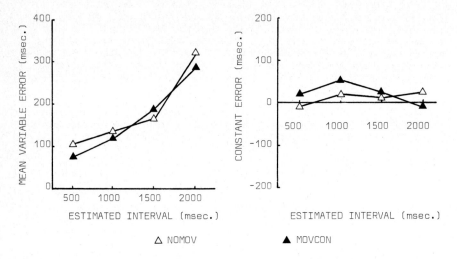

△ NOMOV   ▲ MOVCON

The time interval (TS) main effects was significant for absolute error
(AE) ($F_{3,16}$ = 24.6, $p < 0.01$). Variable error (VE) provided virtually
identical results to those of AE and suggested that under conditions
of relatively long duration movements and no instructional bias in the
movement condition, response variability provided the major error
component whilst constant error (CE) remained close to zero. The linear
trend over this range was significant ($F_{3,16}$ = 16.8, $p < 0.01$) and the
regression of VE on TS was given by VE = 0.14 . TS - 8.3. The movement
condition main effect proved   non-significant on all dependent variables
(e.g. for VE: $F_{1,16}$ = 0.53, $p > 0.25$).

It was concluded from these data that the proprioceptive input hypothesis
was difficult to support when subjects were not specifically instructed
to use movement-generated information to aid their timing. Timing
performance with a substantial movement component was not significantly
better than cognitive strategies such as covert counting. Since AE data
closely reflected VE it seems likely that when timing benefits are
demonstrated, that they are the result of variability reduction. Such
consistency could, in normal movements, arise as a pure output effect.

EXPERIMENT 2

Experiments in the PFB/timing paradigm have suppressed the effects of
mechanical factors by removing the movement component to a separate limb
from that of the timed response. Further, the constraints of linear cursor
and physical endstop meant that timing of fast, short duration movements
have not been studied. Thus, 'unconstrained' movements (Stelmach, Kelso
and Wallace, 1976; Kelso, 1977) were examined, which were not guided
by a linear track and had no physical endstop. The control dynamics were
simply those involved in overcoming the inertial forces of the limb,
in order to cover the given distance in a given time. Timing range
effects for movement distance (5-20 inches) were described for two
movement times (200 and 500 msec). The task was regarded as more akin
to those found in non-laboratory situations (e.g. striking a ball) where
knowledge of the resistive dynamics of the body alone was all that was
required to execute the timed response. Under such conditions, it was
suggested, individual differences in movement control between subjects
would also affect the timing measured. Within-subject minimal movement
time over the given distance was examined as an indicant of 'preferred'
movement capacity which might influence timing. The main results of this
experiment are shown in figure 2.

FIGURE 2   Mean variable error and constant error as a
            function of movement distance and estimated interval

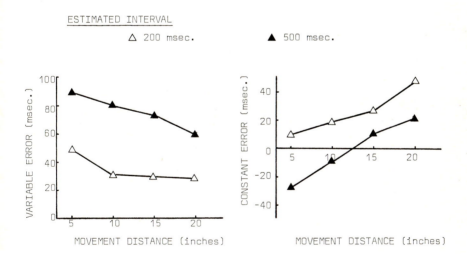

ESTIMATED INTERVAL

△ 200 msec.   ▲ 500 msec.

A wholly positive response bias in the timing of 200 msec. movements
(assumed by default to be under program control) showed a slight increase
with distance moved ($F_{3, 105}$ = 12.8, p < 0.01). However, a 'normal' range
effect with undershooting and overshooting was present only in the 500

msec. estimates ($F_{3,105}$ = 8.9, p < 0.01). The variability of estimates
indicated a steady decrease with distance moved at 500 msec. but at
200 msec., showed a decrease only as the distance increased from 5 to
10 inches. It was concluded that fast, programmed movements over distances
in a range from 10 to 20 inches demonstrate a relatively stable positive
response bias of about + 30 msec. and a within-subject between-trial
standard deviation of also about 30 msec. If the 'knowledge' of these
reliable errors of movement timing is available to the effector
organisation then the complexity of movement control and the degrees
of freedom in decision about what movement best fits the occasion, are
greatly reduced.

The long duration, unconstrained movements demonstrated a timing constant
error range effect which reversed that commonly found in studies of motor
short-term memory for distance. Over long distance, time was overestimated
and over short distances, time was underestimated. This effect can be
interpreted in terms of the subjects' attempts to utilise unreliable
spatial information (from the lack of endstop) to aid temporal anticipation
during the trial.

Subject minimum movement times over the given distances correlated highly
with their timing accuracy on trials which required both high velocity
(e.g. 20 inches in 200 msec.) and low velocity (e.g. 5 inches in 500 msec.).
Thus, it is possible that differential velocity control factors could be
confounding the timing of the very low average velocity movements of the
PFB/timing paradigm (10 inches in 2000 msec.).

Movement velocity, though apparently not a determinant of spatial movement
accuracy, seems to play an important role in establishing the temporal
accuracy. It does not do so through implication of velocity in the timing
decision but as an output effect on the measured timing. Movements within
a central range of velocities demonstrated a response bias of between
+ 10 and + 20 msec. regardless of the distance x time combination that
comprised the movement. If the movement required is slower than the
central range, then errors tend towards increased negativity; if faster,
then the errors tend to increased positivity (see figure 3).

FIGURE 3   Effects of increased average velocity of movement on
            constant error of operative estimates

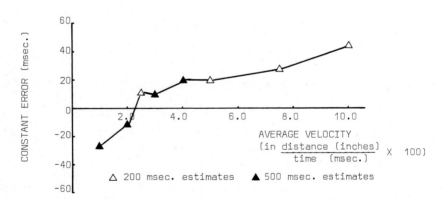

EXPERIMENT 3

As a carry-over from the PFB/timing paradigm, subjects in discrete movement timing experiments continue to operate in the absence of preview. The question thus arises, how do the motor program, visual information and proprioceptive feedback combine to provide adequate anticipation? Christina and Buffan (1976) indicated in a preview/no preview, movement/no movement comparison, that preview led to greater timing accuracy and consistency than did either the no preview or movement alone conditions. However, their study again involved the timing of unreasonably long movements (1.26 seconds) and subjects were predisposed by the task and instructions, to utilise the cue series given first. If proprioception was the initial cue series experienced, then there seems little reason to expect that subjects would not use it. But, in normal situations, subjects experience the visual information first (e.g. the ball flight) and then adapt a suitable movement structure to integrate with the perceived temporal requirements. Thus, two main points were tested: (a) once the subject has experienced the visual sequential dependencies present in the preview, does movement confer any additional timing advantages and (b) after practice with preview plus movement, does removal of the preview create effects which interact with the size of the interval timed?

Three levels of operative estimate (with preview) were established at intervals of 200, 500 and 1000 msec. to provide a range of movements that varied in the functional availability of peripheral information. Subjects were self-paced and initiated the timed interval and the visual display themselves. Subjects operated under only one estimated interval but always acquired this interval in the presence of a reliable dynamic visual display (a spot tracking across an oscilloscope screen) and with a minimal movement response (a switch depression). This acquisition period constituted condition VMM. After performance had become relatively stable under VMM, larger discrete movements to an endstop were integrated into the estimate (condition VM) and after a further period of acquisition, timing compared to the pre-movement levels. In the final two ten-trial blocks (condition MPV), 50% of the trials were, at random, made with the non-appearance of within-trial preview. In this way the relative dependence of the subject at each time interval upon visual information was tested. The results of this experiment are summarised in figure 4.

The results convincingly demonstrated that for both CE and VE timing measures, performance under preview plus integrated limb movement conditions was not superior to performance with preview alone (for the VMM/VM comparison, CE data: $F_{1,22} = 0.31$, $p > 0.25$, and VE data: $F_{1,22} = 1.54$, $p > 0.10$). No noticeable timing benefit or decrement accompanied the addition of a substantial movement to an anticipatory task with preview.

Removal of preview indicated that the shorter duration movements (200 and 500 msec.) were unaffected by either the prior knowledge that their predominant cue source might be absent, or the fact of its absence during the ongoing trial. Although initial acquisition must have taken place with the aid of peripheral visual information, by this stage of learning, control has shifted to another, probably central, timing mechanism.

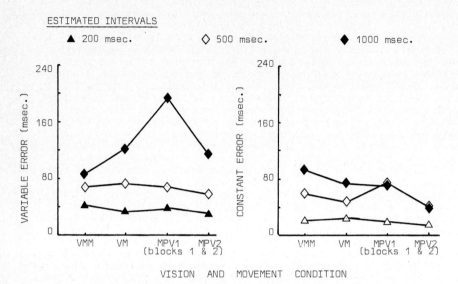

FIGURE 4   Mean variable error and constant error for the various
            vision and movement conditions

ESTIMATED INTERVALS

▲ 200 msec.   ◇ 500 msec.   ◆ 1000 msec.

Over the longer interval (1000 msec) visual information during the trial
appeared to mediate the response timing. Removal of preview had a
significant effect on the variability of estimates as subjects searched
for a new timing strategy ($F_{3, 21}$ = 6.25, p < 0.01). These effects were,
however, short-lived, and within only one ten-trial block VE had
returned to its vision-reliable level. Further comparison indicated that
preview trials under MPV were no less accurate or consistent than those
of the VM phase, when preview was dependably present. The possible absence
of preview did not appear to affect timing. Subjects began each trial
with the expectation that a strategy of visual dependence would be
operable. Vision remained the dominant modality and only when it did not
arrive during long duration movements, did subjects regress to another
strategy.

Timing performance, contrary to earlier views, is not significantly altered
by the presence of a substantial movement of the upper limb which fills the
interval, particularly when the interval has already been experienced
in the presence of preview. Visual plus proprioceptive information does
not appear to confer any marked advantage over visual information alone,
for timing purposes.

EXPERIMENTS 4 AND 5

The final two experiments in the series studied the timing of ballistic
movements in a more ecologically valid situation where highly trained
subjects were free to establish individual strategies to reduce temporal
uncertainty. The first of these experiments is more fully described by

Tyldesley and Whiting (1975). From film analysis of movement organisation in response to a closed, dynamic environment, these authors proposed a second means by which the motor program could assist in anticipatory responding. In addition to the temporal patterning demonstrated by Summers (1975), it appeared that highly trained subjects, when freed from experimental strategy restrictions, could time contact in a ball-striking task through the use of spatially and temporally constant ballistic movements. Least trained subjects were characterised by an inability to produce consistent ballistic movement patterns, which led to timing errors and intermediate subjects could do so, but were unable to locate the chosen pattern adequately in time in relation to the approaching stimulus.

A mechanism of _operational timing_ was proposed which saw a relatively constant 'run-time' for a motor program acting as a means to the reduction of temporal uncertainty. The advantages of such a strategy lay in the reduction of attentional demands, the reduction of the length of interval to be timed by input-based mediation and the easier prior planning of movement sequences.

Important in the strategy of the highly-trained subjects appeared to be the accurate spatial and temporal location of the initiation point (IP) of the ballistic program. In this task it could be operationally defined as the start of the forward movement to contact. The locus of timing decisions of an input form was thus shifted back in time from the point of bat/ball contact to the prediction of IP. The duration over which input-based timing must occur is thus reduced, which (from experiment 2) results in greater accuracy. Operational timing gives expression to the central timing decisions in a reliable and consistent fashion.

But experiment 4 was carried out in a closed environment and could not prove indisputably that subjects were operationally timing, only that a mechanism of consistent movement patterns was available. It remained to experiment 5 to test the hypothesis that temporal consistencies in movement patterning are actually used under normal variable-input conditions. Trialwise stimulus variation was introduced into a table-tennis task similar to that of experiment 4 by programming a machine to project balls on an unpredictable trajectory on each trial. Outcome performance measures were supplemented by fine information regarding the movement organisation. Three kinematic factors (displacement, velocity and acceleration) in two phases of motion (horizontal and vertical) were monitored for two anatomical locations (bat and elbow) and the ball flight, by cine registration and analysis. Two groups (trained and untrained) of three subjects performed a ball-striking task and were recorded for 17 $\pm$ 1 trials at a sampling frequency of 100 f.p.s. Analysis was restricted to a 500 msec. 'window' from 300 msec. before bat/ball contact to 200 msec. after. The 300 msec. period enclosed the initiation point of the forward ballistic movement. Specific research questions were: (a) is the temporal location of IP in relation to the time of bat/ball contact, constant in this open/dynamic environment, and indicative of an operational timing mode? (b) if movement duration consistencies can be identified, does their presence interact with the experience level of the performer? (c) can parameters be identified within the stimulus input (ball flight characteristics) which determine the timing of IP?

A discrete measures approach was adopted, and an initial list of 22
kinematic pattern descriptors, defined according to time during movement,
anatomical location and mechanical property, was refined to 10 variables
for examination of questions (a), (b) and (c). Question (a) was
statistically approached through a simple variance comparison technique,
F_{max}, whilst a multiple linear regression method was used to identify the
input variables controlling the movement organisation and in particular
the temporal location of IP. Both techniques were surprisingly effective,
the F_{max} tests highlighting significant consistency differences between
the two groups, and the multiple regression technique pinpointing parameters within the visual display which governed subjects' movement
organisation strategies. Given an open environment with dynamic stimulus
input, the following observations on timing and movement control could
be made.
1. Despite trialwise variability of input, the timing of the initiation
of ballistic movements was significantly less variable in more experienced
performers (see figure 5a). An operational timing mode appeared to reduce
one of the degrees of freedom of the movement organisation, that of the
movement time. The timing of a portion of the response was thus preprogrammed and prepared before initiation of the ballistic response and
the attentional demands of movement production reduced.

FIGURES 5a AND 5b   Consistency of initiation of ballistic movements (IP)
                    and the ball locations corresponding to IP

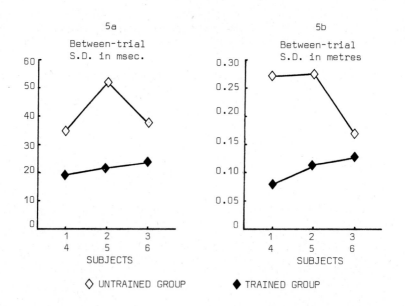

2. In coincidence-anticipation tasks such as this, trained performers chose a constant location of the approaching ball in absolute space, at which to release their programmed movement (see figure 5b). The timing of ballistic movements probably occurs on recognition of a particular ball size in terms of the angle subtended at the subject's eye.
3. Reduced variability, in trained performers, of IP time and the ball displacement corresponding to IP are complemented by increased variability in movement velocity parameters. It appeared that trained subjects in a variable situation reduced the temporal degrees of freedom of their movements and exercised control to match the environment through spatial and velocity factors.
4. Multiple regression techniques indicated that in untrained performers, the timing of IP was significantly related to both displacement and velocity parameters in the input signal (see table 1).

TABLE 1   Beta weights for the various significant independent variables within each IP prediction equation (standard regression method)

| | BALL DISPLACEMENT FEATURES | | BALL VELOCITY FEATURES | | |
	at IP	100 msec. before contact	at projection	at IP	100 msec. before contact
Untrained group					
1	$-1.41^{\dagger\dagger}$	$0.30^{\dagger}$	-	-	$0.30^{\dagger}$
2	$-0.61^{\dagger\dagger}$	-	-	$-0.49^{\dagger\dagger}$	-
3	$-1.07^{\dagger\dagger}$	$0.46^{\dagger\dagger}$	$0.06^{\dagger}$	-	$-0.11^{\dagger\dagger}$
Trained group					
4	$-1.00^{\dagger\dagger}$	$0.13^{\dagger}$	-	-	-
5	$-1.05^{\dagger\dagger}$	$0.50^{\dagger\dagger}$	-	-	$-0.36^{\dagger\dagger}$
6	$-1.06^{\dagger\dagger}$	-	-	-	-

$\dagger$ $p < 0.05$ $\dagger\dagger$ $p < 0.01$

On the other hand, highly trained performers on this ball-striking task appeared to predict IP time solely on displacement parameters in the input. The selection of velocity parameters from early, central and late during the analysis of input ball flight suggest that it is unlikely that input velocity effects in the trained group were missed through inappropriate variables being fed into the predictive equation. The twin possibilities remain that the expert does cognize the velocity information, but chooses

522   D.A. TYLDESLEY

not to use it in his timing decisions or uses it only as a 'check' that
his planned spatial strategy with regard to IP timing will match the
current circumstances.

CONCLUSION

Movement timing is not a straightforward cognitive process but is to a
large extent determined by individual kinematic factors and task
variables which have effects on the output side of the system. The
generalisability of the studies within the PFB/timing paradigm is limited
since in all these experiments, operational timing factors, which
integrate into 'normal' timing strategies, are suppressed. Timing cannot
be viewed simply as imput-governed, but is an 'action-oriented' process
wherein information is extracted to match pre-planned movement structures.

References

(1) Abel, S.M. Discrimination of temporal gaps. Journal of the
      Acoustical Society of America, 1972, 52, 519-524.

(2) Armstrong, T.R. Training for the production of memorized movement
        patterns. University of Michigan, Human Performance Centre,
        (Tech. Report No. 26) Ann Arbor, 1970.

(3) Bartlett, N.R., and Bartlett, S.C. Synchronization of a motor
        response with an anticipated sensory event. Psychological
        Review, 1959, 66, 203-218.

(4) Christina, R.W. Proprioception as the basis for the temporal
        anticipation of motor responses. Journal of Motor Behavior,
        1970, 2, 125-133.

(5) Christina, R.W. Movement-produced feedback as a mechanism for
        the temporal anticipation of motor responses. Journal of
        Motor Behavior, 1971, 3, 97-104.

(6) Christina, R.W. Proprioception as a basis of anticipatory timing
        behavior. In G.E. Stelmach (Ed.), Motor control : Issues
        and trends. London : Academic Press, 1976.

(7) Christina, R.W., and Buffan, J.L. Preview and movement as
        determiners of timing a discrete motor response. Journal
        of Motor Behavior, 1976, 8, 101-112.

(8) Conrad, R. Timing. Occupational Psychology, 1955, 29, 173-181.

(9) Glencross, D.J. Temporal organization in a repetitive speed
        skill. Ergonomics, 1973, 16, 765-776.

(10)Higgins, J.R., and Angel, R.W. Correction of tracking errors
        without sensory feedback. Journal of Experimental Psychology,

(11)Kelso, J.A.S. Planning and efferent components in the coding of
        movement. Journal of Motor Behavior, 1977, 9, 33-47.

(12)Kinchla, J. Duration discrimination of acoustically defined
     intervals in the 1- to 8- second range. Perception and
     Psychophysics, 1972, 12, 318-320.

(13)Neisser, U. Cognition and reality. San Francisco : Freeman, 1976.

(14)Smith, J.L. Kinesthesis : A model for movement feedback. In
     R.C. Brown and B.J. Cratty (Eds.) New perspectives of man
     in action. Englewood Cliffs, N.J. : Prentice-Hall, 1969.

(15)Stelmach, G.E., Kelso, J.A.S., and Wallace, S.A. Preselection in
     short-term motor memory. Journal of Experimental Psychology :
     Human Learning and Memory, 1975, 1, 745-755.

(16) Summers, J.J. The role of timing in motor program representation.
     Journal of Motor Behavior, 1975, 7, 229-241.

(17) Treisman, M. Temporal discrimination and the indifference interval :
     Implications for a model of the internal clock. Psychological
     Monographs, 1963, 77, Whole No. 576.

(18) Tyldesley, D.A., and Whiting, H.T.A. Operational timing. Journal
     of Human Movement Studies, 1975, 1, 172-177.

(19) Vroon, P.A. Divisibility and retention of psychological time.
     Acta Psychologica, 1970, 32, 366-376.

Tutorials in Motor Behavior
G.E. Stelmach and J. Requin (eds.)
© *North-Holland Publishing Company, 1980*

32

SPACE-TIME INVARIANCE IN LEARNED MOTOR SKILLS

P. Viviani and C. Terzuolo

Laboratoire du Physiologie du Travail
C.N.R.S.
Department of Neurosensory Physiology
Paris, France
and
Laboratory of Neurophysiology
University of Minnesota
Minneapolis, Minnesota

The data presented here generalizes the notion of homotetic behavior in the time domain for learned motor sequences, that is, the presence of an invariant structure in such sequences, from typing to handwriting. Furthermore, it extends the principle to the space-time domain for unrestricted, continuous movements. An interpretation of the teleological value of this behavior is provided.

INTRODUCTION

When studying the motor patterns used by professional typists (Terzuolo and Viviani, 1979; Viviani and Terzuolo, 1979), we found that the motor sequence for each word has an invariant and specific structure. More precisely, the ratio of successive time intervals between pairs of strokes is independent of the speed at which the sequence as a whole is executed.

Two questions can then be posed: 1) Is this homotetic behavior a peculiar feature of such a highly constrained task as typing, or is it a general characteristic of learned motor skills? 2) Is such organizational principle confined to the time domain or can it also be found for the space-time domain? This possibility is suggested by the well known phenomenon of "motor equivalence" (Bernstein, 1967; Hebb, 1949; Lashley, 1930) and early data by Freeman (1914) on handwriting. This highly practiced skill which unfolds both in time and space is the obvious choice for providing answers to both questions.

TYPING

In these experiments the measured quantities were the time intervals between successive strokes. It was found that the motor sequences used to type a given text are highly stable and predictable over a period of years (in professional typists).

Words are the basic unit of organization for the motor output (Terzuolo and Viviani, 1979); to each word corresponds a characteristic sequence of time intervals which, as shown in Fig. 1, cannot be accounted for simply on the basis of letter-to-letter transitions.

The homotetic behavior for individual words in the time domain is illustrated in Fig. 2. Part A shows 42 instances of motor sequences used by

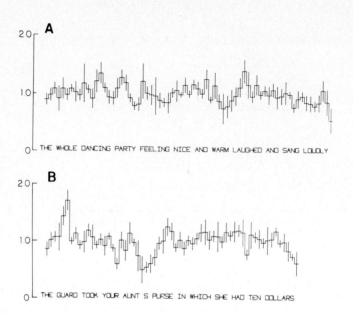

Fig. 1. Each word has a characteristic pattern. The data, from
two subjects, are the ratio between the instantaneous typing
rate for each pair of consecutive letters and the average
instantaneous rate for the same diagram, and subject, as obtained
by using a large number of words which contain the same diagram
and were included in several different texts. The data are
themselves averages of at least 40 repetitions of the same sentence. Vertical bars encompass ± 1 standard deviation. The
conspicuous fluctuations present in the normalized typing rate
demonstrate that, for each word there is a characteristic
sequence of time intervals between strokes, which cannot be
accounted for simply on the basis of letter-to-letter transitions.

one subject to type the word ENCLOSED over a period of two years in different contexts. The instances were ranked according to their total durations and spaced vertically by an amount proportional to their duration
differences. A set of lines originating from a single point adequately
interpolates the time of occurrence of each letter in all instances.
Thus, the set of ratios for all pairs of time intervals is invariant irrespective of the total duration. This invariant structure clearly
emerges when absolute time is disregarded, as in part B and C of the figure. In B one sees that most of the variability across instances (expressed in A as standard deviation) is in fact due to the considerable
variability of total duration. The pattern itself is much more stable.
The standard deviations in all words studied (340) were between 0.1 and 2%
of the average duration of the word; values shown in parentheses in parts

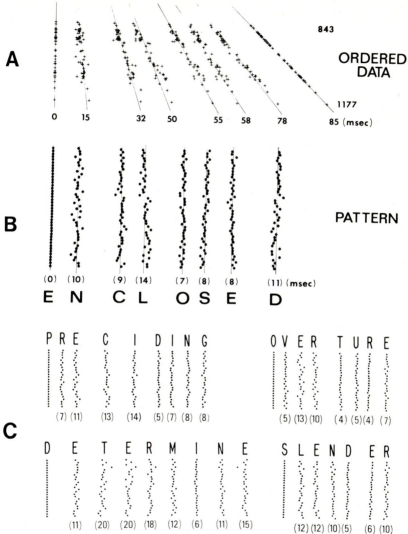

Fig. 2. Homotetic behavior in the time domain. In A is demonstrated
that the motor sequence for a given word retains its temporal structure, as described by the ratios among all time intervals, inspite
of large differences in total duration (given in msec at the right
of the shortest and longest instances). In B the structure of the
sequence (pattern) is demonstrated by normalizing each instance to
the average duration. In C examples of patterns for several words.

Notice that the intrinsic variability across instances (given in
parenthesis in msec) does not increase with the rank order of the
event in the sequence.

B and C of Fig. 2 are typical.

Thus, the presence of homotetic behavior in the time domain is firmly established in the case of typing, that is, for motor sequence composed of discrete events.

HANDWRITING

The horizontal and vertical position of the tip of the pen was recorded by a 622 RP CALCOMP digitizing table (accuracy: 0.025 mm; sampling rate: 100 Hz). This device, which records the movement even when the tip does not touch the page (within one inch), also provides a binary z-axis information. Tangential velocity was then computed to complement the spatial information provided by the position data with a description of the time evolution of the motion. The following features are easily identifiable in this data:

1.   Points when the direction of the movement is inverted (cuspids). Velocity goes to zero at these points.

2.   Points where the sign of the curvature changes (points of inflection).

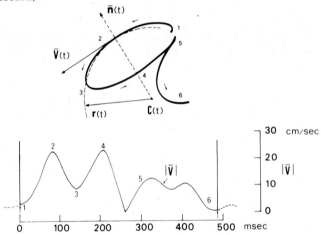

Fig. 3. Dynamic description of handwriting movements. The time course of the modulus of the tangential velocity along the trajectory (lower diagram) is used to characterize the dynamics of handwriting movements. In the example shown, the letter A as written in isolation by one subject, exhibits only one form-related landmark: the cuspid where the velocity goes to zero. However, other features of the velocity profile (identified by corresponding numbers on the trajectory) are easily recognizable and can be used to define a pattern for the movement.

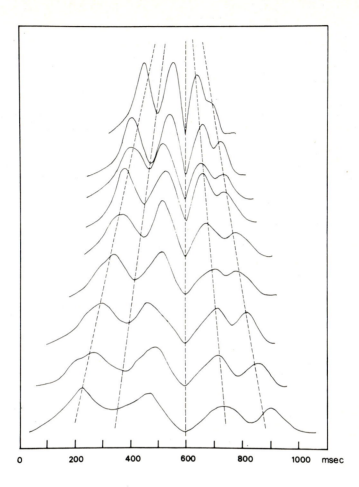

Fig. 4. Homotetic behavior in the time domain for handwriting.
Each record represents the modulus of the tangential velocity
for the same letter and the same subject of Fig. 3. The subject
was instructed to intentionally modify the writing speed while
keeping constant the size of the letter. When the total duration
of the movement decreases, the instantaneous values of the
velocity increase proportionally in such a way as to leave
invariant the ratios among the times of occurrence of the major
features of the profile. This is demonstrated by ranking and
scaling the records as in Fig. 2. The lines interpolating the
times of occurrence of the major features all have a common origin.

Either of these landmarks can be used to divide the movement into identifiable segments (see Fig. 3).

The first question posed in the Introduction was then answered simply by
instructing the subjects to write the same letter or word at different
speeds while keeping the size roughly constant. A typical example of the
results obtained is provided in Fig. 4 which shows the velocity profile
for the same subject and letter as in Fig. 3. Only two segments, as
defined above, are present in this case. The junction between them is
used to align all instances since it is the only unequivocal landmark. (1)
One can then see that the other minima and maxima of the velocity profile
fall along lines which, as in the case of typing converge to a single
point. Thus, we can now fully answer the first of the two questions posed
in the Introduction by stating that homotetic behavior in the time domain
characterizes also unrestrained and continuous, learned movements.

As for the second question, we found that letters generally preserve their
characteristic velocity profiles even when they are welded into words.
Figure 5 provides an example. Thus, the problem of homotetic behavior in

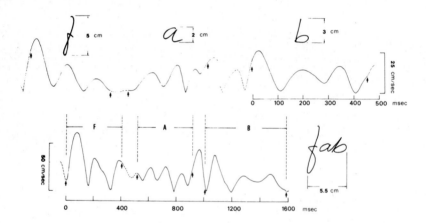

Fig. 5. <u>Composition of individual letters into words</u>. The
upper records show the velocity profiles for the indicated
letters when they are written in isolation. The bottom record
corresponds to the writing of the pseudo-word composed of the
same three letters. The example is typical of most cases in
which the structure of individual letters is not modified by
being welded into words even when, as in the example shown,
the writing speed is changed (note the different scales).
Notice also that the movement is highly structured even when
the pen does not touch the paper (dotted segments of the records).

———————

(1)   In the case of typing instead the most natural landmark is provided
      by the first letter of the word.

the space-time domain can be addressed by using either single letters or longer motor sequences such as words and signatures. Examples of the first case for two subjects, are given in Fig. 6. For each letter, data for three sizes are shown. It can be seen that, whenever the increase in size is accompanied by an increase in total duration, the ratios between the times of occurrence of successive segments are preserved. In several cases, however, naturally occurring increases in speed compensate almost perfectly for the increase in size. Notice that the largest sized letters do require elbow movements, thus changing entirely the bio-mechanics of the movement.

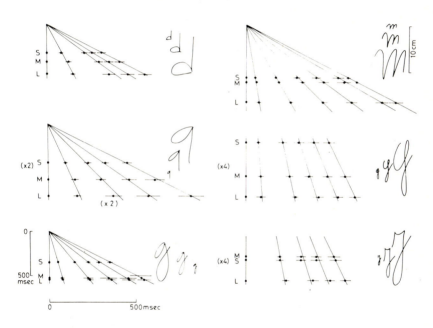

Fig. 6. Space-time invariance in handwriting. Data from two subjects (left and right column). Each diagram compares the results for three grossly different sizes of the same letter (shown aside). The horizontal rows of dots represent the timing pattern established on the basis of a proper choice of features (see text). Horizontal bars encompass ± 1 standard deviations. The patterns were scaled vertically, and lines with a common origin were interpolated (as in Figs. 2 and 4) to demonstrate the presence, also in this case, of homotetic behavior in the time domain. Vertical scales have been adjusted to enhance the differences in total duration. Note that the variability of the time of occurrence of each feature increases far less than linearly with the rank order of the feature in the sequence.

Figure 7 is designed to emphasize space invariance rather than space-time
invariance, in the case of a long and complex motor sequence (signature).
To this end, the records presented were chosen, from a large sample, to be
about equal in total duration inspite of a substantial difference in size.
The actual length of the trajectory as a function of time is also provided.
This choice stresses graphically, in the case of words, the point already
made above for single letters namely that, aside from the velocity scale
factor, the dynamic of the motion can be quite similar for drastically
different sizes.

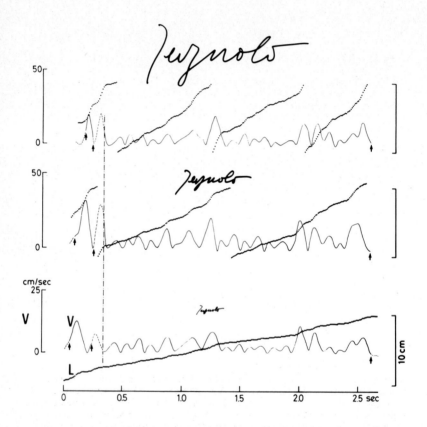

Fig. 7. <u>Space invariance in handwriting</u>. The records describe
the time course of tangential velocity for the indicated signatures.
Dotted lines represent the length of the trajectory as a function
of time. In spite of the large difference in size and in trajectory
length, the duration of the movement is sometimes naturally kept
constant by increasing proportionally the writing speed. In such
instances, as shown in the example, the timing of the motion is
strictly invariant.

CONCULSIONS

The data shown here support the contention that homotetic behavior is a
general organization principle of learned motor skills. Because of the
known relation between amplitude and speed of rectilinear movements stated
in Fitt's law, (Fitts, 1954) one could have suspected that homotetic
behavior in the space-domain, when performing the same movement at different amplitudes, would entail a corresponding homotetis behavior in the
time domain. This we have shown to be the case for such complex movements
as handwriting. In particular, an invariance in the time domain was observed even when the speed of a continuous movement is intentionally
changed while the amplitude is kept constant. Thus, the homotetic transformation in the time domain is not a mere consequence of spatial factors
but is in itself a general organization principle of learned movements.

As for the "raison d'etre" for this principle, we can only offer some
simple speculations. Because the overall speed of the movement can be
affected by endogenous factors as well as by environmental conditions, and
since there is an obvious teleological advantage in having a single central
representation, the possibility of maintaining constant ratios between the
timing of successive motor commands is essential in order to preserve the
continuity and unity of the entire action. Also, a link (in the case of
handwriting) between this organizational principle and the nature of the
central representation of the movement can be hinted. Indeed, if we
postulate that the latter is specified by the spatial aspects of the movements in that a relation exists between speed and form (such as the
curvature), a homotetic behavior would necessarily follow.

ACKNOWLEDGEMENTS

This work was supported by INSERM-ATP Research Grant and by USPHS grants
NS-2567 and NS-15018.

REFERENCES

1) Bernstein, N., The Coordination and Regulation of Movements (Pergamon
   Press, New York, 1967).
2) Fitts, P.M., The information capacity of the human motor system in controlling the amplitude of movements, J. Exp. Psychol. 47 (1954) 381-391.
3) Freeman, F.N., Experimental analysis of the writing movement, Psychol.
   Monogr. 17 (1914) 1-46.
4) Hebb, D.O., The Organization of Behavior, (John Wiley and Sons, Inc.,
   New York, 1949).
5) Lashley, K.S., Basic neuronal mechanisms in behavior, Psychol. Res.
   37 (193) 1-24.
6) Terzuolo, C. and Viviani, P., About the central representation of
   learned motor patterns, in: Talbot, R. and Humphrey, D.R. (eds.),
   Posture and Movement (Raven Press, New York, 1979).
7) Viviani, P. and Terzuolo, C., Emgrammes moteurs dans be traitement de
   l'information Linguistique, in: Requin, L. (ed.), Preparation dans le
   System Nerveux et Processes Psychologigues (in press).

PART VI

COGNITIVE FACTORS
IN MOTOR CONTROL

Tutorials in Motor Behavior
G.E. Stelmach and J. Requin (eds.)
© *North-Holland Publishing Company, 1980*

33

DIMENSIONS OF CONTROL

IN MOTOR LEARNING

H.T.A. Whiting

Interfakulteit Lichamelijke Opvoeding
Vrije Universiteit
Amsterdam, Nederland

Taking as a starting-point, the limited number of
contributions in the literature to motor-learning as
compared with motor control, an attempt is made to indicate
reasons why this should be the case.   This leads to the
conclusion that the majority of paradigms used in motor
control studies and in a high percentage of the limited
number of motor learning studies, are so restricted -
in the terms described - that they have little to
contribute to an understanding of the <u>learning</u> of real-
life skills.   Within this context, the paper explores
the nature of real-life skills and the hierarchical
dimensions of control which might operate.

INTRODUCTION

One of the surest predictions that might be made about any congress or
any book addressed jointly to the problems of motor control <u>and</u> motor
learning is that the proportion of time and/or space devoted to motor
learning would be a relatively minor proportion of the whole.   Since
this would not seem to reflect <u>only</u> a lack of interest or personal bias
on the part of the contributors, it is interesting to consider reasons
for this state of affairs.   Although this is not the specific concern of
this paper, some of the reasons are implicit in the discussion which
follows.

It seems to me, that recently, a number of psychologists are attempting
to present a 'topsy-turvey' world to their readers.   Whether this is
done to capture and hold their attention, or whether they consider -
as did Connolly (1977) with reference to Sperry's (1952) ideas about the
relationship of mental activities to motor behaviour - that turning an
accepted way of looking at the world on its head, is both revealing and
illuminating, is far from clear.

Let me try to explain what I mean.   At one extreme, are those classically
designated 'sensory' processes like perception, imagery, memory etc. being
classified by Weimer (1977) as motor processes or by Saugstad (1977) as
activities.   At the other, recent interpretations of some phases of motor
learning have been in soft-ware terms like the 'cognitive learning of
intentions'.

With these turns of event in mind, I find myself in **some**thing of a dilemma
in having to write an extended tutorial paper about <u>motor</u> learning.   In
this 'topsy-turvey' world, I have problems in trying to understand exactly
what it is I am supposed to be writing about.   The dilemma is not of

course a new one.   The term 'learning' is used now, no more consistently
than the term 'motor' and questions about what is learned and under what
conditions have - in Weimer's (1977) terms - 'dominated Psychology since the
days of Watsonian behaviourism'.   In attempting to explain 'all', such
theories succeeded in explaining very little.   Perhaps, it is with this
kind of hindsight that the majority of the few motor skill learning
researchers of late, have limited their theorising to 'simple, self-paced
graded movements like drawing a line' or to limited classes of schema
controlled movements.   While it is easier to theorise about and research
into, skills in which the 'cognitive' component is removed or reduced to a
minimum, it is to be expected that such theories and research findings
would only find application where cognitive control is not critical.   Under
such constraints, it would not be too surprising to discover man performing
at his most mechanistic level.

While these kinds of consideration do not seem to trouble many workers in
the field, others find difficulty in coming to terms with the meaningfulness
of the findings for real-life skills.   In the present volume for example,
Schaffer focuses some attention on the problems implicit in using simple
movement paradigms as reduced analogues of more complex skills.   In so
doing, he hints not only at problems like how one discovers what simple
analogues to use without a thorough knowledge of the complex skill, but also
to the fact that knowledge of the complex skill might give more information
about the simple skill than the converse.   This kind of 'top-down' approach
would seem to be eminently more meaningful.   The gist of this argument
would be, that theorising based upon more simplistic skills would have
little relevance in Schaffer's case to the musical skills demonstrated by
his pianists or to quote another example, to Taylor's (1978) concept of
craft occupations (e.g. tool-makers and setters, millwrights, fitters and
electricians) i.e. to the messy world of real affairs.

Singleton (1978) points out that during the learning of such skills:

> ...the element times most subject to reduction are those
> where there is 'perceptual load', it seems that it is the
> control function which is subject to change with learning
> rather than the movement itself.

It is to such changes in the dimensions of control that this paper is
ultimately addressed.

Further elaboration of possible limitations of the simple skills to which
reference has been made, comes from the Turvey world (Fowler & Turvey, 1978).
In as far as such models are seen to be general-purpose devices i.e. having
a single general-purpose acquisition strategy, they are:

> ...inapplicable to any skilled performance in which higher-
> order variables of stimulation provide the useful and
> controlling dimensions of information to an actor.

I would like to suggest that such skilled performances are those characteristically encountered in real-life.   Such a viewpoint would endorse
Neisser's (1976) statement that a satisfactory theory of human cognition
cannot be established by experiments that provide inexperienced subjects
with brief opportunities to perform novel and meaningless tasks.

To Fowler and Turvey (1978), learning a skill involves discovering an
optimal self-organisation in the sense of the organising of the musculature

into coordinative structures. Thus, what is altered and will be altered as skill develops, is the relative 'attractiveness' of a particular movement pattern for solving a particular motor problem (Whiting, 1969). The measure of 'attractiveness' may be determined by success in achieving the desired outcome, economy of effort or just personal preference. Each mosaic of meaningless movements or coordinative structures must become assimilated into a meaningful action. It is not only a question of producing coordinated movements, but of producing them at will in an appropriate context. It is wished to emphasise this latter point by questioning some recent theorising about the development of the skills of primitive man, by the physical anthropologist Reynolds (1976) which may have some relevance to the distinction being made between simple and complex skill paradigms. Reynolds proposes that:

> Tool-making could have evolved in a rather stereotyped
> 'animal' way not involving symbolic thought.

Now, can it really be believed that even in a primitive community, the skills to which he refers, were exercised outside a meaningful context and could it reasonably be argued that a person incapable of conceptual and abstract thought could learn to use such movements in an appropriate context? This would indeed entail a very narrow S-R interpretation of learning. The contextual setting is what distinguishes actions from movements and, as Bruner (1979) suggests in relation to language skills:

> ...the rules and maxims for appropriateness are surely no
> less difficult to master than the better-formed rules of
> grammar.

Perhaps, this in itself is an argument for learning movement skills in the context of the actions they are to subserve? Or learning meaningful things (that is to say which have an ecological pay-off) about motor control by studying such movements in their context.

HIERARCHY OF SKILLS

The hierarchical nature of the control of skilled actions is an 'in' phrase and well appreciated but it is still necessary to emphasise that there are hierarchies within hierarchies and that the dimensions of control operating at any one time will be determined by the dominant hierarchy. Let me try to explain what I mean. The French philosopher Ricoeur (1966) in his fascinating book 'Freedom and nature' gives the timely reminder that:

> Our skills are telescoped practical schemata, the highest
> of which are contiguous and continuous with an intention
> or purpose...They contain more precise adjustments (curiosity,
> anger, walking, then movement of the legs etc.). Purpose
> is the persistence of the superior adjustment 'until' an
> appropriate act puts an end to the one and the other. Thus,
> the determining adjustment accounts for variability of sub-
> ordinate movements capable of achieving a purpose.

This is to take a very extensive view of hierarchies - far beyond even the widest viewpoint expressed in the present volume - but more intermediate levels are implicit for example in MacNeillage's concept of speaking style casual or formal (depending on the situation) - which has an effect upon decision-making relevant to subsequent levels of performance. In a similar way, Schaffer refers to the controlling function of the 'interpreta-tion' which a player may need exercise in the performance of a musical score.

It must also be noted that the elaboration of the outer structures of
Ricoeur's nesting hierarchy will extend during the course of ontological
development.   The younger or less experienced the developing person, the
more clear will be the controlling effect of the inner core of such a
hierarchical structure and the more the performance of that person might
be explained in mechanistic terms.

Such a hierarchical concept and its implications for superordinate control
structures is also reflected in modern approaches to decision-making in for
example, games-theory, which - it is claimed - is approached as a multi-
dimensional stimulus and represented as a list of dimensions (in sport
for example, such a list might be 'probability of winning or losing';
'amount to win or lose'; 'risk level'; 'context variables'etc.).   Such
lists may also themselves be hierarchically arranged in terms of the weight
assigned to a particular dimension - and hence its controlling function -
in coming to a decision (Whiting, 1979a).

It is wished to stress, that the developmental progress of the action
systems of man is towards increasingly complex voluntary motor coordinations
dependent upon environmental information which becomes more and more
divorced from primitive imposed stimuli.   The developmental progress (?)
of the experimental laboratory seems to be towards less and less complex
coordinations based upon more and more primitive stimuli.   Perhaps this
mismatch alone, accounts for the lack of relevance of the one for the other.

If the above contention is extended, it is suggested that the experience
of an actor[1] with particular skills, leads to the build-up of a conceptual
model of the system he is controlling ('attunement' in Fowler & Turvey's
(1978) terms).   Such a model is the outcome of successive discoveries about
the structure of the skill (i.e. it is dynamic) - environmental and biokinematic relations that specify the essential features of the skill that
the actor is to perform - which enables him to:

>   ...appreciate the interaction of the main parameters in the
>   system and to predict the consequences of any control action
>   he may take (Whitfield, 1967).

With the kind of simple laboratory skills to which reference has been made,
there is of course not much to discover so that it is not too surprising
to find that within 30-40 trials or so that performance level is asymptotic.

Whitfield (1967) makes the further salient point that:

>   ...operators'[2] use of these conceptual models seems to be more
>   effective in many cases than the attempts of the design
>   engineer to control the process, presumably because of complex
>   interactions which cannot be predicted from theoretical formu-
>   lations.

There is a hint here, of a form of 'knowing' or 'acquaintance' knowledge
which is not translatable and consequently difficult to cater for in any
training programme or theoretical system.   Similarly constructed machines
(e.g. motor cars) are known to have their idiosyncracies which are only
discovered during operation.   Not only are such peculiarities task specific
but they cannot be isolated from the task (Whiting, 1979b).   This idea is
implicit in Polanyi's (1958) concept of 'tacit' knowledge.   He reminds us
that skilful performance is achieved by the observance of a set of rules

which are not known to the person following them.   Singleton (1978) has
recently discussed further, the nature of such models:

> In the cause of economy, these models get more and more
> iconic in that non-essentials are omitted so that the model
> departs from reality, but the real escape from the restrict-
> ions of the immediate environment occurs when the icons become
> entirely symbolic and are connected to reality only by con-
> ventions.   New conventions develop also about the relation-
> ship between symbols: in linguistic terms there are
> syntactics and pragmatics as well as semantics...We can
> manipulate the symbols themselves.   These are the perceptual
> skills we need to develop and control the technological world.

DIMENSIONS OF LEARNING

The wider dimensions of learning implicit in the discussion so far, play
different roles in decision-making and hence the control of human actions.
It would be a pity therefore if simplistic interpretations derived from
the study of only the inner core of Ricoeur's nesting hierarchy should
come to serve as the paradigm for the study of human overt actions.   When
a subject participates in constrained laboratory experiments, he is forced
to behave in an artificial manner often by a limitation of the degrees of
freedom with which he is allowed to operate.   Even when learning becomes
the focus of attention, it is restricted by the simplistic nature of the
skills being performed such that it is generally confined to a limited
number of trials which in totality seldom exceed one experimental session.
It is true that such experiments may demonstrate the subtlety of information processing and movement production that is possible when the subject
is forced or biased towards particular sources of information, but this
should not lead to the belief that this is the way in which he would
operate in the absence of such constraints.   This is not to deny the
potential usefulness of such experimental work towards an understanding
of motor performance, but simply to caution against any assumption that
the information so obtained has more than a very limited explanatory or
carry-over value in relation to real-life skills.

Acquisition, development and learning.

The hierarchical structuring of skills in the manner outlined by Ricoeur
(1966) and Bruner (1974) has implications for the terminology used in
relation to skill. Motor learning is perhaps the term most least likely
to be used. In the sphere of infant skill work for example, it is more
normal to speak about motor development recognising the essential biological progression which together with environmental experience leads to
changes in the capacity for skilled actions of increasing complexity.
This is to be contrasted with learning theory emphasis on the plastic
adaptability of the mind to exnerience leading to a neglect of natural
constraints on mental growth (Trevarthen, 1977).   Such a conception of
learning would of course be counter to the normal definition of learning
in the literature which makes a distinction between learned and maturational
behaviour. But, is it possible to think (with Saugstad, 1978) of any
really meaningful learningwithout the concept of ontogenetic development?
In a similar way, the term 'acquisition of motor skill' occurs frequently
in the literature truly reflecting a state of 'becoming'.   Perhaps, the
French term 'apprentissage', meaning - as it does - a period or course
of learning of a protracted kind better characterises the norms for

meaningful changes in real-life skills.   How many studies of skill
apprenticeship are available?   Although Singleton's (1978) recent book
provides a wide perspective of real-life skills ranging from sewing-
machining to tea-blending, the changing dimensions of control with
apprenticeship are not spelled out.

How can this state of 'becoming' be operationalised?   When for example
can it be said that a person has learned to dance?   When he has mastered
say, the basic steps in the waltz?   When he has learned the waltz,
quickstep, foxtrot and tango?   Or, when he can respond in an appropriate
manner in any situation which demands dance action?   Perhaps, the answer
is all of these depending upon the level of analysis to be specified.
Certainly such different levels imply different dimensions of control
varying from those which are completely task determined to those which
are semi-autonomous.   Laboratory experiments characteristic of research
in motor learning tend to restrict the concept of movement skill to
relatively minor and meaningless actions which quickly become autonomous
in the sense that the performers (not actors) need no longer reflect upon
them.   This is to take a very limited view of movement skill.

>   I know how, I can do!

says Ricoeur (1966).   Skill is a power, a capacity to resolve certain
types of problem according to an available schema: I can play the piano,
I know how to swim.   It is this principle of comprehension with its
contextual embedding in every day living which is so important.   Trial
and error learning is not characteristic of the human species, it is a
method only characteristic of performance in an unpredictable environment:

>   It is an expedient to which man resorts when he cannot
>   understand the problem and when no model (schema) is
>   available to guide the analysis and synthesis of movements
>   (Ricoeur, 1966).

The issue at hand, is exemplified in a short, but amusing and insightful
article by Williams (1977):

>   Consider for a moment what we really mean by riding a
>   bicycle.   There is more to cycling than simply taking a
>   short ride on a machine down a straight road, just as there
>   is more to language than the stereotyped utterances of a
>   parrot.   It is true that animals have been taught to
>   perform certain unnatural acts;   dogs, cats and even
>   elephants have been taught to use scooters and we have all
>   seen the antics of chimpanzees with bicycles.   But we all
>   laugh at the animals' hopeless question 'can you ride
>   tandem?'   Of course she cannot ride tandem!   There is a
>   quiddity to cycling which is in essence human.

As Williams elaborates, it is safe to say that repetition in the sense of
the same person being on the same bike, on the same road in the same
weather conditions etc. is indeed likely to be a unique event.

The point being made was of course well recognised by the syncretic
Russian physiologist Bernstein (1967) who pointed out that one of the
anomalies in training is that it involves repetition without repetition!
That is to say, it involves repeated attempts to solve a problem but
without repeating the same movement (and of course without getting the

same feedback!). To acquire skill in these terms, does not mean to repeat
and consolidate, but to invent, to progress.   Otherwise, what particular
movements would be repeated?   This is only to reiterate Bartlett's (1932)
objections to an interpretation of say, learning to play tennis in terms
of the learning of particular stimulus-response connections.   What is
rememebered in the course of playing such a game in clearly not some
'exact' stroke abstracted from some previous playing experience.   This
would indeed be a very static view of this form of operational memory.
As Bransford, McCarrell, Franks and Nitsch (1977) reiterate:

> ...one would surely not wish to simply <u>equate</u> the ability
> to play tennis with a list of previous memories of tennis
> playing experiences.   Such an equation seems as implausible
> as equating one's knowledge of his native language with a list
> of memories of previously experienced sentences or even
> paraphrases of these sentences. One's ability to remember
> will undoubtedly be related to the nature of the knowledge
> acquired through learning, but it would seem strange to equate
> the problem of learning with the problem of how memories
> are stored and retrieved.

Within this kind of framework, Weimer (1977) emphasises, 'memory' is a
matter of the active, ongoing modulation of information rather than the
retrieval of stored items or particular 'bits'.

The central message apparent from the above statements is the flexibility
of the skilled actor in the sense of his possessing the ability to
generate patterns of movement <u>appropriate</u> to a novel situation.   Motor
skills - like cycling and piano playing - do not grow by a simple addition
of elements, but by structural rearrangement - by analysis and synthesis.
This key principle, is reiterated by Brown (1977) in the context of apraxic
movement disorders:

> ...such impairments indicate that the movement disorder
> reflects a disruption in the development of actions as part
> of, not extrinsic to, the rest of cognition; in other words,
> the substrate of the disorder is not a defective instrumentality
> played upon by more or less intact higher structures but is
> disruption at an earlier cognitive stage.

In these terms, perhaps it is not too surprising that students of motor
learning have recently turned to the linguistic field for ideas about
the generation of novelty and particularly to views about deep structures.
In as far as these are considered to be psychic universals invoked as
an explanation of the way in which language users are able to both generate
and understand an almost limitless range of linguistic expressions (surface
structures) which may have formed no part of their earlier experience,
a possible analogy with movement production and movement perception is
obvious (Gell, 1979).   An explanation of learning in such a framework is
an explanation of how the child progresses from his very limited experience
with surface structures (repertoire of actions) to one of understanding
the deep structure (Connolly, 1977).   While much of this understanding
is based upon knowledge obtained by acting on the environment, what is
often missed, is that the child also has extensive exposure from birth
onwards to humans moving, whether this be the fine detailed movements
involved in speech and non-verbal communication, or gross ambulatory movements concerned with positional changes.   Such information will at least

provide him with an 'Image of an Act' defined in terms of general
properties about space and time which will subserve the development of
an 'Image of Achievement' (the learned prediction of the field of forces
resulting from the production of acts in the past) once he tries to
produce such actions (Den Brinker, 1979).   This kind of developmental
approach parallels an increasing concern of semantically oriented
approaches to language learning to emphasise the primacy of non-verbal
perceptual experience in the initial acquisition of language (Paivio,
1975).   In this respect, it is interesting to consider Gell's (1979)
ideas stemming from Johansson's (1976) fascinating experiments directed at
visual motor perception.   Apparently meaningless patterns of light spots
can be effectively distinguished as 'walking patterns of different sexes'
'two people dancing in the dark' etc.   Gell (1979) speculates:

> If the brain is capable of translating two-dimensional
> displays of moving lights as complex three-dimensional
> movements of solid bodies, it is presumably conceivable
> that the brain could store motor schemas as 'collapsed'
> forms which could be projected as whole-body movement
> in three-dimensional space.   And these collapsed motor
> schemas could be squeezed, stretched, distorted, somewhat
> along the lines of Leach's famous discussion of the
> topological properties of rubber-sheeting...

While such interpretations have an intuitive appeal, research directed
towards an elaboration of such ideas has been limited in nature perhaps,
because of the difficulty of operationalising the postulated concepts.
Or, perhaps the problem is even more basic.   Malcom (1971) for example
argues that Chomsky's internal structures are myths and Saugstad (1978)
adds the rider:

> Indeed one wonders how the claim that they are real might
> be substantiated.

In the linguistic field, progress in the neo-Chomskyan era has perhaps
been more apparent.   Many psycho-linguists now for example consider
that the 'deepest' levels of linguistic structre are 'intentions' to mean
something , not intentions to use certain bits and pieces of syntactic
machinery (Gell, 1979).   It is worth observing at this stage of course
that the learning of intentions alone is rather sterile, because knowing
what one would like to do is of little value unless one is capable of
doing it.   Nevertheless, the learning of intentions as a key factor of
motor learning should not be underplayed.   Many years ago (Whiting, 1969)
I proposed the concept of 'social facilitation' (not in the sense of
audience effects as is commonly used) to imply that in the main, actors
do not 'imitate' (in the sense of copying exactly) the actions of others,
but that a large part of early skill learning is that of being 'made aware
of possibilities' that had not previously occurred to the actor.   In this
sense, he is being socially facilitated by other actors from whom he
learns to construct the 'Image of an Act'.

The more recent ideas on intention from the linguistic field are alluded
to by Bruner (1979) in summarising his growing disenchantment with what
he refers to as this 'rather dry use of language' in favour of a more
functional one:

> Language was concerned, in this dispensation, not simply as a
> set of syntactic rules for generating well-formed sentences

and none that was ill-formed, but rather as a series of
acts designed to achieve the communicative intentions of
the speaker in a given context...In a word then, we are
constantly fulfilling extralinguistic functions by our
choice and timing of utterances and by our skill in
implementing our intentions with appropriate communications
on their behalf...In that deep sense, the use of language is
part of a policy for achieving our intentions.

A similar interpretation might be adopted to account for the growth of
cognitive-motor structures subserving motor learning and performance.
It is not therefore surprising that some workers look to a natural history
of language development and by a similar token to a natural history of
the development of motor skills (c.f. Trevarthen, 1977 ; Bruner, 1974).
Recently, Reynolds (1979) has argued that the only comprehensible way of
describing and accounting for any skilled manual behaviour is via a
two-stage process in which the 'tactical motor system' (which actually
produces the muscular contractions) receives its instructions in a
modularised interlanguage which mediates the strategic intentions of the
intelligent tool user. On this basis, it is possible to suggest that
the 'deep' structures of motor control are not movements, but certain
strategic intentions which are converted into movements via an interlanguage (Gell, 1979).

DIMENSIONS OF CONTROL

A further limitation of much of the work on motor learning, is that of
paying undue attention to surface structures rather than focusing
attention on cognitive changes like the development of information-
processing abilities or the emergence of response strategies.   In addition
the bulk of available data has been based on 'positive' performance measures
which in Wilberg's (1972) terms only describe but do not explain performance.
Since many aspects of learning are qualitative changes which are not
necessarily reflected in performance outcome measures, it is not surprising
that over-attention to such measures has limited conceptual progress in
the motor skill literature. It has been emphasised already, that to acquire
skill does not mean to repeat and consolidate, but to invent, to progress.
This involves the formulation of new strategies of action and the progressive refinement of solutions to motor problems posed by the environment.
So that, it is the usefulness of such positive performance measures which
is being called into question, since they can be stated independently
of the performance of the people concerned i.e. such criteria are not
necessarily related to good performance and, by the same argument, would
be of little use in determining what learning strategies should be
adopted (Whiting, (1975).

Insight into this problem can be obtained by a consideration of the early
findings of plateaux in the performance of motor skills (e.g. Bryan &
Harter, 1897).   The difficulty with many of the performance curves
presented in this and other studies is, not only that they are outcome-
oriented, but that they reflect the results of individuals or groups on
particular positive performance criteria measures in which the experimenter
is interested. Singleton (1979) puts it more strongly when he points out
a discrepancy between factors which it has been fashionable to manipulate
and those which seem important in ordinary work.

Where plateaux do occur in such performance curves, it may well be that
there is a period of no apparent improvement on that particular criterion,
but it does not follow that the subject is not improving his ability to
perform on some other unrecorded variable which might contribute to
total task improvement in the long run. Bruner (1974) puts this viewpoint
rather well:

> Any given programme of skilled voluntary action is gradually
> consolidated within its own restrictions. Its consolidation
> is signalled by the well-known plateau in the learning
> curve. Progress points in the infant's development are
> qualitative rather than quantitative changes of skill.
> These involve not consolidation but the formulation of new
> strategies of action which in turn must be consolidated.

An illustration of this point is provided by individual performance
curves (Fig.1) obtained in a continuous ball-throwing and catching task
(Whiting, 1967; 1972) where plateaux are apparent on the criterion variable
'total-score' - a positive performance measure (reflecting a combination of

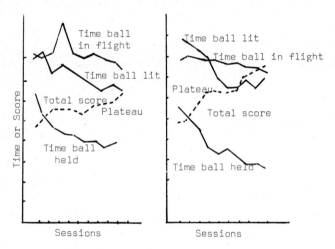

Fig. 1

Individual performance curves on a ball
throwing and catching task (Whiting, 1967)

'number of throws' and 'accuracy') - but other aspects of performance
(e.g. time ball was held, time ball was in flight etc.) continue to show
changes, reflecting - it is suggested - the adoption of changes in strategy
by different subjects. But, these findings also suffer from the fact that
each of these variables is in itself a positive performance measure so
that still little insight is provided into what are the dimensions of
environmental control which lead to these strategy changes. Some information in this respect can be provided - it is suggested - by operational
analyses of real-life skills.

Tyldesley (this volume) in our own laboratories has recently carried out
operational analyses of the movement of table-tennis players when required
to perform forehand drive shots in response to balls fed by a table-tennis
ball projection machine on a relatively unpredictable flight path at the
rate of 55 balls per minute the target being an 18" square on the far
end of the table.   Twenty-two kinematic features describing the ball-
flight (the INPUT features) and the bat movement (the OUTPUT features)
were extracted by operational analysis and formed a 'features x attempts'
matrix for each subject. Earlier work had indicated that one of the most
important output characteristics in this performance was the start time
of the ballistic downswing (IP).   The multiple linear regression evaluated
the partial contribution to the total IP variance of the measured input
features.   It was found possible to account for more than 97% of the total
IP variance in five of the six subjects when only five input features
were included in the equation. Predominant among these factors were
BALL DISPLACEMENT at IP; BALL VELOCITY at IP and BALL PROJECTION VELOCITY
(Table 1).   IP time in non-trained performers appeared to be a function
of both a displacement and a velocity measure with the possible inference
that both distance and its rate of change were important information sources
to the relatively unskilled players (subjects 1, 2 and 3).   In contrast,
the highly trained performers (subjects 4, 5 and 6) indicated a considerably reduced steering function of velocity information with the major
portion of IP variation accounted for by input displacement variations
(Table 1).   These data suggest that the expert is able to time the
ballistic initiation of what is possibly a simpler information basis than
the novice, who is subject to changes in both input velocity and displacement.   Alternative explanations, for example that the expert does
recognise velocity information but does not utilise it in his decision-
making, are also tenable.

Table 1

The partial contribution to the overall variance in
the start-times of ballistic downswings of trained
and untrained table-tennis players on three of the
five kinematic factors identified in multiple regression analysis.

Subjects	Percentage variance in in IP[a] accounted for			Simple correlation with IP[a]			Overall percentage variance accounted for by all equation factors
	BD[b]	BV[c]	BPV[d]	BD[b]	BV[c]	BPV[d]	
Untrained							
1	55	‹1	39	-0.95	0.19	-0.63	97
2	22	40	13	-0.55	0.70	-0.36	83
3	62	‹1	20	-0.90	-0.76	-0.44	99
Trained							
4	82	‹1	13	-0.97	-0.39	-0.37	98
5	73	‹1	1	-0.85	0.04	-0.12	98
6	81	‹1	13	-0.95	0.07	-0.37	98

[a] Start times of ballistic downswing (IP)   [b] Ball displacement (BD)
[c] Ball velocity (BV)   [d] Ball projection velocity (BPV)

SCHEMA THEORY

It would be untoward to conclude a paper on motor learning without reference
to schema theory although it will be appreciated that is has appeared in one
form or another in much that has already been said. Its most recent pro-
ponent has been Schmidt (1976).   Such theories - like the language development analogy previously encountered - have been used to deal with the
'storage' problem implicit in both 'open' and 'closed' loop theories of
motor learning and more importantly the problem with respect to the
'production of novel movements'.   That there have been problems in operationalising such theories is apparent, not the least of the problems being
the number of unconstrained degrees of freedom (Pew & Baron, 1978) and the
difficulty in determining what movements belong to a particular task.   It
is not wished to dwell on these well-known difficulties, but to return
in the present context to the problem of dimensions of control.   One of
the predictions from the schema theory is that a subject who receives
variable practise develops a strong schema for motor production enabling
him to more effectively generate novel movements.   Now, since the schema
refers to a complex set of relations, it would seem for example that in
devising any training programme for schema development, it would make
sense to know which of these relationships is weak i.e. what are the
dimensions of control which the subject currently cannot handle (Van Rossum
1978).   Only when such dimensions are known, does it make sense to
compare constant versus variable training and then only under conditions
of that dimension.   This is only to reiterate Saugstad's (1977) contention
that unless we know how the various activities develop, it is difficult
to say how they are learned.   Earlier, Kay (1970) asked: 'What kind of
system controls human skills?', and concluded that before any answer was
attempted, one must 'say exactly what we are trying to understand...the
beginning lies in a precise description of the essential features of
skilled performance'.

Van Rossum in our own laboratories is currently exploring this issue
in a developmental context.   Whether or not such dimensions can be isolated
by some experimental procedure, or whether they must always remain 'those
dimensions on which the experimenter chooses to focus attention', remains
to be seen.   Some experimental possibilities favouring the former were
presented in the Tyldesley study.

Footnotes

[1]
      Following Fowler and Turvey (1978) the term 'actor' is used
      throughout the paper to refer to people who perform actions.

[2]
      Read 'actor'.

REFERENCES:

Bartlett, F.C.   Remembering: a study in experimental and social psychology (University Press, Cambridge, 1932).

Bernstein, N.   The Coordination and Regulation of Movement (London: Pergamon, 1967).

Bransford, J.D., McCarrell, N.S., Franks, J.J. and Nitsch, K.E. Towards explaining memory, in: Shaw, R. and Bransford, J. (eds.), Perceiving, Acting and Knowing (Wiley, New York, 1977).

Brinker, B. den.   Internal paper.   Department of Psychology, Interfaculty of Physical Education, Free University, Amsterdam, The Netherlands, 1979.

Brown, J.   Mind, Brain and Consciousness: the neurophysiology of cognition (Academic Press, New York, 1977).

Bruner, J.S.   Beyond the Information Given: studies in the psychology of knowing (George, Allen & Unwin, London, 1974).

Bruner, J.S.   Decision-making as discourse, in, Bell, C.R. (ed.), Uncertain Outcomes (MTP Press, Lancaster, 1979).

Bryan, W.L. and Harter, N.   Studies in the physiology and psychology of the telegraphic language, Psychological Review, 4(1897)27.

Connolly, K.   The nature of motor skill development, Journal of Human Movement Studies, 3(1977) 128-143.

Fowler, C.A. and Turvey, M.T.   Skill acquisition: an event approach with special reference to searching for the optimum of a function of several variables, in: Stelmach, G.E. (ed.), Information Processing in Motor Control and learning (Academic Press, New York, 1978).

Gell, A.F.   On dance structures: a reply to Williams, Journal of Human Movement Studies, 5(1979) (in press).

Johansson, A.   Visual motor perception, in, Held, R. and Richards, W. (eds.), Recent Progress in Perception (Freeman, San Francisco, 1976).

Kay, H.   Analysing motor skill performance, in: Connolly, K. (ed.), Mechanisms of Motor Skill Development (Academic Press, London, 1970).

Malcom, N.   The myth of cognitive processes and structures, in, Mischell, T. (ed.), Cognitive Development and Epistemology (Academic Press, New York, 1971).

Neisser, U.   Cognition and Reality (Freeman, San Francisco, 1976).

Paivio, A.   Neomentalism, Canadian Journal of Psychology, 29(1975) 263-291.

Pew, R.W. and Baron, S.   The components of information-processing theory of skilled performance based on an optimal control perspective, in, Stelmach, G.E. (ed.), Information Processing in Motor Control and Learning (Academic Press, New York, 1978).

Polanyi, M.   Personal Knowledge: towards a post-critical philosophy, (Routledge and Kegan Paul, London, 1958).

Reynolds, V.   The Biology of Human Action (Freeman, Reading, 1976).

Reynolds, P.   The programmatic description of simple technologies, Journal of Human Movement Studies, 5(1979) (in press).

Ricoeur, P.   Freedom and Nature: the voluntary and the involuntary
(North-Western University Press, Illinois, 1966).

Rossum, J. van.   Throwing accuracy of children.   Internal report,
Department of Psychology, Interfaculty of Physical Education, Free University
Amsterdam, The Netherlands, 1978.

Saugstad, P.   A Theory of Communication and Use of Language (Global Book
Resources, Oxford, 1977).

Schmidt, R.A.   The schema as a solution to some persistent problems in
motor learning theory, in: Stelmach, G.E. (ed.), Motor Control: issues
and trends (Academic Press, New York, 1976).

Singleton, W.T.   The Analysis of Practical Skills (MTP Press, Lancaster,
1978).

Sperry, R.W.   Neurology and the mind-brain problem, American Scientist,
40(1952) 291-312.

Taylor, R.G.   The metal-working machine tool operator, in: Singleton, W.T.
(ed.), The Analysis of Practical Skills (MTP Press, Lancaster, 1978).

Trevarthen, C.   Descriptive analyses of infant communication behaviour,
in Schaffer, H.R. (ed.), Studies of Mother-Infant Interaction (Academic
Press, London, 1977).

Weimer, W.B.   A conceptual framework for cognitive psychology: motor
theories of the mind, in: Shaw, R. and Bransford, J. (eds.), Perceiving,
Acting and Knowing (Wiley, New York, 1977).

Whitfield, D.   Human skill as a determinant of allocation of function, in:
Singleton, W.J., Easterby, R.S. and Whitfield, D.C. (eds.), The Human
Operator in Complex Systems (Taylor and Francis, London, 1967).

Whiting, H.T.A.   Visual-motor coordination.   Unpublished Ph.D. Thesis,
Department of Psychology, University of Leeds, 1967.

Whiting, H.T.A.   Acquiring Ball Skill: a psychological interpretation
(Bell, London, 1969).

Whiting, H.T.A.   Learning motor skills, in: Kane, J.E. (ed.), Psychology
in Physical Education and Sport (Routledge and Kegan Paul, London, 1972).

Whiting, H.T.A.   Concepts in Skill Learning (Lepus, London, 1975).

Whiting, H.T.A.   Subjective probability in sport, in: Bell, C.R. (ed.),
Uncertain Outcomes (MTP Press, Lancaster, 1979(a)).

Whiting, H.T.A.   Input and perceptual processes in sports skills, in:
Glencross, D.J. (ed.), Psychology and Sport (McGraw-Hill, Roseville,
1979 (b)).

Wilberg, R.B.   Assignment and measurement of performance, Proceedings of
the British Society of Sports Psychology, Leeds, 1972.

Williams, D.   Psychobikistics, Bulletin of the British Psychological
Society, 30(1977) 106-107.

Tutorials in Motor Behavior
G.E. Stelmach and J. Requin (eds.)
© *North-Holland Publishing Company, 1980*

34

LEVELS AND STRATEGIES OF RESPONSE ORGANIZATION

Denis J. Glencross

Department of Psychology
The Flinders University of South Australia
Bedford Park, South Australia

It is proposed that response organization involves a
generative or construction process involving the
transfer of control between a number of levels of
representation (general abstraction, elemental
response units, parameters). In these terms response
organization and production is described as involving
four formats (i) sensory guidance and control (ii)
advance planning and programming (iii) presetting and
tuning (iv) amendment procedures. Finally,
organizational formats and strategies are discussed
in relation to contextual demands and the optimization
of performance.

INTRODUCTION

The issues confronting questions about response organization are strongly
influenced by a number of observations of skilled performance and actions.
Any attempt to describe response organization must offer some understanding of these aspects of motor behaviour, viz (i) motor constancy (ii) the
uniqueness of action (iii) the stability and consistency of action
(iv) the modifiability of action.

(i) Motor Constancy. It is apparent that the motor system can produce a
wide range of purposive movements, that subserve identical or closely
related goals or outcomes, but through the action of different movements
and different muscles. For example a letter or word may be written very
large or very small with either hand, or the foot or presumably any muscle
group which has the mechanical freedom to perform the required range of
movements (Merton, 1973; Turvey, 1977). Because outcomes and actions can
be achieved by a variety of means, we are confronted with the question of
how a vast array of possible movement patterns might be stored, accessed
and retrieved in the brain. Even similar movements, which vary in
starting position, which is a feature of many skilled actions, would each
require a separate stored programme incorporating the precise movement
details and specifications. Surely as Greene (1972) asks, the brain does
not store correspondences between temporal sequences of all of the
possible configurations of all muscles (p.305). If there is not a direct
correspondence between storage and action (which although possible, seems
cumbersome, inefficient and most unlikely), then we are concerned with a
constructional or generative process, whereby responses are constructed or
generated according to a limited set of rules or principles from a wider
range of sub-units or elements, which can be used for a variety of

purposes (Bernstein, 1967; Greene, 1972; Turvey, 1977).

(ii) The Uniqueness of Action. A further feature of motor actions is that
the same response or action pattern is not identical on successive trials
or on subsequent occasions. Not only from performance scores, but also
from detailed analyses of movement patterns from displacement, velocity
and EMG records, a surprising variation is observed. This occurs not only
with discrete actions as in throwing and striking but also in repetitive
and cyclic actions such as walking, cycling and hand cranking (Glencross,
1973a, 1975). There seems to exist a range or 'band width' of variation
or error tolerance which can vary from repetition to repetition without
disrupting overall performance. These variations can occur in metrical
or scalar details, in spatial features, also in terms of phasing (the
temporal relationship between elements within a response) as well as in
timing (the relationship of the response to an external event), (Glencross,
1979).

(iii) The Stability and Consistency of Action. In spite of the apparent
uniqueness of each response, by far the most obvious feature of the
skilled performer is the consistency and stability of performance.
Indeed, this feature enables us to recognise idiosyncratic styles. The
stability of performance of the skilled operator is associated with a
greater consistency in the micro-structure of the response in terms of
displacement and EMG records (Glencross, 1975), as well as the temporal
structure (Glencross, 1973a).

(iv) The Modifiability of Action. Any account of skilled actions, must
include not only the consistent and stable patterns of movement and
outcome, but also incorporate the up-dating, amendment and modification of
action, as a consequence of the changes in information available to the
performer (Neisser, 1976). This is particularly so as a result of the
recognition of the variety of feedback loops and feedforward mechanisms
available (Bizzi & Evarts, 1971; Evarts, 1971). Turvey (1977) in
particular has emphasised that perception and action is continually being
tailored to the current kinematic and environmental contingencies, that is,
it is continually becoming (p.215).

Our consideration of response organization must thus contemplate a system
which can incorporate current display contingencies, within the context of
a response system that does not maintain a direct correspondence between
representation and action, and yet which has remarkable stability over
time. Turvey, Shaw & Mace (1978), Turvey (1977) after Bernstein (1967)
and Greene (1972) have emphasised that there cannot be a direct or even
a remote correspondence between the representation of action and the
detailed form of the movement. There thus must be a representation of
levels whereby the degrees of freedom of the central (controlling) system
is less than the number of degrees of freedom of the mechanical or action
(controlled) system (Turvey, 1977, p.217). Further, the context in which
the movement is to occur will influence the final detailed specifications
and hence outcome of the action. That is the details of the response
(and hence the response organization process) can only be fully understood
in the context of the task demands and specifications, and the desired
outcomes, intentions and expectancies of the performer. Implicit in the
influence of context-specific factors is the interaction of sensory
information with the on-going organization of the motor system.

CONTROL AND STRUCTURAL REPRESENTATIONS

The notion of levels of organization has been central in the discussion of voluntary movement and actions since the time of Bryan & Harter (1899) and Woodworth (1899). Craik (1966) also emphasised that for the rapidity and certainty of skilled actions, it was essential that certain units of activity must be delegated to lower levels (p.38) and that these will then occur automatically when required, with little need for monitoring or direct control. Consequently it became necessary to understand not only the levels of organization, but also the integration of control between these various levels, and so the question of control became the issue of understanding executive ordering and plans for action (Lashley, 1951; Miller, Galanter & Pribram, 1960). Within this context notions of advance planning and programming were consolidated with considerable support from evidence on animal studies (Taub & Berman, 1968; Hinde, 1969). Both Bartlett (1941) and Poulton (1957) had elaborated forms of anticipatory behaviour as a means of facilitating the organization of a number of levels simultaneously. Thus it was necessary not only to understand the operations occurring at each level, but also to understand the time course of such operations. The emphasis of Poulton's (1957) analysis was to direct attention to the emergence and development of organizational formats and strategies related to environment, task and person contingencies. What we are talking about in fact is the transfer of control (Miller, Galanter & Pribram, 1960) between levels. And, as Broadbent (1977) says, why the notion of transfer of control is important, is that it modifies the traditional view of levels and hierarchies. For, rather than higher levels necessarily incorporating and controlling lower levels, we must understand the influence of one level on another, the consequent changes in state and the time-course of operations which may occur independently or in parallel at several levels of complexity.

A solution to degrees of freedom and contextual-specificity problems is to consider responses as being generated or constructed from relatively stable abstract representation of general classes of actions at higher levels with the specification of a relatively few specific details which correspond more directly to the desired outcome at lower levels (Greene, 1972; Turvey, 1977).

(i) General Classes of Action. A general class or equivalence class (Turvey, 1977) of actions refers to an abstract representation of a class of movements or actions which have in common certain predominant general features or attributes, but which are independent of the units of action and may be applied to a variety of situations to achieve a limited range of outcomes. Recognising classes of actions, common attributes and boundary specifications will help in the understanding of this level of abstraction. Investigations of the motor constancy phenomenon and in particular the transfer of performance and learning between and within such classes (as well as between and within levels) offers to shed some light on this question. In particular the investigation of the transfer of handwriting between muscle and movement groups, including bilateral transfer, and analysing spatial and temporal consistencies should be particularly rewarding (Wing, 1978). Milisen & Riper (1939) reported bilateral transfer in learning a novel task, tracking a clover-leaf maze. Bi-lateral reminiscence effects lend support to the notion of a general representation. Irion & Gustafson (1952) have demonstrated reminiscence using the koerth pursuit-rotor. A group of subjects which had a rest period after training trials on the right hand, showed greater transfer to

the left hand, than a group that had no rest period. Similarly Grice &
Reynolds (1952) reported bilateral reminiscence effects using a rotary
pursuit task. Further investigations of this type, using appropriate
controls and varying systematically, spatial, temporal and parametric
details in novel tasks should be of great value in unravelling the
specifications of general representations of classes of movement.

More recently, Rosenbaum (1977) has used the negative transfer paradigm to
investigate the general representation of a variety of arm actions. He
has argued that selective adaptation (of the neural representation) by
continued use of a general programme for action will result in negative
transfer to the same action, but performed by different musculature.
Using a variety of arm movements (hand cranking, gear shifting, arm
twisting) Rosenbaum demonstrated that using a specific muscle pattern,
with one arm led to a fall off in performance of the identical pattern
(and the same task) but on the other arm. Such a decrement did not occur
if the second task was different (but still involving the same muscles)
from the first task (e.g., cranking v gear shift). Although the effect
was small and there are difficulties in controlling motivation, this
approach could be further developed to identify spatial and perhaps
temporal attributes within and between classes of movements.

(ii) Response Units or Elements. A consequence of proposing a general
abstract representation of a movement class, is that lower levels of
representation each more specific and corresponding more closely to the
context, must be specified finally in terms of forces and muscles.
Although there has been considerable speculation as to the form of the
'letters and words' of the motor language, it seems unlikely that unitary
muscles or movements form the basic building blocks of action. Bernstein
(1967) has argued that the topological properties of space are represented
at the unitary level. However Evarts (1967) has demonstrated that forces
may be the units of action. Action becomes possible, because movements
are specified or attuned to the field of external forces (Pribram, 1971).
The reflex has played a ubiquitous role in motor control. But as
Bernstein (1969) has pointed out the reflex is not an element of an action,
but rather an elementary action (p.443), and that the reflex loop is an
integral part of movement organization. Bruner & Bruner (1968) reach
the same conclusion in the study of the emergence of voluntary action in
the infant, and stress that in no sense are the reflexes the paving
blocks from which skilled programmes of action are constructed, but
rather they provide the directional specifications for the construction
of voluntary actions (p.18). Easton (1972) has proposed that locomotory
behaviour of some animals can be accurately specified by the way in which
short and long spinal, supra-spinal and other high level reflexes are
commanded in terms of sequence and rhythm. More recently, however,
Easton (1977) has proposed, "It seems quite clear that the CNS composes
movements not by commanding single muscle contractions or even joint
movements, but rather by commanding units of motor activity of some kind"
(p.64). Such units of motor activity have been termed coordinative
structures (Easton, 1977; Turvey, 1977; Fitch & Turvey, 1978) as the
functional combination of reflexes and that their primary feature is
relative autonomy. An alternative view which does not place the emphasis
on the reflex is that of muscle synergies, and that coordinative action
involves the harmonious interplay of agonists and antagonists, fixators
and stabilizers which operate as synergistic units. Kots & Syrovegin
(1966) demonstrated what they called 'motor letters' involving the muscle
synergies about the wrist and elbow joints, these took the form of a

relatively few of the possible range of speed ratios (speed of wrist movement/speed of elbow movement), and that these few speed ratios represented a learned constraints in the motor action. Although such an idea of a learned modular constraint is an elegant organizational format and represents a novel interpretation of the elements or units of action, it does lack convincing empirical support. A recent replication of the same procedure and techniques failed to support Kots & Syrovegin's data and conclusions (Bishop & Harrison, 1977).

An alternative view of response elements is to consider them as control specifications of rules or instructions. Thus for example response elements have been specified as sub-routines (Bruner, 1970; Connolly, 1970, 1978), instructions (Glencross, 1978) and as speech 'stress' units (Sternberg, Monsell, Knoll & Wright, 1978). Bruner & Connolly proposed that a sub-routine is "... an act, the performance of which is a necessary but not sufficient condition for the execution of some more complex hierarchically organized sequence of sub-routines in which it is embedded" (Connolly, 1978, p.7), and that the sub-routine gains its significance as an act from the context in which it occurs. A number of sources of evidence have suggested that the elemental components of a response are a consequence of the contextual significance of an event. One example of this notion comes from the organization of speech responses. Although there is general support for a syllable effect in the latency of a spoken response, there has also been a pattern of conflicting findings (see for example Erikson, Pollack & Montague, 1970; Klapp, 1971; Henderson, Coltheart & Woodhouse, 1973). A clarification of this conflict is suggested by Sternberg, Monsell, Knoll & Wright (1978) who suggested that the syllable structure may not be the appropriate elemental or response unit, but rather the stress unit of speech.

Sternberg's et al (1978) results showed that the increase in latency with list length was related to the number of words in the list with primary stress, leading the authors to conclude that the basic unit or element was the articulatory 'stress group' viz a segment of speech associated with a primary stress. In a similar way, it has been proposed that manual responses are a composite of elements that relate to significant changes or instructions in the movement pattern. In a number of manual tasks the latency of the response seemed to be more closely related to these 'instruction events' than to the mechanical features of the action (Glencross, 1978). It is of course possible that instruction-based elements are higher order representations of the movement-based elements.

(iii) Parameters. According to Brooks (1978) much debate has accumulated around the question of programming movement parameters ... Are there separate control programmes for parameters such as force, speed or displacement? (p.32). It is likely that parametric specification involves 'lower' level mechanisms and occurs relatively late in the organizational sequence. A consequence of a parametric change would be that speed of action would change, but that the relative structural and spatial features would remain the same. Such seemed to be the case in the sequential organization of hand cranking (Glencross, 1975). When the resistance or load was changed progressively it was not until the load changed by a factor or two, that any appreciable reordering of temporal and spatial features occurred. Another line of evidence suggests that changes of speed may be achieved relatively rapidly without any change in serial ordering. Thus Vince & Welford (1967) showed that a slow movement could be speeded up in response to a second signal closely following a first

signal in a psychological refractory period paradigm, without the usual
refractory period delays. However amendment to a rapid movement to slow
it down, took relatively longer to accomplish as though the serial order
now incorporating antagonist activity had to be structured and initiated.
On the other hand speeding up the action required no serial reorganization
but rather 'amplification' of the existing structure. Megaw (1974)
supports this conclusion, suggesting that lower levels of the organization
may be easier to modify or up-date and that quantitative features seem to
be the most rapidly amendable details. Further support for this notion
comes from a study by Glencross (1973b) who showed that the latency for
short rapid movements was not related to the resistance or load to be
moved, but did change as the sequence of movements became more complex.
That is latency and hence programming time was related to changes in
spatial and temporal organization, but not to changes in gain or
amplification. Finally, there is some evidence that the metrical
properties of the response may be pre-set and subject to rapid servo
control. For example Crago, Houk & Hasan (1976) have proposed that it is
likely that the spinal motor servo may be pre-set, and that this servo
guides the limb through simultaneous adjustments of force, length and
velocity.

RESPONSE PRODUCTION

Response production is a generative process contingent not only upon the
integration and ordering of the levels of representation but also upon the
contextual changes of the task environment. In describing response
production in these terms we are concerned with two extremes of
organization, on the one hand direct sensory guidance and on the other
advance planning of the whole response. With the former an unpredictable
series of environmental requirements needs to be matched very closely by a
precise series of movements. At the other extreme the response as a whole
is planned in advance, and is executed without the need for any feedback
control, (Keele, 1968). To account for these forms of actions four basic
organizational processes are involved; (i) sensory guidance and control
(ii) advance planning and programming (iii) presetting and tuning
(iv) amendment procedures. In response production these processes may be
closely related and the final combination of processes will be a
consequence of the strategy of the operator.

(i) Sensory Guidance and Control. Direct sensory guidance is a fundamental
form of control in the production of very precise movements to a changing
display. When there cannot be perceptual, receptor or effector
anticipation (of any significance) then resort must be made to such a
guidance system (Poulton, 1957). However it is clear as far as the
production of skilled actions is concerned that direct sensory control is
not only too slow, but provides an inadequate description of the serial
ordering of actions that typify most skilled behaviour. This issue will
not be discussed here but has been extensively reviewed by Lashley (1951),
Miller, Galanter & Pribram (1960), Keele (1968) and Glencross (1977). But
what needs to be understood is when sensory control becomes necessary, that
is when the transfer of controls demands or requires that direct sensory
information is needed to produce the required response precision or pattern
to achieve the desired outcome. This is beyond the immediate scope of this
paper, but will be referred to in section iv, amendment procedures.

(ii) Advance Planning and Programming. There are two extreme views
regarding advance planning, on the one hand a strict motor programming

interpretation specifies that all details are planned in advance and that once initiated the programme will run its full course without sensory intervention (Keele, 1968; Hinde, 1969). On the other hand Arbib (1972) and Greene (1972) proposed that the response need only be planned in general and that the final specification of detail is a consequence of presetting and tuning in the periphery. However the 'ball-park' response must be a sufficiently close approximation to the final response so that the tuning capabilities are not exceeded. The elegance of this notion within a limited capacity system is that much of the precise detail may be 'off-loaded' by the attention and capacity demanding systems and so transfer the control to other aspects of the task. The crucial issue seems to be, how general (or specific) can a 'ball-park' response be? Although such notions seem attractive they may be applicable only to a limited range of movements, not demanding precision and speeded organization. The support for this form of organization comes indirectly from the demonstration of a variety of presetting and tuning mechanisms to be discussed in section (iii).

The important point about the programming concept was not that feedback is not involved in some role, but rather that feedback was not necessary in eliciting many patterned movements. More recently Keele (in press) has re-emphasised this, a motor programme is "a central representation of a skill that can lead to patterned movement in the absence of feedback" (p.28). There is considerable evidence from animal studies that patterned movement occurs in animals with sensory blockage or deafferentation, viz swallowing movements in mammals, bird vocalizations, the flight action of locust's wings and climbing, locomotion and grasping in monkeys (reviewed in Hinde, 1969; Glencross, 1977). But detailed analyses of performance has frequently revealed   some disruption, for example with the bird song, tonality and syllable structure was affected, in the deafferentation studies the elegance of movement was lost.

However some evidence on the complete programming of detail comes from a study of Bizzi, Polit & Morasso (1976), using normal and deafferented monkeys in a head alignment task. Animals had to learn to rotate their heads to a position in space (30° or 40°). It was found that without visual, kinesthetic and vestibular feedback, the head located the learnt position. When a spring resistance was applied, the head stopped short, but moves to the learnt position immediately when it was released. Similarly, with an applied weight, it overshot the position and then returned to the learnt location, when unloaded. These results suggested that the peripheral adjustments were achieved without any sensory feedback, but that it is the mechanical properties of agonist and antagonist sets of muscles which adjust to the final programmed head position, "the central pattern of neural impulses establishing final head position is pre-programmed and it is not reset by the afferent proprioceptive impulses generated during the intended movement" (Bizzi et al, 1976, p.443). The accuracy of the final head position is dependent in the first instance on the coding of the motor output signal in terms of the tensions of agonists and antagonists related to the desired spatial location.

Let us consider further what details of the response may be planned in advance;

(a) Programming Serial Order. There is considerable evidence that quite long sequences of movements (without rigid accuracy constraints) may be programmed in advance. For example in the original Henry (1960) study,

subjects were required to make rapid movements to strike a target. In the
simpler movement, involving an arm sweep and ball grasp, RT = 200 msec and
MT = 112 msec. For the complex movement involving an arm sweep to a ball,
reversal, sweep, reversal, sweep to a ball, RT = 212 msec and MT = 516
msec. It is unlikely that visual information, although available could be
used for control purposes as it would be out of phase with the appropriate
movement. Glencross (1972, 1973b) showed a similar pattern of results for
reversing and tapping movements (with minimal accuracy constraints). For
sequences involving two taps, RT = 276 msec, MT = 702 msec and for three
taps, RT = 291 msec and MT = 833 msec. In a related series of studies
Glencross (1978) used probe RT procedures. Comparing a simple arm sweep, a
one tap and a two tap movement, lengthening of the probe RT was related to
this increasing complexity of serial order. The delays to the probes were
greatest during the latency phase of the primary movement. Further the
pattern of probe RT's was essentially the same for visual and non-visual
(blind) trials, providing support that the movements were programmed in
advance.

(b) Programming Precision. There seems to be considerable restrictions on
the complete advance planning of precise rapid movements to a target, and
this seems dependent upon the distance travelled, target size, speed of
movement, force exerted and the permissable error (Fitts, 1954; Keele,
1968; Schmidt, Zelaznik & Frank, 1978). In the line of Henry's (1960)
argument, Fitts & Peterson (1964) reported for discrete movements, that
there was only a small increase in RT with changes in accuracy constraint,
5.4 msec/BIT. Glencross (1976) studying rapid aiming movements to
varying sized targets found an increase of 9.5 msec when target size was
changed from 2 ins to 0.5 ins, however there was also a significant
increase in error rate. For the small target condition MT = 285 msec and
so it was possible for vision to be used for control in the latter stages
of the movement. Klapp (1975) has provided some support for the complete
programming of very small movements (2mm) to targets ranging from 2 to 64
mm. The extreme latencies were 374 msec to the small targets and 304 to
the large targets. For long movements to corresponding targets the
latencies ranged from 323 to 329 msec. Somewhat surprisingly, when vision
was removed the error rate in the 2mm condition increased six times.

Rapid aiming movements, where the target is located during the movement,
rather than at the end of movement, as in many kicking and striking skills,
may be planned in advance. Using probe RT procedures, Glencross & Gould
(1979) reported that the lengthening of probe RT was closely related to
target size and that this was most significant for the probes presented
during the latency phase of a 'rapid' aiming movement, where the target
was mid-cycle. However there were also significant increases in probe RT
during the actual movement phase. The movement times to the target were
approximately 100 msec and 175 msec for the 2cm and 1cm targets
respectively, suggesting that visual feedback could not be used in the
first phase of the movement for control purposes. The lengthening of
probe RT in the region of the target may reflect attention being directed
for up-dating rather than immediate control purposes. It would seem that
some very rapid movements to relatively small targets, must be planned in
advance for the speed of movement is such that feedback will always be
out-of-phase with the action. Such rapid actions as striking with a golf
club or baseball bat to hit relatively small targets at speed have not
been fully investigated and may prove to be a special class of movement in
terms of their organization and control.

(iii) Presetting and Tuning. The issues concerning presetting and tuning
relate not to the demonstration that such mechanisms in fact exist, but
rather to what detailed amendments or shaping such mechanisms can achieve
(Kots, 1969; Mitchie, Clarke, Sinden & Glue, 1975). There is some
evidence of general and specific changes at spinal and central levels,
which occur prior to specified responses. This comes from studies in
which the excitability of the monosynaptic tendon and Hoffman reflexes
have been studied in relation to preparation to respond. Requin, Bonnet &
Semjen (1977) were unable to show strong evidence of specific preparation or presetting. With the Hoffman reflex following a warning
signal, there was not a clear differential modulation of the motor spinal
structure reactively during preparation (p.164). In a study similar to
that of Requin et al (1977), but in which a long foreperiod (4 secs) was
used, Brunia & Vuister (1979) also reported no specific motor preparation
process, using the Hoffman reflex, although there was evidence of a
generalized change.

There is some evidence supporting the notion of presetting in studies by
Evarts & Tanji (1974) and Tanji & Evarts (1976). Recorded neurons of the
motor cortex showed a differential effect to two instructions ('push' or
'pull') such that the motor cortex was in a different state some 200 msec
after the instruction had been given. The authors suggest that this may
be the bases underlying the presetting of spinal cord reflex mechanisms.
Again within the same temporal phase Gailland (1978) provides evidence
that the terminal CNV is contingent on a motor response and that the
amplitude of this wave reflects the level of motor preparation.

Although there is considerable evidence of changes in spinal and motor
cortex neurons immediately prior to movement, it is as yet difficult to
relate these changes to specific preparatory stages and levels of motor
control and in particular to tuning functions that are specifically
related to the task outcome. However Tanji & Evarts (1976) conclude,
"Since motor cortex PTN axons end in alpha and gamma motor neurons and on
interneurons of the spinal cord, changes of PTN activity with 'intention'
or 'motor set' provide a mechanism for suprasegmental control and presetting of spinal cord reflex excitability specific to the nature of an
impending movement" (p.1062).

(iv) Amendment Procedures. With many forms of response, amendment and
error correction procedures are an important part of the organizational
process. It is proposed that such procedures should be viewed as an
integral part of the organizational process.

Error detection and correction based largely on visual feedback is a major
amendment procedure. However typically such amendments are relatively
slow and usually involve a major modification of the ongoing response, or
provides the basis for up-dating the subsequent responses. For example,
Keele & Posner (1968) investigated the processing of visual feedback in a
rapid aiming movement. The visual feedback did not facilitate accuracy
when the movement time was less than 190 msec. But accuracy was enhanced
when the movement time was in the order of 260 msec. That is a visually
based amendment took in the order of 200-250 msec to be implemented. In
situations in which there is considerable input uncertainty as well as a
range of response possibilities the latency of the visual feedback system
may be considerably longer than this.

Aiming movements have been a convenient vehicle for studying feedback
based amendments and corrections and in particular the time course of such
amendments. This approach was enhanced by the work of Fitts and the
designation of a speed/accuracy relationship which came to be known as
Fitts Law (1954), although little effort was made to understand the
conceptual basis of the motor control involved. However Annett, Golby &
Kay (1958) had shown that with a peg-hole aiming task over 8.0 ins, the
time taken to traverse 7.5 ins remained approximately constant, but that
the time taken over the last 0.5 ins was related to accuracy and
assumedly to visual guidance of the peg into the hole. There is some
contention as to whether one or a series of corrections take place in this
type of task. Both Crossman & Goodeve (1963) and Keele (1968) had
proposed a series of sub-movement adjustments each of the order of 250
msec, until the movement falls within the target area. More typically,
only one correction is made (Vince, 1948; Langolf, Chaffin & Foulke, 1976).
However the point is that there exist a range of strategies that can be
used, depending upon the specific task, the instructions by the
experimenter, the intentions of the subject and possibly the level of
skill. For example in the Langolf et al (1976) study, as the accuracy
constraints became greater, the whole movement was slowed down. Again
Howarth, Beggs & Bowden (1971) found that subjects slowed down the whole
movement as the targets became smaller and then when the subject is in the
proximity of the target a single correction is made. Keele (in press) has
suggested that optimization is achieved by adopting a strategy for
achieving greater terminal accuracy, by slowing the speed of the limb to
bring the responding limb closer to the target at the time of a final
single visually-based correction (p.14). However, what we need to know is
under what conditions does the subject use a particular strategy and how
the strategy adopted relates to optimizing performance.

Kinesthetically based amendments and corrections may be faster than visual
amendments. Reacting to changes in kinesthetic stimulation, as in
responding to the release of supported arm, produces reaction times in the
order of 125 msec to 150 msec (Chernikoff & Taylor, 1952; Glencross &
Koreman, in press). Kinesthetic and tactile choice reactions are also
faster than visual reactions (Leonard, 1959; Oldfield, 1976; Glencross &
Koreman, in press). Corrective movements, in pursuit tracking, based on
unexpected changes in lever resistance have latencies, in the order of 200
msec (Vince, 1948). There have also been consistently reported a variety
of error correction responses with latencies in the order of 60-110 msec
in tracking type of situations (Gibbs, 1965; Higgins & Angel, 1970; Megaw,
1974). Gibbs (1965) using a step-input tracking task reported mean error
correction times of 110 msec, after considerable learning, and proposed
that these corrections were based on kinesthetic monitoring. In a series
of similar experiments Higgins & Angel (1970) reported amendment times in
pursuit tracking significantly faster than correct responses and
kinesthetic RT's derived in the same manner. They suggested that subjects
make use of short latency control processes in correcting such motor
errors and that sensory feedback, visual or kinesthetic is not involved.
However, of course, there is no direct evidence for this and the short
latency may be related to processing sensory feedback more directly or
that alternative responses may have been partially activated and can be
implemented rapidly (Rabbitt & Rodgers, 1979). Rabbitt & Vyas (1970) and
Welford (1974) have suggested that error correction times might be
related to the stage of organization and level of representation of the
programme. Megaw (1974) also supports this proposal, suggesting for
example that if the modifications are quantitative involving parametric

changes that these could be achieved relatively rapidly. But if at the elemental level there were changes in spatial and/or temporal organization, these would take longer to implement.

There is considerable evidence that a variety of movement amendments and adjustments are reflex based, although the precise nature of these processes is not fully understood (Matthews, 1972; Crago, Houk & Hasan, 1976). They may also be closely related to the presetting and tuning notions discussed earlier. According to Mathews (1972), with the normal co-activation of the alpha and gamma motoneurones, if an external resistance or force is encountered so that the extrafusal and intrafusal fibres are not 'counterbalanced', then the stretch receptor will increase its discharge reflecting the change in external load. A subsequent adjustment can be made reflexly in the order of 50-60 msec (Hammond, 1956; Marsden, Merton & Morton, 1972). This stretch reflex however seems to be influenced by cortical connections. Hammond (1956) had demonstrated that the 50 msec EMG response (assumedly the stretch reflex) was influenced by the prior instructions to the subject (the instruction to let go in elbow flexion abolished the 50 msec EMG response). More recently Evarts & Tanji (1974) and Tanji & Evarts (1976) have provided supporting evidence. However additional evidence by Crago, Houk & Hasan (1976) suggests that these observed modifications to the stretch reflex may be a result of the superimposed movements (triggered reactions), and are not produced by servo action acting to change the gain of the stretch reflex.

The point of reporting these details is that they emphasise the variety of amendment procedures that are available and that can be matched to the contextual demands of the movement and task and thus must be considered in the overall organization of the response.

ORGANIZATIONAL STRATEGIES

The purpose of this review has been not only to identify organizational processes but also to emphasise that there are a variety of organizational procedures which need to be matched to the task demands to optimize performance. What we need to understand is under what conditions is each organizational format used and also what organizational strategy should be used to optimize a particular outcome. We have described a number of studies where a similar task or end result has been achieved by different organizational strategies. For example Bizzi, Kalil & Tagliasco (1971), studying eye-head coordination in monkeys reported two patterns of eye-head coordination to a target depending on whether the target was randomly or non-randomly presented. For randomly presented targets, the sequence involved a visual saccade followed by a head movement and then a compensatory eye movement. With non-randomly presented targets, the head moved before the target presentation, together with compensatory eye movements, then a saccade occurs followed by a second compensatory eye movement. Further a variety of movement patterns have been reported for aiming movements to a target (Annett, Golby & Kay, 1958; Keele, 1968; Klapp, 1975; Langolf, Chaffin & Foulke, 1976; Glencross & Gould, 1979). An initial programmed phase may be followed by several visually based corrections, alternatively the initial response is slowed down followed by a single adjustment close to the target. If the movement is very short or the accuracy constraints minimal or if the whole movement is very rapid, then the whole movement may be programmed in advance. A final example relates to the incorporation of error correction strategies in an ongoing sequence of movements. Pew (1966) used a tracking task that required the appropriate timing of alternating key presses of the two hands. Three

strategies were observed; subjects allowed the misalignment to gradually
increase and then eventually made one discrete error correction; other
subjects changed the relative time of activity of the right and left keys,
so that over a series of responses the target gradually drifted back to
the target; a further group of subjects made a response, waited for the
feedback and then initiated a second response on the basis of the
perceived discrepancy.

There seems to have been in the past considerable attention directed
towards competing views of central versus peripheral control mechanisms.
However what needs to be understood is the interaction of central and
peripheral mechanisms in the organization of meaningful patterns of
movement. More specifically under what conditions is a particular
organizational format used or preferred? The answer seems to lie in an
understanding of organizational strategies related to the transfer of
control between the various levels of representation such that the
behaviour may be organized at a number of levels of complexity
simultaneously.

ACKNOWLEDGEMENTS

I am most grateful to Steve Keele for discussions on many of the issues
raised in this paper. Support was provided by the Study Leave Committee
of the Flinders University of South Australia and the paper was prepared
whilst the author was a visitor at the University of Western Australia.
I am grateful to the support provided by Aubrey Yates and Alan Morton at
the University of Western Australia.

REFERENCES

[1] Annett, J., Golby, C.W. and Kay, H., The measurement of elements on
     an assembly task - the information output of the human motor system,
     Quar. J. Exper. Psychol., 10 (1958), 1-11.
[2] Arbib, M.A., The metaphorical brain: An introduction to cybernetics
     as artificial intelligence and brain theory (New York, Wiley, 1972).
[3] Bartlett, F.C., Fatigue following highly skilled work, Prac. Roy. Soc.
     Lond. Bull., 131 (1941), 247-257.
[4] Bernstein, N.A., The coordination and regulation of movement (London,
     Pergamon Press, 1967).
[5] Bernstein, N.A., Methods for developing physiology as related to the
     problems of cybernetics, in: Cole, M. and Maltzman, I. (ed.),
     Handbook of Contemporary Soviet Psychology (New York, Basic Books,
     1969).
[6] Bishop, A. and Harrison, A., Kots and Syrovegin (1966) - A
     demonstration of modular units in motor programming? J. Hum.
     Movement Studies, 3 (1977), 99-109.
[7] Bizzi, E. and Evarts, E.V., Translational mechanisms between input
     and output, Neurosci. Res. Prog. Bull. 9 (1971), 31-59.
[8] Bizzi, E., Kalil, R.E. and Tagliasco, V., Eye-head coordination in
     monkeys: evidence for centrally patterned organization, Science,
     1973 (1971), 452-454.
[9] Bizzi, E., Polit, A. and Morasso, P., Mechanisms underlying achieve-
     ment of final head position, J. Neurophysiol., 39 (1976), 435-444.
[10] Broadbent, D.E., Levels, hierarchies and locus of control, Quar. J.
     Exper. Psychol., 29 (1977), 181-201.

[11] Brooks, V.B., Motor programmes revisited, in: Talbott, R.E., and
      Humphrey, D.R. (eds.), Posture and movement: perspective for
      integrating sensory and motor research on the mammalian nervous
      system (Raven Press, 1978).
[12] Bruner, J.S., The growth and structure of skill, in: Connolly, K.J.
      (ed.), Mechanisms of motor skill development (London, Academic Press,
      1970).
[13] Bruner, J.S. and Bruner, B.M., On voluntary action and its
      hierarchical structure. Paper presented at the Symposium on New
      Perspectives in the Sciences of Man, Alpbach, Austria, 1968.
[14] Brunia, C.H.M. and Vuister, F.M., Spinal reflexes as motor indicator
      of motor preparation in man (unpublished paper, 1979).
[15] Bryan, W.L. and Harter, N., Studies on the telegraphic language.
      The acquisition of a hierarchy of habits, Psych. Rev., 6 (1899),
      345-375.
[16] Chernikoff, R. and Taylor, F., Reaction times to kinaesthetic
      stimulation resulting from sudden arm displacement, J. Exper.
      Psychol., 43 (1952), 1-8.
[17] Connolly, K.J., Skill development problems and plans, in: Connolly,
      K.J. (ed.), Mechanisms of motor skill development (London, Academic
      Press, 1970).
[18] Connolly, K., The development of motor skills in children, in:
      Glencross, D.J. (ed.), Psychology and Sport (Sydney, McGraw-Hill,
      1978).
[19] Crago, P.E., Houk, J.C. and Hasan, Z., Regulatory actions of human
      stretch reflex, J. Neurophysiol., 39 (1976), 925-935.
[20] Craik, K.J.W., The nature of explanation (Cambridge, Cambridge
      University Press, 1966).
[21] Crossman, E.R.F.W. and Goodeve, P.J., Feedback control of hand-
      movement and Fitt's Law, Proceedings of the Experimental Society
      (Oxford, 1963).
[22] Easton, T.A., On the normal use of reflexes, Amer. Scientist, 60
      (1972), 591-599.
[23] Easton, T.A., Coordinative structures - The basis for a motor
      programme, in: Landers, D.M. and Christina, R.W. (eds.), Psychology
      of motor behavior and sport (Champaign, Illinois, Human Kinetic
      Publishers, 1978).
[24] Erikson, C.W., Pollack, M.D. and Montague, W.E., Implicit speech:
      mechanism in perceptual encoding? J. Exper. Psychol., 84 (1970),
      502-507.
[25] Evarts, E.V., Representation of movements and muscles by pyramidal
      tract neurons of the precentral motor cortex, in: Hahr, M.D. and
      Purpura, D.P. (eds.), Neurophysiological basis of normal and
      abnormal motor activities (New York, Raven Press, 1967).
[26] Evarts, E.V., Feedback and corollary discharge: a merging of the
      concepts, Neurosc. Res. Prog. Bull., 9 (1971), 86-112.
[27] Evarts, E.V. and Tanji, J., Gating of motor cortex reflexes by prior
      instruction, Brain Res., 71 (1974), 479-494.
[28] Fitch, H.L. and Turvey, M.T., On the control of activity: some
      remarks from an ecological point of view, in: Landers, D.M. and
      Christina, R.W. (eds.), Psychology of Motor Behavior and Sport
      (Champaign, Illinois, Human Kinetic Publishers, 1978).
[29] Fitts, P.M., The information capacity of the human motor system in
      controlling the amplitude of movement, J. Exper. Psychol., 47 (1954),
      381-391.
[30] Fitts, P.M. and Peterson, J.R., Information capacity of discrete
      motor responses, J. Exper. Psychol., 67 (1964), 103-112.

[31] Gaillard, A., Slow brain potentials preceding task performance
      (Amsterdam, Institute for Perception TNO, 1978).
[32] Gibbs, C.B., Probability learning in step-input tracking, Br. J.
      Psychol., 56 (1965), 233-242.
[33] Glencross, D.J., Latency and response complexity, J. Motor Behav.,
      4 (1972), 251-256.
[34] Glencross, D.J., Temporal organization in a repetitive speed skill,
      Ergonomics, 16 (1973a), 765-776).
[35] Glencross, D.J., Response complexity and the latency of different
      movement patterns, J. Motor Behav., 5 (1973b), 95-104.
[36] Glencross, D.J., The effects of changes in task conditions on the
      temporal organization of a repetitive speed skill, Ergonomics, 18
      (1975), 17-28.
[37] Glencross, D.J., The latency of aiming movements, J. Motor Behav.,
      8 (1976), 27-34.
[38] Glencross, D.J., The control of skilled movements, Psychol. Bull.,
      84 (1977), 14-29.
[39] Glencross, D.J., Output and response processes in skilled
      performance, in: Roberts, G.C. and Newell, K.M. (ed.), Psychology
      of Motor Behavior and Sport (Champaign, Illinois, Human Kinetic
      Publishers, 1979).
[40] Glencross, D.J., Response planning and the organization of speed
      movements, Paper presented at Attention and Performance VIII,
      Princeton, N.J., 1978.
[41] Glencross, D.J. and Gould, J.H., The planning of precision movements,
      J. Motor Behav., 11 (1979), 1-9.
[42] Glencross, D.J. and Koreman, M.M., The processing of proprioceptive
      signals, Neuropsych., in press.
[43] Greene, P.H., Problems of organization of motor system, in: Rosen,
      R. and Snell, F.M. (eds.), Progress in theoretical biology, Vol. 2
      (New York, Academic Press, 1972.
[44] Grice, G.R. and Reynolds, B., Effect of varying amounts of rest in
      conventional and bilateral transfer "reminiscence", J. Exper.
      Psychol., 44 (1952), 247-252.
[45] Hammond, P.H., The influence of prior instruction to the subject on
      an apparently neuromuscular response, J. Physiol., 132 (1956),
      17-18P.
[46] Henderson, L., Coltheart, M. and Woodhouse, D., Failure to find a
      syllabic-effect in number-naming, Mem. and Cog., 1 (1973), 304-306.
[47] Henry, F.M., Increased response latency for complicated movements
      and a "memory drum" theory of neuromotor reaction, Res. Quar., 30
      (1960), 448-459.
[48] Higgins, J.R. and Angel, R.W., Corrections of tracking errors
      without sensory feedback, J. Exper. Psychol., 84 (1970), 412-416.
[49] Hinde, R.A., Control of movement patterns in animals, Quar. J. Exp.
      Psychol., 21 (1969), 105-126.
[50] Howarth, C.I., Beggs, W.D.A. and Bowden, J.M., The relationship
      between speed and accuracy of movement aimed at a target, Acta
      Psychol., 35 (1971), 207-218.
[51] Irion, A.L. and Gustafson, L.M., "Reminiscence" in bilateral
      transfer, J. Exp. Psychol., 43 (1952), 321-323.
[52] Keele, S.W., Movement control in skilled motor performance, Psychol.
      Bull., 70 (1968), 387-403.
[53] Keele, S.W., Behavioral analysis of motor control, in: Brooks, V.
      (ed.), Handbook of Physiology: Motor Control (in press).
[54] Keele, S.W. and Posner, M.I., Processing of visual feedback in rapid
      movements, J. Exp. Psychol., 77 (1968), 155-158.

[55] Klapp, S.T., Implicit speech inferred from response latencies in same-different decisions, J. Exper. Psychol., 91 (1971), 262-267.

[56] Klapp, S.T., Feedback versus motor programming in the control of aimed movements, J. Exper. Psychol. Human Perc. and Perf., 104 (1975), 147-153.

[57] Kots, Y.A.M. Supraspinal control of the segmental centres of muscle antagonists in man I. Reflex excitability of the motor neurones of muscle antagonists in the period of organization of voluntary movement, Biofizika, 14 (1969), 167-172.

[58] Kots, Y.A.M., and Syrovegin, A.V., Fixed sets of variants of inter-actions in the muscles of two joints in the execution of simple voluntary movements, Biophysics, 11 (1966), 1212-1219.

[59] Langolf, G.D., Chaffin, D.B. and Foulke, J.A., An investigation of Fitt's Law using a wide range of movement amplitudes, J. Motor Behav., 8 (1976), 113-128.

[60] Lashley, K.S., The problem of serial order in behavior, in: Jeffress, L.A. (ed.), Cerebral Mechanisms in Behavior (New York, Wiley and Sons, 1951).

[61] Leonard, J.A., Tactual choice reactions: I, Quar. J. Exper. Psychol., 11 (1959), 76-83.

[62] Marsden, C.D., Merton, P.A. and Morton, H.B., Servo action in human voluntary movement, Nature, 238 (1972), 140-143.

[63] Matthews, P.B.C., Mammalian muscle receptors and their central action (Baltimore, Williams and Wilkins, 1972).

[64] Megaw, E.D., Possible modification to a rapid ongoing programmed manual response, Brain Res., 71 (1974), 425-441.

[65] Merton, P.A., How we control the contraction of our muscles, Sci. Am. 288 (1973), 30-37.

[66] Milisen, R. and Riper, C. Van., Differential transfer of training in a rotary activity, J. Exper. Psychol., 24 (1939), 640-646.

[67] Miller, G.A., Galanter, E. and Pribram, K.H., Plans and the structure of behavior (New York, Holt, 1960).

[68] Mitchie, P.T., Clarke, A.M., Sinden, J.D. and Glue, L.C.T., Lateral facilitation of Hoffmann reflexes prior to voluntary movement in a choice reaction time task, Appl. Neurophysiol., 38 (1975), 191-196.

[69] Neisser, U., Cognition and Reality (San Francisco, Freeman, 1976).

[70] Oldfield, S.R., Hemispheric and attentional effects on the transmission of somatosensory information, unpublished Ph.D. Thesis, Australian National University, 1976.

[71] Pew, R.W., Acquisition of hierarchical control over the temporal acquisition of skill, J. Exp. Psych., 71 (1966), 764-771.

[72] Poulton, E.C., On prediction in skilled movements, Psychol. Bull., 54 (1957), 67-78.

[73] Pribram, K.H., Languages of the Brain (New Jersey, Prentice-Hall, 1971).

[74] Rabbitt, P.M.A. and Rodgers, B., What does a man do after he makes an error? An analysis of response programming, Quar. J. Exper. Psychol., 29 (1977), 727-743.

[75] Rabbitt, P.M.A. and Vyas, S.M., An elementary preliminary taxonomy for some errors in laboratory choice RT tasks, Acta Psychol., 33 (1970), 56-76.

[76] Requin, J., Bonnet, M. and Semjen, A., Is there a specificity in the supraspinal control of motor structures during preparation, in: Dornic, S. (ed.), Attention and Performance, VI (Hillsdale, New Jersey, Erlbaum Associates, 1977).

[77] Rosenbaum, D.A., Selective adaptation of "command neurons" in the human motor system, Neuropsychol., 15 (1977), 81-91.

566   D.J. GLENCROSS

[78] Schmidt, R.A., Zelaznik, H.N. and Frank, J.S., Sources of inaccuracy in rapid movement, in: Stelmach, G.E. (ed.), Information Processing in Motor Control and Learning (New York, Academic Press, 1978).

[79] Sternberg, S., Monsell, S., Knoll, R.L. and Wright, C.E., The latency and duration of rapid movement sequences: comparisons of speech and typewriting, in: Stelmach, G.E., Information Processing in Motor Control and Learning (New York, Academic Press, 1978).

[80] Tanji, J. and Evarts, E.V., Anticipatory activity of motor cortex neurons in relation to direction of an intended movement, J. Neurophysiol., 39 (1976), 1062-1068.

[81] Taub, E. and Berman, A.J., Movement and learning in the absence of sensory feedback, in: Freedman, S.J. (ed.), The Neuropsychology of Spatially oriented Behavior (Homewood, Illinois, Dorsey Press, 1968).

[82] Turvey, M.T., Preliminaries to a theory of action with reference to vision, in: Shaw, R. and Bransford, J. (eds.), Perceiving, Acting and Knowing: Toward an Ecological Psychology (Hillsdale, New Jersey, Lawrence Erlbaum Association, 1977).

[83] Turvey, M.T., Shaw, R. and Mace, W., Issues in the theory of action: degrees of freedom, coordinative structures and coalitions, in: Requin, J. (ed.), Attention and Performance, Vol. 7 (Hillsdale, New Jersey, Erlbaum, 1978).

[84] Vince, M.A., Corrective movements in a pursuit task, Quar. J. Exper. Psychol., 1 (1948), 85-103.

[85] Vince, M.A. and Welford, A.T., Time taken to change the speed of a response, Nature, 213 (1967), 532-533.

[86] Welford, A.T., On the sequencing of action, Brain Res., 71 (1974), 381-392.

[87] Wing, A.M., Response timing in handwriting, in: Stelmach, G.E. (ed.), Information Processing in Motor Control and Learning (New York, Academic Press, 1978).

[88] Woodworth, R.S., The accuracy of voluntary movement, Psychol. Rev., Monograph. Suppl. 13 (1899), 1-114.

Tutorials in Motor Behavior
G.E. Stelmach and J. Requin (eds.)
© *North-Holland Publishing Company, 1980*

35

HANDWRITING AND DRAWING:
A TWO STAGE MODEL OF
COMPLEX MOTOR BEHAVIOR

Gerard P. van Galen
Psychological Laboratory of
the University of Nijmegen
Erasmuslaan 16
6525 GG Nijmegen
The Netherlands

This paper is on the execution stage of complex motor behavior.
In our view handwriting and drawing, and more generally response
execution of all internally monitored motor behavior, must be
considered as containing two structurally different stages: A
'focal' stage of motor pattern selection, in which stage an
abstract representation of the selected goal response is
retrieved from a dynamic long term motor memory, and a second,
'ambient' stage of parameter estimation for actual muscle
innervation. In two experiments, one with young children and
the other with normal, right-handed subjects we tested some of
the implications of the Two Stage Model. Specifically it could
be shown that repetition of a grapheme within a serial choice
reaction time drawing task results in a significant reduction
of response latency but not in any change of the motor time.
The results are interpreted as giving support to the proposition
of a sustained, focal process of motor pattern retrieval, followed
by a transient process of ambient parameter estimation.

INTRODUCTION

Handwriting and drawing are examples 'pur sang' of psychomotor tasks, with
all of the components of traditional psychology: Perception and imagery;
response planning and control; feedback and knowledge of results;
information processing about space and form. Yet the number of references
in the literature on this type of psychomotor behavior is extremely small.
We know something about developmental aspects (Søvik, 1975). A small
number of experimental studies has been published on typical constancies
of force and timing patterns in handwriting (Denier van der Gon & Thuring,
1965; Vredenbregt & Koster, 1971; Wing, 1979), and Goodnow & Levine (1973)
have proven the usefulness of the concept of 'movement grammar' by showing
constant strategies in the performance of drawing and writing strokes.

There are, however, in our view, no systematic studies in which it has
been tried to describe drawing and handwriting in terms of the dominant
concepts of the psychology of motor behavior. Partly an explanation for
this situation is to be found in the specific nature of both handwriting
and drawing, a feature which is also typical for speech and making
gestures. What these four psychomotor behaviors have in common is that the

pattern of spatial and temporal muscular adaptations is dictated not by
spatial relations in the outside world (like e.g. in pointing and
grasping) but by a discrete, inner representation of a motor pattern. It
is this patternlike character of drawing and handwriting that we wish to
consider as a specific class of movement behavior. For reasons to be
explained further on we shall call it 'focal' behavior. This latter
category of psychomotor tasks is in contrast to 'ambient' psychomotor
adaptation which loads on moment – to – moment adaptations to spatial and
temporal changes in the physical surrounding. Walking, pointing, grasping,
ocular pursuit may serve as typical ambient behaviors.

Before mentioning something of the theoretical and empirical considerations
in favor of the focal/ambient distinction, and before presenting our view
on the relation of handwriting to these modes of information processing,
it should be made clear that the introduction of a theoretical distinction
between focal and ambient psychomotor tasks is not to say that focal tasks
have no ambient components and, likewise, ambient tasks do not start with
the selection of a specific, internally represented, movement scheme. The
difference is in the relative load either on choice between discrete motor
memory states or on spatial (and temporal) adaption to the perceived
surroundings.

The relevance in making this difference is that it can make clear that
handwriting is more than the production of associations of strokes, either
linked together by feedback of foregoing elements, or held together by as
vague a concept as a generalized motor scheme. On the other hand we feel
that in most of the theoretical explanations and empirical work on motor
behavior many interesting things have been said about the realisation of
spatial goals (e.g. by intervention of a recall schema that makes it
possible to generalize past experiences with spatial goals, muscle
innervations and limb position feedback to new spatial conditions) without
in any way discussing how a subject selects the basic proficient movement
pattern. A basketball player, before being able either to catch or to
avoid the ball, must choose to approach or to avoid it.

Let us now go back to the origin of the focal/ambient distinction. In 1968
Trevarthen (and a couple of colleagues) published, in the papers of a
symposium, the proposition that evolution has brought about two
fundamentally different ways of information processing. One, the ambient
mode, is associated with phylogenetically older brain structures and is
functionally responsible for spatial adaptations like locomotion and
transport movement. The other, focal, mode has evolved with the development
of the neocortical structures and is concerned with pattern perception and
patternlike movement production, such as manipulation and speech. Evidence
for this "Boston Group" view has been provided mainly by animal studies of
the effects of brain lesions and animal conditioning studies (Held, 1968;
Ingle, 1968; Schneider, 1968; Humphrey, 1974).

Semmes (1968) and Sperry, Gazzaniga & Bogen (1969) produced data from
neurosurgical patients which are to be considered as positive evidence for
the usefulness of the 'two modes' of information processing view in the
field of human psychology. Van Galen (1974) proposed formulating the focal

and ambient modes in the terminology of human experimental psychology. In
that study was added, to the discriminating features of Trevarthen, the
Single Channel, discrete memory character of the focal mode and the
Parallel Processing, analog production rules of the ambient mode. With the
former traits we mean that focal information is retrieved and processed
one chunk at a time because incoming information has to be retrieved or to
be compared with discrete memory states. With the latter characteristics
(parallel processing with the aid of analog rules) is meant that ambient
adaptations can be realised simultaneously and independently and that the
realisation of certain output states in answer to specific input values is
found by application of general rules which apply to the whole range of
possible input and output values. (c.f. the recall schema and the
recognition schema of Schmidt (1976) as analogous to these ambient motor
production rules.) Experimental support for this theorising was found in a
series of experiments on RT with the double stimulation paradigm. (See
also Van Galen & Ten Hoopen, 1976.) In the meantime the idea of multiple
modes of information processing has received further attention in the work
of Pick (1978) who reviews the basic idea within the context of different
sensory modalities. As far as we know, however, modes of perception have
had far more consideration than modes of movement production. We now
present a model of movement organisation, specified with regard to
handwriting but in principal extendible to motor behavior in general, which
gives room to a focal as well an ambient stage.

THE TWO STAGE MODEL OF RESPONSE EXECUTION

Stage analysis of psychomotor behavior is nearly as old as experimental
psychology itself. Donders (1968) and his apprentice De Jaager (1865) may
be considered as the founders of a theoretical model which considers
reaction processes as the additive and consecutive sum of stages into
which the total psychomotor behavior can be partitioned. Recently Sternberg
(1969) has added a new era to this component processes analysis by
introducing a statistical technique for differentiating new stages. In the
past ten years a view on psychomotor behavior has crystallized out (see
e.g. Sanders, 1977) in which every sensorimotor behavior contains the
following stages: Stimulus representation, characterized by the 'hardware'
features of the sensory system; Stimulus coding, determined by the 'soft
ware' programming of the perceptual systems; Response selection, programmed
by the long term and short term instructions to the subjects; Response
execution and control, i.e. the actual carrying out of a motoric response.

It is this latter stage, that is relatively least worked out in the human
performance literature. It must be allowed that there is a huge literature
on feedback and control processes, but apart from studies in some
circumscribed areas such as speech (e.g. MacNeilage, 1970) very few of
those studies put the question of how a selected response goal is carried
out in an ever changing ambient work field and in never recurring
biomechanical circumstances. Our tentative answer to this issue is to
introduce, on both logical and empirical grounds, a model of response
execution that makes a distinction between two structurally different
stages in ongoing motor behavior. The first stage we will call 'the focal
stage of motor pattern retrieval'. The second stage has been termed 'the

ambient stage of temporo-spatial parameter estimation'. The basic
assumptions of and predictions from the model are described in the next
paragraphs.

A. Motor pattern retrieval

Every motor act starts with an internally or externally given command to
retrieve from motor memory the most adequate motor pattern for the given
situation. This motor pattern is a description of an ordered sequence of
goal (or intended) movements, in which description only the relations
between temporal and spatial parameters are defined; but not their common
units of measurement for time and translation. The memory description only
contains formal values $\underline{t}$ and $\underline{x}$ for time and translation.

As an illustration of this idea we consider the hypothetical
representation of the writing pattern of the letter b. We can think of
the motor pattern for this letter as an ordered sequence of two goal
movements, one downgoing ($\downarrow$) and one going around rightways ($\circlearrowright$). If we
put the unity of translation at the (dummy) value of $\underline{x}$ then it is
possible to define the characteristic ratio between the extent of the
downgoing movement and the radius of the around-going movement as
$p\underline{x} : q\underline{x}$, where for p and q can be filled in arbitrary values under
the condition that e.g. $p > 2q$. In other words, retrieving the motor
pattern for the letter b is the same as retrieving from motor memory a
plan that says: draw a vertical line followed by an around-going line in
such a way that the vertical line is longer than the height of the
circle.

Typically for this kind or representation is that

1. A whole series of different b's can be produced under slight variations
   of one general pattern description.
   Examples are: b, b, b, b, · · ·
   What is varying here are the parameters p and q.
2. The representation of the motor pattern is independent of extent of the
   movement actually needed. For the absolute size of the pattern varies
   with x.
3. This description is only a partial one, i.e. to actually carry out such
   a motor plan the system needs real numbers for the values of the
   parameters and the choice of units of measurements. In our model these
   values are provided by the above mentioned second stage, of ambient
   parameter estimation.

About the first, focal, stage of motor pattern retrieval we further propose
that separate motor pattern descriptions are stored as a dynamic and
hierarchically organized set of discrete descriptions. The term discrete
refers to the discontinuous borderlines between different patterns. Every
motor pattern has its own discrete place in the memory structure. The
dynamic and hierarchic character of the 'memory building' has to do with
the ever changing number of stored motor patterns and with the ever
changing retrievability of pattern by frequency and recency mechanisms. We
assume that frequently used patterns get an 'outstanding' place in the
memory (frequency principle) and that recently activated patterns have some

profit on a next repeated retrieval from fading rest activity in the
memory structure (recency principle). In some respects these features of
the motor memory are comparable with Morton's logogen model of speech
recognition (Morton, 1969). We will meet the recency and the frequency
principle again in the section on experimental predictions where we state
that the retrieval-time for a grapheme, i.e. the latency between getting
the command to write and the actual start of movement will be shorter if
that grapheme has occured more often and/or more recently.

Concluding the section on the focal retrieval stage: it seems to be
necessary to state some limiting remarks with regard to the character of
the model which until now has remained very hypothetical. Some of the
uncertainties are very clear but are not necessarily disastrous. We know
very little about the structural elements of motor patterns. Is the letter
b really stored in terms of vertical and around-going movements? What is
also very uncertain is how we should think of the relation between visual
imagery and motor memory. How far can we consider drawing as tracking a
cognitive image? An empirical answer to this question may be found if we
are able to define a motor specific measure of structural complexity of
motor programs. The beginnings of this have been made by Restle & Burnside
(1972) and by Sternberg, Monsell, Knoll & Wright (1969). However their
measures of complexity do not consider the aggregation of motor elements
as different from cognitive structures in general.

B. Ambient parameter estimation

Like Schmidt (In Stelmach, 1976), who proposes his recall and recognition
scheme as a solution for the excess of memory load caused by the 'Novelty
phenomenon' of motor behavior, we assume that actual temporal and spatial
parameters of a motor act are not stored in, and retrieved from memory,
but computed with the aid of general rules, which are analogous to
Schmidt's recall schema. The computation of these performance parameters
is supervised by a hypothetical 'ambient' monitor, who fills in spatial
and temporal parameters, given the actual starting position of the limbs.
These computations are of only ad hoc value, i.e. the result of each
computation is only valid at one moment, for one place.

We look on the ambient parameter estimation typically as a transient
process, quite contrary to the long-lasting focal memory. To be clear,
what is meant here is that the outcome of the ambient process is transient.
The rules which make the computations possible are stored and can therefore
be considered as a kind of motor memory. But this memory structure is very
different from the focal memory for patterns. The ambient memory does build
in rules which describe a whole range of relations between given starting
positions, desired goals and actual innervations. This is exactly what, in
Schmidt's theory, the recall schema does. The ambient memory, also like the
recall scheme, gives a solution for the apparent contradiction between a
common 'pattern character' of graphemes and the ever changing modes of
execution. We differ, with respect to Schmidt's theory, in that our view is
that spatio-temporal rules are only part of the history, a part which is
meaningless without the definition of motor patterns.

TESTING THE TWO STAGE MODEL

Some of the evidence for a distinction between the retrieval of an
abstract motor program and the actual figuring out of movement parameters
comes from the literature. Klapp (1977), using Sternberg's (1969) additive-
factor method showed that response programming starts before muscle
selection has been completed. In the field of speech production MacNeilage
(1970) has produced evidence for the view that speech programs are
represented in terms of articulatory goal positions of the speech organ
and not as specific articulatory movements. Vredenbregt & Koster (1971),
in a timing analysis of handwriting, showed that the ratios of time
intervals for different segments of the same letter were remarkable
constant over subjects. Earlier Katz (1951) had produced similar findings
for subjects drawing letters at different scales.

We have chosen, for an empirical test of the two stage execution model, an
analysis of repetition effects in a serial reaction time task. The subject
in our experiments has to perform a series of drawing tasks with optimum
speed and accuracy. Within a series there is a limited number of drawing
commands ordered in a quasi-random sequence such that each grapheme
appears in an unpredictable way in groups of 1 , 2 , 3 or 4 repetitions
of the same grapheme. The subject's task is to draw, as quickly as
possible after the appearance of the next command, the corresponding
drawing. We measured response latency (time elapsing between appearance of
the command and the first drawing movements) and movement time (time from
beginning the drawing until completing it). We assume that response
latency reflects mainly the time needed for retrieving the focal motor
pattern and preparing the very first stroke of the drawing and that
movement time stands for the ambient proces of actual movement execution.

In our model a task like this asks on each trial the retrieval of an
abstract and focal motor pattern from the subject, and the estimation of
the ambient parameters for actual muscle innervation. The focal pattern is
retrieved from a Long Term Memory, which is a dynamic system of abstract
representations of descrete motor patterns. The dynamic character of this
system becomes visible in learning and context effects: The more recent
and the more frequent the pattern is used the more easily it is retrieved.
Therefore, we predict that response latency will be smaller for repeated
than for new responses. As we stated above, the status of the ambient
movement execution stage is quite different. It is in the first place
performed by an ever-adapting, transient system. Ambient parameters for
muscle innervation are really the moment - to - moment adaptions of a
transient system, whose transient character is just the core of its
adaptability. We do not, therefore, predict at the same time any short
term repetition effect with respect to movement times.

A SERIAL DRAWING TASK WITH FOUR, FIVE AND SIX YEARS OLD CHILDREN

In this experiment we studied the effect of repeated drawing of the same
figure within a serial Choice Reaction Time task with a group of 15
children of ages 4.3 through 6.5 year. The subject's task was to draw a
series of simple, geometrical figures, like circle, square and triangle.

Within a series the level of repetition of the same drawing instruction
was varied systematically such that groups of single, double and triple
presentations of the same instruction were randomly and equally spread over
a series. The commands, which were given orally by E   were either to draw
a circle, or a square,or a triangle, in an unpredictable order of
presentation. The number of alternations and repetitions of the figures
were counterbalanced. Drawing latencies and drawing performance times were
measured by means of a videotape recording of the drawing session with a
digital millisecond counter within view of the camera. Afterwards
latencies and movement times were determined through a slow motion play
back of the tapes. Latency was defined as time elapsing between giving the
command and starting the drawing movement. Movement time was the time
between beginning and stopping the drawing movement.

For reasons of interest in the developmental aspects of the long term motor
memory and the growth of ambient adaption we divided our group of subjects
in two subgroups, relatively to their motor development. As a criterion
for this latter subject variable we observed post hoc the degree of usage
of distal and proximal muscle groups in the drawing task. In such a manner
we could arrange two groups of six subjects, one performing mainly
proximally, and one performing distally. For different reasons three out of
the initial group of 15 subjects had to be discarded. Our predictions were
that there would be savings of drawing latency with repeated drawing,
without any such saving for the movement times. We furthermore hypothesized
that this saving of movement latency would be more pronounced in distally
performing, and therefore motorically more mature, children.

Analyses of variance of the data for distinct figures revealed no
significant interactions between the variables figures and repetitions.
Therefore data for the different figures we,re combined and analysed over
subjects and repetitions. A pictorial representation of the latency-data
is given in figure 1, and of the movement times in figure 2.

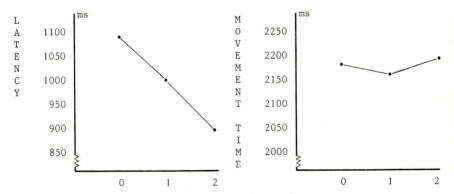

Figure 1. Mean drawing latencies
          for 12 subjects (proximal
          and distal groups combined)
          with 0, 1 or 2 repetitions
          of the same drawing.

Figure 2. Mean movement times for 12
          subjects (proximal and
          distal groups combined)
          with 0, 1 or 2 repetitions
          of the same drawing.

As can been seen the picture is quite in agreement with the predictions.
Latencies profit from repetitions, whereas movement times do not. Analyses
of variance of the latency data showed a significant $(F = 4.975; p < .05)$
effect of repetition. The same variable was not significant with the
movement times $(F = .612; n < .557)$. Further analyses revealed that the
significant latency effect of repetition was mainly to be contributed to
the distally performing group $(F = 5.442; p < .013)$ and less to the
proximal group $(F = 2.084; p < .15)$.

It is to be concluded, in our view, that the analyses of reaction and
movement times in this serial drawing task are in agreement with our two
stage execution model. To collect more evidence and to replicate the
repetition effect on latencies we ran a second, analogous, experiment with
adults.

A SERIAL DRAWING TASK WITH TWO NEW GRAPHEMES WITH ADULT SUBJECTS

A basic problem in studying complex motor behavior with known graphemes is
the uncontrolled level of usage in individual subjects. Therefore we
designed an experiment in which we studied the effect of recency on
latencies and movement times in a serial drawing task with two new
graphemes. These graphemes (See figure 3 and 4) were constructed by the
experimentor, using a number of rules on motoric complexity, to be
published elsewhere (Teulings, Van Galen & Thomassen in prep).

Figure 3.   Grapheme 1   Figure 4.   Grapheme 2

Ten subjects (5 male, and 5 female students from different faculties, ages
ranging 20 and 32) trained, for five days, about one hour a day, to draw
the graphemes as quickly and as accurate as possible. During the first
three sessions drawing instructions were given by presenting in an
alternating random order of single, double, triple or quadruple
tachistoscopic exposures of each of both graphemes. Each tachistoscopic
exposure (duration 160 milliseconds) gave a picture of the figure to be
drawn and the number code of the figure ('1' or '2'). During the fourth
and fifth session only the number codes were given as drawing commands.
Tachistoscopic presentation was used to press the subject to draw the
figures from memory and the number codes were introduced to stress the
internally monitored character of the task.
The subject was instructed to draw as quickly and as accurately as possible,
on appearance of the command stimulus, the corresponding figure. In the
instructions the subject was stressed to preserve the structure of the

figure and to pursue during the whole experiment as constant a level of
accuracy as possible.
Each subject drew nine series of 52 trials each. Within a series the number
of alternations and repetitions of figures was varied systematically. There
were equal numbers of single, double and triple presentations of the same
grapheme. Within a series four sets of quadruple presentation were added
as catch **trials to prevent the subject from being sure of a next**
alternation after three presentations of the same command.
At the beginning and halfway through each session the subject got two
series of eight presentations each of either figure to help the subject to
remember the correct outline of each figure.
Each of the experimental trials started with an acoustic warning signal
followed 1.75 seconds later by the command signal. Upon the appearance of
the drawing command started a three second data sampling period, during
which we measured movement latency (RT), movement time (MT), and movement
distance (D).
Technically this procedure was possible by application of an X-Y drawing
and writing tablet (Vector General Data Tablet, VG 101065), connected with
a 32 K laboratory computer (PDP 11-45). The drawing commands were exposed
by a Vector General display (VG 101056). Apparatus development and
applications are described in Van Galen, Teulings & Thomassen (1979).

For this paper our primary interest was in the predicted pattern of
repetition effects on RT and MT. Figure 5 describes the RT of grapheme 1
(solid line) and grapheme 2 (dotted line) for all ten subjects after 0, 1,
or 2 repetitions of the same drawing. With both graphemes there is a
general reduction of movement latency with increasing level of repetition.

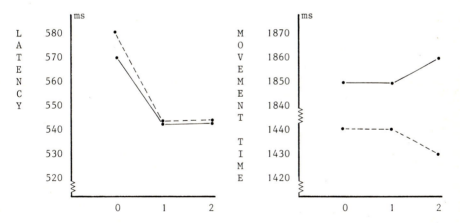

Figure 5. Means of the medians of   Figure 6. Means of the medians of
          RT's of 10 subjects on   MT's of 10 subjects on
          the first, second and   the first, second and
          third presentations of   third presentations of
          the same drawing command.   the same drawing command.

Analysis of variance of the RT and MT data revealed a very significant effect (of repetitions on the RT (F = 16.52, p = 0.0002) but no effect on the MT data. The RT decreased by 50 and 30 milliseconds respectively on the first repetition. There was no more saving on the second repetition, possibly because of a ceiling effect. This result confirms our earlier findings that short term, within-series repetition effects work on movement latency but not on movement execution time. To be sure that repetition effects were really motoric, and not stimulus repetition effects, we ran a control series of trials on each subject, containing the same random sequence of first, second or third order repetitions of the drawing command. This time the subject's task was a very simple discrimination task. Half the subject moved the pen a small distance to the right on appearance of the first code and an equal distance to the left on appearance of the second code. The other half of the group did it the other way around. We again analysed the repetition effect for stimulus one and two but now there was not any significant effect.

The outcome of the experiment is consistent with the view that motor programs are discrete elements in a hierarchic and dynamic motor memory. Assuming the abstract nature of these motor programs (c.f. Klapp, 1977) we postulated a transient ambient system, which fits in, from moment to moment, the actual values for the spatial and temporal parameters. While the motor program selection corresponds with the movement latency is the stage of ambient parameter estimation reflected in the movement execution time. It is clear that this variable is not influenced by short term repetition effects, which is in agreement with its transient character.

DISCUSSION

Evaluating both serial drawing experiments we have strong evidence for the independent behavior of latency and movement time data. We think that these outcomes give support to theories of movement which make separate provisions for active storage and retrieval of abstract motor programs and for mechanisms for actual parameter estimation with respect to the ever changing, ambient behavioral field. Concerning the nature of both stages we know quite a lot more about the ambient than about the focal stage. All the ideas and empirical materials that have evolved in the last years, within the context of the schema theory of Schmidt and other related theories, have to do with finding the correct motor instructions in varying ambient conditions. How we store and retrieve the correct focal plan is yet to be studied. We feel that this study can profit a great deal from the study of cognitive psychology in related areas like language and pattern perception. In both these fields the idea of a dynamic and hierarchic memory, containing abstract stimulus representations, has been proposed (See e.g. Leeuwenberg, 1971).

AKNOWLEDGMENTS

I wish to thank my students, Edward van Aarle and Harry Knippenberg, for the important and extensive work they did in running the first experiment. Further I am most grateful to Hans-Leo Teulings who did really pioneer work in designing all the computer software for sampling and analysing the subjects' drawing data, and ran a great part of the second experiment. Finally I appreciate Patrick Hudson's help in correcting the text.

REFERENCES:

[1] Denier van der Gon, J.J. and Thuring, J.Th., The guiding of human writing movements, Kybernetik 2 (1965) 145-148.

[2] Donders, F.C., Over de snelheid van psychische processen [On the speed of mental processes], Utrecht, 1868, (Translated by W.G. Koster), in: Koster, W.G. (ed.), Attention and Performance II (North-Holland, Amsterdam, 1969).

[3] Held, R., Dissociation of visual functions by deprivation and rearrangement, Psychologische Forschung. 31 (1968) 338-348.

[4] Humphrey, N.K., Functional role of the mid-brain visual areas in primates, European Training Program in Brain and Behaviour Research, Zuoz (Sw.), 1974.

[5] Ingle, D., Two visual mechanisms underlying the behaviour of fish, Psychologische Forschung. 31 (1968) 44-51.

[6] De Jaager, J.J., Reaction Time and Mental Processes (1865) (De Graaf, Nieuwkoop, 1972).

[7] Katz, D., Gestalt Psychology (Methuen, London, 1951).

[8] Klapp, S.T., Reaction time analysis of programmed control, Exercise and Sport Sciences Review 5 (1977) 231-251.

[9] Leeuwenberg, E., A perceptual coding language for visual and auditory patterns, American Journal of Psychology. 84 (1971) 307-349.

[10] MacNeilage, P.F., The motor control of serial ordering of speech, Psychological Review. 77 (1970) 182-196.

[11] Morton, J., Interaction of information in word recognition, Psychological Review. 76 (1969) 165-178.

[12] Pick, H.L.JR. and Saltzman, E., Modes of perceiving and processing information (LEA, New York, 1978).

[13] Restle, F. and Burnside, B.L., Tracking of serial patterns. Journal of Experimental Psychology. 95 (1972) 299-307.

[14] Sanders, A.F., Structural and functional aspects of the reaction process, in: Dornic, S. (ed.), Attention and Performance VI (LEA, Hillsdale N.J., 1977).

[15] Schneider, G.E., Contrasting visuomotor functions of tectum and cortex in the golden hamster, Psychologische Forschung. 31 (1968) 52-62.

[16] Semmes, J., Hemispheric specialization: a possible clue to mechanism, Neuropsychologia. 6 (1968) 11-26.

[17] Søvik, N., Developmental Cybernetics of Handwriting and Graphic Behavior (Universitetsforlaget, Oslo, 1975).

[18] Sperry, R.W., Gazzaniga, M.S. and Bogen, J.E., Interhemispheric relationships: The neocortical commissures; syndromes of hemisphere dysconnection, in: Vinken, J.J. and Bruyn, G.W. (eds.), Handbook of Clinical Neurology, Vol. 4 (North-Holland, Amsterdam, 1969).

[19] Stelmach, G.E. (ed.), Motor Control: Issues and trends (Academic Press, New York, 1976).

[20] Sternberg, S., The discovery of processing stages: Extension of Donders' method, in: Koster, W.G. (ed.), Attention and Performance II (North-Holland, Amsterdam, 1969).

[21] Sternberg, S., Monsell, S., Knoll, R.L. and Wright, C.E., The latency and duration of rapid movement sequences: Comparisons of speech and typewriting, in: Stelmach, G.E. (ed.), Information Processing in Motor Control and Learning (Academic Press, New York, 1979).

[22] Trevarthen, C., Two mechanisms of vision in primates, Psychologische Forschung. 31 (1968) 299-337.

[23] Van Galen, G.P., Ambient versus focal information processing and single-channelness, Ph.D. Thesis, University of Nijmegen (April 1974).

[24] Van Galen, G.P. and Ten Hoopen, G., Speech control and single-channelness, Acta Psychologica. 40 (1976) 245-255.

[25] Van Galen, G.P., Teulings, J.L.H.M. and Thomassen, A.J.W.M., Micro analysis of drawing and writing behavior with some applications in the field of clinical neurology, Proceedings of the 20th Dutch Federation of Medical Research Associations, Groningen, 1979.

[26] Vredenbregt, J. and Koster, W.G., Analysis and synthesis of handwriting, Philips Technical Review. 32 (1971) 73-78.

[27] Wing, A.M., Response timing in handwriting, in: Stelmach, G.E. (ed.), Information Processing in Motor Control and Learning (Academic Press, New York, 1979).

Tutorials in Motor Behavior
G.E. Stelmach and J. Requin (eds.)
© *North-Holland Publishing Company, 1980*

36

WHAT CAN PROBE RT TELL US ABOUT THE
ATTENTIONAL DEMANDS OF MOVEMENT?

Peter McLeod
MRC Applied Psychology Unit
15 Chaucer Road
Cambridge, CB2 2EF
ENGLAND

Previous attempts to assess the attentional demands of movement have involved the interpretation of probe reaction times
plotted as a function of the time of probe stimulus arrival.

(i)   It will be argued that this method cannot answer most
      of the questions which its users ask.

(ii) It will be shown that some of these questions can be
      answered if the probe reaction time by stimulus arri-
      val function is combined with information gained by
      plotting probe reaction time as a function of the time
      of probe response production.

(iii) It will also be demonstrated that changing the res-
      ponse modality for the probe from manual to vocal
      completely changes the pattern of probe/movement
      interference. Thus it seems that previous studies
      using manual probes have not discovered absolute pro-
      perties of movement, but properties relative to
      competing manual tasks.

(iv) A technique for unconfounding the effects of
      expectancy from those of capacity limitations in deter-
      mining probe reaction time will be demonstrated.

Over the past 10 years there have been a number of attempts to measure
the attentional demand of movement using the probe technique. |E.g. Posner
and Keele, 1969; Ells, 1973; Kerr, 1975; Klein, 1978; Glencross and Gould,
1979| The measure universally used to infer the attentional demand of the
movement has been probe RT plotted as a function of the time of arrival of
the probe stimulus. Underlying this method lies the assumption that the
system producing the movement and the probe response can be represented in a
manner similar to that shown in Figure 1.

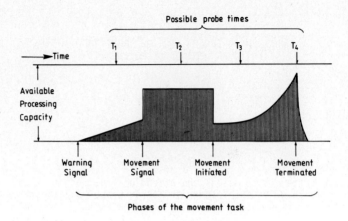

Figure 1

Figure 1 represents a possible distribution of processing capacity (or processing resource or attention according to taste) in a system common to both the probe and movement tasks during the time when a movement is being produced. Different phases of the movement such as preparing for the movement signal, selecting the response, initialising, executing or terminating the movement are presumed to make different demands on the system. The relative demand of different phases is represented by different heights of the shaded area. The reaction time to the probe stimulus is assumed to reflect the amount of processing capacity remaining after that allocated to the movement task has been taken - the less taken by a particular phase of the movement task the faster the probes occurring during that phase are presumed to be executed.

First I shall give two reasons why I think it is impossible to deduce the shape of the profile of attentional demand by plotting the probe RTs as a function of the time of arrival of the probe stimuli. Then I shall describe an experiment which introduces a new way of analysing the probe RTs which may eventually lead to a better understanding of the attentional demands of movement.

The first problem with interpreting the conventional measure of probe RT by stimulus arrival is that the response to the probe stimulus does not occur until several hundred milliseconds after the stimulus. Thus the reaction time to the stimulus is a measure of the time integral of available capacity over a period of several hundred milliseconds and not of the available capacity at any single point such as the time when the stimulus arrives.

This point is fairly obvious but I think that the force of the difficulties it creates have not always been fully appreciated. To demonstrate the problem I will analyse one paper from the attention and movement field where conclusions appear to be based on the assumption that probe RT indicates available capacity at the moment of stimulus arrival. I will show that its data are equally consistent with diametrically opposite conclusions when it is realised that probe RT is a measure of the time integral of interference between stimulus presentation and response. The paper I have chosen is Ells, 1973. This should not be taken as criticism specifically of this one work. Ells' paper is simply being used as a vehicle for demonstrating the difficulty of interpreting the traditional measure used in probe studies. The same analysis could have been made of other papers using this measure.

Ells manipulated two variables in his movement task - directional uncertainty and target width. On every trial he presented a probe (an auditory tone requiring a 1-choice response with the left hand) in one of nine positions. These are demonstrated in Figure 2.

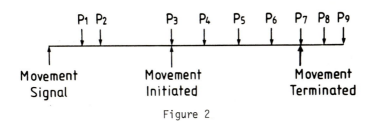

Figure 2

Three conclusions from Ells, 1973.

(i)   Ells observed a monotonic decline in probe RT going from probe 3 to probe 7. From this he concluded, assuming that probe RT measures available capacity at probe arrival time, that 'movement execution requires relatively more attention early in the movement than later in the movement'.

It is clear that probes which arrive later overlap the movement task less and thus would be responded to more quickly than those arriving earlier. Figure 3 demonstrates the effect, with the attentional demand of the movement represented by the height of the shaded area. Figure 3 shows that Ells' observation equally supports the view that attentional demand is constant throughout the movement. In fact, virtually any distribution of attentional demand through the movement would yield the monotonic decline which Ells observed.

(ii)   Ells also observed that the reaction time to probes arriving in positions 3 to 7 were always faster when they accompanied a movement to a wide target. The data are shown in Figure 4. From this Ells concluded that the attention demand of movements to wide targets must be less than that of movements to narrow targets.

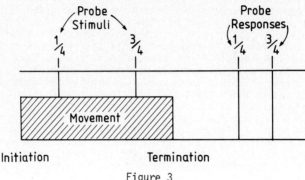

Figure 3

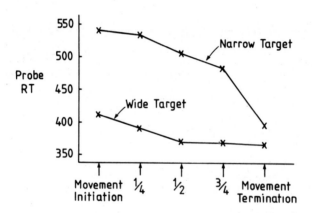

Figure 4

However, a consideration of the movement times involved shows that the
observation is equally consistent with the view that the attentional demand
of a movement is independent of the width of the target. The argument is
demonstrated in Figure 5, with movement to a narrow target shown in the upper part of the figure, and to a wide one in the lower part. This shows
what happens when a probe arrives simultaneously with the onset of the movement. The attentional demand of the movement is represented by the height
of the 'movement' box. The attentional demand has been represented as equal
in the two conditions. It is clear that the slower probes in the narrow condition are caused by the fact that the movement takes much longer in that
condition, thus ensuring more overlap between probe and movement. It is
clear that for movements of such different duration probes will be faster
when accompanying the quicker movements irrespective of their relative attentional demand. Indeed, if the attentional demand was greater for movement to a wide target the same result would probably have been obtained.

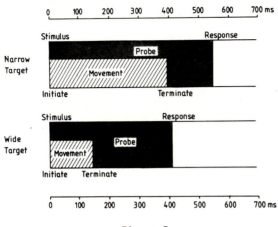

Figure 5

(iii) Ells also noted that RTs to probes occurring during response selection (positions 1 & 2) are shorter when the number of possible signals which might occur is reduced. He interpreted this as meaning that the attentional demand of response selection increased with the number of possible responses. His data are shown in the upper part of Figure 6. The reason why this conclusion cannot be drawn is demonstrated below. The relative time taken by response selection, movement and reaction to the probe are shown for a probe arriving 100 ms after a 3-choice signal or a 2-choice signal. Since the probe overlaps both selection and movement phases, and neither the absolute or the relative demand of either phase is known, it is not possible to interpret a change in probe RT as caused uniquely by a change in the demand of either selection or movement phase. It could be caused by a change in either of the phases in isolation, or both together.

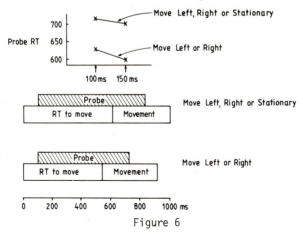

Figure 6

In summary then, I am not saying that Ells' conclusions are wrong, simply that his data cannot distinguish them from equally likely alternatives. The traditional measure of probe RT plotted as a function of stimulus arrival cannot give an unambiguous answer when it is used to interpret attentional differences between (i) different phases of a single movement or (ii) corresponding phases of different movements when the probe overlaps a different temporal extent of the two phases.

A further problem with the conventional use of the probe technique is demonstrated in Figure 7. This represents a movement, some aspect of which makes a demand on the common channel. The object of the experiment is to determine where the demand is located. A probe stimulus is presented at various times during the movement and the reaction time to it plotted at the point in the movement where the probe stimulus occurred. The kind of function that this procedure will produce is demonstrated by the solid line above the movement. Although the exact shape of this function will obviously depend on the movement and the length of the probe reaction time, the crucial point is that the bulge of increased probe RTs will always occur before the time in the movement task when the demand actually occurs.

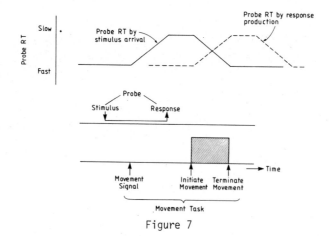

Figure 7

Thus in the hypothetical example shown in Figure 7 it would appear that it is processes occurring during the selection of the response which are 'demanding' because that is where the probe RTs are raised, while in fact the demand only starts during the execution of the movement. Although the back end of the bulge is a reasonable indication of where the demand in the movement task ends (because the probe RT returns to its resting level as soon as the stimulus end of the probe task is clear of the disturbance), the front end of the bulge in probe reaction times gives a very misleading impression of where the demand of the movement task starts. If we take the same data, the probe reaction times, and plot them as a function of when the probe response occurred (rather than when the probe stimulus arrived) the opposite effect is produced (the dashed line in Figure 7). The bulge in the probe reaction time function always occurs after the disturbance caused by the movement task. In this case the front edge of the bulge gives a reason-

ably good indication of where the disturbance starts (because the increase
in probe reaction times occurs as soon as the response end of the probe task
starts to overlap the disturbance) but the rear end of the bulge **gives**
a very misleading indication of where the demand **ends.**   However, **if we**
combine both sources of information then we can arrive at a more accurate
estimate of where the disturbance occurs than we could with either one alone.
The duration and temporal position of the disturbance is given by the time
during which <u>both</u> probe RT by stimulus arrival <u>and</u> probe RT by response
production <u>are above</u> their resting level. By com<u>bin</u>ing these two functions
we lose the misleading front end of the stimulus arrival distribution and
the misleading tail-end of the response production distribution.

Experiment 1

Both the difference between the conventional stimulus arrival function and
the response production function, and the misleading nature of the former
are demonstrated in Experiment 1, a conventional movement plus probe task.
The subjects, 4 right-handed women, average age 30, sat facing a CRT display,
holding a pen in their right hand. Following a fixation warning signal
(a cross) an arrow pointing either left or right appeared. They moved the
pen to hit a target 1 cm wide 10 cm away from the rest position. After returning to the home square (1 cm wide) there was an interval of 1430 ms
before the next warning signal appeared. The probe task consisted of a 2-
choice tone (300 or 2000 Hz) presented over headphones, to which the subject
responded on buttons with two fingers of her left hand - left for the low
tone and right for the high tone. 490 ms after each response on the 2-
choice task the next tone stimulus arrived, and so on throughout the 50
movement trials which constituted each block. Thus tone stimuli occurred
throughout the movement task rather than being time locked to specific
points as in conventional. The advantage of this technical novely is that
it keeps the probability of a stimulus constant throughout the task. Previous research on probe RT has been bedevilled by the fact that both expectancy and capacity limitations determine probe RT (see Salmoni, Sullivan and
Starkes, 1976). By keeping probe probability constant expectancy effects
are removed and it becomes possible to see the effects of capacity limitations alone. Typical temporal relationships between the two tasks are
demonstrated in Figure 8.

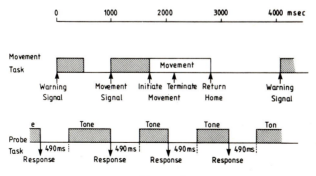

Figure 8

Design: Each subject came for one session lasting approximately 1¼ hours
during which she performed 12 blocks of trials with feedback and a pause
between each block. Each block involving movement lasted for 50 movements.
A probe only block lasted for 50 probe responses.

Block

1	Movement only	
2	Probe only	Practice
3 & 4	Movement and probe	
5	Movement only	Single Task Control Data
6	Probe only	
7-10	Movement and probe	Dual Task Data
11	Movement only	Single Task Control Data
12	Probe only	

After each block there was feed-back on probe RT, movement RT and movement
time, with encouragement to go faster. Sessions 7-10, which provided the
dual task data, yielded 200 movements and approximately 700 probe responses
per subject.

Results: Figure 9 shows that the probe RTs plotted in two ways. The solid
line shows the conventional fashion, where each probe reaction time contributes to the mean at the point where the probe stimulus arrived. The plot
obtained is broadly similar to that obtained by other workers with the technique and its interpretation would cause no problem. The demand of the
movement task starts to rise during response selection and reaches its peak
around the time when the response is initiated. It then falls steadily
during the execution of the movement.

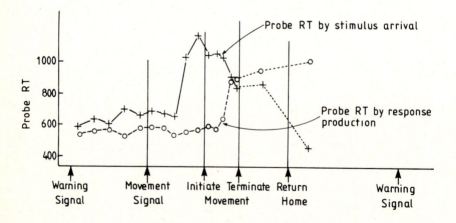

Figure 9

However, the demonstration in Figure 7 showed that this method must produce
a peak to the left of the real outset of demand in the movement. If we now
look at the plot of probe RTs by time of response production (the dashed
line in Figure 9) it becomes clear that the conclusions based on the conventional stimulus arrival plot are untenable. The data show that a response
produced on the probe task is just as fast during the selection and initiation of the movement as it is during the time prior to the movement signal.
Clearly the conclusion, based on the probe RT by stimulus arrival plot, that
response selection and initiation are the demanding phase of the movement,
is wrong.

In the discussion of Figure 7 I claimed that the front end of the demand
phase of the movement task could not be identified by the probe RT by
stimulus arrival plot, but was indicated by the point at which the probe RT
by response production plot started to rise. This would suggest that for
this particular movement the only demanding phase is the response termination. Of course, I am not concluding that response selection never demands
attention. This result is, presumably, determined by the very natural relationship between movement stimulus and corresponding action used in this
experiment. To initiate a movement to the left in response to an arrow
pointing left is a stimulus-response relationship which every subject probably brings into the laboratory with her. The point which I wish to make
is that what I believe to be the correct conclusion to draw from this experiment, that the selection and initiation of the movement investigated
do   not demand attention, would not have been drawn using the method which
has been used by all probe RT studies to date of only plotting probe RTs by
stimulus arrival.

Experiment 2

If the previous conclusion is correct, that it is only the termination and
not the selection of the movement which is demanding, then it appears that
the main source of interaction between probe and movement is in the peripheral motor components of the tasks rather than in any central stage. If
this were true then changing the response modality of the probe task from
manual to vocal should change the pattern of interference between the tasks.
Certainly the increase in probe RT for responses produced near the termination of the movement should vanish. Experiment 2 investigated this prediction by replacing the manual probe response with a vocal one - saying 'High'
to the high tone and 'Low' to the low tone. In all other respects the two
experiments were identical. The subjects were five right-handed women,
average age 29.

It might be argued that in some sense saying 'High' to a tone is more
natural or easier than pressing a button. It is difficult to prove this
point one way or the other but there are two lines of argument against it.
Firstly, in the probe alone conditions, the button response group were
faster than the voice response. Secondly, there is nothing naturally 'high'
about a tone of 2000 Hz. Had I used 2000 and 4000 Hz, then 'low' would
have the appropriate response. An arbitrary experimenter defined relationship between stimulus and response has to be learnt by both groups.

Results: Figure 10 shows the distribution of probe response times (by response production) for the vocal group (dotted line) compared to the same
data for the manual group in Experiment 1. It is clear that there is no

phase of the movement task which causes any change in the speed at which
the subjects respond to the probe stimulus. This supports the conclusion
reached in the first experiment that there was no central attentional demand of the movement studied. It reinforces the warning given after Experiment 1 that there was no way in which the conventional method of analysing
probe RTs could have reached this conclusion.

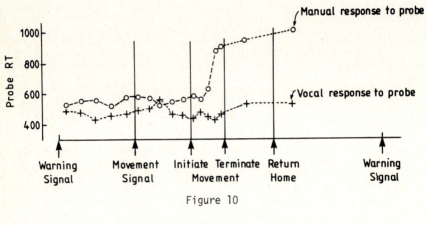

Figure 10

Conclusions

Two conclusions about the use of the probe technique to study movement can
be drawn from these experiments.

Firstly, the dramatic difference between the pattern of probe RTs for vocal
and manual responses shows that movements do not have an absolute attentional demand which can be measured by any one sort of probe.(Amplification of
this point is a slightly different paradigm can be found in McLeod, 1978.)
So the first question to be asked in studying a movement is not 'how much'
interference with a probe, but 'what sort' of interference. By following
the appearance and disappearance of interference with different sorts of
probe it can be inferred which of the CNS's independent structures are involved in the control of a particular movement. (Justification for the
rather bold dismissal of the limited-capacity approach to understanding the
control of movement which is implicit in the last paragraph can be found in
Allport, 1979.)

Secondly, it was shown that where a probe task has been found which does
interact with the movement task, this interaction cannot be understood by
analysing the probe RT as a function of stimulus arrival alone. As a first
step towards a better understanding it has been demonstrated that probe RT
plotted by response production produces an estimate of the onset of the demand phase of the movement task, a time which the stimulus arrival function
does not produce.

Finally, a method for deconfounding expectancy effects and capacity limitations in determining probe RTs has been demonstrated.

Reaction Time Data (ms)

	Alone			Dual Task		
	Movt. Time	Movt. RT	Probe RT	Movt. Time	Movt. RT	Probe RT
Button Response	390	407	350	451	723	779
Vocal Response	332	386	400	371	500	516

References

|1| Allport, D.A., Attention and Performance, in: Claxton, G. (ed.)
       New Directions in Cognitive Psychology (London, Routledge and Kegan
       Paul, 1979)

|2| Ells, J.G., Analysis of temporal and attentional aspects of movement
       control. Journal of Experimental Psychology 99 (1973) 10-21.

|3| Glencross, D.J. and Gould, J.H., The planning of precision movements.
       Journal of Motor Behaviour 11 (1979) 1-9.

|4| Kerr, B., Processing demands during movement. Journal of Motor
       Behaviour 7 (1975) 15-27.

|5| Klein, R.M., Attention and Movement, in: Stelmach, G. (ed.)
       Motor Control: Issues and Trends (New York, Academic Press, 1976)

|6| McLeod, P.D., Does probe RT measure central processing demand?
       Quarterly Journal of Experimental Psychology 80 (1978) 83-89.

|7| Posner, M.I. and Keele, S.W., Attentional demands of movement.
       In: Proceedings of the 17th Congress of Applied Psychology (1969).

|8| Salmoni, A.W., Sullivan, S.J., and Starkes, J.L., The attentional
       demands of movement: A critique of the probe technique. Journal of
       Motor Behaviour 8 (1976) 161-169.

Tutorials in Motor Behavior
G.E. Stelmach and J. Requin (eds.)
© *North-Holland Publishing Company, 1980*

37

MOTOR BEHAVIOR AND THE ROLE OF COGNITIVE PROCESSES AND LEARNER STRATEGIES[1]

ROBERT N. SINGER

Movement Science-Physical Education Department
Florida State University, Tallahassee
U. S. A.

Abstract

It is quite meaningful for instructional and self-learning purposes to determine those processes that may be under the conscious control of the learner. Correspondingly, the most effective strategies need to be identified that can enhance the operation of these processes. The use of appropriate strategies should facilitate the acquisition of skill, as well as retention and transfer. Learners, it is posited, will be better performers when they can associate pertinent strategies with certain kinds of tasks, and learn to use self-managed strategies more and externally-imposed strategies less.

INTRODUCTION

The focus in this paper is on cognitive processes and learner strategies, and their involvement in the learning and performance of motor skills. A perusal of the recent psychological literature reveals an abundance of studies in which learner strategies are examined in the acquisition of verbal materials. Conceptual and practical concerns are addressed. A plea has been made elsewhere (Singer, 1978) for a similar approach with motor skills.

For instance, from a practical perspective, most training programs emphasize what to do, in terms of content and skills to be mastered. But imposed training often fails to teach learners to think, to evaluate, to develop alternative responses, and to problem solve. Since a limited amount of content can be directed toward specifics within the time appropriated to a typical training program, the question is: What kinds of learner processes can and should be activated, what can the learner learn how to do, in order to generalize to and accommodate future demands?

This question and many others suggest that more needs to be known about the role of cognitive processes in motor performance, and how learners can maximize the involvement or detachment of cognitions during learning/performance (Singer & Gerson, in press). Better strategies should enhance the selection and processing of information, as well as decision making, in acquisition, retention, and transfer situations. The plan in this paper is to: (a) describe the nature of cognitive processes, control, and learner strategies; (b) suggest a relationship among these terms; and (c) review research findings with regard to the use of strategies in acquisition, retention, and transfer situations.

COGNITIVE PROCESSES AND MOTOR BEHAVIOR

Some form of control can be potentially exerted by the learner/performer from the time information enters the system until it is transformed and responded to in the form of movement activity. A great deal of information processing occurs, possibly under severe time constraints, when people attempt to learn/ perform complex motor activities. The desirability of exerting deliberate conscious control will depend on many factors. One of the primary differences between the highly skilled and the lesser skilled is the degree and type of conscious involvment prior to, during, and following motor performance (cf. Singer, Gerson, & Kim, 1979). Therefore, conscious planning, focus, and/or intervention at a particular stage must be determined according to task demands and the capabilities of the person.

The term cognitive processes, or cognitions, has been defined in many ways. Interpretations have varied (e.g., Battig, 1975; Hunt & Lansman, 1975; Norman & Rumelhart, 1975), as have the contexts in which the term has been applied. For purposes here, a cognitive process is defined as a control process, that is self-generated, transient, situationally determined conscious activity a learner uses to organize and to regulate received and transmitted information, and ultimately, behavior.

However, the person does not totally influence any situation, nor does the reverse probably happen. Whereas behaviorists might lead us to view human behavior as passively controlled by situational dictates, cognitive psychologists would suggest that people actively control their environments. The truth probably lies somewhere in a middle position. Behaviors are not produced without cues or stimuli, and these behaviors are directed accordingly. But all people do not respond similarly to the same events, thereby demonstrating some degree of self-determination. In a sense, then, associationistic behaviors are indeed developed, but in a person's own way.

Mechanisms can be identified that appear to be activated sequentially in stages or in parallel as information is processed leading to complex motoric behavior. A mechanism is defined here as a real or hypothesized "location" or "structure" associated with the nervous system in which specified unique control processes and functions occur. The deliberate use of certain conscious control processes, or the capability of activating certain desirable subconscious control processes, will improve the functional capabilites of one or several of the hypothesized mechanisms in the human behaving system (cf. Belmont & Butterfield, 1977; Butterfield & Dickerson, 1976), such as increasing the capacity of the short-term store by imposing an organizational structure to information being processed in that mechanism (Rigney, 1978). A definite relationship is hypothesized to exist between a particular mechanism and associated cognitive processes (see Table 1). Although a one-to-one relationship between a mechanism and a cognitive process may exist, it should be realized that several cognitive processes may also be associated with a given mechanism.

The effective operation of a particular control process for a given task reduces the amount of information that must be transmitted through the mechanism associated with it (cf. Butterfield & Dickerson, 1976). Accuracy would be truer and processing quicker than otherwise. Due to the existence of this relationship between cognitions and stages of processing (Trabasso, 1973), the learner is probably capable of developing a hierarchy of processing skills corresponding to each mechanism (Schaeffer, 1975). The hierarchy is based on the complexity of the cognition or processing operations the learner must employ to transform and to transmit information through the system. Thus, as information passes through each stage, the corresponding control processes must be adapted by the learner to meet the changing task requirements, so that information may continue to be transmitted through the system.

To integrate some ideas expressed so far, the learner/performer may invoke cognitive processes to perceive the nature of the task in the context of the environment, to recognize similiarities between the present task and previous experiences, and to selectively attend to and to identify the most relevant, yet minimal number of cues necessary for a response to occur. In addition, a person may utilize cognitive processes to enhance goal-expectancy formations, to enhance goal-image formation, or to finalize movement decisions made in the short-term store. Cognitions may be used to permanently store evaluative feedback and causal reasons for a performance outcome for future use, information that will influence future behavior in the same situation. Cognitive processes should be facilitated by the learner's activation and implementation of the appropriate strategies.

LEARNER STRATEGIES AND SKILL ACQUISITION, RETENTION, AND TRANSFER

An effective strategy has been described as the simplest and most efficient means of processing the information inherent in a situation (Newell & Simon, 1972). Rigney (1978) has stated that a strategy may be interpreted as signifying operations and procedures that a learner may use to acquire, to retain, and to retrieve different kinds of knowledge. To Gagné (1974), a strategy is a skill of self-management that the learner acquires to govern the processes of attending, learning, and thinking, while Gagné and Briggs (1974) have suggested that a cognitive strategy is an internally organized skill which governs the learner's own behavior.

A strategy is interpreted here as a self-initiated or externally imposed way of directing information leading to decisions for purposeful behavior. A learner imposes some type of structure on movement information so that it is learned and retrieved more efficiently. Performance is either dependent upon the experimental structuring of the task in which the totality of the relations among the movement cues is emphasized (Gentile & Nacson, 1976), or the subjective organization of the information, in which a structural context corresponding to

TABLE 1

THE CONCEPTUAL RELATIONSHIP OF MECHANISMS, POTENTIAL COGNITIVE PROCESSES, AND FUNCTIONS IN COMPLEX MOTOR BEHAVIORS

Mechanisms	Cognitive Processes	Functions and Purposes
1. sensory storage*	receive	briefly hold information
	transmit	forward it to LTS for memory contact or directly to perceptual mechanism

*Cognitive processes do not directly influence sensory storage but can affect orientation to stimulli.

2. perceptual mechanism	detect	realize existence of signal
	alert	anticipate
	selectively attend	filter
	recognize	analyze features
		..... match (present cues with stored information)
		..... make meaning of information
	transmit	forward information to STS for action
3. short term storage (STS)	rehearse and process information temporarily	...... retain information for immediate use and decision making
	compare	retrieve information from LTS for analysis, decision making, and attributions following feedback
	transform	organize (chunk)
		..... make more functional space available
		..... provide additional meaning
	appraise situation	form performance and goal expectancies
		..... establish emotional state
	select programs from LTS	transmit programs to movement generator
	plan program execution	determine parameters (location, speed, direction, timing, amplitude, force, effort) in which program is to operate
	transmit information	transfer information to long term storage to establish learning

4. long term storage   store information
   (LTS)   permanently........................make information avail-
                                                                  able for future use,
                                                                  establish pertinence,
                                                                  aid in anticipation,
                                                                  expectancies, and
                                                                  perception

5. movement generator   initiate program for
                              motor behavior....................cue appropriate
                                                                  musculature to execute
                                                                  within response
                                                                  parameters
                              initiate corollary
                              discharge............................ alert sensory center of
                                                                  the brain, anticipate
                                                                  movement

6. effectors   receive command............... execute observable
                                                                  performance
                              activate feedback
                              sources .... provide information
                                                                  for future usage
                                                                  (comparison, recognition)
                                                                  by making it available
                                                                  for long term storage
                                                            ..... provide information to
                                                                  peripheral organs to help
                                                                  regulate ongoing
                                                                  behavior, to adapt
                                                                  behavior to situational
                                                                  demands
                                                            ..... provide information to
                                                                  influence arousal and
                                                                  attitudinal states

the learner's cognitive capabilities is imposed on the movement cues. Thus, the development of organizational strategies occurs in one of two ways.

An instructional strategy which is imposed by the instructor on the learner may be designed to help the learner to acquire a skill as quickly as possible, or to facilitate transfer effectiveness or problem solving in the future. While some imposed strategies may increase the rate of initial skill acquisition (Singer & Pease, 1976, 1978), they may not facilitate learning in transfer situations in which no instructor is present (Singer & Gaines, 1975). In the latter case, this can only be achieved when a learner becomes capable of self-generating strategies, whether they have been initially externally-directed or self-generated.

A self-initiated strategy is one in which the learner is capable of determining a procedure which is compatible with personal cognitive capabilities and cognitive style for the learning of a task or a category of related tasks. Strategy choice is partially determined by the particular situation (Bruner, Goodnow, & Austin, 1956), so a sound procedure would appear to be to initially instruct learners in the use of learning strategies if they are ignorant about them. Once a learner comprehends the nature of and the reasons for the use of particular strategies for the acquisition of skill, he or she should be capable of self-generating strategies in related future learning environments.

The learning experience is governed by the use of strategies, which in turn activate conscious and, perhaps subsequently, subconscious processes. The hypothesized relationships would be that situations activate particular strategies that influenced cognitive processes associated with particular mechanisms:

    1.   A situation activates potential alternative strategies.

    2.   A particular appropriate strategy influences a corresponding cognitive process.

    3.   A particular cognitive process is associated with a corresponding mechanism or stage in performance.

    4.   Situation ⟶ Strategy ⟶ Process ⟶ Mechanism

The learning of a motor skill, or a verbal skill, reflects a problem which must be solved. The behaviors involved in acquiring both types of skills are very similar (Adams, 1971) in that the learner must identify and interpret the problem, utilize strategies to facilitate the processing of information so a plan may be devised which will lead to possible solutions, produce those solutions, and then decide which is the best solution (Posner, 1973).

Some generalizations may be made about strategies. For instance, strategies characteristically: (1) involve systematic analysis and processing; (2) require repeated attempts at a solution; and (3) involve the development of rules, to be applied to the same or similar situations.

Experts use effective strategies; novices use inefficient strategies. However, even experts may not use the same strategies to the same degree. Likewise, it is possible that different strategies are used by experts and novices. Or, they use the same ones, only the experts apply them more effectively. In this light, it is well-documented that individuals have preferential modes of interpreting and responding, and this premise has led to a body of literature entitled ATI (Aptitude and Treatment Interaction). One type of aptitude is cognitive style or approach to learning, and a particular style may suggest the desirability of the use of one strategy over alternatives.

So far, the nature of cognitive processes and learner strategies has been discussed somewhat descriptively. With regard to experimental findings, pertinent learner strategies have been shown to facilitate the acquisition and retention of verbal skills (e.g., Campione & Brown, 1974) and motor skills (Hagenbeck, 1978; Ho & Shea, 1978; Shea, 1977). The acquisition, storage, and retrieval of verbal information has been facilitated by appropriate learner strategies in many investigations.

For example, mnemonic techniques, encoding instructions, or instructions in the use of particular strategies (Belmont & Butterfield, 1971; Craik & Lockhart, 1972; Weinstein, 1978) have had positive effects on performance. Most researchers in this area indicate the importance of involving the learner in the development of organizational strategies. Such strategies are helpful to the learner in storing information and retrieving it when desirable. The more frequently investigated techniques, and those that have appeared to demonstrate consistent and significant improvement in the learning process, include rehearsal, chunking, imagery, mnemonics, and elaboration.

Many cognitive strategies have been analyzed by researchers and used successfully by subjects in verbal learning situations. Strategies in the learning of verbal material have been typically characterized as: (1) possessing a heavy cognitive component; (2) serving the ultimate purpose of reducing learner dependence on external cues and maximizing self-directedness in using strategies; (3) a means of controlling the processing of information; (4) an operation that alters data that enters the system, thereby enhancing the meaningfulness of stimuli; and (5) learning techniques that may be generalized in different learning situations and with various types of subject matter. The subsequent effect of strategy usage is to improve the processes involved in learning to learn, retention, and the retrieval of information. Perhaps most important is that these processes appear to be of equal importance for psychomotor behaviors.

In conjunction with motor skill acquisition, imposed strategies have required subjects to: (1) "think about" or "imagine" motor responses or movement patterns; (2) attach verbal labels to each of a series of movements; (3) selectively attend to relevant components of a task; (4) verbally rhythmize a sequence within a movement pattern; (5) organize information so that new learnings can be tied to old learnings, thereby enhancing meaningfulness to novel stimuli; (6) demonstrate comprehension of a skill through the verbal communication of newly acquired knowledge and skills; and (7) use rules which, when acknowledged, allow greater recall of information and/or skills.

While the short-term effects of strategy usage has been reasonably well documented (at least in the verbal area), knowledge of long-range effects is minimal. In fact, there is little supportive evidence that strategies used in one situation are applicable and facilitatory in a future situation (Brown, 1978). However, strategies that enhance skill acquisition and short-term retention also have the potential to transfer to the learning of a skill in a new situation with similar parameters.

Strategy transfer usually cannot occur unless the learning environment includes some reference to the transfer situation (Bransford, Franks, Morris, & Stein, 1978; Campione & Brown, 1974; Morris, Bransford, & Franks, 1977); e.g., the temporal structuring of the components within each task are similar (Keele & Summers, 1976). Another factor that has an influence on strategy generalizability is the compatibility of a particular strategy with a learner's cognitive processing capabilities. If a strategy is effective but incompatible, the learner would tend to reject it in lieu of some other, less efficient strategy. This less efficient strategy may facilitate initial acquisition, but it would probably have a detrimental effect in a transfer situation. The decrement in transfer learning would be the result of the limited applicability of the self-imposed strategy.

To train a person to be aware of the potential to activate strategies for skill acquisition is not sufficient. Externally imposed strategies may produce the same positive effect on immediate learning as will internally generated strategies. The training of this potential must also be geared to the utility of those abilities in future retention and transfer situations (Duncan, 1953). In this way, a person can enter new learning environments, acquire the necessary skills prescribed in that environment, and do so with a minimal amount of external guidance.

For effective transfer to occur, both the instructor and the learner must understand the original training task and the transfer task (Belmont & Butterfield, 1977; Morris et al., 1977). The components of both tasks must be similar enough so the learner is able to determine the relationship between the two tasks. Performance decrements on the transfer task are often due to the trainee's inability to comprehend these relationships, but inferior performance may be due to the differences between the demands of the two tasks which neither the instructor nor the learner realized (Brown, 1978). When transfer is not demonstrated because of differential task requirements, it is not due to a deficiency in the learner's cognitive capabilities. The lack of transfer is a result of the change in the processing activities required by the two tasks (Morris et al., 1977).

A POSSIBLE RESEARCH ORIENTATION AND METHODOLOGY

The analysis of the effectiveness of various learner strategies in influencing processes associated with the acquisition, retention, and/or transfer of motor skills can be handled in many experimental paradigms. A number of topics need to be addressed. The following list is suggestive but not conclusive:

   1.   effectiveness of instructor-imposed versus self-generated
strategies;

   2.   effectiveness of different types of strategies for different types of
tasks;

   3.   influence of strategies on acquisition versus retention versus
transfer;

   4.   individual differences (e.g., cognitive styles) and relationship
to strategy effect on learning;

   5.   high versus low-skilled performers and differences in the usage
of strategies;

   6.   the training of low-skilled performers with strategies typically
adopted by the highly-skilled;

   7.   the development of strategy learning modules (self learning) for
different categories of tasks;

   8.   effects of informed choice of multiple strategies on learning.

During the past year, we have been interested in the relative effectiveness of
different strategies with three types of tasks. They are computer-managed and
are referred to as the Serial Positioning Apparatus (SPA), the Serial Manipulation Apparatus (SMA), a procedural task, and the Visual Tracking Apparatus
(VTA). Each makes different demands on subjects and may be considered as
representative of three categories of tasks.

Five groups have been used in each experiment: three different strategy
groups, an informed choice group, and a control group. Strategies are decided
on dependent upon their apparent association with successful performance in
the task.

In one of the first studies (Singer, Gerson, & Ridsdale, 1979), a curvilinear
repositioning apparatus--not computer-managed--was used. Subjects were
required to replicate 6 limb movements to predetermined criterion locations.
Imagery, kinesthetic emphasis, and labeling were the three strategies selected.
Analysis for AE, CE, VE, and percent of correct responses revealed "imagers"
to be more accurate and less variable in their responses than the subjects in
the four other groups. However, the control subjects performed better than
the other three groups, possibly suggesting the importance of implementing
strategies that are compatible with individual cognitive styles, or the irrele-
vance of labeling and kinesthetic emphasis to achievement in this task.

In another study with the same task (Hagenbeck, Singer, & Gerson, 1979),
imagery again was found to be the most effective strategy technique. The
serial position curve was obtained, with a strong primacy effect and a slight
recency effect for the imagery, relevant labeling, and kinesthetic groups.

Nevertheless, the first two strategies elevated the response scores in the middle positions of the curve significantly more than was the case with the other groups. The indication is that not only will different strategy conditions possibly lead to different levels of skill acquisition, retention, and transfer, but also differential effects on the serial position curve.

The computer-managed tasks have not provided us with clear-cut trends as yet. We have learned that much more time needs to be spent on general instructions orienting the learner to the task as well as to the particular strategy condition. These tasks are quite complex. Information overload or underload must be considered, and we are refining our procedures. With the SMA (described in its earlier form elsewhere by Singer, 1976), imagers performed better than chunking, verbalization, and informed-choice groups on both acquisition and transfer tasks (Singer, Ridsdale, & Korienek, 1979a). No strategy (imagery, rhythmic, or anticipatory) was more effective than the other with the VTA. However, the rhythmic strategy group was superior to the control group in performance (Singer, Ridsdale, & Korienek, 1979b).

With the SPA (Singer, Ridsdale, & Korienek, 1979c), and 10 positions, the typical primacy-recency effect generally exhibited during serial recall was not demonstrated. If anything, performance seemed to become increasingly worse with each position across trials. No performance differences were noted among the groups, the strategies being rhythmic, imagery, and chunking. In spite of such disappointing data, we are quite optimistic that we can redesign our tasks and instructions and produce more interesting data.

Each experiment is not designed to improve the performance in a specific motor skill. Rather, the search is for methods that will enable learners to self-generate problem-solving strategies and techniques in order that success may be realized more readily in categories of skills. The development of analytical and adaptation processes within a learner should lead to the creation of self-instructional environments. If the person possesses the strategies and skills to produce a solution to a problem, then the amount of external guidance necessary for learning is reduced. Additionally, the acquired skill is probably retained to a greater degree since the learner is more involved in the learning experience.

FOOTNOTE

[1] Preparation of this work has been supported through contract #MDA903-77-C-0200 with the Defense Advanced Research Projects Agency. Special appreciation is extended to Dr. Richard F. Gerson, for his assistance with this project. In addition, many individuals helped to generate ideas, and I am indebted to Dr. Ronald G. Marteniuk, Dr. Richard A. Schmidt, Dr. Geroge E. Stelmach, Ms. Susan Ridsdale, and Mr. Gene Korienek.

REFERENCES

(1)   Adams, J.A., A closed-loop theory of motor learning, Journal of Motor
        Behavior 3 (1971) 111-150.

(2)   Battig, W.F., Within-individual differences in "cognitive" processes, in:
        R.L. Solso (ed.), Information Processing and Cognition: The Loyola
        Symposium (Erlbaum, Hillsdale, N.J., 1975).

(3)   Belmont, J.M., & Butterfield, E.C., Learning strategies as determinants
        of memory deficiencies, Cognitive Psychology 2 (1971) 411-420.

(4)   Belmont, J.M., & Butterfield, E.C., The instructional approach to
        developmental cognitive research, in: R. Kail & J. Hagen (eds.),
        Perspectives On The Development of Memory and Cognition (Erlbaum,
        Hillsdale, N.J., 1977).

(5)   Bransford, J.D., Franks, J.J., Morris, C.D., & Stein, B.S., Some
        general constraints on learning and memory research, in: F.I.M.
        Craik & L.S. Cermak (eds.), Levels of Processing and Theories of
        Memory (Erlbaum, Hillsdale, N.J., 1978).

(6)   Brown, A.L., Knowing when, where, and how to remember: A
        problem of metacognition, in: R. Glaser (ed.), Advances in Instruc-
        tional Psychology (Erlbaum, Hillsdale, N.J., 1978).

(7)   Butterfield, E.C., & Dickerson, D.J., Cognitive theory and mental
        development, in: N.R. Ellis (ed.), International Review of Research
        in Mental Retardation (Academic Press, N.Y., 1976).

(8)   Campione, J.C., & Brown, A.L., The effects of contextual changes
        and degree of component mastery on transfer training, in: H.W.
        Reese (ed.), Advances in Child Development and Behavior (Acadmic
        Press, N.Y., 1974).

(9)   Craik, F.I.M., & Lockhart, R.S., Levels of processing: A frame-
        work for memory research, Journal of Verbal Learning and Verbal
        Behavior 11 (1972 671-684.

(10)   Duncan, C.P., Transfer in motor learning as a function of degree of
        first-task learning and intertask similarity, Journal of Experimental
        Psychology 45 (1953) 1-11.

(11)   Gagné, R.M., Educational technology and the learning process,
        Educational Researcher 3 (1974) 3-8.

(12)   Gagné, R.M., & Briggs, L., Principles of Instructional Design (Holt,
        Rinehart & Winston, N.Y., 1974).

(13) Gentile, A.M., & Nacson, J., Organizational processes in motor con-
      trol, in: J. Keogh & R.S. Hutton (eds.), Exercise and Sport Sciences
      Reviews Volume 4 (Journal Publishing Affiliates, Santa Barbara, Ca.,
      1976).

(14) Hagenbeck, F., The effect of strategies upon the performance of a
      serial motor task, Masters Thesis, Florida State University (1978).

(15) Hagenbeck, F., Singer, R.N., & Gerson, R.F., Strategy enhance-
      ment of serial motor skill acquisition, Manuscript submitted for pub-
      lication (1979).

(16) Ho, L., & Shea, J.B., Levels of processing and the coding of position
      cues in motor short-term memory, Journal of Motor Behavior 10 (1978)
      113-121.

(17) Hunt, E., & Lansman, M., Individual differences, in: W.K. Estes (ed.),
      Handbook of Learning and Cognitive Processes (Erlbaum, Hillsdale, N.J.,
      1975).

(18) Keele, S.W., & Summers, J.J., The structure of motor programs, in:
      G.E. Stelmach (ed.), Motor Control: Issues and Trends (Academic
      Press, N.Y., 1976).

(19) Morris, C.D., Bransford, J.D., & Franks, J.J., Levels of processing
      versus transfer appropriate processing, Journal of Verbal Learning and
      Verbal Behavior 16 (1977) 519-533.

(20) Newell, A., & Simon, H.A., Human Problem Solving (Prentice-Hall,
      Englewood Cliffs, N.J., 1972).

(21) Norman, D.A., & Rumelhart, D.E., Explorations in Cognition (W.H. Free-
      man & Co., San Francisco, 1975).

(22) Posner, M.I., Cognition: An Introduction (Scott, Foresman & Co., Glen-
      view, Ill., 1973).

(23) Rigney, J. W., Learning strategies: A theoretical perspective, in: H.F.
      O'Neil, Jr. (ed.), Learning Strategies I (Academic Press, N.Y., 1978).

(24) Schaeffer, B., Skill integration during cognitive development, in: A.
      Kennedy & A. Wilkes (eds.), Studies in Long-Term Memory (John Wiley
      & Sons, N.Y., 1975).

(25) Shea, J.B., Effects of labeling on motor short-term memory, Journal of
      Experimental Psychology: Human Learning and Memory 3 (1977) 92-99.

(26) Singer, R.N., The serial manipulation apparatus, Journal of Motor
      Behavior 8 (1976) 69-73.

(27) Singer, R.N., Motor skills and learning strategies, in: H.F. O'Neil, Jr. (ed.), Learning Strategies I (Academic Press, N.Y., 1978).

(28) Singer, R.N., & Gaines, L., Effect of prompted and trial-and-error learning on transfer performance of a serial motor task, American Educational Research Journal 12 (1975) 295-403.

(29) Singer, R.N., Gerson, R.F., & Kim, K., Information processing capabilities in performers differing in levels of motor skill, (Tech. Rep. TR-79-A4), (Florida State University, Motor Behavior Resource Center, Tallahassee, Fla., January, 1979).

(30) Singer. R.N., Gerson, R.F., & Ridsdale, S., The effect of various strategies on the acquisition, retention, and transfer of a serial positioning task, (Tech. Rep. #4), (Florida State University, Motor Behavior Resource Center, Tallahassee, Fla., April, 1979).

(31) Singer, R.N., & Pease. D., The effect of different instructional strategies on learning, retention and transfer of a serial motor task, Research Quarterly 47 (1976) 788-796.

(32) Singer, R.N., & Pease, D., Effect of guided vs. discovery learning strategies on initial motor task learning, transfer, and retention, Research Quarterly 49 (1978) 206-217.

(33) Singer, R.N., Ridsdale, S., & Korienek, G.G., The influence of learning strategies in the acquisition, retention, and transfer of a visual tracking task, (Tech. Rep. #5), (Florida State University, Motor Behavior Resource Center, Tallahassee, Fla., June, 1979 (a)).

(34) Singer, R.N., Ridsdale, S., & Korienek, G.G., The influence of learning strategies, in the acquisition, retention, and transfer of a procedural task, (Tech. Rep. #6), (Florida State University, Motor Behavior Resource Center, Tallahassee, Fla., June, 1979 (b)).

(35) Singer, R.N., Ridsdale, S., & Korienek, G.G., Achievement in a serial positioning task and the role of learner strategies, (Tech. Rep. #7), (Florida State University, Motor Behavior Resource Center, Tallahassee, Fla., July, 1979 (c)).

(36) Trabasso, T., Discussion of the papers by Bransford and Johnson; and Clark, Carpenter and Just: Language and cognition, in: W.G. Chase (ed.), Visual Information Processing (Academic Press, N.Y., 1973).

(37) Weinstein, C., Elaboration skills as a learning strategy, in: H.F. O'Neil, Jr. (ed.), Learning Strategies I (Academic Press, N.Y., 1978).

PART VII

EMERGING CONCEPTS
IN SPEECH CONTROL

Tutorials in Motor Behavior
G.E. Stelmach and J. Requin (eds.)
© *North-Holland Publishing Company, 1980*

38

DISTINCTIVE PROPERTIES
OF SPEECH MOTOR CONTROL

Peter F. MacNeilage
University of Texas
Austin, Texas 78712

Language has a dualistic structure: a meaning level formed by morphemes, words and syntactic rules, and a sound level, at which
concatenations of a limited number of basic
sounds (segments, phonemes) are used to form
the lexical items of our mental dictionary.
This dualistic structure constrains speech
motor control theories. They must account for:
1. effects of segmental context on movements
for a given segment, and; 2. semantic, syntactic and lexical effects, such as semantic
focus, signalled by sentence stress, intonation, syntactic boundary effects, signalled
by segment duration, and lexical stress effects.
Additional constraints arise from nonlinguistic
factors such as variations of speaking style
and speaking rate, 'compression' effects of
utterance size on segment duration and the
great ability of the production mechanism to
adapt to postural variations, either self
imposed or experimenter imposed. Consideration of these constraints plus speech errors
suggests a tripartite structure to the speech
production process consisting of 1. establishment of semantic and syntactic structure and
choice of lexical items, 2. serial arrangement of a set of segments in short term store,
and 3. implementation of motor control algorithms responding to segmental specification
and current linguistic and nonlinguistic
constraints. Theoretical approaches to
speech motor control have consisted primarily
of unsatisfactory attempts to use the concepts of spatial or auditory target, a spring
analogy, and the concept of coordinative
structure to account for the maintainence
of invariance in segment production. The
main general hypothesis pertaining to control of segment durations--that there is
a mechanism tending to produce equal intervals between stressed syllables in English
(Stress Timing) is also unsatisfactory.

OUTLINE OF THE SPEECH PRODUCTION PROCESS

Speech is produced by the combined operation of three sets of structures: the respiratory structures -- the lungs and the surrounding tissue; the laryngeal structures -- the vocal folds and the collection of cartilages and muscles which surrounds them; and the articulatory structures -- in particular the tongue, lips, jaw and soft palate.

The main role of the respiratory structures in speech is to maintain a relatively constant excess of air pressure in the lungs over air pressure in the atmosphere during the expiratory phase of respiration. This results in a relatively constant outward flow of air through the speech production apparatus, and modulation of this air flow results in the sounds of speech. The main role of the laryngeal structures is to provide an alternation between periods of vocal fold vibration (called voicing) the major sound source for speech, and periods of voicelessness when air is allowed to pass relatively unimpeded between vocal folds. The articulatory structures have two major roles. First, by modifying the shape of the vocal tract which they surround, they are capable of varying the resonance properties of the tract and thus producing different speech sounds. Secondly, by producing a close approximation between two structures on each side of the airway the articulatory structures can produce turbulent air flow, resulting in "Fricatives" as for example, in the first sound in the English word "set". During speech production the articulatory structures tend to alternate between producing a relatively open configuration of the vocal tract and a relatively closed one. The open configuration is characteristic of vowels which are virtually always voiced sounds, and the relatively closed configurations are characteristic of consonants, which may be either voiced or voiceless. Vowels and consonants are usually described as speech segments and form the segmental level of speech production. There is in addition a so-called suprasegmental level characterized by a number of phenomena. First, there is the phenomenon of Stress, which typically relates to the energy level applied to a syllable. Two kinds of stress can be distinguished. First, lexical stress, or stress specified for a single lexical item or word. For example, in English the noun "object" and the verb "object" differ from each other. In the former case stress is placed on the first of the two syllables of the word, and in the latter case the second. Second, sentence stress; a single stress placed on one syllable of an utterance, usually a syllable bearing important semantic weight in the utterance. A second major suprasegmental phenomenon is Intonation which refers to patterns of variation in the rate of vocal fold vibration (termed "fundamental frequency") across an utterance. For example, in English one can distinguish between the statement "John's here" in which the fundamental frequency falls toward the end of the utterance (and is heard as a falling pitch) and the question "John's here?" in which the fundamental frequency increases towards the end of the utterance. An additional suprasegmental phenomenon is termed Quantity. This refers to the tendency in certain languages to make a distinction between 2 or 3 forms of a vowel or consonant with a single quality, (that is, single vocal tract shape) by producing forms of the segment with different durations. Finally, there is the phenomenon termed tone. This refers to the fact that in certain languages single vowels, and sometimes consonants, are distinguished from each other in terms of the fundamental frequency accompanying the vowel or consonant alone. Many Asian languages fall into this category.

THE MESSAGE: LINGUISTIC STRUCTURE, AND ITS IMPLICATIONS FOR MOTOR CONTROL

The role of speech production is to transmit a linguistic message from a speaker to a listener. In order to fully understand the motor control of speech production, it is necessary to consider the nature of the linguistic message and, of course, the process by which the message is turned into a speech signal, rather than, for example, in the case of writing, where it is turned into a series of visual signals.

An extremely important property of the linguistic message is that of Duality (Hockett, 1960). Language has both a sound level and a meaning level (semantic level). A limited set of sounds (Phonemes) can form an enormously large number of words by being ordered in various ways -- the words "tack", "cat" and "act" can be considered to be constructed of the same sounds in different orders. An additional aspect of the message structure of language is its syntax often conceived of as the system by which meanings and sounds are related (Chomsky, 1965). Words are ordered in various ways by rule.

My choice of the phoneme as a plausible unit of the sound level of message structure is influenced partly by linguistic analyses but mostly by the observation that phoneme-sized units are much more frequently involved in the permutations observed in spoonerisms (e.g. night life → knife light) than other possible sound units such as the syllable or the distinctive feature (Fromkin, 1971; MacNeilage, 1979b).

In so far as the linguist's conceptions are related to the actual behavior of the speaker the notions of duality, and of syntax, are of interest for students of speech motor control in that a given phoneme is subject to a wide variety of context effects both within words and within syntactically determined multiword utterances. A crucial question is, how does a model of speech production incorporate these contextual constraints. Consider first the constraints on segments determined by the immediate context provided by adjacent segments, and then constraints from syntactic, semantic and lexical structure.

CONSTRAINTS ON MOTOR CONTROL FROM SEGMENTAL CONTEXT

With the exception of a few phonemes each phoneme can be

characterized by a single shape of all or part of the vocal
tract which is at least approximated at some point in each
production of that phoneme. This is a context independent
aspect of phonemes. However, this shape must be achieved by
different movements in different contexts. For example, in
the production /t/, which involves placing the tongue on the
gum ridge immediately behind the top teeth, a different motor
control gesture is required if the previous vowel involved
a low back tongue position, (for example, /a/), than if the
previous vowel involved a high front tongue position, (for
example, /i/). It has also been observed that not only the
previous segment but the following segment influences the
form of the movement for a given segment. These so-called
Coarticulation effects (Kent and Minifie, 1977) can even
spread over several segments. For example in French the
lip rounding gesture for a rounded vowel can be initiated
up to 7 segments before the segment for which the rounding
is required (Benguerel and Cowan, 1974). An extremely complicated picture emerges in which lip rounding can be
initiated at various times prior to the rounded vowel itself
depending on the precise nature of the segmental sequence.
Such rounding is typically not blocked by higher order
boundaries such as syllable and word boundaries. An additional complication arises from the fact that rounding and
other forms of coarticulation are not totally determined by
universal articulatory constraints but can vary in form
from language to language.

The duration of segments is also conditioned by their segmental environment. For example, consonants are shorter when
they abut other consonants than when they abut vowels.
Vowels are shorter before voiceless consonants than before
voiced consonants.

At what level of the control system is the information for
implementing these context effects represented? Should it
be represented with the lexical items which constitute the
mental lexicon, (mental dictionary)? We have relatively
little understanding of the mental lexicon. Perhaps the
most useful information for present purposes comes from a
study of the tip of the tongue phenomenon -- the situation
we periodically encounter in which we know something about
the word we are trying to recall without being able to
recall it (Brown and McNeil, 1966). This study showed that
we typically have some idea of the initial sounds of the word,
the number of syllables, and the position of the stressed
syllable. Although this result shows there is some common-
ality between the word as a motor control entity at the
sound level and the word as a stored meaning unit, it tells
us nothing about whether context-conditioned aspects of
the segments of the to-be-produced word are represented in
the mental lexicon.

However, on other grounds it seems unlikely that context
conditioned aspects of segments are represented in the mental
lexicon. Consider again the segmental spoonerism. It is

assumed that when segments from 2 successive words permute, those words were temporarily represented in proximity to each other perhaps in some kind of short term storage device. Thus the error is deemed to occur after the words have been accessed from the mental lexicon and not in the lexicon itself. But note that spoonerisms are typically fluent, that is, they are produced with acceptable durations and vocal tract shapes. For a spoonerism (such as; take the cap → cake the tap) to be produced fluently, a different transitional movement from the transposed consonants to their 'new' following vowels would be required than that called for within the correct lexical items. Thus if the information appropriate for control of the transitional movement was represented in the correct items in the mental lexicon it would have to be replaced by a new set of information appropriate to the new transitional movement following the spoonerism. Such a dual mode of establishing the means of control of transitional movements seems extremely uneconomical, and instead one is encouraged to believe that the means of control of transitions are established only 'below' the level at which the spoonerism occurred.

At the very least this must be true of the transitions across word boundaries in continuous speech. The means of control of these could not be stored with individual lexical items as their choice depends on the choice of order of words, which we assume is made afresh for each utterance. As movement transitions across boundaries are typically analagous to those between the same two segments within words, and as there can be about as many types of segment sequence across word boundaries as within words, there would appear to exist a capacity sufficient for achieving transitions, below the level of the mental lexicon.

SYNTACTIC SEMANTIC AND LEXICAL CONSTRAINTS ON MOTOR CONTROL

There are a number of consequences for motor control of segments, which follow from a choice of a semantic and syntactic structure of an utterance and of a set of lexical items. As pointed out earlier, one of these is sentence stress, involving an increase in duration (by 10-20%), intensity and fundamental frequency placed on the main lexically stressed syllable of the word which carries the semantic focus. Also mentioned earlier was the sentence intonation contour, which involves a systematic pattern of change in fundamental frequency which must be superimposed on the alternation of vocal fold abduction and adduction associated with segmental distinctions between voiced and voiceless sounds. Decisions about sentence stress and intonation must be made relatively early in the construction of an utterance as they involve the entire sentence, and a number of necessary details of syntactic structure of an utterance depend upon these earlier decisions. On the other hand the control values for the implementation of these effects in the motor system must be assigned relatively late, in order to allow spoonerisms to be fluent with respect to sentence stress and intonation.

For example consider the following spoonerism (Fromkin, 1971):
What we need is a computer in our own laboratory→ What we
need is a laboratory in our own computer. In this case
the motor control parameters for sentence stress must have
been assigned (to the last word) after the permutation or
they would have shifted with the correct word (laboratory).
As in the case of segmental context effects, it seems uneconomical to suppose that the motor control prerequisites
were assigned before the spoonerism, and that a second
assignment was made after the spoonerism.

Other effects involve segment durations at syntactic boundaries. In English, though not in many other languages, the
last syllable of the final word in a sentence is considerably
longer (about 100 ms) than that same syllable within the
utterance. The final word of a sentence has similar durational characteristics to the same word spoken in isolation.
This lenthening mainly involves the vowel and any consonants
following it which do not involve total occlusion of the
vocal tract. Of course a sentence is usually followed by
a silence or pause. In addition pauses within a sentence at
major syntactic boundaries such as clause or phrase boundaries are accompanied by similar lenthening to that observed
in sentence final syllables. And even when there is no
pause at clause and phrase boundaries there is some final
syllable lenthening (approximately 30%). In fact some final
syllable lengthening has often been observed even in words
within a syntactic phrase (Klatt, 1976).

As in the case of other context effects, discussed earlier,
these timing effects must be implemented at a relatively
late stage of the production process to allow for fluent
spoonerisms that involve units at syntactic boundaries, e.g.
give my back a hot bath→ bath a hot back. As to the
mechanism of the timing effects, Fowler, 1977 has suggested
that prepausal lengthening is an inertial effect inherent
in the termination of sequences of events by the motor
system. This would seem unlikely in the light of the very
great cross language differences in the scope of these
effects (Oller, 1973; Hutchinson, 1973). A more plausible
though speculative explanation arises from the fact that
prepausal words are similar in duration to those words
spoken in isolation. Perhaps the 'initial' specification
of words for duration is the one observed when words are
spoken in isolation. Then a shortening adjustment follows
from the determination that the word will not be followed
by a pause, and a further shortening adjustment is made
when the word does not terminate a major syntactic boundary.
Note, however, that whereas a pause following a sentence is
obligatory and therefore grammatically determined, pauses
following phrase and clause boundaries are optional and
therefore determined by performance constraints, not by
the linguistic code. But however plausible a theory of non-
pausal shortening might be, there is at present no empirical
justification for preferring it to a pausal lengthening
hypothesis.

A constraint on segments arising from lexical items in addition to that provided by their phoneme sequences is the degree of stress placed on each syllable of the item. Although there is no agreement as to how many degrees of stress are appropriate for English lexical items, there is agreement that higher levels of stress are signalled by higher fundmental frequency, higher intensity, longer segment duration, especially of the vowel, and a closer approach of articulators to their goals. Although it was mentioned earlier that stress can be thought of in terms of the level of energy applied to a syllable, this is at present more a metaphor than a documented fact.

NONLINGUISTIC CONSTRAINTS ON MOTOR CONTROL

A theory of motor control of speech must also take into account a number of nonlinguistic constraints; that is constraints that do not arise from the structure of the language. Different speaking styles used by the same speaker in different social contexts result in differences in the entire organization of utterances. The difference between casual conversational speech and speech e.g. to a respected superior, is reflected in types of syntactic structures chosen, selection of vocabulary items and rules of sound production. For example at the sound level some sounds used in careful speech may simply be eliminated and others changed in a manner apparently determined by context: "did you eat yet" becomes "gee chet". Obviously much of the necessary difference in style must be introduced at a very early stage of utterance production. Virtually nothing is known about how to characterize these style differences in terms of the mechanism of their production and they remain a formidable barrier to theories of speech production at any level.

One nonlinguistic variable that is operative in speech style differences but can also be studied under more controlled experimental conditions is speaking rate, defined in terms of number of segments per second. The hope that rate changes could be simply explained in terms of quantitative changes in some single control variable such as rate of movement or duration of movement has not been realized (MacNeilage, 1979b). One very important datum, at present refractory to explanation, is that that vowel durations are more sensitive to changes in overall speaking rate than consonant durations. This appears to call for a dual control mechanism. A complication of speaking rate studies is that there is more than one way to change speaking rate. It has been observed that subjects can increase rates of articulator movement and achieve the same positional goals as in normal speech (Kuehn and Moll, 1976), they can keep rates of articulator movement constant, and 'undershoot' normal goals (Kuehn and Moll, 1976), and they can even decrease articulator movement rates (Kozhevnikov and Chistovich, 1965). The particular method of rate increase which is adopted may depend on implicit demands of particular

experimental situations or on the whim of the individual
subject.

An additional nonlinguistic property of languages is a
tendency towards the decrease in duration of each component
of an utterance with an increase in the number of components
in the utterance (Lehiste, 1970). For instance within single
syllables segment durations (particularly vowel durations)
decrease as the number of segments in the syllable increases.
Within multisyllabic words, syllable durations decrease
with an increase in number of syllables. These decreases
are not uniformly spread throughout the word. For example
Lindblom and Rapp (1973) note that in Swedish, decrease is
proportional to both the number of preceding syllables and
the number of following syllables (that is, most marked for
word medial syllables) with the number of following syllables
having the greater effect. The situation is not nearly as
clear cut for multiword utterances, although some analagous
shortening effects of number of components in the utterance
have been reported. One hypothesis (Lindblom, et al, 1977)
is that the word and utterance effects are explicable in
terms of the properties of short term motor memory.

A final nonlinguistic constraint is that arising from what
can be called postural restrictions, both those voluntarily
imposed on a speaker by himself and those imposed by an
experimenter in the form of perturbations for which the
speaker must compensate. As to our great ability to cope
with self-imposed restrictions, I quote from an earlier
paper (MacNeilage, 1979a): "Compensation is the normal
mode of operation of the system. We don't typically talk
while sitting otherwise motionless in front of a microphone,
but in the context of intermittent changes in what can be
loosely called the postural configuration of the speech
apparatus. We talk equally well standing up and lying down,
and as Hixon et al (1976) have shown we can preserve comparable subglottal pressure levels under the two conditions,
even though the effect of gravity, particularly on the abdom-
inal contents, requires two quite different motor control
patterns for the 2 different postures. A lecturer can
"speak across" sizeable updown movements of the head if
he is reading text, and sizeable lateral head movements if
he is using a blackboard. Lateral head movements are typical
in speakers in a small group. I could go on and on citing
the changes we choose to impose on ourselves while speaking.
It is possible that to some extent these changes are simply
superimposed on the ongoing speech control and produce
acoustic perturbations that the perceptual system can sur-
mount. But I believe many of them require off-line feedforward compensatory strategies in the production control
mechanism. The fact that the mechanism has chosen to solve
this problem is one of the most central facts we have in
attempting to constrain a speech production control model.
It certainly constrains us to reject models in which the
means of speech production control have a simple and fixed
relation to either underlying linguistically defined units

on the one hand, or observable ends of the production process
on the other."

In recent years a number of studies have involved experimenter
induced perturbations of the speech production apparatus.
These studies have revealed a great ability of the control
mechanism to compensate for disturbance in signalling segmental aspects of the message. The 'segmental' goals of
the production mechanism are typically achieved despite
the perturbations. A prominent example is the study of
Lindblom et al (1979) which showed that immediately following insertion of bite blocks 25 mm in size between the teeth,
subjects were able to produce acoustical representations of
vowels which were correct at the onset of voicing. Results
such as these require a specification of invariant underlying goals at some stage of the control process. This
specification is capable of guiding an elaborate set of
compensatory mechanisms.

The constraints on the motor control process discussed so
far require at least a tripartite structure to the speech
production process. Many writers (e.g. Fromkin, 1971, Garrett,
1975, Foss and Hakes, 1978) including this author (MacNeilage
and MacNeilage, 1973) have presented block diagrams with
many more stages. But although these multistage models have
merit, the present emphasis on motor control, and the
increasing difficulty of separating and ordering stages as
one increases them confine me to the structure presented in
figure 1. The figure is intended to summarize much of the
preceding discussion. I have already argued extensively for
the separation of these 3 stages and for their order -- at
least for the order of the last 2.

HYPOTHESES ABOUT SEGMENTAL MOTOR CONTROL

Having outlined some of the main phenomena that a theory of
speech motor control must encompass let us now consider some
theoretical approaches. More effort has been expended in
attempting to account for the achievement of more or less
invariant segmental articulatory goals in the face of context
constraints and postural perturbations, than in attempts to
account for control of segment durations.

One possibility suggested by a number of writers was that
goal achievement in segmental production was guided by the
specification of targets, perhaps in an internalized 3 dimensional spatial representation of the vocal tract (MacNeilage,
1970). This view was encouraged by the analogy available
in visual motor coordination, where the attainment of pre-
viewed goals by movements without on-line visual support,
seems to demand an ability to represent targets in terms
of internalized representation of spatial coordinates. Problems with the target concept in speech include its apparent
lack of testability, and the fact that it throws no light on
how the articulators might approximate targets. Fowler (1977)
has attempted to partially solve the latter problem by a

UTTERANCE STRUCTURE GENERATION

Semantic and syntactic
structure established.
Lexical items chosen.

↓

SERIAL ORGANIZATION

Segments arranged in
serial order in short
term store.

↓

MOTOR CONTROL

Control algorithms respond
to segmental specification
and linguistic and nonlinguistic
constraints.

Figure 1.   Stages of the speech production process.

suggestion that for vowels the tongue may be able to
temporarily assume the properties of a spring-mass system
with a resting configuration or "zero state" equivalent to
a target position for a particular vowel. This suggestion
was made by analogy with the behavior of subjects in experiments by Asatryan and Fel'dman (1965) who were capable of
voluntarily centering on a certain fixed joint angle at the
elbow in the presence of various loading conditions.

Like the target hypothesis, the spring-mass hypothesis awaits
test. But some data already available make it clear that
neither hypothesis will provide a satisfactory explanation
for all segmental phenomena. These data show that a single
articulatory configuration for a given segment is not always
approximated. For example the voicelessness associated with
English /p/ between two vowels is produced by vocal fold
abduction, but in a [p] preceding a voiced stop (e.g. in
"upbringing") some subjects adduct the vocal folds
(MacNeilage, 1979b). Thus the production of the same
underlying segment in two environments is achieved by opposite
movements and opposite end states of the production apparatus.
In addition, in an experiment in which Folkins and Abbs
(1975) unpredictably impeded jaw elevation movements and
therefore lower lip closure movements for /p/, the upper
lip responded with active compensatory lowering resulting
in lip closure at a different (lower) point in space than
normally observed.

An additional problem for these hypotheses is the likelihood
that not all the goals of the articulatory system are
specified as positions. For example in some diphthongs the
tongue is in continuous movement, and some data suggests
that the rate of movement for a diphthong is invariant across
speaking rates (Gay, 1968). A further problem for these
hypotheses comes from an experiment by Riordan (1977). In
a study of French speakers she observed that if lip protrusion for the production of rounded vowels is mechanically
prevented, subjects lower the larynx as an alternative
means of producing the increase in length of the vocal tract
required to produce the correct sound for the vowel. This
result suggests that the speakers can produce more than one
adequate vocal tract configuration for a vowel, though they
normally only use one particular means.

None of these problems for the spatial target and spring-mass
hypotheses are necessarily problems for a hypothesis based
on auditory targets. Auditory properties of speech production are obviously primary in the sense that the auditory
information provided by our language community is by far
the main source of goals for our acquisition of speech production (MacNeilage, 1979b). Auditory properties also seem
to be a potential link between the signal and message levels
of speech production, judging from the accessibility of the
first sounds of words by subjects suffering from the tip
of the tongue phenomenon. However, as with the spatial
target and spring-mass hypothesis, appropriate tests of
this hypothesis are not yet available, and it shares the
inability of the spatial target hypothesis to generate consequences for the control of actual movements.

In the past few years an attempt has been made to apply the
concept of Coordinative Structure to the speech control
process (Fowler, 1977) (See also the paper by Kelso and
Turvey in this volume). A coordinative structure is defined
as a set of muscles, often spanning many joints that is constrained to act as a unit.   (Turvey et al, 1978). This concept is basically an attempt to formalize the fact of coordination, and would appear to have potential explanatory
value in cases where articulators reach relatively invariant
end points in varying circumstances. Gay and Turvey (1979)
have recently attempted to apply this concept to the results
of an experiment including the conditions of bite block,
surface oral anesthesia, and temporomandibular joint anesthesia
They reasoned that only in the presence of both the bite
block and anesthesia, would atttainment of articulatory
targets be impaired. They argued that if some components
of a coordinative structure "cannot vary (due to a bite
block) and their values are not communicated within the
system (due to anesthetization) then fulfilling the equa-
tion(s) of constraint will not be possible and successful
vowel production would be seriously hindered." Although this
prediction was confirmed, acceptance of an explanation in
terms of coordinative structures should nevertheless await
information on precisely what the equations of constraint are,

618   P.F. MacNEILAGE

and in what terms they should be stated in the context of
such a complex multidimensional sensorimotor apparatus.   In
addition the concept, as stated, did not account for the
remarkable fact that after a few initial unsuccessful
attempts, subjects did manage to produce the vowels accept-
ably.

As was pointed out earlier, relatively little effort has
been made to account for the control of segment durations.
An obvious problem for a unified theory of durational control
is the diversity of origins of durational effects.   Semantic,
syntactic, phonotactic (sound order) and nonlinguistic
variables are all involved.   Perhaps most attention has
been given to the possibility of a durational influence in
addition to the ones already discussed.   Considering the
pervasiveness of rhythmic systems in motor control it is
not surprising that efforts have been made to detect global
rhythmic properties of speech production (Allen, 1975).   The
simplest rhythmic event is perhaps a cyclic activity with
a fixed period.   The intuition of Pike (1945) shared by many
other linguists was that many languages possessed either one
or the other of two simple rhythms of this type.   He called
them stress timed and syllable timed languages.   In the
former, of which English is an example the time interval
between the onsets of successive stressed syllables was
considered to be approximately equal.   In the latter, of
which Spanish is an example, the intervals between successive
syllable onsets was considered to be approximately equal.
Of course in English, the interval between successive stressed syllables does not remain absolutely equal.   Because of
the distribution of stressed and unstressed syllables in
different lexical items an actual utterance might include
between zero and 4 unstressed syllables between successive
stressed syllables.   For example in the sentence:

     John's innocent of the charges.

There are no unstressed syllables between John's and inn--
but there are 4 unstressed syllables between inn-- and char--.
Differences of this kind in the number of syllables between
stressed syllables definitely affect the size of the interval
(Lehiste, 1977).   However some theorists have contended that
there may nevertheless be a tendency towards stress timing in
the sense that more intervening unstressed syllables would
produce more compression of the speech material within the
interstress interval.   This is an interesting hypothesis
because it would involve a mechanism that 'looks at' a body
of material after it has been chosen for delivery and makes
adjustments contingent on the properties of that material.
Tests of this hypothesis typically involve measurement of a
stressed vowel in an interval containing different numbers
of unstressed syllables with the expectation that this vowel
would get shorter as the number of unstressed syllables in
the interval increased.   Results of such tests have been
disappointing.   Although some successes have been claimed,
(e.g. Huggins, 1975) more often negative results have been

reported (e.g. Lea, 1974; Lehiste, 1977). Furthermore, even in the successful cases, differences are only in the order of a few milliseconds and there are some reasons to believe that the studies may have had methodological problems which rendered their results equivocal. Thus there is relatively little evidence at present for the existence of a rhythmic constraint operating across entire utterances in English, other than that provided by the incidence of stressed and unstressed syllables in the lexical items chosen for an utterance.

In conclusion it may be worthwhile to note major topics that have been neglected in this survey, and to list alternative sources of information on these topics whenever possible. Control of fundamental frequency has not been considered, either in relation to intonation (Liberman, 1975) or to tone languages (Fromkin, 1977). The integration of the operation of the 3 speech production subsystems has not been considered (Ohala, 1974; Fujisaki, 1977). And finally scant reference has been made to cross-language differences in motor control. The question: which aspects of speech motor control are universal and which aspects are language specific, (Lehiste, 1976; Lindblom, 1979) is obviously crucial to a theory of speech motor control. Unfortunately an answer to this question is just beginning to be provided.

References

1   Allen, G., Speech rhythm: its relation to performance universals and articulatory timing, Journal of Phonetics 4 (1975) 75-86.
2   Asatryan, D. and Fel'dman, A., Functional tuning of the nervous system with control of movement or maintenance of a steady posture -- I. Mechanographic analyses of the work of the joint on execution of a postural task, Biophysics 10 (1965) 925-935.
3   Benguerel, A.-P. and Cowan, H.A., Coarticulation of upper lip protrusion in French, Phonetica 30 (1974) 41-55.
4   Brown, R. and McNeill, D., The "tip of the tongue" phenomenon, Journal of Verbal Learning and Verbal Behavior 5 (1966) 325-337.
5   Chomsky, N., Aspects of the theory of syntax (M.I.T. Press, Cambridge, 1965).
6   Folkins, J.W. and Abbs, J. H., Lip and jaw motor control during speech responses to resistive loading of the jaw, Journal of Speech and Hearing Research 18 (1975) 207-220.
7   Foss, D.J. and Hakes, D.T., Psycholinguistics: An introduction to the psychology of language (Prentice-Hall, Englewood Cliffs, 1978).
8   Fowler, C.A., Timing control in speech production, Ph.D. thesis, Dept. of Linguistics, Dartmouth College (November, 1977).
9   Fromkin, V., The non-anomalous nature of anomalous utterances, Language 47 (1971) 27-52.

10   Fromkin, V.A. (Ed.), Tone: A linguistic survey,
        (Academic Press, New York, 1978).
11   Fujisaki, H., Functional models of articulatory and
        phonatory dynamics, in: Sawashima, M. and Cooper, F.S.
        (eds.), Dynamic Aspects of Speech Production (U. of
        Tokyo Press, Tokyo, 1977).
12   Garrett, M., The analysis of sentence production, in:
        G. Bower (ed.), The psychology of learning and motiva-
        tion (Academic Press, New York, 1977).
13   Gay, T., Effect of speaking rate on diphthong formant
        movements, J. Acoust. Soc. Amer. 44 (1968) 1570-1573.
14   Gay, T. and Turvey, M., Effects of efferent and
        afferent interference on speech production: implica-
        tions for a generative theory of motor control,
        Proceedings of the 9th International Conference of
        Phonetic Sciences, Copenhagen, August 6-11, 1979.
15   Hixon, T.J., Mead, J. and Goldman, M.D., Dynamics of
        the chest wall during speech production: Function of
        the thorax, rib cage, diaphragm, and abdomen, JSHR
        19 (1976) 297-356.
16   Hockett, C., Logical considerations in the study of
        animal communcation, in: Lanyon, W. E. and Tavolga,
        W. N. (Eds.), Animal sounds and communication (American
        Institute of Biological Sciences, Washington, D.C.,
        1960).
17   Huggins, A.W.F.,,, On isochrony and syntax, in: Fant,
        G. and Tatham, M.A.A. (eds.), Auditory analysis and
        perception of speech, Academic Press, London, 1975).
18   Hutchison, S., An objective index of the English-
        Spanish pronounciation dimension, Masters Thesis,
        University of Texas at Austin. (1973).
19   Kent, R.D. and Minifie, F.D., Coarticulation in recent
        speech production models, JPh 5 (1977) 115-134.
20   Klatt, D., The linguistic uses of segment duration in
        English: Acoustic and perceptual evidence, JASA 59
        (1976) 1208-1221.
21   Kozhevnikov, V.A. and Chistovich, L.A., Speech articu-
        lation and perception, J.P.R.S 30 (1965) 543.
22   Kuehn, D. P. and Moll, K., A cineradiographic study
        of VC and CV articulatory velocities, J. Phonetics 4
        (1976) 303-320.
23   Lea, W.A., Prosodic aids to speech recognition: IV
        A general strategy for prosodically guided speech
        understanding, Univac Report No. PX10791, St. Paul,
        Minn., Sperry Univac, DSD.
24   Lehiste, I., Suprasegmentals (Cambridge, M.I.T. Press,
        1970).
25   Lehiste, I., Suprasegmental features of speech, in:
        Lass, N.J. (ed.), Contemporary issues in experimental
        phonetics (Academic Press, New York, 1976).
26   Lehiste, I., Isochrony reconsidered, J. Phonetics 5
        (1977) 253-263.
27   Liberman, M.Y., The intonation of American English,
        Ph.D. Thesis, Dept. of Ling., M.I.T., (1975)
28   Lindblom, B.E.F., Some phonetic null hypotheses for a
        biological theory of language. Proceedings of the 9th

International Congress of Phonetic Sciences, Copenhagen, August 6-11, 1979.

29   Lindblom, B.E.F. and Rapp, K., Some temporal regulari-
      ties of spoken Swedish, P.I.L.U.S. 21 (1973) 1-59.
30   Lindblom, B., Lyberg, B., and Holmgren, K., Durational
      patterns of Swedish phonology: Do they reflect short
      term motor memory processes? (Unpublished manuscript,
      1977).
31   Lindblom, B., Lubker, J., and Gay, T., Formant fre-
      quencies of some fixed-mandible vowels and a model of
      speech motor programing by predictive simulation,
      J. Phonetics 7 (1979) 147-162.
32   MacNeilage, P.F., Motor control of serial ordering of
      speech, Psychological Review 77 (1970) 182-196.
33   MacNeilage, P.F., The control of speech production,
      Proceedings of the conference on Child Phonology:
      Perception, Production and Deviation, Yeni-Komshian,
      G.H., Kavanagh, J.F. and Ferguson, C.A. (eds.).   (In
      preparation, 1979)
34   MacNeilage, P.F., Speech production, Proceedings of
      the 9th International Congress of Phonetic Sciences,
      Copenhagen, August 6-11, 1979.
35   MacNeilage, P.F. and MacNeilage, L.A., Central processes
      controlling speech production during sleep and waking,
      in: McGuigan, F. J. and Schoonover, R.A. (eds.),
      The psychophysiology of thinking (Academic Press, New
      York, 1973).
36   Ohala, J.A., Mathematical model of speech aerodynamics,
      in: Fant, G. (ed.), Proceedings of the Speech Commu-
      nication Seminar (Stockholm, Almqvist and Wiksell, 1974).
37   Oller, D.K., The effect of position in utterance on
      speech segment duration in English, J.A.S.A. 54 (1973)
      1235-1246.
38   Pike, K., Intonation of American English, (University
      of Michigan Press, Ann Arbor, 1945).
39   Riordan, C. J., Control of vocal-tract length in speech,
      J.A.S.A. 62 (1977), 998-1002.
40   Turvey, M.T., Shaw, R.E., and Mace, W., Issues in the
      theory of action, in: Requin, J. (ed.), Attention and
      performance VII (Erlbaum, Hillsdale, N.J., 1978)

Tutorials in Motor Behavior
G.E. Stelmach and J. Requin (eds.)
© North-Holland Publishing Company, 1980

39

LANGUAGE AND SPEECH PRODUCTION
FROM A
NEUROPSYCHOLOGICAL PERSPECTIVE

Oscar S. M. Marin and Barry Gordon
Departments of Neurology
Baltimore City Hospitals
and
The Johns Hopkins University School of Medicine
Baltimore, Maryland

ABSTRACT

Neuropsychologic analysis of the abnormalities of speech and
language production in patients with cerebral lesions reveals
clear dissociations between different processes. These dissociations are similar to ones predicted by linguistic theory,
lending further support to the validity of linguistic theoretical constructs. Moreover, the specific relation of certain
types of disruptions to certain areas or types of brain damage
suggests that different processes are subserved by separable
neuronal subsystems. Distinct disorders range from those involving purely phonological motor mechanisms (dysarthrias) through
those involving syntactic processes (agrammatism), the semantic-
lexical interface (anomia), and general semantic pre-verbal
processes (some cases of dementia). In addition, disorders
of the supralinguistic process of planning for speech intentions are seen in some other cases of dementia and in lesions
of the frontal lobes.

Parallelisms and divergencies between motor acts and speech
production are briefly discussed.

While speech represents a very specialized form of motor behavior, it shares
many requirements with other forms: it must operate quickly and accurately
in real time, and it needs considerable preplanning for proper execution.
Because of these similarities, the processes involved in language and
speech production should be of interest to those studying motor behavior in
a more general context (see 1,2,3). We will briefly discuss some of these
possible mechanisms in the context of showing how they can be separated
from each other by brain pathology. There may be quite distinct mechanisms
for these functions, and they may depend on distinct portions of the brain.
Under certain circumstances, they may even operate relatively independently
from the rest of our cognitive machinery. However, there are two major
language functions -- paralleling those in motor behavior -- that cannot be
understood solely from the basic motor apparatus of speech: (1) The ultimate use of language for the expression of thoughts, emotions, intentions,
and purposes; and (2) the metaprogramming of the semantic, lexical and
syntactic form of the speech expression itself in order to convey these ulterior motives to the listener. Green (4) has called this latter planning
"expressive pragmatics," and it is similar to what Bernstein (5) and others
have considered to be "plans" for motor action. As we will discuss, even
these functions may be differentially affected by certain types of brain
pathology.

The validity of studying aphasic language dissociations has been well documented (6,7,8,9,10). While we feel that this approach is impressively
useful, we are obliged to warn the reader of three major limitations of
this type of research: (1) Neuropsychologic dissociations are the chance
results of disease states or accidents. Therefore, truly informative cases
are uncommon. So the usual scientific skepticism about "irreproducible"
results has to be tempered by practical considerations. (2) By themselves,
neuropsychologic dissociations do not provide information about the timing
or sequence of neural operations. (3) While neuropsychology has profited
from the empirical and theoretical frameworks of psychology and linguistics, there is no comparably detailed processing model of the central
nervous system. We have relatively little idea of the nervous system's
natural subdivisions and modes of information storage and transmission
beyond relatively intuitive notions based on anatomic connectivity. Despite
these cautions, we hope to demonstrate the usefulness of neuropsychologic
evaluation of speech production disorders.

Our framework for analysis will be based on hypothetical stages of speech
production suggested by psychology and linguistics, which we will show receive impressive support from pathologic dissociations. We conceive of
speech production as requiring at least these stages: (1) The intent to
initiate speech; (2) The plan of what is to be conveyed by the speech,
which we conceptualize as a pre-verbal semantic schema; (3) The ability to
choose the proper lexical items ("abstract" words) to represent the semantic intentions; (4) Selection of the correct syntactic lexical items,
perhaps with (5) Concurrent selection of the appropriate phonologic encoding, finally followed by (6) articulatory expression.

A. Semantic and Semantic-lexical Dissociations

W.P. is a patient whose illness illustrates two of these stages: Early in
her course, the semantic-to-lexical selection stage was primarily affected
but later the pre-verbal "semantic intention" stage was impaired as well.
At age 62 this previously normal woman developed a progressive senile dementia (Alzheimer's disease). (For complete details see Schwartz, Marin,
and Saffran [11].) In her spontaneous language she began to show some
naming difficulties for which she occasionally compensated by circumlocutions or by vague lexical fillers. (See section B (Anomia) below) This,
for example is W.P. talking about her family at the beginning of her illness: "But...Oh Lord, my other...ah! girl, you know, my girl that I have,
she says, 'Mom, now you tell me something...'". At the end of two and one-
half years, her speech production was still well articulated with preserved
syntax, but lexically restricted to a few reiterated items or emotional expressions: "Oh, my Lord! All of a sudden he says, 'I'll get the shopping
center' and I said Oh good! and then I went, but she said, Oh shopping
center, and there, and he's dead...."

It became apparent that her spontaneous lexical difficulties (anomia) were
not due to deficient phonological knowledge of the words but rather to a
deeper semantic-lexical disorganization. Schwartz et al were able to demonstrate that this patient had difficulties in assigning the proper lexical labels to the correct referential pictures. Thus, W.P. made 51 errors
in naming simple objects or animals represented in 140 pictures. Forty-six
of these errors were induced by semantic distractors. Further analysis of
her lexical-referential confusion for specific semantic categories showed
that she tended to erase categorical boundaries and to overextend some

categories at the expense of others. Thus, she correctly labeled all pictures of dogs "dog," but she also called 5 out of 7 pictures of cats "dog" as well. The mislableing was confined to atypical cats (cf. [12]). We demonstrated that the disorder was not necessarily a verbal one by showing that similar over-extensions were found when the patient was asked just to match pictures of dogs and cats without verbal labels.

Despite this semantic-lexical disorganization, W.P.'s remaining language abilities were remarkable. She was able to correctly read aloud a sizeable corpus; she was even correct on the many items for which she had already lost the semantic referents, and which she did not use spontaneously any longer. She was able to correctly select orthographically regular English words from items that were not regular English constructions (in this she was more successful than when judging whether an orthographically regular lexical item was a real word or a pseudo-word). She was able to select the proper orthography of homophones according to their lexical function, and consequently, would write "nose" in the case of "my/noz/" and "knows" in the case of "he/noz/". She successfully disambiguated homophones in semantically related triads, such as "priest-pope-/nun/" versus "some-many-/nun/". W.P. was able, until late in her illness, to correctly read outloud words having both regular and irregular orthographic-phonologic correspondence. Only when her illness became advanced did she begin making more reading errors on words that had markedly irregular print-to-sound correspondence, which she still tended to tead following the rules of regular English. She remained able to judge and to correct the grammaticality of sentences. Thus, to the sentence "The boy was been hit by the girl," she repeated "The boy has been hit by the girl." W.P.'s case shows how a clearcut dissociation may exist between normal higher linguistic levels and intact underlying instrumentalities of speech operation.

B. Lexical Selection: The Problem of the Anomias

As we outlined, for speech production some lexical choice has to be made from our semantic intentions. At first glance, all patients with anomia seem to illustrate disorders of this lexical selection stage. Anomic speech is characterized by the absence of content words (particularly nouns). They are replaced by silences or vague circumlocutions, so sentences convey little meaning. However, speech is syntactically correct, well-constructed, and well articulated:

(The patient is attempting to describe a picture:) "No, tell me...Yeah! I know what it is but I can't say it. No, no...Yep!...Didn't I do it? I know but I can't....I know what it is right there but I can't do it..A little bit, you got to go a little bit more though. That's it...No. Start again...I can almost do it all the way. I am sorry. There you go. Woops!"

Actually, anomia represents a mixed group of disorders (see [8]). In some, the anomia seems to result from faulty input processes (perceptual or agnosic). Other anomias are relatively straightforward output problems. One such case of ours (8) clearly had an intact lexicon and an intact internal phonological representation of words, but this information seemed to be disconnected from her speech motor mechanisms resulting in markedly anomic speech.

Most anomic patients do not have such clear-cut input or output disorders. Recently, there has been an increasing awareness that the lexical defect in anomias may be related to a deeper lexical-semantic disorganization (13,14, 15). There has also been a growing consensus that anomias are closely linked with other abnormalities of language production such as the para- phasias and neologisms of Wernicke's aphasia, possibly reflecting the same underlying disruption. There is much circumstantial evidence for this re- lationship. Anatomically, the sites of the two syndromes overlap exten- sively (16, 17). Functionally, naming difficulty is often the earliest sign of disturbances that evolve into Wernicke's aphasia. Conversely, a- nomia is often the fate of a recovered Wernicke's aphasic. In both anomia and Wernicke's aphasia, there are severe lexical abnormalities, with rela- tive preservation of syntax and articulation (16,18). Furthermore, as Buckingham (19) notes, the words most affected in the anomias are nouns, and they are also the words most affected by phonemic paraphasias in Wernicke's aphasia as well. Phonemic paraphasias occur in nouns and lexi- cal stems, rarely in syntactic morphemes. This suggests that there is a prephonological disturbance of nouns as a primary defect in both disorders, despite what appears to be on the surface a phonemic disorder (paraphasias). This conclusion, based on neuropsychologic evidence, is consistent with that of many psychologists and linguists who have also assigned nouns the pre- eminent position in the semantic and lexical stages. In this view, nouns act as pivotal content words around which the other forms of lexical selec- tion take place. Phonological expression depends on the semantic processes and not the other way around. This sequence, which makes phonologic pro- cesses relatively unimportant in word selection, is supported by clinical observation. Although anomics constantly struggle searching for words, they do not seem to use a phonemic strategy nor are the helped by phonemic cues as much as normals. In word-finding tasks, the anomics seem to access the word by gradually accumulating semantic features; giving them the "sound" of the word alone (by using it in a different semantic context or by saying it accidentally) is often useless. One of our patients could not name "the item that we drink from" even though she could report that a window pane was made of "glass" and could correctly give the other word for "spectacles" as "glasses".

One problem with assigning a semantic-lexical breakdown as the determinant factor in paraphasic productions is that some paraphasias (phonemic para- phasias) clearly involve phonological disruptions (transpositions, dele- tions, or substitutions) which generally obey seemingly pure phonological rules. However, it is very likely that such paraphasias do arise from a phonologic mechanism, but only because it is not receiving proper guidance. It is not hard to imagine that the phonological-articulatory mechanism can function quasi- independently of the semantic-lexical one (20). Echolalic patients (21) are the most convincing examples of pure, independent phone- mic articulatory performance, where understanding of language is lost or severely impaired. Normal subjects can also allow these mechanisms to operate in isolation when reading syllabically or when pronouncing nonsense words.

In summary, the data for anomia and related disorders suggests that the dis- order in most anomic patients is at the semantic-lexical level, involving mainly nouns. Their defect is not really a phonological one, but the fact that their paraphasias are governed by phonological rules suggests that phonemic processing is going on independently of the impaired lexical input. (We recognize that the phonological-articulatory mechanism may also be damaged in some cases.) We conceive of the final expression of a sentence

as the result of processes that operate simultaneously at multiple levels.
Operations are guided by higher levels (i.e., semantics), with each lower
level performing more stereotyped and limited operations within its compe-
tance. Each of the lower levels depends on its superiors only for general
guidance; it is relatively independent as it solves its specific problems
by its specific mechanisms. Higher levels monitor the results of these
operations and provide redirection and backup in case production turns out
incorrectly.

C. Syntactic Organization; Agrammatic Language Production.

The speech of a patient with Broca's aphasia is slow, reduced in quantity,
effortful, halting and hesitant. Not only are there obvious difficulties
in his articulation, but there is a conspicuous disorganization of word
order, absence of functors, omission or mistaken use of inflections -- what
in summary has been described as agrammatism (Pick [22]): "Like the door..
crash...like, pants...shirt..shoes..the boy the dress. Do you do window?..
Does...you do window?...Like, the boy is window..." What remains are irregular juxtapositions of content words, mostly nouns and adjectives, that
give the overall impression of a telegrammatic style. Verbs appear in
their infinitive or gerundive forms, the latter more often functioning as
nominal rather than progressive forms.

Studies by numerous authors, notably Goodglass et al (23), Scholes (18),
Andreewsky and Seron (24), Zurif and Caramazza (25), and by our group (6,
26, 27), have confirmed that agrammatic patients have specific difficulties
in applying the proper functional syntactic morphemes to lexical stems, and
in selecting the right prepositions or other modifiers. The syntactic
difficulty is compounded by a strong ambiguity in choosing the grammatical
role of specific words. These patients hesitate, for example, when determining whether a particular word should function as a noun, verb or other
element.

Zurif and Caramazza (25) demonstrated that agrammatic production in these
patients was accompanied by a parallel defect in syntactic comprehension,
particularly noticeable with sentences in which semantic clues were eliminated. Schwartz et al (26,27) further demonstrated that with these
patients one could sometimes distinguish between pragmatic knowledge of the
meaning of the elements and grammatical use of the elements. Some of the
patients studied by Schwartz et al were able to give the meanings of loca-
tive prepositions and some verbs, although they were unable to use them.
This was particularly clear with reversible sentences in which there were
no semantic cues as to the most likely word order (e.g., "The triangle is
on the circle" vs. "The circle is on the triangle").

The main syntactic strategies of language are the use of word order and the
use of syntactic functors. In most agrammatic patients, abnormal word
order strategies coexist with abnormal use of syntactic markers. But not
infrequently, patients disassociate these two strategies, suggesting that
they have separate mechanisms. Among many examples, this is one of our
agrammatics describing a picture of a woman loading a washing machine:
"The lady...thelady launders the...the lady puts the washes...wash on..puts
on the wash with the laundry." A picture of a woman kissing a man was
described as "the kiss..the lady kissed..the lady is...the lady and the man
and the lady...kissing." (See Saffran et al [27] for details.) While it
is not certain what is influencing the production of syntactic morphemes,
Saffran et al (27) showed that word order was semantically determined.

Although it is not clear what is fundamentally wrong with agrammatics, the distinctive role of word order, syntactic morphemes, and functors in comparative studies of language development (28) suggests that these agrammatics have a primary psycholinguistic abnormality. (Word order difficulties present a major problem (but not the only one) in trying to attribute agrammatic performance to a defect in phonologic representation [cf. Kean (29)].)

D. Articulation of Speech and the Problem of Anarthrias.

After the lexical selection is phonologically determined, and the syntactic markers are specified and applied, articulatory execution remains. In many other motor acts, this central programming overlaps with execution; there are complex feedback controls and re-adjustments all throughout. In contrast, the linguistic articulatory programs seem to be encoded in a motor keyboard that operates predominantly on a feedforward, ballistic style (30,31,32). Alajouanine and his colleagues (33,34) analyzed the characteristics of anarthric speech. They distinguished three aspects: (a) a "paretic" component, marked by insufficiency of breath and weakness of articulation; (b) a "dystonic" aspect revealed by exaggerated, abnormal tension or spasticity of the articulatory structures; and (c) an "apraxic" factor expressed in impaired sequentiality of movements. This latter component was sometimes associated with a bucco-facial apraxia, inducing some authors to postulate an intimate relationship between speech and motor praxis (2,3). Alajouanine and Lhermitte (35), while acknowledging the association between anarthria and apraxia, refused to accept the existence of a common basic defect.

From audio tape and speech sonographic recordings of anarthric patients vocalizing isolated phonemes or articulating vowel combinations, we (36) were able to discriminate two major problems: First, the intensity, steadiness and pitch of the utterance were affected, corresponding to the paretic and dystonic difficulties found by Alajouanine et al. Secondly, there was inaccuracy in reaching target vowels and in moving from one vowel to the next. Our patients tried to correct their vocalizations, albeit slowly and often incorrectly, by guiding themselves auditorily. In bi-vowel articulations between distant sounds, such as "i-a", patients tended to slowly slide along all intermediate sounds to reach the final target: "i-e-oe-ae-a". This probably corresponds to Alajouanine et al's apraxic component.

Luria (37) has also distinguished two major components in dysarthria: One, at a phonemic level, is the result of an instantaneous postural disorder; the other is from a disorganization of the sequence of phonemes. More recently Derousne, Beauvois and Ranty (38) have re-examined this hypothesis and, by asking patients to perform articulatory tasks that require instantaneous postures or sequential changes, were able to confirm that the two operations may dissociate in different patients suggesting independent components of speech production.

Lecours and Lhermitte (39) were able to verify the anatomical localization of one of the cases of phonemic disintegration originally studied by Alajouanine, Ombredane and Durand (33). At age 63, this patient suffered from a cerebral infarct leaving him with severely dysprosodic and dysarthric speech that obliged him to slowly and consciously utter the syllables

of words one by one. Other aspects of oral and written language were
normal. No bucco-facial apraxia was observed. The disorder consisted
mainly of inconstant anomalies of the actual production of phonemes. The
authors considered the speech defect as phonetic in nature, and the anarthria as corresponding to what Alajouanine et al classified as dystonic.
This, in physiological terms, most likely represents the effect of post
paralytic spasticity. The patient's brain had cortical and subcortical
damage localized on the left exactly in the dominant hemisphere's primary
cortical representation of the face, mouth and tongue. The variable nature
of the disorder and the fact that the defective functional units were so
closely tied to the specific function of speech should have hardly sur-
prised us. There is a great deal of other evidence showing that such high
levels of function are represented at the cortical motor level, a point
originally made by Jackson and implicit in most physiological interpretations of cortical motor organization.

The articulatory disorder resulting from left lower frontal lesions (ro-
landic operculum) is rarely very severe or permanent (40, 41). Permanent,
severe inability to articulate speech (mutism) generally requires bilateral
infarcts affecting both cortical or subcortical opercular regions of the
brain in most cases. Only then does a complete bucco-lingual voluntary
paralysis exist, concomitant with the total abolition of speech articulation. All this suggests that lateralization of language production is
actually a consequence of lateralized programmative higher-order mechanisms, not of lateralization at the level of final articulatory pathways.
This problem deserves further study because of its direct bearing on the
overall problem of dexterity and hemispheral dominance, as well as its
relevance to speech mechanisms.

E. Initiation of Speech: Mutisms

Mutism and/or akinesia occuring in full wakefulness suggests the existence
of triggering mechanisms for the initiation of motor action and speech.
These problems are seen in cases of frontal lobe and thalamic/hypothalamic
damage. Both motor and verbal behavior are blocked or significantly slowed
down. Luria (42) described patients with left frontal lesions who, in
spite of otherwise totally normal language facilities, had great difficulties in initiating and sustaining verbal communication. The problem was
particularly evident during narrative speech. A number of authors (see
[43] for other references) have described cases of transient verbal block
or mutism unaccompanied by generalized akinesia. Lesions affected the inner aspects of the frontal lobe of the major hemisphere, near to or directly affecting the supplementary motor area. These cases, while not true
aphasias, strongly suggest that the left frontal lobe contains mechanisms
that regulate the initiation and sustenance of speech behavior.

F. The Speaker and the Uses of Language. Language Production in Frontal
Lobe Lesions and Dementias.

While we have outlined "stages" of language production, we hardly conceive
of the process of sentence construction as merely a free-running assembly
line where semantic, lexical, syntactic, and phonological components are
successively welded together. What guides sentence production at each step
has to be some sort of anticipated plan for the whole, much as Bernstein
and others (5,44,45) have suggested is necessary for motor acts. There

must not only be an overall plan for the cognitive contents of the intended communication but also for the nuances that allow the sentence to
express the emotions, motives, desires, and ulterior intentions of the
speaker. As Fillmore, Green and others (4,46) have argued, one must distinguish between the speaker's knowledge of the options available in the
language (a concept close to that of competence) and his knowledge or
ability to choose among those options to best express his full intentions.
Some refinements of the speaker's intentions are obviously resolved by
careful lexical selection, but a number of the subleties of direction and
stress expressing intentions, motives or attitudes depend upon syntactic
changes. We feel that it is not coincidental that these more subtle disorders of syntactic organization are found in aphasics with predominantly
anterior lesions and patients with frontal lobe lesions.

In these patients the expressive and regulatory aspects of the personality
are disorganized, with relative sparing of the more posteriorly located
perceptual and cognitive functions. One of our presenile demented
patients showed a remarkable accuracy of perceptual description in contrast
to a total inability to integrate components into a coherent, meaningful
whole:

(Describing the Broken Window picture [47]:) "The man comes out; the door
is open; the girl goes to school...my daughter is a school teacher...the
window is broken; the boy is hiding...there are some bushes..." (Ex: What
do you think is going on in this picture?) "The man comes out..." (Ex.:
Is he angry with somebody?). "He points with both hands (Imitates gesture)". (Ex: What is going on in this picture?). "The door is open, the
window is broken...the girl...". In frontal lobe lesions, propositional
language and the organization of complex motor acts often both disinte-
grate in parallel. Some patients are perseverative in language and in
movement; others are incoherent, fragmented and impoverished in their
linguistic productions and equally unable to organize motor complex acts
or are apraxic in their gait. Some are overtly echolalic as if no longer
in control of their speech phonological-articulatory loop (8) or they may,
more subtly, answer with sentences that imitate the interlocutor's questions and move as the examiner does. Yet others are emotionally blunted,
have concrete linguistic production, and are devoid of gestures and motor
spontaneity and unable to mimic motor acts. These disturbances all may be
related to the role the frontal lobes play in the dynamic, executive aspects of behavior.

Luria (48) described two basic perseverative disorders of executive behavior: (a) the inability to turn off the initial motor components of an
act to allow for subsequent processing and (b) the inability to initiate
another complex program of action. Barbizet et al (49) have demonstrated
how similar propositional aspects of language production are affected by
frontal lesions. More recently, Shallice and Evans (50) described similar
abnormalities in tasks that require cognitive selection, judgment and
planning.

Luria (48,51) and others have attempted to correlate the specific behavioral abnormalities of frontal lobe patients with the localization of their
lesions, but the correlation is uncertain in most cases because of the extent of the damage. Anatomically. it is of interest that the orbito-basal
aspects of the frontal cortex are closely related to thalamic (dorso-medial

nucleus) and hypothalamic non-specific activating pathways, while the dorso-lateral cortex is more an intracortical associative region. The medial frontal cortex is related to projections from the anterior group of thalamic nuclei and hence to the limbic system. If these differences in cortical connectivities are behaviorally important, then one should expect that arousal, attentional, emotional, and possibly general cognitive abnormalities would result from damage to basal and medial frontal areas or to their corresponding subcortical or thalamic nuclei. More specific patterns of cognitive deficits would be present in dorsolateral frontal damage, with different types of deficits depending on the side of the lesion. The clinical evidence seems, in general, to confirm these correlations. Left frontal lesions impair verbal and sequential processes and/or memories while those on the right impair visuo-spatial and holistic functions (52).

References

(1) Liepmann, H., Drei Aufsatze Aus Den Apraxiegeibeit Vol. 1 (Krager, Berlin, 1908).

(2) Kimura, D., The neural basis of language qua gesture, in: Whitaker, H. and Whitaker, H.A. (eds.) Studies in Neurolinguistics, Vol. 2 (Academic Press, New York, 1976).

(3) Lomas, J. and Kimura, D. Intrahemispheric interaction between speaking and sequential manual activity, Neuropsychologia 14 (1976) 23-33.

(4) Green, G.M., Linguistics and the Pragmatics of Language Use, paper read at the Program in Cognitive Science, "Neurolinguistics and Cognition" conference, University of California, San Diego (March 1979).

(5) Bernstein, N., The coordination and regulation of movements (Pergammon Press, London, 1967).

(6) Marin, O.S.M., Saffran, E.M. and Schwartz, M.F. Dissociations of Language in Aphasia: Implications for normal function, Annals of the New York Academy of Science 280 (1976) 868-884.

(7) Marin, O.S.M. Neurobiology of Language: an overview, Annals of the New York Academy of Science 280 (1976) 900-912.

(8) Marin, O.S.M. and Gordon, B. Neuropsychologic aspects of aphasia: an approach for the study of speech and language processes, in: Tyler, H.R. and Dawson, D.M. (eds.) Current Neurology Vol. 2 (Houghton Mifflin, Boston, in press)

(9) Marshall, J.C. Disorders in the expression of language, in: Morton, J. and Marshall, J.C. (eds.) Psycholinguistics Series 1: Developmental and Pathological (Elek Science, London, 1977).

(10) Saffran, E.M., Schwartz, M.F. and Marin. O.S.M. Evidence from aphasia: isolating the components of a production model, in: Butterworth, B. (ed.) Language Production (Academic Press, New York, in press).

(11) Schwartz, M.F., Marin, O.S.M. and Saffran, E.M., Dissociations of language function in dementia: a case study, Brain and Language (in press, 1979).

(12) Rosch, E., Principles of Categorization, in: Rosch, E. and Lloyd, B.B. (eds.), Cognition and Categorizaton (Erlbaum, Hillsdale, N.J. 1978).

(13) Marin, O.S.M. and Saffran, E.M., Agnostic behavior in anomia: a case of pathologic verbal dominance, Cortex 11 (1975) 83-89.

(14) Goodglass, H. and Baker, E., Semantic field, naming, and auditory comprehension in aphasia, Brain and Language 3 (1976) 359-374.

(15) Coughlan, A.K. and Warrington, E.K., Word-comprehension and word-retrieval in patients with localized cerebral lesions, Brain 101 (1978 163-185.

(16) Naeser, M.A. and Hayward, R.W., Lesion localizations in aphasia with cranial computed tomography and Boston Diagnostic Aphasia Exam, Neurology 28 (1978) 545-551.

(17) Kertesz, A., Lesk, D., and McCabe, P., Isotope localization of infarcts in aphasia, Arch. Neurol. 34 (1977) 590-601.

(18) Scholes, R., Syntactic and lexical components of sentence comprehension, in: Caramazza, A. and Zurif, E. (eds.) The Acquisition and Breakdown of Language (Johns Hopkins, Baltimore, 1978).

(19) Buckingham, H.W., The conduction theory and neologistic jargon, Language and Speech 20 (1977) 174-184.

(20) Fromkin, V.A. The non-anomalous nature of anomalous utterances, Language 47 (1971) 17-52.

(21) Geschwind, N., Quadfasel, F. and Segarra, J., Isolation of the speech area, Neuropsychologia 6 (1965) 327-340.

(22) Pick, A., Aphasia in: Brown, J.W. (trans. and ed.) Aphasia (C.C. Thomas, Chicago, 1973).

(23) Goodglass, H., Agrammatism, in: Whitaker, H. and Whitaker, H.A. (eds) Studies in Neurolinguistics Vol. 1 (Academic Press, New York, 1976).

(24) Andreewsky, E. and Seron, X., Implicit processing of grammatical rules in a classical case of agrammaticism, Cortex 11 (1975) 379-390.

(25) Zurif, E.B. and Caramazza, A., Psycholinguistic structures in aphasia: Studies in syntax and semantics, in: Whitaker, H. and Whitaker, H.A. (eds.) Studies in Neurolinguistics Vol. 1 (Academic Press, New York, 1976).

(26) Schwartz, M.F., Saffran, E.M., and Marin, O.S.M. The word order problem in agrammatism I: Comprehension (Brain and Language, in press).

(27) Saffran, E.M., Schwartz, M.F., and Marin, O.S.M. The word order problem in agrammatism II: Production (Brain and Language, in press).

(28) Slobin, D.I., Universals and particulars in the acquisition of language, paper presented at conference on "Language Acquisition: States of the Art (University of Pennsylvania, 1978).

(29) Kean, M.L., The linguistic interpretation of aphasic syndromes: agrammatism in Broca's aphasia, Cognition 5 (1977) 9-46.

(30) Anderson, S.W. Ballistic control of rhythmic articulatory movements in natural speech, Annals of the New York Academy of Science 263 (1975) 236-243.

(31) MacNeilage, P., Motor control of serial ordering of speech, Psychological Review 77 (1970) 182-196.

(32) Fowler, C.A., Timing control in speech production, Ph.D. Thesis, Indiana University (1977).

(33) Alajouanine, Th., Ombredane, A. and Durand, M., Le syndrome de desintegration phonetique dans l'aphasie (Masson Ed, Paris, 1939).

(34) Alajouanine, Th., Verbal realization in aphasia, Brain 79 (1956) 1-28.

(35) Alajouanine, Th. and Lhermitte, F., Les troubles des activities expressives du langage dans l'aphasie: Leurs relations avec les apraxies Rev. Neurol. 102 (1960) 604-633.

(36) Marin, O.S.M. and Bernales, M., Unpubished observations (1967).

(37) Luria, A.R. Higher Cortical Functions in Man (Tavistock, London, 1966)

(38) Derouesne, J., Beauvois, M.F., and Ranty, C., Deux composantes dans l'articulation du language oral, Neuropsychologia 15 (1977) 143-153.

(39) Lecours, A.R. and Lhermitte, F., The "pure form" of the phonemic disintegration syndrome (pure anarthria): anatomo-clinical report of an historical case, Brain and Language 3 (1976) 88-113.

(40) Bruyn, G.W. and Gathier, J.C., The opercular syndrome, in: Vinken, P. J. and Bruyn, G.W. (eds.) Handbook of Clinical Neurology Vol. 2 North Holland-Elsevier, Amsterdam, 1969).

(41) Mohr, J.P., Broca's area and Broca's aphasia, in: Whitaker, H. and Whitaker, H.A. (eds.), Studies in Neurolinguistics, Vol. 1 (Academic Press, New York, 1976).
(42) Luria, A.R., Basic problems of neurolinguistics (Mouton, The Hague, 1976).
(43) Masdeu, J.C., Schoene, W.C. and Funkensetin, H., Aphasia following infarction of the left supplementary motor area, Neurology 28 (1978) 1220-1223.
(44) Turvey, M.T., Shaw, R.E. and Mace, W., Issues in the theory of action: degrees of freedom, coordinative structures, and coalitions, in: Requin, J. (ed.), Attention and Performance VII (Erlbaum, Hillsdale, N.J., 1978).
(45) Shaw, R. and McIntyre, M., Alogoristic foundations to cognitive psychology, in: Weimer, W.B. and Palermo, D.S. (eds.) Cognition and the Symbolic Processes (Erlbaum, Hillsdäle, N.J., 1974).
(46) Fillmore, C.J., Frame semantics and the nature of language, Annals of the New York Academy of Science 280 (1976) 20-32.
(47) Wells, F.L. and Reusch, J., Mental Examiner's Handbook (The Psychological Corporation, New York, 1945).
(48) Luria, A.R., Two kinds of motor perseveration in massive injury of the frontal lobes, Brain 88 (1965) 1-10.
(49) Barbizet, J., Duizabo, P. and Flavigny, R., Role des lobes frontaux dans le langage, Rev. Neurol. 131 (1975) 525-544.
(50) Shallice, T. and Evans, M.E., The involvement of the frontal lobes in cognitive estimation, Cortex 14 (1978) 294-303.
(51) Luria, A.R., The frontal lobes and the regulation of behavior, in: Pribram, K.H. and Luria, A.R. (eds.) Psychopathology of the Frontal lobes (Academic Press, New York, 1973).
(52) Milner, B., Hemispheric Specialization: scope and limits, in: Schmitt, F.O. and Worder, F.G. (eds.) The Neurosciences - Third Study Program (MIT Press, Boston, 1974).

Tutorials in Motor Behavior
G.E. Stelmach and J. Requin (eds.)
© *North-Holland Publishing Company, 1980*

40

CHANGE IN PHONEME TARGETS WITH DIFFERENT PHONATION TYPES

PETER HOWELL
Department of Psychology,
University College London,
Gower Street, London WC1E 6BT.

Between speaker variations in the rate of vibration of the
vocal cords (pitch) are associated with differences in the
size of the vocal tract and, thereby, with differences in
the formant frequencies. Pitch is considered incidental to
production because the same speaker can speak at different
pitches and produce intelligible productions with no vocal
cord vibration (whispering). The former observation assumes
that subjects do not move their articulators when speaking
at different pitches and the latter that there is no pitch
in whispered speech. Subjects can, however, whisper at
different pitches.

In an experiment subjects produced vowels at different
pitches and acoustic analyses were performed to determine
the speech output and articulatory configurations used to
produce them. The implications of the results for the
nature of the specified target in speech are discussed.

INTRODUCTION

Some current research in speech production has been addressed to the
systematic differences which occur in speech produced with differences in
stress or at different speaking rates, Lindblom, (1). These variations
represent situations in which the vocal output is most constant for a
given linguistic input and might shed light on the properties of the
speech production mechanism. The present chapter starts by examining
why we might expect systematic differences in vowel formant frequencies
when they are spoken on different pitches, reports an experiment that
shows that these differences do occur and discusses their implications
for theories of speech production.

In considering theories of speech production it is often assumed that
lower order linguistic units are organized serially to generate a given
sound pattern. Producing a speech message involves, among other things,
continuously changing the shape of the vocal tract which in turn changes
the acoustic output. The movements of the resonant frequencies of the
vocal tract (formants) over time are the prime source of information
available to the listener to determine the string of linguistic segments
the speaker intended. One aim of the spectrographic studies first
performed during the 1950's was to determine the acoustic properties of
the speech message. It soon became apparent that there are few, if any,
invariant formant relationships for a given speech sound especially
considered over different speakers.

Supported by a grant from the S.R.C. I would like to express my thanks
to Prof. R.J. Audley and Drs. N. Harvey, A.R. Jonkheere & S.M. Rosen.

Acoustical considerations lead us to expect that if the articulators are
positioned in corresponding positions in different vocal tracts when
producing a given linguistic segment, that as vocal tract size decreases
the formants move to higher frequencies for the same intended production.
The formant frequencies are not invariant across speakers and information
about the size of the speaker's vocal tract needs to be extracted from the
signal to determine what production the speaker intended. One source of
information simultaneously available with the formant information for
voiced sounds which might give a clue about the dimensions of a speaker's
vocal tract is the voice pitch (F_0). The vocal folds are thinner and
shorter in females than in males and vibrate at different F_0's,
Sonesson, (2). Plotting measured formant frequencies against F_0 for a
given vowel reveals a positive correlation between the formant frequencies
and F_0, Potter & Steinberg, (3). It can be shown that F_0 information
improves the classification of this data as the intended vowel. When the
Potter & Steinberg (3) data were reanalyzed by multiple linear regression with a dependent variable which represents group membership
(discriminant analysis), it was found that 67.6% of the vowels were
correctly classified if the first two formants were used as discriminating variables but this improved to 82.4% if F_0 was included too. Note
that not all the improvement in classification is attributable to the inclusion of F_0 since an extra degree of freedom is taken out of the data,
and some improvement in the classification would be expected on this
basis alone.

A perceptual experiment by Miller (4) shows that subjects may use F_0
information to identify vowels. A two-formant steady-state vowel
presented in an /s/-vowel-/t/ frame may be perceived as two different
vowels depending on which pitch it is presented at. See also Fant,
Carlson & Granstrom, (5), Howell, (6), and Wendahl, (7).

Clearly any particular speaker uses many different pitches and thus we
might ask do formant frequencies change when a speaker speaks at different pitches in the same way as they change between different speakers.
This issue has not previously been considered. One reason for this
omission seems to be the fact that perfectly intelligible speech can
be produced with no movement of the vocal cords at all (whispered speech).
Whispered speech is produced with a partly open glottis and the vocal
tract is more occluded than in normally voiced speech. A subsidiary aim
of the present study is to determine whether, with these differences in
production, speakers can still achieve the same formant frequencies as in
voiced vowels. A speaker is able to whisper at different pitches and
under these circumstances the formant frequencies move up in frequency
with increasing pitch, Meyer-Eppler, (8). Whatever the mechanism of
pitch variation is in whispered speech, it too may be associated with
compensatory changes in the vocal tract to position the formant frequencies contingent of the pitch he intended to produce.

To summarize, it is known on the one hand what acoustic effect the speaker
would try to achieve if he were organizing his articulatory gestures on
the basis of both pitch and formant frequencies. In the experiment to be
reported the acoustic output and articulatory positions used to achieve
them were estimated from the speech of subjects who spoke and whispered
vowels at different pitches. The questions to be addressed are whether
the acoustic output is compensated when a speaker speaks at different
voiced and whispered pitches and whether and how he achieves the same
formant frequencies for whispered vowels as for spoken vowels.

METHOD

Subjects. Five male speakers of British English were screened by a
phonetician for their ability to produce vowels in the same register at
three different pitches. All male subjects were used because there is
evidence that the ratio of mouth to pharynx cavity size may differ between the sexes, Fant, (9) and may therefore require different articulatory compensations.

Stimuli. The vowels to be spoken were /ɪ, I, ɛ, æ, ɔ, ʋ, and u/ in an
/h/-/d/ frame. These included two of the point vowels, /i and /u
which, for a given set of formant frequencies, have unique vocal tract
area functions associated with them and it might be supposed that a
speaker would be better able to hold them constant at different pitches,
Lindblom and Sundberg, (10), Stevens, (11). The words were presented to
subjects on a card in the order they were required to speak them. This
order was the same for a subject whether the words were to be spoken or
whispered but differed from speaker to speaker. The subject performed
all the voiced or all the whispered words before the other phonation
condition. The order of phonation conditions was counterbalanced across
subjects.

Recordings. The subject was seated in a comfortable chair in a sound-
treated room with a moving coil microphone (Beyerdynamic M 88 N)
positioned about 7 cm from his lips. The electrodes of a laryngograph
were secured firmly but comfortably around his neck at the level of his
larynx to determine the pitch of the voice by sensing impedance changes
across the vocal folds, Fourcin & Abberton, (12). The recordings of the
microphone and laryngograph outputs went to separate tracks of a two-
track Revox tape recorder (model A77).

Subjects were given the card and instructed to speak or whisper each word
at three steady-state pitches which increased in pitch from the first to
the last before proceeding to the next word. An ascending pitch was used
in order to keep subjects phonating in the same register, Lerman & Duffy,
(13). The first sequence of words of each phonation type was not recorded but used to adjust the gain on the tape recorder and to familiarize
the subject with the task. After he had performed one phonation type,
the gain on the tape recorder was readjusted while he practiced the other
phonation sequence.

Listening Tests. To determine the intelligibility of both spoken and
whispered productions and the rated pitch of the whispered speech eight
volunteers were given two tests. The words were digitally sampled and
stored on a PDP-12 computer at 8 kHz after filtering at 3.5 kHz (48
dB/octave). All of a speakers productions were randomized (i.e., the 3
productions of each of the 7 vowels) and recorded with 1.75 sec between
them. The productions of the other subjects were recorded sequentially
in the same manner. These were presented to subjects over headphones for
identification. In order to determine whether the pitch of the whispered
speech was perceived as intended, subjects were given a two-interval
forced choice task. The 6 different pairings of a subject's 3 whispered
productions of a particular vowel were randomized with the pairings of the
other vowels and recorded with 1/2 sec between the members of the pair
and with 1.75 sec before the next pair. The listener's task was to

indicate the interval in which a specified pitch (high or low) occurred. The subject was not concerned with vowel identity in the task because the two vowels were the same. Half the subjects indicated the interval in which the lower pitch occurred and the other half the interval in which the higher pitch occurred.

ANALYSIS PROCEDURE.

Formant Frequency Analysis.

Linear prediction analysis was performed on a PDP-11 computer using speech recorded like that of the listening tests. The vowel section was located visually. For each production a number of frames of 256 consecutive points were available and these were analyzed frame by frame. The voiced data were differentiated as an approximate way of removing the spectral slope of the excitation source and a Hanning window was applied. The Fourier Transform of each 256-point data frame was calculated, and an eighth-order autocorrelation function and model spectrum for the discrete values were computed. The formants were calculated by interpolating the model spectrum and picking the peaks from these values. The estimated formant frequencies were checked against spectrograms. The program occasionally failed to detect one of the formants (7% voiced, 7.6% whispered) because the formant was poorly defined. No difficulty was found in detecting the low frequency resonances of the whispered speech. The pitch of the voiced sounds was calculated by determining the period of the zero crossings in the laryngograph output.

For the whispered sounds the same procedure was employed except that the data were not differentiated or windowed. Note that two approximations were made; first, voiced but not whispered speech was differentiated. This is a crude form of pre-emphasis. A more precise pre-emphasis would involve putting the data through a single zero filter in which the co-efficients are determined by the first two autocorrelation coefficients, Rathjen, (14). Second, application of an all-pole model is less applicable for unvoiced speech, but Markel & Gray (15) state that it provides a satisfactory approximation.

Articulatory Analysis.

Area functions of the acoustic tubes were estimated from Wakita's model, Markel & Gray, (15). A 35-th order autocorrelation analysis was employed which gives 35 sections. Assuming that a male's vocal tract with a lowered larynx is 17.5 cm, this gives an estimate of the area every 1/2 cm. Two statistics were estimated from the area function: area of lip opening, and the radius of the tube at the point of tongue construction.

RESULTS AND DISCUSSION.

Formant Frequencies.

The formant frequencies of the spoken and whispered vowels are presented in Figures 1 and 2 respectively. The data are presented averaged over subjects for their low, medium and high pitch productions.

Compensations at Different Pitches for the Two Phonation Types

For the voiced vowels an analysis of covariance was performed for each formant and for each vowel (21 analyses) with F_o as a supplementary measure and subjects as groups to determine whether the regression of formants on F_o was significant. Such a result would indicate whether

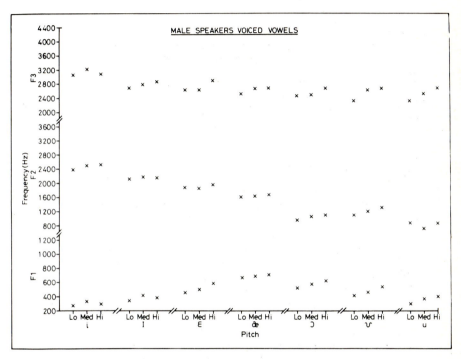

Figure 1. Formant frequencies of the vowels arranged
           as explained in the text.

the subject changed his formant frequencies with F_o, and whether or not the slopes were the same between subjects. As in all analyses reported in this chapter, the mean observation value was entered for a subject when he had missing data points. The regression of formants on F_o was significant at the 5% level or better in all but 7 cases. The Bernoulli probability of getting 14 failures in 21 independent trials is 0.039. The slopes differed between subjects on only one occasion. Note that shifts in the formant frequencies occur for the two point vowels. This indicates that the subject was not retaining a unique vocal tract shape for these vowels. This analysis leads to the conclusion that there is a significant increase in the frequencies of the formants with pitch. The fact that the slopes were not significantly different between subjects indicates that the shifts in formant frequencies that a particular subject was producing was the same as those which occur between the speakers in this study.

The data for the whispered vowels cannot be analyzed by covariance analysis because the pitch of the different productions are only measured on an ordinal scale. A non-parametric test for related observations (productions from the same subjects) in which a trend is predicted (Page's L test) was employed to test the hypothesis that the formant frequencies increase with the intended pitch. The trend was significant at the 5% level or better in 14 cases out of 21 (Bernoulli probability 0.039). No equivalent test of the hypothesis that the shifts a speaker was achieving were the

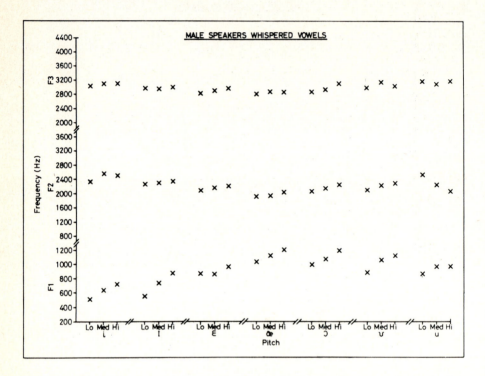

Figure 2. Formant frequencies of the vowels arranged
            as explained in the text.

same within a subject as between the subjects was performed because there is no criterion for determining the pitch range produced with the whispered vowels.

The normal mechanisms available to the speaker to change his formant frequencies to produce a different vowel are point and degree of constriction of the vocal tract. The point at which the subject constricts his vocal tract changes the formant frequencies by changing the area function of the vocal tract. Changes in positioning the constriction with pitch could not be evaluated because changes in pitch are associated with upward movement of the larynx and this narrows the pharynx cavity,

Sundberg & Nordstrom, (16) and reduces its length, Ohala & Ewan, (17).
In addition changes in tongue height change the larynx position, Petersen,
(18). Because of the upward movement associated with pitch and tongue
height and the absence of data available to correct for these differences,
the point of constriction in the vocal tract cannot be estimated by assuming a constant vocal tract length.

There are several known acoustical effects associated with deformation of
the vocal tract by constriction at a particular point. First, a resonance
will rise if the vocal tract is constricted at a point of volume velocity
maximum for that resonance mode and conversely fall if the vocal tract is
expanded at that point, Chiba & Kajiyama, (19). Second, expansion of the
vocal tract at a particular point will cause frequencies to rise if there
is an excess of potential energy at that point, Fant & Pauli, (20).

For the normally spoken speech, analysis of covariance was performed with
radius of constriction and vowels as factors and pitch as the covariate.
There was a significant difference in the radius of constriction between
vowels and pitch was a significant covariate. This analysis indicates
that the radius of constriction was being changed with pitch. The
analysis cannot be performed for the whispered speech because of the
ordinal measurement of pitch. Inspection of the whispered speech showed
that overall the radii of constrictions were less.

Increasing the area of lip opening has been shown to be a maneuver employed by adult actresses to mimic children's speech, Kirikae, Sawashima,
Hirose & Fujisaki, (21). An acoustical explanation of this is available
in Fant (22) who shows that the effect of lip rounding (decrease in area
or protrusion of the lips) is to lower the first four formants or more
precisely those which are below one quarter wavelength resonance of the
lip cavity. Opening the lips as observed by Kirikae et. al., (21) would,
then, increase the formant frequencies as required if they are trying to
imitate children's speech.

To check whether the speakers used this manoeuvre analysis of covariance
for the lip opening data was performed in the same way as with the radius
of constriction data. There were differences in lip opening for the
different vowels and pitch was a significant covariate. Inspection of
the data revealed that there was some increase in lip opening with increasing pitch.

Compensations across Phonation Types.

A comparison of the mean formant frequencies across spoken and whispered
vowels shows that the formant frequencies for the whispered productions
are higher than their voiced counterparts. The difference in formant
frequencies is not constant across vowels but is greater for the back
vowels. To determine the extent to which the formant frequencies differ
between the phonation types discriminant analysis was performed with vowel
as the grouping variable and F_1, F_2 and F_3 as the independent variables.
When both whispered and voiced vowels were included with their appropriate
group designation only 29.5% were correctly classified. This is surprisingly low even though variations which occur as a consequence of differences in pitch were not included in the analysis. The whispered productions were next entered as unclassified cases after discriminant
analysis had been performed for the voiced sounds. On this analysis

63.81% of the normally spoken vowels were classified correctly. The
categories which the whispered vowels had been assigned to were next
examined and it was found that only 18.095% of the whispered productions
were correctly classified. Similar patterns of results were found when
the discriminating functions were set for the whispered productions and
the voiced tokens entered as unclassified cases. The discriminating
functions classified 43.27% of the whispered productions but on inspection
it was found that only 21.91% of the spoken vowels were assigned to the
correct category. Despite the large differences between the formant
frequencies of the two phonation types, there was a surprisingly high
level of correct identification and this was about as good for the two
phonation types (number of errors was 60 for the voiced and 74 for the
whispered speech out of 840 responses each). Thus the formant frequencies
differ with phonation type but this does not impair perception. Subglottal and laryngeal effects might account for the higher formant frequencies in the whispered vowels. Fant, Ishizaka, Lindqvist & Sundberg,
(23), have shown that F_1 and F_2 of aspirated sounds appear to move up a
few hundred Hertz as a consequence of the subglottal cavities being
coupled when the vocal cords are open. This and the occluded back cavity
caused by increasing the tongue constriction result in selected frequencies not being transmitted. The coupling of the cavities below the
tongue constriction is made more complex because of the differences in
tongue constriction for the different vowels and amount of opening of the
vocal folds which differs between strong and weak whispered speech and
which may occur here too van den Berg, (24).

Mechanisms of Pitch Variation in Whispered Speech.

It could be claimed that since there is no identified means of varying
pitch for the whispered vowels, formant frequency shifts are perceived as
differences in pitch. For the time being this remains an open question.
It is to be noted that even if this were the case the whispered data
would be of interest to the production theorist. The formant frequency
shifts would then be effected to indicate pitch for the same linguistic
input and again indicate a shifting target specification.

GENERAL DISCUSSION.

Analysis of the acoustic tubes of a particular vowel shows that there is a
difference in the radius of the tube at the point of tongue constriction
with increasing pitch and that lip opening increases with pitch. One
problem with these data is that these measures are indirect and may not
be the actual configuration used because many different configurations
give the same low frequency output, Mermelstein, (25). With this proviso,
the results are next discussed with respect to their implications for
theories of speech production.

One possible explanation is that these changes in formant frequencies with
pitch are coincidental concomitants of mechanisms which change the voice
pitch. One such effect, mentioned above, is the upward movement of the
larynx which reduces the overall vocal tract length and the pharynx cavity
dimensions in particular. The changes in larynx height associated with
pitch might be a mechanism which is actively employed to change the voice
pitch, Stevens, (26), but is incidentally involved in changing the vocal
tract length. It has been reported that changes in larynx height have an

effect of 2% or less on the formant frequencies, Lindblom & Sundberg, (27), Wood, (28) and even then not always up in frequency. This particular effect could not explain the observed differences.

Most current theories of speech production propose that a central control mechanism issues executive instructions to the periphery. For example, one of the most influential models was proposed by MacNeilage, (29), where an articulatory target is issued to the periphery where it is achieved by gamma-loop control. Nooteboom, (30) offered two criticisms of this model; first, he argued that the same acoustic output can be achieved in different ways and this implicates acoustic representations and second, gamma-loop control, by which muscles reach a constant length, could only operate provided that the articulatory environment was constant. MacNeilage (31) later recognized that acoustic considerations need to be taken into account at the level of the target specifications. If the target was acoustic then a speaker could take account of the rules which apply to the speech of different speakers. This explanation might be extended to explain why the whispered data could be recognized by the listeners: the constraints in their production could be undone by the perceptual mechanism. The weak point of this explanation is that it dodges the acoustic to articulatory transformation which has to be performed and deflects the problem of explaining the present data to the perceptual theorist.

Theories such as those of MacNeilage, (29) have recently come under attack by Fowler, Rubin, Remez & Turvey, (32). They propose that instead of a "translation" of central instructions, central processes involve organizing "co-ordinative structures". A co-ordinative structure is defined as "a set of muscles, ..., that is constrained to act as a unit", Turvey, Shaw & Mace, (33). Co-ordinative structures can be nested from complex higher level sentential structures to more specific ones for vowels. For vowels Fowler et. al., (32) propose four co-ordinative structures, - one for vocal tract lengthening, one for vocal tract shortening, one for tongue shape and one for tongue position. In order to explain the present data, these co-ordinative structures would need to be organized in different ways depending on the pitch of the speech sound. This could occur at the level of the higher order co-ordinative structures when prosodic information like pitch might be organized or it might be a modulable property of the lower order co-ordinative structure for vowels.

In summary, the present results show a systematic difference in the production of vowels which is not coincidental. Translation theories would need to specify in detail the nature of acoustic to articulatory transformations to adequately explain these data. The action theory of Fowler et. al., (32) needs to specify the nature of the co-ordinative structures in more detail before it can be evaluated.

References

(1) Lindblom, B.E.F., Spectrographic study of vowel reduction, Jrnl. Acoust. Soc. Amer. 35 (1963) 1773-1781.
(2) Sonesson, B., On the anatomy and vibratory pattern of the human vocal folds, Acta Oto-Laryngologica. 156 (1960) whole issue.

(3) Potter, R.K. and Steinberg, J.C., Towards the specification of speech,
     Jrnl. Acoust. Soc. Amer. 22 (1950) 807-820.
(4) Miller, R.L., Auditory tests with synthetic vowels, Jrnl. Acoust.
     Soc. Amer. 25 (1953) 114-121.
(5) Fant, G., Carlson, R. and Granstrom B., The [ö]-[ø] ambiguity,
     Speech Communication Seminar, Stockholm, Aug. 1-3 1974.
(6) Howell, P., Pitch as a phonemic cue, Memory and Cognition, in press.
(7) Wendahl, R.W., Fundamental frequency and absolute vowel identifi-
     cation, Jrnl. Acoust. Soc. Amer. 31 (1959) 109-110.
(8) Meyer-Eppler, W., Realization of prosodic features in whispered speech,
     Jrnl. Acoust. Soc. Amer. 29 (1957) 104-106.
(9) Fant, G., A note on vocal tract size factors and nonuniform F-pattern
     scalings, STL-QPSR. (1966/4) 22-30.
(10) Lindblom, B.E.F. and Sundberg, J., A quantitative model of vowel
     production and the distinctive features of Swedish vowels. STL-
     QPSR (1969/1) 14-32.
(11) Stevens, K.N., The quantal nature of speech: Evidence from articula-
     tory - acoustic data, in David, E.E., and Denes, P.B. (eds), Human
     communication: A unified view (McGraw Hill, 1972).
(12) Fourcin, A.J., and Abberton, E., First applications of a new laryngo-
     graph, Medical and Biological Illustrations, 21 (1971) 172-182.
(13) Lerman, J.W., and Duffy, R.J., Recognition of falsetto voice quality,
     Folia Phoniatrica, 22 (1970) 21-27.
(14) Rathjen, J., Numerische und experimentelle Methoden der linearen
     Pradiktion Zur Datenreduktion von Sprachsignalen, Inst. fur Phonetik
     arbeitserichte, 11 (1969) 3-133.
(15) Markel, J.D., and Gray, A.H., Linear prediction of speech (Springer-
     Verlag, 1976).
(16) Sundberg, J., and Nordstrom, P.E., Raised and lowered Larynz - the
     effect on vowel formant frequencies, STL-QPSR, (1976/2-3) 35-39.
(17) Ohala, J.J., and Ewan, W.G., Speed of pitch change, Jrnl. Acoust.
     Soc. Amer. 53 (1973) 345.
(18) Petersen, N.R., Intrinsic fundamental frequency of Danish vowels,
     Aripuc, 10 (1976) 1-27.
(19) Chiba, T., and Kajiyama, M., The vowel - its nature and structure
     (Tokyo University, 1941).
(20) Fant, G., and Pauli, S., Spectral characteristics of vocal tract
     resonance modes, Speech Communication Seminar, Stockholm, Aug. 1-3,
     1974.
(21) Kirikae, I., Sawashima, M., Hirose, H., and Fujisaki, H., Simulation
     of children's speech by adult actresses, An. Res. Bull. Inst. Log.
     Phon. 11 (1977) 51-55.
(22) Fant, C.G.M., Acoustic theory of speech production (Mouton, 1960).
(23) Fant, G., Ishizaka, K., Lindqvist, J., and Sundberg, J., Subglottal
     formants, STL-QPSR, (1972/1) 1-12.
(24) van den Berg, Jw., Mechanisms of the larynx and the laryngeal
     vibrations, in Malmberg, B. (ed), Manual of Phonetics.
(25) Mermelstein, P., Determination of the vocal-tract shape from measured
     formant frequencies, Jrnl. Acoust. Soc. Amer. 41 (1967) 1283-1294.
(26) Stevens, K.N., Physics of laryngeal behavior and larynx modes,
     Phonetica, 34 (1977) 264-279.
(27) Lindblom, B.E.F., and Sundberg, J.E.F., Acoustical consequences of
     lip, tongue, jaw and larynx movement, Jrnl. Acoust. Soc. Amer.
     50 (1971) 1116-1179.

(28) Wood, S., Tense and lax vowels - degree of constriction or pharyngeal volume? Working papers Department of Linguistics Lund University, 11 (1975) 109-134.
(29) MacNeilage, P.F., Motor control of serial ordering of speech, Psychol. Rev. 77 (1970) 182-196.
(30) Nooteboom, S.G., The target theory of speech production, IPO Annual progress report, 5 (1970) 51-55.
(31) NacNeilage, P.F., Speech physiology in Gilbert, J.H. (ed), Speech and cortical functioning (Academic Press, 1972).
(32) Fowler, C.A., Rubin, P., Remez, R.E., and Turvey, M.T., Implications for speech production of a general theory of action, In Butterworth, B. (ed) Language Production (Academic Press, in press).
(33) Turvey, M.T., Shaw, R.E., and Mace, W., Issues in the theory of action In J. Requin. (ed) Attention and Performance VII (Erlbaum, 1978).

Tutorials in Motor Behavior
G.E. Stelmach and J. Requin (eds.)
© *North-Holland Publishing Company, 1980*

41

PEGGY BABCOCK'S RELATIVES

Brian Butterworth and Steve Whittaker
Department of Experimental Psychology
University of Cambridge
Cambridge

Control of speaking breaks down in tongue twisters. This
study explored some of the variables which contribute to
making a legitimate English sequence error-prone. Three
experiments are reported, all using two syllable items,
which looked at the effects of segmental similarity and
syllable structure. It turned out that both variables affected performance, and that the kinds of errors produced
have not been previously reported in the 'slips' literature.
The results are discussed in terms of the model framework
proposed by Shaffer (1976).

INTRODUCTION

In speaking, a linguistic plan has to be realised by a sequence of articulatory
movements. It is widely, and often tacitly, held that there is a final form
of this plan, its most detailed version, and it is this version which will
be translated into muscle commands to the articulatory system. One way of
exploring the nature of this linguistic plan and its relation to articulatory movements is to find cases of processing asymmetry - for instance,
where linguistic form is unproblematic but articulation in particularly
error-prone. Tongue-twisters are a case in point. They are entirely ortho-
dox linguistically, but of course cause abnormally many errors.

The principles underlying tongue-twister ('TT' henceforth) design are not
well understood since they've not been studied systematically. Most, but
not all, consist of the repetition of similar phonemes (Schourup, 1973).
Even less understood are the kinds and causes of errors produced. In our
preliminary studies, using traditional TTs, it appeared that errors were at
least systematic. Thus subjects repeating the notorious Peggy Babcock erred
in just a few of the large number of theoretically possible ways: Peggy →
Pebby, Babcock → Bagcock, Bagpock, or Bagpop. Moreover, error types seemed
similar to some 'slips of the tongue' in spontaneous speech: whole segments
(/p/, /b/, /g/) move into locations intendedly occupied by others, usually
similar segments, rather than the intrusion of new segments, or the amalga-
mation or distortion of segments. The resultant form, though incorrect,
nevertheless obeys the rules of English phonotactics - segments and their
sequencing - (Fromkin, 1971; Garrett, 1979; Meringer and Mayer, 1895). If
TTs do replicate certain classes of spontaneous slips, then they can be employed with advantage in the investigation of processes currently accessible
only through the happy chance of error and investigator being in the same
place at the same time (with all the methodological issues that raises).

Although many authors have described regularities in segmental errors
(Fromkin, 1971; Garrett, 1979; Meringer and Mayer, 1895; etc.), only two,
to our knowledge, have offered models which attempt to show how these come
about. One, MacKay (1970), predicts that stressed segments will tend to
substitute for unstressed segments; whereas, in fact, interaction is more
likely between elements of equal stress. The second, Shaffer (1976), seems
to make the correct predictions (or retrodictions) about segmental error
types. The structure of Shaffer's model is outlined in Figure 1:

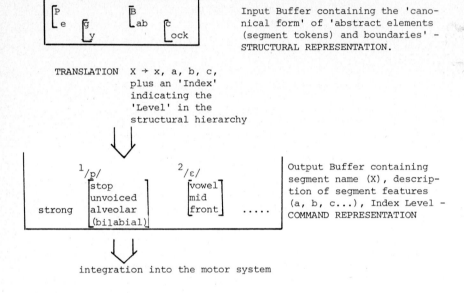

Input Buffer containing the 'canonical form' of 'abstract elements
(segment tokens) and boundaries' -
STRUCTURAL REPRESENTATION.

TRANSLATION X → x, a, b, c,
plus an 'Index'
indicating the
'Level' in the
structural hierarchy

Output Buffer containing
segment name (X), description of segment features
(a, b, c...), Index Level -
COMMAND REPRESENTATION

integration into the motor system

Figure 1: Shaffer's model of speech control

The 'structural representation' (SR) consists of abstract phoneme symbols
organised hierarchically by stress level and syllable position. Pe- has
strong stress, and /p/ is top of the syllable hierarchy because it's syllable initial. Syllable and word boundaries are marked in SR. The 'translation' takes these abstract phoneme symbols and defines them in terms of
(articulatory?) features making appropriate adjustments for syllable contexts - that is, it forms the appropriate allophone (e.g. [pʰ], aspirated
/p/, which is always the initial /p/ in English; final or medial /p/, [p⁻],
is generally not aspirated). This property entails that the translation is
language-specific. (Spanish, for example, has initial [p⁻], so the allophonic form cannot be simply a function of coarticulation). The 'command representation' contains all the information required by the motor system: a specification of phonetic features, syllable position given by the Index Level
- e.g. '¹X' will be syllable initial, '³X' will be syllable final - though
the nature of these hierarchical indices is not spelled out in much detail
in Shaffer (1976). As far as we can judge, the relation between CR and motor
activity is meant to be straightforwardly homologous - elements do not shift
position in this later translation. Control of output is governed by SR. A
'pointer' moves through the SR associating an element of the SR with the
appropriate element(s) of CR, and then outputting that CR element. (We leave

aside, in this outline, timing and prosodic properties of the model.)

Shaffer claims that this model explains the following types of error which
are found in spontaneous slips of the tongue.
1. Faults of index assignment by confusion of indices, the pointer finds,
   say, the wrong Level 1 in the CR: hence, immigration of segments to
   homologous syllable positions - e.g. heft lemisphere (Fromkin, 1973).
2. Faults of pointer control, where the pointer repeats or omits a segment
   erroneously - e.g. tone movement → tonement (Fromkin, 1973), and stut-
   tering.
3. Faults of execution; presumably slurring, mumbling etc.
4. Faults of translation, perhaps where elements of CR changes names; i.e.
   if X → Y, a, b, c and Y → X, x, y, z. Diagnostically, this seems to be
   a residual category if 1, 2, or 3 won't explain the error.

The results we have obtained from TTs do not fit the model as presented
here; since these results are rather complicated and since modifications
within the model framework can account for parts of the results, we shall
present them in a somewhat unorthodox manner. A version of the model will
be stated, patterns of errors inexplicable by this version will be given
and then a modification of the version offered. In all we will offer four
versions of the model, each of which turns out to satisfy only a part of
the data. Our negative conclusions may be interpreted in two ways: either
the model framework is fundamentally misconceived, or that the authors
haven't the imagination to figure out the appropriate version.

Materials

Since this was, to our knowledge, the first systematic study of TTs, we
wanted to keep the number of experimental variables to a minimum but to
investigate thoroughly the variables we did choose. Peggy Babcock herself
has two levels of stress - strong on peg and bab, weak on gy and cock -
four vowels - /ɛ, i, æ, ɔ/ - and four consonants - /p, g, b, k/. We used
instead, just two syllables, one vowels per syllable pair, two consonants
and one level of stress. Pretesting with traditional TTs indicated that repeating just two syllables would, in some cases, be sufficient to generate
errors.

There were three separate experiments, all using two-syllable items as follows.
Expt. I   # C_1 V_1 (C_2) # C_3 V_1 (C_2) #   (# = word boundary)

            e.g. nick sick, tee zee. 66 stimulus items.
Expt. II   #/? C_1 V_1 C_2 #/? C_3 V_1 C_2 #/?

            e.g. fav sav, vat zat. (rhyming words and nonsense syllables,
            all with the vowel /æ/) 40 items.
Expt. III #/? C_1 V_1 C_2 #/? C_3 V_1 C_2 #/?

            e.g. fab fak, tab tag. (words and nonsense syllables differing
            just in the final consonant, all with the vowel /æ/) 40 items.

Procedure

Subjects were asked to read aloud the two syllables with equal stress on
each syllable. When the experimenter ensured that the reading was correct,
the speaker had to repeat the syllables as quickly as possible until 15sec.s

had elapsed or an error had been detected by the experimenter. The session was tape-recorded for subsequent analysis.

The dependent measures were (1) error type (what kind of error was committed); (2) the number of correct repetitions before an error. (Had we used the number of errors committed in the 15sec.s it would have been impossible to disentangle the effects of correctly repeated items from the effects of incorrectly repeated items. It would have been equivalent to increasing the number and kind of stimulus items in an unplanned way.) A more detailed account of the design of the stimulus materials will be given with the relevant results sections.

Results 1: errors predicted by Model 1

TYPE	EXPT.	EXAMPLE stimulus	error	PERCENT OF ALL ERRORS
(1) anticipations	I	mat rat →	rat rat	23
	II	bav pag →	gav gav	22
	III	pab pag →	pag pag	30
(2) perseverations	I	puck duck →	puck puck	29
	II	bav gav →	bav bav	16
	III	zab zag →	zab zab	18
(3) transpositions	I	bus gus →	gus bus	2.5
	II	paz kaz →	kaz paz	4
	III	pap pak →	pak pap	9.2
(4) feature moves	I	tee zee →	dee see [± voicing]	<1
	II	vat zat →	vad zad [± voicing]	<1
	III	sav saz →	zav zaz [± voicing]	<1
(5) feature changes	I	zip rip →	[zʉp rʉp] (front→central)	<1
	II	faf saf →	raf zaf [+ voicing]	<1
	III	mav maz →	mav mas [− voicing]	<1

Table 1: error predicted by Model 1

Model 1 allows anticipations, perseverations and transpositions of whole segments in either the SR ('structural representation') or the CR ('command representation'); feature movements can occur only where phonetic features are represented, i.e. in the CR. Feature changes are not explicitly discussed, but presumably information loss or alteration can occur, infrequently, at the appropriate level.

Results 2: error patterns not predicted by Model 1

In the design of Experiment I we systematically varied the similarity of the initial consonants in terms of a metric derived from Ladefoged's articulatory feature system (Ladefoged, 1975). Consonants can be classified on three dimensions: manner of articulation, place of articulation and voicing.

Manner: stop (e.g. p), fricative (s), nasal (m), approximant (l)

Place: bilabial (b), labiodental (f), dental (th /θ,ð/), alveolar (t), palato-alveolar (sh /ʃ/), velar (k)

Voicing: voiced (b), unvoiced (p).

If consonants differed on just one dimension they were treated as differing by one feature, on two dimensions by two features and on all three dimensions, by three features. (That is, we regarded /b/ as being as different from /d/ as from /g/.)

Model 1 states that the conditions on segmental movement will be a function solely of the 'index'. In SR segments are quite abstract, featureless; in CR segments are described by their abstract name, index and features, but again movement will be conditioned just by the index.

Similarity Measure	N of items	Mean no. correct before error
1. Feature different	33	13.0
(Voicing, e.g. pit bit	6	9.0
Place, e.g. pick tick	16	14.8
Manner, e.g. bit mit	11	12.8)
2. Features different	22	14.8
e.g. puck duck		
3. Features different	5	25.3

Table 2: Effects of initial segment similarity in Expt. 1

A Kruskall-Wallis one-way ANOVA by ranks distinguished reliably the 1, 2 and 3 Features groups ($\chi^2 = 6.84$; 2df, $P<0.05$) and between the Voice, Manner and Place Features ($\chi^2 = 6.28$; 2df, $P<0.05$). (So our feature system does not list features of equal value: syllables with initial consonants differing just on voicing lead more quickly to error, than those differing in either place or manner.)

Model 2

There are three ways in which the data in Table 2 may be handled within the model framework. First, the segment symbols could be less abstract and amenable to some non-featural similarity metric (cf. MacNeilage, this volume). Second, segments in SR could be fully specified as to their features. Third, a system later than the CR, perhaps, the motor system itself could scan the CR feature matrices index level by index level. That is, transduce all feature matrices on Level 1, then all feature matrices on Level 2, etc. into a motor representation or similar. This allows feature similarity to lead to confusability at a given Index Level, though how this comes about needs further elaboration.

The first option is unsatisfactory, since similarity still needs to be defined appropriately (acoustically, articulatorily or what?). The second option would either make the two-representation and translation scheme irrelevant, since everything in CR would be already specified in SR. So option three gets the vote as Model 2. (Shaffer, this volume, now proposes something along these lines anyway: his 'motor scan'.)

Results 3: error patterns not predicted by Model 2

In the design of the stimulus materials for Expt. II the manner, place and voicing features of initial and final consonants were systematically varied (see Table 3). According to Model 2, which transduces CR Index Level by Index Level, the nature of the Final consonant (Level 3) should have no effect

```
EXPT. II              INITIAL SEGMENTS
              STOPS                 FRICATIVES
         VOICED   UNVOICED     VOICED     UNVOICED

           b, g      p, k        v, z       f, s

                    FINAL SEGMENTS
              STOPS              FRICATIVES        NASALS
         VOICED   UNVOICED    VOICED   UNVOICED    VOICED

           b, g     p, k       v, z      f, s       m, n
```

EXPT. III   Same consonants, but FINALS and INITIALS reversed.

Table 3: design of materials for Expt. II and Expt. III

on overall performance for a given initial consonant (Level 1). (A parametric ANOVA was carried out on normalised data.) This showed that the number of correct repetitions for initial stops with a stop in the final position (e.g. bad gad) was reliably smaller than for initial stops with final
fricatives (baz gaz) or with final nasals (bam gam). Similarly, for initial
fricatives, performance is worse with final fricatives than with final stops
or nasals. That is, errors are more likely when all consonants have the
same manner of production (all stops or all fricatives), than when they are
mixed. There is no consistent effect of voicing or place.

Paradoxically, the role of final consonants was not reflected in the type
of errors produced. Only 13 out of 400 errors could be interpreted as the
interaction of final and initial consonants - that is, where a final segment moves into an initial position (or vice versa), e.g. bap gap → bag gap
or bap gag.

Model 3

In order to allow two Index Levels to interact to affect performance, the
'motor scan' must operate in parallel on at least Index Level 1 (= initial
segments) and on Index Level 3 (final segments). There's still the paradox
of an effect without an apparent interaction between the two levels; perhaps an intrinsic property of the feature specification maintains output
homology. One way this might work would be, as Shaffer suggests, CR specification distinguishes allophones, say, initial p's [p^h] (aspirated) from final p's [p$^-$] (unaspirated).

Results 4: error patterns not predicted by Model 3

Both allophonic specification and the idea of language specificity in the
transductions between representations postulated in Model 1 and carried
through to Models 2 and 3 predict that non-English sequences will not be
produced.

```
EXPT. II          bat gat    →    gbat gat
                             →    bat bgat
                  baz gaz    →    gbaz gaz
                             →    baz bgaz
```

(NB. These sound like genuine cluster, not, for example, [gəbæt].)
            Table 4: error clusters in Expts I and II

EXPT. I   nick sick   →   nick nsick
                    kill sill   →   kill ksill
                    tin shin   →   tin [tʃɪn]

cluster errors
as percent of   II   25.5%
total errors   I   28.6%

Table 4 (cont.): error clusters in Expts I and II

As can be seen, these cluster errors constitute a sizable fraction of all
errors - better than one-quarter in each experiment (27.9% in Expt. III,
see below). Moreover, each speaker produces cluster errors, and most of the
items in Expt. I and 39 out of 40 of the items in Expt. II result in a cluster error from at least one speaker. So these errors cannot be discussed as
a small or idiosyncratic effect.

Not only are these clusters common, but in Expt.s I and II, they are formed
in just two ways:

(1) C_1 V_1 C_2 C_3 V_1 C_2

Homology is preserved in that initial segments only form initial clusters,
(incidentally, there was no strong tendency to produce clusters on C_1 (N=64)
rather than C_3 (N=45)) but rules of English segment sequencing are violated.
This is particularly striking in examples like nick nsick and kill ksill
(Table 4) where homologous, regular, word-forming clusters - snick, skill -
are not produced, even though one might expect language habits to overrule
the observed cluster formation scheme in (1).

A second problem for Model 3 (and its antecedents) is that items in Expt.
III are much harder than those in Expt. II. Recall that the only difference
between items in Expt. II and Expt. III is that the segments within syllables are in the reverse order (II: bat gat; III: tab tag). In Expt. II
the mean number of correct repetitions before an error was 6.4, whereas
in III it was 3.2. Nothing in the Model predicts this asymmetry.

Model 4

Suppose that the 'motor scan' of CR produces a 'motor representation' (MR),
and suppose further that an analogue to Shaffer's 'pointer system' between
SR and CR, operates between CR and MR. In Shaffer's model (Model 1), the
pointer works through, essentially, positional addressing; but it could
work through content addressing instead - utilising both segment description
and index level. We would, in addition, need to postulate that the CR-MR
translation - 'motor scam' - is not language specific.

The motor scan will still translate all segments in a syllable in parallel,
and some (unspecified) process will still make syllables with segments of
the same manner - e.g. all stops - more error-prone. However, the pointer
will operate on the basis of the segment description as well as Index Level,
so when two syllables have the same or similar consonant description(s)
associated with the same Index Levels, they will be more confusable; we may
further hypothesize that to economize on syllable addressing the pointer
makes use of the initial segment only (or at least gives it special weight).
Thus the CR of tab tag will be more confusable than that of bat gat, since
[^{1}t-] will be more similar to [^{1}t-] than [^{1}b-] will be to [^{1}g-]. So, when

the motor scan uses CR descriptors to initiate output of MR, it will be
more likely to start on the second (incorrect) syllable in the tab tag case.

Results 5: clusters in Expt. III not predicted by Model 4

The cluster formed in Expt. III show a quite different pattern from those
in Expt.s I and II.

Cluster Location	Syllable position of moved segment	Error examples	N
First syllable	Homologous	(a) mab mag → mabg mag bap bak → bapk bak	5
		(b) vap vak → vakp vak daf das → dasf das	3
	Nonhomologous	(c) nab nag → gnab nag	3
		(d) saf sas → fsas sas zav zaz → vzav zaz	8
Second syllable	Homologous	(e) fap fak → fap fapk pav paz → pav pavz	22
	Nonhomologous	(f) nap nak → nap knak	1
		Others	3
			45

Table 5: cluster patterns in Expt. III

In addition to the errors in Table 5, there were 15 clusters formed using
the last segment of the first syllable and the first segment of the second
syllable. For example,

(2)   sap sak → sap psak
        dab dag → dab bdag

Unlike Expt. II the second consonant is the most likely to move: in eight
cases to the initial position (d, Table 5) and in 22 cases to a location
just in front of the final segment of the second syllable (e, Table 5). Notice that, even discounting clusters like (2), 12 out of the 45 involve
segments moving into nonhomologous syllable locations and thereby violating
Index Level constraints.

Finally, speakers produced clusters involving an intrusive segment, or a
feature change on the moved segment, e.g.

(3)   tab tag → ptab tag [-voicing]
        nab nag → knab nag [-voicing]
        dav daz → dafs daz [-voicing]

        zab zag → vzab zag [stop → fricative?].

Now these clusters are by no means random. Most theoretically possible clusters just do not occur. So tab tag does not, for example, give the error
types tatb tag, tabt tag, tab tagt, tbat tag, tab tbag, tgab tag, etc. even
though these seem just as likely as the errors in Table 5. Actually, none
of the errors fall into these types: the initial segment of either syllable
never moves, and no segment moves into the final position of the second syl-

lable following the last intended segment. (In Expt. II, the final segments never moved. That is, repeated segments hold their positions.)

Discussion

Model 4 will also have to be modified, but it is not clear to us what modification would be satisfactory. Some method of allowing Index Level constraints to be violated would need to be incorporated, such that in appropriate conditions, and just these, nonhomologous movements would be allowed. Completely abandoning index levels would mean that the bulk of errors involving homologous segment movements are left unexplained.

Another possibility is that Shaffer's treatment of syllable structure is wrong. If so, this would seem to have serious consequences for linguistics. Most recent work has utilised a kind of hierarchical structure for syllables very similar to Shaffer's - e.g. Liberman and Prince (1977), Vergnaud, Halle et al. (1979). In this last account Level 1 - 'onset' and Levels 2 and 3 - 'rhyme' and 'coda' are distinguished ((onset)(rhyme(coda))) and constraints of segment sequencing are defined on these positions rather than between them. Thus non-English initial clusters violate 'onset' structure constraints, and nonhomologous movements violate hierarchy constraints - i.e. codas move to onset positions and vice versa.

To 'save the phenomenon', such errors would have to be considered as taking place at a stage in the process where linguistic information no longer affects processing; that is, the articulatory or motor system would have to be thought of as language independent.

Such errors would then be constrained by the general properties of motor systems, and we would expect to find similar error patterns in sequences of nonlinguistic motor behaviour. Alternatively, constraints, though independent of the speaker's language, may be linguistically universal. So speakers would only commit errors which are legal sequences in some language or other.

Finally, it could be argued that TTs have little or nothing to do with ordinary speaking. Against this it should be remembered that nearly three-fourths of the errors are just like reported spontaneous slips, and that hearing the remaining one-fourth is by no means easy.

Acknowledgements

The first author.thanks the following people who have been generous with their time listening to the arguments and suggesting further studies. Alas none of them could solve the theoretical problem. At this conference: Peters Howell, MacNeilage and McLeod, and especially John Long and Henry Shaffer; at MIT, Merrill Garrett, Jay Keyser and Ed Walker; at the Boston Veteran's Administration Hospital, Edgar Zurif.

References

[1] Fromkin, V., The nonanomalous nature of anomalous utterances. Language 47 (1971) 27-52.
[2] Fromkin, V., Speech Errors as Linguistic Evidence. (Mouton, The Hague,

1973).

[3] Garrett, M.F., The analysis of sentence production, in Bower, G.H. (ed.), The Psychology of Learning and Motivation 9 (Academic Press, New York, 1975).

[4] Garrett, M.F., Levels of processing in sentence production, in Butterworth, B.L. (ed.), Language Production Vol. 1: Speech and Talk (Academic Press, New York, 1979).

[5] Ladefoged, P., A Course in Phonetics (Harcourt, Brace, Jovanovich, New York, 1975).

[6] Liberman, M. and Prince, A., On stress and linguistic rhythm, Linguistic Inquiry 8 (1977) 249-336.

[7] MacKay, D.G., Spoonerisms: the structure of errors in the serial order of speech, Neuropsychologia 8 (1970) 323-350.

[8] Meringer, R. and Mayer, C., Versprechen und Verlesen: eine Psychologisch-Linguistiche Studie (G.J. Göschen'sche Verlagshandlung, Stuttgart, 1895).

[9] Schourup, L., Unique New York unique New York unique New York, Chicago Linguistic Society, Ninth Regional Meeting (1973) 587-596.

[10] Shaffer, L.H., Intention and performance, Psychological Review 83 (1976) 375-393.

[11] Vergnaud, J.R., Halle, M., et al., Metrical structures in phonology (a fragment of a draft), MIT Internal Report.

AUTHOR INDEX

SUBJECT INDEX

A

Accuracy, 154-160, 203-206
  and mass variability, 154-159
  and movement amplitude, 153-156, 203-206
  and spring-tension variability, 160
Action, 553-554, 647-648, 653
  classes of, 553-554
  plans of, 523, 647-648, 653
Action-perception cycle, 72
Additive factor method, 331-350, 375, 379, 434
  overadditive, 336
  underadditive, 336-340
Afference, 50, 61, 65, 91, 106
  see also Feedback; Proprioception system, 141
Agramatism, 627
Alarm clock model, 487, 498
  alternative models, 490-493
  Clock Setting models, 493-498
Algorithms, 3, 73
Alpha motorneurons, 105, 135
Alpha gamma coactivation, 162, 167, 226-227
  linkage, 91, 106
Amplitude errors, 176-180
Anararthria, 628
Anomia, 624-626
  input and output processes, 625
  lexical selection, 625
Anticipation, 511-521
  errors, 244
  timing, 511-521
  see also Timing

Aphasia, 624, 626-627
Arousal, 346-347
Attention, 243-248, 255, 374, 430-431, 440, 479-489
  and control of movement, 243-248
  and response selection, 583-584
  capacity, 246-248, 440, 580-581
  demands, 579-589
Automata, 3
Autonomous system, 17, 19

B

"Ball parking", 75
Basal ganglia, 315-325
  globus pallidus, 315-325
Bereitschaft's potential (BP), 399-400, 411, 414, 416-417
Bernstein's problem, 1-2, 18, 20, 32, 66
  see also Degrees of freedom
Bimanual movements, 151-152, 185-196
  interference, 186, 192, 195
  kinematic analysis, 189
  location errors, 188
  model of coordination, 185, 193-196
  MT, 192
  RT, 191
Broadman's area, 7, 118-125

C

Catastrophes, 26-27
Candate nucleus, 118
Central control, 131, 315-325, 457-458, 460

673

C. Ulat.